Carl
404 W. Catawissa
Nesquehoning, Pa. 18240
1-717-669-9195

ELECTRONIC CONNECTIONS

ELECTRONIC CONNECTIONS

Home and Car Entertainment Systems

Martin Clifford

PRENTICE-HALL, INC.
Englewood Cliffs, New Jersey 07632

Library of Congress Cataloging-in-Publication Data

Clifford, Martin, (date)
Electronic connections.

Includes index.
1. Electric cables. 2. Electric connectors.
3. Stereophonic sound systems. 4. Home video
systems. 5. Automobiles—Audio equipment. I. Title.
TK3301.C55 1987 621.388'332 86-12217
ISBN 0-13-250499-5

Editorial/production supervision: *Denise Gannon*
Cover design: *George Cornell*
Manufacturing buyer: *Gordon Osbourne*

Printed in the United States of America

10 9 8 7 6 5 4 3 2 1

ISBN 0-13-250499-5 025

Prentice-Hall International (UK) Limited, *London*
Prentice-Hall of Australia Pty. Limited, *Sydney*
Prentice-Hall Canada Inc., *Toronto*
Prentice-Hall Hispanoamericana, S.A., *Mexico*
Prentice-Hall of India Private Limited, *New Delhi*
Prentice-Hall of Japan, Inc., *Tokyo*
Prentice-Hall of Southeast Asia Pte. Ltd., *Singapore*
Editora Prentice-Hall do Brasil, Ltda., *Rio de Janeiro*

CONTENTS

PREFACE

The use of electronic connections has had a long, eventful history. Today electronic component connections have become an integral part of in-home video, high-fidelity, and satellite TV systems, and they are essential in autos, vans, and recreational vehicles. Electronic connections are slowly being recognized as having an importance comparable to that of the components themselves.

Electronic connections started with the growth of radio, circa 1919. Crystal sets were used, as the average cost of a vacuum tube was equivalent to almost a week's pay for many. Several connections were required for the receiver: a downlead from the antenna (an outside antenna was a must), a good ground, and a pair of headphones. The headphone cords terminated in small, nickel-plated pins that were attached to the set's earphone terminals, a pair of Fahnestock clips, a spring-like connector.

As tubes came down in price, radio receivers became vacuum-tube oriented, as these tubes could supply amplification. Because they were battery operated, connecting wires were needed to the batteries. Also needed were a 6-volt storage unit for the tube's filaments, three 45-volt battery blocks interconnected with insulated single-wire conductors and then wire-connected to the receiver, and a C-battery for bias.

With increased sound volume possible from receivers, headphones were replaced by a single external speaker connected to the output of the radio by a pair of wires. When power supplies were substituted for batteries, connections became simpler. At first positioned outside the radio, the power supply was gradually incorporated within it. As speakers became smaller, they, too, were placed inside the radio. As tubes were made more sensitive, the antenna and its downlead gradually disappeared, and the antenna also moved into the radio receiver in the form of a loopstick.

The result of all this was that connections for in-home AC-operated radios just about disappeared, with the exception of the power cord. When solid-state technology came along, portables became practical and for such receivers the power cord also went into the electronic attic. We finally had radio receivers that required no connections at all!

Early TV sets were electromechanical, using a spinning disc, but when these were replaced by purely electronic TV the only connection required was a downlead from an outdoor antenna. It, too, needed a minimum of connections. Radios joined this march of progress and in-home entertainment systems were offered consisting of a radio receiver, a record player (subsequently called a turntable) and speakers—all factory interconnected, and supplied in a console.

Restless radio (especially FM, and this was about 1950) began to realize the possibilities of quality sound, and yielded to the birth of component systems in which the integrated receiver was separated into a tuner and an integrated amplifier, and then into a tuner, a preamplifier, and a power amplifier. When stereo sound came along, the speakers came out of their radio receivers and were used as separate components. Component interconnections were again needed and with the passage of the years high-fidelity systems began to consist of a fairly large number of components: tuner, preamplifier, power amplifier, open-reel tape deck, audio cassette deck, equalizer, electronic crossovers, a single pair of left-and-right stereo speakers, and then several such pairs, turntable, microphone, and one or more headphones. All of these, as they are individual units, require connections.

While all this was happening, TV plodded along in the same old way. TV sets were integrated units, with only the downlead from an outside antenna. The sound supplied by these TV receivers was barely adequate—tinny, distorted, and strictly monophonic, but all that is now in the process of change.

Within the past decade video has begun to replace television. *Video* means a component system with television as the picture display for that system. The television receiver has evolved into three different forms: the TV receiver, a monitor, and a TV receiver/monitor. By itself, the TV receiver is wholly inadequate as far as signal inputs are concerned. The TV set has only two inputs—for VHF and UHF signals. Further, these signals must be RF, that is, modulated. Baseband signals (video signals without modulation) cannot be accepted by those input terminals, unless they are modulated by some external component. Further, most TV sets are input oriented only; they have no output ports. Even here, however, the winds of change are blowing and we are now getting TV sets equipped with audio and video output ports.

With the help of switchers, RF modulators, and components that do contain modulators, the TV set is now becoming part of a video system. To overcome the usual TV set's lack of input ports, we now have TV receiver/monitors and monitor-only components that are far better equipped for accepting either unmodulated audio and video signals or those that are modulated.

Video systems include outboard components such as video cassette recorder/players, video cameras, tuners, image enhancers, satellite TV systems, video disc players, dynamic noise filters, commercial killers, single-channel and block converters, decoders, plus a host of add-ons.

With TV broadcast and video cassette recorders now beginning to supply stereo sound, the TV receiver—with its built-in monophonic-only amplifier and its pathetic little speaker—is gradually being displaced by the long-delayed union between video and audio. Connections have had a tremendous resurgence, especially with the emergence of the two-, three-, and four-set family.

The purpose of this book is to show you how to make the needed connections. Most of the connections are on the rear apron, hidden from view, but their function is as essential as that of the components they join.

North Lauderdale, FL 33068 MARTIN CLIFFORD

My thanks to the Coral Springs Branch of the Broward County Library System for the use of their resources and the support of the staff.

ACKNOWLEDGMENTS

This book is the result of cooperative effort, with a number of electronics companies graciously opening their files and supplying me with data. I acknowledge their substantial contribution and their awareness of the growing need for published information on electronic connections.

Alpine Electronics of America, Inc.
Avantek, Inc.
BP Electronics, Inc.
Channel Master, Div. Avnet, Inc.
Discwasher, Div. International Jensen, Inc.
Fujitsu Ten Ltd.
GC Electronics
Gemini Industries, Inc.
General Electric
Kloss Video Corp.
Marshall Electronics, Inc.
McCullough Satellite Equipment, Inc.
MFJ Enterprises, Inc.
Pfanstiehl Corp.
Pioneer Electronics [USA] Corp.
Precision Satellite Systems
RCA
Recoton Corporation
Rhoades National Corp.

RMS Electronics, Inc.
Sharp Electronics Corp.
Signet
Sparkomatic Corporation
Vidline Video Accessories
Winegard Co.
Yamaha Electronics Corp.

ELECTRONIC CONNECTIONS

1

WIRE AND CABLES

Wire for work in electronics is a solid copper or copper-plated steel conductor. It is used for delivering a varying signal voltage, a DC voltage, and a direct or alternating current. It can be bare or covered with some kind of insulating material, possibly enamel, cotton, silk, rubber, or plastic. Wire can be single or made up of a number of strands twirled around each other. The purity of the copper in wire is an unknown factor as far as the user is concerned, although a manufacturer may make a claim for a high degree of purity without accompanying data. Unlike the fairly rigid wire used for electrical purposes, wire for electronics is flexible—an advantage when interconnecting components.

WIRE GAUGE

The diameter of a wire is indicated by its gauge number; the lower the gauge number, the thicker the wire. There are a number of different wire gauges, including American Wire Gauge (AWG) and Brown & Sharpe (B & S); these are used for copper wire, and others are used for brass, iron, and sheet metal. AWG is standard for wire used in electronics and its gauge numbers range from the thickest wire, gauge 0000, to gauge 40. Gauge 0000 has a thickness of 0.460 inch and gauge 40 has a thickness of 0.0031 inch. The most commonly used wires in electronics are wire gauges 16 to 22 (Fig. 1-1). The wire used in electronics usually has an even gauge number (16, 18, 20), but wire with odd gauge numbers is available.

Size, Approx. (AWG)	Uninsulated Conductor				Finished Wire
	Number of Strands	Strand Diameter, Nominal (Inches)	Strand Area (Circular Mils)	Conductor Diameter, Average (Inches)	DC Resistance (Ohms/1000 ft)
32	7	0.0031	67	0.010	183.0
30	7	0.0040	112	0.013	109.9
28	7	0.0050	175	0.016	70.4
26	1	0.0159	253		46.3
26	7	0.0063	278	0.020	44.3
24	1	0.0201	404		28.3
24	7	0.0080	448	0.025	27.5
24	19	0.0050	475	0.026	25.7
22	1	0.0253	640		17.9
22	7	0.0100	700	0.031	17.6
22	19	0.0063	754	0.032	16.3
20	1	0.0320	1024		11.2
20	7	0.0126	1111	0.038	10.9
20	10	0.0100	1000	0.038	12.3
20	19	0.0080	1216	0.041	10.1
18	1	0.0403	1624		7.05
18	7	0.0159	1770	0.048	6.89
18	16	0.0100	1600	0.048	7.69
18	19	0.0100	1900	0.051	6.48
16	1	0.0508	2581		4.43
16	19	0.0113	2426	0.058	5.02
16	26	0.0100	2600	0.061	4.73
14	1	0.0641	4109		2.79
14	19	0.0142	3831	0.072	3.18
14	41	0.0100	4100	0.076	3.00
12	1	0.0808	6529		1.76
12	19	0.0179	6088	0.090	2.00
12	65	0.0100	6500	0.096	1.89
10	104	0.0100	10380	0.121	1.16

Figure 1-1. AWG wire table.

DC WIRE RESISTANCE

The DC resistance of a wire—its opposition to the flow of a direct current through it—is generally measured per thousand feet at 68° F (20° C). As temperature increases, so does resistance. In terms of gauge numbers, the resistance of copper wire becomes larger for each increase in gauge number. If you know the resistance of a thousand feet of any wire, it is possible to calculate the resistance of a thousand feet of wire of the next larger gauge number. Thus, the resistance of a thousand feet of gauge 20 wire is 10.15 ohms. Multiplying this by 1.26 supplies a resistance of 12.789 ohms for 21-gauge wire. Conversely, to find the resistance of 1000 feet of the next lower gauge number, divide by 1.26. The resistance of smaller lengths can be calculated by multiplying or dividing by some factor such as 10 or 1000. Thus, the resistance of

300 feet of 30-gauge stranded wire is (300/1000) × 109.9 = 32.97 ohms. 109.9 ohms is the resistance of 1000 feet of this wire. The resistance of a wire is proportional to its length in feet and inversely proportional to its cross-sectional area.

WIRE DIAMETER

Wire size isn't specified by its length, which is indeterminate, but by its cross-sectional area, since for any length of wire this is constant. The cross-sectional area of a wire is measured in circular mils (CM). A circular mil is the cross-sectional area of a wire whose diameter is 1 mil (a thousandth of an inch or 0.001 inch). The diameter of the thickest wire, gauge 0000, is 460 mils, and that of the thinnest, gauge 40, is 3.1 mils.

To determine the cross-sectional area of a wire in circular mils, square its diameter in mils. Gauge 18 wire has a diameter of 40.0 mils and its cross-sectional area in circular mils is 1600.

Circular Mil Area of Stranded Wire

Stranded wire, commonly consisting of seven strands of bare copper wire twirled to form the equivalent of a single solid conductor, is used extensively in making electronic connections. Assume you have a wire consisting of seven strands of 32-gauge wire (identified as 7/32 wire) each of which has a diameter of 3.1 mils. Each of these wires will then have a circular mil area of 3.1 × 3.1 = 9.61 circular mils. As there are seven wires, the total area is 7 × 9.61 = 67.27 circular mils.

The cross-sectional area of a wire doubles for every three gauge numbers, and the current carrying capacity is also doubled. The cross-sectional area of wire is given in circular or square mils (Fig. 1–2). The circular mil area is equal to the square of the diameter; square mil area to the dimension of any side multiplied by itself.

Square wire was used at one time in making connections between parts in radio receivers. It may still find applications in power panels for large cur-

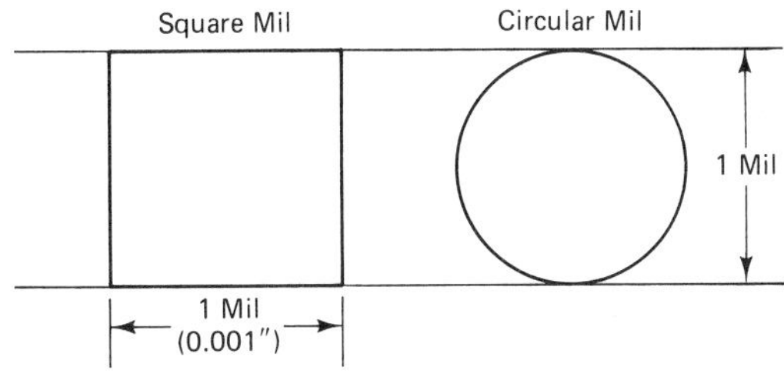

Figure 1–2. Square mil vs. circular mil.

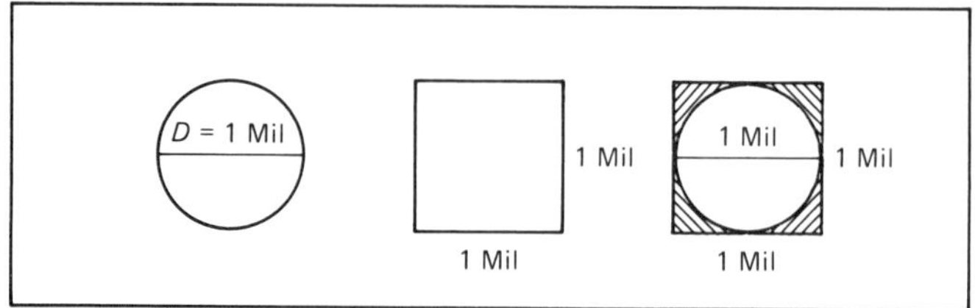

Figure 1–3. The area of a circular mil is approximately 78.5 percent of a square mil. The shaded section indicates the greater area of the square wire.

rents. A circular mil is equivalent to 78.5 percent of a square mil. Thus square mils = circular mils multiplied by 0.7854; circular mils = square mils divided by 0.7854. The resistance of a wire is proportional to its length in feet and inversely proportional to its cross-sectional area in circular mils (see Fig. 1–3).

IDENTIFYING WIRE

Wire can be categorized in a number of different ways: by gauge number, by the type of insulation used, by whether it is stranded or solid, and sometimes by the components it connects. Still another way is by voltage. Wire used for interconnecting audio and video components is sometimes referred to as low-voltage wire; low-voltage means any voltage that is less than 30.

The low-voltage wire interconnecting video and audio components is neither a fire nor a shock hazard, but it is not wise to open audio and video components and poke around. In-home components can be battery or power-line operated, and the AC power line is not to be considered low-voltage. In a television receiver, the voltage for the picture tube is measured in kilovolts. It is one thing to interconnect audio and video components; manufacturers expect you to and sometimes supply the wire, but you should not tamper with the interior of their components, as you could nullify the warranty.

With the exception of wires connecting high-fidelity power amplifiers to speakers and power-line cords connecting components to AC outlets, wires joining components in in-home video or high-fidelity systems carry very small amounts of current. Using a larger than necessary wire will only reduce wire flexibility and will not improve the system.

Bell Wire

It is sometimes necessary to connect a single point on a component to another single point, such as the ground terminal on one component to the ground terminal on another. Even if a component does not have a ground

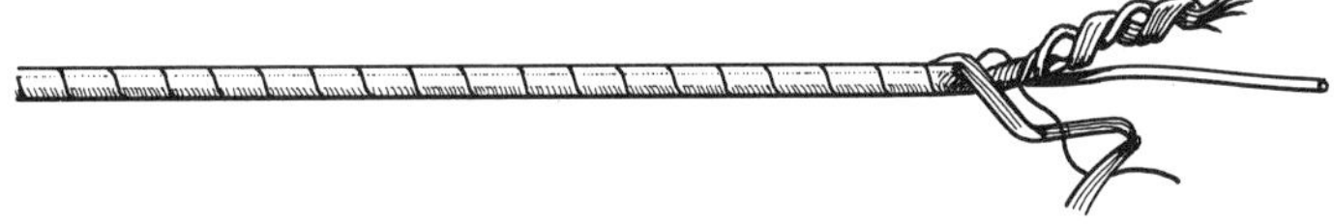

Figure 1-4. Bell wire.

terminal, it may be desirable to wire one metal chassis to another to put all units at the same ground potential.

Bell wire (also known at one time as annunciator wire), as shown in Fig. 1-4, can be used for these purposes. It consists of a single conductor, most often solid copper wire. It isn't insulated with plastic or rubber but has a double layer of cotton, with each layer wound in opposite directions, and the layers impregnated in paraffin. The copper conductor isn't enameled and it can be used as it is for making connections. It is sometimes called pushback wire because of the ease with which the insulating covering can be pushed back to expose the bare wire.

Single-Wire Line

Single-wire line (Fig. 1-5A) is almost like Bell wire except for its insulation, often plastic and available in different colors. Unlike that of Bell wire, the insulation isn't a pushback type, but can be removed by using a sharp, single-edge razor blade and then making a circumferential cut about 3/8 inch in from the end. Diagonal cutters or a wire stripper can also be used.

Twisted Pair

Twisted pair consists of two intertwined insulated conductors, as shown in Fig. 1-5B. Conductors in cables for interconnecting electronic components are parallel to each other and do not use the twisted arrangement.

Litzendraht Wire

Litzendraht wire, or Litz, is stranded wire, with each strand insulated from the others. The effect is an increase in total surface area with a reduction in AC resistance. At their ends, all the individual strands of Litz wire are joined, forming a parallel connection. Litz wire is effective up to about 1 MHz

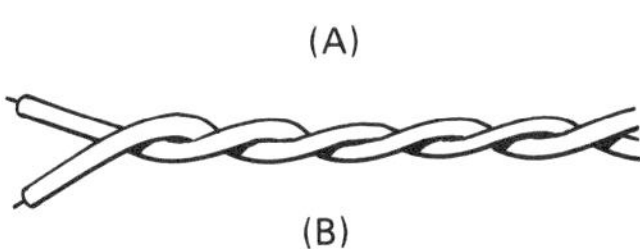

Figure 1-5. Single-wire line (A) and twisted pair (B).

and is used for connecting receivers and amplifiers to speakers (but not too often because of its cost). Removing the insulation from each individual strand presents connection problems.

Litz wire is sometimes used in phonograph cartridges, but again, not often because of its cost.

Tinned Wire

Some wires, most often single insulated conductors, are sometimes supplied with tinned surfaces. A tinned surface is a fine, extremely thin layer of tin, and is desirable because it makes soldering wires much easier, producing a good electrical connection.

Lamp Cord

Lamp cord, also known as zip cord since its individual conductors can be pulled or "zipped" apart, is used extensively for fans, small electrical appliances, and, of course, for lamps (Fig. 1–6). It is also commonly used for connecting the output of an audio power amplifier to speakers. It may consist of two solid conductors of 18-gauge wire but more often is made of seven strands of wire whose total cross-sectional area is the equivalent of 18-gauge or 20-gauge wire.

Lamp cord may be polarized (not all lamp cords are); that is, each conductor may be identified in some way. One of the conductor pairs may have a ridge above it, or may be covered with a silver- or copper-colored plastic.

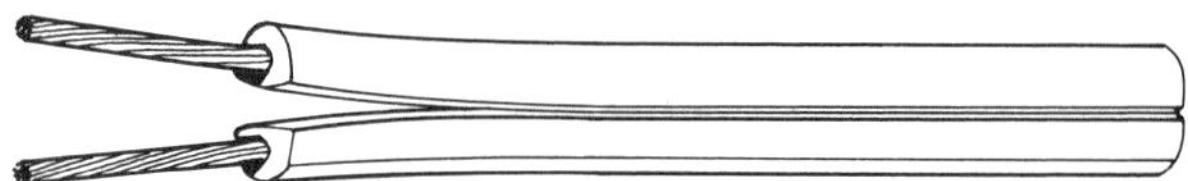

Figure 1–6. Lamp cord, also called zip cord, can be separated easily to facilitate stripping the wire ends.

AC WIRE RESISTANCE

The resistance of a wire to the flow of current through it can be measured with an ohmmeter. At zero frequency, that is, DC, the entire volume of the wire is used for the passage of current. (This assumes no variation of current, which you would find in pulsating DC.)

Skin Effect

Skin effect, also known as AC resistance, is the tendency of an electric current to flow near or on the surface of a conductor with an increase in frequency. At a frequency of zero (DC) the current flows through the entire volume of the conductor. At a frequency as low as 1 kHz the current flows through the outside skin only to a depth of 0.09 cm. At 1 MHz the skin depth through which the current flows is only 0.007 cm deep. Stranded wire is often used in preference to solid conductors for radio-frequency currents, as the surface area is much larger than that of a comparable solid wire. Thus, skin effect is equivalent to a reduction of the volume of copper through which a current flows.

WIRE STRIPPING

When you make a connection to a wire, its ends must be stripped or the insulation must be punctured to permit metal contact to the conductor below it.

Wire stripping can be done in three ways: by removing the insulation with a sharp knife or single-edge razor blade, by using a pair of diagonal cutters, or by using a tool known as a wire stripper. The wire stripper is the best and fastest of these three and is supplied with replaceable cutter blades for removing the insulation from wire of different gauges. The one shown in Fig. 1-7 can strip wires from gauge 14 to gauge 20.

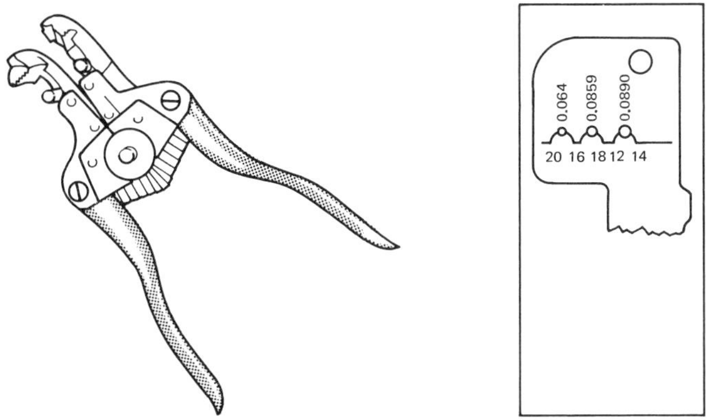

Figure 1-7. Wire stripper and replaceable blade. (*Courtesy GC Electronics*)

CONNECTING SINGLE CONDUCTORS

Joining single conductors is usually a two-step operation. The initial step is the formation of a good mechanical connection followed by soldering. To make a *wire splice,* as shown in Fig. 1-8A, first make sure the stripped ends are shiny bright by scraping the conductors with a knife. Twist one wire around the other as shown on the left. Continue wrapping until the two wires form

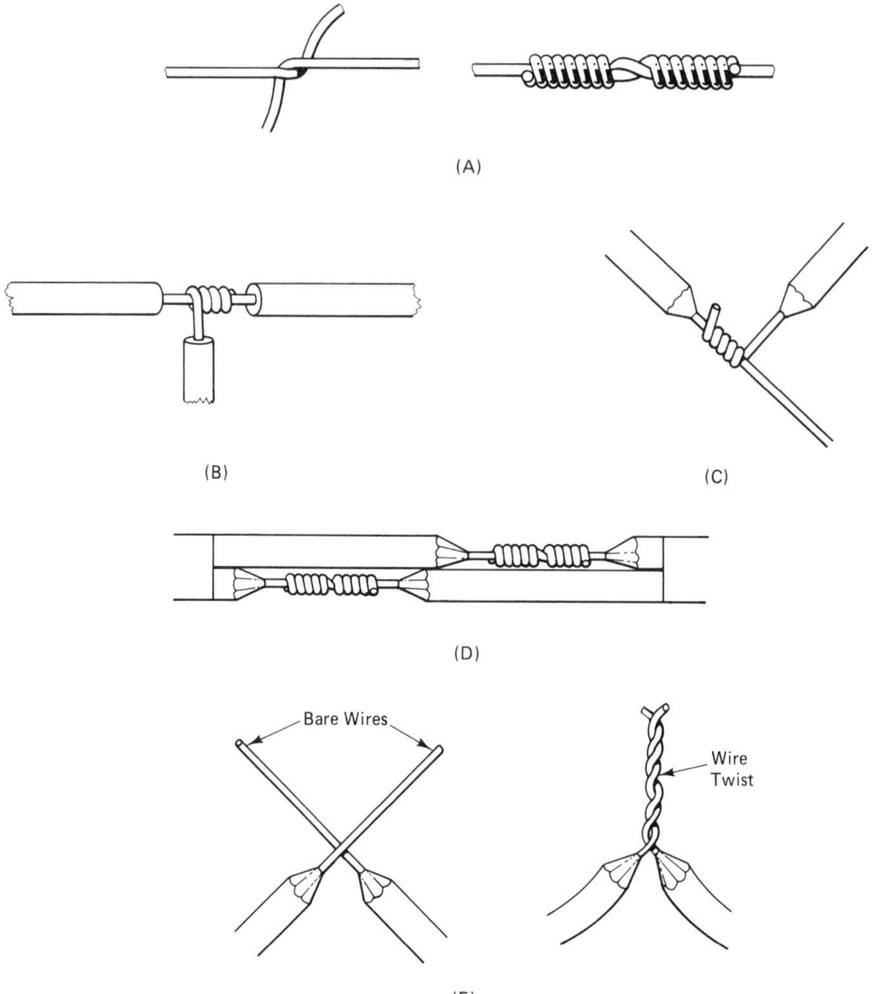

Figure 1–8. Mechanical methods of joining wires: wire splice (A); tap strip (B); Western Union splice (C); staggered splice (D); rattail joint (E).

a mechanical joint, as illustrated at the right. The best tools to use are a vise and a pair of pliers. Mount the two wires in the vise and twist with the pliers. To insulate the exposed wire ends, cover them with shrink wrap and heat until the wrap covers the wires.

To form a *tap,* strip one of the wires anywhere along its length, exposing the conductor. Strip the other wire about 1/2 in. from its end and wrap it around the first wire, as in Fig. 1–8B. When the tap strip is completed, the two wires will be at right angles to each other.

Figure 1-8C shows another method, known as the *Western Union splice.* One of the stripped wire ends remains as it is, with the other wire wrapped around it.

Figure 1-8D is a *staggered splice.* When the splicing is completed there is less chance of one of the wires shorting against the other.

The drawing in Fig. 1-8E shows the formation of a *rattail joint.* The two exposed wire ends are tightly twisted together. Before joining wires, regardless of the type of connection being made, rub the exposed wires with sandpaper. This will facilitate soldering, but be sure to wipe the wires with a clean cloth before doing so.

WIRE CABLING

One of the problems with home entertainment systems is the large number of wires and cables behind the components. If the system is working well and is not expected to be changed in the near future, a more professional appearance can be had by using cable ties for keeping the wires together. Don't join the wires tightly; instead, try a cable tie wrap or a plastic-covered twist tie intended for kitchen use (Fig. 1-9). Try to avoid cabling input and output leads to eliminate the possibility of signal feedback.

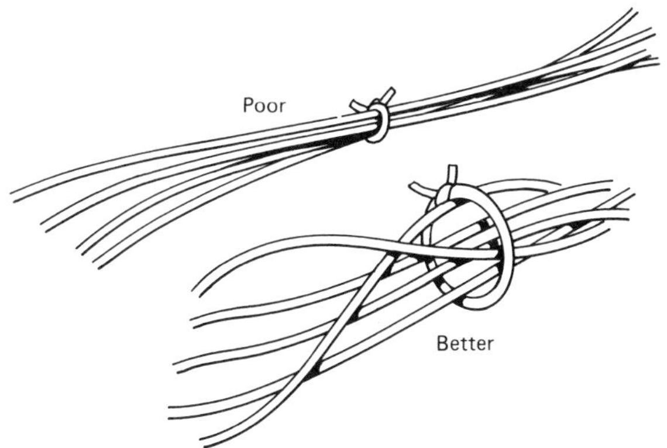

Figure 1-9. Methods of cabling connectors.

Don't cable the wires together, but form them into groups. If the system is on shelves instead of in a rack, follow the technique shown in the lower drawing of Fig. 1-9. If the system is on a shelf there may be a temptation to lace all wires tightly to keep them out of sight. Instead of using wire ties, support them with a hook. (Fig. 1-10).

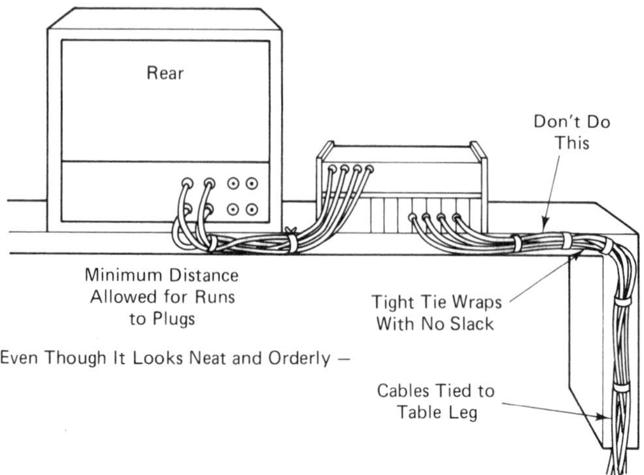

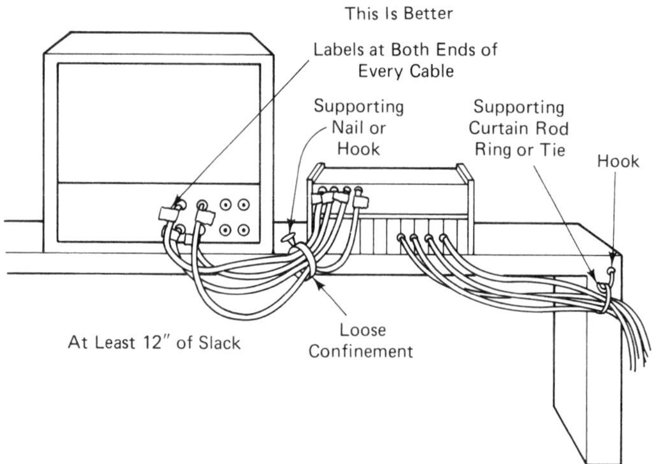

Figure 1-10. Using hooks for wire support.

CABLES

Single wires have limited applications in making connections for use in electronics. The ground wire supplied with a turntable for connection to ground is a single conductor. The lead-in from an outside antenna to the antenna terminal on an AM receiver is a single wire. The wire interconnecting the chassis of components is also a single wire. But other than these few examples, most wiring in video and high-fidelity systems is in wire pairs.

The simultaneous use of two wires or more is called a *cable.* In some instances the insulation of the wires is unitized, forming a joined or twinned pair with the wires independent of each other, but often enough the wires are separate. The cables may be round and they are most often used for audio and video installations, while flat cable is the preferred type for computers; it is used to connect a computer to a disk drive and to a printer. Flat cable (Fig. 1-11) also known as ribbon cable, may or may not be color coded, and it terminates in a special type of connector plug.

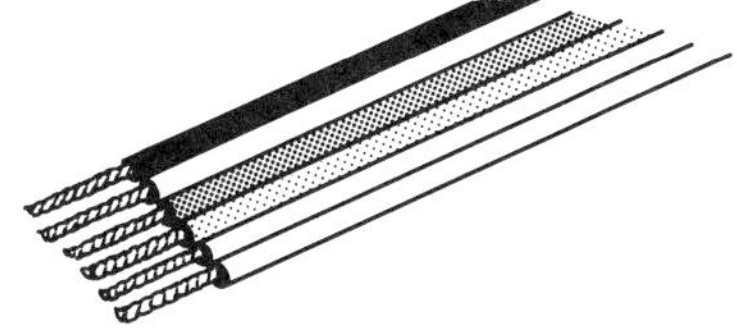

Figure 1-11. Flat (ribbon) cable. This type is usually supplied with a mounted connector.

Various other types of flat cable are shown in Fig. 1-12—the mainspring cable, the rollup cable, and the accordion cable.

Multiconductor Cable

Multiconductor cable is sometimes used when one of the wires, a white wire, as shown in Fig. 1-13, is to be a signal-carrying wire; the other white wire the "hot" lead for supplying a DC voltage, and the black lead a common, ground, or negative lead. The stripped, exposed ends of these leads are often terminated by wrapping them around a captive screw. This cable is supplied round or flat.

Any group consisting of wires only or one or more wires plus shield braid is known as multiconductor cable. The wires can be color coded red, black, or white; two of the wires may be white and one black; or they may be no particular color, as in coaxial cable. White or red is generally considered the plus, positive, or "hot" lead; black the minus, negative, ground, or "cold" lead. The words *hot* and *cold* as used here do not refer to temperature. A cold lead is a ground lead and can be used as a voltage reference point. For DC, a hot lead is one that is at a higher positive or negative potential when measured with respect to ground.

The color coding of multiconductor cable is exactly the opposite of the wire polarity used for electrical wiring. In house wiring, for the transmission of electrical power the black lead is the hot, or positive, conductor, the white lead is the ground.

Video Cassette Recorder Cables

Cables are sometimes named by the equipment with which they are used. Cables used by VHS video cassette recorders are sometimes called VHS cables; those for Beta sometimes referred to as Beta cables. While this associates the

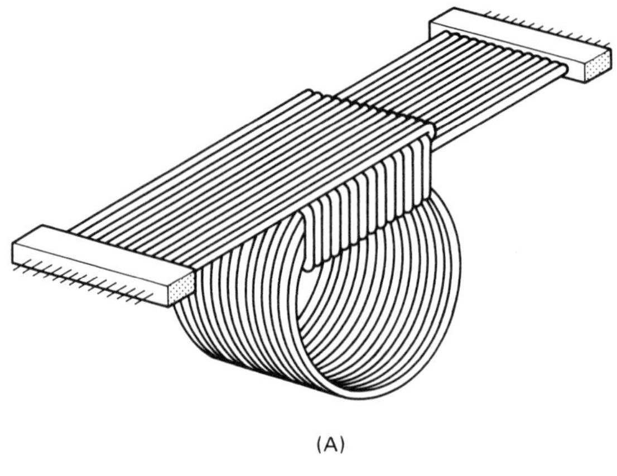

(A)

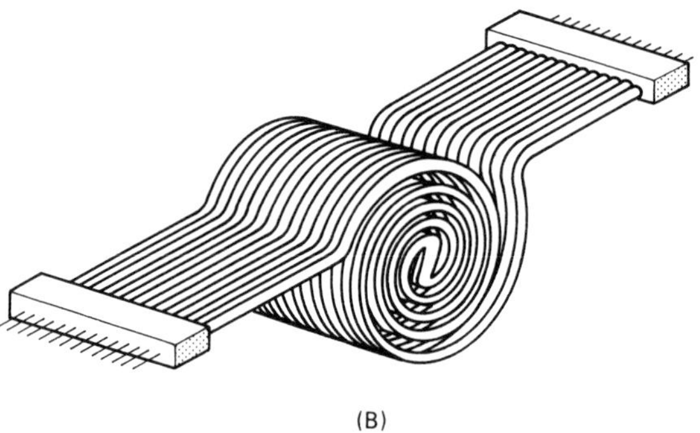

(B)

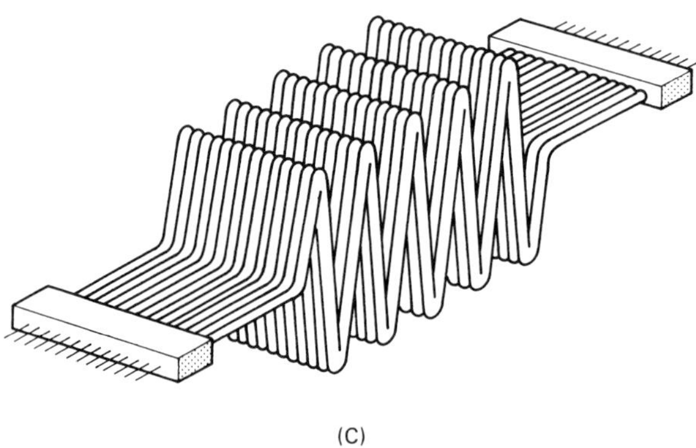

(C)

Figure 1-12. Flexible (flat) cable: mainspring (A); rollup (B); accordion (C).

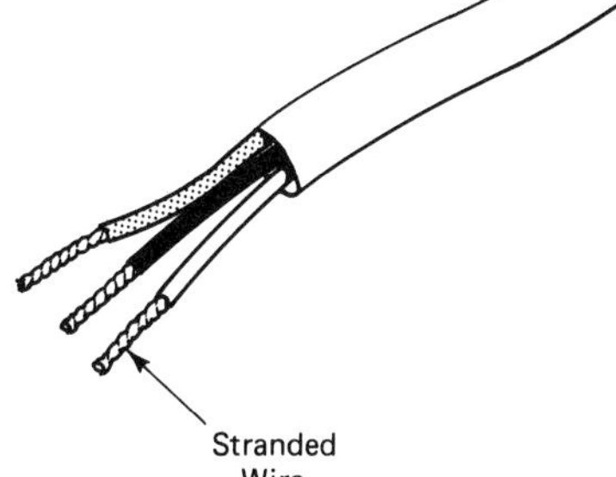

Figure 1-13. Multiconductor cable.

cable with either one or the other of the two most commonly used video cassette recorders, it is inadequate as a specific cable identification.

Rotor Cables

There are two options for the reception of VHF and UHF television signals, and for FM broadcast. One is to use three separate antennas—a desirable arrangement, as each of the antennas can be individually adjusted for best reception of its particular range of signals. A further benefit is that each of these antennas can be optimum, that is, have the highest gain. The disadvantage is the need for three transmission lines, downleads from these antennas.

The second option is a combined VHF/UHF/FM antenna, which is popular, as just a single installation is required, plus the use of a single downlead. The problem of having the antenna face broadside to the transmitting station can be overcome by using a rotor, a small motor mounted on the antenna shaft and controlled from indoors using a circular scale marked in north, south, east, and west divisions. Adjustment of a center control turns the motor on and that motor continues rotating until it stops automatically at the user-selected position on the in-house control.

Rotor cables can be three- or four-conductor, using 20-gauge wire. The wire is stranded and is covered by a black vinyl insulation. Rotor cables can be flat or round and each of these is obtainable in suitable lengths (Fig. 1-14). Connections are made to the motor's small terminal block, corresponding to a similar terminal block on the control unit. The wires can be slit apart at their ends to permit stripping the wire ends prior to making connections. For greater cable flexibility, stranded wire is used. The round cable, shown in the lower part of the illustration, does have an advantage, as not only are the individual wires insulated, but the wire group is then covered with an additional layer, offering better weather-proof protection. The wires in the round cable are color coded, with one black and the other wire or wires white. The flat cable isn't color coded but one of the wires has a larger layer of insulation

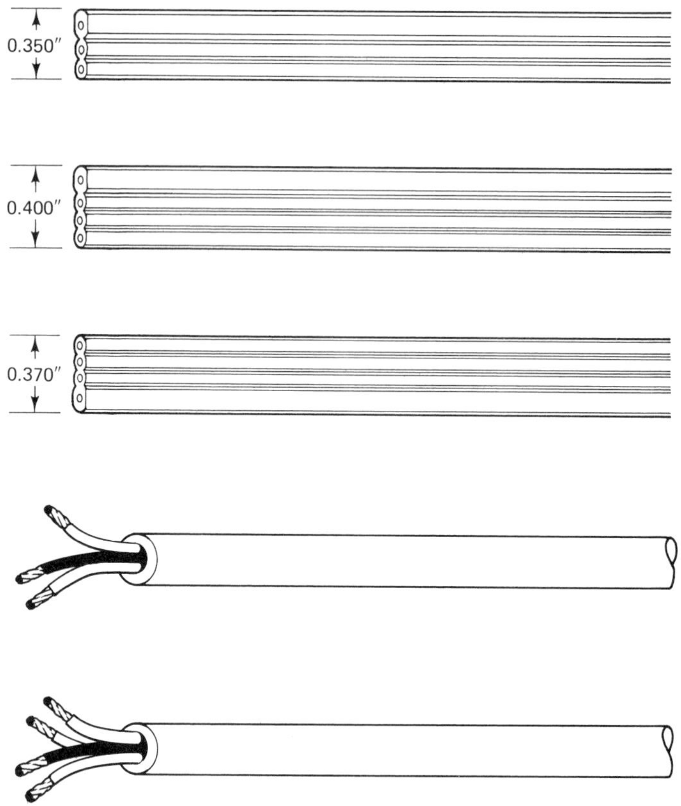

Figure 1-14. Rotor cables (*Courtesy Channel Master, Div. Avnet, Inc.*)

than the others and this can be used for wire identification. Each wire can be recognized by its position with respect to the thickest wire. The wire used in the cable consists of seven strands of 20 gauge.

Double-Receptacle Connector Cable

This type of cable permits the operation of two components at the same time from a single battery. The total current drain is the sum of the current loads of the individual items. Both components must have the same DC voltage requirements but can have different current needs.

Extension Cord

This cable is intended for plugging into the cigarette lighter of a vehicle. The cord must be sufficiently long to permit components to be operated at some distance from the car. Typical cord length is 25 feet. The thicker the wires in the cable (the lower their wire gauge number), the better. The voltage drop across the cable may be large enough so that connected components either will not function or will do so intermittently. Extension cables can be used for operating a portable video camera.

Dubbing Cable

Cable can be used for transferring video and audio signals from one VCR to another, a technique known as dubbing. The cable is a twinned or joined cable (Fig. 1-15). A dedicated cable—used only for dubbing—it is twinned for the greater part of its length, but the individual conductors are separated a few inches from their connectors (plugs).

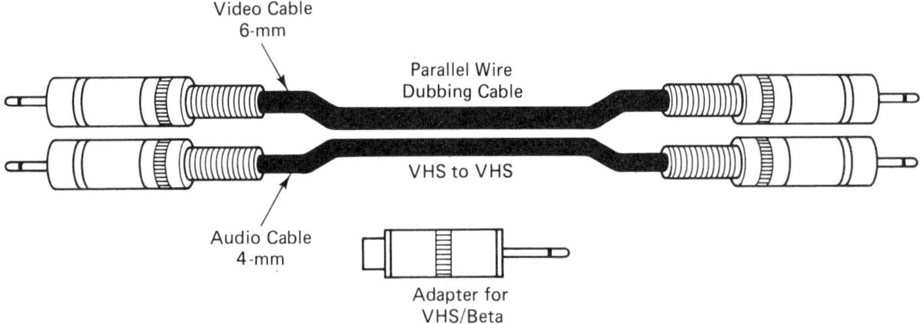

Figure 1-15. Dedicated dubbing cable.

TRANSMISSION LINE

A transmission line is a closed system for carrying a signal from one point to another. Although not ordinarily regarded as such, a power-line cord of the type used to connect an appliance to an AC wall outlet is a kind of transmission line, linking the source (AC line voltage) to a load (a TV receiver or audio amplifier). Although both the source and the load have impedances, these are disregarded and the main factor of interest is the current-carrying ability of the line cord.

Transmission line, also called downlead, is a cable connecting an antenna with the input terminals on a receiver, television tuner, television receiver/monitor, or a video cassette recorder. The ideal transmission line is one that delivers all signals from an antenna without modifying them in any way and without any decrease in signal amplitude.

There are three types of transmission lines used for audio, radio, and television: single-wire line, twin lead, and coaxial cable. The line having the least loss, that is, the smallest voltage drop across the full length of the line, is the single-wire lead. Such a wire could be used as the downlead from an antenna to an AM receiver, but it has its limitations. If it is used with an AM receiver whose front end mixer or converter circuit is not preceded by an RF (radio frequency) amplifier—whether tuned or untuned—there is always the chance of signal radiation from the receiver's front end, and the possibility of causing interference to other radio receivers.

Transmission Line Velocity Factor

The velocity of a wave, such as an RF modulated composite video signal, is dependent on the medium through which is travels. It is not only different when the wave is unguided, as in the case of a broadcast TV signal traveling through space, but varies from one type of transmission line to another. The ratio of the actual velocity of the wave to its velocity in space is the velocity factor. In space, the velocity or speed of a radio wave is the same as that of the speed of light, approximately 186,000 miles per second. The velocity of radio waves in transmission lines is always less than this. Figure 1–16 shows the velocity factor for radio waves in different types of transmission lines.

Type of Transmission Line	Velocity Factor (V)
Coaxial Line (Air Dielectric)	0.85
Coaxial Line (Solid Plastic Dielectric)	0.66
Two-wire Line (Wire with Plastic Dielectric)	0.68–0.82
Twisted-pair Line (Rubber Dielectric)	0.56–0.65

Figure 1–16. Velocity of radio waves in transmission lines.

TWIN LEAD

Twin lead, also known as two-wire line or 300-ohm line is used primarily as the transmission line or downlead from an antenna. Short lengths of twin lead, when connected to the antenna input terminals of a TV set, can also be used as an interfering signal trap. Some small components, such as radio-frequency transformers, also use twin lead as connecting wires.

The impedance is 300 ohms regardless of length, but the greater the length, the larger the signal loss. Each of the two conductors in twin lead is made of parallel lengths of stranded wire, generally seven strands of gauge 28 wire, with the conductors jointly forming the equivalent of gauge 20 solid wire (Fig. 1–17).

Twin lead is a passive device, and as such it introduces signal losses, expressed in decibels per 100 feet. The loss increases with frequency and the condition of the line, whether dry or wet. It has a greater signal loss than single-wire line. Further, this loss increases with age as the plastic begins to

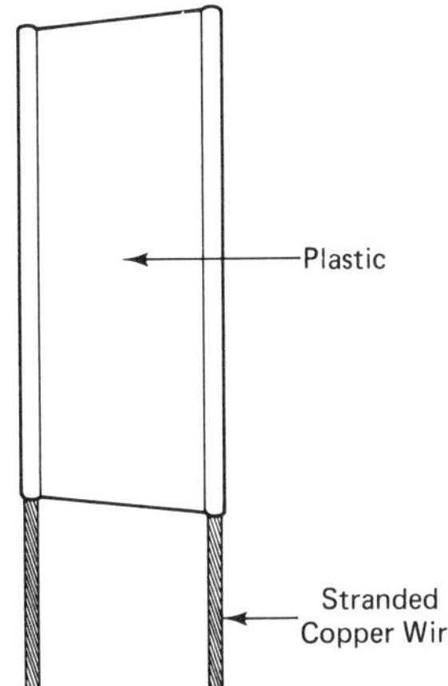

Figure 1–17. Two-wire transmission line, also known as twin lead. The conductors usually consist of seven strands of 28-gauge wire.

weather from outside use. In the home, twin lead is sometimes painted over, increasing deterioration and capacitance effect.

The two conductors of twin lead, separated by plastic (sometimes called a dielectric), behave like a capacitor. As in any other capacitor, its reactance varies inversely with frequency, and so twin lead's capacitance has a bypassing effect on high audio and video frequencies. The effects are even more noticeable at higher frequencies, particularly UHF. When used outdoors, twin lead is subject to stress from the collection of water, which may subsequently freeze. The water may also contain various mineral salts, or it may be contaminated.

Ordinarily, the dielectric material, the plastic between the two conductors, serves a dual purpose. It helps maintain those conductors at a uniform distance from each other throughout the entire length of the transmission line so the electrical characteristics of the line remain the same. The dielectric also works as a protective covering, keeping the conductors from being exposed to the elements. In some instances, though, an additional covering, a polyethylene jacket, is placed over the dielectric, reinforcing the transmission line and serving as further protection against the weather (Fig. 1–18).

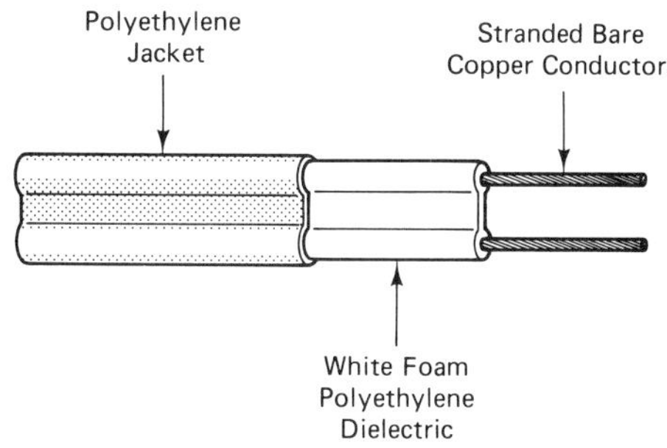

Figure 1–18. Double-covered twin lead.

The disadvantage of unshielded twin lead is that while it is intended to transfer a signal from an antenna to a TV set or video cassette recorder (VCR) it can also work as an antenna. In this capacity it picks up not only unwanted interfering broadcast signals but also signals produced by noise voltages, possibly generated by electric motors, fluorescent and neon lighting, or passing cars. On the positive side, twin lead is inexpensive compared to other types of cables, light weight, easy to handle, and easy to install. Its stripped ends can readily be equipped with spade lugs, making connections easy and convenient (Fig. 1-19A).

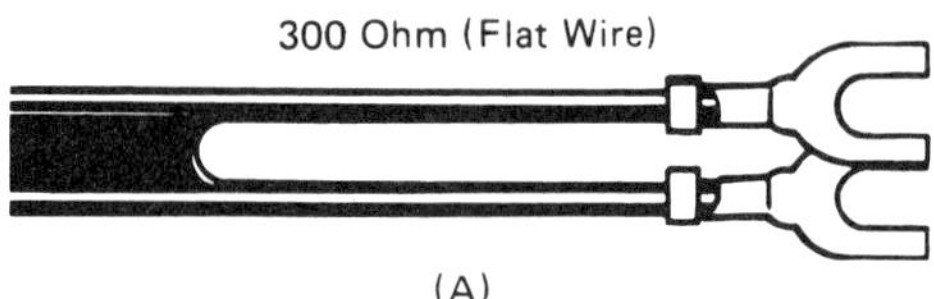

Figure 1-19A. Twin lead transmission line equipped with open spade lugs. (*Courtesy General Electric.*)

Both types of transmission line, twin lead or coaxial cable, can be connected directly to the antenna terminals of a TV set (Fig. 1-19B).

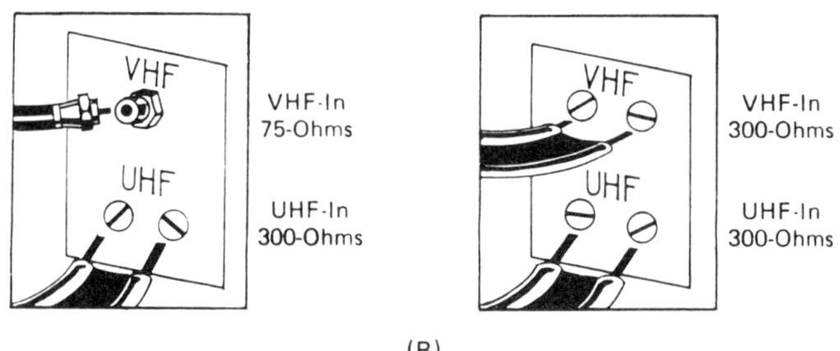

Figure 1-19B. Possible transmission line connections to the antenna block of a TV receiver. (*Courtesy GC Electronics*)

Shielded Twin Lead

Noise pickup can be overcome by shielded twin lead (Fig. 1-20). Like unshielded twin lead, it consists of a pair of conductors made up of seven strands of bare, twisted copper wire. The wire is insulated with plastic and then covered with a foil sheathing. Running along the foil is a bare wire that can be used as a separate ground lead. The assembly of the twin conductors, the ground wire, and the metallic sheath is covered with a layer of plastic, such as Mylar.

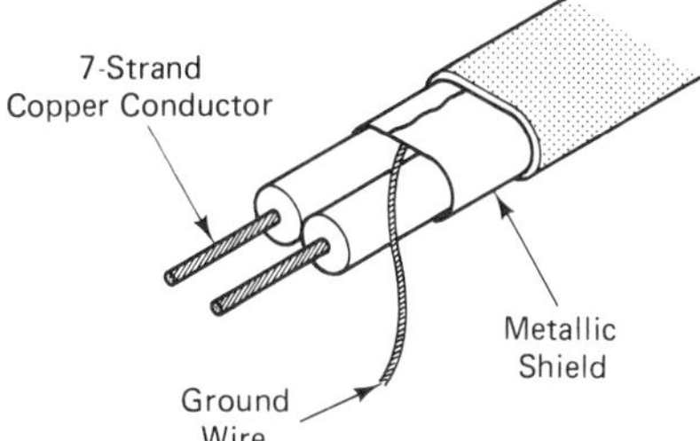

Figure 1-20. Shielded twin lead.

Shielded twin lead is a little thicker and a little heavier; it costs more than twin lead and is more difficult to handle, but its anti-electrical noise characteristic makes it desirable in areas plagued with electrical interference. Both types of twin lead, shielded and unshielded, are installed in the same way and both could be called balanced cable, as two independent conductors are used for signal transmission. The shield works solely as a protection against electrical noise pickup.

STANDOUTS AND PLASTER STRAPS

In its route from the antenna to the TV receiver two-wire transmission line, or twin lead, can be held in place by small fastening devices known as standouts or standoffs. A standout is a small metallic device with wood screw threads or a clamp on one end and a circular loop (eye) with slotted insulating material on the other. Its purpose is not only to prevent unshielded transmission line from vibrating in the wind but also to keep it away from metal gutters, walls, or other surfaces.

Plaster strap is also a nonmetallic fastener used to secure wall connectors for 300-ohm line. Metal straps should not be used with twin lead because they can affect its signal-handling characteristics. This precaution does not apply to coaxial cable.

COAXIAL CABLE

In addition to two-wire line, coaxial cable (coax) works as a downlead from an antenna to receiver or VCR inputs, and as a connecting link between components. Coaxial cable is also used in satellite TV systems, connecting a dish-mounted downconverter to an in-home satellite receiver.

There are two types of video coaxial cable, balanced and unbalanced, with unbalanced coax the more widely used.

Unbalanced Coaxial Cable

Unbalanced cable (Fig. 1-21) consists of a central conductor of solid or stranded conductor and is made of pure copper—that is, copper without other conducting materials mixed in with it—or of copper-plated steel. It is the hot lead, and is surrounded by a layer of insulating material made of polyethylene plastic (Fig. 1-22). The dielectric can be foam or solid, but the foam is preferred for VHF and UHF signals. Around it is a jacket of wire mesh or braid, or sometimes just a wire wrap in the form of a continuous loop. The braid serves as a double purpose. It works as a conducting lead—the ground, or cold, lead. The braid and the center lead form the two conductors required for the transfer of a signal.

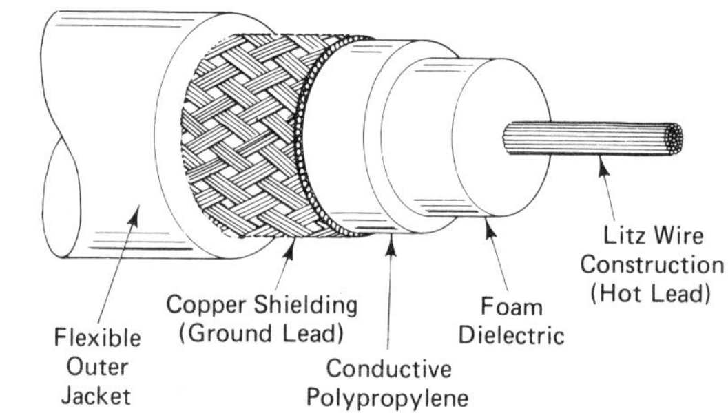

Figure 1-21. Unbalanced coaxial cable.

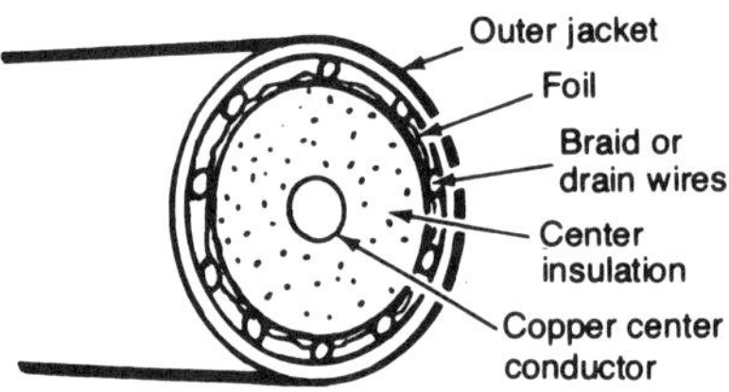

Figure 1-22. Cross-section of unbalanced coaxial cable (*Courtesy Winegard Co.*)

It may seem strange to call the insulating plastic a dielectric, but any metallic material separated by an insulating substance forms a capacitor, and the separating material is the dielectric. Thus, every coaxial cable has capacitance, similar to the electrical behavior of twin lead (Fig. 1-23). This applies to coaxial cable used for video or audio. In audio, the hot lead and the shield braid are much closer to each other than in coaxial cable made for video. This can be tolerated, even though such construction increases the capacitance of the cable. Cable capacitance is much less significant at audio frequencies than at video.

In some coaxial cables, additional shielding is obtained by covering the braid with metal foil. The shielding, whether by braid alone or braid with foil,

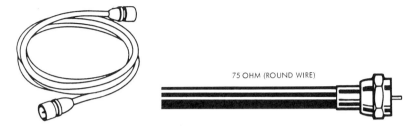

Figure 1-23. Coaxial cable with connectors. (*Courtesy General Electric*)

isn't as effective at audio frequencies as at the frequencies used for VHF and UHF.

The outer jacket around coaxial cable not only protects it against the weather and indoor abuse by users, but also helps in maintaining a uniform distance between the shield braid and the center conductor. Coaxial cable isn't as easy to install or use as two-wire transmission line and is somewhat more costly, but it is often preferred because of its signal-shielding ability.

In some types of coaxial cable, there is an aluminum foil shield, beneath which there is a separate wire used as the ground lead. Coaxial cables used by cable TV companies for the delivery of programs to their subscribers may use solid metal instead of braid as the outer shield.

The impedance of coaxial cable used in video is 75 ohms, although coaxial cable is available with other impedance values. Like twin lead, the impedance is independent of length and is 75 ohms for any section. Coaxial cable is used as a downlead from an antenna to the antenna input terminals of a VCR or TV receiver and is also for interconnecting components.

Twin lead is generally supplied in bulk in lengths of 25 feet, 50 feet, and 100 feet, but it is not equipped with connectors. Coaxial cable is available, connector equipped, in short lengths of 3 feet, 6 feet, and 10 feet—and also in bulk form, without connectors.

Types of Unbalanced Coaxial Cable

Not all unbalanced coaxial cables are alike, differing principally in modifications of their basic structure. The coax shown in Fig. 1-24A uses a single layer of braid while that shown in B has a layer of foil beneath the braid to supply more effective shielding against unwanted signals. The coaxial cable in C is quite unusual (and more expensive); it uses Litz wire to help overcome skin effect and has a double layer of shield braid, with the outer braid silver-coated. The silver coating supplies greater conductivity than ordinary copper braid. The coaxial cable illustrated in A is most widely used.

Dual coaxial cable. Sometimes two signals must be transferred independently. In that case twinned, or dual, coaxial cable is available (Fig.

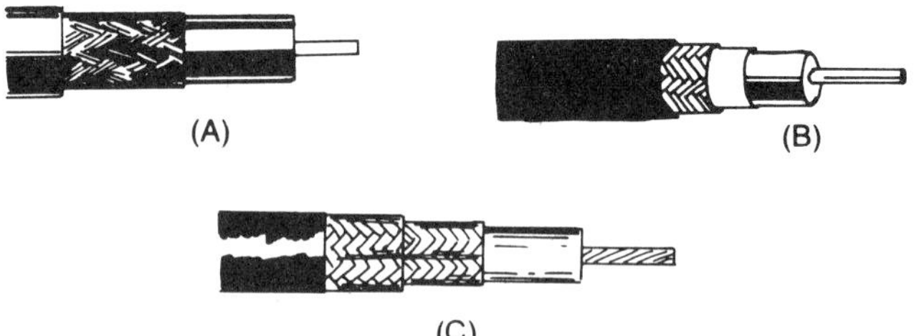

Figure 1-24. Unbalanced coaxial cable: single layer of braid (A); layer of foil beneath braid for better shielding (B); silver-coated double braid (C). (*Courtesy Precision Satellite Systems*)

1-25). Each of the two cables is unbalanced, and the two cables use a common protective outer covering. Aside from dual signal independence, such cable has the advantage of greater ease in installation when two cables must be used.

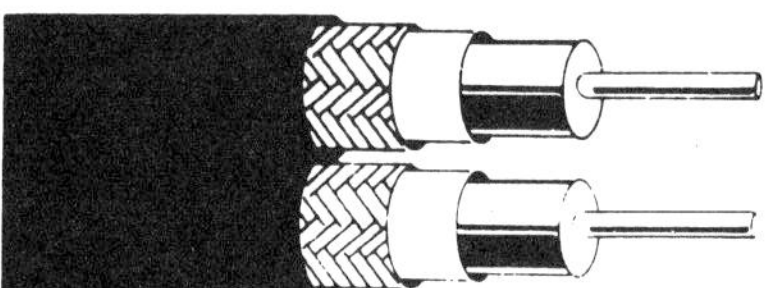

Figure 1-25. Dual coaxial cable. (*Courtesy Precision Satellite Systems*)

Messenger cable. For in-home satellite TV installations, it is not only necessary to supply coaxial cable for bringing the signal indoors, but also to use wiring to supply DC operating voltages for the dish motor—and also for the low-noise amplifier and downconverter, the solid-state components mounted on the dish structure. Unbalanced coaxial cable is used to handle the signal, and a single conductor can deliver the DC voltage. This can be done by using messenger cable (Fig. 1-26). The single conductor, either solid or stranded wire, is housed in its own coating of insulating material and is then joined to the coaxial cable. The single wire is the positive (plus) conductor for DC while the shield braid is used as the negative (minus) lead. The shield braid also works as the negative lead for the coaxial cable. The advantage of this arrangement is not only greater ease in installation, but the elimination of a separate ground lead for the DC voltage.

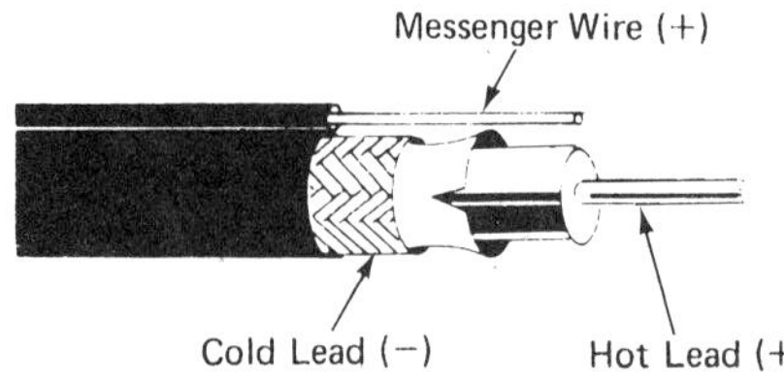

Figure 1-26. Messenger cable. (*Courtesy Precision Satellite Systems*)

Hardline. This is a type of unbalanced coaxial cable using a solid outside metallic shield instead of flexible conductive braid. Aside from this physical characteristic, hardline works much the same way as ordinary coax. It is used only for special applications, not including in-home entertainment systems.

Siamese cable. Siamese cable (Fig. 1–27) carries the concept of messenger cable an additional step and is used in connection with TVROs (television receive-only systems) in satellite TV. It consists of coaxial cable, plus three additional wires, two of which are color-coded white, the other black. The conductors and the cable are independent but are housed in a single jacket.

The black wire, sometimes called a drain, is the ground lead, so this arrangement does not make use of the shield braid as a common wire. One of the white wires is used for supplying a DC voltage to the low-noise amplifier and also to the downconverter mounted on the dish structure. The remaining white wire is used for supplying a DC voltage for a voltage-tuned oscillator (VTO). A VTO is a circuit whose frequency can be changed by the application of DC. The DC voltage is supplied by a satellite receiver in the home, and is used for channel selection.

Two of the white wires deliver DC; one must supply a constant voltage, usually 22 volts, to the low-noise amplifier and the downconverter, while the VTO supply is 8 volts, and is used intermittently.

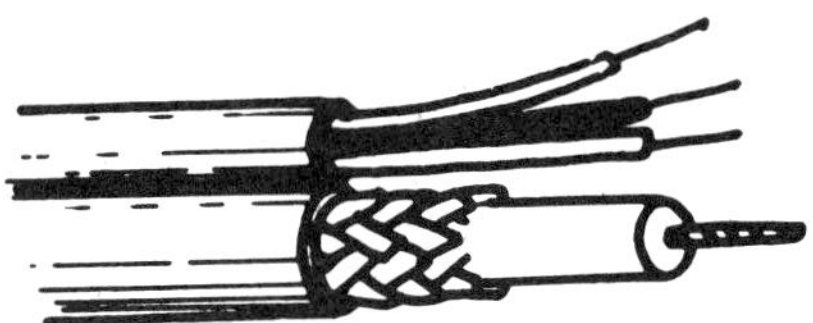

Figure 1–27. Siamese cable using RG-59 coax, plus two-conductor shielded wire and drain wire as the ground lead. (*Courtesy Precision Satellite Systems*)

Balanced Coaxial Cable

Balanced coaxial cable consists of two independent conductors in parallel throughout the length of the cable (Fig. 1–28). These are covered by plastic which, in turn, is surrounded by flexible metal braid. The two conductors

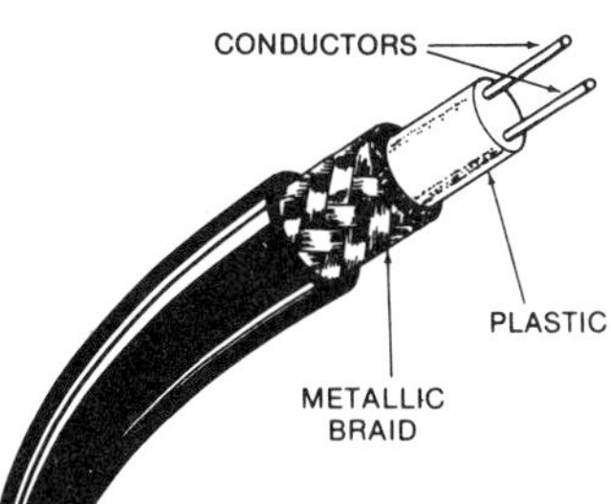

Figure 1–28. Balanced coaxial cable.

Type	Jacket O.D. Inch (mm)	Jacket Type	Shield	Dielectric O.D. & Type Inch (mm)	Center Conductor (mm)	pF/ft. (pF/m)	Nom. Imp. Ohms	Nominal Attenuation dB	
								MHz	100 ft.
59/U	.242 (6.15)	Black Vinyl	Bare copper 95% coverage	.146PE (3.71)	22 Ga. (.643) copperweld	21 (68.9)	73	100 200 400	3.4 4.9 7.1
59/U	.242 (6.15)	Black Vinyl	Bare copper 80% coverage	.146PE (3.71)	22 Ga. (.643) copperweld	21 (68.0)	73	100 200 400	3.4 4.9 7.1
59/U Stranded Center	.242	Black Vinyl	Bare copper 95% coverage	.146FPE (3.71)	22 Ga. 7×30 (.76) bare copper	17.37 (56.8)	75	100 200 400	3.0 4.4 6.5
59/U cable for 'F' 59 Connectors	.242 (6.15)	Black	Bonded aluminum +60% Alum. braid 100% coverage	.146FPE (3.71)	22 Ga. (.81) copperweld	17.3 (56.8)	75	50 100 200 500 900	1.8 2.6 3.8 6.2 8.4
62A/U	.242 (6.15)		Bare copper 95% coverage	.146SSPE (3.71)	22 Ga. (.81)	13.5 (44.3)	93	100 200 400 900	3.1 4.4 6.3 11.0
Video Double Braid	.304 (7.72)	Non-contaminating vinyl	Tinned copper double braid 98% coverage	.200PE (5.08)	20 Ga. (.813) bare copper	21 (68.9)	75	.01 .10 1 4.5 10 100	.06 .08 .25 .45 .78 2.70
213/U	.405 (10.29)	Black Vinyl	Bare copper 97% coverage	.285PE (7.24)	13 Ga. (2.17) bare copper	30.8 (101)	50	100 200 400 900	2.0 3.0 4.7 7.8
214/U	.425 (10.80)	Black Jacket	2 Silver coated copper 98% coverage	.285PE (7.24)	13 Ga. (2.26) silver coated copper	30.8 (101)	50	100 200 400 900	2.0 3.0 4.7 7.8
Dual RG/59 Coax Cable	.242 × .505	Black PVC	Bare copper 95% coverage	.146PE (3.71)	22 Ga. (.570) copperweld	20.5 (67.3)	75	100 200 400	3.5 5.1 7.5

Figure 1–29. Commonly used coaxial cables and their characteristics. (*Courtesy Marshall Electronics, Inc.*)

are used for carrying signals, and the braid serves as a shield against electrical noise and extraneous signals. The braid is usually grounded.

Coaxial Cable Identification

Coaxial cable is identified by type number, with each type having different physical and electrical characteristics (Fig. 1–29). For television work, the most commonly used cable is RG-59/U, simply indicated as 59/U. Quite often the center conductor is 22 gauge, adequate for in-home entertainment systems. Heavier wire gauges are used for commercial installations, such as the coaxial cable installed by television companies from their studios to their customers' homes.

SIGNAL LOSS

Signal loss in a transmission line because of weather depends on whether the transmission line is twin lead or coaxial cable. Signal loss in coaxial cable is the same whether the cable is wet or dry (Fig. 1–30), but twin lead is more affected by wet weather (Fig. 1–31). For twin lead, the closer the spacing of the two conductors, the greater the signal loss—whether the two-wire line is dry or wet—and the closer these conductors, the greater the capacitance of the line.

Signal loss in a cable is a function of its length. This is DC resistance loss and is caused by the ohmic resistance of the cable. For a limited frequency range this type of loss is not selective. Thus the DC resistance loss for a 50-MHz signal and for one of 55 MHz will be the same; it will also be the same for any of the frequencies in a band extending from 50 MHz to 55 MHz.

Another type of loss is frequency-selective. The inner conductor and the shield behave like any other capacitor; the higher the frequency, the lower the capacitive reactance. Consequently, if a band of frequencies is to be sent through a coaxial cable, and the passage of a band is usually the case, the

	MHz	57	85	177	213	500	650	800	900
dB Loss Per 100 Feet	Dry	2.1	2.5	3.6	3.8	5.9	6.8	7.7	8.0
	Wet	2.1	2.5	3.6	3.8	5.9	6.8	7.7	8.0

Figure 1–30. Signal loss in decibels for RG-59 coaxial cable. The loss does not change, whether the cable is dry or wet. (*Courtesy Channel Master, Div. Avnet, Inc.*)

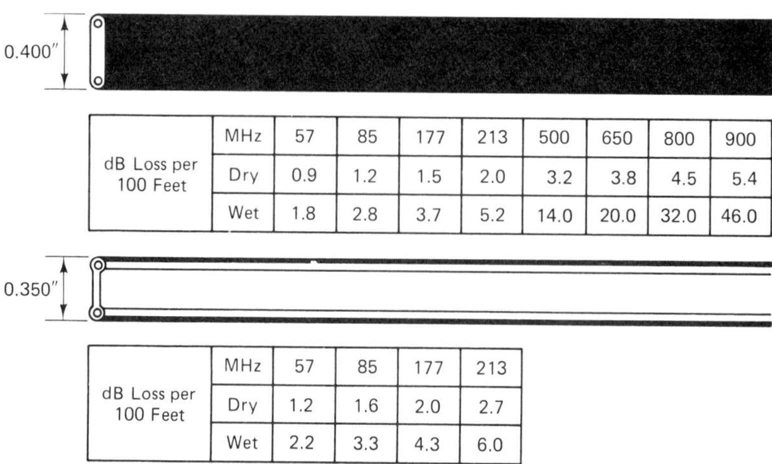

dB Loss per 100 Feet	MHz	57	85	177	213	500	650	800	900
	Dry	0.9	1.2	1.5	2.0	3.2	3.8	4.5	5.4
	Wet	1.8	2.8	3.7	5.2	14.0	20.0	32.0	46.0

dB Loss per 100 Feet	MHz	57	85	177	213
	Dry	1.2	1.6	2.0	2.7
	Wet	2.2	3.3	4.3	6.0

Figure 1-31. Signal losses in twin lead. (*Courtesy Channel Master, Div. Avnet, Inc.*)

bypassing action of the cable will be more effective at the high-frequency end of that band. As a result the higher frequencies may undergo some attenuation, while there will be very little loss for the lower frequencies. For audio frequencies whose range extends from 20 Hz to 20,000 Hz, the high-frequency loss will be insignificant. But for video frequencies whose upper frequency limit is 4.2 MHz the loss at this high-frequency end will result in degradation of fine picture detail. The amount of loss, then, depends on these four factors: DC resistance loss; amount of cable capacitance, usually supplied in picofarads; signal frequency; and losses in the dielectric.

Coaxial Cable Dielectric

The best dielectric to use in a coaxial cable is a vacuum, but this isn't a practical solution. A more realistic approach is to use air, but this leaves the problem of supporting the center conductor. In some earlier coaxial cables, a combination of plastic and air was used, with the shield braid concentrically supported by a series of rings made of plastic. As a result of this design, most of the dielectric was air, except for these plastic spacers.

Another technique is the use of foam, a dielectric containing a large percentage of air. Not all foam materials are alike; at the time the coaxial cable is made, plastic is mixed with air. The smaller the air bubbles, and the more numerous, the lower the possible dielectric signal loss.

Dielectric signal loss is as applicable to twin lead as it is to coaxial cable. And, as in coax, foam-filled twin lead can be used instead of solid plastic.

Coaxial Cable Attenuation

The four factors resulting in cable signal loss, described above, depend on the type of cable used, the frequency, and the length of the cable. RG-59/U, the type of coaxial cable most commonly used for video, has a signal loss of 2.6 dB per 100 feet for channel 2, increasing to 10.3 dB for UHF channel 60, for the same length of cable (Fig. 1-32). Note the smaller attenuation figures for the same cable but one that is foam filled instead of using a solid plastic dielectric.

The coaxial cable having the lowest attenuation is .500 cable, a type indicated by its outside dimension (one-half inch) and not by any specific cable number. For channel 2, this cable has an attenuation of 0.52 dB per 100 feet. However, the cable is more expensive than the other types and is more difficult to handle.

Twin lead has a smaller attenuation level than coaxial cable and this is evident whether the twin lead is wet or dry.

Cable Characteristics									
Nominal Attenuation dB Per 100 Feet									
Cable	Ch. 2	Ch. 6	Ch. 7	Ch. 13	Ch. 20	Ch. 30	Ch. 40	Ch. 50	Ch. 60
Color Duct	2.3	2.7	3.8	4.2	6.5	7.0	7.5	7.8	8.0
Foam Color Duct	2.1	2.5	3.3	3.8	5.9	6.3	6.7	7.0	7.3
RG-59/U	2.6	3.5	4.9	5.4	8.3	8.8	9.2	9.7	10.3
RG-59/U Foam	2.3	2.7	3.8	4.2	6.2	6.6	6.8	7.1	7.3
RG-6 Foam	1.7	1.9	2.8	3.0	4.8	5.2	5.6	5.9	6.2
RG-11/U	1.4	1.7	2.2	3.2	5.1	5.3	5.5	5.7	6.1
RG-11/U Foam	1.1	1.4	1.6	2.3	3.9	4.0	4.1	4.2	4.4
.412 Cable	.74	1.0	1.4	1.5	2.5	2.6	2.7	2.9	3.1
.500 Cable	.52	.67	.72	1.1	1.5	1.8	2.1	2.4	2.7

Figure 1-32. Attenuation of various types of coaxial cable for specific channels.

Associated Transmission Line Losses

There are other losses in the use of transmission lines such as twin lead and coaxial cable. These losses cannot really be charged to the line but to the way in which the line is used and to passive devices inserted in the line. The losses can be due to impedance mismatching and the use of add-on parts such as transformers.

ELECTRICAL CHARACTERISTICS OF COAXIAL CABLE

The electrical characteristics of coaxial cable can be categorized as attenuation, capacitance, insulation voltage rating, and current-carrying capacity. For in-home video systems, the insulation voltage rating and current-carrying capacity are not of interest, as the signal voltage and signal currents are so low as to be well within limits. The two remaining factors, capacitance and attenuation, are significant.

Coaxial cables meet the definition of a capacitor; that is, any pair of metal plates separated by a dielectric. In the case of cable the metal plates are the central conductor; and the shield braid, with the separating material, is the dielectric. When a video signal is delivered to coaxial cable, the first requirement is that the capacitance of the cable must be charged. The capacitance of the cable takes signal precedence over the load and must be charged before the load can receive its full signal voltage. If the cable capacitance is large enough, the load may never receive its full voltage and in this instance the capacitance behaves somewhat like a filter. The capacitance of the cable can also degenerate the shape of the signal waveforms. To keep the cable capacitance at a minimum, it is preferable for the cable to have a low dielectric constant (k). This characteristic is usually measured at a selected temperature, often 25° C. The dielectric constant may decrease with an increase in frequency, although for some dielectrics it remains fairly uniform.

The dielectric constant for dry air is 1, for polystyrene 2.5, for glass 4.3, for mica and porcelain, 5.5; for pure water it is 81. The dielectric constant can also vary depending on the purity of the dielectric—temperature, moisture, and voltage. Because the outer jacket of coaxial cable is fairly impervious to water, its dielectric constant remains steady over a wide frequency range. This does not apply to twin lead.

Polyethylene is frequently used, as its dielectric constant is about 2.23 compared to vinyl, which may be from less than 3 to more than 6.

The attenuation of coaxial cable can be lowered by using conductors with greater thickness, by using metals having higher orders of conductivity, and by low-loss insulation. The hot lead of coaxial cables, used by cable companies for the delivery of signals to their subscribers, is much thicker than that in coaxial cable used as the downlead in a home TV system.

HIGH-DEFINITION CABLES

Advertising claims for cables are sometimes noted more for their enthusiasm than for their accuracy, and some connecting cables used for video are sometimes described as high-definition cables. However, as all cables are passive devices, no cable can improve any signal. The best any cable can do is not deteriorate the signals significantly at the high-frequency end. Signal losses can occur in a cable because of its DC resistance, its high-frequency resistance, and its overall capacitance. DC resistance and connector resistance due to oxidation produce a loss at all frequencies and result in a uniform voltage drop along the cable, hence the best cable is the shortest cable. High-frequency resistance, in which current tends to flow more along the outer portion of the conductor, also causes a loss. Cable capacitance produces a variable bypassing effect, increasing with frequency. Presumably, a high-definition cable is one that has a minimum amount of capacitance per foot and low DC resistance, and it will supply a large conducting surface for reducing high-frequency resistance. Manufacturing coaxial cable is a matter of a trade-off between what is desirable and what is practical. A coaxial cable might have very low capacitance, very low DC resistance, and very low high-frequency resistance, but it might be so bulky that it would be impossible to install or connect to components. Claims for coaxial cable can be checked by comparing the specifications (specs) of one cable with those of another for use in the same application.

AUDIO CABLES

There are coaxial cables for video, and there are similar cables for audio. Such cables use a central conductor surrounded by plastic, which, in turn, is surrounded by shield braid (Fig. 1-33). The shield braid has an outer covering of a plastic material. While audio cables are constructed along the lines of coaxial cable, they are seldom referred to as such. The signal bypassing effect due to cable capacitance isn't a problem, as audio signals are at a much lower frequency than video signals. Similarly, the DC resistance isn't very significant, as audio cables, with a few exceptions, are quite short.

Audio cables do not include extra wires such as Siamese or messenger cables. For connecting audio components, for instance, a turntable, to the input of a receiver or preamplifier, shielded wire is used. These cables are supplied in convenient lengths, starting at about three feet, often preattached.

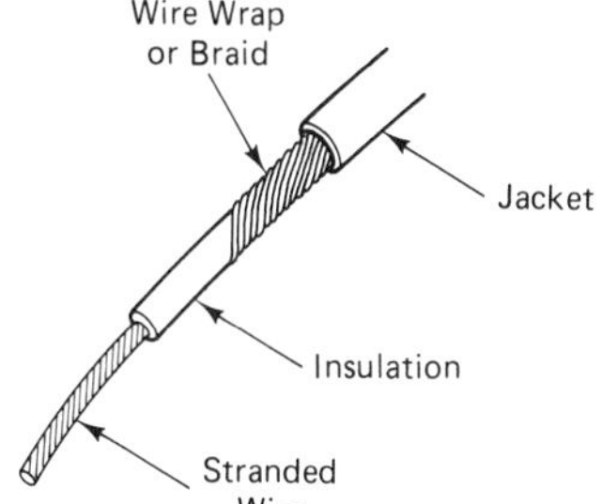

Figure 1-33. Audio cable.

CABLE TYPES

Audio cables are available in a great variety—variety in quality as well as in other characteristics. It is practically impossible to determine the quality of a cable just by looking at it, but superior types of audio cable have a cotton wrap over the center hot conductor, helping to keep that conductor from shorting against the cold, or ground, metal braid that surrounds it. This is a possibility if the insulating material between the center conductor and the shield braid degenerates because of age or flexing. The outermost insulating layer may be rubber but polyethylene is used more often. Rubber is a vegetable product and while antioxidants are used in its manufacture it will, in time, become brittle and crack. Polyethylene isn't as flexible as rubber, but doesn't have its aging characteristic. Further, it is a more economical material. Some cables use so-called chrome vinyl as the outer covering or jacket, a material characterized by its shiny appearance. It, too, is less flexible than rubber.

Microphone Cables

Microphone cables can be balanced or unbalanced, and, like audio or video cables, they are available in a number of grades of quality. Microphone cables are members of the audio coaxial cable family but in this instance are identified by their use.

The lower grades of microphone cable have a center conductor covered with thermoplastic insulation. The shield, instead of braid, is a spiral wrap of wire. This is a more economical manufacturing method and uses less material than shield braid. The wire wrap is covered with a vinyl jacket. The difficulty of using this material for the jacket is that it is rather stiff, making the cable difficult to handle when long runs are to be used. Quality cables cost more but in the long run are less troublesome and need replacement less often.

If a microphone is to be fixed in position, mounted permanently on a lectern or on a microphone stand, cables having a diameter of 1/4 inch to 5/16 inch can be used, but this thickness makes the cable stiffer, and consequently more difficult to handle. If the microphone is to be carried, the cable should be flexible, with a thickness of about 3/16 inch.

If cables are in an area where there is pedestrian traffic, and this is possible on a stage or outdoors, arrange the cables so they are out of the way of foot movement.

Speaker Cables

Speaker wires are often zip cord (lamp cord). It is essential that speaker wires be coded, as the polarity of the connections on the output of an amplifier must match the polarity of the connections on the speaker enclosure. Further details on cables and their connections to speakers are supplied in Chapter 6.

Jones Cable

The Jones cable, also known as a TV control cable, is characterized by an 8-pin plug for carrying both video and audio signals. A Jones cable belongs to the multiconductor family. TV receiver/monitors may be equipped with 8-pin sockets for a Jones cable connection. Jones cables are also used for connecting a video cassette recorder to a TV receiver-monitor.

Adapter Cable

The adapter cable is an accessory cable that permits the connection of a video cassette recorder to a video camera when these have incompatible terminals. Cameras and portable VCRs sometimes cannot be connected when these components are made by different manufacturers. The fact that a cable plug will fit into a jack does not necessarily indicate compatibility.

CABLE LENGTH

In a few instances, cable length must be a variable. For an outdoor concert or for a limited-performance indoor concert the required lengths of the audio cables connecting the microphones to a mixer will depend on location. Similarly, the cables connecting the power amps to the speakers will not always be the same. For an outdoor demonstration of a satellite TV system, the length of the coaxial cable from the dish to a satellite receiver may be an unknown variable. All of these are temporary situations, so the cables may be much longer than is desirable.

For an in-home installation, most of the wiring is behind a rack holding audio and video components. The longest run of cable is from the antenna (or antennas) into the home. Here, if the cable is too long, there may be a tendency to roll up the excess and hide it behind a rack. Not only could this damage the cable, but the stress put on it could produce a difficult-to-find intermittent.

With an increasing number of components in an audio-video system, the cabling network behind the rack can become a region of complete confusion. Excess unshielded twin lead from an antenna can only make the mess worse. It is also possible for the wire to work as an antenna, picking up extraneous signals, a problem difficult to pinpoint when connections have been made and a system is operating.

Ideally, a signal shouldn't need to travel any distance from one component to another. This kind of thinking, while correct, can lead to some impractical wiring situations. If a number of components are to be interfaced, the connecting cables behind a rack should be slack enough so that any one of the components can be turned around, independently of all the others, for examination of the wiring, if the rack cannot be swung around for this purpose. If there is no cable slack, it may be necessary to disconnect some or all of the cables, and this can be a nuisance when the cables must be reconnected.

IDENTIFYING CABLES

When it becomes necessary to interconnect a number of components or to reconnect them at some later date when one or more units are added, the large number of connecting leads, particularly if they are similarly color coded, can be confusing, making it quite possible to join components that should not interface. A simple solution is to put an identifying label on each cable, at its beginning and at its end. As a memory aid, keep a sketch or at least a list of the wiring, including a very brief description of the components that are connected.

CABLE CARE

The care required by cables depends on several factors: climate (whether humid or not); area (whether near large bodies of salt water); whether used indoors or out; and amount of handling, if any.

Cables used on a stage, or for connecting microphones to some remote mixer (indoors or outdoors), and cables of unusual length require much more handling than short lengths permanently connected and used only indoors. Cables that must be repeatedly connected and disconnected are going to suffer much more abuse. But even under poor environmental and operating conditions, cables should last for many years if they are properly used and handled.

If the cables are in an area where there is pedestrian traffic, and this is possible on a stage or outdoors, arrange the cables so they are out of the way of foot movement.

CABLE QUALITY

Not all cables are alike, even though a physical examination may not reveal any differences. Poorer quality cables may have a spiral wire wrap instead of braid. A quality cable will have minimum DC resistance from one end of the cable to the other. It will also have low capacitance, measured in picofarads (pF) per foot. It is advisable to avoid cables whose specs indicate a capacitance of 25 pF or more.

A better-grade cable will have a noncompressible insulating material between the center conductor and the braid. If a compressible material is used, crimping the cable, necessary when putting on its connectors, may permit the central conductor to cut through the foam material, shorting the cable.

Many cables use a central conductor made only of stranded copper wire. Copper is a good electrical conductor, but it does lack strength if the cable is repeatedly flexed. This is not a problem for an in-home installation, as cables remain fixed in position, but it can cause difficulties for on-location work. A better cable consists of a seven-strand steel-plated copper.

IMPEDANCE

Impedance is one of the most widely used words in describing the connections of electronics components. These can have an output impedance only, an input impedance only, input and output impedance, or a variety of both input and output impedances.

The greater the impedance of a device, the smaller the current flow. However, for the most part components used in home entertainment systems are voltage operated as far as signal inputs and outputs are concerned. Thus, for an antenna, we are interested in the signal voltage it delivers. For a tuner, our interest is in signal voltage input and output. For a TV, set the input is a signal voltage and a signal voltage is delivered to the picture tube. The main exception is the loudspeaker; it is a current-operated device, and what we want here is low impedance.

Impedance of Coaxial Cable

Coaxial cable has an electrical property referred to variously as *characteristic* or *surge impedance,* but this specification, indicated in ohms and represented by the letter *Z,* is independent of length and is due to the distributed inductance and capacitance of the cable (Fig. 1–34). Generally, the amount of capacitance is shown in cable specifications in picofarads per foot, but inductance is often ignored. Characteristic impedance in terms of a formula is:

$$Z = \sqrt{L/C}$$

In which *Z* is the impedance in ohms, *L* the inductance in henries and *C* the capacitance in farads. The inductance and the capacitance are assumed to be uniformly distributed along the length of the cable, and the characteristic impedance is the same for any amount of cable. A cable having an impedance of 75 ohms has the same impedance for a length of 10 feet or 300 feet, or any other length.

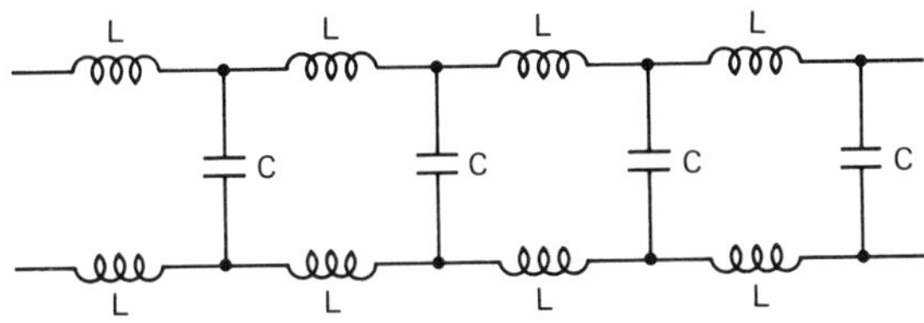

Figure 1–34. Distributed capacitance and inductance of coaxial cable.

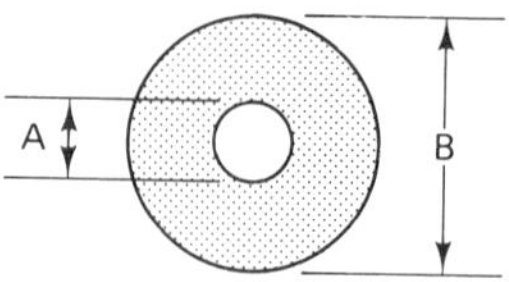

Figure 1-35. Physical characteristics of coaxial cable for the calculation of surge impedance.

Impedance is the vector sum of resistance and reactance, but in the generalized formula just supplied, resistance is ignored. Its value is so small compared to that of reactance that it can be disregarded.

The characteristic impedance is a factor determined prior to manufacturing and is directly dependent on the physical dimensions of the cable (Fig. 1-35). In this drawing, *A* represents the outside diameter of the inner conductor (the hot lead) while *B* is the inside diameter of the shield (the cold lead). When you know these dimensions, the impedance can be calculated.

$$Z = 138 \log_{10} (B/A)$$

Z is the characteristic impedance in ohms, while *A* and *B* can be any measurement units, provided they are the same (that is, inches, centimeters, and so on).

The selection of 75 ohms as the characteristic impedance for cables for video is no accident. Experiments have indicated that the ratio of B to A in the formula for characteristic impedance should have a value of 3.6 for obtaining the lowest cable losses. Using 3.6 as the ratio results in an impedance of 76.77 ohms but it is more convenient to refer to the cable as 75 ohms. However, coaxial cables having other impedances ranging from 50 ohms to 150 ohms are used for other applications when certain physical characteristics of the cable are more significant than the impedance.

This formula for impedance is empirical—derived experimentally. It is based solely on the dimensions of the cable and does not take inductive reactance, capacitive reactance, or resistance (whether AC or DC) into consideration.

While impedance is measured or calculated in ohms, the characteristic impedance of a coaxial line cannot be measured with an ohmmeter, for that instrument will only measure the DC resistance of the conductors. Further, in the case of unbalanced coaxial cable these two conductors, the inner wire and the outside shield, can have different values of resistance when measured individually. However, since the ohmmeter is DC operated the value of resistance obtained is the DC resistance—interesting, but not too significant, as the coaxial cable is used for high-frequency currents. Consequently, the AC resistance, immeasurable with the ohmmeter, is not the same as the DC resistance and, depending on frequency, can be higher.

The DC resistance of coaxial cable can be calculated from:

$$R_0 = P_0 L/s$$

R_0 is the resistance in ohms; P_0 is the coefficient of resistance for the kind of material used as the conductor; L is the length of the conductor measured in meters, and s is the cross-sectional area of the conductor in square meters. For a solid conductor such as the center conductor of unbalanced coaxial cable, the use of the formula is simple enough, but the wire mesh constituting the outer shield isn't as easily calculated. However, the formula does supply a good approximation for DC and very low frequency currents up to 60 Hz.

One of the problems involved in measuring the resistance of coaxial cable is that of skin effect (described earlier), a tendency of high-frequency currents to move toward the surface of the conductor. In effect, the inner material of the conductor plays no role in the passage of the current; that is best exemplified in waveguide, a type of transmission line in which no central conductor is used at all.

There is a formula that takes both frequency and physical characteristics into consideration:

$$R_s = (4.16)10^{-8} \times \sqrt{f\left(\frac{1}{A} + \frac{1}{B}\right)}$$

Rs is the calculated value of resistance in ohms/meter at the skin effect frequency, *f*, and *A* and *B* are the dimensions of the cable conductors as indicated earlier.

Impedance of Twin Lead

The characteristic impedance of two-wire transmission line can be calculated from:

$$Z = \frac{275}{\sqrt{K}} \log_{10} \frac{b}{a}$$

K is the dielectric constant of the material between the parallel conductors and its value is 1 for air. When polyethylene is used the value of K is 0.675. The characteristic impedance of twin lead usually ranges from 50 to 300 ohms, but for TV the impedance chosen is generally 300 ohms, selected to match the impedance of the antenna and the 300-ohm input impedance at the antenna terminals of the television set. In the formula supplied above, *b* is the spacing, center to center of the conductors, and *a* is the diameter of the conductors (see Fig. 1–36).

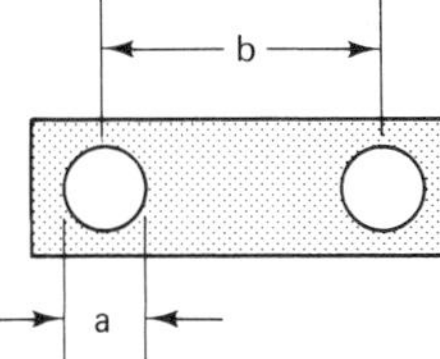

Figure 1–36. Physical characteristics for determining the impedance of two-wire line.

Cable length is not included in the formula. The impedance of the line is independent of length, just as in the case of coaxial cable. A section of this line would be 300 ohms for a 1-foot piece or for a length of 200 feet, assuming both are cut from the same reel. However, the DC resistance of the line increases linearly with length. Consequently, the longer the line, the greater the signal loss.

Impedance Variations

Since the impedance of coaxial cable and of twin lead is the same anywhere along its length, its input impedance—the points at which it receives signal voltage from the antenna—and its output impedance—the component terminals to which it is connected—are identical. However, a component, such as a receiver, can have one impedance at its input, another at its output. A receiver used in a high-fidelity system could have an input impedance at its antenna terminals of 300 ohms, and an output impedance of 8 ohms, the points at which it is connected to a speaker. A TV set can have a pair of input impedances, one of 75 ohms, the other 300 ohms.

IMPEDANCE MATCHING

To obtain the maximum signal from the antenna and to minimize or eliminate ghosts, the connecting link between the antenna and the antenna input terminals of the TV set—the downlead or transmission line—must match both impedances, that of the antenna and that of the TV set.

Figure 1-37A is an example of automatic impedance matching. The folded dipole has an output impedance of 300 ohms. These are the terminals on the antenna to which the 300-ohm transmission line, the downlead, is connected. No impedance matching devices are required, as both devices have the same impedance: the output impedance of the antenna and the input impedance of the downlead. At the TV receiver, the impedance across the input terminals is also 300 ohms. Note that we are concerned with impedance matching at two places: between the antenna and the transmission line, and between the transmission line and the TV set.

The same situation exists in drawing B, where a 75-ohm open dipole antenna is connected by coaxial cable to a TV set. The dipole has an output impedance of 75 ohms and so does the coaxial cable to which it is connected. At the receiver the antenna input terminals are 75 ohms. As in drawing A, we have automatic impedance matching throughout. In both examples this type of impedance matching is best and easiest to connect; it results in the maximum transfer of signal from the antenna to the transmission line, and from the transmission line to the TV receiver.

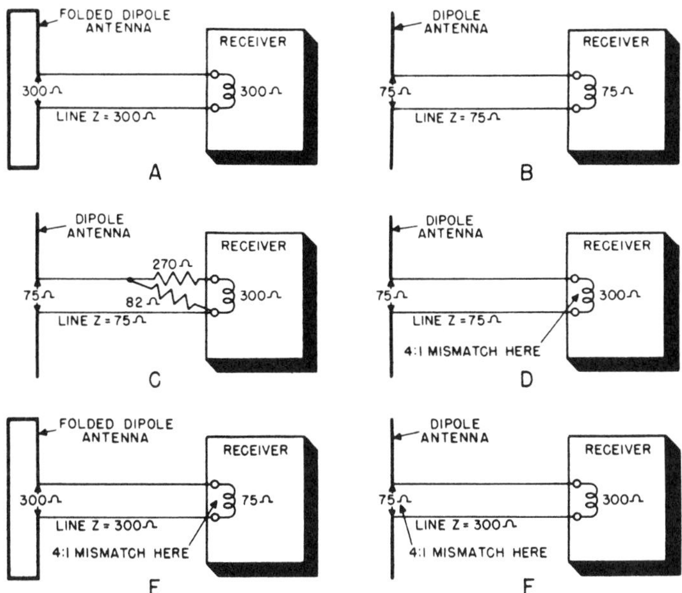

Figure 1–37. Matched and mismatched impedances.

The transmission line has both an input impedance and an output impedance, consequently the line must be matched at both ends. This leads to several possibilities. It may be matched at both ends, or at just one end, or at neither end.

In drawing C, the 75-ohm impedance of the open dipole antenna matches the 75-ohm impedance of the coaxial cable connected to it. However, the input impedance of the TV receiver is 300 ohms. To effect an impedance match here, the antenna terminals of the receiver are shunted by a 270-ohm resistor in series with one having a value of 82 ohms. While this network does provide impedance matching, there is signal loss in a resistive arrangement. A preferable arrangement is to use a 75-ohm-to-300-ohm matching transformer, an add-on unit described in more detail in Chapter 3.

If, as is indicated in drawing D, a 75-ohm coaxial cable connects to a 75-ohm dipole, impedances will be matched at the antenna. Since the receiver has a 300-ohm input there will be a 4:1 mismatch.

In drawing E, the 300-ohm folded dipole is correctly impedance matched to the 300-ohm two-wire transmission line, but there is a 4:1 mismatch at the 75-ohm input of the receiver. Drawing F shows a 300-ohm two-wire transmission line correctly matched to the 300-ohm input of the TV receiver, but there is a 4:1 mismatch at the dipole antenna.

Matching and Mismatching Impedances

Devices are said to be impedance matched when the maximum available signal is transferred between a pair of interfacing devices. Mismatching is a reference to the lack of impedance matching between interfacing units. Impedance mismatching reduces the amount of signal transfer.

LOW *Z* AND HIGH *Z*

Although the impedance of 75-ohm line and 300-ohm line are approximations, they are fairly accurate. However, there are instances when general impedance values are used. Thus the output impedance of a microphone is often specified as low impedance or high impedance. Low-impedance, moving-coil microphones have typical impedance values in the range of 50 to 250 ohms, but more commonly 150 to 200 ohms. For high-impedance microphones the values are approximately 50,000 ohms. Instead of indicating these generalized amounts, microphones are more often referred to as low impedance or low *Z*, or high impedance or high *Z*.

VOLTAGE STANDING-WAVE-RATIO

The voltage standing wave ratio, abbreviated as the VSWR of a transmission line is the difference between the maximum and the minimum voltage along that line. Ideally, the best VSWR is unity, a ratio of 1:1. VSWR is also an indication of the loss of signal energy along a transmission line due to reflected signal energy from the load to the source. This can happen, for example, if the impedance of a transmission line is not matched by the impedance across the antenna terminals of a TV set. Some of the signal is accepted by the TV receiver, working as a load, but the remainder of the signal energy will be reflected along the transmission line, back to the antenna. At that point it will be returned via the transmission line to the TV set. This reflected signal, plus the original signal, will be delivered to the antenna terminals. Since two signals have now been presented, the reflected signal will appear as ghost, displaced on the screen because of the travel time of the reflected signal from the antenna terminals, back to the antenna, and then back to the receiver again.

Because of the impedance mismatch, the process is a repetitive one, and it is possible to have a number of ghost signals appearing on the TV screen.

Figure 1–38 shows a chart indicating various values of VSWR. Note that the poorer the VSWR, the greater the percentage of signal reflection.

VSWR	Reflection Coefficient	Percentage Reflection	VSWR	Reflection Coefficient	Percentage Reflection
8.71	0.790	79%	1.110	0.050	5.0%
4.42	0.630	63%	1.080	0.040	4.0%
3.01	0.500	50%	1.070	0.032	3.2%
2.32	0.400	40%	1.050	0.025	2.5%
1.92	0.320	32%	1.040	0.020	2.0%
1.67	0.250	25%	1.032	0.016	1.6%
1.50	0.200	20%	1.026	0.013	1.3%
1.37	0.160	16%	1.020	0.010	1.0%
1.28	0.130	13%	1.010	0.005	0.5%
1.22	0.100	10%	1.006	0.003	0.3%
1.17	0.079	7.9%	1.004	0.002	0.2%
1.13	0.063	6.3%	1.002	0.001	0.1%

Figure 1-38. Return loss/VSWR chart.

If, as is indicated in Fig. 1-39, we could make the transmission line infinitely long, there would be no wave reflections, as the signal would never reach the load—in this case the antenna terminals of the TV set. However, when the impedance of the TV receiver's input matches the impedance of the transmission line, the effect is just as though we had made that line infinitely long.

As an example, a TV receiver having an input impedance of 300 ohms can match a transmission line also having this impedance. All of the signal is delivered to the TV receiver and none of it is returned to the antenna. The same result could be achieved by disconnecting the receiver from the transmission line and substituting a 300-ohm resistor for it. The signals developed across the resistor would be in the form of heat, and none of the signal would be returned to the antenna. The amount of heat produced, of course, would be slight, so much so that it could not possibly be detected by touching.

WAVEGUIDE

We can categorize waves as guided or unguided. A guided wave is one that is conducted from one point to another via some type of transmission line such as twin lead, coaxial cable, or waveguide. An unguided wave is any wave that is broadcast—a wave that is transmitted by and received by antennas and that travels through space.

When the magnetic field accompanying an unguided wave cuts across an antenna, it induces a voltage across it. This is the signal voltage that is delivered to the signal input terminals of a component such as a TV set or a VCR via a transmission line.

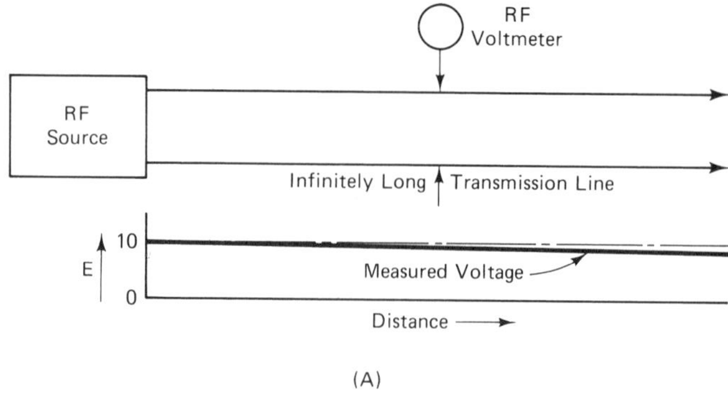

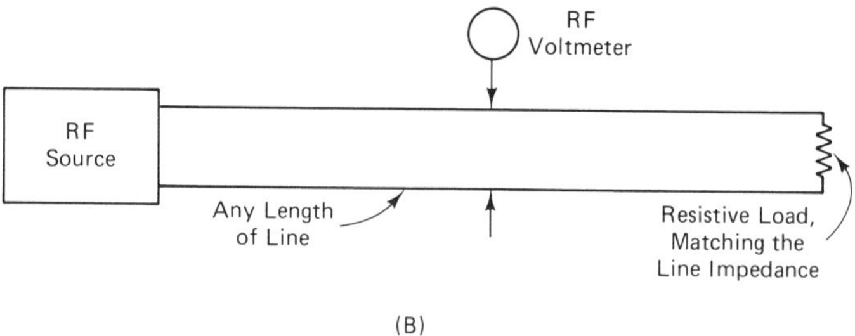

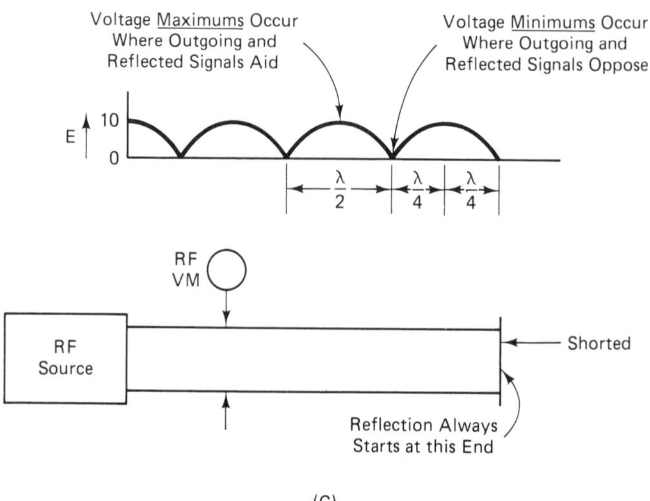

Figure 1–39. If transmission line is infinitely long (A) there are no wave reflections. Resistive load (B) that matches the surge impedance of the line makes the line behave as if it were infinitely long. Signal reflections (C) always start at the load.

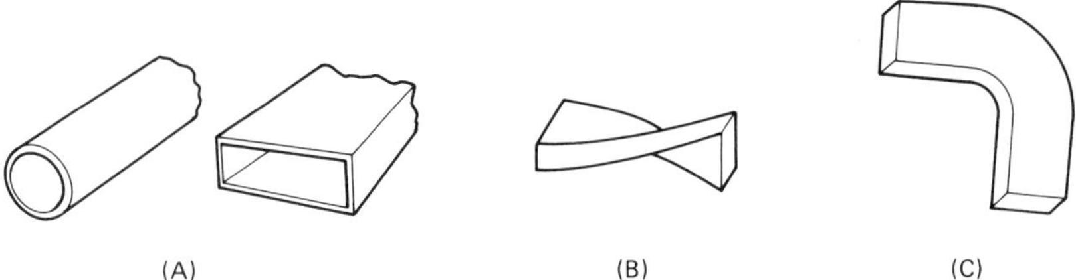

Figure 1-40. Waveguide (A) can be rectangular or tubular; twisted (B); or bent to a right angle (C).

There is another type of transmission line, in addition to twin lead or coaxial cable, and it is known as *waveguide.* Waveguide looks like a piece of rectangular or tubular pipe, as is shown in Fig. 1-40A. And, just like twin lead or coaxial cable it can be twisted (drawing B) or can be made to assume a right angle (C). As with other transmission lines, the input impedance of a section of waveguide can be changed by modifying its shape and this can be done in various ways. Drawing A in Fig. 1-41 shows a flared waveguide; B shows another impedance matching technique, and C shows how impedance matching is accomplished with flared tubular waveguide.

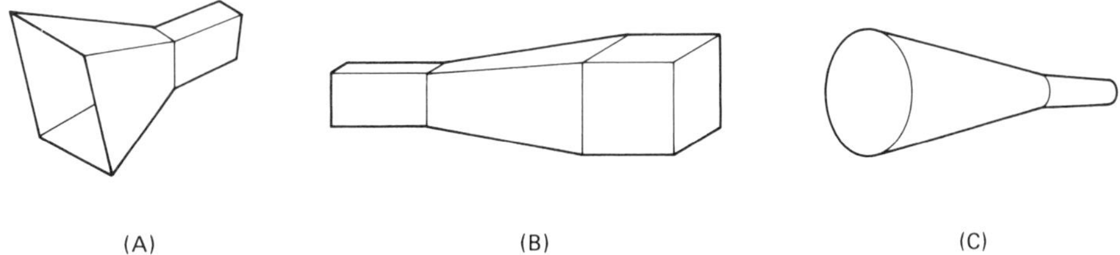

Figure 1-41. Flared waveguide (A); impedance matching section (B); flared tubular waveguide (C).

Waveguide is used for in-home satellite TV systems (described more fully in Chapter 8). As is shown in Fig. 1-42, the magnetic field of a transmitted signal is directed toward the input of the waveguide. This magnetic field moves down the waveguide until it cuts across the small exposed end of the hot lead of a section of coaxial cable. This end of the coaxial cable extends into the open space of the waveguide, and the shield braid of the cable makes good electrical contact with its outside surface. A signal voltage is developed across the small open portion of the coaxial cable, working as an antenna. This voltage is then delivered via the coaxial cable to a preamplifier and ultimately to an in-home satellite TV receiver.

The advantage of waveguide is that it can be used as a transmission line at extremely high frequencies, in the gigahertz (GHz) region, frequencies at

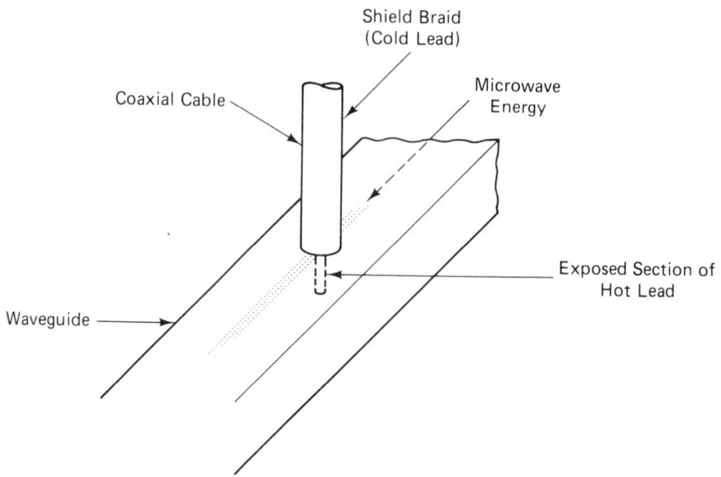

Figure 1–42. Junction of coaxial cable and waveguide, with cable's exposed hot lead functioning as an antenna.

which twin lead or coaxial cable would have tremendous signal losses. The use of waveguide as a transmission line will become more important as ever higher frequencies are used for signal transmission.

G-String Waveguide

Hollow waveguides are commonly used for extremely high radio frequencies, but there are other types not as commonplace. One of these, known as a *G-string,* is a single conductor sometimes used as waveguide.

Microwave Strip

This is a relatively unknown type of waveguide consisting of a flat conducting strip having a certain amount of spacing relative to a ground plane. Neither the G-string waveguide nor the microwave strip are presently being used as transmission lines for the delivery of signals to an in-home entertainment system. For that matter, neither rectangular nor tubular waveguides were used at one time for TV and audio signals, but now they are quite common.

DIAGRAMS

Some in-home entertainment systems are so elementary and use so few components that wiring is practically no problem at all. An in-home entertainment system can be quite complex, but it can also consist of nothing more than a single TV receiver. This unit comes equipped with a built-in antenna—a telescoping type for VHF reception, and a circular type for UHF. All that is necessary is to plug the unit into the nearest convenient AC power outlet and the TV system is ready to function. This is a minimum setup and is limited to broadcast TV, while the two built-in antennas provide minimum, marginal reception. Other systems, especially combined audio/video and some of the newer complete in-home control systems, are so elaborate that some sort of electronic road map—a diagram—is needed. There are a number of different kinds of diagrams. Some require no knowledge of electronics. Others are more complex and assume a technical background on the part of the user.

The Block Diagram

The block diagram consists of a series of rectangular blocks with each block representing some component of a system or circuit (Fig. 1-43). The advantage of such a diagram is that it shows the relationship of the electronic components to one another.

Usually the blocks are connected by single lines, even though the actual connection may require a pair of conductors. Further, the block diagram does not supply information about the kinds of connecting wires to use; that is, whether that wire is shielded or not, nor is data given about the types of connectors. When components are added, a block diagram of an existing system may indicate a possible number of positions for the inclusion of the component. For interconnecting the components of a video or high-fidelity system, the block diagram often indicates the path a signal will take from the input of a system to its output.

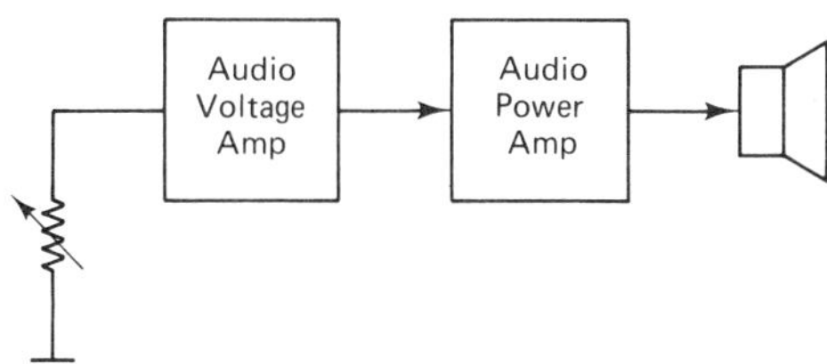

Figure 1-43. Block diagram.

The Pictorial Diagram

A pictorial diagram is a diagram that makes use of drawings or photos, or some combination of the two, with lines drawn to indicate the interconnections (Fig. 1-44). In this respect it is very much like the block diagram, but because of its picture form it is easier to identify each component. Like the block diagram, the pictorial does not supply information about the cables and their connectors. The pictorial diagram, however, is ideal for those who

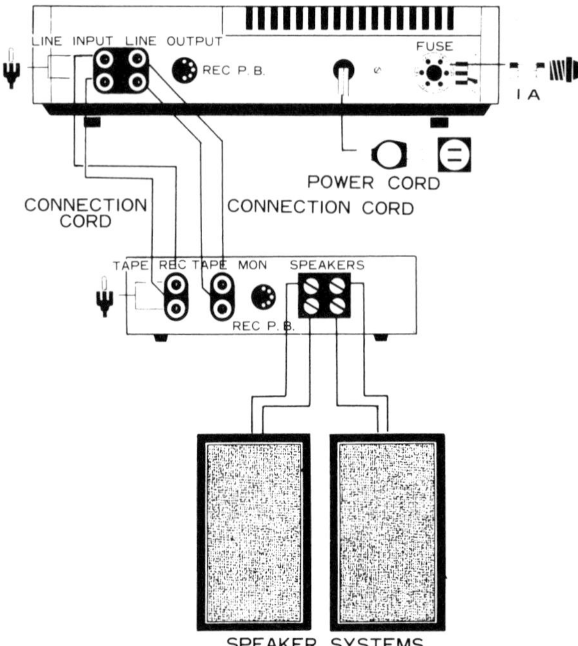

Figure 1-44. Pictorial diagram. (*Courtesy Pioneer Electronics* [*USA*], *Corp.*)

have a limited knowledge of electronic components and feel more comfortable with a pictorial form.

Manufacturers prefer pictorial diagrams and often include them in the operating instructions supplied with a component. The diagram may show the front view of one or more units, while a back view will identify the way in which connections are to be made.

The Wiring Diagram

This type of diagram, shown in Fig. 1-45, illustrates the connections between components, usually in pictorial form. Often, the type of wire used is marked on the diagram and in some instances a view of the terminal points, such as the antenna input block on the back of a TV set, is supplied.

Diagrams aren't always used on a one-alone basis. You may want to examine a block diagram to get an idea of the relationships of the components to each other or possibly a concept of signal movement through a system, followed by a pictorial to identify those components, and finally, a wiring diagram as an aid in making connections.

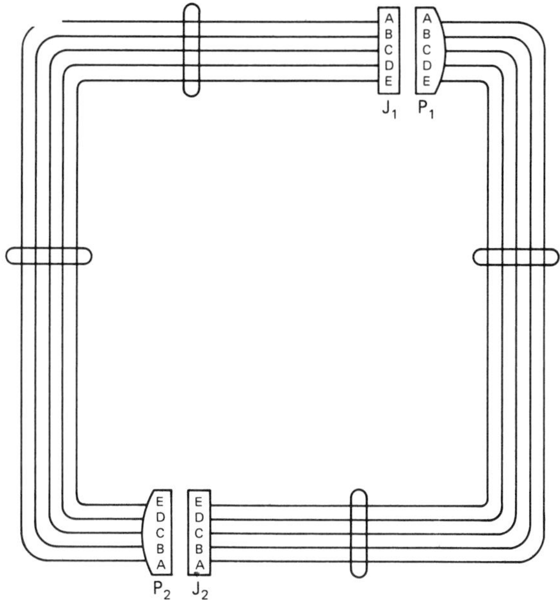

Figure 1–45. Wiring diagram for flat cable.

The Circuit Diagram

Of all the diagrams, the circuit diagram (Fig. 1–46) is the most complex, requiring a knowledge of the symbols used to represent parts plus an understanding of electronics. Such a diagram isn't suitable for wiring components, for interwiring information isn't supplied. The diagrams do show the various inputs and outputs and switching arrangements, if any. They often supply parts values and voltages at various points and are useful when repairs are to be made. A circuit diagram can supply information about the movement of the signal voltage, and the kinds of circuits that are used. It may also show the internal wiring, sections in which printed circuit (PC) boards are used, and the types of transistors or integrated circuits (ICs). However, connecting components to each other to form a system does not require a knowledge of electronics, just as an understanding of the internal combustion engine isn't needed for driving a car.

Mixed Diagrams

In some instances, possibly for the sake of clarity or for drawing convenience, you may see a mix of the different kinds of circuits. A mixed diagram may consist of a block diagram, a wiring diagram, and circuit diagrams.

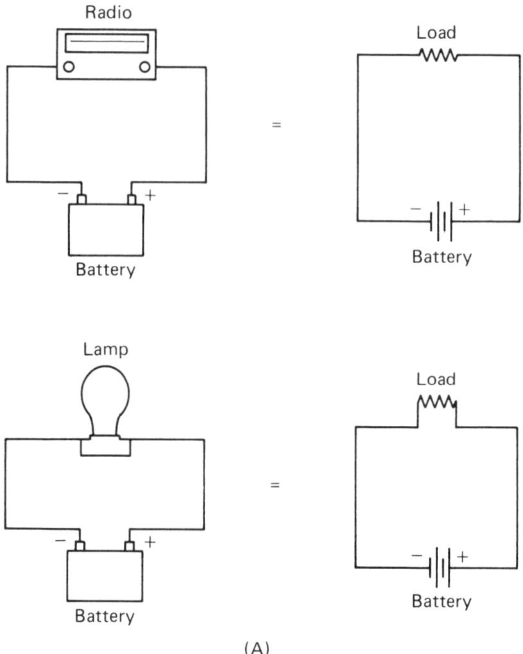

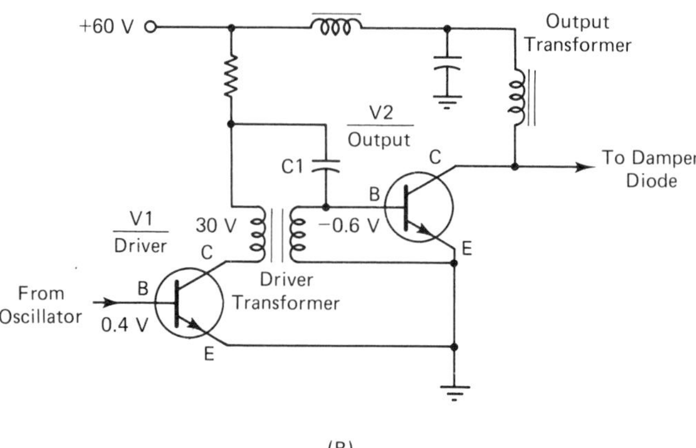

Figure 1–46. Pictorial diagram (left) and equivalent circuit diagram (right) shown in drawing A. Partial circuit diagram (also called a schematic diagram) in drawing B.

An electronics technician or engineer may be interested only in a selected circuit, and this will be shown in circuit-diagram form, possibly preceded and followed by block diagrams. This makes the diagram easier to produce and less complicated, as extraneous material is omitted. In some instances, individual electronic symbols may be used, together with a block diagram. Antenna and ground symbols are commonly used, together with a block diagram, the antenna to indicate a signal source and the ground symbol to indicate a common connection between the different components.

2

CONNECTORS

Wire and cables are used to interlink components, but to do so they must have some kind of connecting device attached to their ends, or else they must have some other means of permitting the unhindered movement of a signal from one component to another. A pair of wires may be joined at their ends to form a connection, but leading a signal into a component requires some other method. Most often, this is supplied by a plug—sometimes called a male connector—at the end of the wire or cable and a jack—sometimes called a female connector or a port—mounted on the front panel or the rear apron of a component. Jacks may also be found on cables.

An astonishing number of plugs and jacks is available, but unless these can be made to join, no connection will be made between components. There is no plug and jack standardization, as each manufacturer has the option of selecting any type of jack for his components. Sometimes different jacks are used by different component models made by the same manufacturer.

TWISTING, SOLDERING, AND CRIMPING

There are three ways of joining wires or mounting them on connectors. The simplest connection is the joining of a pair of wires whose ends have been stripped for that purpose. The wire ends can be twisted together, forming a mechanical connection. It can lead to problems if the connection becomes loose or the wires separate. Soldering the connection is more desirable, as the combination twist action and solder results in a mechanical and electrical joining of the wires. Soldering, though, while the best method, isn't always feasible if the connection is to be made in a hard-to-reach place, or if the job is to be done in a hurry. Soldering requires some expertise if the insulation around the wire ends isn't to crawl away from the heat of the iron. Shrink wrap, heated after the connection is made, can be used to cover the joint with a layer of insulation.

Crimping is a method of joining a connector to a wire with that connector squeezed into a holding position by pliers or a special crimping tool. Whether, or when, to use wire twisting, soldering, or crimping is a matter of personal choice.

Soldering

Soldering isn't difficult, but it does require patience and cleanliness. There are many types of soldering irons, ranging from the 30-watt pencil iron—so called because it looks like, and is held like a pencil—to 100-watt, 200-watt, and 500-watt irons, then to soldering guns. For wiring in-home systems, any iron from about 35 watts to 100 watts can be used, but the 100-watt iron is preferable. The soldering gun is convenient because the tip becomes hot very quickly. Further, the soldering gun is finger-trigger controlled, and thus the heat of the tip can be made the equivalent of a low-wattage iron, such as a 35-watt type, to as much as a 200-watt iron. Because it is so versatile, the soldering gun can be used for many different kinds of soldering jobs.

The tip of the iron should have a clean, silvery finish, which is obtained by tinning the iron. It is possible to buy an iron that is pretinned, so no initial tinning is required. An iron with a silver-plated tip is highly desirable, but it is expensive and may be difficult to obtain.

If the tip of the iron looks black and does not have a smooth finish of solder it will not work. Use a file with fine teeth or rub the faces of the soldering iron tip against a fine sandpaper block. Continue to do so until the copper surface of the tip is exposed, and until all black areas are removed. It takes a long time to wear out a tip, and they are usually replaceable.

Plug the iron into an AC outlet and let the iron get hot. Use a soldering iron stand, or crimp an empty tin can to work as a soldering iron support.

As the iron gets hot, the shiny coppery-looking surfaces of the tip will become dark brown or may even tend to blacken. Using a thick cloth, such as an old, but clean, towel, rub the tip surfaces against the cloth. If the black spots or areas aren't removed, rub the tips with a file or sandpaper until they disappear. Then wipe the tip with the cloth.

An easier method is to dip the hot iron tip into a tin of acid soldering paste, again wiping the tip thoroughly by rubbing it against a thick cloth. (This is an old technique and it may be difficult to get the paste.)

Apply rosin-core solder to the soldering iron tip. At first the solder may form a ball and roll off but some of it will adhere. Rub the tip with the cloth and keep reapplying solder until all the faces of the soldering iron have a shiny, silvery appearance. The soldering iron is now ready for use.

The kind of solder to use. Solder is a mixture of lead and tin with a core of rosin. The metal ratio is either 50 percent tin, 50 percent lead or 60 percent tin, 40 percent lead. To solder connections of cables for home entertainment equipment, the 60:40 ratio is suitable. Like wire, solder is available in different gauges, some of which require high-wattage irons. Buy a rosin-core solder designed to be used with the wattage rating of your iron. Solder gauges range from 16 to 20. For irons rated at 15 to 30 watts, use 20-gauge; for 100 watt irons, use 18-gauge; and for soldering guns, use either 16-gauge or 18-gauge.

Before using the iron, which by now should be amply hot, apply solder to the tips. The solder should melt smoothly and quickly, forming balls of solder. Do not remove these by shaking the iron (a dangerous practice). Instead, clean the tip of the iron with the cloth. Now apply the tip of the iron to the work (Fig. 2–1) until the joint is hot enough to melt the solder. Apply just enough solder to the joint (not to the iron) and let a small amount of solder flow onto it. A large amount of solder is undesirable; use just enough to make a connection. The solder on the connection should be smooth, not lumpy.

In soldering it is essential that the joint being soldered remain motionless. Let the joint cool and after a minute or two, giving the soldered joint enough time to lose its heat, tug on the connected wires to make sure the solder doesn't pull away. It may be necessary to clean the joint with a cloth if there is any residue of rosin.

An important point to remember is that the purpose of soldering is to make an electrical, not a mechanical connection. Make the mechanical connection first, and then do the soldering. When you are finished soldering,

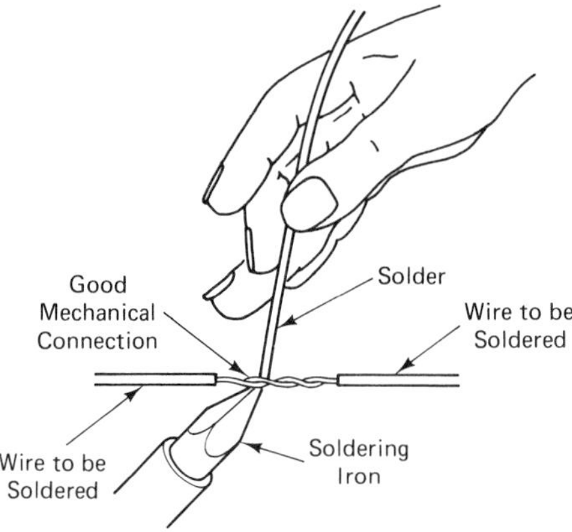

Figure 2–1. Soldering technique.

never cool the iron with water. Instead, let the iron rest on a large metal surface.

Protecting the Insulation

Insulation, particularly that made of plastic, has a fairly low melting point and so will crawl away from the hot tip of the soldering iron. This may expose more of the wire and could lead to a short circuit. To prevent this, use a heat sink, which can be a pair of pliers whose jaws are positioned between the joint being soldered and the insulation. The jaws can be kept closed by using a rubber band around the handles.

Whenever a soldered joint is made, it is like an exposed wire. To protect it, slip a section of heat shrink tubing over either of the wires to be connected. When the wire splice is completed and the soldered connection is cold, slide the heat shrink tubing over the joint. Heat the tubing, using either a match, or bring the soldering iron close to, but not touching, the tubing. Special accessories are also available for heating shrink tubing. Heat will cause the tubing to shrink by about 50 percent, making a tight, insulated coating around the connection. If heat shrink isn't available, use plastic rubber, available in a tube in hardware stores. A thin coating will dry in about a half hour; it will never dry out and become brittle. If one coating doesn't seem enough, wait about fifteen minutes and apply another.

It isn't advisable to use electrical tape around a soldered connection. Such tape, whether plastic or cloth, eventually becomes dry, then the tape's adhesiveness is no longer tacky, and the tape gradually unravels. Further, the tape makes a much bulkier wrapping than heat shrink tubing and is generally unsightly.

Connectors can be positioned on the front or rear of components or on the exposed ends of wires or cables. Wherever they may be located, connectors are essential for joining individual wires or cables to components.

Alligator Clips

Alligator clips are spring-loaded devices and are handy for making temporary connections. The associated conductor is usually flexible, insulated, stranded wire. The clips can be solderless, like the one shown in Fig. 2–2A. The connecting wire is stripped about 1/4 inch from its end, with the strands twirled to form the equivalent of a single wire, and then secured in place to the clip by bending a pair of triangular points at the end of the clip, using pliers. No part of the wire insulation should extend into the clip. The typical length of a clip is 2 inches, but miniature clips only 1-1/8 inch long are available.

A better method of making a connection to an alligator clip is to use a machine screw mounted on the body of the clip, as in drawing B. Bring the

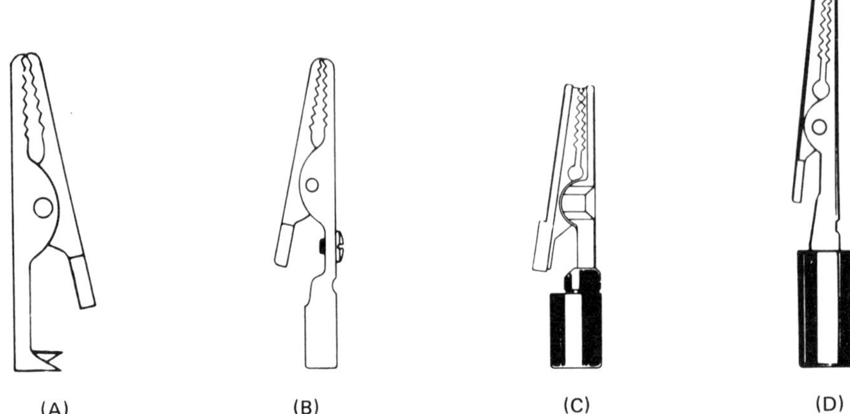

Figure 2-2. Alligator clips. Clip has sharp points for making a solderless connection (A); clip with screw for wire connection (B); clip equipped with an adapter (C); alligator clip with insulated end (D). *(Courtesy GC Electronics)*

exposed wire through the tubular end of the clip, wrap it clockwise around the screw, and tighten it.

Some alligator clips are equipped with an adapter, as in C. The adapter permits the insertion of various kinds of plugs to permit connecting the wire to points not equipped with jacks. When not used this way, the adapter can be removed.

Some alligator clips (D) are supplied with insulated ends. This is a useful feature, as it protects the user against accidental shock when the clip is to be connected to a voltage point. This alligator clip can be used with or without an adapter.

The best arrangement for joining a wire to an alligator clip is to fasten the wire to the clip mechanically and then to solder the wire to the clip. When using stranded wire, make sure none of the strands extend beyond the clip.

Lugs

A lug, as shown in Fig. 2-3, is one of the simplest types of connectors. It can be soldered to a conductor or it can be a solderless type held in place by crimping. Lugs are available in a variety of styles, but those most commonly used for in-home electronic connections are the spade lug and the ring

Figure 2-3. Open spade lug. In a ring lug the ends are closed.

lug. The spade lug permits quick insertion of the lug onto a binding post; the ring lug, because it surrounds the screw of a binding post, makes a more permanent connection, one that will not fall off.

Lugs are designed to mate with screw terminals (Fig. 2–4). They are often used as connectors with two-wire transmission line for attachment to the 300-ohm antenna input of a television receiver. Indoor TV antennas, such as rabbit ears, are usually equipped with a short length of twin lead that is terminated with spade lugs.

Insulated Crimp Terminals

The word *crimp* immediately implies that the connection of the wire to a terminal is to be handled mechanically only. Crimping can be done with pliers or a special crimping tool. The purpose is to apply sufficient pressure to the terminal so it makes a tight grip on the wire to which it is being connected.

Insulated crimp terminals are ring and spade terminals, with one end consisting of an insulating sleeve. Insulated crimp terminals can be used as connectors or as splices for any bare wires to be joined.

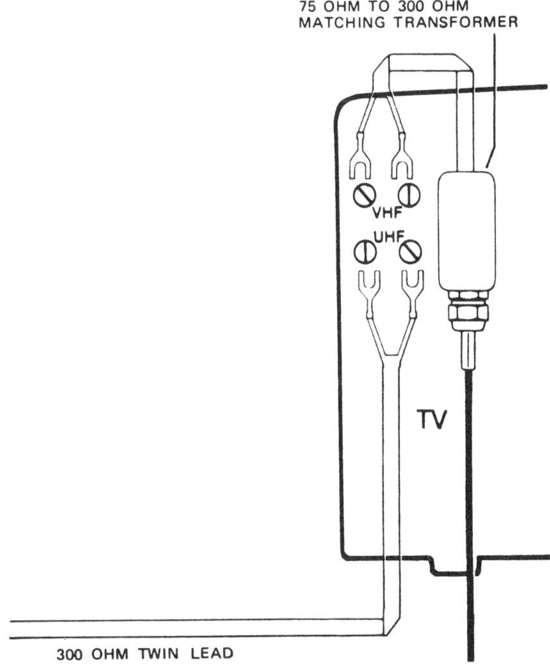

Figure 2–4. Open spade lugs on twin lead for connection to antenna terminal block of TV set.

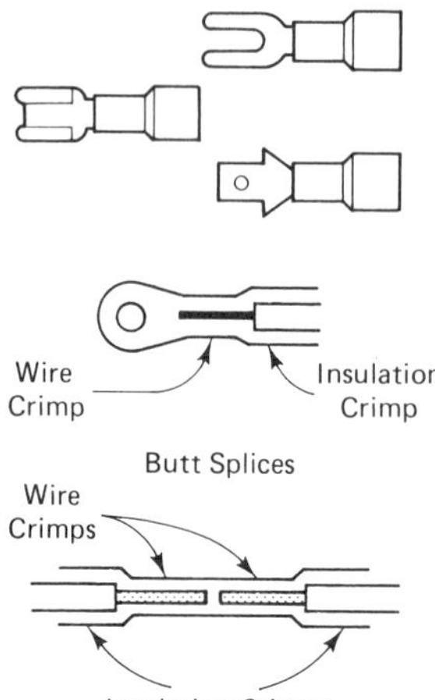

Figure 2-5. Mounting insulated lugs by crimping. (*Courtesy General Electric*)

To mount an insulated crimp terminal, strip the insulation from the wire approximately 1/4 inch. If the wire is stranded, twirl the exposed bare ends to form the equivalent of a single, solid wire (see Fig. 2-5). Insert the bare wire copper conductor into the terminal barrel so it protrudes about 1/32 inch. For butt splices, used when two lengths of wire are to be joined, insert the bare copper conductors into each end to the midpoint of the splice. Crimp the barrel tightly over the insulation. After completion, tug on the connection to make sure the crimp is tight.

Crimp terminals are available in different models depending on the wire gauge to be pushed through the insulating sleeve. The size of the wire the terminal can accommodate is indicated by the color of the terminal: a red terminal means that wire sizes from 22 to 18 AWG can be accepted; blue is for wire gauges from 16 to 14 AWG; while yellow is for wires 12 to 10 AWG. For electronics work, terminals color coded red are the most commonly used. The lugs are also marked with the size of the wire gauge the insulating barrel will accept.

TWIN-LEAD CONNECTIONS

Twin lead has several uses. It can be made to work as an indoor FM or TV antenna, it is often supplied as a folded doublet type of antenna, and it is packed in with receivers for this purpose. Its most important use, though, is as a downlead, a transmission line delivering a signal to a television set or an FM receiver from an outside antenna.

There are two ways of connecting twin lead. The first, the quickest but by no means the better way, is simply to strip the wire ends of each of the multistrand twin-lead conductors, twirl the exposed ends of the wires, and

Figure 2–6. Connecting twin lead. Screw terminals are always used for this type of conductor.

then wrap them around the antenna connections of the receiver. These connections are a pair of captive machine screws. Wrap each wire around the two individual screws clockwise and then tighten the screws. Make sure the wire wrap goes completely around the body of the screw and not partially around it, nor should the wire simply be put across the body of the screw.

Figure 2–6 is a method of using self-piercing screws, but a small change is made: Remove 3/8 inch of insulation from the wires and then fold the exposed wires back, forming a small loop. Remove the screws and slide the wire loops over the screw shafts. Then tighten the screws until the screw teeth bite into and through the plastic. The advantage of this method is that double contact is obtained: from the biting action of the screws, and from the exposed wires pressed against the screws.

You can use spade lugs, either a solder or crimp lug, but solder the exposed leads of the two conductors to spade lugs, as these will make a positive connection to the antenna terminals. Alternatively, the lug can be crimped onto the bare ends of the wires (Fig. 2–7). The best approach is to use both methods: crimping to supply a good mechanical connection; soldering to supply a good electrical connection. If both crimping and soldering are to be used, crimp the connection in place first, to make sure the wire and the connector are tightly in place; then solder the wire and the lug. A large amount of solder isn't needed, for it isn't the function of the solder to hold the wire and lug together.

The terminals in Fig. 2–7 have a pair of "ears," ending in sharp points.

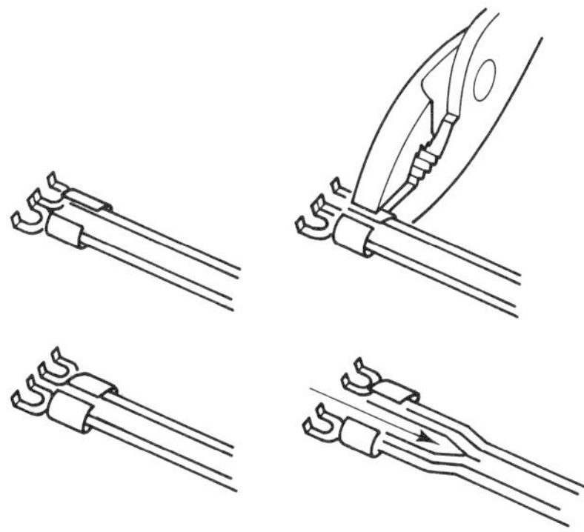

Figure 2–7. Crimping open spade lug to twin lead. (*Courtesy General Electric*)

Use a pair of terminals, one for each twin-lead conductor. The twin lead need not be stripped but can have its end squared off. Mount a pair of lugs on the twin lead, one for each conductor. Tighten the ears with pliers, as shown. The points of the lug will pierce the plastic insulation and will make contact with the conductors. After mounting the lugs, separate the conductors by splicing the plastic with a sharp knife or single-edge razor blade. Do not use this crimping method with foam-filled twin lead. Also note that the open ends of the lug aren't straight but have an upward twist. This will keep the lug from sliding off the machine screw to which it will be attached, should that screw become loosened.

Screw Connectors

Machine screws used for making connections to 300-ohm twin lead are common on TV sets and VCRs. There are several different types and one of these is the ordinary flat-head machine screw. It depends for contact with the wire of two-wire line by the flat surface underneath the head of the screw.

Another type, known as a captive screw, is like the flat-head machine screw, except that it can be loosened only a certain distance, just far enough to permit the wire of the transmission line to be wrapped around the shaft of the screw. The purpose of this design is to keep the screw from falling out.

Still another is the self-piercing screw. Beneath the head of the screw is a washer, which may be loose or which can be made part of the underneath surface of the screw. This washer is serrated and has numerous sawteeth around its circumference. When the screw is fastened, these teeth bite into the conductors of two-wire line, making contact with them.

With self-piercing screws, it should not be necessary to remove any of the plastic surrounding the twin conductors. Cut diagonally across the twin lead and make sure no wires protrude from either of the conductors. Insert the transmission line between the two screws and then tighten them securely, making sure the sawteeth cut into and through the plastic. Using self-piercing screws makes the connection to the terminals easier and quicker, and eliminates the possibility of individual strands of wire being cut away or reaching over to short the terminals. It is, however, not the most desirable form of connection, as much better electrical contact is made by a lug.

Connecting Indoor AM and FM Antennas

An indoor FM antenna can be connected to the FM antenna terminals on a receiver with the twin lead terminated in spade lugs, as shown in Fig. 2-8. An indoor AM antenna can be handled in the same way. Either spade lugs or ring lugs can be used, crimped or soldered (or both) to the wires.

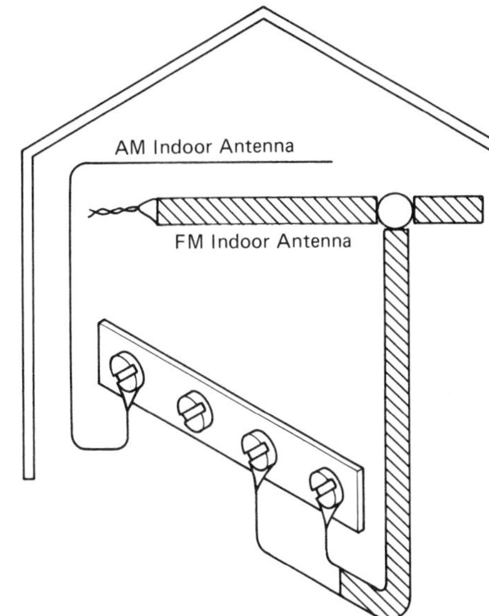

Figure 2–8. Connections for indoor AM and FM antennas.

Binding Posts

Binding posts are used wherever a single conductor is to be connected to some component such as a speaker. Where two wires are to be connected, a pair of such posts are used or else a dual binding post, as in Fig. 2–9A.

Binding posts used on speakers can be spring loaded. With this binding post, the head of the post is depressed, the wire inserted, and the head released. Contact is maintained through the pressure of the built-in spring (B). Another type of binding post is shown in C. Here the wire to be connected is wrapped around the body screw of the post in a clockwise direction. The head

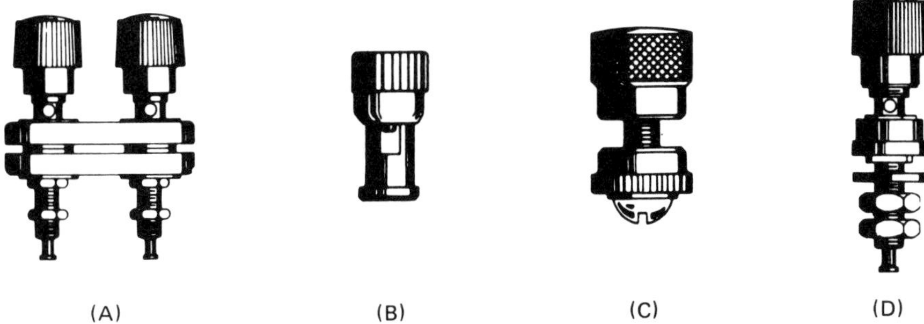

Figure 2–9. Types of binding posts: double (A); spring-loaded (B); screw (C); through-hole (D). (*Courtesy GC Electronics*)

of the post is then tightened. The fourth type (D) has a hole drilled in the body screw. The wire is inserted through this hole and then the head of the post is tightened. Note that the dual binding post in drawing A also has the through-hole method of connecting wires.

When you use a through-hole binding post, twirl the individual wires of the conducting cable if twisted wire is being used before pushing the wire through the binding post hole. This problem doesn't arise if solid conductor is used. In either case, the conductors should not extend more than about 1/16 inch beyond the binding post after the connection has been made. If the wire is an insulated type, no part of the insulation should be pushed through the hole. If a wrap-around type of binding post is used, no part of the insulation should be around the center screw.

Gold Binding Posts

Gold binding posts are sometimes used on more expensive speakers. These aren't solid gold, of course, for gold is not only costly but a relatively soft material. The posts are actually gold plated. Aside from being a status symbol, gold does have advantages. It does not corrode or tarnish, desirable qualities in a connector material. In some instances plugs are also gold plated. Ideally, a gold-plated plug should be used with a gold-plated jack.

Twin-Lead Wiring

The twin lead used for bringing signals into the home and through the home to a TV set and an FM receiver is low-voltage, lightweight, and very flexible. Because it is a low-voltage wire, there is no danger of electrical shock (unless it somehow contacts a power line) and it does not represent a fire hazard.

The advantage of twin lead is that it can be tacked to a baseboard, concealed in molding around the walls of a room, and hidden under carpeting. The disadvantage of routing twin lead along a baseboard is that painting the baseboard also leads to painting the twin lead. This can increase the capacitance between the conductors, causing some signal loss at the high-frequency end of the signal, producing less signal detail. The paint, in time, can cause the plastic of the twin lead to deteriorate. A better arrangement is to use duct molding (Fig. 2–10). Made of vinyl, it will not change the twin lead's electrical characteristics and is self-extinguishing in the event of excessive heat or flame. The vinyl can be painted to match the baseboard without affecting the twin lead.

You don't need a license as an electrician to route such wiring through walls or closets, for there will be no violation of municipal fire codes. This low-voltage wiring can be brought into the home from an antenna, possibly routed down the side of the building.

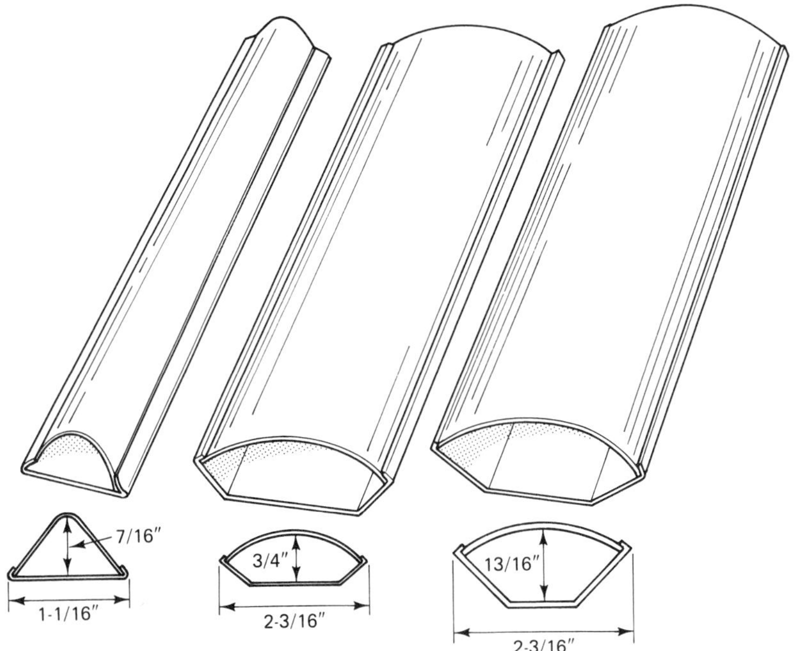

Figure 2–10. Duct molding for twin-lead installation. (*Courtesy RMS Electronics, Inc.*)

Using an outside antenna means the twin lead will need to come through a wall. One technique is to bring the transmission line in through an attic louver, and then down through an inside wall. A downlead can also be brought in through a window by drilling through the bottom portion of a window frame. Another method is to use a wall tube (Fig. 2–11). Make a hole in both outside and inside walls and then pass the tube through them. Use a rubber grommet on the outside wall to seal out the weather and a wall plate on the inside wall. The two-wire line is terminated at this plate.

When you use a wall tube, slant the tube slightly downward from the inside to the outside to avoid providing a path for water that may somehow manage to get past the outside grommet. If a wall tube isn't available, make one from a length of plastic tubing. Seal the outside with liquid rubber. What-

Figure 2–11. Wall tube can accommodate twin lead or coaxial cable. One end uses a rubber grommet to seal out weather; the in-house end terminates in a wall plate.

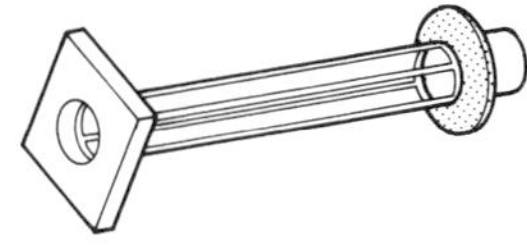

ever method is used to bring the antenna downlead into the home, that wiring must somehow be brought over to the television set or to a video cassette recorder, if one is being used. Once the twin lead has been brought into the room, it can be continued along the baseboard until it reaches the component to which it is to be connected.

A more professional installation is to bring the downlead through the wall to a wall plate. From the wall plate the twin lead can be continued along the baseboard. It may also be possible to nudge the wire under the end of carpeting if wall-to-wall carpeting is being used.

If the wiring installation is such that the twin lead must not just go through a wall, but pass through the inside of the wall for some distance, it could be helpful to consult or use the services of an electrician. While an electrician may be more accustomed to working with power-line wiring, bringing twin lead in from the outside, up, down and through walls, is not so different.

Wall Plates

There are two types of wall plates. One of these is the surface mount (Fig. 2–12). This type of plate is mounted directly on the wall and extends somewhat beyond it. Make a small hole in the wall so the stripped ends of the transmission line can be brought into the plate. The other type of plate is the flush mount. With this type the plate does not extend beyond the wall, but is flush with it. The connecting terminals of the flush mount plate extend into the wall area so some space must be cut out of the wall. Both types of plates, flush and surface, work in the same way. The surface plate is easier to install, but you may consider it unsightly. The flush plate is less obtrusive, but its installation requires more work.

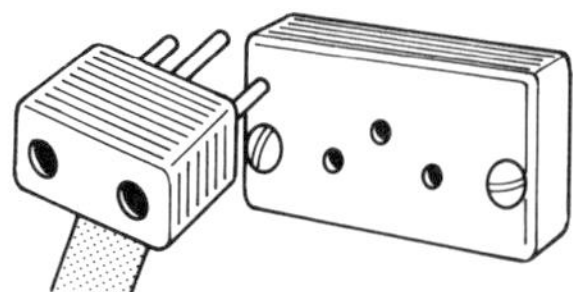

Figure 2–12. Plug for connecting indoor twin lead to a surface mount wall plate.

The technique used for twin lead is also applicable to coaxial cable. The cable can be brought into the home, through the walls, with a final connection to a wall plate (Fig. 2–13). Unlike twin lead, which can be tacked along a wall, or hidden under a rug or in a duct, coaxial cable isn't handled this way. Instead, a length of coaxial cable, equipped with suitable coaxial connectors, will run directly from the VCR or TV set to the wall plate. This means the wall plate should be placed somewhere behind the component to which the connection is to be made.

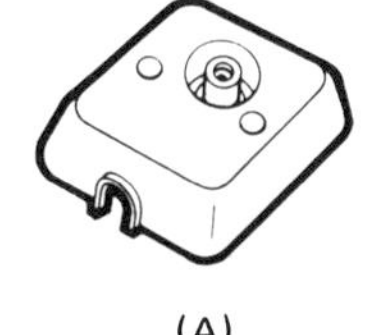
(A)

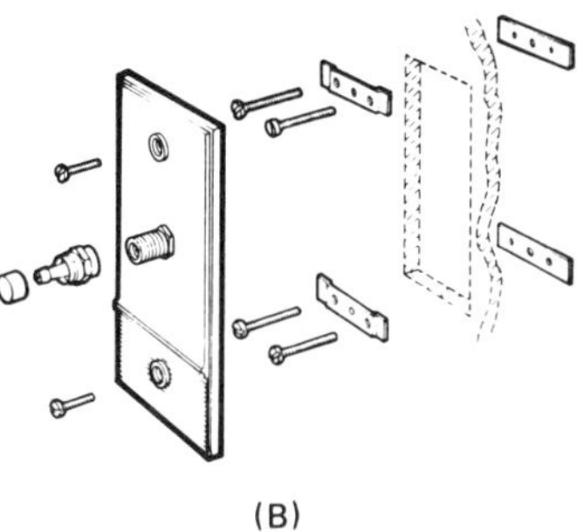
(B)

Figure 2–13. Surface mount wall plate for use with a quick connect push-on transformer or push-on F-plug (A). Flush wall plate for connecting 75-ohm cable (B). The flush unit requires a rectangular cutout in the wall; the surface wall plate requires only a fairly small through hole. *(Courtesy Gemini Industries, Inc.)*

PLUGS

A plug is a convenient way of joining wires and cables from outside a component to some circuit located inside. The plug is inserted into a jack positioned on the front or rear of the component. Plugs and jacks are members of the connector family.

A large number of plugs are available, and even a specific type of plug can have variations in shape, style, and color.

Banana Plugs

Banana plugs are used for connecting single, unshielded wires. These plugs should be made to standard industry dimensions and mate with jacks having a bore of 0.161 inch. The joining of a wire to a banana plug can be a solderless or soldered connection. In some solderless banana plugs the wire connection is via a set screw mounted in the plastic handle (Fig. 2–14A). When a pair of wires is required, a dual banana plug (drawing B) can be used, with polarity indicated on the top and side. The mating jack must be 3/4 inch on centers. The midget banana plug (C) is used where economy of space is wanted. The right-angle banana plug (D) is commonly used for connecting probes to a test instrument. The connecting wire is soldered to the body of the plug. Like all other plugs in this family, this plug has a standard sized tip with a diameter ranging from 0.170 inch to 0.180 inch.

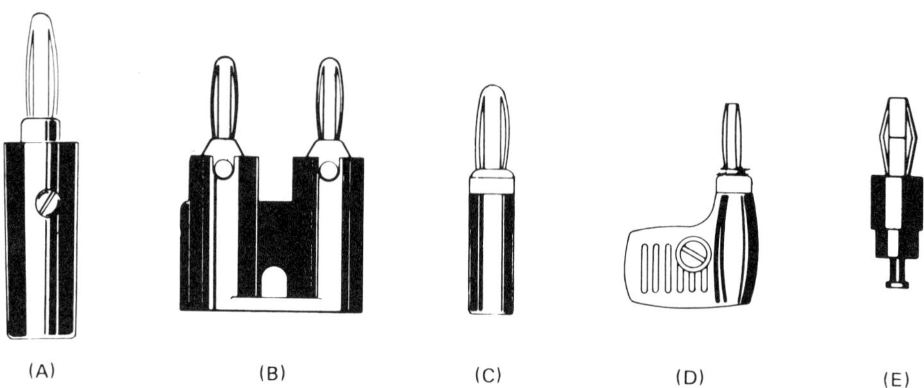

Figure 2-14. Banana plugs: plug with wire connection through screw on plug body (A); twin plug (B); midget (C); right-angle plug (D); subminiature (E). (*Courtesy GC Electronics*).

Banana plugs are equipped with four-leaved, phosphor bronze or beryllium copper nickel-plated spring tips. The springs are compressed to fit into the opening of the mating jack. Because of the difference in the dimensions of the plug and jack, the plug makes a force fit, but the springiness of the four leaves of the tip permits easy removal.

While the typical banana plug has a standard tip diameter, a subminiature plug is available with a tip diameter that is only 0.120 inch (drawing E). This type of banana jack, used for printed circuit connections, is riveted to a terminal board with the connecting wire soldered to the turret terminal of the plug. The mating jack should have a diameter of 0.104-inch inside diameter. The four leaves forming the tip of the subminiature banana plug are made of beryllium copper and are silver plated to supply a connection having minimum ohmic resistance.

Tip Plugs

Unlike banana plugs, which depend on a metallic spring leaf structure for making good contact with a mating jack, tip plugs have solid metallic tips made according to standard industry specifications of 0.080-inch diameter. Because there is no spring action, as in the case of banana plugs, the tips of these plugs must be machined to very close tolerances. The connecting wire to the solid tip plug can be soldered to the plug or the connection can be solderless.

The tip plug shown in Fig. 2-15A is solderless, with the connecting wire tightened securely under the knurled collar. The tip plug in drawing B differs from the others, as its tip is hollow. However, its tip diameter is the same as that of other tip plugs. The tip plug in drawing C is a right-angle type. The plastic handle consists of a pair of mating halves that can be assembled with

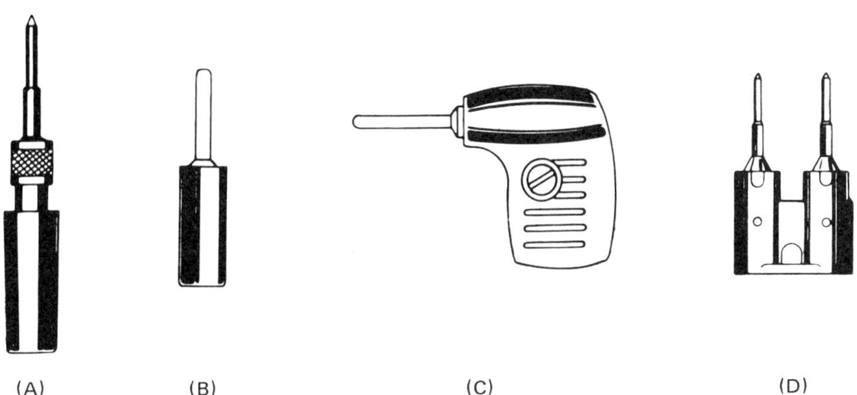

Figure 2–15. Tip plugs: solderless type (A); hollow tip (B); right-angle (C); double plug (D). (*Courtesy GC Electronics*)

one machine screw and nut. The right-angle tip plug is popularly used for meter test leads. Tip plugs are also available as dual units (D). This is solderless, and plugs into a corresponding pair of jacks having a spacing of 3/4 inch on centers.

The Mini Plug

This plug is used to make connections to Beta format VCRs, as these are equipped with mini jacks (Fig. 2–16). The mini plug accepts wire using shield braid. The tip of the plug makes contact with the center conductor of the wire, while the cylindrical metal extension (also called a barrel) of the plug makes contact with the shield braid. The wire has some resemblance to unbalanced coax, but in this case the shield braid is not coaxial with the central hot lead. In coaxial cable the insulation around the hot lead is such that the central conductor is equidistant from its surrounding shield braid. Such is not the case with ordinary shielded wire used in audio applications.

When a barrel is internally threaded, as some of them are, it is identified by its diameter and the number of threads per inch. In its specs, a barrel could be 5/8 × 27 TPI (5/8 inch diameter; 27 threads per inch).

Phone Plug

The phone plug is a larger version of the mini plug and is sometimes used as the terminating element for cables joining audio components. The mini plug is used with Beta format VCRs and the phone plug is used with the VHS.

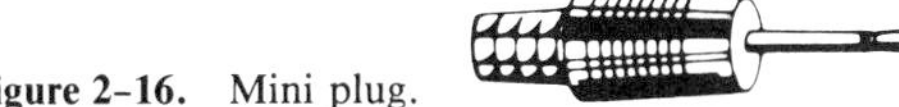

Figure 2–16. Mini plug.

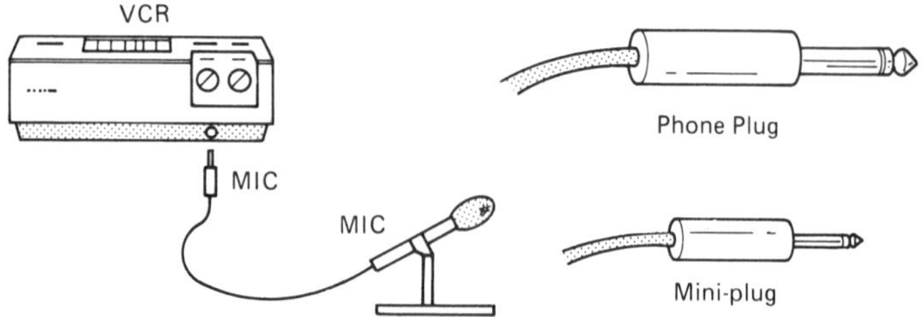

Figure 2–17. Mini plug is used with Beta format VCRs, phone plug with VHS.

The phone plug looks just like its smaller version, the mini. It is a two- or three-element type and has a barrel that is 1-1/4 inch (31.8 mm) long. Microphone cables use either of these two plugs for connection to VCRs (Fig. 2–17).

Both plugs, the mini and the phone, can be either monophonic or stereophonic (Fig. 2–18). The phone plug is so called because it was originally used as a connector for telephone switchboards. Some of these plugs have an insulated casing, and others use metal, which not only adds strength to the plug, but works as a shield as well. It is also possible to obtain these plugs in right-angle form.

How to Connect Audio Cable to a Phone Plug

Turn the casing of the phone plug counterclockwise and it will come off, revealing screw terminals for the connection of the audio cable. For a mono connection there will be two screws on the interior of the plug, one for the hot lead and the other for a connection to the shield braid. No soldering is

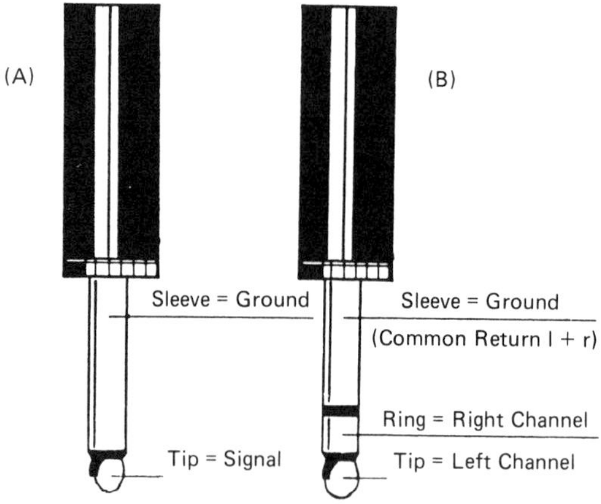

Figure 2–18. Phone plugs: mono (A) and stereo (B).

required. The attachments to the stereo plug are similar, using three connections instead of two.

The Phono Plug (RCA Plug)

The names for these two different plugs, phone and phono, are so similar they are often confused. A phono plug, also called an RCA plug or a pin plug (Fig. 2-19) is commonly used as a connector for audio components.

Figure 2-19. RCA molded phono pin plug.

Plug Adapters

Ordinarily a mini plug would mate with a mini jack, a phone plug with a phone jack and a phono plug with a phono jack. A problem arises, though, if a cable is equipped with one type of plug while the component to which it must deliver a signal has a completely different type of jack. There are various solutions. The existing plug can be removed, the jack can be changed, or you can try to get a cable with the right kind of plug. By far the easiest (and fastest) technique is to use an adapter.

The three plugs shown in Fig. 2-20—the phone plug, the phono plug (it's less confusing to call it an RCA plug), and the mini plug—have adapters available so they can be made to join with other types of jacks. As is indicated at the top of the drawing, a phone plug that would ordinarily require a phone jack can be made to mate with an RCA jack. Along the same lines, an RCA plug can join with a phone jack and a mini plug with a phone jack. Adapters for other types of plugs are also available. This does not mean a cable with the right kind of plugs isn't desirable—it is, but a cable with one kind of plug at one end and a different type on the other end isn't always easy to get. A possible alternative is to customize your own, starting with bulk cable and mounting the specific plugs required.

Connecting an RCA Plug to Audio Cable

To connect shielded audio cable to an RCA plug strip about 1-1/4 inch of the outer jacket by cutting around that jacket with a sharp (preferably new) single-edge razor blade (Fig. 2-21). Try not to nick or cut the shield braid directly beneath the jacket. Slide this small section of jacket off the cable, but if it will not come off freely, cut it lengthwise.

Carefully cut along the length of the exposed braid and then pull it back. Twist the braid so it resembles a single conductor. Strip back about 1/4 inch of the vinyl insulation surrounding the center conductor and discard it. To do

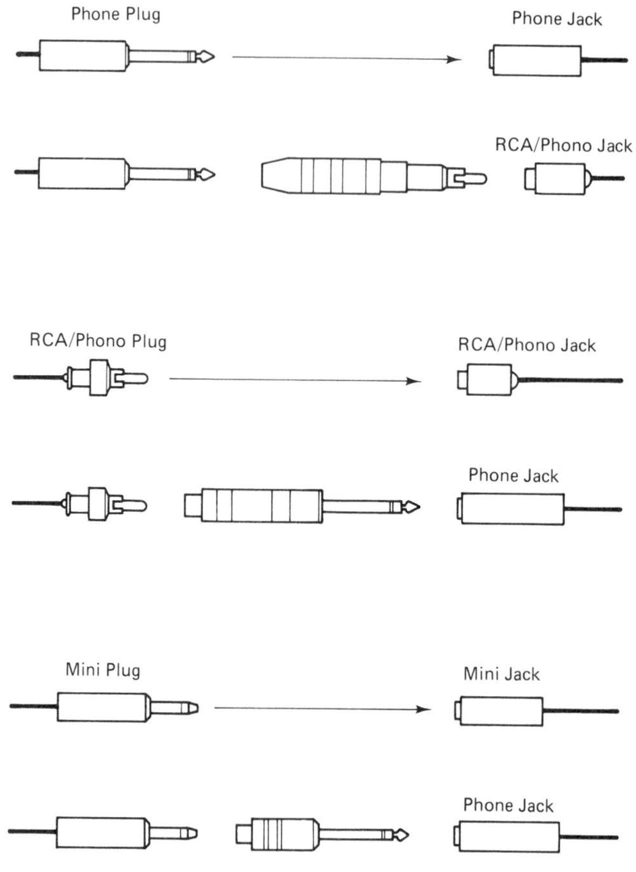

Figure 2–20. Plug adapters.

so you will need to cut that insulation with the razor blade, but be careful not to damage any of the conductors directly beneath it. The conductors will consist of seven strands of fairly fine wire. Twirl the exposed ends and then tin them, covering the entire length with a fine, thin coating of solder. The center conductor will now resemble a single, solid wire having a silvery finish.

Now insert it into the plug until about 1/16 inch is exposed from the front end of the tip. Solder the inner conductor to the tip's end. Since you have tinned the center conductor, you should be able to do so very easily. Use a very small amount of solder. As a final step, solder the shield braid to the outer collar of the plug. As a check, insert the plug into an RCA jack. The plug should go in easily making, a fairly tight fit, but be sure to insert the plug as far as it will go. Rotate the plug once completely, first in one direction, then in the other.

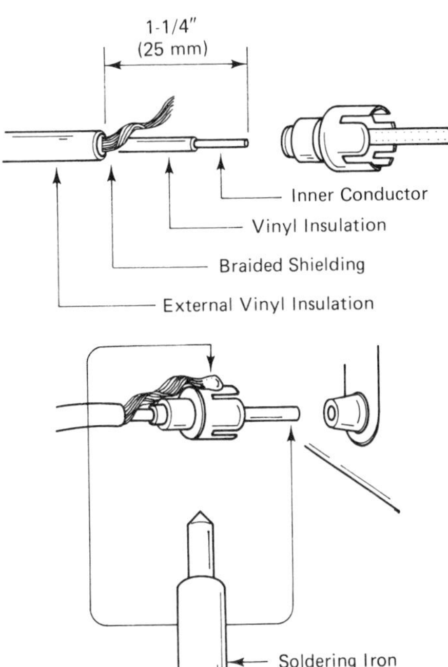

Figure 2–21. Connecting an RCA plug.

Plug Quality

As is true of cables, all plugs are not of equal quality. A gold-plated plug, for example, is superior to one that doesn't have this feature, for it will not corrode. How it is constructed in other ways is another matter, but at least in this one respect it is better.

Figure 2–22 shows some of the physical characteristics of a quality RCA plug. The wire strands are made of steel-plated copper and are covered by a noncompressible insulating material. The copper supplies conductivity and the steel adds strength. Since the steel is simply a coating there is just a small reduction in cable flexibility.

In some of the poorer-grade cables the shield consists of a wire wrap instead of braid. In Fig. 2–22, the cable is fully braided and is soldered to the four-leaved grounding shell completely around its circumference. This ground shell must make good, positive contact with the corresponding jack. The plug must not just slide into the jack but must be pushed in. If the plug feels loose when mounted in the jack, use a pair of pliers to tighten the four leaves of the plug.

The tip of the plug should be solder dipped to ensure good electrical contact between it and the central conductor. If this contact should break, the result could be intermittent operation. Reheat the tip with a soldering iron

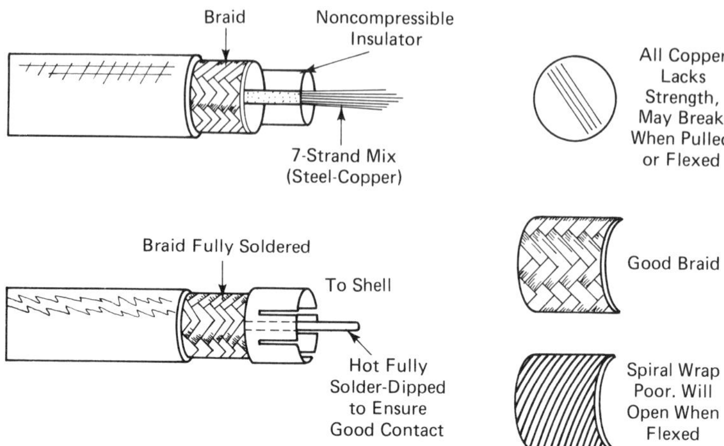

Figure 2–22. Physical characteristics of a quality connector.

without adding solder to see if the connection can be reformed. If solder is needed, add it sparingly. Too much will prevent the plug from entering the jack.

The advantage of a noncompressible insulator around the central conductor is that it helps maintain a uniform distance between that lead and the shield braid.

Figure 2–23 shows RCA plugs mounted on twinned cable. The cables are joined for almost their complete length, with separation near the connectors. If further separation is required, simply pull the cables apart. Using twinned cables has several advantages: the installation will be neater and it will be easier to trace the connection if it becomes necessary to do so. Further, it avoids the exasperation of losing one cable of a pair.

The outer body of the plug is sometimes covered with an insulating material color coded as an aid in observing polarity. If the plugs are the same color, the symbol (+) may sometimes be stamped on a corresponding pair of input and output plugs. Color-coded plugs, often using black for the negative lead and red for the positive lead, are preferable, as colors permit quick identification. Stamped polarity symbols are difficult to read.

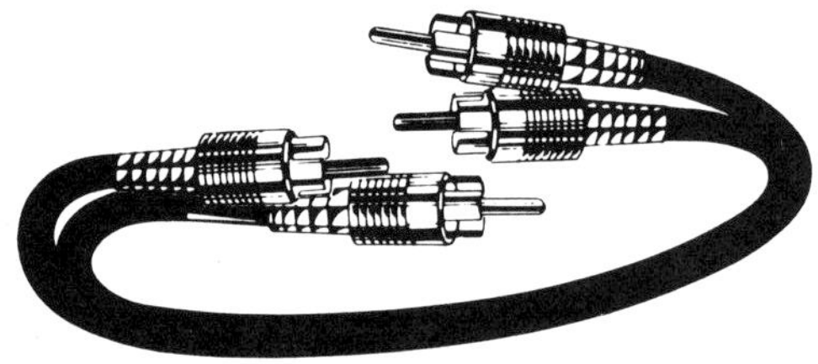

Figure 2–23. RCA connectors for a hi-fi system. (*Courtesy Recoton Corporation*)

Belling & Lee Plug

The plug in Fig. 2–24 is a push-in connector, attached to coaxial cable. It is a standard type used in Europe, Africa, the Middle East, and Great Britain.

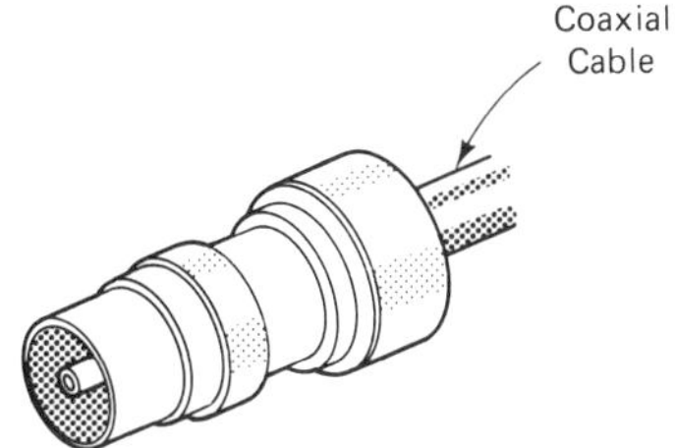

Figure 2–24. Belling & Lee plug.

Motorola Plug

This plug, shown in Fig. 2–25, is used to connect video components to a corresponding Motorola jack, used in a wall plate with connections to a master antenna. This is part of a television system used in high-rise apartment houses.

Figure 2–25. Motorola plug.

The F-Plug

There are numerous kinds of plugs, but the F-plug (Fig. 2–26) is one of the most widely used, and this plug is available in a wide assortment. It can be straight or it can have a right-angle bend to keep a cable close to the equipment. It is used with unbalanced coaxial cable, which can be the downlead from an antenna or consist of short lengths for interconnecting video components.

You will find the F-plug on cables connecting a video cassette recorder and a TV set, between switchers and the equipment to which the switchers are attached, on accessory devices such as baluns (impedance-matching transformers), on band separators, on signal splitters, and so on. It is used for connecting 75-ohm cable to the antenna input terminals of a TV set or a VCR.

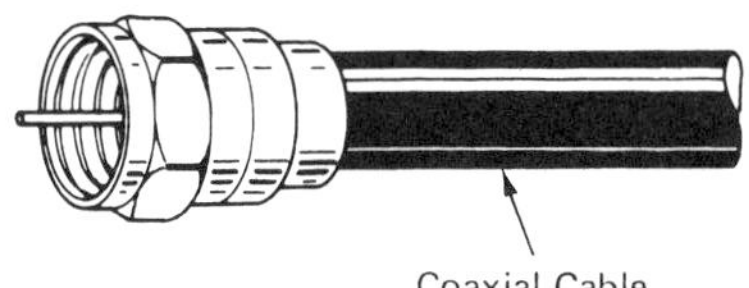

Figure 2–26. F-plug.

F-connectors may be threaded or push-on. The advantage of the threaded F-plugs is that the connection is tighter and more secure. They are less likely to contribute to cable intermittents, often difficult to find during servicing. However, if for some reason a cable must be disconnected fairly often, using a screw-on connector can be a nuisance. The push-on connector, as its name implies, forms a connection when the plug is pushed into its mating jack. This plug is held in place simply by physical contact.

Connecting the F-plug to coaxial cable. Connecting the F-plug to coaxial cable isn't difficult, but until you acquire some experience, it does take a little time and patience. Figure 2–27 shows the steps required.

As a first step, remove a small portion of the outer jacket. The amount of jacket to be cut away isn't critical and can be from about 3/8 inch to 5/8 inch. This will be a circumferential cut, and you can use a sharp knife or a single-edge razor blade. Special cable-cutting tools are sold for this purpose. When making this cut be careful not to nick the shield braid beneath the jacket.

Slide the small section of jacket off the cable and, as shown in Fig. 2–27A, the shield braid will now be exposed. Push the shield braid completely back, as in B. If the cable is equipped with a drain wire (a separate ground wire), push this back with the braid.

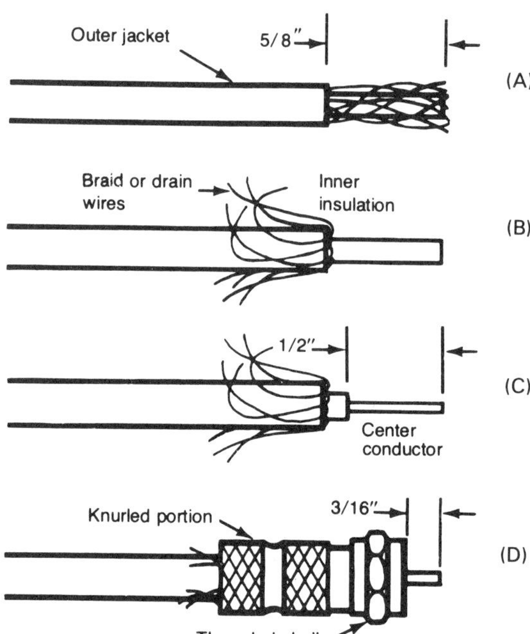

Figure 2–27. Method of connecting coaxial cable to an F-plug. (*Courtesy Winegard Co.*)

Now cut away about 1/4 inch to 1/2 inch (the exact amount isn't critical) of the insulation covering the center lead, as in C. Be careful not to damage the center conductor.

Slide the F-plug over the cable (D) so about 3/16 inch to 1/4 inch of the center conductor extends beyond the end of the plug. If the F-plug is equipped with a crimping ring, squeeze it with a pair of pliers or with a special crimping tool made for this purpose. Finally, using a pair of diagonal cutters, cut away any part of the shield braid extending beyond the back of the plug.

Not all F-plugs have a built-in section to be crimped. The plug shown in Fig. 2–28 has a separate crimping ring. With this type of connector, mount the crimping ring on the cable before putting on the plug. After the plug is on, slide the crimping ring over the connector's sleeve and pinch it with a pair of pliers or a crimping tool.

BNC Plug

The purpose of a plug and jack is to ensure a good transfer of a signal or a DC voltage; therefore, the plug and its mating jack must make a good fit. To ensure the fit, some plugs are equipped with rotatable rings that are threaded so the plug can be screwed into place. Other plugs depend on good manufacturing tolerances so the plug and its jack can make a force fit. A

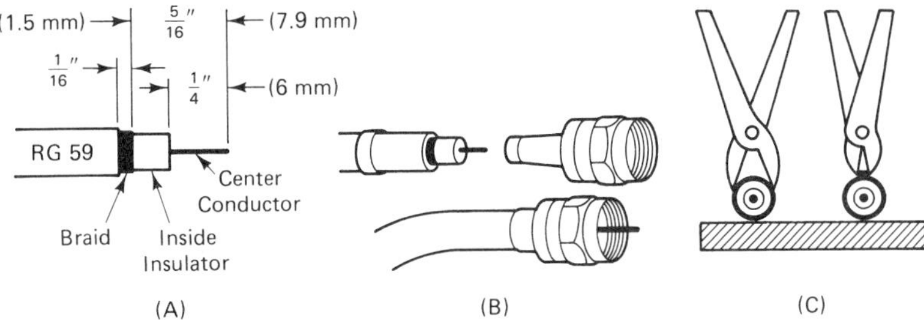

Cut off 5/16" (7.9 mm) piece of jacket and braid. Do not damage inside insulator (A).

Carefully remove a 1/4" (6 mm) section of the inside insulator. Avoid damage to the center conductor.

Carefully remove 1/16" (1.5 mm) of the outside jacket without damaging or nicking braid. Fan braid or foil back against the outside jacket.

Place crimping ring over cable. Push on small end of the connector sleeve between the braid and inside insulator (B).

After connector is fully pushed forward, slide crimp ring over the connector's sleeve (B).

Pinch the crimp ring with a pair of pliers (C).

Screw F-type cable connector onto the chassis connector.

Figure 2–28. F-plug mounting details.

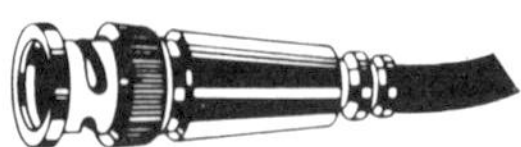

Figure 2–29. BNC plug connector. It has an outside diameter of 0.25 inch and is used with coaxial cable. (*Courtesy Recoton Corporation.*)

compromise between these two extremes is the BNC plug shown in Fig. 2–29. Comparable to a twist-on bayonet bulb, this plug requires a partial turn to lock the plug into position. It has the advantage of permitting a quick connection, plus one that is positive in its action. Figure 2–30 shows a pair of BNC plugs terminating both ends of a length of coaxial cable.

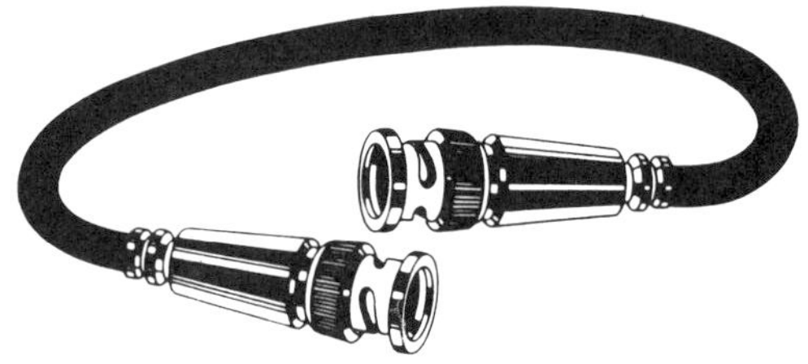

Figure 2–30. Coaxial cable with BNC connectors on both ends. (*Courtesy Recoton Corporation.*)

Connecting the BNC plug to coaxial cable. Figure 2–31 shows how to connect the BNC plug to coaxial cable. Make a circumferential cut around the jacket of the cable removing it to a length of about 9/16 inch. If the cut is clean, the section of cut jacket should slide off fairly easily. Beneath the jacket is the shield braid. Cut away a 9/16-inch section. It isn't easy to make a clean cut of braid so it is best to use a new single-edge razor blade. Slide the braid off the cable and if there are any dangling threads cut them away with diagonal cutters.

The insulation surrounding the center conductor will now be exposed. As in the case of the jacket and the braid, cut away a 9/16-inch section. You will find the plastic cuts much more easily than the braid or jacket. When you make this cut, be careful not to damage the center conductor that is right beneath the plastic insulation. If all has gone well, you will now have an exposed length of inner conductor.

Cut away another section of the outer jacket to a length of 1/4 inch, as indicated in Fig. 2–31A. The outer braid is fairly flexible, so twist it in a clockwise direction (B). When you finish, about 1/32 inch of the inner dielectric will be exposed. The braid you have just twisted should be flat. Make sure there are no loose or stray wires from the braid, as these could possibly cause a short.

The cable is now ready for the BNC plug. Insert the center conductor down into the back end of the connector, guiding the hot lead into the center

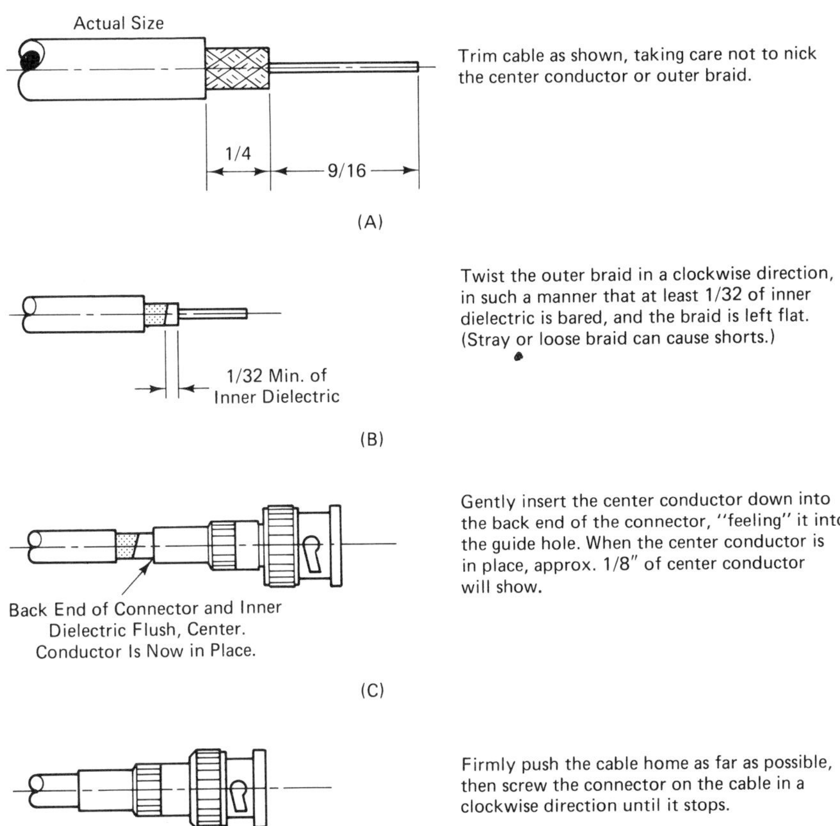

Actual Size
1/4
9/16
Trim cable as shown, taking care not to nick the center conductor or outer braid.
(A)
1/32 Min. of Inner Dielectric
Twist the outer braid in a clockwise direction, in such a manner that at least 1/32 of inner dielectric is bared, and the braid is left flat. (Stray or loose braid can cause shorts.)
(B)
Back End of Connector and Inner Dielectric Flush, Center. Conductor Is Now in Place.
Gently insert the center conductor down into the back end of the connector, "feeling" it into the guide hole. When the center conductor is in place, approx. 1/8" of center conductor will show.
(C)
Firmly push the cable home as far as possible, then screw the connector on the cable in a clockwise direction until it stops.
(D)

Figure 2-31. Method of connecting a BNC plug: (A) trim cable; (B) twist outer braid clockwise; (C) insert cable into plug; (D) screw connector onto the cable. (*Courtesy Marshall Electronics, Inc.*)

hole (see drawing C). Finally, push the cable firmly as far forward as possible. Then screw the connector on the cable in a clockwise direction until it can go no further (D).

Note that no crimping was used with this method. There are some F-plugs that have a separate crimping sleeve and for these a pair of pliers or a crimping tool will be required.

The T-Connector

It is sometimes necessary to make a connection to coaxial (coax) cable somewhere along its length. For this a special connector is needed (Fig. 2-32). Although generally referred to as a plug, it is a hybrid, composed of two jacks

Figure 2–32. T-connector.

and a plug. Two ends of coaxial cable with F-type male connectors are plugged into the sides, while an F-type jack is connected to the remaining port at the center.

PL-259 Plug

Another type of plug is the PL-259, also known as a UHF plug, used with RG-59/U coaxial cable. This is a standard UHF connector often supplied with a screw-on lock. It is also available as a solderless push-on type, with the connector screwed onto its connecting cable.

Test Instrument Connectors

Plugs are used for making connections to test instruments such as a volt-ohm-milliameter (VOM) (Fig. 2–33). The leads can be terminated in a pair of insulated alligator clips or in a pair of needle-point test prods. The plugs used with test leads are often pin or banana plugs. The plugs can be straight or right-angle units.

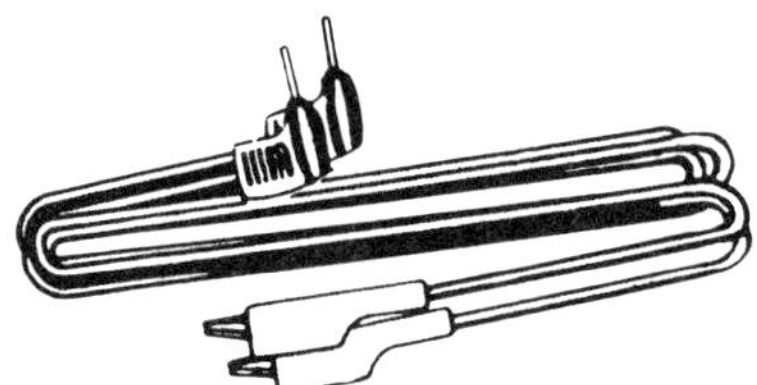

Figure 2–33. Test leads for a volt-ohm-milliammeter (VOM). The leads are terminated in a pair of insulated alligator clips at one end and either pin plugs or banana jacks at the other. (*Courtesy GC Electronics*)

CABLE CONNECTORS

Different components can have identical jacks, in which case the cable used to connect them will have identical plugs, one at each end of the cable. However, jacks on one component are often different from those on another, especially if the components are made by different manufacturers. As a result, a cable may have different plugs at each end.

In Fig. 2–34, drawing A shows a cable with a pair of F-plugs indicating that each of the components to be connected is equipped with F-jacks. This cable can be used to interface a pair of video components. Drawing B is a

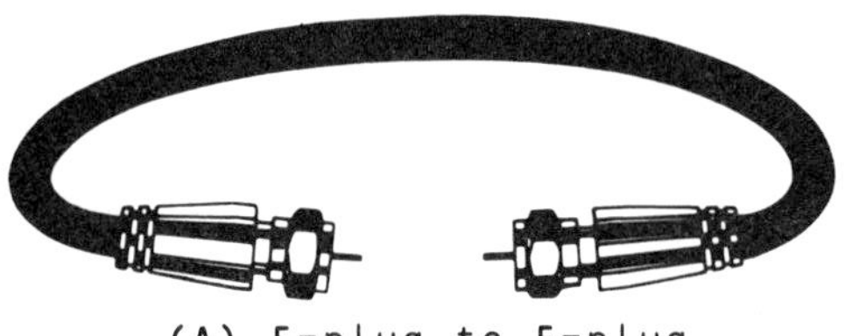

(A) F-plug to F-plug

(B) RCA plug to RCA plug

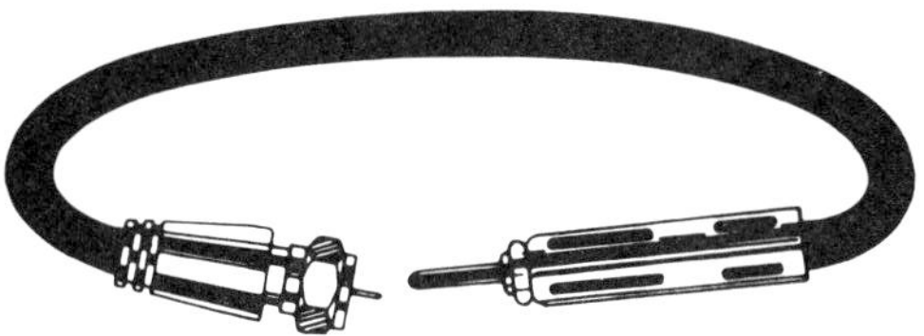

(C) F-plug to Motorola plug

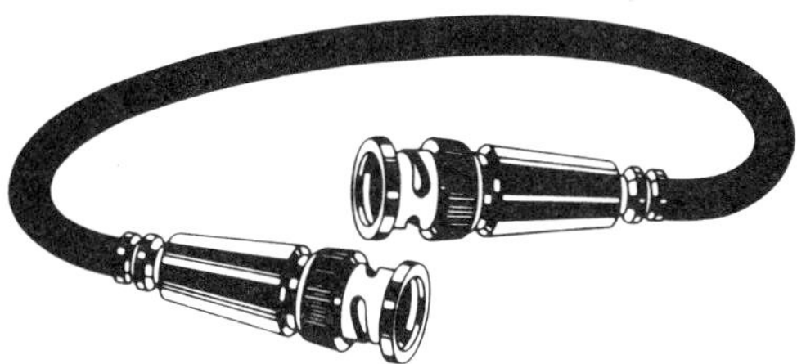

(D) BNC plug to BNC plug

(E) Right-angle quick connect F-plug to F-plug

Figure 2-34. Adapter plugs. (*Courtesy Recoton Corporation*)

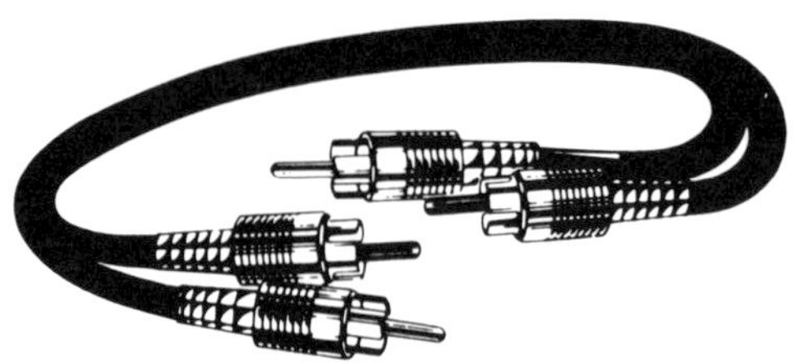

(F) Two RCA plugs to two RCA plugs

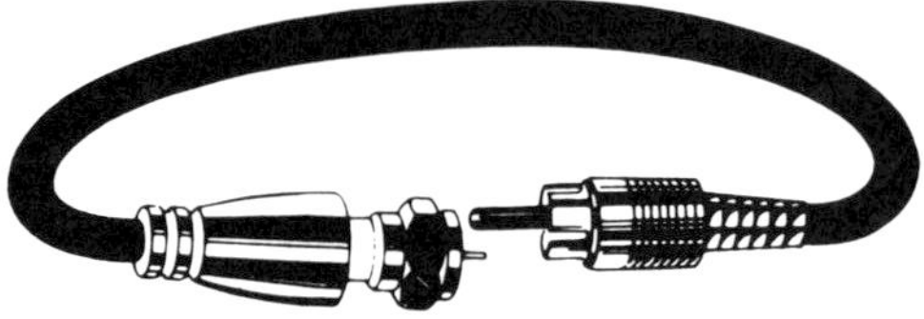

(G) F-plug to RCA plug

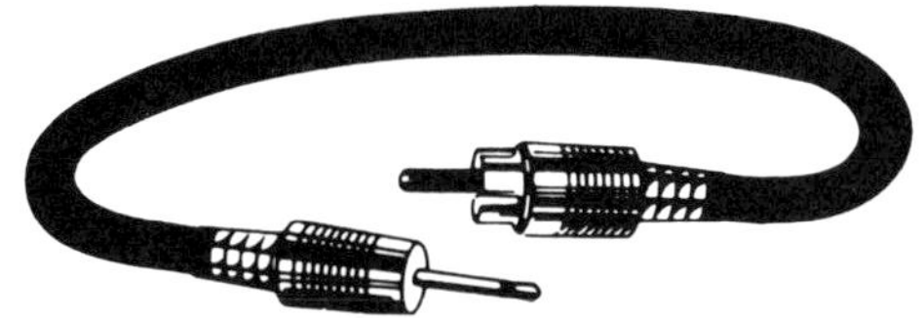

(H) RCA plug to 3.5-mm mini plug

Figure 2-34. *(continued)*

cable using RCA plugs on both ends. This type of connector is frequently used to interconnect audio components. The cable is audio coax but more frequently called audio cable. In C, the cable has an F-plug at one end and a Motorola plug at the other. The Motorola plug connects to a wall plate wired to a master antenna, and the F-plug is used to connect the coaxial cable to a television set. Drawing D shows a cable with a pair of BNC plugs. As indicated earlier, these are twist-lock types and come somewhere between a push-on plug and a screw-on plug. Drawing E shows a pair of F-plugs, and though they may look different, they are identical and vary only in construction. Both are F-plugs, but one is a right-angle type. A right-angle plug is useful if the cable is to go straight up or down from the component to which it is connected. Drawing F shows a paired (twinned) set of plugs, RCA to RCA, an arrangement commonly used for connecting high-fidelity components. Drawing G illustrates an F-plug to RCA plug cable, and H shows an RCA plug connected to a 3.5 mm mini plug.

Plugs and Impedance

The connection of a plug to a cable does not change the impedance of the cable in any way. Plugs do not have impedance. If one of them is called a 75-ohm plug all this means is that the cable to which it is attached is a 75-ohm cable. Similarly, spade lugs connected to 300-ohm line do not affect the impedance of that line.

The DIN Connector

All of the plugs previously described involve the use of a single cable. Since a component may have a number of jacks, a relatively large collection of cables may be required, especially if a number of components are involved. As a result, the area behind a rack housing those components can look like a wiring maze. Not only is it unsightly, but it can lead to making wrong connections and also makes it difficult to locate and trace individual cables.

One solution is the use of a DIN cable for interconnecting audio components. Another is flat cable of the type widely used for connecting computer units, consisting of four or more wires so that multiple connections can be made with a single cable. The flat cable has had very limited application for audio components, but the DIN connector is used more often. DIN is an abbreviation for Deutsche Industrie Normen. DIN cables usually have three wires or five wires. Figure 2–35 shows a DIN plug. Five-pin DIN connectors can be used for interfacing open reel tape decks or cassette decks to a receiver or integrated amplifier. Because the ports (jacks) for the input and output of a tape deck are often identified in different ways, it is sometimes easy to transpose the connectors. Since the DIN connector has a keyway, the connection becomes certain and wiring errors are eliminated. Not only does the DIN arrangement make it impossible to transpose input and output connections, but polarity is followed automatically. With separate cables you must be careful to identify which line is left channel and which is right channel when signal polarity is important. The difficulty with a DIN cable is that manufacturers can assign different functions to the various wires inside the cable. Thus, the fact that a DIN plug will fit into a DIN jack is no guarantee of connection success. Fortunately, manufacturers often supply DIN cables with their equipment. Further, components such as tape decks are often supplied with two

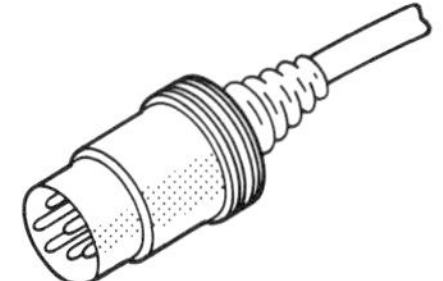

Figure 2–35. DIN connector.

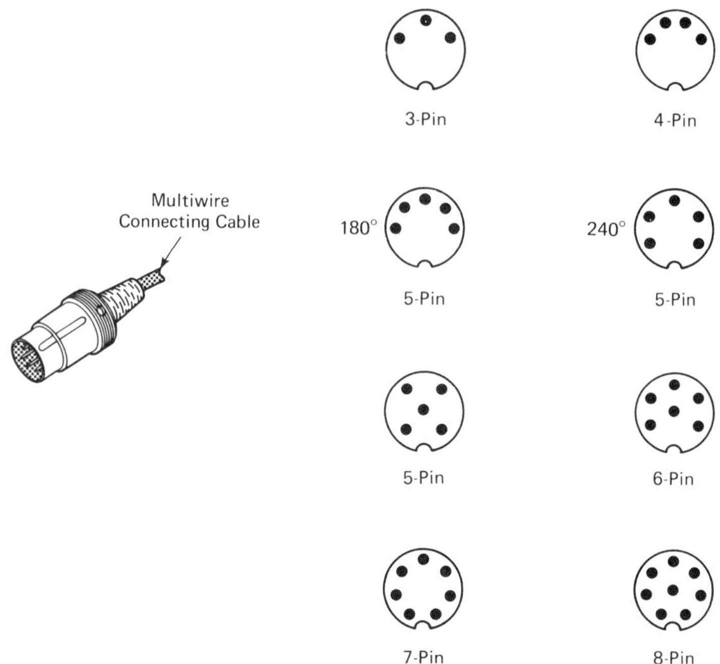

Figure 2–36. Multiple-pin DIN connectors.

types of ports: one for a DIN connector and other ports for the use of RCA plugs.

Three- and five-pin DIN connectors are common, but they can range to as many as eight pins (Fig. 2–36). Not all DIN pin arrangements are the same. Note in the drawing the differences in the five-pin types.

DIN plugs may also be straight or right-angle. The right-angle DIN plug permits the cable to form an angle of 90 degrees with the equipment to which it is connected. DIN connectors are look-alikes, and a three-pin DIN can have the same outward appearance as an eight-pin DIN. To determine the type it is necessary to count the number of pins.

The XLR Plug

XLR plugs, sometimes called Cannon plugs (Fig. 2–37) are used with microphone cables and, as shown in Fig. 2–38, are three- and five-contact keyed plugs, so it is possible to insert the plug in its jack in only one way.

XLR plugs and DIN connectors are functionally and physically different. The DIN connector uses wire pairs to carry signals to and from a component. The XLR is intended only for carrying signals from a microphone to some component, such as a mixer.

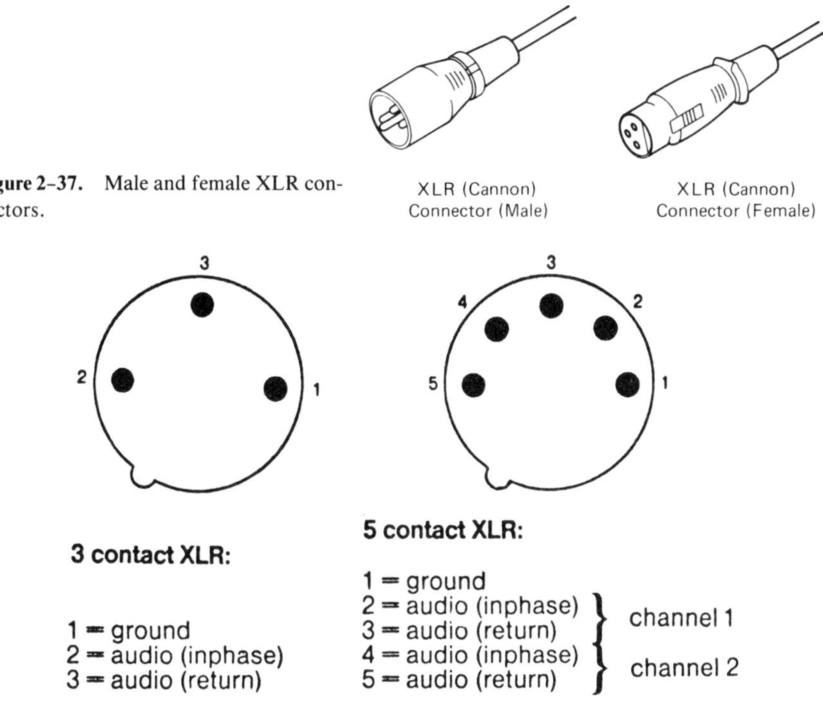

Figure 2–37. Male and female XLR connectors.

Figure 2–38. Three- and five-contact XLR connectors.

The outer shell is held in place by a machine screw, as shown in the open view in Fig. 2–39A. Toward the end of the shell, a pair of screw-mounted clamps keep the shell in place—at the same time securing the assembly to its connecting cable. Drawing B is an assembled view of its mating jack.

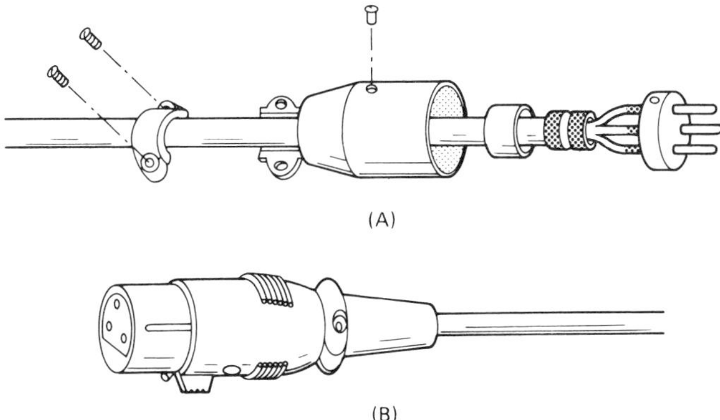

Figure 2–39. Three-pin XLR connector: exposed view of the plug (A); assembled view of the jack (B).

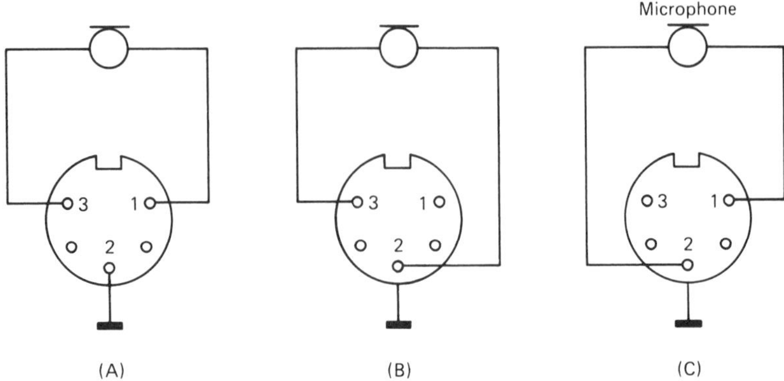

Figure 2–40. Alternative XLR three-pin connections.

The numbering of the pin positions on the plug or jack (sometimes called a socket) is clockwise when the plug or jack is held as shown in Fig. 2–40. (Sometimes, though, to make connections more confusing, the XLR pins are numbered counterclockwise.) There is no standardization as to the way in which the wires of the cable are connected to the terminal points of the plug or jack. Drawing A shows the connections for balanced cable, and drawing B illustrates how an unbalanced cable can be connected. As there are only two connections for unbalanced cable the center, or hot, lead is wired to terminal 3 while the shield, which also works as a signal conductor, is wired to terminal 2. Note that terminal 1 is unused. For a three-pin XLR you can use pin 2 as the grounded shield connection, with either pin 1 or pin 3 for the hot lead. Drawing C shows the alternate connections for unbalanced cable.

Figure 2–41 shows the connections for a three-pin XLR. Note that the terminals are not numbered as are those shown in Fig. 2–40. Drawing A is an end view of either the plug or the jack, and B shows the wiring arrangement for unbalanced cable. Drawing C indicates the connections for balanced coaxial cable, and D illustrates an unbalanced to a balanced output, using a center-tapped transformer. Terminals 2 and 3 of the output side of the transformer are the signal leads; the center tap connection is grounded.

While there is no agreement on XLR connections, a standard for the three-pin XLR does exist and it is IEC 268-12. Using this standard, pin 1 is common, pin 2 is positive, and pin 3 is negative.

Multipin Plugs

The output of a video camera consists of video and audio signals, and these alone require a total of four wires. An additional wire is needed for switching the accompanying portable VCR, plus a ground wire, plus a wire for DC voltage. Connectors are usually either ten- or fourteen-pin plugs, but

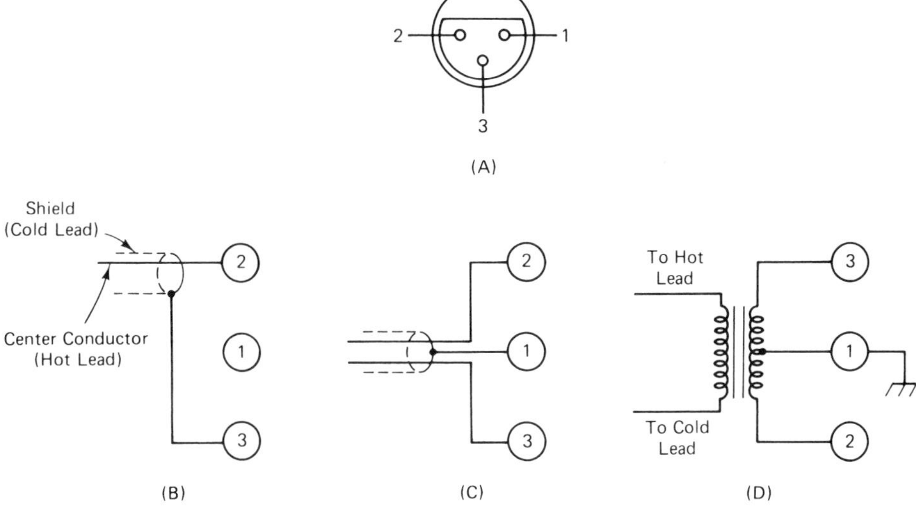

Figure 2–41. The three-pin XLR connector: end view of plug or jack (A); unbalanced connection (B); balanced connection (C); unbalanced-to-balanced connection (D).

eight-pin and twelve-pin connectors are also available. VHS portable video cassette recorders use the ten-pin; Beta format uses the fourteen-pin. Figure 2–42 shows a ten-pin quick-fit connector for portable VHS units. Because of the difference between VHS and Beta, their cables are not interchangeable.

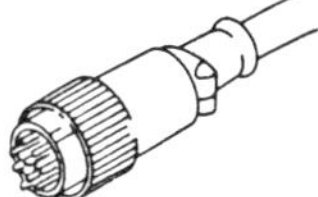

Figure 2–42. Ten-pin quick-fit connector for portable VHS recorders.

Video Camera Connectors

Connectors for video cameras are often ten-pin types but some are also fourteen pins. There is no standardization for such connectors used to form a link between the camera and its associated portable video cassette recorder (VCR). The fact that a connector will fit does not automatically mean it is the correct one, as manufacturers may assign different circuits to the wiring.

The connectors in Fig. 2–43 are quick-fit connectors. Video home system (VHS) units use the ten-pin type more often, and Beta format portable VCRs use the fourteen-pin connectors. For VHS recorders, the power supply terminal is a seven-pin DIN; the camera terminal is a round ten-pin connector.

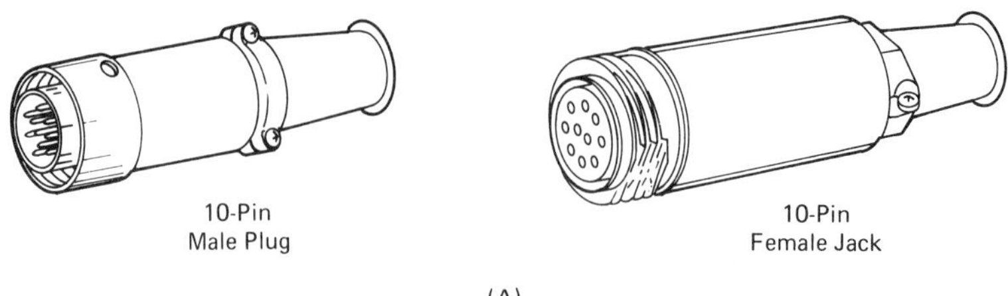

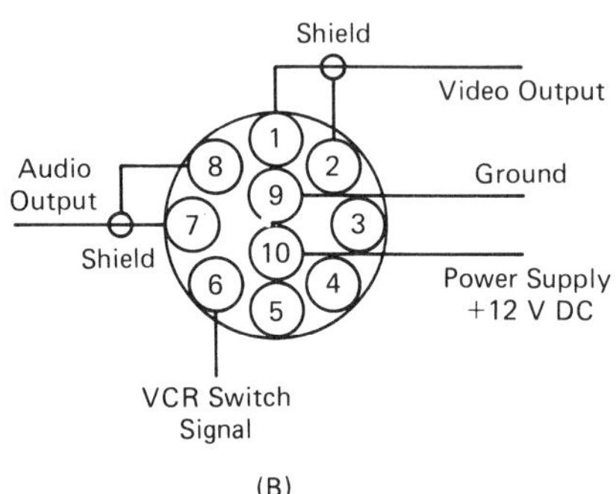

Figure 2–43. Ten pin male and female VCR/camera connectors (A) and wiring diagram (B).

Some video camera manufacturers supply interfacing cables to permit their cameras to be used with just about any VCR. Typical cable length is about five feet, but longer extension cables are available. Professional video cameras can use connectors having as many as fifty pins.

Modem Connections

Computer data can be delivered via telephone lines using a device called a modem, an acronym derived from the words *modulate/demodulate*. Modulation is associated with signal transmission; demodulation with signal reception.

There are two basic modem techniques: the acoustic mode and the direct mode. Figure 2–44 is an illustration of the use of the acoustic mode. The telephone handset is removed from its cradle and is positioned in the modem. The modem is connected to the keyboard of the computer via a four-foot (1220 mm) cable. The other end of this cable fits into a jack at the rear of the modem. The cable is keyed so it can fit one way only. The telephone is connected to a telephone outlet and this can be done by using either a modular jack or a standard phone jack.

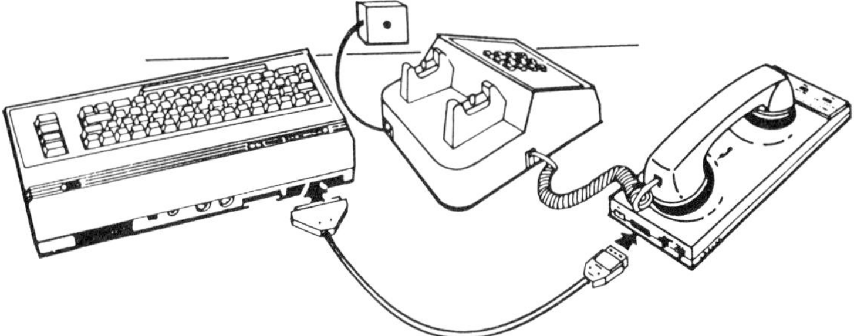

Figure 2–44. Modem in acoustic mode. (*Courtesy General Electric*)

In the direct mode, the telephone handset remains in its cradle (Fig. 2–45). The modem is plugged into the telephone line while the cable connection between the computer keyboard and the modem is the same as that shown in Fig. 2–44. In order for your computer to communicate over the telephone line you must first load a terminal program into your computer. To place the modem on line, run the program.

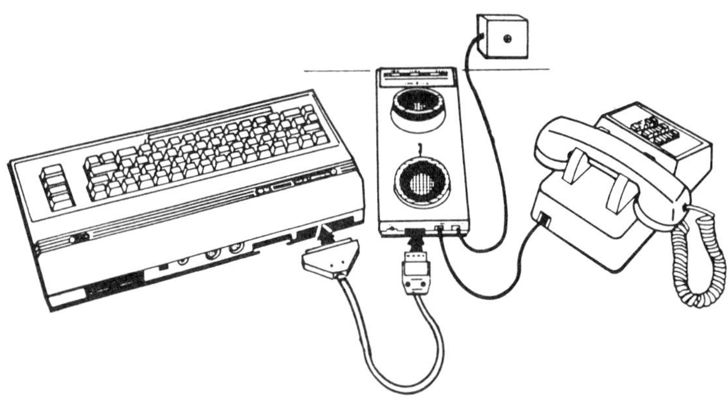

Figure 2–45. Modem in direct mode. (*Courtesy General Electric*)

Printed Circuit Board Connections

At one time, all components used point-to-point wiring, which has now been replaced by the wiring on a printed circuit (PC) board. The conductors etched into the board can terminate in a series of connectors (Fig. 2–46). These connectors can be joined to a jack, which can then mate with a plug having corresponding pins.

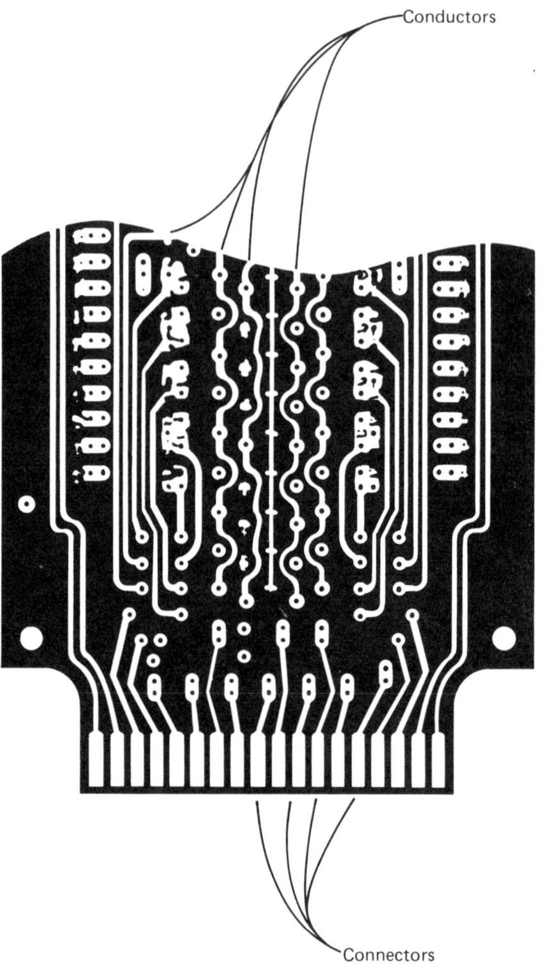

Figure 2–46. Printed circuit (PC) board connections.

TERMINATORS

A terminator is a resistor used to match coaxial cable to its characteristic (surge) impedance. When installed at the ends of a coaxial line, it prevents signal reflections back along the line. Since the terminator is resistive, it results in some signal loss across the resistive element, but because it improves the standing wave ratio, it suffers less transmission line loss. A terminator also minimizes or eliminates picture ghosting due to transmission signal line reflections.

A component may have one or more unused output signal ports. It is generally expected that all these ports will be utilized, but this isn't always the

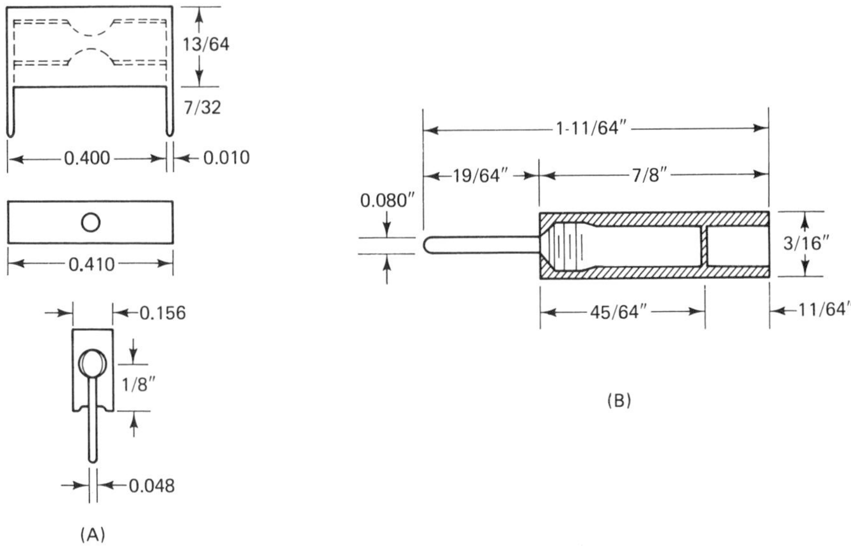

Figure 2-47. Jack and plug for printed circuit boards: miniature horizontal jack (A) and plug (B). (*Courtesy GC Electronics*)

case. To avoid signal reflections, a terminator is used—a resistor mounted in a plug that supplies a fixed load. If the signal output port is 75 ohms, the terminator resistor will have this value. Connect the terminator plug and forget about it until you can make use of the available port.

Semistandardization

There is not much standardization in the world of connectors. The astonishing number of noninterchangeable plugs and jacks testifies to the lack of standardization: plugs and jacks on equipment made by different manufacturers sometimes cannot interface directly; and different models of components made by the same manufacturer sometimes cannot interface. However, this sorry state of affairs is modified by the use of jack and plug adapters. Further, all plugs and jacks are standardized within their class—all phono plugs of a particular size are interchangeable, even though made by different manufacturers. Even this small concession is marred by some lack of standardization in cables. For instance, the three-pin XLR can be connected with wires going to different pins, so there is no assurance, even if an XLR plug fits an XLR jack, that the correct connections have been made.

There is one small bit of comfort, and it is possibly the only rationalization for the absence of plug standardization—competition is at work supplying plugs and jacks for every conceivable connection need. It does mean the jacks and plugs we have are the best obtainable and that designers of plugs and jacks, and inventors of new kinds, know they must meet the competition of an open market. Some amount of plug and jack confusion is the price we pay for the opportunity to get the best.

JACKS

Making a connection from one component to another involves plugs and jacks; the plugs are mounted on cables, the jacks on the equipment and sometimes on cables as well.

Plugs and Jacks for Printed Circuit Boards

Printed circuit (PC) boards can make use of plugs and jacks specifically designed for them. Figure 2-47A is a dimensional drawing of a miniature horizontal jack. It can accept a tip plug of 0.080-inch diameter in either end, or from the top or bottom. This jack has a width of 0.400 inch and a depth of 0.156 inch. The contact is silver-plated beryllium copper and has a current capacity of five amperes maximum.

A miniature tip plug that can be used with miniature horizontal and vertical jacks having a standard 0.080-inch diameter is shown in Fig. 2-47B. This plug requires a soldered connection of the wire lead.

Banana and Tip Jacks

These jacks are mounted on the chassis of components or on the rear apron, although some, such as jacks for microphones or headphones, are positioned on the front for user convenience. A typical banana jack is shown in Fig. 2-48A. The threaded jack is held in place by a hex nut, and the internal connection is made to a soldering lug positioned between the hex nut and the front of the jack. In banana jacks the bore must be such that it will accommodate all standard banana plugs. The bore is smooth. As the banana plug is inserted in its jack the four-spring metal leaves of the plug are compressed, forcing good contact between the plug and the jack. Figure 2-48B shows the jack for a tip plug.

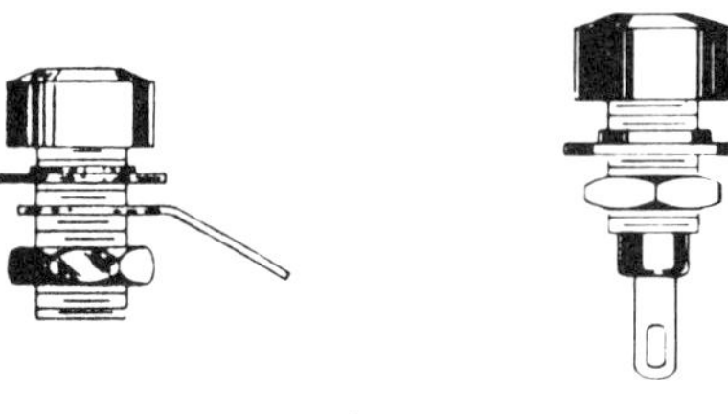

Figure 2-48. Banana jack (A); tip jack (B). (*Courtesy GC Electronics*)

Jack for Unbalanced Connector

Figure 2–49 shows the details for an unbalanced phone jack. (The phone plug for this jack was shown in Fig. 2–18A.) This jack has two connecting elements. One is the tip connector that makes contact with the tip of the plug and is the connection for the hot lead. The other is the sleeve connector and this element of the jack contacts the sleeve of the plug, which, in turn, is attached to the cable's shield braid. Inside the component on which the jack is mounted, the sleeve connector is automatically grounded to the chassis. A contact on the tip connector is wired to a circuit using a small length of shielded cable. The shield of that cable is also grounded to the chassis.

The phone jack shown in Fig. 2–49A, and its accompanying plug in 2–49B, are intended for monophonic signal use only.

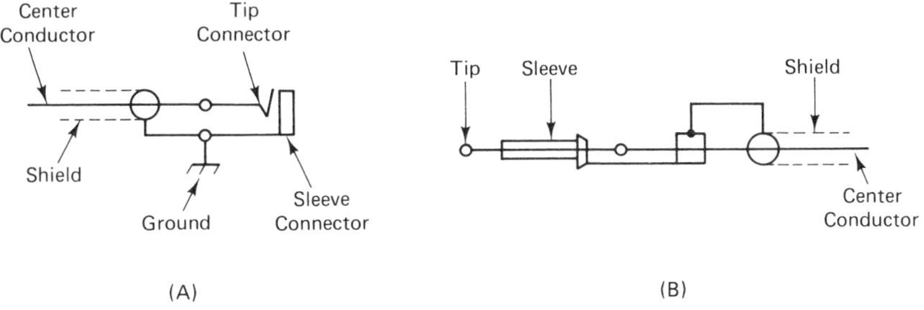

Figure 2–49. Connection details for a phone jack (A) and plug (B).

Balanced Connectors

Figure 2–50 shows the arrangement for two-wire balanced connections for a jack. (The phone plug for this jack was shown in Fig. 2–18B.) This jack has separate contacts for the tip and the ring of the mating plug. The metal frame of the jack makes contact with the long sleeve of the plug and is the ground connection. The tip and the ring are insulated from each other and

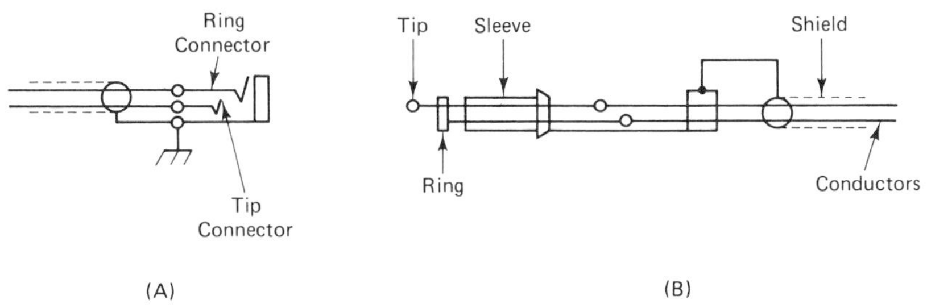

Figure 2–50. Jack (A) and plug (B) connections for balanced cable.

from the shield of the plug. The tip and the ring, however, are connected to the two hot lead conductors in the plug.

Shorting and Nonshorting Jacks

Jacks can be categorized in various ways; but one is whether the jack is a shorting or nonshorting type. Figure 2–51A illustrates a nonshorting jack, and B shows a shorting jack. In the nonshorting jack, the hot lead connector remains "floating," that is, it remains open. In the shorting type in drawing B, note that the two upper terminals make contact and that this contact is broken when the plug is inserted. The shorting arrangement can put a resistive load across the hot connection, killing any possible unwanted signal pickup, such as a hum or noise voltage, by the hot lead. The jack in drawing B is sometimes called a closed-circuit jack; the others, such as those in Fig. 2–49 and Fig. 2–50 are open-circuit jacks.

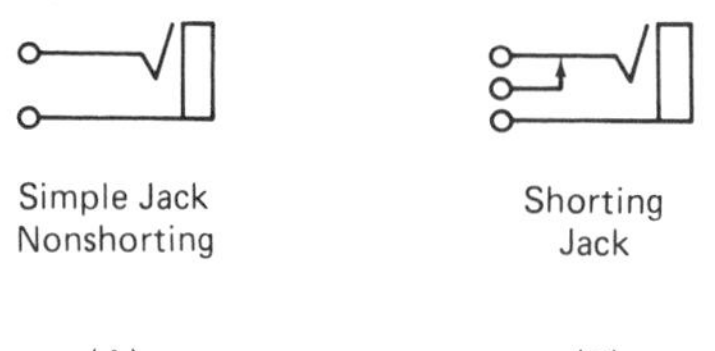

Figure 2–51. Nonshorting (A) and shorting (B) jacks.

Inline and Open-Frame Jacks

Jacks can be mounted on cables. Known as inline jacks, they are completely shielded, protecting the wiring of the cables to which they are attached. Jacks used on components such as receivers and amplifiers are open-frame, so called because they have no need of a surrounding shell like that used by inline jacks. Inline jacks use a small machine screw for making connections; open-frame jacks have soldering terminals. Another type of jack used to replace the open-frame type is the enclosed jack. Electrically, the connections are the same as those used with the open-frame type but the jack's metal enclosure protects the jack against unwanted signal pickup.

Jack Adapters

Because of the diversity of plugs and jacks, adapters are needed. Thus a component equipped with an RCA jack can be connected to some other component using a BNC jack. Many other variations are possible.

Figure 2–20 showed the use of adapters for plugs. Adapters can also be used for jacks and some of these appear in Fig. 2–52. Drawing A shows an F-jack to F-jack adapter. The input to this adapter can be a cable equipped with an F-jack, as can its output. An adapter can be a combined plug-jack,

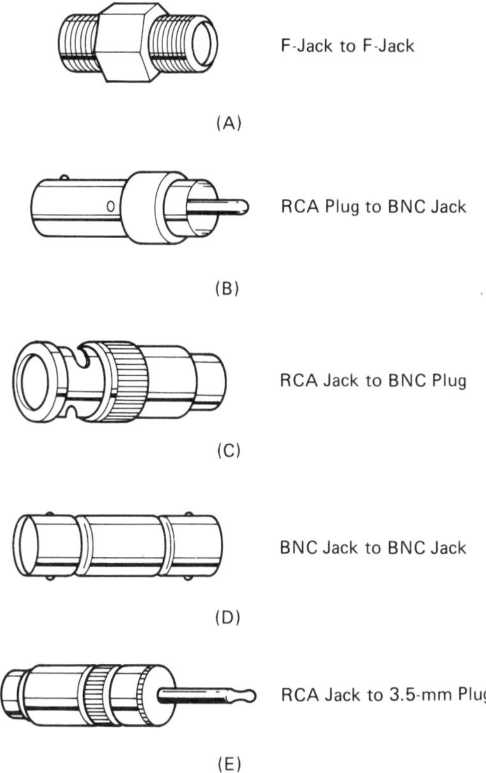

Figure 2–52. Jack adapters: F-jack to F-jack (A); RCA plug to BNC jack (B); RCA jack to BNC plug (C); BNC jack to BNC jack (D); RCA jack to 3.5 mm plug (E).

as in B. Here the input is a BNC jack; the output is an RCA plug. This adapter could be used, for example, if a connecting cable was equipped with a BNC plug. It would be inserted into the BNC jack portion of the adapter. The end of the plug equipped with the RCA plug could then be inserted into an RCA jack.

Drawing C indicates connections that are exactly the opposite of those in B. Here the RCA jack can accommodate a cable equipped with an RCA plug. The BNC plug output of the adapter can then be inserted into a BNC jack.

Drawing D is a BNC jack to BNC jack adapter. An adapter of this kind could be used when a cable equipped with BNC plugs is to be extended. Finally, in drawing E there is an RCA jack to a 3.5 mm plug adapter. This adapter could be used with a cable equipped with an RCA plug. This plug could be inserted into the RCA jack end of the adapter while the 3.5 mm plug could be inserted into the corresponding jack mounted on some component.

CABLE-HANDLING PRECAUTIONS

When removing a plug from its jack, hold the body of the plug firmly and pull. Do not pull on the cable. Some plugs are easy to insert; others, such as the multipin types, must line up exactly with the corresponding connectors in the jack. In some instances the plug and jack may have a keyway to help make the correct connection, or else the connectors may be arranged asymmetrically. If the plug has a number of fine connectors, proceed with caution. Bending one or more may require a plug replacement.

Do not assume, because a plug and jack fit easily, that the connection will be satisfactory. The purpose of a plug and jack is to connect wires that should be connected, but in multiwire cables, manufacturers are at liberty to use any arrangement they wish.

PLUG AND JACK CARE

Plugs are made of brass, plated with nickel or cadmium. These metals can tarnish, get dirty or rusty, or all three. The tarnish is a light, invisible film of oil obtained from the fingers during handling, and it acts as an insulating material. The dirt and oxidation (rust) also degrade the conducting qualities of the plug. Use fine sandpaper or steel wool to clean, or you might try the eraser on the end of a pencil. After treatment, rub it with a cloth and make sure all particles from the sandpaper, steel wool, or eraser are removed. The more expensive connectors use very thin gold plating. The advantage is that these do not corrode but they can still become contaminated by tarnish and dirt. Do not use any abrasives on these, as the gold layer removes easily. Simply wipe with a tissue.

When the cleaning is finished, wash the connectors with pure isopropyl alcohol, obtainable in drug stores. Do not use ordinary rubbing alcohol.

Tarnish and dirt are easy enough to remove; rust is another matter. When the connectors of a cable rust, the contact between the jack and the plug never gets better, always worse. The result is a high-resistance connection, reducing signal strength and raising the noise level. The best cure for rust is prevention. From time to time, possibly every six months or so, remove plugs from their jacks, but do so only one at a time to avoid confusion about which plug goes into which jack. Use the cleaning methods described. If this does not help, replace the cable and its plugs. It is generally not worthwhile to salvage the connecting cable and replace the end connectors.

Examine the jacks (you may need a flashlight to do so). If you see evidence of rust and you cannot remove it, take the unit in to a qualified service technician or to an official service station of the manufacturer. How long jacks will last before new ones are needed depends on the amount of moisture in the air. In humid regions, connectors—with the exception of those that are gold plated—rust more quickly.

When you insert a plug into a jack, do not do so with a straightforward motion. Instead, rotate the plug once completely. The advantage of doing so is that it will help clean the recessed portion of the jack, and that is fairly inaccessible. After the plug has been inserted into the jack, it should be secure. Pull gently on the plug to make sure the connection is tight. If there is any play between the plug and the jack, the plug and its cable may need to be replaced.

Cleaning plugs is easier than cleaning jacks because plugs are accessible and can be examined from all sides. Jacks are mounted on the front panel or the rear apron of components and are not only awkward to get at, but difficult to inspect. However, unless the jack is a gold-plated type it is safe to assume that corrosion has probably set in after a year following installation.

You can remove oxide coatings and other accumulations from the metal surface of jacks by using a commercial product which not only cleans but supplies a conductive lubricating film that acts to protect the jack in the future.

A special tool, made of a stiff foam resin material, is supplied with the cleaner (Fig. 2–53). Move the tool repeatedly over the jack's surface but do not apply excessive force. The cleaner can also be used on plugs.

It may be tempting to repair a short length of cable equipped with a pair of pin or phono connectors. The time and effort required make such a project hardly worthwhile. It is better to get a replacement.

Total Cable Resistance

Total cable resistance is usually considered the resistance from the pin or tip of the plug connected to the hot lead to the corresponding tip of the connector at the other end of the cable. However, this is not total resistance but just the sum of the plug and cable resistance. Total resistance is that mea-

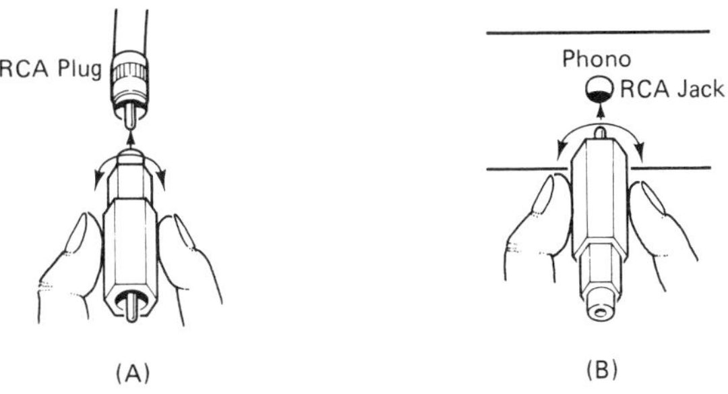

Figure 2–53. Method of cleaning a plug (A) and a jack (B). (*Courtesy Signet*)

sured from the jack of one component to the jack of the other component to which it is connected. This test includes the resistance of the contact between the connector pins of the plugs and their mating jacks. Measuring that resistance is beyond the scope of the in-home user. It requires a test instrument capable of measuring extremely tiny fractions of an ohm. Further, it assumes a test made with the jack exposed, something that can only be done by taking the component out of its case. This isn't recommended for the component owner, as such an action would nullify the warranty of the component. If the jack or its plug is corroded, the contact resistance could easily be much higher than the resistance of the cable alone.

TESTING CABLES

Because they are out of the way, and are so simple and so inexpensive compared to components, there is a tendency to ignore cables as a contributing factor to an audio or video system's failure to operate properly, or in some cases, not at all.

All cables are passive devices. They do not amplify—and in the best of cases they attenuate the signal only slightly—but no system can be any better than its cables. They must make sure, positive contact and they should not change their physical or electrical characteristics at any time and under any normal operating conditions.

The first test of any cable should be a visual one. Examine the connectors at both ends. Do they show signs of rust; are they obviously oily or dirty? Replace any cable that shows these symptoms for if they aren't troublemakers, they soon will be. Examine the full length of the cable for any obvious signs of age or damage. If the cable covering shows cracks or splits, if it seems to be nicked or cut, get rid of it. Examine the connectors. The hot lead should be soldered to the tip of the plug. If you can see the hot lead and can move it, retouch the tip with a soldering iron.

When you insert a plug into a jack, wiggle the plug back and forth and up and down. There should be no looseness or play. The plug should not be able to fall into its jack; it must require pushing.

The easiest test for any cable is replacement with a cable known to be in good operating order, but if you want verification it isn't difficult to test cables; there are several resistance checks you can make. One is from the center plug of the connector to the shield braid. Using an inexpensive instrument such as a volt-ohm-milliammeter equipped with test leads ending in alligator clips, attach one to the shield of the connector, the other to the center pin. Flex the cable. The resistance reading should be maximum for any setting of the resistance control of the test instrument; R × 1, R × 10, R × 100. The resistance reading should indicate an open circuit condition.

The next test is from the center pin of one connector to the center pin of the connector at the other end of the cable. This should indicate zero resistance, or very close to it. While you are doing this, flex the cable. There should be no change in the meter reading. Repeat the same test with the meter leads attached to the ground portion of both plugs. Again, the reading should be a short (zero resistance), regardless of the flexing of the cable.

If brand-new connectors are being used, it is reasonable to assume that the cable and its connectors are in good condition. But it is always well to be suspicious and with a system that is noisy, intermittent, or inoperative, it is logical to check the cable. If the cable was used, and is being drafted as a replacement, it is also sensible to check it for defects.

Passive vs. Active Testing

The visual inspection of connectors and cables and the use of a volt-ohm-milliammeter for checking cable and connector opens and shorts are passive tests. However a test instrument isn't needed if a system is operative, for the connectors and cables can be subjected to an active test.

In an active test, the cable (or cables) being checked must have the plugs inserted into the proper jacks and the system turned on. Use a signal source, preferably one that starts at the front end of the system, such as a TV broadcast signal. Set the volume control so the signal can be heard, but at a low-to-moderate level. Flex all cables and move all connectors involved in the flow of the signals from the input end to the output. At no time should the sound or picture level be affected by cable movement. Repeat with the connectors used for the tape decks and for other sound sources or signal processors. The important thing to remember is that the cables and connectors being checked must be in the sound or picture path and that both of these must be active.

These tests can be done even if the system is intermittent or there is no sound, or no picture, or both. With the system turned on, flex the cables and try moving the connectors. If just the sound is involved, concentrate on those cables in the sound path; if just the picture is missing or intermittent, work on those cables in the picture path. As a final test, check all cables, as picture and sound sometimes travel together.

3

ADD-ON DEVICES

An *add-on device* is a component that is put on line with a television or high-fidelity system. The term is sometimes used synonymously, but incorrectly, with *accessory* (also described in this chapter). The purpose of an add-on device is to supply some additional feature, or features, to an in-home entertainment system.

One type of add-on is any device incorporated into an audio or video system to permit the correct interconnection of components. A matching transformer for impedance-matching an antenna to a transmission line is an add-on. A switcher, a unit that permits the selection of one of a number of possible signal inputs, is an add-on. Some add-ons are integrated into components but many others must be included by the user.

ACTIVE AND PASSIVE DEVICES

An active device is a component either used on-line or added to a video system to supply some desired feature, but it also supplies some signal amplification. An antenna downlead is a passive device. It not only does not supply a signal gain; it results in a signal loss.

A unit can be either active or passive, but in some instances a component that is normally passive can be made active through the addition of an amplifier. Any length of connecting cable, regardless of the kind of connectors is uses, is passive. An impedance terminator is passive. Although not ordinarily regarded as such, a loudspeaker is passive, for it not only does not supply signal gain, but always operates at a loss.

ACCESSORIES

An accessory is any device used for the maintenance of a system, whether that system is video or audio, or a combination of the two. A video head cleaner for a video cassette recorder is an accessory. The cleaner does not become part of the system but assists in its correct functioning. A section of shrink wrap used for covering and insulating a wire joint is an accessory; the wrap remains on the wires, but it does not become part of the system—it supplies a protective function only.

PROTOCOL

An active or passive component that observes previously agreed-upon standards is said to be following protocol. Protocol is important. If several manufacturers are engaged in the manufacture of an item such as an F-plug, all the plugs they produce will be interchangeable, as these different manufacturers will all have used the same manufacturing specifications. There may be some minor external differences in color or material quality.

SWITCHERS

A basic switcher can be nothing more than the equivalent of a four-pole, double-throw switch (often called an A/B switch), giving the user a choice of two signal sources, or the ability to route a signal into one or the other of two possible paths.

There is a difference, though, for switchers are also impedance-matching devices. The source impedance for the input of a switcher can be 75 ohms or 300 ohms, and the outputs can both be 75 ohms, or 300 ohms, or 75 ohms and 300 ohms. This is illustrated in Fig. 3-1. The switcher at the left has two 75-ohm inputs and a 75-ohm output. The one in the center has a 75-ohm input, a 300-ohm input, and a 300-ohm output. The switcher at the right has a pair of 75-ohm inputs and a 300-ohm output.

Figure 3-2 shows the use of an A/B switch. There are two possible signal inputs in this example, a video game or computer, and TV broadcast signals from an antenna. Either one of these signals can be selected by the A/B switch for delivery to the TV set. Note that impedances aren't indicated for either of the two inputs or for the output. Because the antenna input is split, as shown

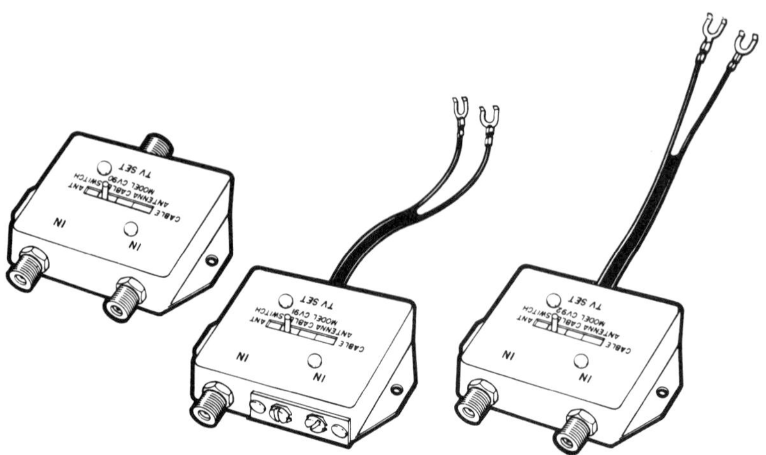

Figure 3-1. Types of A/B switchers: left—75 ohms in, 75 ohms out; center—75 ohms and 300 ohms in, 300 ohms out; right—75 ohms in, 300 ohms out. A/B switchers have two inputs, one output. (*Courtesy Gemini Industries, Inc.*)

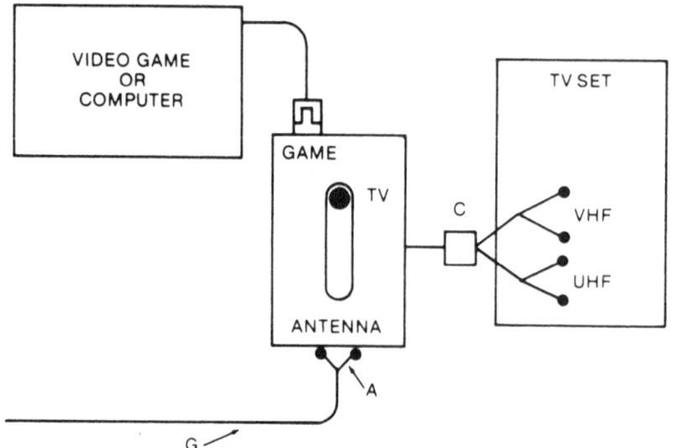

Figure 3-2. A/B switcher for antenna or video game (or computer). (*Courtesy Pfanstiehl Corp.*)

at point A, presumably the downlead is 300 ohms. The input for the game or computer appears to be 75 ohms. Item C is a band separator, dividing the signal into its VHF and UHF bands.

The impedances of the various ports on an A/B switch are determined by the components to which it will be attached. Impedance matching then becomes the responsibility of the in-home entertainment system owner, who must select switchers whose impedances match those of the components, or else use matching transformers.

Some wiring installations use just one A/B switch but others require two. The TV/game switcher in Fig. 3-3 is a slide type, but some use pushbuttons

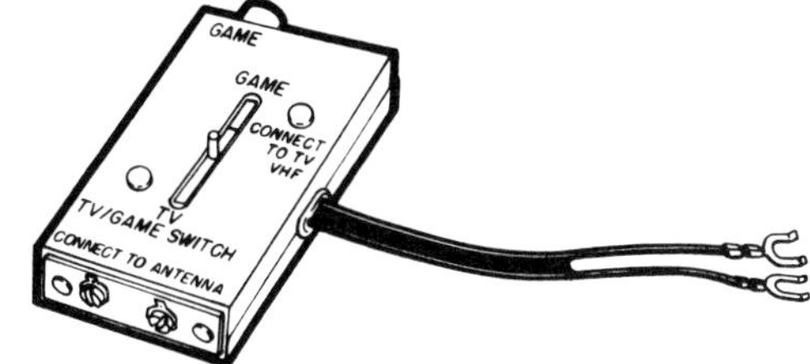

Figure 3-3. TV/game switch. (*Courtesy Gemini Industries, Inc.*)

(Fig. 3–4). The type of switch isn't of any great importance. What is more significant is to have the least amount of signal leakage from one of the internal switches to the other.

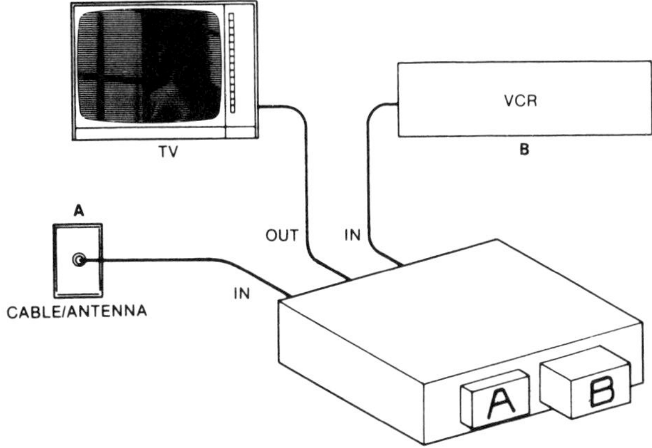

Figure 3–4. A/B switcher. (*Courtesy GC Electronics*)

A/B switches (or switchers) are lightweight and easily mounted on the rear of a TV set, and manufacturers often supply mounting screws packed in with the switcher just for this purpose. Sometimes the unit is allowed to hang from the antenna terminals of the TV set. Since the switch will be manipulated for program changes it will be less of a strain and less subject to damage if it is supported in some way. Some are supplied with a back plate having mounting holes (Fig. 3–5).

Switcher Input and Output Ports

The input and output ports on video switchers may be intended for either 75-ohm or 300-ohm connecting lines, or for some combination of the two. They use connectors for 75 ohms and spade lugs for 300 ohms. Video games require a phono jack (an RCA jack), as they have conductors equipped with phono plugs.

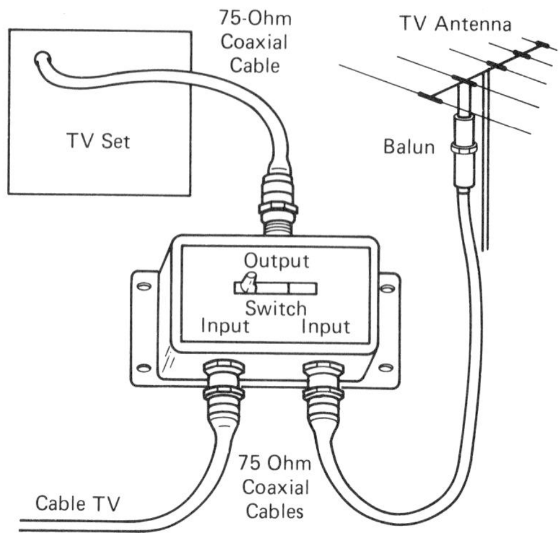

Figure 3–5. TV antenna-cable TV coaxial A/B switch. (*Courtesy RMS Electronics, Inc.*)

Switching Devices

Rotary switching devices, used for audio switching, are avoided for video, as they supply too much crosstalk—that is, signal leakage from one switch to the other at the much higher frequencies used in video.

Some TV tuners are supplied with audio/video switchers integrated into the units and these are controllable by a remote switching device. This does not increase the ability of the TV tuner to handle additional signals by much, so an add-on switch will probably be required. Ultimately, with the growth of signal sources requiring the use of the TV set's signal input terminals, switchers may be integrated into that component rather than selected as an outboard add-on. The problem with integrating switchers with TV sets is that it adds more controls and may make them less user friendly, especially for those who are satisfied with nothing more than broadcast TV signal input.

The simplest type of switcher is the A/B, giving the user a choice of two signal inputs. This doesn't sound like much but it does double the signal selection choice.

One of the more sophisticated switchers is shown in Fig. 3–6. This is a mechanical switcher using pushbuttons on its front panel. This switcher permits recording one channel while watching another, it permits remote control of the TV set, and also allows the inclusion of a second recorder. All of the ports are for 75-ohm coaxial cable, so if some of the components to be connected are 300 ohms, one or more impedance-matching transformers will be needed. As is shown in the drawing, the unit can switch a pair of TV sets, one of which could be a remote unit. It connects to a VCR, a video game, an antenna, and either cable TV or subscription TV (STV). This is a scrambled

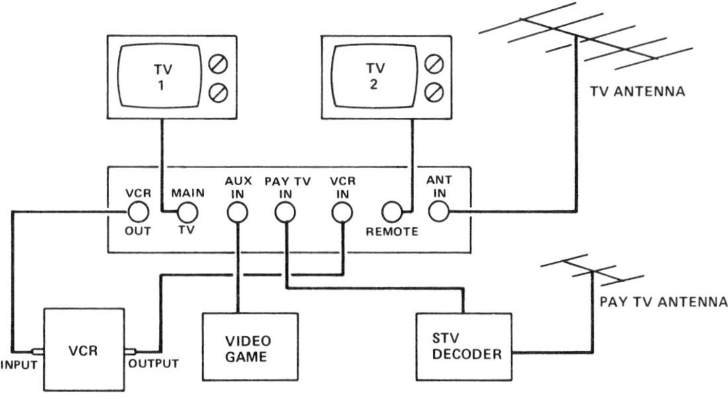

Figure 3–6. Video control center. (*Courtesy Channel Master, Div. Avnet, Inc.*)

TV broadcast signal, and requires the use of a decoder. STV is user supported and the programs carry no advertising.

Some switchers have no mechanical or moving parts, but have a face plate that is a membrane type. More elaborate switchers of this type can provide instant switching of six inputs by a single touch. Instead of using mechanical switching, these more sophisticated units are electronic, and one type has an illuminated control panel with six LED (light-emitting diode) indicator lights. As an input is activated, a LED immediately indicates which input has been selected. The switch operates on AC and will switch any of six RF inputs to a television set.

Switch Identification

Sometimes a switch will be identified by the way in which it may be used, but such identification does not mean it is restricted. Thus even if a switch is known as a cable/VCR switch, one of its inputs could be a signal from a master antenna TV.

Coaxial Switch

The term *coaxial switch* refers to a switch that is equipped with coaxial inputs and a coaxial output. However, the term is used very loosely and has come to mean any switch that has at least one 75-ohm port.

The Switcher as an Add-On

Until fairly recently, in-home entertainment systems consisted of a TV set, used only for TV broadcast reception. With the growing popularity of VCRs, personal computers, video games, and video discs, the TV set has become the display device for all of these. Switchers have become an important add-on component, for the unpleasant alternative was constantly connecting and disconnecting cables to allow the use of different signal sources. The problem of signal-source selection centered entirely on the TV set, designed to accept only two signals—both broadcast—with one VHF, the other UHF. The switcher has overcome this TV set input limitation.

The useful frequency limit of a switcher can extend as high as 900 MHz, well within the range of various program sources. Switching isolation is sometimes as low as 40 dB but more commonly is either 50 dB or 60 dB. The higher this rating, the better.

The switcher is usually a passive device, so there is some insertion loss. Typically, the loss ranges from 3.5 dB to about 10 dB. This loss is also dependent on frequency and is a few dB greater for UHF signals than for VHF. Some switchers have built-in amplifiers, changing them from passive to active devices, and of course these indicate a gain instead of a loss. The gain can be as much as 10 dB.

Switchers are not AC-operated devices, so no power-line cord connection is needed. The exception, of course, is the switcher with a built-in amplifier. Such amplifiers are solid-state and require very little operating power.

Switching Matrix

The term *switching matrix* describes a measure of the unit's switching capability, indicating the total number of possible inputs and outputs. A 4 × 2 matrix means the switcher can accept four inputs and has two outputs. Typical matrices are 4 × 4; 4 × 2; 2 × 4; 6 × 3; 6 × 1; 5 × 2; 4 × 3; 5 × 1; 1 × 2 and 5 × 6.

The Signal and Impedance Switch

There are two considerations when selecting a switch. The first is the number of signals that are to be selected and the other is the matter of impedance matching. Some switches do both, as does the one illustrated in Fig. 3-7. Like all A/B switches, this unit allows the choice of two signal inputs, and in this example the inputs are broadcast TV and cable TV. The unit is also impedance switchable. Thus the input from an outside antenna can be via twin lead, and that is always 300 ohms, or through the use of coaxial cable as the downlead, and that is always 75 ohms. A slide switch permits the selection of either of these two impedances.

The second signal input is cable TV, and here no impedance choice is necessary, as this signal source is always 75 ohms. There is also a switch on this unit for the selection of either cable TV or broadcast TV as the desired signal source. The output of the switch can be 300 ohms for a TV set whose

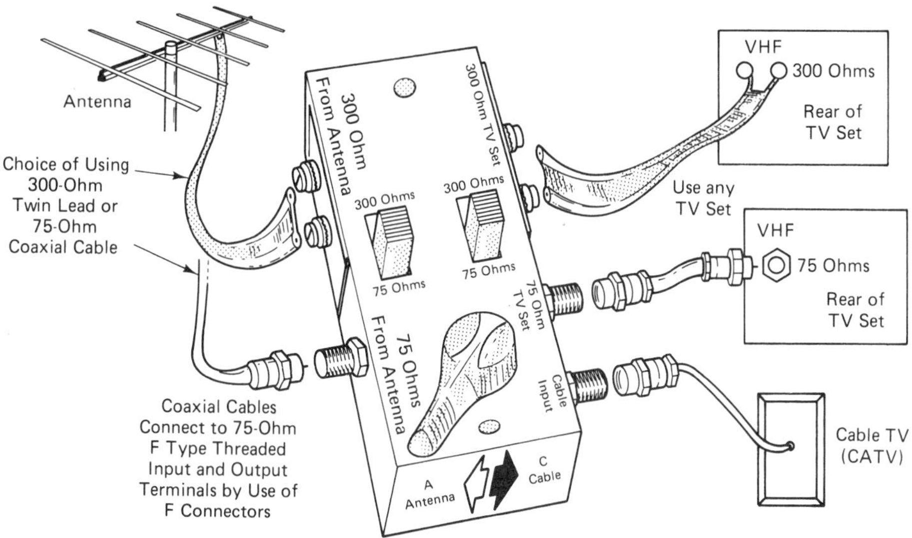

Figure 3–7. Combined A/B switch and impedance switch. (*Courtesy RMS Electronics, Inc.*)

VHF input is 300 ohms or a different TV set whose VHF input is 75 ohms. Thus, with this single switch, either one or the other of two signal sources can be chosen with no concern about impedance matching, as that can be handled by the switcher. With this unit no special impedance-matching transformers are needed. The unit can be mounted out of sight, fastened by screws to the rear of the TV set.

Connecting a Two-Way Switch

Figure 3–8 shows the wiring diagram for a two-way switch, so called because it can select one or the other of two signal sources. The switch is a true coaxial type, as its two inputs and single output are all 75 ohms. The downlead from the antenna is coaxial cable and so is the connecting cable to the video game. The output impedance is 75 ohms, and this could be connected directly to the antenna terminals of the TV receiver if they also had the same impedance. In this example, those antenna terminals are 300 ohms, so a matching transformer is used between the switch and the TV set. This transformer has an input of 75 ohms; an output of 300 ohms.

With this very simple wiring arrangement using nothing more than a two-way switch, and possibly an impedance-matching transformer, the system can use the TV set as a display for either TV broadcasts or a video game. The switch does not interfere with the way the TV set is operated. Stations can be

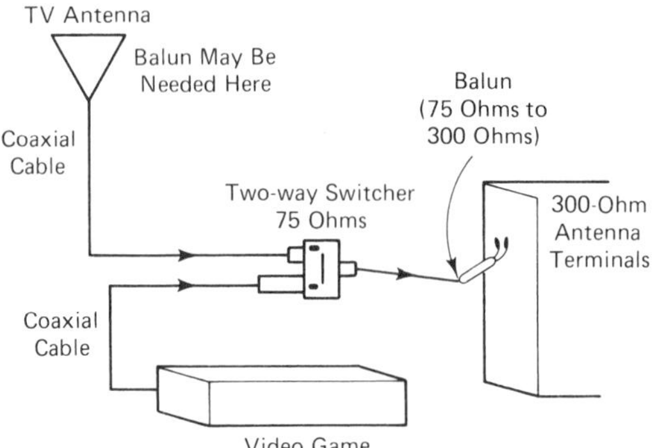

Figure 3-8. Coaxial A/B switcher.

selected manually or with the help of a wireless remote control if the set is remote-control equipped.

Multiple-Signal Input Switchers

A multiple-signal switch (or switcher) is desirable when there is a much wider choice of possible input signals. One of these is shown in Fig. 3-9. Here the choice consists of broadcast TV, a video game, a personal computer, and an input marked *aux* (for auxiliary). An aux input could be any component that needs to use the TV set as a display device. For example, at some future date a videodisc player could be added, and could be connected using the aux input.

The antenna shown in this drawing is a combined VHF/UHF antenna having an output impedance of 300 ohms, supplying TV signals to a very short length of twin lead. Somewhere along this line a balun (an acronym for balanced-to-unbalanced) is used. This is simply an impedance-matching transformer, and in this case it matches the impedance of the short length of 300-ohm line at the antenna to a length of coaxial cable that will be used as the downlead, the transmission line to the VCR.

The signals traveling along this transmission line consist of both VHF and UHF. These will be separated by a small add-on known as a band separator. The VHF and UHF signals will then be delivered to the antenna input terminals of the VCR. From the VCR the UHF signals will be supplied directly to the UHF terminals of the TV set, and the VHF signal output will be routed to terminal 1 of the switcher.

There is one problem with a drawing of this kind; it does not supply enough information. There is no indication of the output impedances of the VCR, nor is there any data supplied about the impedance of either the VHF

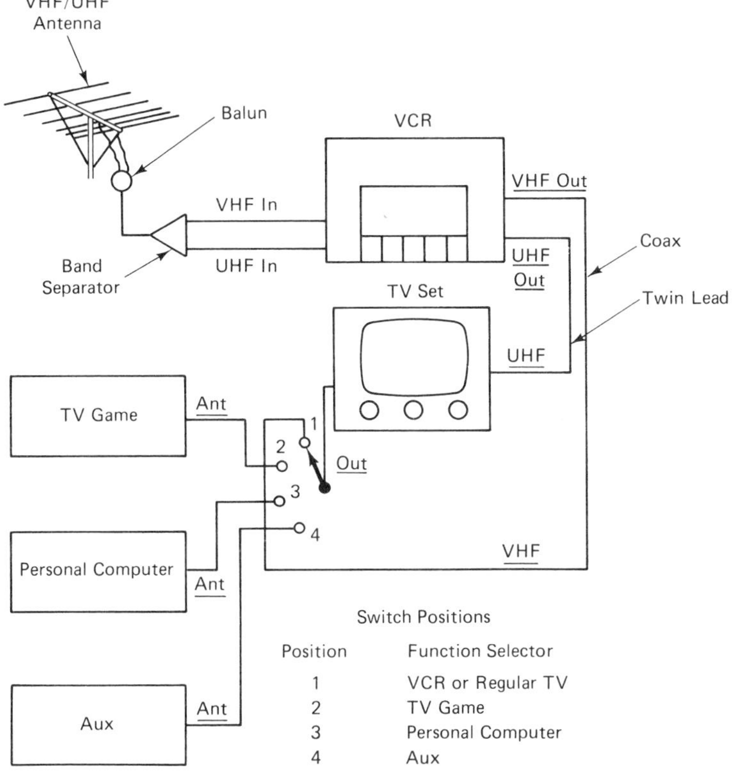

Figure 3-9. Multiple video switcher replaces several A/B switchers.

or UHF terminals on the TV set. If this information is already known or will be supplied, a diagram such as this is an aid in making the required connections. There is also no information furnished as to whether the VCR can record one channel while the TV set is used for watching another.

Figure 3-10 shows a system using a switcher that is even more sophisticated. This setup uses two TV sets—one a main unit and the other a remote. The rear of the switcher has eight ports, all accommodating 75-ohm inputs. The aux port can be used for either a video game or a videodisc player.

The output to both TV sets, the main and the remote, is via a length of coaxial cable but this cable carries both TV broadcast signals—VHF and UHF. Consequently, somewhere between the TV output of the switcher and the TV a band separator will be required. The band separator, as its name implies, separates the VHF and UHF television bands so these signals can be fed to their independent inputs on the antenna terminal block on the back of the TV set. (Band separators are described in greater detail later in this chapter.)

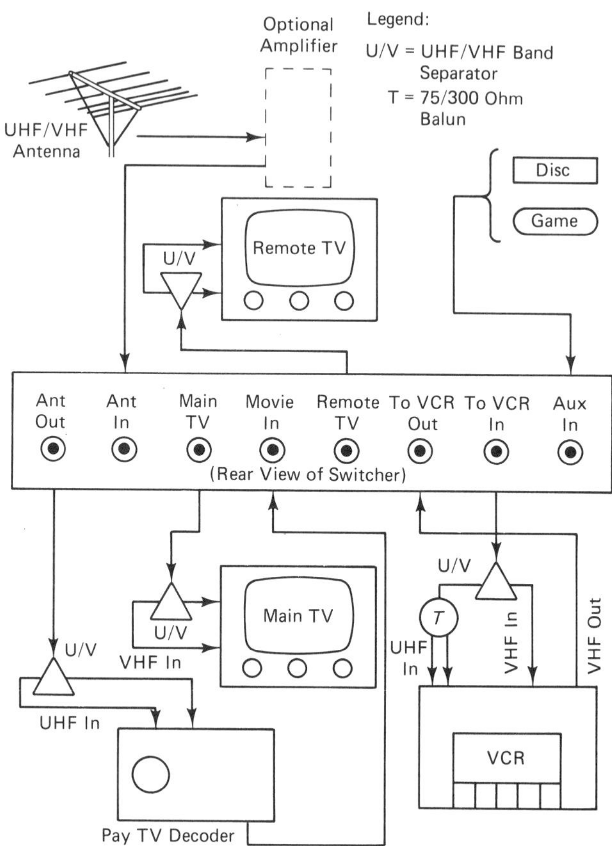

Figure 3–10. Multiple switcher (Fig. 3–9) with different connections.

The arrangement in Figure 3–10 uses a combined VHF/UHF antenna as one of its signal inputs. However, the same switcher (Fig. 3–11A) can also use a cable TV signal. With cable TV some of the signals may be encoded (scrambled), so a decoder (unscrambler) is used. The decoder shown in the illustration is identified as a pay TV decoder. Figure 3–11B shows the hookup details for a video control center.

Choosing a Switcher

The simple A/B switcher is a moderately priced component, is easy to connect, and can be mounted out of sight on the rear of the TV set. All that is needed is to reach behind the set to operate the switch; it isn't necessary to see the switch, as with a little use, putting the control arm of the switch in either of the desired positions will become completely automatic.

Like plugs and jacks, switchers may be subject to corrosion because of

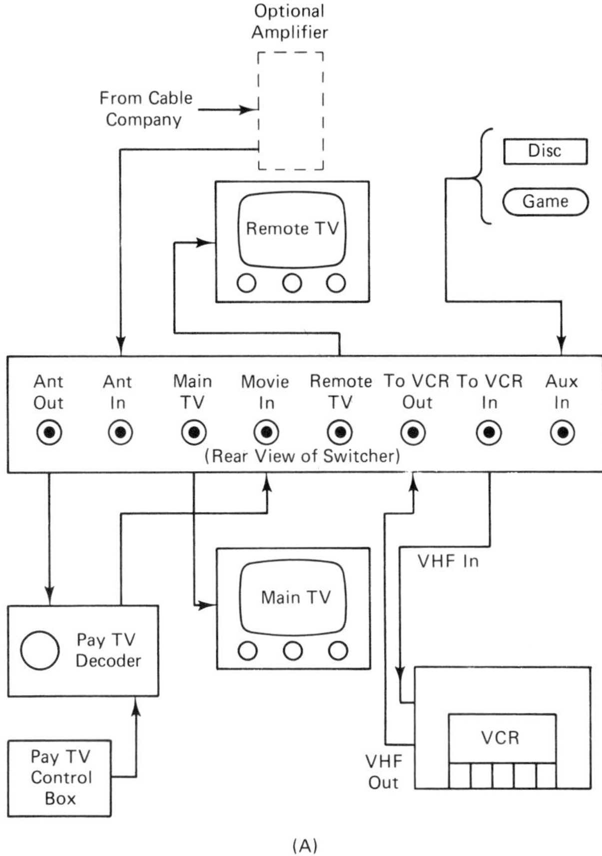

Figure 3–11A. Multiple switcher can deliver signals to two TV sets.

humidity. However, there is a difference. The switcher is completely enclosed; plugs and jacks are not. Some switchers are made with gold-plated contacts and while these eliminate the corrosion problem it is doubtful whether the extra cost is justified.

The great disadvantage of the A/B switcher is its limitation to two signal choices. Multiple signal switchers do not have this disadvantage but unlike the two-way switchers are much larger and must be positioned where their front panel controls can be seen and used. This may be a problem for rack-mounted components. The multiple switcher, of course, is a much higher priced item than the A/B. However, when obtaining the multiple switcher it is advisable to get one that has as many switching ports as possible. Even if all ports are not used, those that are vacant can be kept in reserve to allow for future expansion of the in-home entertainment system.

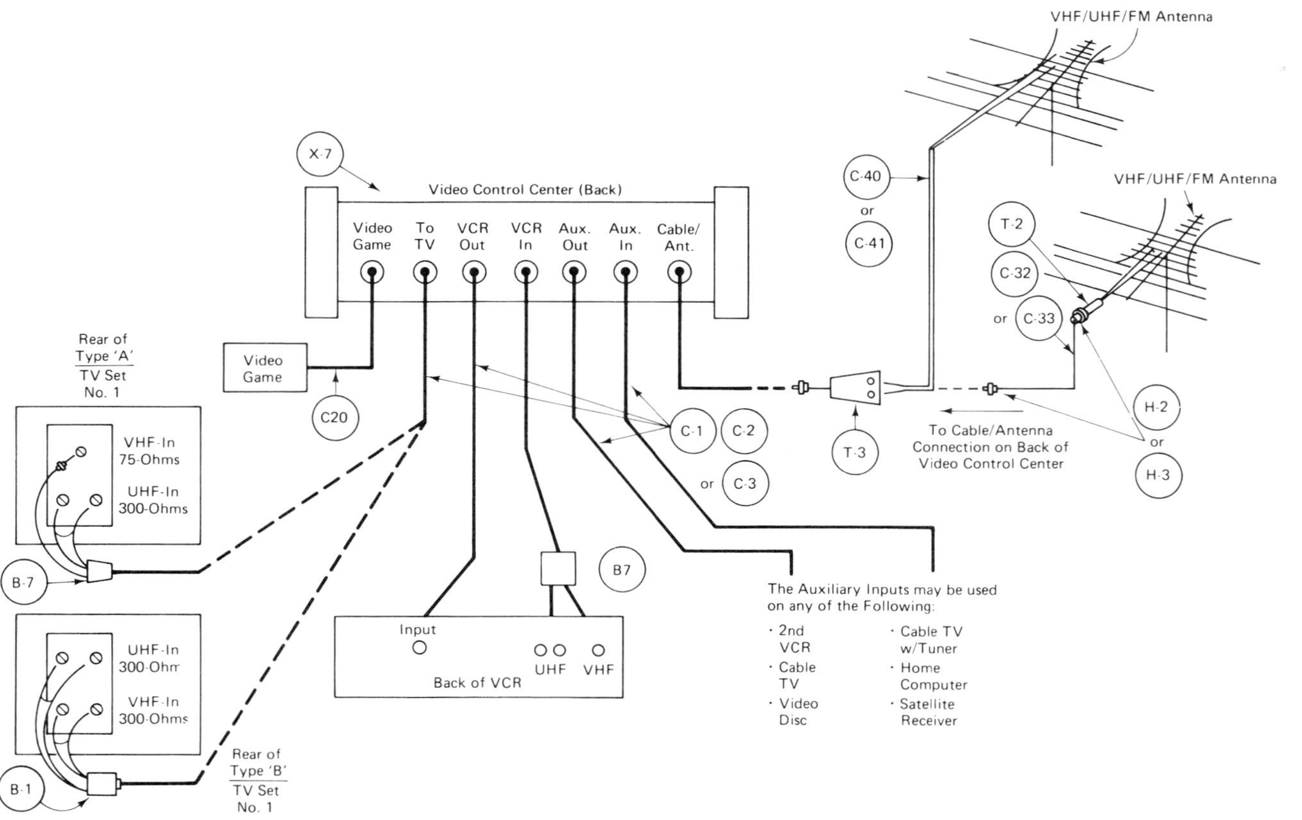

Figure 3–11B. Hookup for video control center. (*Courtesy GC Electronics*)

TV Hookup 'A'

Qty.	Part	Description
1	C-40 or C-41	50 ft., or 75 ft., Bulk 300-Ohm Foam-filled Twin-lead Down-lead Cable.
1	T-3	300 to 75-Ohm Matching Transformer.
1	C-20	6 ft., Round Coaxial Cable with Phono (RCA-Type) Plugs on Both Ends.
2	B-7	75 to 75/300-Ohm Transformer and VHF/UHF Band Separator.
5	C-1 C-2 or C-3	3 ft., 6 ft., or 12 ft., Round 75-Ohm Coaxial Cables with 'F'-Plugs on Both Ends.
1	X-7	Video Control Center.
		VHF 75 Ohms; UHF 300 Ohms

Qty.	Part	Description
1	T-2 32-3010	300 to 75-Ohm Outdoor Matching Transformer.
1	C-32 or C-33	25 ft., or 50 ft., Bulk 75-Ohm Coaxial Down-lead Cable (Without Connectors).
1	C-20	6 ft., Round Coaxial Cable with Phono (RCA-Type) Plugs on Both Ends.
2	B-7	75 to 75/300-Ohm Transformer and VHF/UHF Band Separator.
5	C-1 C-2 or C-3	3 ft., 6 ft., or 12 ft., Round 75-Ohm Coaxial Cables with 'F'-Plugs on Both Ends.
2	H-2	'F'-Type Crimp-on Plugs for Round Coaxial TV Cable (Above).
	*or	
2	H-3	'F'-Type Twist-on Plugs for Round Coaxial TV Cable (Above).
1	X-7	Video Control Center.
		VHF 75 Ohms; UHF 300 Ohms

TV Hookup 'B'

Qty.	Part	Description
1	C-40 or C-41	50 ft., or 75 ft., Bulk 300-Ohm Foam-filled Twin-lead Down-lead Cable.
1	C-20	6 ft., Round Coaxial Cable with Phono (RCA-Type) Plugs on Both Ends.
1	B-7	75 to 75/300-Ohm Transformer and VHF/UHF Band Separator.
5	C1 C-2 or C-3	3 ft., 6 ft., or 12 ft., Round 75-Ohm Coaxial Cables with 'F'-Plugs on Both Ends.
1	T-3	300 to 75-Ohm Matching Transformer
1	B-1	75 to 300-Ohm Transformer with UHF/VHF Band Separator.
1	X-7	Video Control Center.
		VHF 300 Ohms; UHF 300 Ohms

Qty.	Part	Description
1	B-1	75 to 300-Ohm Transformer with UHF/VHF Band Separator.
1	B-7	75 to 75/300-Ohm Transformer (Balun) and VHF/UHF Band Separator.
5	C-1 C-2 or C-3	3 ft., 6 ft., or 12 ft., Round 75-Ohm Coaxial Cables with 'F'-Plugs on Both Ends.
1	C-32 or C-33	25 ft., or 50 ft., Bulk 75-Ohm Coaxial Down-lead Cable (without Connectors).
1	T-2	300-Ohm to 75-Ohm Outdoor Matching Transformer.
1	C-20	6 ft., Round Coaxial Cable with Phono (RCA-Type) Plugs on Both Ends.
2	H-2	'F'-Type Crimp-on Plugs for Round Coaxial TV Cable (Above).
	*or	
2	H-3	'F'-Type Twist-on Plugs for Round Coaxial TV Cable (Above).
1	X-7	Video Control Center.
		VHF 300 Ohms; UHF 300 Ohms

(B)

Figure 3–11B. *(continued)*

Switchers and System Versatility

One of the great advantages of a multiple switcher over the simpler A/B type is the system versatility that can be obtained with the multiple unit. This is demonstrated by the three different setups shown in Fig. 3–12 using the same switcher. The drawings are similar in some respects. The TV output terminal of the switcher is used to drive either one or two TV sets. Whether two-TV-set operation will be possible will depend on the strength of the input signals routed to those sets. As the sets share the input signals, these are effectively divided in half.

Drawing A uses subscription TV (STV), a form of broadcast TV whose transmitted signals are scrambled, thus requiring the use of a decoder at the reception end. Drawing B does not make use of broadcast TV but relies entirely on cable TV for its signals. The first input, identified as cable one, is for cable signals that have not been scrambled. No converter box is shown, as the TV sets used here are cable ready. There is another cable TV input, cable two, and this makes use of a cable-company-supplied converter which is actually a combined converter/decoder, and is intended for receiving (and unscrambling) encoded signals. The switcher is able to select either of the two kinds of cable TV signals.

The third drawing, C, indicates that the signal input can be either cable TV or that supplied by an antenna. If cable TV is used, only unscrambled signals will be viewable, as there is no decoder in this wiring arrangement. Note also that the aux input is now being used by a videodisc player.

Using Two A/B Switchers

The difficulty with the A/B switcher is that it permits a selection between two signal sources only. If three signal sources are available, such as broadcast TV, a videodisc, and a video game, then a pair of A/B switchers can be used. Under these circumstances, it would be helpful to have a written card posted near the system listing the switching possibilities. Circuits involving two A/B switchers are shown in the next chapter.

Mounting the A/B Switcher

Some switchers have a base plate with holes for screw mounting to the rear of a TV set (Fig. 3–13). This unit gives the user a choice of broadcast or cable signals. The inputs are 75 ohms, while the output has a small section of twin lead for connection to the 300-ohm terminals of the TV set.

Multiple switchers cannot be mounted this way and are often placed on top of the TV receiver or close by.

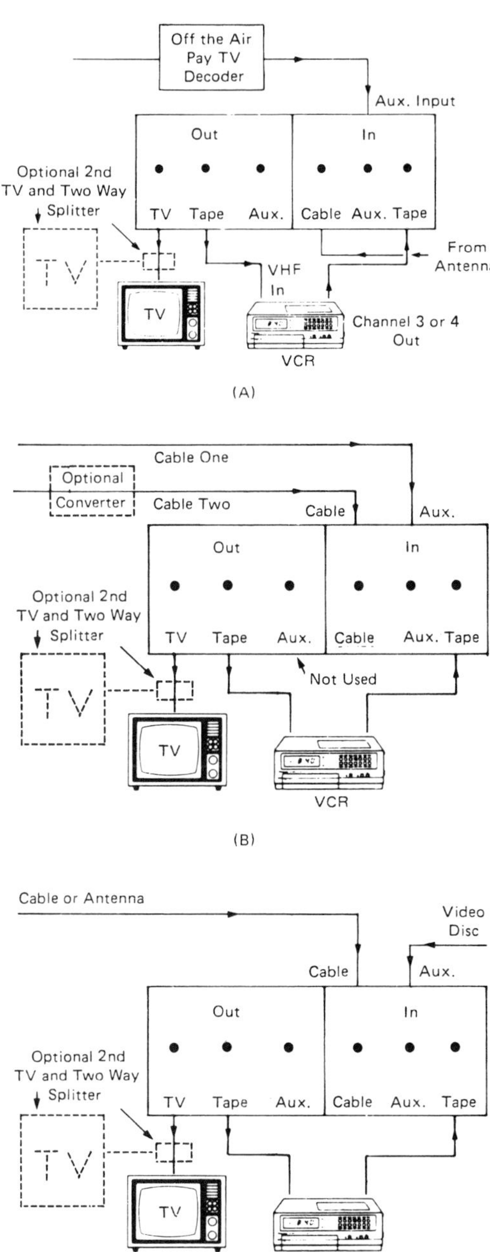

Figure 3-12. (A) One or two TVs and VCR connected to antenna and over-the-air pay TV. (B) One or two TVs and VCR hooked to two-cable system. (C) One or two TVs, a VCR, and a video-disc. (*Courtesy Rhoades National Corp.*)

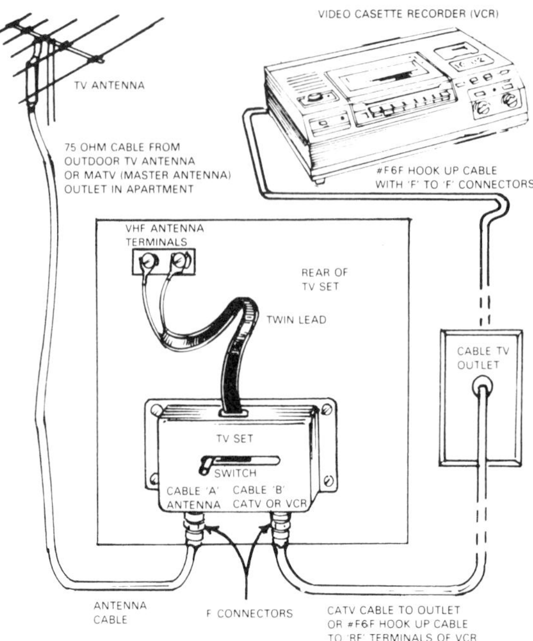

Figure 3–13. A/B switcher mounted on rear of TV set. (*Courtesy RMS Electronics, Inc.*)

SPLICING BOX

Running a 300-ohm downlead from an antenna to a receiver can be one of the annoyances of connection if that line, after installation, is found to be several feet short. The line can be spliced onto a small section to complete the connection, but this means stripping four stranded conductors with a good possibility of accidentally cutting away one or more of the strands. Further, after the connection is finally made, the joined wires are exposed and should be covered. Don't use electrical tape for this, because in time the tape will unravel, and it is always unsightly.

A better technique is to use a splicing box (Fig. 3–14). No wire stripping is required. Cut straight across the twin lead so none of the strands of wire are exposed. Position one of the twin leads to be joined between one pair of

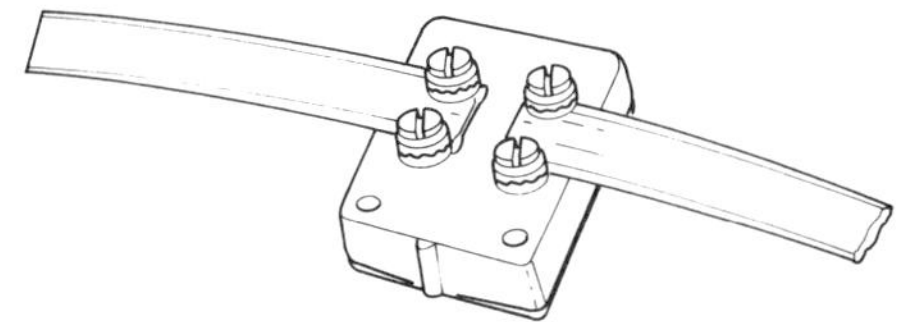

Figure 3–14. A 300-ohm splice box. (*Courtesy RMS Electronics, Inc.*)

screws on the splicing box and then tighten them. The screws are equipped with a penetrating sawtooth washer beneath the screw head and their sharp points will bite into the twin lead, making contact with the conductors. Repeat this procedure with the other section of twin lead. The two sections of twin lead are separated, but they are actually connected by conductors inside the box. The box can be mounted by a pair of screws or by using a self-adhering base.

SYNTHETIC STEREO

Sound sources—ranging from TV to many FM stations, video cameras, and VCRs still produce monophonic sound. This is no great loss if the sound is reproduced by the speakers in a TV receiver, but it is unfortunate if the sound is supplied to a high-fidelity system.

One way of obtaining synthetic stereo is to use a Y-adapter, a length of audio cable having a single input terminal and a pair of output terminals identified as *L* (left) and *R* (right). The Y-adapter could be called a signal splitter, for some of the audio signal is supplied to the left input terminal of a preamplifier or integrated amplifier, and some of the signal to the right input terminal. The audio signal, not always easy or convenient to obtain, is supplied by the TV set.

The Y-adapter consists of a length of audio cable with RCA plugs on both ends. With this arrangement, some of the audio signal will go through the left channel of the high-fidelity system and some through the right channel. If an integrated amplifier or a stereo receiver is used instead of a preamplifier these components must be equipped with aux ports.

When you operate this system, sound will also come out of the TV's speaker. Some TV sets are equipped with a speaker kill plug, which cuts off the TV speaker's sound while permitting the sound signal to travel to the high-fidelity system to be heard through its speakers. The best that can be said of the Y-adapter is that the sound is supplied by the left and right speakers of the high-fidelity system. The result isn't stereo but rather two-speaker monophonic sound.

Another pseudostereo technique uses two sound inputs. One of these is the audio output of a VCR; the other is the earphone output of a TV receiver, with those outputs not always available. The output of the adapter is brought into the aux input of a stereo preamp or an integrated amplifier.

Stereo synthesizers are available and, like the Y-adapter, can operate with just a single, left- or right-channel audio signal. Figure 3–15 shows the wiring arrangement. The audio is supplied by the audio output of the earphone jack of a TV set, although the sound could also be tapped off the voice coil terminals of the TV's speaker. The output of the synthesizer is delivered via audio cable equipped with RCA plugs to the tape or aux inputs of a stereo amplifier.

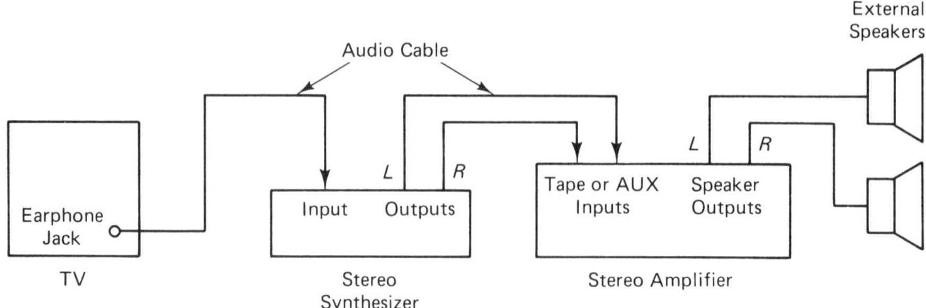

Figure 3–15. Connections for stereo synthesizer. (*Courtesy MFJ Enterprises, Inc.*)

Figure 3–16 is the same concept but shown in more detail, with the sound signal supplied by the audio output terminal of a VCR. Again, this is monophonic sound and is supplied to the input jack of the stereo synthesizer. The video output of the VCR is delivered to a video enhancer. The video is a baseband signal only, hence must be modulated before it is routed to the antenna input terminals of the TV set. The modulation carrier is generally that of either channel 3 or channel 4, and the TV set's tuning control must be positioned to either one of these channels. All channel selection is handled by the VCR.

Figure 3–17 gives the details of a synthesizer. The mono signal is supplied to a noninverting amplifier, indicating that the phase of the signal is the same at its output as its input. The output of the amplifier feeds three circuits: a right-channel mixer, a left-channel mixer, and a three-stage phase shifter. Following the right-channel mixer is an inverting amplifier, which shifts the phase of the audio signal by 180 degrees. Thus, the left-channel output and the right-channel output are completely out of phase. Pseudostereo is obtained as a result of this phase shift.

BALUNS

A balun is a transformer specifically designed to work with video signals. The word *balun* is a contraction of *balanced to unbalanced.* It is a device that can connect a *bal*anced line to an *un*balanced line or an unbalanced line—such as single-center conductor coaxial cable—to two-wire line, such as 300-ohm twin lead. A balun is a transformer and can be used as a step up (75 ohms to 300 ohms) or as a step down (300 ohms to 75 ohms). Baluns are commonly used for impedance matching; for example, connecting the output of a 300-ohm antenna to 75-ohm coaxial downlead, or for connecting a 75-ohm picture signal source to the 300-ohm antenna input terminal of a TV set. There are only two basic types: the step up and the step down, but there are a number of variations and combinations.

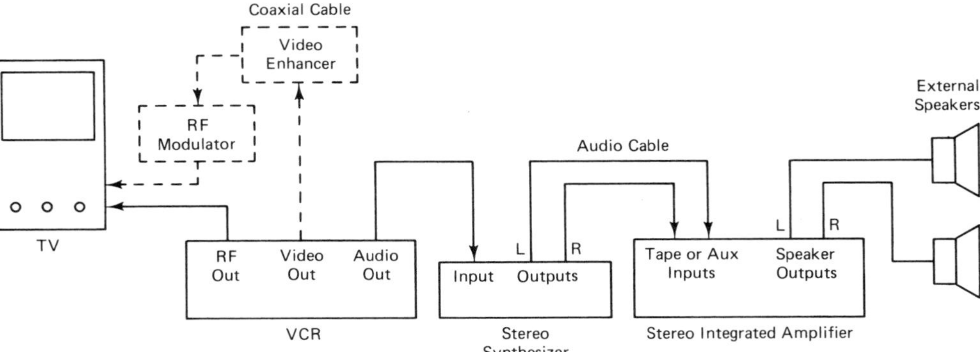

Figure 3–16. Method of adding pseudostereo to a VCR. (*Courtesy MFJ Enterprises, Inc.*)

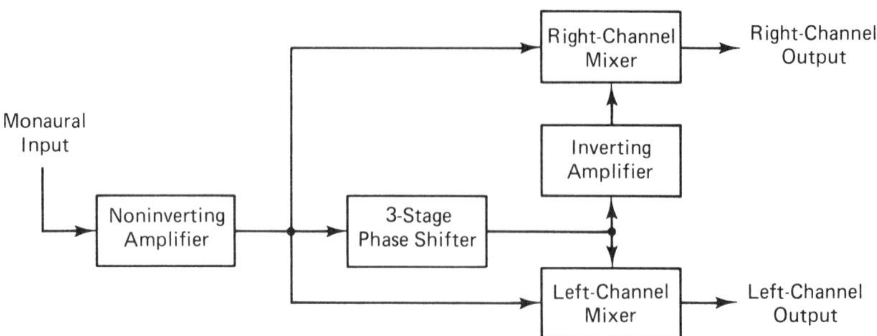

Figure 3–17. Circuit arrangement of pseudostereo system.

Circuit Arrangement of a Balun

Figure 3–18 shows a step-up balun having an input of 75 ohms and an output of 300 ohms. A circuit of the balun is shown directly below its picture. The markings 6T and 12T do not indicate the actual number of turns of wire of the primary and the secondary (6T = 6 turns) but rather the turns ratio. The turns ratio is 2 to 1, supplying an impedance ratio of 4 to 1. A balun of this kind could be used to connect a coaxial downlead to the 300-ohm input terminals of a TV set. A balun is always used for impedance matching, and is sometimes known as an impedance-matching transformer.

Baluns are reversible. The input can be the 300-ohm side; the output the 75-ohm side, or the connections to the balun can be transposed. In that case the 75-ohm side is the input; 300 ohms the output. The 300-ohm side is balanced, that is, always connected to a balanced cable such as twin lead. The 75-ohm side is always connected to unbalanced coax.

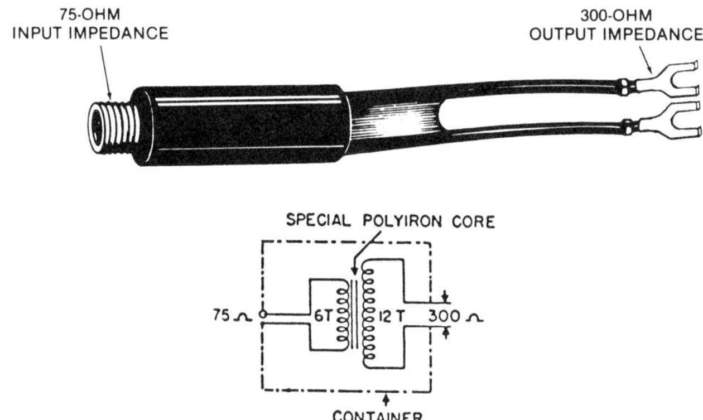

Figure 3–18. A 75-ohm to 300-ohm balun: 6T and 12T indicate the turns ratio, not the number of turns. This type of balun is reversible; the input can be used as an output, and the output as an input.

As is shown by the threads on the 75-ohm connector in Fig. 3–18, one side of this balun is screw-on. A variation of this balun is shown in Fig. 3–19. This add-on also has 300-ohm and 75-ohm ports, but there are some differences. The 75-ohm connector is a push-on type, depending on a force fit between the plug and its jack. The output terminals consist of a pair of captive machine screws.

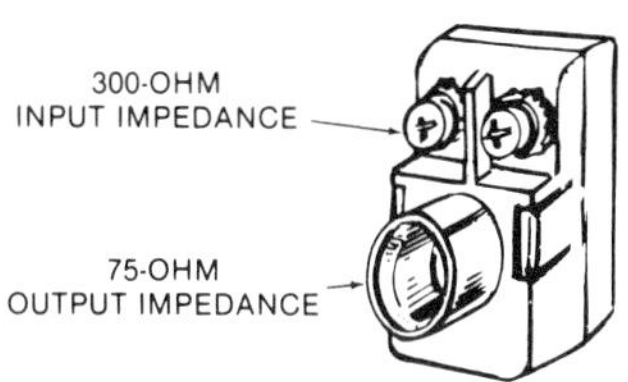

Figure 3–19. Quick-connect, push-on balun with 300-ohm input, 75-ohm output. (*Courtesy Vidline Video Accessories*)

One advantage of this balun is that it can impedance-match coaxial cable and twin lead when these two are at right angles to each other. While twin lead can bend easily enough, coaxial cable cannot, so in this instance this is a desirable balun. Its disadvantage is that the twin lead must have its ends stripped for connection to the screws. If the twin lead is supplied equipped with open-end spade lugs, then connecting the 300-ohm side is no problem.

Figure 3–20 shows one application of the right-angle balun. In this case the 75-ohm connector is a screw-on type instead of using a force fit. Twin lead, such as a transmission line from the antenna, is connected to the 300-ohm terminals of the balun. The twin wires are stripped, twirled, and wrapped clockwise around the balun screws. The cap of the 75-ohm connector is screwed onto the threaded coax antenna terminal of the receivers.

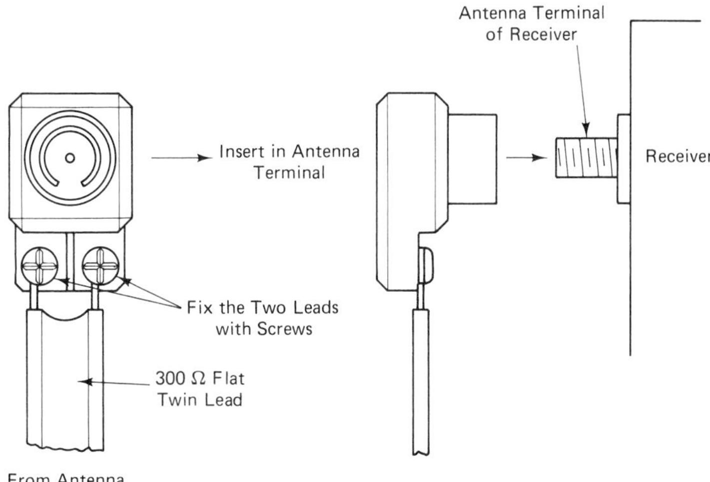

Figure 3–20. Right-angle, quick-connect 300-ohm to 75-ohm transformer.

The Dedicated Balun

A dedicated balun is one that is used for impedance transformation only. It will have one input and one output, either one of which can be 75 ohms or 300 ohms. Baluns are used only for the video section of a system, not for the high-fidelity portion that may be associated with it. If the impedances are not marked on the balun, the 75-ohm side can always be recognized, as it will have an F-jack for connection to coaxial cable. The 300-ohm side will always have a pair of machine screws for connection to twin lead.

A nondedicated balun is integrated with a band separator, described in the following section.

Using the Balun

Figure 3–21 shows the use of a dedicated balun. The problem is how to connect the VHF output of an indoor antenna to the 75-ohm VHF input antenna terminal on a TV receiver. The VHF and UHF outputs of a pair of rabbit ears are 300 ohms, indicated by two short lengths of twin lead connected to the antenna. The VHF output twin lead is connected to a pair of machine screws on one side of the balun. The other side of the balun uses a length of coaxial cable equipped with F-plugs on both ends with one end connected to the balun and the other to the 75-ohm input F-type VHF terminal on the TV set.

If the downlead from an antenna is 75 ohms and the input to the TV set is 300 ohms, simply reverse the balun.

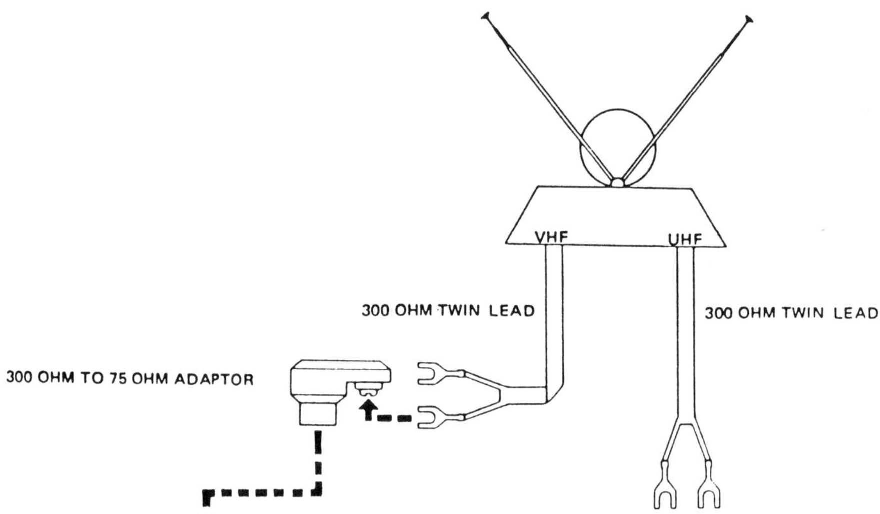

Figure 3–21. Use of dedicated balun. (*Courtesy Sharp Electronics Corp.*)

STUBS

While a balun is a convenient and practical way of matching antenna, transmission line, and TV receiver input impedances, there is another method that involves the use of a quarter-wave matching stub. A quarter-wave stub functions as a transformer. The length of the stub, a spare section of 300-ohm line, can have its length (*L*) calculated thus:

$$L = 246/f$$

L is the length in feet and *f* is the frequency in MHz. In the example shown in Fig. 3–22, the stub is being used to match a 75-ohm open dipole antenna to a transmission line that is 300 ohms, with the receiver's input impedance, also 300 ohms. Since the downlead is 300 ohms and the antenna input at the TV receiver is also 300 ohms, transmission line to receiver input impedance is obtained automatically. The stub, however, can be used to match the 75-ohm output impedance of the antenna to the transmission line.

The correct impedance can be gauged by watching the picture on the TV screen for optimum signal and minimum ghosting. A small amount of experimentation may be needed. This can be done by tapping the transmission line up or down on the stub. It will be necessary to pierce the plastic surrounding the conductors of the stub. Use a pair of screws equipped with washers having triangular pointed teeth pointing downward. When tapping down on the stub be sure to maintain equal distances on both conductors from the end of the stub.

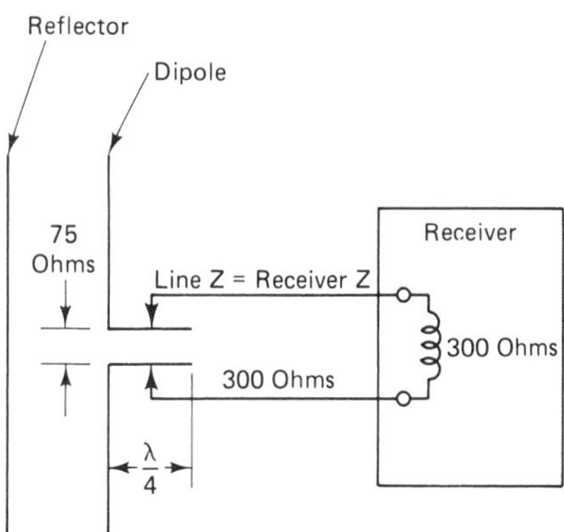

Figure 3–22. Use of quarter-wave stub to match transmission line to antenna.

GHOSTS

A ghost is a picture that follows or precedes the wanted image on the television screen. The ghost is usually a fainter image and may be a single picture or a series and can be either leading or trailing. A leading ghost is one that precedes the main image on the screen; a trailing ghost is one that follows it.

A leading ghost is caused by signal pickup in the twin lead transmission line when it is used as the downlead, or if it is coiled up behind the TV set. There is less opportunity for ghost formation if the twin lead is in a vertical line from the antenna to the receiver. If any part of the twin lead is horizontal, outdoors or indoors, it is then capable of acting like an antenna, picking up broadcast TV signals. To avoid such interference, position the twin lead vertically insofar as possible or replace it with either coaxial cable or shielded twin lead. In either case, make sure the shield of the transmission line is grounded. Regardless of the type of transmission line used, it may need to be impedance-matched, at the antenna, at the receiver, or both.

Trailing ghosts are more difficult to eliminate, as they are the result of TV signals' being reflected from buildings and terrain. Such signals arrive after the direct signal and appear on the screen as an image or a series of images following the main image. Such ghosts can also be caused by mismatched impedances at the antenna, the receiver, or both.

Using a balun at the antenna and/or at the receiver will not only help eliminate ghosts but may result in a stronger picture signal. This may not be evident if the signal is a strong one to begin with, but it will be helpful if the signal is marginal. If ghosts are caused by the pickup of reflected signals, they may be minimized by using a rotator at the antenna for best ghost-free signal pickup. A rotator, however, is no substitute for one or more baluns.

SWITCHABLE IMPEDANCES

The VHF and UHF antenna input terminals on the back of a TV set can both be 300 ohms or 75 ohms. Alternatively, one can be 75 ohms, and the other 300 ohms. There is no standardization. More recent TV sets have a switchable VHF input that can be set to 75 ohms or 300 ohms. The VHF input consists of two ports instead of just one, so either coaxial cable or twin lead can be connected. A slide switch positioned alongside these terminals can switch impedances to either 75 ohms or 300 ohms. If the connection is via twin lead the switch is set to 300 ohms and to 75 ohms if coaxial cable is used. While this eliminates the need for a balun for VHF signals, a matching transformer may still be required for the UHF signal. A balun may still be needed at the antenna.

BAND SEPARATORS

A band separator divides one band of signals from another. Thus, a VHF/UHF band separator divides VHF and UHF signals that have been combined at some point. There are also VHF/UHF/FM band separators that can supply these as individual bands. As an example, some multiband antennas are three-

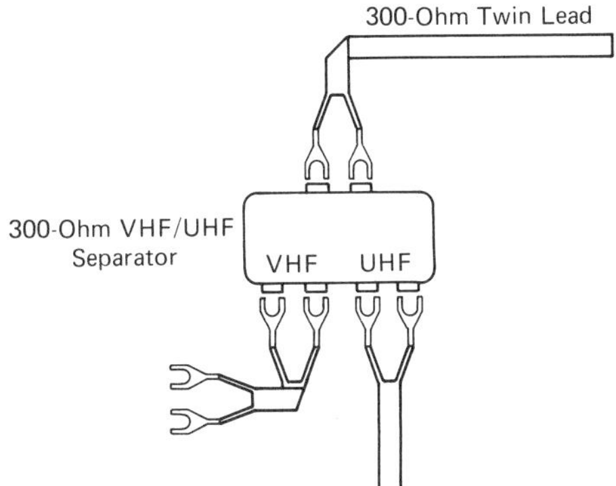

Figure 3-23. Two-way band separator.

band types capable of receiving VHF, UHF, and FM signals. The advantage is the use of a single downlead. Prior to the antenna input terminals, the three different bands are separated (by the band separator), with the FM signals routed to the antenna terminals on the FM receiver, and the individual VHF and UHF signals delivered to their respective terminals on the TV set.

Figure 3-23 is an illustration of a two-way band separator, which separates two bands only—VHF and UHF. The signal input is from a 300-ohm downlead connected to a TV antenna. The two individual outputs are both 300 ohms. If an antenna is also capable of picking up FM signals, then a three-way separator, such as the one shown in Fig. 3-24, can be used. Like the

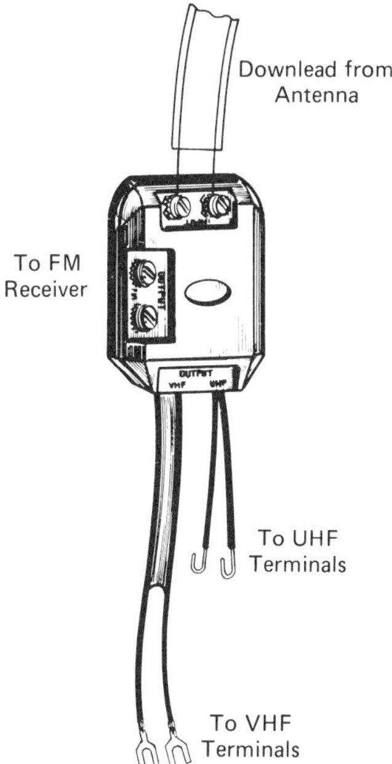

Figure 3-24. Three-way band separator.

separator shown in Fig. 3–23, this unit is 300 ohms throughout, at its input and at its three outputs. Since the input is 300 ohms, as well as the outputs, no transformer action is required and the input and outputs are impedance-matched automatically.

One assumption in the use of the band separators of Figures 3–23 and 3–24 concerns impedance matching. If the downlead is 75 ohms and either or both of the TV inputs are also 75 ohms, one or more baluns will be required.

You will find a variety of balun-band separators that combine transformer function with band separation. The one shown in Fig. 3–25 separates incoming VHF and UHF signals from a multiband antenna and is used for a TV set that has 300-ohm and 75-ohm inputs for these signals. The input for this balun-band separator is 75 ohms and it also has provision for connections to an FM receiver.

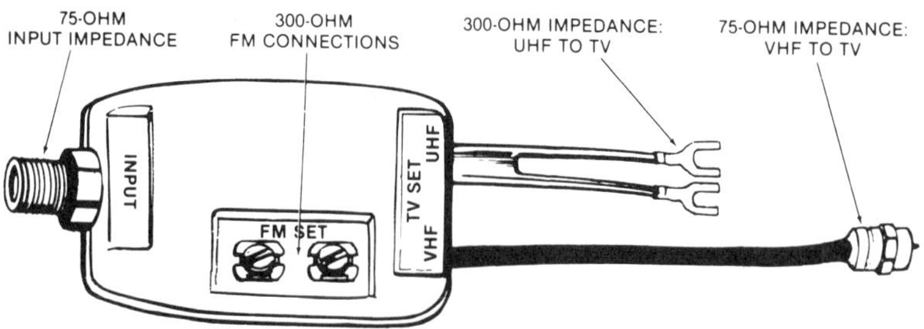

Figure 3–25. A 75-ohm balun VHF/UHF separator with 300-ohm output for an FM receiver. (*Courtesy Vidline Video Accessories*)

The Dedicated Band Separator

Most band separators are dual function, combining band separation with impedance matching. However, as it is possible to have a dedicated balun, it is also possible to have a dedicated band separator. Such a unit is one that does no impedance transformation, but band separation only.

Figure 3–26 shows a half-dozen variations of band separators. Those that have identical impedance inputs and outputs are dedicated types. Thus, if a band separator has a 75-ohm input and all its outputs are 75 ohms, the unit is dedicated. It is also dedicated if all its ports are 300 ohms.

Band separators are not only used at the antenna terminals of a TV set, but as add-ons elsewhere in a system where it is sometimes convenient to combine bands and then to separate them. A band separator is also used to supply signals to a VCR (Fig. 3–27).

Band separators are sometimes mistakenly referred to as splitters. However, signal splitters, described later in this chapter, and band separators are completely different and one is not a substitute for the other.

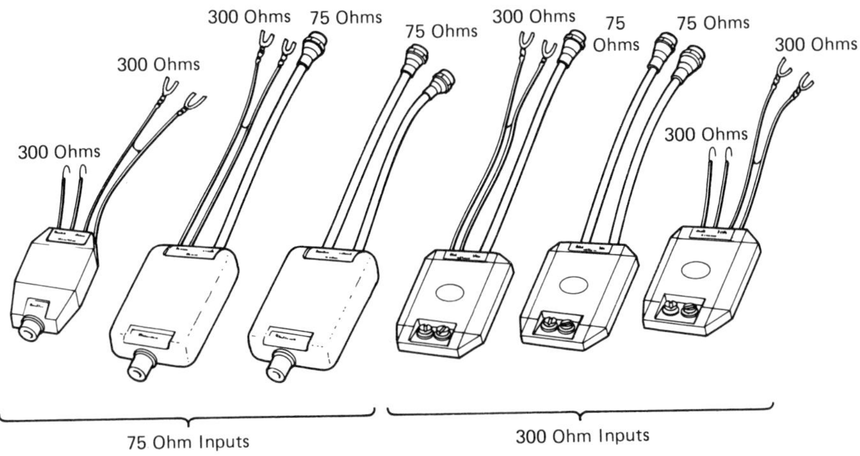

Figure 3–26. Types of band separators. Inputs and outputs can be 75 ohms or 300 ohms or any combination. (*Courtesy Gemini Industries, Inc.*)

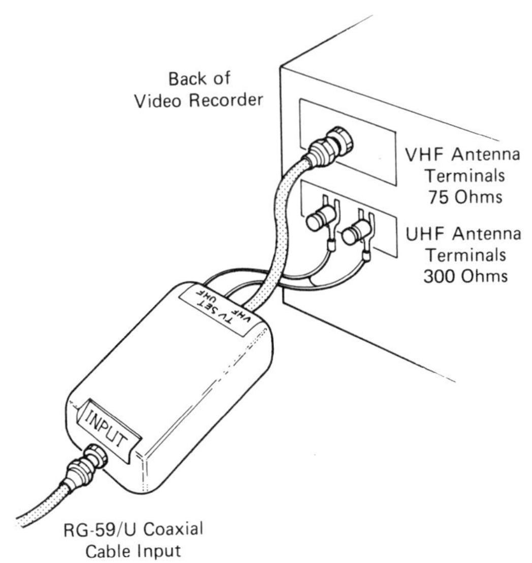

Figure 3–27. Band separator connected to a VCR. (*Courtesy Marshall Electronics, Inc.*)

Band Separator Differences

Band separators can be unlike internally as well as externally. If the input and output impedances are different, impedance step up or step down is obtained with the use of a transformer.

When the band separator has identical input and output impedances,

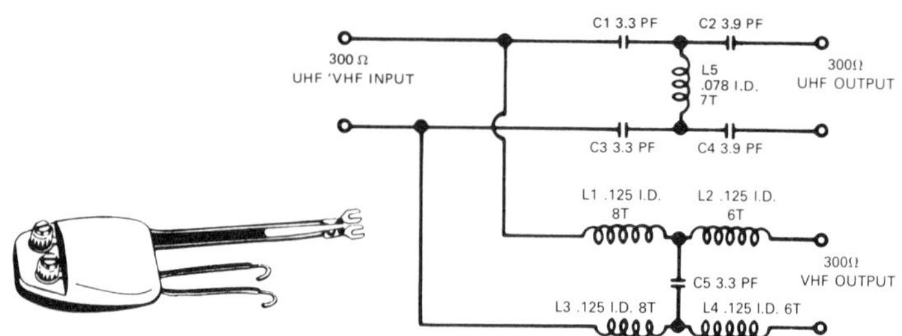

Figure 3–28. When input and output impedances are identical, separator uses band-pass filters. (*Courtesy Channel Master, Div. Avnet, Inc.*)

transformers aren't required, and all that are needed in such separators are band-pass filters. These are *L* (inductance) and *C* (capacitance) types (Fig. 3–28).

BAND COMBINERS

When multiband antennas are used, a band separator is needed; it follows the downlead to route VHF and UHF signals to the antenna terminals of a TV receiver, and FM signals to an FM receiver. When individual antennas are used for picking up VHF, UHF, and FM signals, separate downleads are required for each of the bands, but a band combiner can permit the use of a single transmission line.

A combiner can also be used when you are making connections between components (Fig. 3–29). This illustration shows that the separate VHF and UHF outputs of the VCR are to be delivered to a pair of TV sets. These separate signals are brought into a combiner, marked CV65, permitting the use of a single cable. You might think the combiner in this illustration could have been omitted, but its use was dictated by the necessity to split the UHF and VHF signals, as they were to drive a pair of TV sets.

Band combiners are used to combine a pair of bands, such as VHF and UHF, or three bands, the third one being FM. While three antennas are used, they can all be mounted on the same pole, with each of the antennas adjusted separately for best signal reception for its particular band. The best location for the combiner is right at the antenna outputs—a feature that permits the use of a single downlead.

SIGNAL SPLITTERS

The term *signal splitter* is sometimes used synonymously with band separator, but they are different. A signal splitter takes an existing signal, such as a VHF signal, and divides it into two approximately equal parts. Thus, to operate two

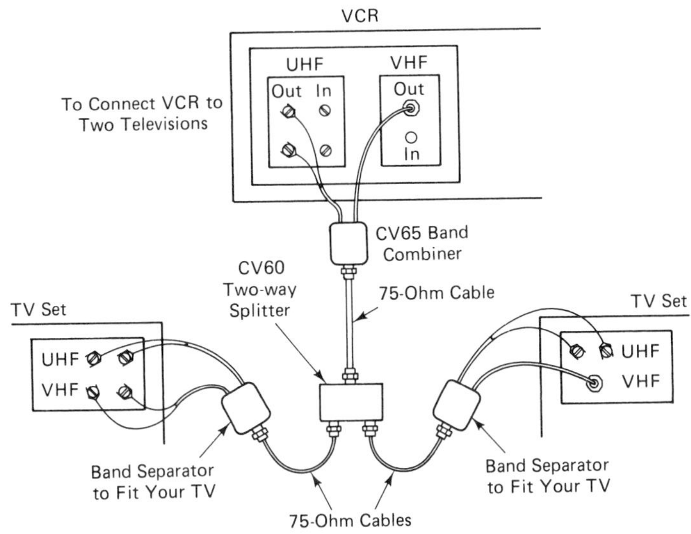

Figure 3–29. Connections for a band combiner. (*Courtesy Gemini Industries, Inc.*)

TV sets from a single antenna, a signal splitter is inserted between the antenna's transmission line and the inputs to the two TV sets.

Figure 3–30 shows the connections for a signal splitter. The signal, picked up by an antenna, or delivered from a VCR, is brought into a balun, identified by the letter *B*. The balun may or may not be necessary. If the downlead from the antenna or the cable from the VCR is 75-ohms, and if the input to the splitter is also 75 ohms, no balun is required.

The splitter takes the existing signal and divides it into two approximately equal parts. In this way, two TV sets can be operated from a single signal source. The signal reaching the two TV sets is weaker than that received by the antenna for two reasons: (1) The signal has been split into two parts so each receiver gets no more than half; and (2) there is always some signal loss in a balun and also in the splitter. The setup shown in Fig. 3–30 can be

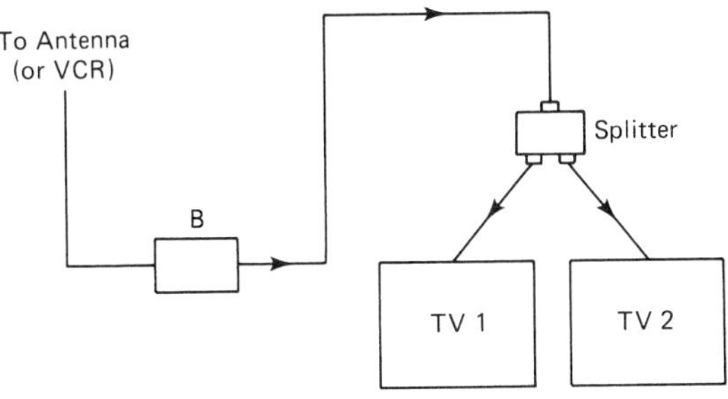

Figure 3–30. Use of a signal splitter.

used to connect one VCR to two TV sets or the input signal from a cable wallplate to the two TV receivers.

Splitters, like baluns, are inserted on line and must match impedances. Baluns may be needed at the input and the output of the signal splitter.

Signal splitters can be two-way, three-way, or four-way for operating two, three, or four TV sets. Usually, if the signal is split more than two ways, one or more preamplifiers are needed.

Splitter Characteristics

The use of a signal splitter, whether two-way, three-way, or four-way, results in some signal loss—often referred to as insertion loss. The amount of loss depends on the bands and is greater for higher frequencies. For VHF it is about 3.5 dB, and it is about 4 dB for UHF. The operating frequency range for splitters is from 0 Hz to 900 MHz for commercial types used outdoors or 5 MHz to 300 MHz for noncommercial applications. Splitters can be used indoors or outdoors. Those intended for outdoors are enclosed in a weatherproof die-cast housing. Those for in-home use are nickel-plated as protection against corrosion.

An important spec is the isolation between the separated bands, a measure of the amount of possible leakage from one band to the other. The isolation from port to port ranges from 20 dB to 30 dB, and the higher this number, the better.

The impedance is 75 ohms for all the ports, whether input or output. The ports are F-jacks, usually of the screw type, which extend from the body of the splitter. The screw type is used, as the connections are expected to remain on permanently.

The number of ports depends on whether the unit is two-way, three-way, or four-way (Fig. 3–31). A two-way splitter will have three ports, a three-way will have four ports, and so forth.

Signal splitters can also be active devices, containing a built-in signal amplifier. These are desirable when weak signals are to be distributed or when a number of TV sets, possibly four or more, are to be wired to a single antenna transmission line. Assuming equal input impedances, each connected TV set will get its proportionate share of the signal. If there are four such receivers, each will get one-fourth of the TV signal, assuming that each set imposes an equivalent load. Figure 3–32 shows the use of a three-way splitter.

The Signal Coupler

There is a lack of standardization in plugs, jacks, and cables, and different words are also used to describe some add-ons. A signal splitter is sometimes referred to as a coupler, as, with its use, two or more TV sets can be

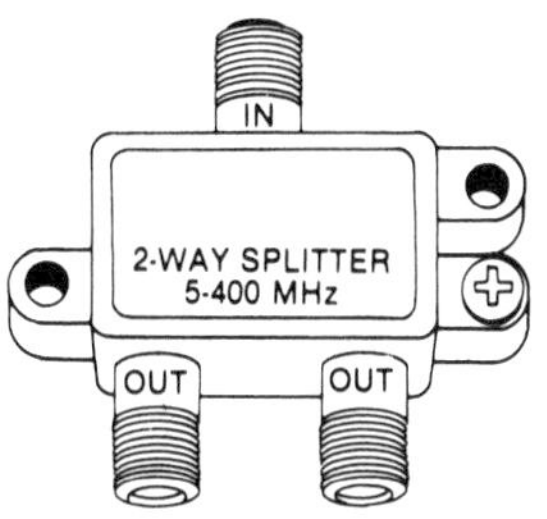

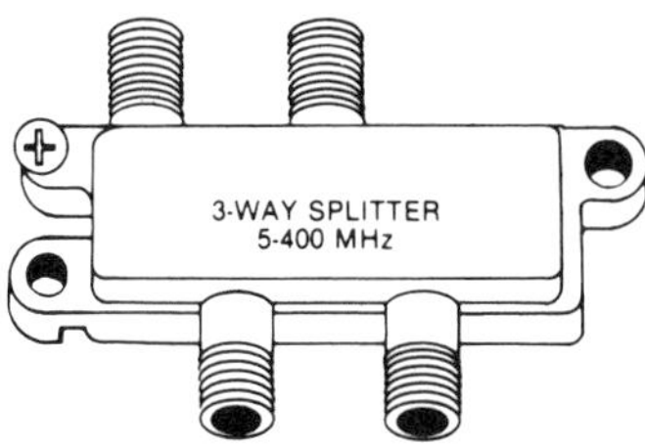

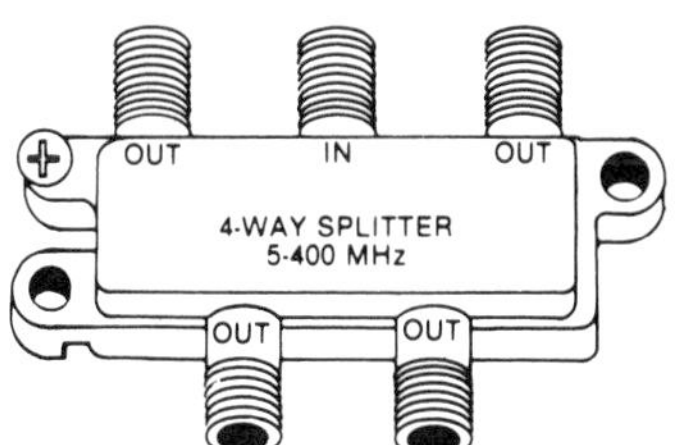

Figure 3–31. Two-way, three-way, and four-way splitters. (*Courtesy BP Electronics, Inc.*)

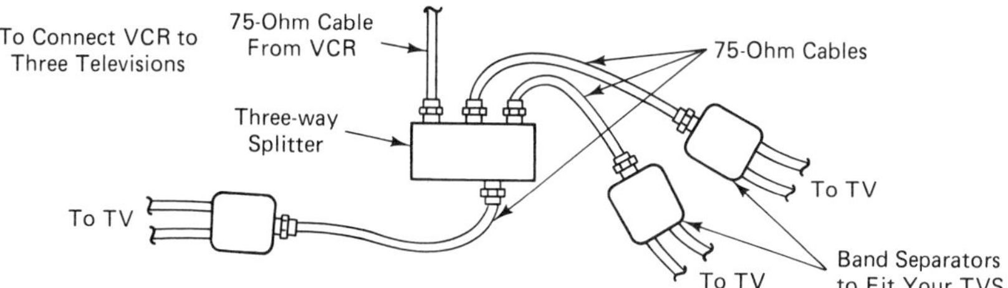

Figure 3–32. Three-way splitter used with band separators. (*Courtesy Gemini Industries, Inc.*)

coupled to the same signal source. However, *signal splitter* is much more widely used than *signal coupler.*

ANTENNA, DOWNLEAD, AND TV SET IMPEDANCE MATCHING

The ideal antenna and TV receiver installation is one that requires no impedance matching, something best done before an antenna and a TV set are purchased. Figure 3–33 shows one of the possibilities of automatic impedance matching without the use of transformers. The antenna (A) is a folded dipole and as such has an output impedance of 300 ohms. It is directly connected to a twin-lead transmission line and since its impedance is also 300 ohms, no balun is needed. The transmission line is attached to the 300-ohm antenna terminals of a TV set. This arrangement, plus all the others shown in this illustration, assumes single-band input, generally VHF. For combined VHF and UHF, a band separator would be required. Drawing B shows a similar transformerless arrangement, but this time the impedances are 75 ohms throughout. The 75-ohm dipole is directly connected to a coaxial cable downlead which, in turn, is connected to the 75-ohm input of the TV set. Usually, the downlead terminates in a 75-ohm plug connected to a 75-ohm jack on the set. Either unbalanced or balanced coaxial cable can be used. If it is unbalanced, one of the connectors is to the center conductor of the cable, the other to the shield braid. If balanced coaxial cable is used, the two conductors of the cable are connected to the free ends of the antenna. The shield can be grounded at the antenna or in the home.

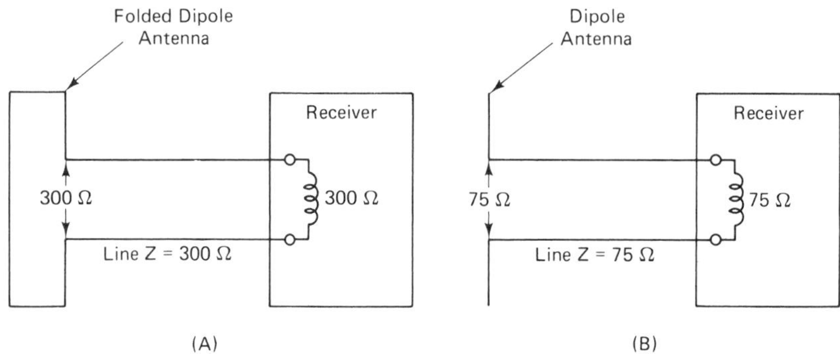

Figure 3–33. Automatic impedance matching: 300 ohms (A); 75 ohms (B).

MULTI-TV SET INSTALLATION

Baluns, band combiners, band separators, and signal splitters are used extensively for multi-TV set installations, usually involving more than two TV sets. But if that multiset installation also involves a VCR, there is always the question of whether the VCR can record the channel being watched, or a different channel; if the VCR can be used only in real time, or whether time shifting is possible; and whether the TV sets can be operated independently of each other and of the VCR. Consequently, multi-TV set operation with at least one VCR on line involves more than just impedance matching, but also the way in which the components are connected.

Figure 3–34A shows an in-home installation using four TV sets—a straightforward wiring setup—somewhat simple because a VCR isn't being used. Baluns are not shown in the drawing, but one or more (most likely more)

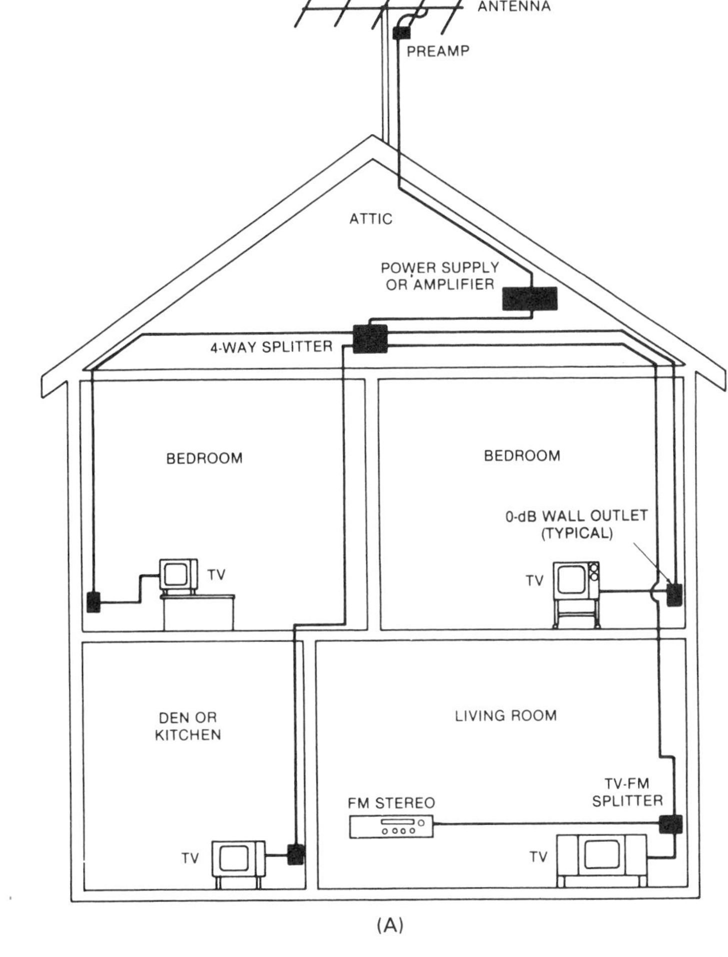

Figure 3–34A. In-home entertainment system using four TV sets. (*Courtesy Channel Master, Div. Avnet, Inc.*)

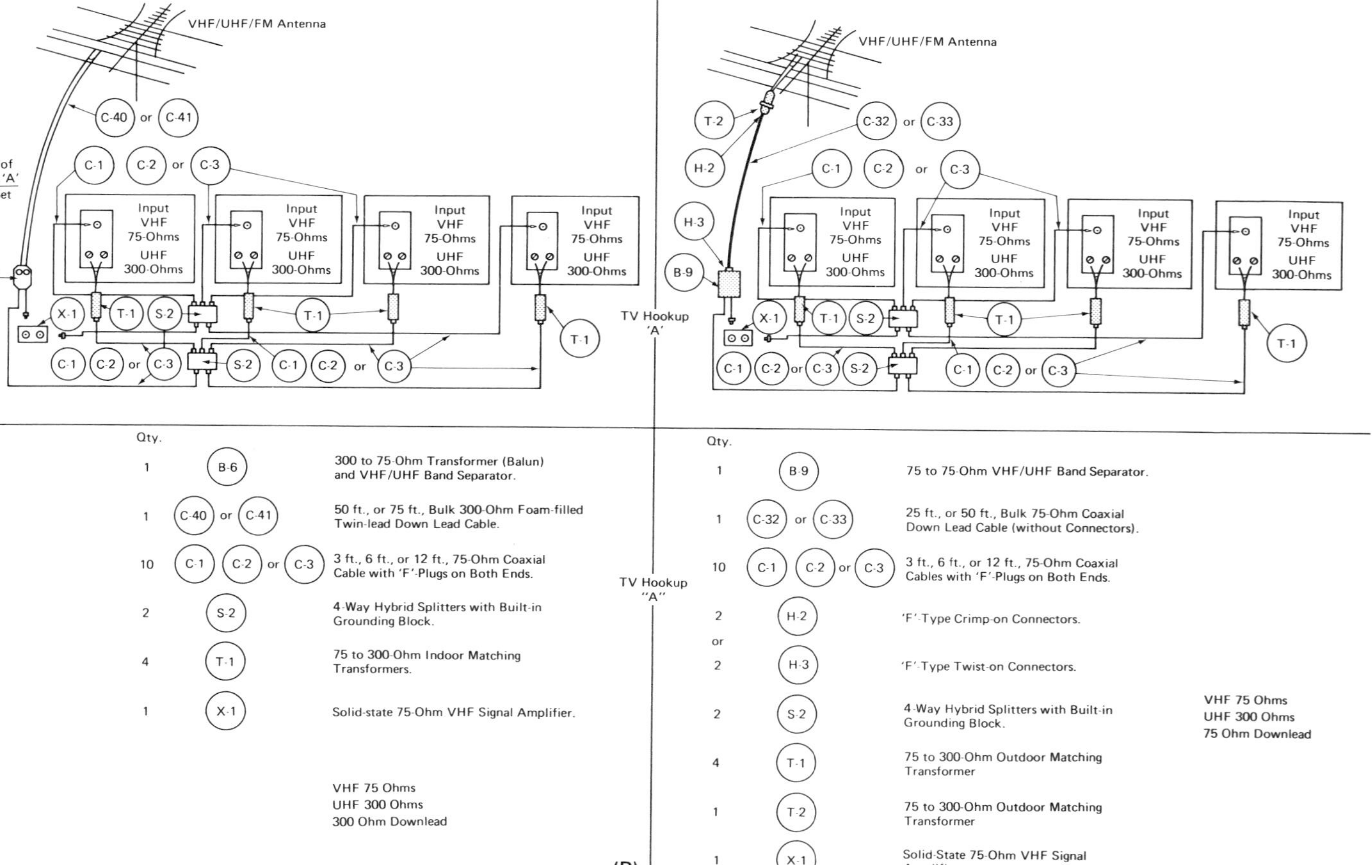

VHF/UHF/FM Antenna
Rear of Type 'A' TV Set
B-6
C-40 or C-41
C-1 C-2 or C-3
Input VHF 75-Ohms UHF 300-Ohms
X-1 T-1 S-2
T-1
C-1 C-2 or C-3 S-2 C-1 C-2 or C-3
T-1
Qty.
1 B-6 300 to 75-Ohm Transformer (Balun) and VHF/UHF Band Separator.
1 C-40 or C-41 50 ft., or 75 ft., Bulk 300-Ohm Foam-filled Twin-lead Down Lead Cable.
10 C-1 C-2 or C-3 3 ft., 6 ft., or 12 ft., 75-Ohm Coaxial Cable with 'F'-Plugs on Both Ends.
2 S-2 4-Way Hybrid Splitters with Built-in Grounding Block.
4 T-1 75 to 300-Ohm Indoor Matching Transformers.
1 X-1 Solid-state 75-Ohm VHF Signal Amplifier.
VHF 75 Ohms
UHF 300 Ohms
300 Ohm Download
(B)
TV Hookup 'A'
TV Hookup "A"
VHF/UHF/FM Antenna
T-2
H-2
C-32 or C-33
C-1 C-2 or C-3
H-3
B-9
Input VHF 75-Ohms UHF 300-Ohms
X-1 T-1 S-2
T-1
C-1 C-2 or C-3 S-2 C-1 C-2 or C-3
T-1
Qty.
1 B-9 75 to 75-Ohm VHF/UHF Band Separator.
1 C-32 or C-33 25 ft., or 50 ft., Bulk 75-Ohm Coaxial Down Lead Cable (without Connectors).
10 C-1 C-2 or C-3 3 ft., 6 ft., or 12 ft., 75-Ohm Coaxial Cables with 'F'-Plugs on Both Ends.
2 H-2 'F'-Type Crimp-on Connectors.
or
2 H-3 'F'-Type Twist-on Connectors.
2 S-2 4-Way Hybrid Splitters with Built-in Grounding Block.
4 T-1 75 to 300-Ohm Outdoor Matching Transformer
1 T-2 75 to 300-Ohm Outdoor Matching Transformer
1 X-1 Solid-State 75-Ohm VHF Signal Amplifier.
VHF 75 Ohms
UHF 300 Ohms
75 Ohm Downlead

Figure 3–34B. Details of four TV set hookup. (*Courtesy GC Electronics*)

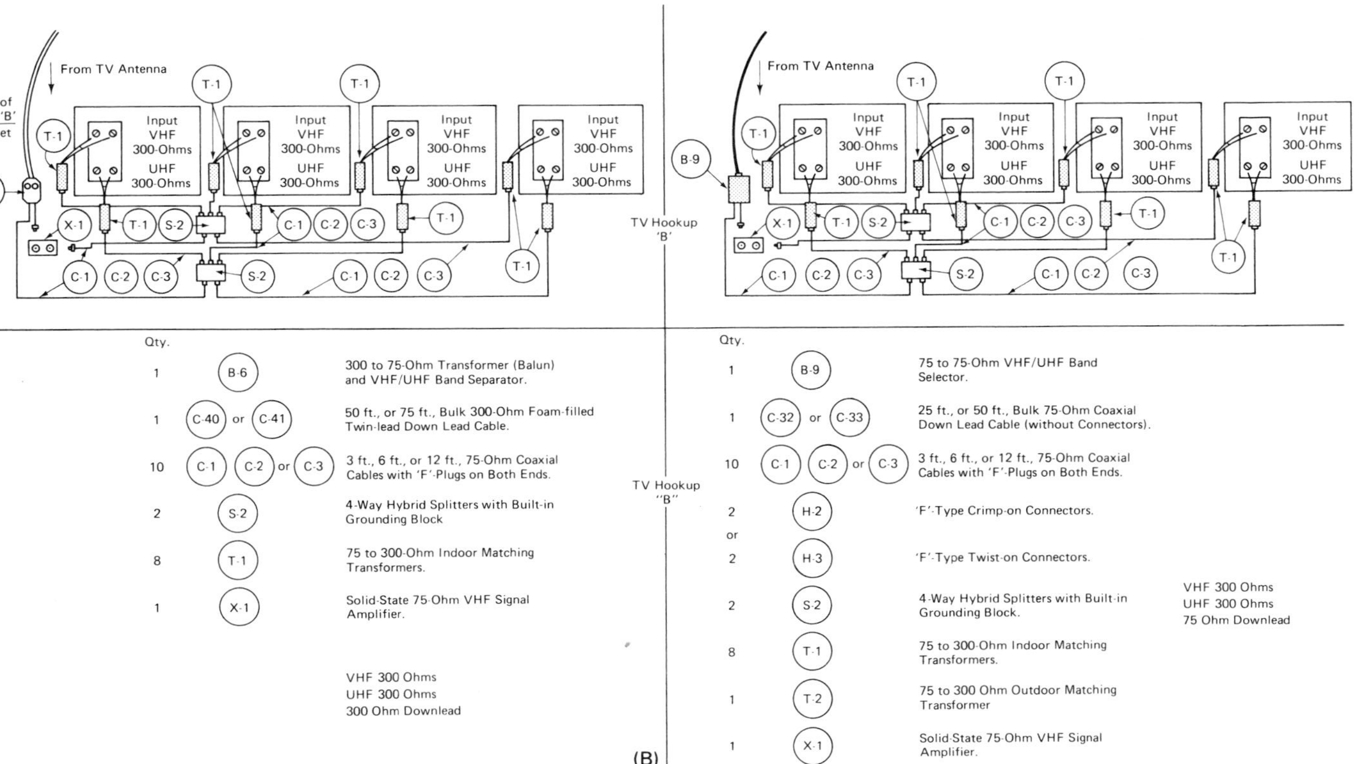

Figure 3–34B. *(continued)*

will be required. The antenna signal is delivered to a preamplifier mounted on the antenna mast, with the output of the preamp delivered directly to another amplifier in the home. The output of the second preamp is delivered to a four-way splitter. The wiring for the four TV sets is snaked through the walls and ends in wall plates in the various rooms. A separate splitter is also used to supply FM to an FM receiver. Not shown in the drawing are band separators to be used with each of the TV sets, assuming the antenna is multiband. Each of the TV receivers can operate independently and can be used to select VHF or UHF programs. Figure 3–34A is an overall view—not a detailed diagram. Figure 3–34B is a detailed drawing of a four TV set hookup.

Figure 3–35 also illustrates a four-TV set connection but note two important differences from Fig. 3–34. A VCR is now being included and, as the add-ons are shown, we now have a specific drawing.

The wiring arrangement of Fig. 3–35 permits every one of the TV sets to be used to watch any channel being received. The system also permits playback or recording of any channel on the VCR at the same time. However, the requirement for this setup is that channels 3 or 4 are not being received by the antenna.

The combined signal is first picked up by the antenna and routed through an antenna balun. This balun may or may not be required, depending on the output impedance of the antenna and the impedance of the transmission line. In this example the assumption is that the antenna is a 300-ohm type and that 75-ohm coaxial cable is used as the downlead.

The rectangular block shown at point 1 is a device that has two inputs and one output, working as an A/B switcher. It receives signals from the antenna and from the VCR. The combined VHF/UHF signals travel from the switcher at 1 to a splitter (point 2). The splitter at 2 can be two-way or four-way. The solid lines show two-set operation; the solid and dashed lines, four-way.

The first splitter is followed by a two-way splitter, also identified by the number *2*. This splitter divides the antenna signal into two parts, half for the first TV set, the other half for the VCR. Band separators will be required for all four TV sets, plus baluns, depending on the input impedances of the receivers. Installation will be simplified if combined band separator–baluns are used.

The signal output from the VCR is routed to the A/B switch and from there through the first signal splitter and then to two or four TV sets.

With this wiring arrangement, and if neither channel 3 nor channel 4 is being received by the TV antenna, set the output of the VCR on channel 3. If the TV channels being received by the antenna are weak—this will show as snow in the picture—it will be helpful to use one or more preamplifiers for the pictures received from the antenna. If the pictures from the VCR are snowy, insert a preamplifier in the output of that component.

If channel 3 or channel 4 is being received by the antenna, the wiring

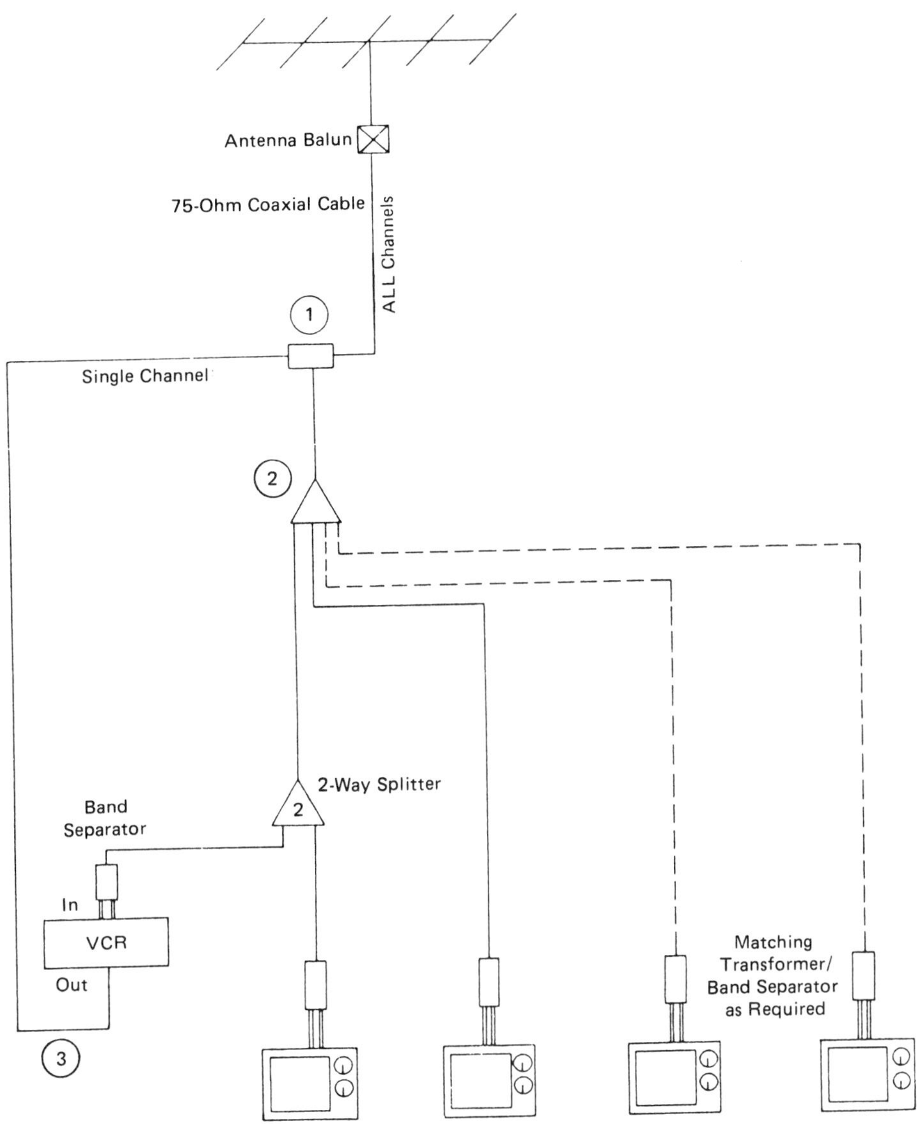

Figure 3–35. Two- or four-set operation. Channels 3 and 4 are not being received by the antenna. (*Courtesy Channel Master, Div. Avnet, Inc.*)

diagram of Fig. 3–35 can be modified to look like that in Fig. 3–36. Two signals are supplied to the inverted triangle (2), an A/B switch. One of these is the signal from the VCR, the other from the antenna. From the switch, the signal is routed toward either a two-way or a four-way splitter, also identified by the number *2*. From here, the antenna signal can be routed to either two

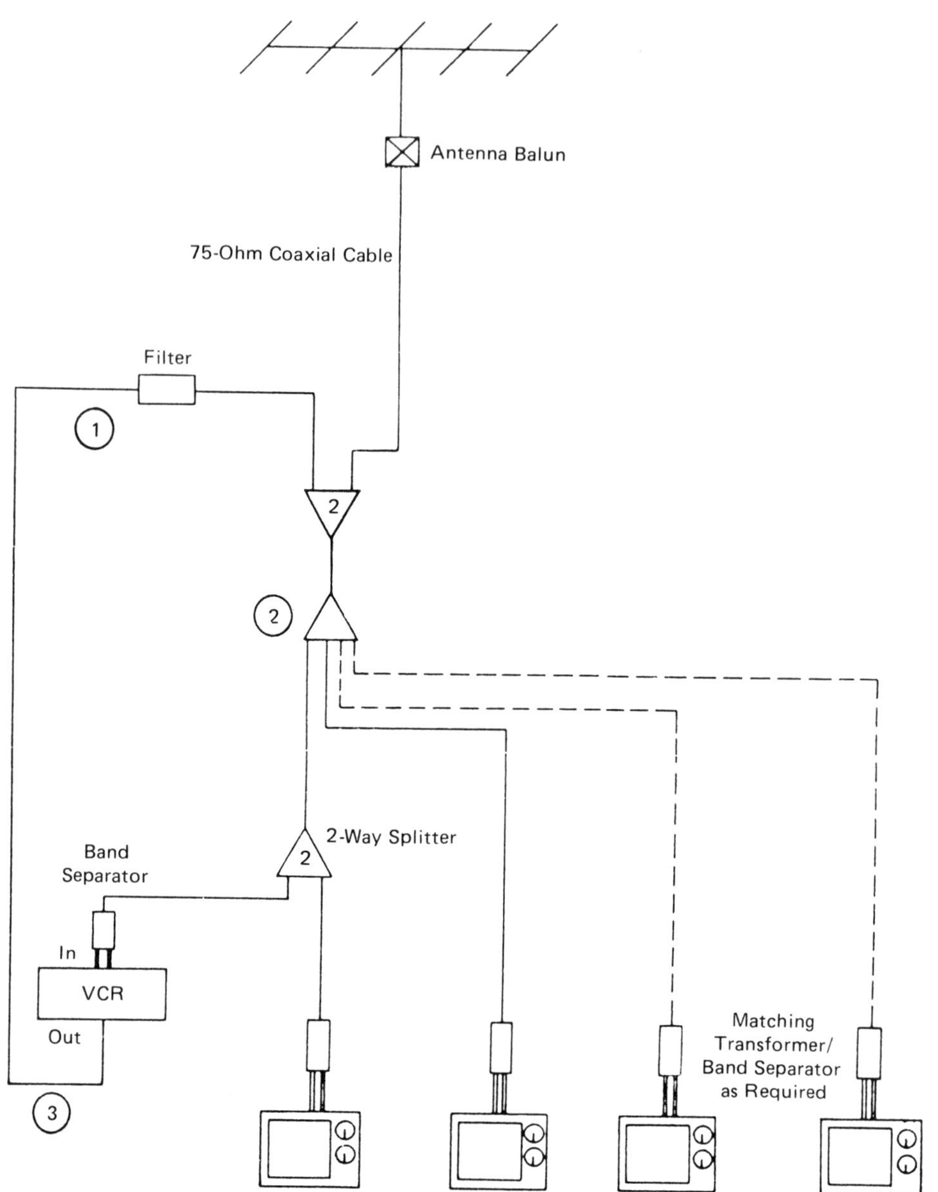

Figure 3–36. Two- or four-set operation. Channel 3 or Channel 4 being received by antenna. (*Courtesy Channel Master, Div. Avnet, Inc.*)

or four TV sets or to the VCR. The output signal from the VCR is directed toward the switcher, first passing through unit 1, a filter installed to reduce potential interference on channels 2 and 4. This is a nonswitchable add-on.

With this arrangement, either channel 3 or channel 4 can be received by the antenna. When channel 4 is received from the antenna the output of the VCR should be set to channel 3.

Figure 3–37 shows how this type of wiring can be used for either antenna signal input or cable TV. At the left of the drawing, the input can be a TV antenna or cable TV. If the wiring at the left is used and the input is cable TV, the TV sets should be cable ready. The signal from the antenna is brought into a two-way splitter, with part of the signal output delivered to an A/B switch, and the other part to a band separator. The band separator delivers VHF and UHF signals to the VCR whose output is supplied to the A terminal of the switch. With the help of this switch either the antenna or VCR signals

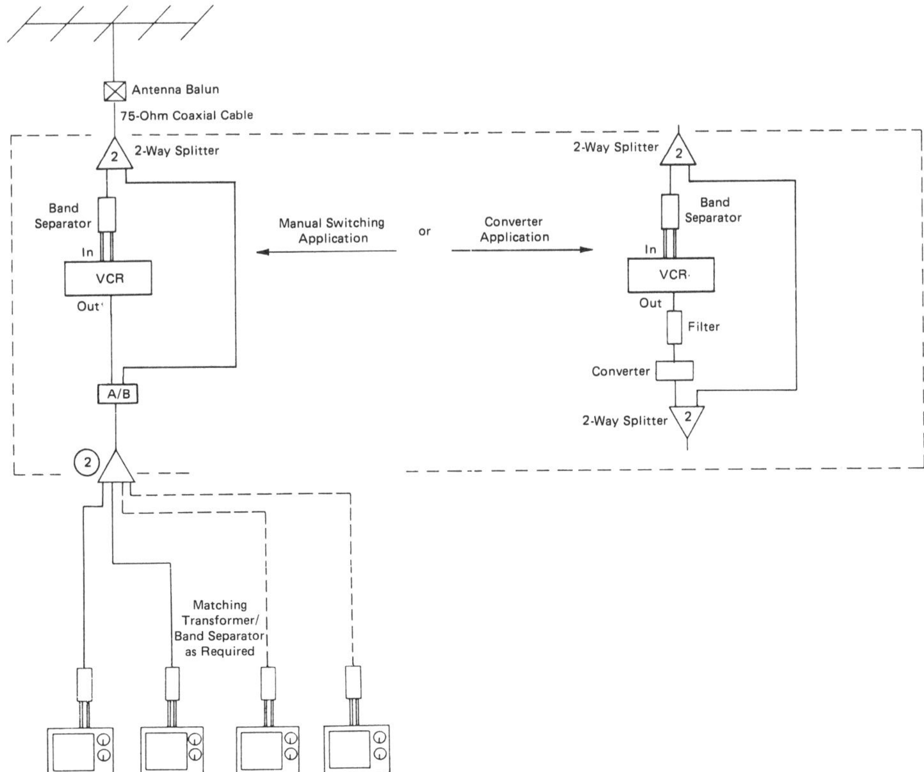

Figure 3–37. Multiple TV set operation when channels 3 and 4 are being received by the antenna or cable TV input. (*Courtesy Channel Master, Div. Avnet, Inc.*)

are delivered to the two or four TV sets. The TV sets are preceded by a two- or four-way splitter depending on the number of TV sets to receive the signals.

Note that, from the antenna all the way to the TV sets, the VHF and UHF signals are combined, hence band separators are needed before connections are made to the antenna terminal blocks of the receivers.

If the input is from cable TV and a separate block converter is to be used, the changed wiring is shown enclosed in dashed lines. All the other connections remain the same. The wiring of Fig. 3–37 can be used when both channels 3 and 4 are being received by the antenna or cable TV input.

CATV DIRECTIONAL TAP

For an in-home installation, the transmission line takes a fairly direct route to the antenna input terminals on a VCR or TV set. However, for CATV (cable TV) when a large number of sets are to receive input signals from a common source, the coaxial cable may branch off in various directions. To enable it to do so, a directional tap is used.

A directional tap is not the same as a signal splitter. The tap does not divide the signal but permits the signal to move in a number of different directions. The directional tap is used before the coaxial cable reaches the in-home wall plate. Once the cable signal is in the home, that is, following the wall plate, a signal splitter may be used to deliver the cable TV signal to a VCR and a TV set, or a pair of TV receivers.

MULTIPLE PREAMPLIFIERS

The best location for a preamplifier, as indicated previously, is in the downlead as close to the antenna as possible. This preamplifier has a single input (from the antenna) and a single output (to the downlead). However, in a multiple TV system one or more of the sets may require signal preamplification.

Figure 3–38 shows three types of preamplifiers. The one at the left is single input, single output, and can be used to supply one TV set with a stronger signal or, if inserted in the transmission line, an amplified signal for all the sets. The unit shown in the center can deliver an amplified signal to a pair of TV sets, while the add-on at the top right can be used for four sets.

All preamplifiers are power-line operated, require very little operating current, and can remain plugged in permanently. The input signal is 75 ohms and so are all the outputs. If the transmission line is 300 ohms, a 300-ohm to 75-ohm balun will be needed before the input. All the outputs are coaxial cable connected to the 75-ohm inputs of the TV sets, but a 75-ohm to 300-ohm balun will be required for those receivers that have 300-ohm input terminals.

The preamplifiers are mounted on a base plate for attachment to the back of a TV set. The jacks shown in the illustration are for screw-on F-

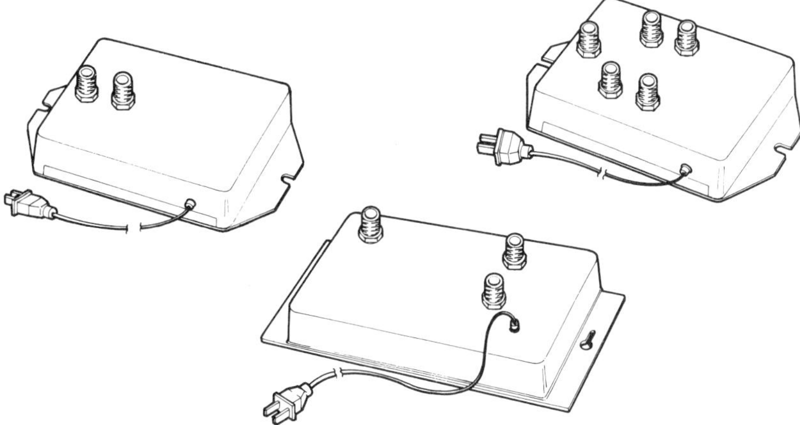

Figure 3–38. Multiple output preamps. (*Courtesy Gemini Industries, Inc.*)

connectors, which can be straight or right-angle. Screw-on connectors are used, as the connections, once made, are most often permanent.

THE AC OUTLET PROBLEM

One of the problems in looking at diagrams showing active devices is that these often omit an important connection, that of a line going to an AC outlet. A video system requires a surprising number of outlets, especially as active add-ons and components are gradually included. Unfortunately, most homes do not have enough baseboard outlets, and even when these are supplied, they are often at some uncomfortable distance from the in-home entertainment system. Cube taps (Fig. 3–39) are not the answer. This problem was solved a

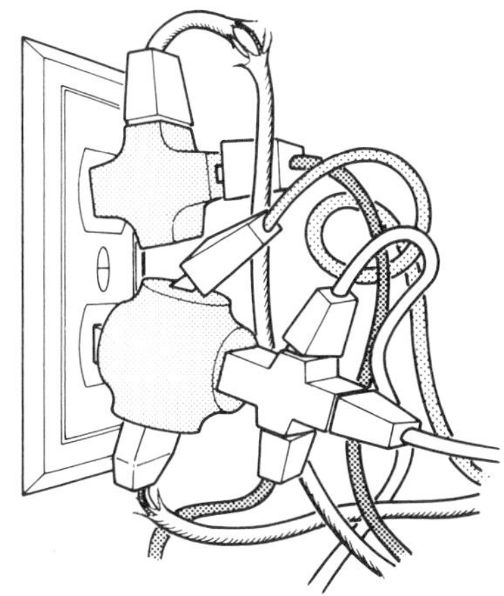

Figure 3–39. No!

long time ago for audio when manufacturers of high-fidelity equipment began including convenience outlets, switched and unswitched, on the rear apron of their components. That state of advanced thinking has not yet reached manufacturers of video equipment.

The solution is to select an outlet nearest the system and connect a multiple outlet to it. Use a multiple outlet that has a master switch so all the outlets can be shut off at the same time. It should also be equipped with an on-off warning light.

CONNECTING A BLOCK CONVERTER

Converters supplied by cable TV companies are most often single-channel with pushbuttons for the selection of channels. However, instead of using a single channel converter it is possible to use a combined VHF-cable block converter.

With this block converter it is possible to pick up all VHF cable channels as well as the midband and superband channels being used by many cable companies. It also permits the use of a VCR for recording and viewing midband and superband channels at the same time. A feature of this add-on is that all switching is done at the receiver. The advantage here is that this permits remote control of the receiver, assuming that it is so equipped.

With the block converter, the midband and superband cable channels are converted to UHF frequencies and are then supplied to the UHF tuner of the TV set, or the VCR, or both.

This component can convert up to 36 channels, including the VHF, midband, and superband channels. The VHF channels can be tuned directly by the VHF tuner of the TV set. Unlike the single-band converter, the block converter does not have tuning pushbuttons. Connections are shown in Fig. 3–40. There is one input port for the cable TV signal and two output ports: one for VHF, the other for UHF. All three ports use coaxial connectors. Since the UHF input on TV sets is usually 300 ohms, the UHF output is connected via a short length of coaxial cable to a 75-ohm to 300-ohm matching transformer. The VHF output cable is shown as 75 ohms, but if the input to the TV set is 300 ohms, a matching transformer will be required here as well.

The block converter can be used in addition to the primary converter supplied by the cable TV company, adding channels A through W to regular TV sets. The block converter has no tuning pushbuttons, and as it uses so little electrical power, is not equipped with an on/off switch. The converter in Fig. 3–41 can be mounted behind the TV set. Once it is installed, connected, and plugged into the AC power line, no further attention is required. The advantage of the block converter is that you can use your VCR to its maximum capability. You can record VHF, UHF, cable, or pay TV while watching other TV broadcasts or prerecorded VCR tapes.

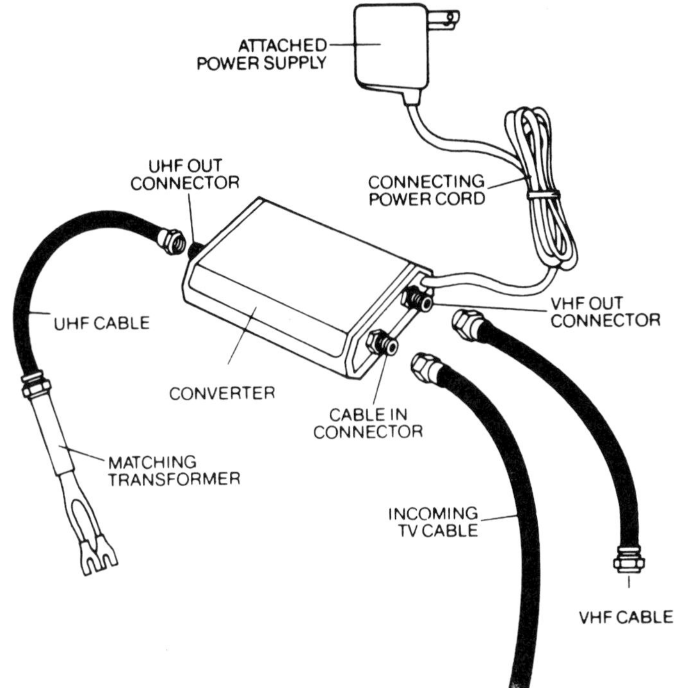

Figure 3–40. Connections for a block converter. (*Courtesy Rhoades National Corp.*)

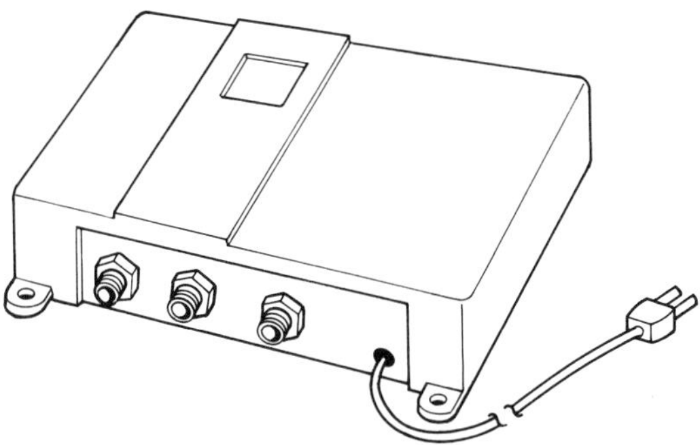

Figure 3–41. Block converter can be mounted behind TV set. (*Courtesy Gemini Industries, Inc.*)

ATTENUATORS

A fairly common problem for TV receivers is inadequate signal strength and it is for this reason that preamplifiers are so widely used. The other side of this coin is that signal strength is sometimes excessive. This could be for a combination of reasons, such as using a high-gain antenna with a TV set having a higher-than-usual input sensitivity, and a location fairly close to the TV broadcast antenna. In some instances the problem may be due to a strong signal lobe of the TV station's signal pattern. In this case the signal can be so strong as to overload the input circuits of the TV receiver. This problem can be solved by using an attenuator. The attenuator is connected by screwing it into an F-type antenna jack equipped with inside threads and then by using the opposite end of the attenuator as the input terminal for the downlead.

Since both ends of the attenuator are designed for 75-ohm input and 75-ohm output, a matching transformer may be required at one end or both, depending on the impedance of the downlead and that of the antenna input terminal on the TV set. This add-on is available in units that can supply an attenuation of 3 dB, 6 dB, or 10 dB.

An attenuator, sometimes referred to as a pad or an attenuator pad, is a passive network. Pads can be fixed or variable, but the fixed pad is the one used for in-home systems. They are fairly small and lightweight, and—as they require no adjustments—can be positioned in any convenient spot between the downlead and the antenna input jacks. The rear of the TV set is a suitable location.

The problem with attenuators is that they are made of resistive elements and are not frequency selective. As a result, all incoming signals will be weakened to the same extent, whether those signals are weak or strong.

Attenuators are available under a variety of different names, often dependent on the function the attenuator is to perform. A coaxial line attenuator is used on line in series with coaxial cable. A flap or fin attenuator is used with waveguide. In this case, a flap or fin is moved into the opening of the waveguide with a resultant power absorption. Another type of waveguide attenuator is the transverse film, in which a film of conducting material is positioned transverse to the axis of the waveguide.

RADIO-FREQUENCY INTERFERENCE

Abbreviated as RFI, radio-frequency interference is sometimes used synonymously with TVI (television interference). These are any naturally occurring or man-made signals that interfere with picture or audio reception, or both. RFI can exist as snow, confetti, or sparklies. Snow is interference with a monochrome signal; confetti is interference with a color TV signal; and sparklies are microwave interference in satellite TV reception.

Harmonic	Frequency (MHz)	Channel No.	Frequency Range (MHz)
20	71.60	4	66-72
21	75.18	5	76-82
23	82.34	6	82-88
49	175.42	7	174-180
57	204.06	11	198-204
58	207.64	12	204-210
60	214.80	13	210-216

Figure 3–42. Harmonics of the color-burst signal that can cause TVI.

Harmonics of the color-burst signal in a TV set can result in interference. Figure 3–42 shows the channels most often responsible for TVI. The color-burst signal for all color TV sets is 3.58 MHz. It is their harmonics, ranging from the twentieth to the sixtieth, that produce RFI. For example, the twentieth harmonic of 3.58 MHz is 71.6 MHz; and this will produce interference in channel 4, whose frequency range is 66 MHz to 72 MHz.

Traps

A trap is a frequency-sensitive device used to attenuate signals that cause interference. Sometimes known as a wave trap, it is a circuit that may be series tuned, shunt tuned, or some combination of the two. Traps are ordinarily fixed tuned although there are some that are variable. Traps are L-C (inductor-capacitor) circuits adjusted to a particular frequency or to a band of frequencies. Depending on their circuit configuration, traps are either high- or low-impedance.

High-Pass Filter

A high-pass filter is an arrangement of resistors, capacitors, and inductors connected between a transmission line and the antenna input terminals of a TV receiver for removing interfering signals whose frequencies are below those in the TV bands. High-pass filters are used to eliminate or minimize amateur radio and citizens' band interference.

4

TV AND VCR CONNECTIONS

It is sometimes necessary to understand the special language used by manufacturers before making connections, and sometimes interpretation is necessary. The word *monophonic,* as clear and specific as a word can be, is referred to as normal sound, implying that any other kind of sound is abnormal. Stereophonic sound is termed *hi-fi audio* but many kinds of stereo are better called *low-fi.*

Connecting a high-fidelity system, or a video system, or some combination of the two presupposes an understanding of wire, cables, connectors, and accessories. The next logical step is to show how these are used in conjunction with components. Of all those available, the TV set and the video cassette recorder (VCR) are a good starting point for video systems, as either one of these is the first component to receive picture signals.

THE INTEGRATED SYSTEM

An integrated system is one in which the various components of a system are housed in a single enclosure, with the components prewired to each other, eliminating the need for making interconnections. Quite often the integrated components are mounted on a single chassis, although there are exceptions. A television set is an integrated system. A high-fidelity receiver is an integrated system. The only connections needed for these are an antenna and AC line power. There may be a terminal for a ground connection but this is generally ignored.

The disadvantage of such a system, whether audio or video, is that the user is locked in. To update, the entire system must be discarded, the price paid for the convenience of not making component connections. Buying an integrated system is always a matter of trading convenience for desirable features. In addition to convenience, an integrated system is often user friendly.

THE COMPONENT SYSTEM

A component system is one made up of individual units. In a video system, this could consist of a TV tuner, a monitor, speakers, a video camera, an image enhancer, a VCR, and a videodisc player. All of these units must be connected. The plugs and jacks may not be compatible if the components are supplied by different manufacturers—and sometimes even if they are made by the same manufacturer.

The advantage of a component system, whether in video or high-fidelity sound, is that the outboard units may supply wanted features and are easy to put on line. Each individual component can be selected for optimum performance. Upgrading means replacing a single component, or adding a component from time to time.

Of course there are disadvantages. A multiplicity of components means that a rack is needed to house them. The number of operating controls becomes awesome, and the wiring behind the rack looks like, and is, a maze.

The Antenna Terminal Block

A TV set is very limited in inputs, with these located on the antenna terminal block on the rear of the receiver. There are only two inputs—for VHF- and UHF-modulated video signals. These two are used as the entry ports, not only for broadcast TV (for which the TV set was originally intended), but also for VCR signals, microwave TV, low-power TV, video games, computers, satellite TV, and videodisc players, resulting in an electronic traffic blockage.

The problem is countered in three ways. The first is to switch signal input cables manually, a time-consuming nuisance that can damage the cables and their connectors. A better method is to have a TV set with a built-in automatic switcher, with the changeover from one video signal source to another handled by a remote control unit. The most widely used technique is to install an outboard signal switcher.

The word *standardization* is inapplicable to antenna terminal blocks. That block can consist of 300-ohm inputs only, 75-ohm inputs only, or a combination of 300-ohm and 75-ohm inputs. The 300-ohm input can always be recognized by its use of machine screws. The 75-ohm input is an F-jack.

RF versus Video Signals

These two inputs, 75 ohms or 300 ohms, can accept only one kind of signal—the standard NTSC (National Television Systems Committee) signal. This is a composite video signal consisting of video, audio, and various pulses. Further, this signal must be modulated onto a carrier wave. It is called a radio-frequency signal (RF) to distinguish it from a video signal. The video signal has all the characteristics of the RF signal except that it is unmodulated. Because of this lack of modulation, a video signal cannot be injected into the VHF or UHF terminals of the TV set. This can be done, however, if the video signal is modulated by some component external to the TV set, such as a video cassette recorder. The carrier frequency selected is that of a VHF channel, either 3 or 4, depending on which of these is not used for TV broadcast reception. Other channel frequencies can be used.

MONITORS

The component approach to a high-fidelity system has been available for many years but it is only fairly recently that the same technique has been applied to video. Further, video systems have now been joined to high-fidelity systems, and we now have home-entertainment systems with a high order of electronic sophistication.

A TV receiver consists of two basic components: a tuner or front-end section, and a video section. The video section includes the high-voltage circuitry, the picture tube, and all sweep circuits.

One possible advantage of using a monitor is that it may have a better-quality picture display. (However, a monitor doesn't automatically qualify it for a better picture, as some display pictures no better than average.) In a TV set, the phosphor used by the picture tube is commercial grade. A better-quality phosphor may be used in a monitor, supplying superior resolution. The monitor may also have circuitry giving better picture definition.

A monitor looks like a television set; it has a screen but cannot be tuned, as it has no front end. Consequently, the monitor can only display the video signals delivered to it, but not if they are in RF form.

Monitors are used in closed-circuit television (CCTV), with the video signal supplied by a camera. Such monitors often have much better horizontal resolution than either TV sets or monitors used for in-home entertainment. A monitor for CCTV could have a horizontal resolution of 700 lines at the center of the screen, with a monochrome picture. While a monitor can be connected to a TV tuner, it can also be hooked up to a VCR if it has a video output terminal. The video output is connected to the monitor via a suitable length of coaxial cable, usually equipped with F-connectors. The signal is NTSC, that is, complete with the various sync and blanking pulses, but it is not modulated on an RF carrier. In this respect it is similar to the signal in a TV receiver following the demodulator stage.

ANTENNA CONNECTIONS

The starting point for a TV system could be at the antenna terminal block on the receiver. The set has only two connections—one for VHF, the other for UHF. These could each have input impedances of 300 ohms as shown in Fig. 4-1, or 75 ohms and 300 ohms as in Fig. 4-2.

The input to an FM receiver is usually 300 ohms, and the connections

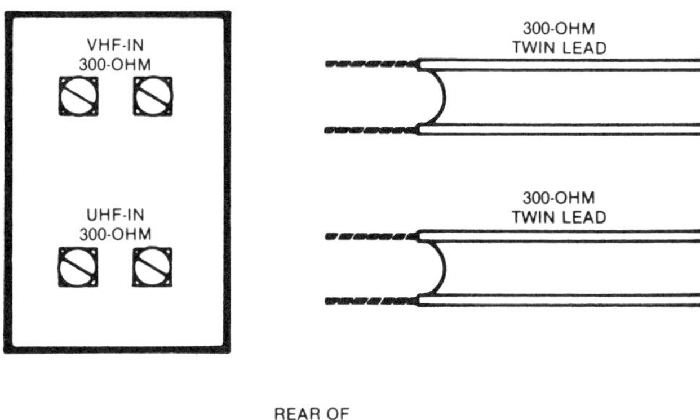

Figure 4–1. TV receiver antenna terminal block with 300-ohm inputs for VHF and UHF. (*Courtesy GC Electronics*)

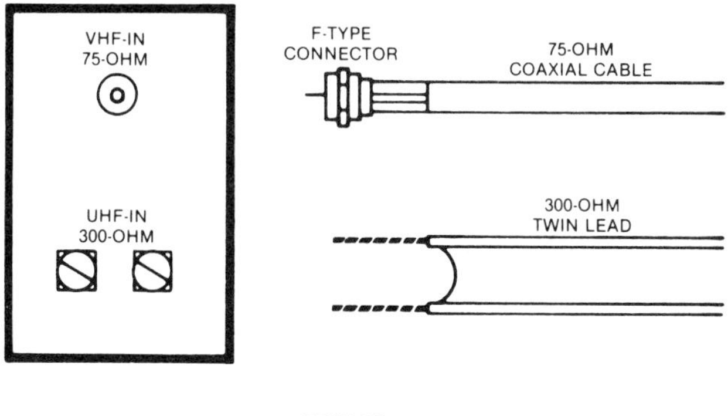

Figure 4–2. TV receiver antenna terminal block with 75-ohm input for VHF; 300-ohm input for UHF. (*Courtesy GC Electronics*)

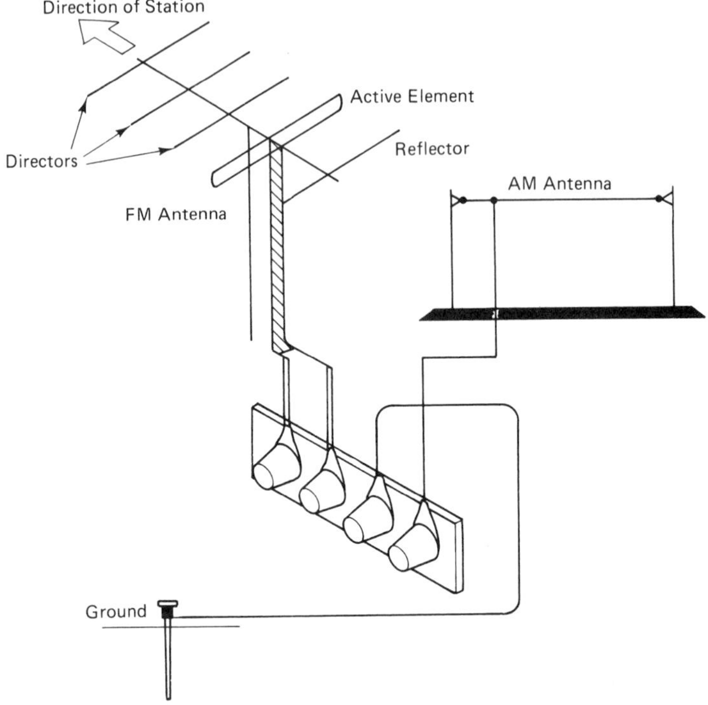

Figure 4–3. Connections for outdoor AM and FM antennas.

to it can be straightforward, as shown in Fig. 4–3. In this drawing, the antenna has an output impedance of 300 ohms; the transmission line is 300-ohm twin lead. No matching transformers are needed and even the connectors are simple spade lugs. The AM connection is a single-wire downlead from an antenna and here no impedance matching is required.

ANTENNAS

There are two types of antennas—single, and composite or multiple. Both types are used and both have their advantages and disadvantages.

The Single VHF/UHF/FM Antenna

A combined VHF/UHF/FM antenna is commonly used for pickup of these three signals. The advantage is the use of a single downlead, but impedance matching is still essential. In addition, a band separator is required to route the signals to their respective receivers. If you select a band separator whose output ports have impedances matching the input impedances of the

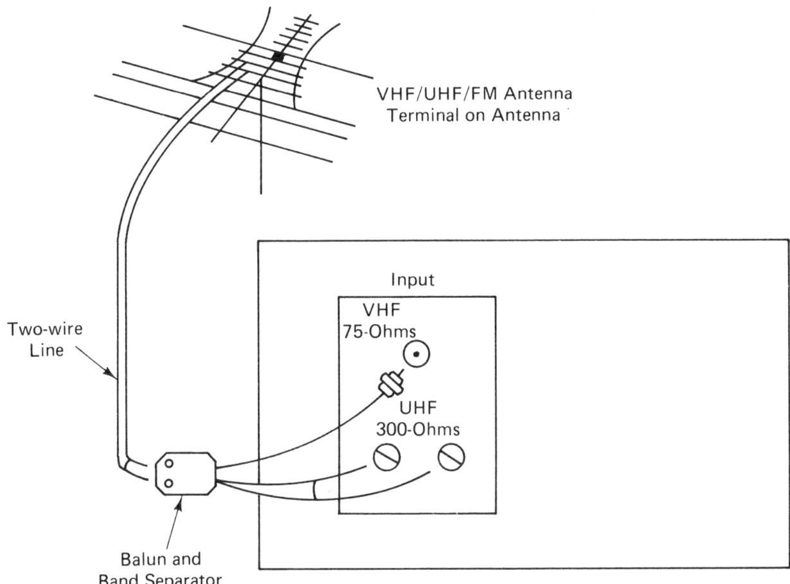

Figure 4–4. A 300-ohm line connected to a 300-ohm antenna. A balun band separator is used to separate VHF from UHF, and also to match the different input impedances of the TV set. (*Courtesy GC Electronics*)

TV and FM sets, no matching transformers will be needed. A matching transformer may still be required at the antenna, to match the antenna impedance to that of the transmission line.

Figure 4–4 shows how an antenna is connected to a TV set. In this example, the antenna has an output impedance of 300 ohms and the downlead is also 300 ohms, so no impedance matching is required at the antenna. The accessory used at the input to the TV set is a combined balun-band separator, which is convenient because otherwise a separate matching transformer and band separator would be required. The balun portion of this add-on has a 300-ohm input, and a pair of outputs, 75 ohms and 300 ohms. The band separator section divides the input signal into its VHF and UHF bands. The balun-band separator connects the VHF signals via a short length of coaxial cable, while the 300-ohm UHF input uses a small piece of twin lead.

The connections at the TV set in Fig. 4–5 are exactly the same, but there are some modifications prior to that terminal. The antenna is still one that has 300-ohm output, but since coaxial cable is to be used as the downlead, a 300-ohm to 75-ohm matching transformer is needed. The coaxial cable leads into a combined balun and band separator. This balun is not the same as that in Fig. 4–4; it has a 75-ohm input. However, its outputs are the same.

If an FM receiver is to be used, the only change necessary will be in the selection of the balun-band separator. It will need to have three outputs: dual

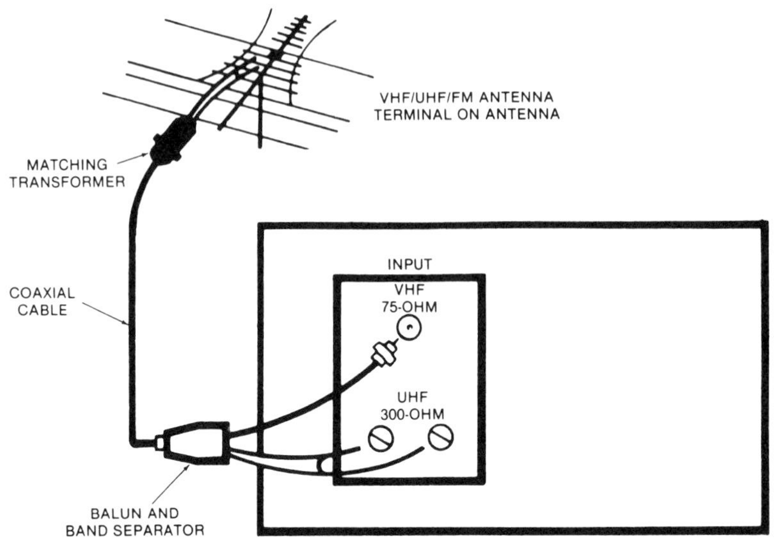

Figure 4–5. This is the same arrangement as that in Fig. 4–4, except that a coaxial line is used as the downlead. (*Courtesy GC Electronics*)

300 ohms, and a single 75 ohm. The band separator will be a type that will be able to split the three bands: VHF, UHF, and FM.

The connections in Figs. 4–4 and 4–5 assume two different impedances at the antenna terminal block of the TV set. However, quite commonly a TV set will have 300-ohm inputs only for both VHF and UHF. That is no great problem, whether the downlead is 75 ohms or 300 ohms. Figure 4–6 shows both possibilities. The upper drawing shows the use of twin lead; the lower drawing coaxial cable, but there is an important distinction. If the downlead is 300 ohms and the inputs are both 300 ohms, no balun is required, and the only accessory required is a band separator. In the lower drawing, however, the downlead is coaxial cable, and a combined balun-band separator must be used.

Multiple Antennas

In a multiple antenna setup, separate antennas are used for each of the bands: VHF, UHF, and FM, with individual downleads for each. While this may seem somewhat of a nuisance, not all users want three bands, or three bands may not be available. It also has the advantage that all three antennas (if three are used) can be individually adjusted for best reception.

How to Connect a VHF-Only Antenna to a Single TV Set. In some areas only VHF reception is available and so the antenna may be for VHF

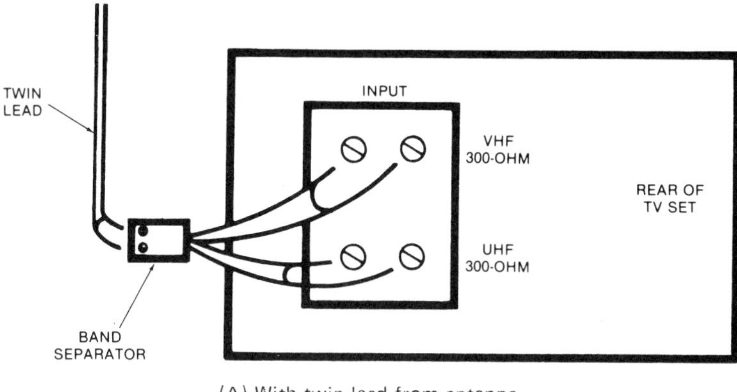

(A) With twin lead from antenna

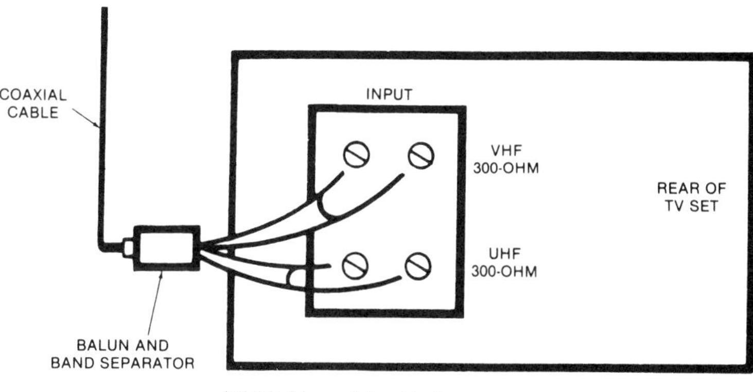

(B) With coaxial cable from antenna

Figure 4–6. Substitution of coaxial cable for twin lead will require a balun at the antenna and a balun-band separator at the TV set. (*Courtesy GC Electronics*)

only. Even when UHF transmission can be received, some older antennas are VHF only. If the antenna is a 300-ohm unit, a 300-ohm to 75-ohm balun should be used at the antenna, if coaxial cable is preferred as the downlead. If the VHF terminal on the TV set is 75 ohms, the coaxial cable can be connected directly to that terminal by using an F-connector. If the input to the TV set is 300 ohms, a 75-ohm to 300-ohm matching transformer will be needed.

Using a VCR with a VHF-only antenna is equally simple (Fig. 4–7). The VCR has been inserted on line between the antenna and the TV receiver. The coaxial cable lead-in from the 75-ohm antenna is connected to the VHF antenna input terminal on the VCR. The output port of the VCR is connected to the 75-ohm VHF port on the antenna terminal block of the TV set.

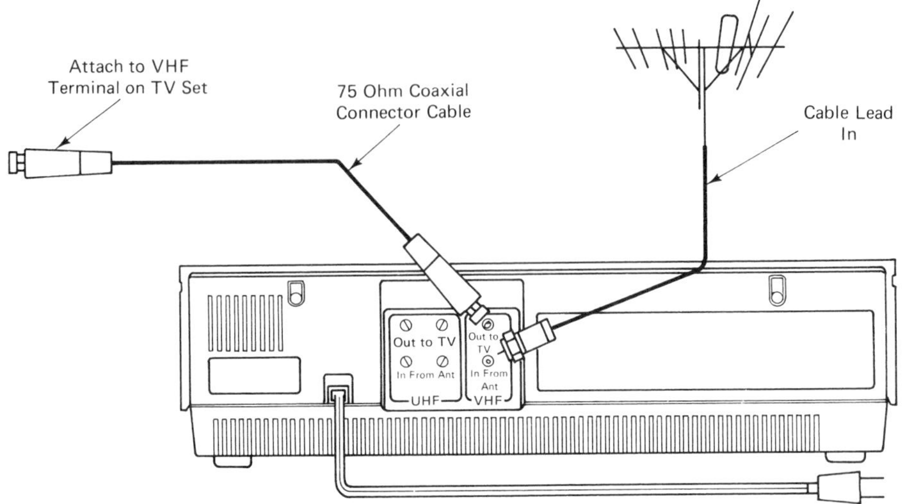

Figure 4-7. Connections for a VHF-only antenna using coaxial cable throughout. (*Courtesy RCA*)

Figure 4-8 shows a comparable wiring arrangement except that the antenna is 300-ohms. The downlead is twin lead, but as the antenna input port of the VCR is 75 ohms, a 300-ohm to 75-ohm matching transformer is needed. The output of the VCR is 75 ohms and so is connected via a short length of coaxial cable to the 75-ohm VHF input port of the TV set. If that port should happen to be 300 ohms, a 75-ohm to 300-ohm matching transformer would be required here.

How to Connect a UHF Antenna. In some areas only UHF television broadcasts can be received. If the antenna is UHF only, having a 300-ohm output, the antenna can be wired directly to the UHF terminals on a TV set, using twin lead.

If a VCR is to be used (Fig. 4-9), the twin lead can be wired directly to its 300-ohm UHF input terminals. The UHF output terminals of the VCR, also 300 ohms, can be wired to the TV set with a suitable length of twin lead. Note that no baluns are required, and as only one TV band is involved (and no FM band) there is no need for a band separator either.

Connecting Two TV Sets to One Antenna. Two TV sets can be operated from an antenna following either of the wiring arrangements shown in Fig. 4-10. A television signal isn't an inexhaustible supply of energy, and if two TV sets are used and they have equal sensitivity, the signal will be divided in two, approximately. There is no further problem if the signal is adequate, but if not, a video preamplifier can be used. The preferable location

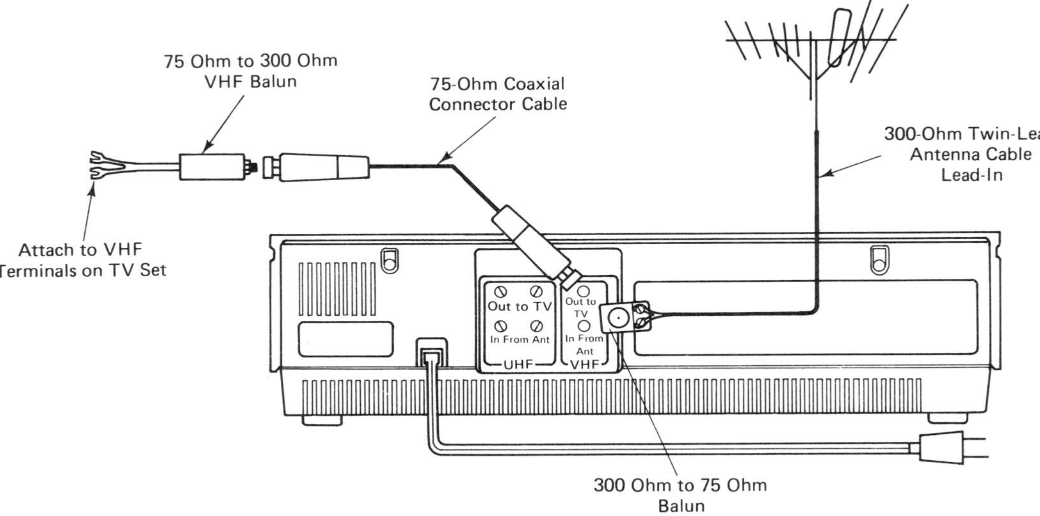

Figure 4–8. Connections for a VHF-only antenna using 300-ohm downlead. (*Courtesy RCA*)

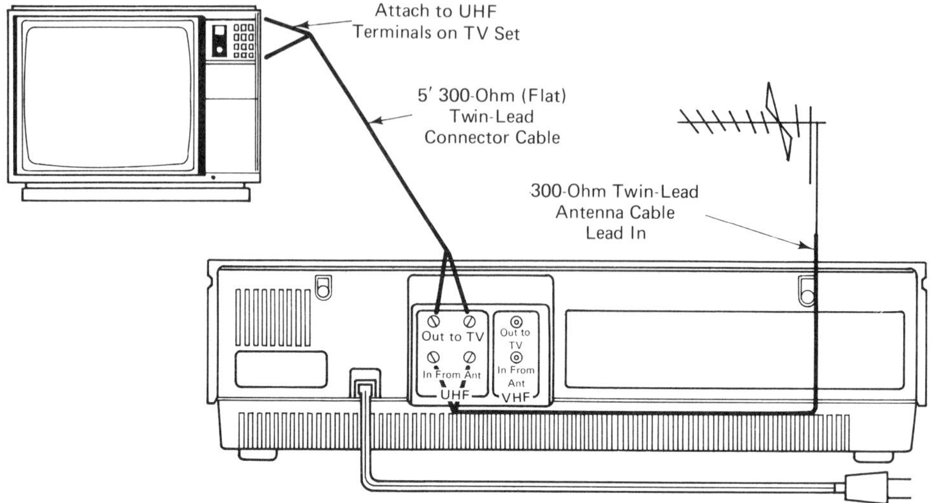

Figure 4–9. Connections for a UHF-only antenna to a VCR and TV set. (*Courtesy RCA*)

is right at the antenna with the unit mounted to the mast, a position that supplies the best signal-to-noise ratio. If not, then the preamp can be put at the point where the downlead enters the home. For a good picture, the signal strength at the antenna input terminals of a TV receiver should be approximately 1000 microvolts or 0 dBmV.

The 300-ohm antenna used in Fig. 4–10 is a multiband antenna supplying VHF/UHF and FM signals. The coaxial cable downlead is connected to the antenna by a 300-ohm to 75-ohm transformer in the upper drawing. Since two TV sets are to be driven by the signal, it is necessary to divide that signal into two parts and this is done by a signal splitter, identified as S1. Note that the signal splitter does not do any impedance changing. Its input is 75 ohms and its two outputs are also 75 ohms. These two outputs are connected to the two TV sets in exactly the same way, assuming that both TV sets have identical antenna blocks. The lines marked C1, C2, or C3 are suitable lengths of coaxial cable and ordinarily are 3-ft., 6-ft., or 12-ft. lengths of coaxial cable having F-plugs at both ends.

The unit marked B1 is a 75-ohm to 300-ohm matching transformer. However, the matching transformer, identified as B7 in the upper drawing, has two different outputs. One is 75 ohms; the other 300.

USING THE SIGNAL SPLITTER

Connections for a video system can be fairly simple, even in multiple TV setups; however, careful planning prior to installation is necessary. The first proviso is the use of a single-band antenna instead of a multiple type. That an-

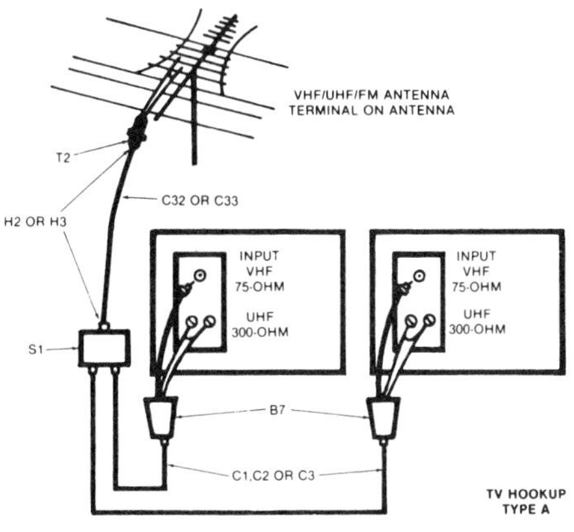

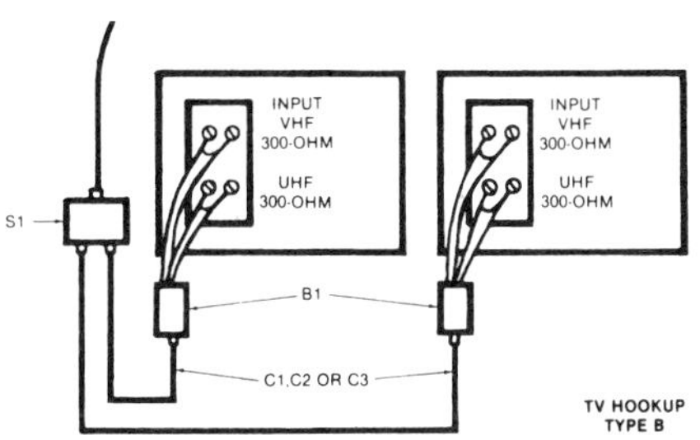

TV HOOKUP TYPE A — VHF 75-OHM, UHF 300-OHM | **ANTENNA HOOKUP — 75-OHM COAXIAL CABLE DOWN CABLE**

QUANTITY	CODE	COMPONENTS REQUIRED
2	B7	75- TO 75/300-OHM TRANSFORMER (BALUN) AND VHF/UHF BAND SEPARATOR
1	C32 OR C33	25-ft. OR 50-ft. BULK 75-OHM COAXIAL DOWN-LEAD CABLE (WITHOUT CONNECTORS)
2	H2	F TYPE CRIMP-ON CONNECTORS
OR		
2	H3	F TYPE TWIST-ON CONNECTORS
2	C1,C2 OR C3	3-ft, 6-ft, OR 12-ft 75-OHM COAXIAL CABLES WITH F TYPE PLUGS AT BOTH ENDS
1	T2	300- TO 75-OHM OUTDOOR MATCHING TRANSFORMER
1	S1	2-WAY HYBRID SPLITTER WITH BUILT-IN GROUNDING BLOCK

TV HOOKUP TYPE B — VHF 300-OHM, UHF 300-OHM | **ANTENNA HOOKUP — 75-OHM COAXIAL CABLE DOWN LEAD**

QUANTITY	CODE	COMPONENTS REQUIRED
2	B1	75- TO 300-OHM TRANSFORMER (BALUN) AND VHF/UHF BAND SPLITTER
1	C32 OR C33	25-ft. OR 50-ft. BULK 75-OHM COAXIAL DOWN-LEAD CABLE (WITHOUT CONNECTORS)
2	H2	F TYPE CRIMP-ON CONNECTORS
OR		
2	H3	F TYPE TWIST-ON CONNECTORS
2	C1,C2 OR C3	3-ft, 6-ft, OR 12-ft 75-OHM COAXIAL CABLES WITH F TYPE PLUGS ON BOTH ENDS
1	T2	300- TO 75-OHM OUTDOOR MATCHING TRANSFORMER
1	S1	2-WAY HYBRID SPLITTER WITH BUILT-IN GROUNDING BLOCK

Figure 4–10. Multiband antenna driving two TV sets. (*Courtesy GC Electronics*)

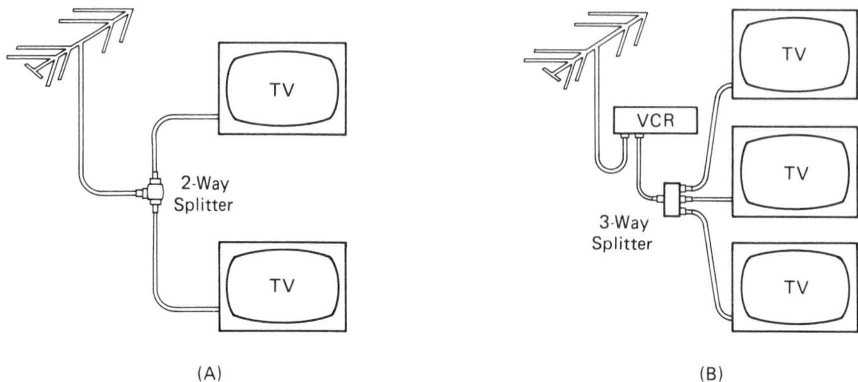

Figure 4–11. Antenna signal driving two sets (A). Antenna delivers signals to VCR, which supplies three TV sets (B).

tenna should have an impedance that directly matches that of the downlead without the need for a balun. As the signal is to be divided, the signal splitter should have input and output impedances that match that of the downlead and also the input impedance of the TV set.

Figure 4–11 shows how this arrangement can be used to drive two TV sets in drawing A. Drawing B illustrates how the same hookup can be used with a VCR and three TV receivers. Unfortunately, the larger the number of components to be connected, the less likely it is that input and output impedances will allow avoidance of add-ons. One reason is that impedances aren't touted as features, and the potential buyer of an antenna, a transmission line, a VCR, or two or three television sets isn't aware of the need for add-ons until the components are unpacked and ready for installation.

Using Cable TV to Drive Two TV Sets

One of the great advantages of cable TV is that it can simplify in-home installations by reducing the number of needed add-ons. Figure 4–12 shows one possible arrangement. Since cable TV connections are 75 ohms, wiring is simplified if the VCR is also rated at 75 ohms for both VHF input and output, and this is usually the case. Still another reason for wiring simplification is that the VCR is supplying a TV signal for one band only—VHF.

Since two TV sets are to be operated, a two-way signal splitter is required. If both of the sets have a 75-ohm VHF antenna terminal, all that is required is a short length of coaxial cable equipped with F-connectors. In Fig. 4–12, however, the TV set in the lower part has a 300-ohm input, so a 75-ohm to 300-ohm matching transformer is needed.

For connections of this kind, there are three possibilities as far as the TV

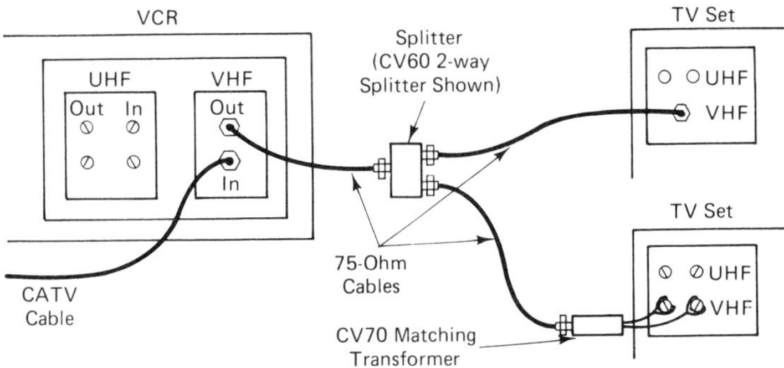

Figure 4–12. Cable TV supplying signals to two TV sets. (*Courtesy Gemini Industries, Inc.*)

sets are concerned: both sets could have 300-ohm VHF inputs, or both could have 75-ohm inputs, or, as shown in the illustration, one could be 300 ohms, the other 75 ohms.

Connections for Two-Band Operation

The greater the demand imposed on a system for a larger number of signal sources, the greater the number of add-ons required. Figure 4–13 differs from Fig. 4–12, as it delivers both VHF and UHF signals.

Typically, a VCR will have 300-ohm outputs for UHF and 75-ohm outputs for VHF, although there are exceptions. The first add-on following the outputs of the VCR is a band combiner, identified as CV65.

In a wiring setup, it is entirely possible for two or three bands to be separated and combined several times. Thus, in Fig. 4–13A, we have no knowledge of the type of antenna, or antennas, used. If a single antenna is used, a band separator is needed prior to the input of the VCR, as the VCR has separate inputs for VHF and UHF. If separate antennas are used, one for VHF, the other for UHF, the downleads can be connected directly to the VCR, assuming the use of twin lead for UHF signals and coaxial cable for VHF signals. If twin lead is not used, then matching transformers could be required prior to the inputs to the VCR.

After the band combiner (CV65) whose output is 75 ohms, coaxial cable is used for connection to a two-way signal splitter. You can always be sure that if a band combiner is used in a system, sooner or later a band separator will be needed. Similarly, if two or more TV sets are to be operated, a signal splitter will be required.

Following the splitter equipped with a pair of 75-ohm outputs, each output leads into a band separator. Note the difference between these band sep-

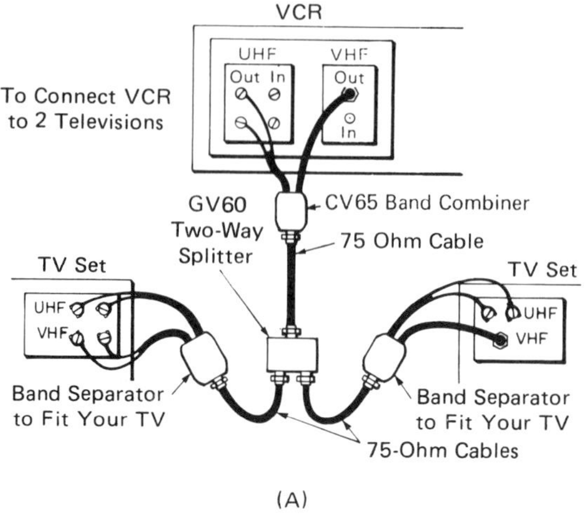

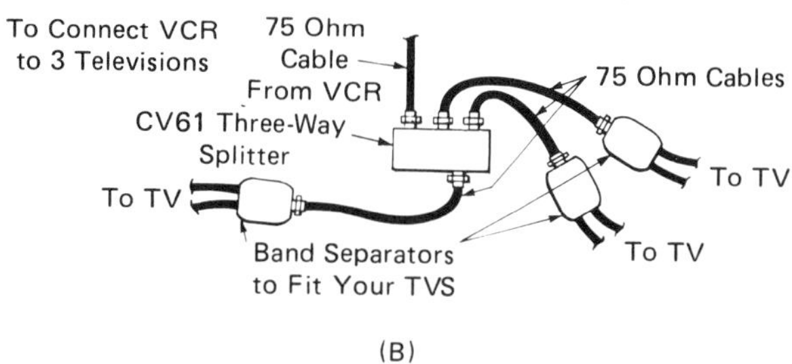

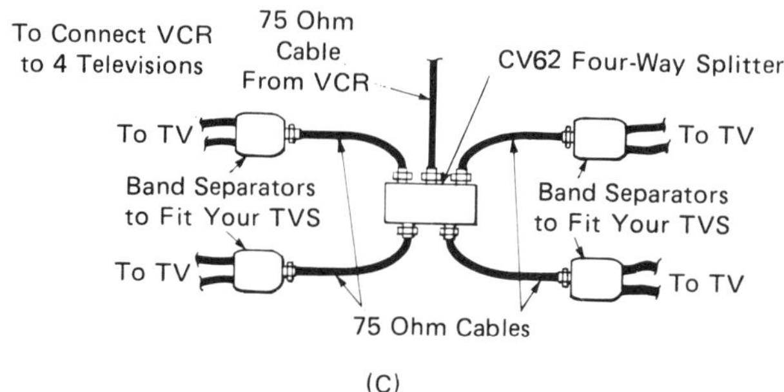

Figure 4-13. VCR operating two TV sets (A); three sets (B); and four sets (C). (*Courtesy Gemini Industries, Inc.*)

arators—they are not identical as far as outputs are concerned. The one at the left has a pair of 300-ohm outputs; that at the right, 75 ohms and 300 ohms.

The same technique can be used to drive three TV sets as that shown in drawing B. The difference is in the use of a three-way instead of a two-way signal splitter. The splitter has a single input and three outputs. The three outputs are coaxial cable connected to three band separators. The kinds of band separators used will be determined by the input impedances of the three TV sets.

The wiring of Fig. 4–13 could be extended to four TV sets (drawing C) or more, following the same general procedure. However, this assumes that the original signal strength is adequate, and that may or may not be the case. It is probably not adequate to operate three TV sets. This does not mean the wiring arrangement must be abandoned. All that is required is the use of a signal preamplifier, and if one of the TV sets is characterized by low sensitivity, it may need a preamplifier of its own.

Before you interconnect components, it would be helpful to prepare a plan, a wiring diagram of the work to be done. Since the inclusion of each and every add-on in such a diagram tends to make it look complex, you might find it helpful to consider an overall view, omitting add-ons (Fig. 4–14). You can use a diagram like this and then block in signal splitters, band combiners, and band separators as required, plus an impedance-matching device at the antenna, if needed. Each of your diagrams may well be different, depending on the various impedances of all the components. Several RF preamplifiers are shown in Fig. 4–14, but they have been included more as a reminder. One could be positioned at the antenna or placed immediately following the VCR, or in any one or all of the lines going to the TV sets. In its present location, the first preamplifier strengthens all signals for all the TV sets. You may prefer to have such a component used in connection with just one of the TV receivers or with all of them. Also, mark the impedances at various points on the diagram.

With the connections shown in Fig. 4–14, it is possible to record any channel on the VCR. Each of the TV sets can be tuned independently to any channel, or the VCR can be used as the signal source and a videotape can be watched on any or all of the TV sets. While Fig. 4–14 shows VHF input and output only, the system can also respond to UHF. With VHF only, band com-

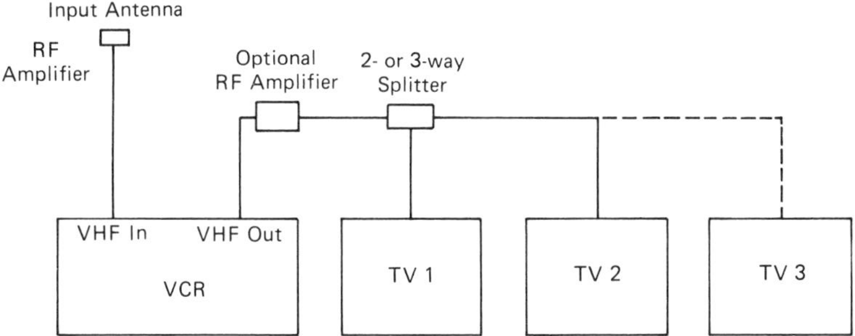

Figure 4–14. Overview of two- or three-TV-set operation. If you use the VCR for tape playback, it is possible to watch the recording on any set or on all of them.

biners and separators aren't needed. With both bands, VHF and UHF, they are.

The Independent TV Set

All the TV sets in Fig. 4-14 are dependent on the VCR, that is, the VCR must be turned on for the TV sets to receive a signal. It is possible, as shown in Fig. 4-15, to operate two TV sets and have one of them independent of the VCR. The video signal from the antenna first passes through a splitter. A pair of band separators is used: one for TV 2, the other for the VCR. Since TV 2 gets its signal directly from the antenna, even though it is via a splitter and band separator, is can be turned on or off, and also tuned independently of the VCR. TV 1, however, gets is signal input from the VCR, and so for TV 1 to display a picture, the VCR must be turned on.

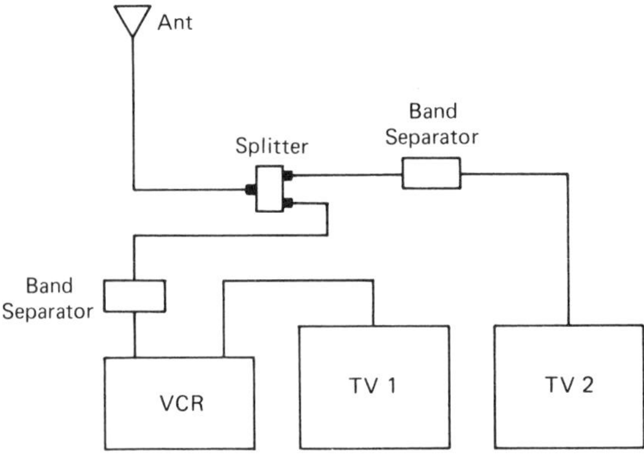

Figure 4-15. TV 1 works through the VCR. TV 2 receives broadcast signals only.

THE VIDEO CASSETTE RECORDER

The video cassette recorder (VCR) is an electromechanical component, equipped with a tuner section for the reception of RF signals plus circuitry for the demodulation and remodulation of video signals; hence it contains a demodulator and a remodulator. All broadcast TV signals received by the VCR are stripped of their carriers (demodulation) resulting in a combined video-audio signal. That signal is then superimposed on a carrier whose frequency is that of channel 3 or channel 4, a process called remodulation. A VCR can accept either modulated or unmodulated signals. In the case of a video camera, the signal is unmodulated when it is supplied by the camera. The VCR modulates this signal onto a carrier whose frequency is that of either channel

3 or channel 4, with the channel frequency selectable by the user. This arrangement of demodulation and remodulation is essential, as the output of the VCR is supplied to a TV set, equipped only for modulated video signals—that is, RF signals. In the demodulation or remodulation process, only the carriers are affected; they are either eliminated or changed. Thus a VCR may have a video port for supplying unmodulated signals and another port for those that are modulated.

The modulator in the VCR produces a radio-frequency carrier on which video and audio signals can be superimposed, but this carrier is a miniature broadcasting station. If a VCR is incorrectly connected to a TV antenna, the signal produced by the VCR can be transmitted, and not only can that be a nuisance, but it is also illegal. The use of a preamplifier between the antenna and the VCR is helpful in blocking such signal transmission.

Unlike a TV set, a VCR has ports for both input and output connections. The 300-ohm terminals use machine screws; the 75-ohm terminal an F-jack.

VHS and Beta Connections

These two video tape recorders (VTRs) are incompatible, but the connections to them from antennas and other signal sources and their wiring to TV sets are made in the same way. An impedance of 75 ohms or 300 ohms is not affected by the fact that a recorder is VHS or Beta. Consequently, all connections described for VCRs in general, are applicable to both, and the VCRs are not identified as to format. (*VTR* as a designation is gradually being replaced by *VCR*.)

The VCR and Remote Control

When a VCR is connected to a TV set, the receiver must remain tuned to either channel 3 or channel 4, determined by a switch setting that is usually on the rear of the recorder. The TV set's remote control is then of no use except for the initial selection of channel 3 or channel 4. Manual selection of these channels is preferable, with the remote control turned off. Some remote control devices are very touch sensitive and it is possible to change the TV set's tuner accidentally.

Clear Channel

A TV broadcast channel that cannot be picked up by a receiver is referred to as a clear channel. Clear channels are either 3 or 4, hence one or the other of these channels can be used for input from some other signal source, such as a VCR.

RADIO-FREQUENCY MODULATOR

A radio-frequency (RF) modulator is an add-on unit that generates a carrier frequency equivalent to that used by VHF channels 3 or 4. The signal input to the modulator is a baseband signal (video, sync, and blanking pulses). This composite signal is used to amplitude-modulate a carrier. The modulating signal may or may not include audio, but if it does, it will be frequency modulated. If channel 3 is chosen, from 60 to 66 MHz, the frequency of the video carrier will be 61.25 MHz and that of the audio carrier will be 65.75 MHz. For channel 4, 66 MHz to 72 MHz, the video carrier will be 67.25 MHz while the sound carrier will be 71.75 MHz. The output of the modulator is an RF signal. With the help of an RF modulator, a TV receiver will accept video and audio signals from any video component. This allows the user to connect a camera, computer, or image enhancer directly to the antenna input terminals of a TV receiver.

The RF modulator is equipped with F-jacks for input and output for connection to coaxial cable. The output is wired to the VHF antenna terminal on a TV receiver. If that terminal is intended for 300-ohm input, it is necessary to use a 75-ohm to 300-ohm matching transformer at the output of the RF modulator.

If a VCR is used, a separate RF modulator is not required, as the VCR contains its own modulator circuitry.

CABLE TV

Cable TV had its inception in 1950, and was originally known as community antenna television (CATV). TV set owners were able to abandon individual receiving antennas in favor of one centrally located antenna in a high location that allowed it to pick up signals that would otherwise be blocked by terrain or buildings.

Cable TV services are provided by private corporations, which must usually obtain some agreement or franchise from a municipal government, with payment by the cable company to that government. The agreement specifies not only the amount and method of payment, but also the amount and kind of programming. In some arrangements, the cable group must supply educational programs to schools without charge.

In its early days, cable supplied TV reception services to subscribers in areas that could not receive television or that were limited in TV reception. However, cable is now also being used in cities to overcome the problems of ghosting caused by multiple signal reflections from buildings.

A cable system is defined by the FCC as:

> . . . a nonbroadcast facility consisting of a set of transmission paths and associated signal generator, reception and control equipment, under common own-

> ership and control, that distributes or is designed to distribute to subscribers, the signals of one or more TV broadcast stations, but said term shall not include (1) any facility that serves fewer than 50 subscribers, or (2) any facility that serves or will serve only subscribers in one or more multiple unit dwellings under common ownership, control or management.

The FCC does not license cable TV systems. Its jurisdiction over cable TV does not stem from any statutory provision in the Communications Act; instead it derives from its general regulatory authority over television broadcasting. Accordingly, it has even less authority to regulate program content on cable systems than in the broadcast area.

Although the Commission does issue certain construction permits, licenses, or other authorizations for communication facilities (Multipoint Distribution Service, Microwave Radio, Subscription Television Service, and Cable Television Service) used to distribute pay TV programming, it does not regulate the contents of such programming.

Cable systems operators are required to carry all VHF and UHF programs that can normally be seen in their franchise area. Beyond these requirements, the choice of which cable program services are to be offered is determined by the operator.

The cable company can pick up, via its master antenna, the signals of a number of TV stations. These signals are then amplified, frequency converted, and then fed into a mixing arrangement. The cable company has the option of scrambling (encoding) the signals. The signals are amplified further, equalized, and routed to the homes of subscribers via coaxial cable.

Tiered Service

This is an arrangement of programming services supplied by cable TV in groups or tiers. The lowest tier is the least expensive, the highest tier the most costly. The highest tier may consist of special sports events, possibly not available on regular TV broadcasts, or recent full-run movies not interrupted by advertising commercials. The lowest tier is sometimes offered as basic services supplied by a cable company in exchange for a minimum fee.

CABLE TV CHANNELS

Broadcast TV channels are divided into groups: VHF and UHF. Cable TV channels are also divided.

Midband Channels

As is shown in Fig. 4–16, cable TV starts at 120 MHz and has nine channels with the last channel ending at 174 MHz. Each channel has a bandwidth of 6 MHz (just like any broadcast channel) and so these nine channels occupy

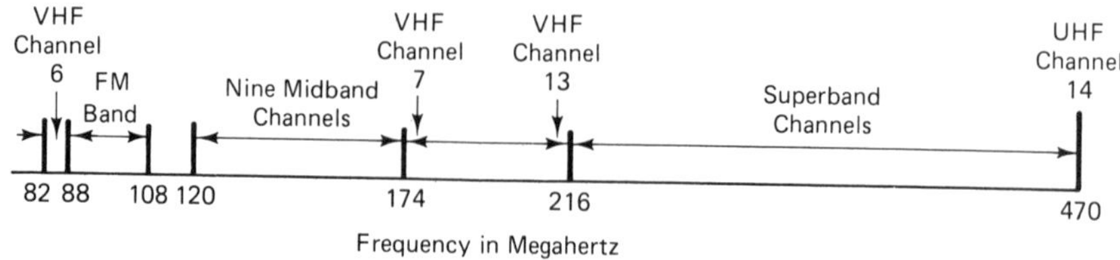

Figure 4–16. Midband and superband cable TV channels.

a total bandwidth of 54 MHz (120 MHz + 54 MHz = 174 MHz). These are sometimes referred to as the midband channels (Fig. 4–17), but instead of being numbered, each is assigned an identifying letter. The first band from 120 to 126 MHz is channel A; that from 126 to 132 MHz is channel B, and so on. In some instances the audio and video carriers are inverted, a method of scrambling.

Superband Channels

The next group of cable channels begins at 216 MHz—and these are called the superband channels. The upper limit of the cable superband channels is at 470 MHz, which represents the beginning of the UHF broadcast TV channels. Thus, the superband channels, extending from 216 MHz to 470 MHz, have a total available bandwidth of 470 − 216, or 254 MHz, enough to accommodate forty-two channels, each having a bandwidth of 6 MHz. Actually, there is more than enough space, as 254 ÷ 6 = 42 MHz, with 2 MHz left over. The number of channels selected by any cable company and their frequencies can differ from one cable company to another.

Channel Number	Frequency Limits of Channel	Center Frequency of Carrier	
	120 MHz		
A		Picture Sound	121.25 125.75
	126 MHz		
B		Picture Sound	127.25 131.75
	132 MHz		
C		Picture Sound	133.25 137.75
	138 MHz		
D		Picture Sound	139.25 143.75
	144 MHz		
E		Picture Sound	145.25 149.75
	150 MHz		
F		Picture Sound	151.25 155.75
	156 MHz		
G		Picture Sound	157.25 161.75
	162 MHz		
H		Picture Sound	163.25 167.75
	168 MHz		
I		Picture Sound	169.25 173.75
	174 MHz		

Figure 4–17. Midband channels, identified by letters.

Subchannels

There is also a group of three video channels, known as subchannels (Fig. 4–18) and identified as A, C, and E for cable TV use. To avoid any confusion with midband channels, they are sometimes known as T-9, T-11, and T-13 respectively.

These channels start at 18 MHz and continue in 6-MHz steps to 48 MHz, the upper frequency limit of channel E (T-13). There is a separation of 6 MHz between the subchannels. In each, the picture and sound carriers are separated by 4.5 MHz, following the arrangement used by VHF and UHF channels. However, the picture carrier is only 1 MHz above the bottom frequency of the channel.

Thus, for subchannel A, the width of the channel extends from 18 MHz to 24 MHz. However, the picture carrier for this channel is at 19 MHz. For channel C, the low-frequency is 30 MHz, but the picture carrier is 31 MHz. For VHF channels (and also for UHF channels) the picture carrier is 1.25 MHz above the low-frequency end of each channel.

Channel E (T-13) extends from 42 MHz to 48 MHz, a total of 6 MHz. The picture carrier is 43 MHz; the sound carrier 47.5 MHz.

Channel Number	Frequency Limits of Channel	Center Frequency of Carrier		CATV
Subchannel				
A	18 MHz 24 MHz	Picture Sound	19.0 MHz 23.5 MHz	T-9
C	30 MHz 36 MHz	Picture Sound	31.0 MHz 35.5 MHz	T-11
E	42 MHz 48 MHz	Picture Sound	43.0 MHz 47.5 MHz	T-13

Figure 4–18. Subchannel frequencies. (*Courtesy Winegard Co.*)

SIGNAL SCRAMBLING

Cable companies supply two types of signals: basic, also referred to as unscrambled, and premium, also called encoded or scrambled. There are various techniques for scrambling a signal. The video portion can be *inverted* so that pictures appear as negatives on the TV screen. Another method is *sync pulse compression,* so the picture does not remain locked in.

Encryption Algorithm

This is a recursive procedure for encoding a program to prevent unauthorized viewing or recording of a video program. With this technique, the video signal is scrambled in a random manner, possibly by processing various time-amplitude elements in the composite video signal, with the encoding changed as often as desired and varied with time under computer control. To be effective, the decoder must produce an action equal and opposite to that of the encoding procedure, both in amount and time.

CABLE TV—ADVANTAGES AND DISADVANTAGES

Cable TV eliminates many of the disadvantages of broadcast TV. Cable supplies an improved signal with uniform strength for all channels, so there is no difficulty with channels that supply marginal broadcast reception. Ghosts due to improper impedance matching between the antenna and transmission line, or between the transmission line and the TV set, are eliminated. So are ghosts due to signal pickup by unshielded transmission line. Cable TV also supplies many more channels than are available through broadcast.

Cable TV also has its problems. It requires the use of a converter, and even if a TV set or a VCR is cable ready, a special converter is needed if the TV signals are scrambled. Cable TV also requires the payment of a monthly fee, which is larger for premium programs.

The Cable-Ready TV or VCR

A cable-ready TV set or VCR can utilize a nonscrambled (nonencoded) program through any cable hookup without an external converter box. The TV set or VCR can tune in the various channels on cable TV without a converter by making the TV set's UHF channel selector perform a double function. This is advantageous, as it makes possible the use of a wireless remote control for cable channel selection.

Cable-ready TV sets do not work with all cable systems, as these have nonstandardized channels. Cable-ready TV sets cannot be used to decode scrambled signals requiring a special decoder.

A cable-ready TV receiver is not a television set used exclusively for cable TV signals, for such receivers can still tune in any of the regular 82 VHF/UHF channels. Even if a receiver is touted as cable ready, a local cable company may still require the use of its converter for receiving some or all channels.

The emphasis by manufacturers of cable-ready tuners or receivers or VCRs is on the number of channels that can be received by those who are subscribers to a cable TV service. A typical number is 133. This does not mean the TV receiver will pick up 133 channels from the cable service. It does mean the number supplied is the sum of all broadcast VHF channels, UHF channels, and cable channels. Further, there is no assurance that all these channels are active in any particular area, and it would be surprising if they were. It does mean if all the channels are active and available, the cable-ready tuner or receiver is equipped to process them.

The total channel capability can vary from one cable-ready TV set to the next. A unit with a 104-channel capability will be able to receive all 68 VHF/UHF channels, plus 36 cable channels. There are 12 VHF channels and 68 UHF channels.

The 12 VHF channels are included in the cable channel count, for they can be delivered via cable. A total count for cable could be 12 VHF channels, 9 midband channels, 10 superband channels, 14 translator band channels, and 3 subchannels. The translator band channels consist of a group of TV channels that were formerly part of the UHF band comprising channels 70 through 83. They extend from 806 MHz, the beginning of channel 70, through channel 83, whose upper frequency limit is 890 MHz.

CONVERTERS

A cable converter is a device that can be a separate add-on unit or built into a TV receiver or VCR for use by cable TV subscribers. There are two types of add-on converters, the single-channel and the block converter.

The converter changes the midband and superband channels to standard UHF frequencies. UHF is used because there is less possibility of interference from adjacent UHF channels. A representative converter will change VHF channels 2 through 6 to UHF channels 42 through 46; midband channels to UHF channels 54 through 62; VHF channels 7 through 13 to UHF channels 63 through 69; and superband channels to UHF channels 70 through 78.

There is no converter standardization, consequently not all cable companies follow the same frequency conversion routine.

RF Converters

Add-on converters, whether supplied by a cable company or a separate purchase, are known as cable TV converters. A converter built into a TV set or VCR is called an RF converter. There are also some add-on converters, not intended for cable use, and these are also RF converters.

An RF converter is a circuit arrangement for using baseband signals, such as sound and video information, for modulating a radio-frequency (RF) carrier. In a video cassette recorder, the baseband audio and video signals are modulated onto a radio-frequency carrier, that of VHF channels 3 or 4. Less often, the carrier frequencies of channels 5 and 6 are used. For audio signals, frequency modulation is used; for video, amplitude modulation. Add-on RF converters are used with any component supplying baseband signals that are to be connected to the antenna input terminals of a TV set.

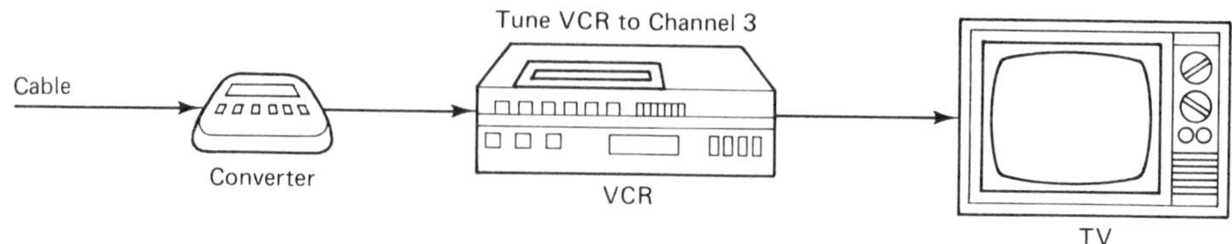

Figure 4–19. Basic system using converter.

Converters are commonly used by video system owners who are cable TV subscribers, with the converter either built into a TV set or VCR, or made available by a cable company as an outboard or add-on component (Fig. 4–19). Unlike a broadcast TV station, which has only one assigned carrier frequency so as not to interfere with other TV stations, a cable studio sends all its programs along a single wire, a substantially sized coaxial cable. With the help of signal splitters, each subscriber gets a portion of the original video/audio signal. Those signals undergo substantial amplification prior to delivery.

The TV set in the home is designed only for the reception of channels that are either VHF or UHF, and the TV set's tuner has no provision for accepting cable TV channels directly (with the exception of cable-ready TV sets). The converter changes cable frequencies to those acceptable by a TV receiver. It may seem strange that a cable TV company can put so many different programs into a single cable without having these programs interfering with each other. The answer lies in the fact that each of the programs has a different carrier frequency. One carrier may have a frequency of 120 MHz; the next 126 MHz; the next 132 MHz, and so on.

Figure 4–20 shows the connections for an outboard converter. This converter has two output ports, both 75 ohms. Its input port is connected via a short length of coaxial cable ending in F-plugs at both ends. One of these is inserted into a wall plate supplied by the cable company, while the other end is put into an F-jack on the converter. The outputs of the converter are also 75 ohms and are connected to input ports on the VCR.

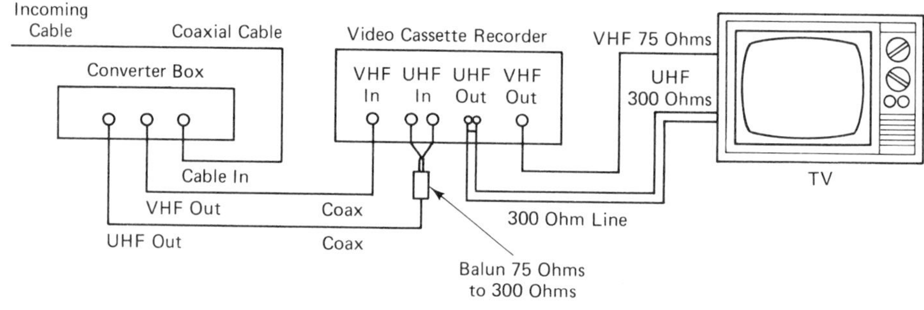

Figure 4–20. Cable TV converter.

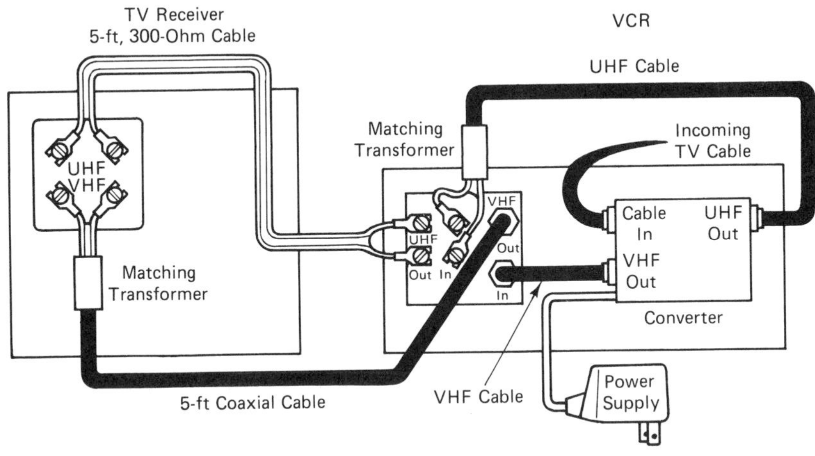

Figure 4–21. All cable signals, with the exception of those that are VHF, are converted to UHF.

Figure 4–21 shows the converter connections in a little more detail. The incoming cable is connected to the converter at a port labeled "cable in." The converter in this example has two outputs—VHF and UHF. Both outputs are 75 ohms and supply VHF and UHF signals. The VHF input of the VCR is 75 ohms, so a direct connection can be made. The UHF input, however, is 300 ohms, and to effect an impedance match, a 75-ohm to 300-ohm balun is used. The outputs of this VCR are 75 ohms for VHF and 300 ohms for UHF.

The Direct Cable Connection

A converter does not always have to be used with a VCR, and the connections are then simpler (Fig. 4-22). Here we have a TV set connected to a cable converter. No antenna is used, either inside or outside, and cable is the only signal source. Seventy-five-ohm coaxial cable is used for making the con-

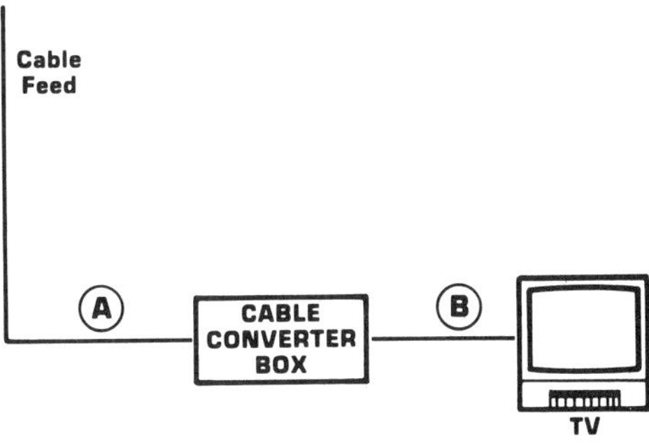

Figure 4–22. Cable TV connection without a VCR. Line A is coaxial cable equipped with F-connectors. Output of converter box (B) is coaxial cable. (*Courtesy Discwasher, Div. International Jensen, Inc.*)

nections throughout, from the cable converter to the coaxial cable wall plate (A) and from the cable converter to the TV set. The only accessory required is a 75-ohm to 300-ohm balun inserted at point B, and this would be most likely since many TV sets are designed for 300-ohm VHF input.

The advantage of the connections in Fig. 4–22 is simplicity, in the absence of additional signal options, but note the limitations. The TV is completely dependent on cable and there is no way of recording any program. There are other disadvantages as well. All signals must be selected through the cable converter, so any remote control unit, whether wired or wireless, is useless. Finally, only one channel can be received at a time.

The Cable/VCR Connection

A VCR can be put on line, and, as shown in Fig. 4–23, is put in series between the cable converter and the TV set. This means the connections have become a little more elaborate than the basic setup of Fig. 4–22, but not by much. All connections to the VCR are 75-ohm coaxial cable, assuming the input port of the VCR is 75 ohms, and this is quite usual. The connection from the VCR to the TV receiver can also be coaxial cable, but this assumes a 75-ohm input to the TV set. Otherwise, a 75-ohm to 300-ohm balun should be inserted at point C.

Point A is a coaxial cable connection from the cable feed. Points B and C are also coaxial cable lines. This arrangement allows watching a recorded tape or a channel while recording it. Channels must be selected manually through the cable converter box. Remote control isn't possible, nor is it pos-

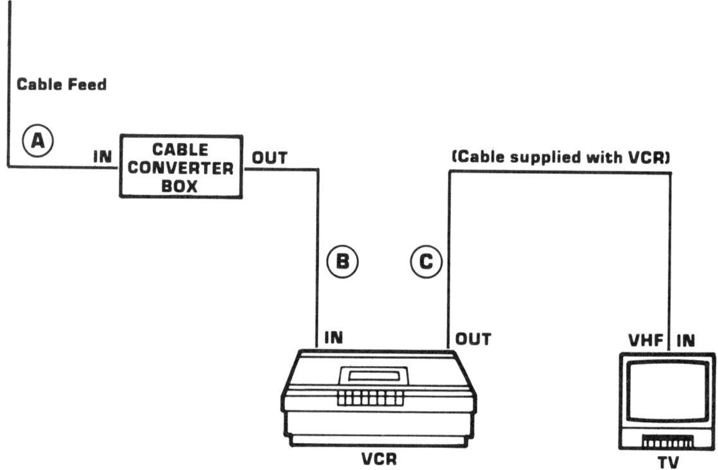

Figure 4–23. Connections for a VCR and cable converter. (*Courtesy Discwasher, Div. International Jensen, Inc.*)

sible to watch one channel while recording another. VCR programmability is limited to time shifting. Only one channel at a time can be received.

The inclusion of the VCR has now made the system more versatile at the cost of the added component plus additional wiring. The user can now watch a prerecorded video tape and also watch a program as it is being recorded, either in real time or by time shifting. As in the wiring setup of Fig. 4-21, all channels must be selected manually through the cable converter. It is true the VCR is equipped with a tuner (and so is the TV set), but both of these tuners have been made useless by the wiring setup. Even though a VCR is used, it isn't possible to watch one program while recording another. Only one channel at a time can be used. Note that with only one signal source available the user is completely dependent on cable for program material. If, for any reason, the cable company discontinues its services, or has a system failure, no TV viewing is possible. To become independent of cable TV for programming it is desirable to utilize broadcast TV through the use of an outside antenna and an A/B switch (Fig. 4-24).

Cable and Antenna Connections

First consider the A/B switch in its A position. The antenna is then automatically excluded and we are then right back to the wiring arrangement shown in Fig. 4-23. When the switch is in its B position, the cable converter and the VCR are removed and the TV set is directly connected to the antenna. What we have here, then, is a "one-or-the-other" setup, but still there are advantages. With the switch in its B position, the VCR can be used to record

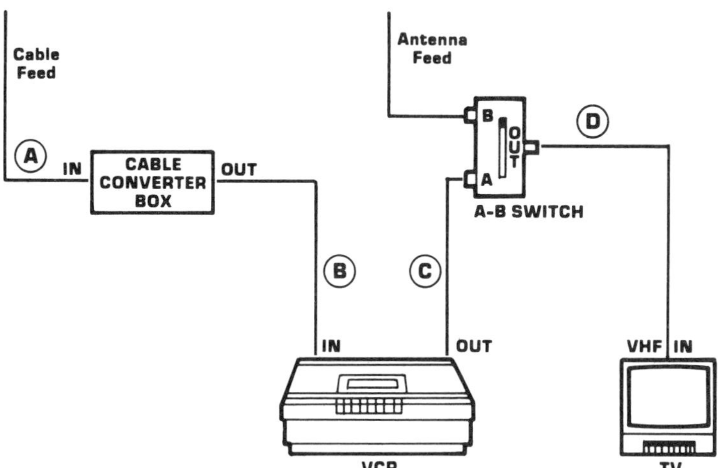

Figure 4-24. With this hookup it is possible to watch and record the same cable channel simultaneously. (*Courtesy Discwasher, Div. International Jensen, Inc.*)

a cable program. Thus is has become possible to record one program, via cable, while watching another program, via broadcast TV. However, the only channels that can be recorded are those received via cable and, with the switch in its A position, it still isn't possible to use a remote control device. However, remote control can be used when the switch is at B, or station selection can be had by using the tuner of the TV set.

The drawing of Fig. 4-24 has been simplified, as add-ons have been omitted. The antenna feed can be 300-ohm line or coaxial cable. The type of A/B switch to be used will depend on the input and output impedances wanted, and that will be determined by the impedances of the lines arriving at the signal input ports and the input impedance of the TV set. To make practical use of such a wiring diagram, mark the impedances at the inputs and outputs of all the components plus that of the A/B switch.

In Fig. 4-24, A and B are coaxial lines; C is also a coaxial line connected to the A/B switcher, and D is a coaxial line or a length of twin lead. If the VHF input of the TV set is 300 ohms, it would be better to have an A/B switcher with a 300-ohm port. With this arrangement it is possible to watch a broadcast TV signal while the VCR records a selected channel.

Recording One Channel and Watching Another

The disadvantages of the connections shown earlier can be overcome by the addition of a signal splitter and an A/B switch (Fig. 4-25). With this diagram, we are back to using a single signal source, cable TV, but the operation of the system has become more versatile. The wiring, however, is on its way to becoming more complex.

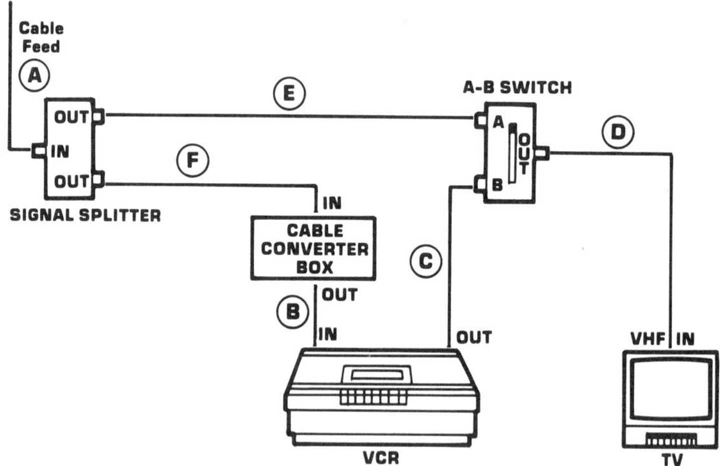

Figure 4-25. This arrangement permits watching any basic cable channel while recording any other channel. (*Courtesy Discwasher, Div. International Jensen, Inc.*)

The cable TV signal is split into two approximately equal parts by the signal splitter. These two outputs, identified as E and F, are wired to the A/B switch and the cable converter. With the A/B switch in its A position, the TV set is connected directly to the signal splitter, and has direct access to the cable TV signal. This means you can select cable TV signals without the use of the external cable converter. However, a requirement here is that the TV set must be cable ready. If the TV set isn't cable ready, VHF channels 2 to 13 would still be available.

Note that the VCR precedes the A/B switch, so cable TV signals are available to it at all times. With the switch in its B position those signals are viewable. Consequently, using the channel selector on the cable converter, you can record any cable signal while watching a different channel on the TV set; that is, you can record one channel while watching another. You can also use a remote control device for the TV set or select the channels manually. The wiring arrangement of Fig. 4–25 is such that the VCR has lost its programmability. All channel selection must be made through the cable converter when the VCR is used.

Connections for VCR Control

An improvement can be made simply by changing the wiring position of the cable converter (Fig. 4–26). The converter has now been inserted in line between the signal splitter and the A/B switch. Note that in this wiring arrangement the VCR has direct access to the cable TV signal. There is a dif-

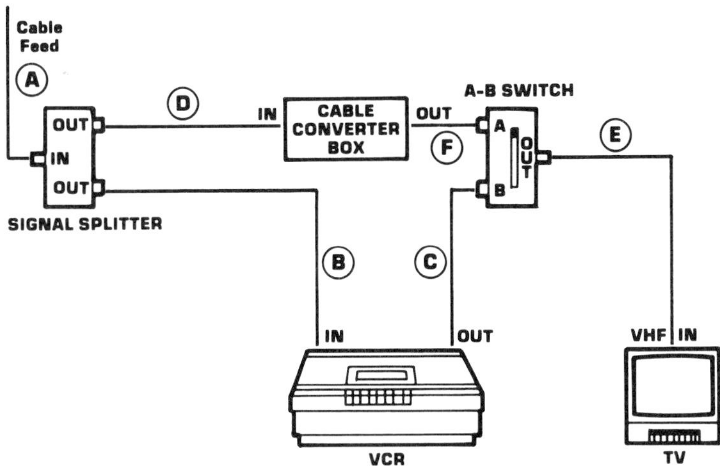

Figure 4–26. With this wiring arrangement it is possible to utilize the full programming capabilities of the VCR. (*Courtesy Discwasher, Div. International Jensen, Inc.*)

ference in VCRs, though. The one shown in Fig. 4–25 was not cable ready; the one in Fig. 4–26 is. However, even if the VCR is not cable ready, all the VHF signals can be handled.

When the A/B switch is in its A position the cable converter is in the circuit with the TV set then displaying cable TV signals. However, even with the switch in this position, the VCR is still connected to the cable signal, getting its share of the signal from the signal splitter.

There are two types of cable signals—premium and basic. A premium program isn't necessarily better than a basic program. It may be a very recent movie or a sports event that may not be available via broadcast TV. To be frank about it, a premium program is one for which cable subscribers have to pay a premium. No premium is required for basic programs. With the connections shown in Fig. 4–26, it is possible to watch either a premium or basic cable channel while recording another basic channel. Watching a premium channel requires a combined converter/decoder. If the VCR has a remote control, it can be used to select basic cable channels. Finally, it is possible to view a recorded tape.

The so-called premium signal is one that has been scrambled, or encoded. Such a signal can be unscrambled or decoded, but it requires an outboard unscrambler or decoder, or the cable converter box may have the decoder built in.

When the A/B switch is set to its B position, the TV set works through the VCR rather than through the converter.

Connections Using an Unscrambler

Cable companies aren't under any particular obligation to use a specific type of scrambling, and they can use any kind they wish. The scrambling may have the picture fall out of synchronization (sync) by using sync pulse compression, by inverting the polarity of the signal so that the picture looks like a film negative, or by using a combination of these methods. Scrambling may also involve changing the encoding method, making it erratic rather than regular, in an effort to thwart those who want to construct or buy their own unscramblers to avoid payment of fees for watching premium programs.

There is no such thing as a "standard" descrambler box; the scrambling method is selected by the program originators. Subscribers to one cable system may not necessarily use the same unscramblers as subscribers to a completely different cable system.

Whether it contains an unscrambler or not, the output of the converter box is a short length of coaxial cable equipped with an F-connector at its output end. This connector is usually a screw-on, to make sure any attachment to it is secure.

Connecting Two TV Sets to One VCR

By using the wiring setup shown in Fig. 4–27A, you can connect two TV sets to one VCR. The obvious step is to make use of a signal splitter, in effect producing two signals from the cable outlet. The output of the VCR is brought to the input port of the signal splitter. One of the outputs of this splitter is fed into the first receiver, TV 1. The second output, identified by the letter E, could be brought directly into the second receiver, marked TV 2. The disadvantage, as described earlier, would be reliance on just a single signal source for TV pictures. To avoid this, an A/B switch can be used, with one of its input terminals connected to the cable signal splitter; the other to the downlead from an antenna.

When the A/B switcher is in its A position, TV 2 has access to the VCR. The first TV is always wired to the VCR; the second TV only when the A/B switch is in its A position. When the A/B switcher is in its B position, the second TV is connected to the antenna.

This arrangement, like others, has its advantages and its disadvantages. The second TV set can be remotely controlled when the A/B switch is at B. Under these conditions the wiring is such that TV 2 is directly connected to the antenna. At the same time, the first TV set, TV 1, can pick up a signal via cable TV, so separate programs can be watched on the two receivers.

If the converter box contains a decoder, it is possible to watch either a basic or a premium cable program. If a prerecorded tape is inserted into the

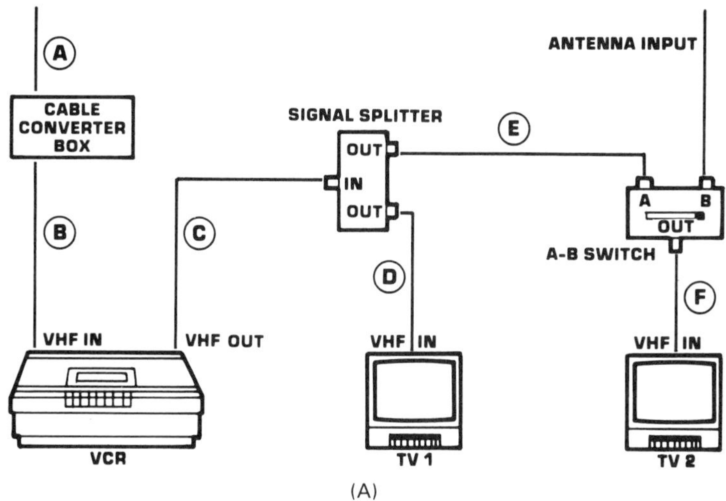

(A)

Figure 4–27A. Two-TV receiver setup for watching either cable or broadcast TV. (*Courtesy Discwasher, Div. International Jensen, Inc.*)

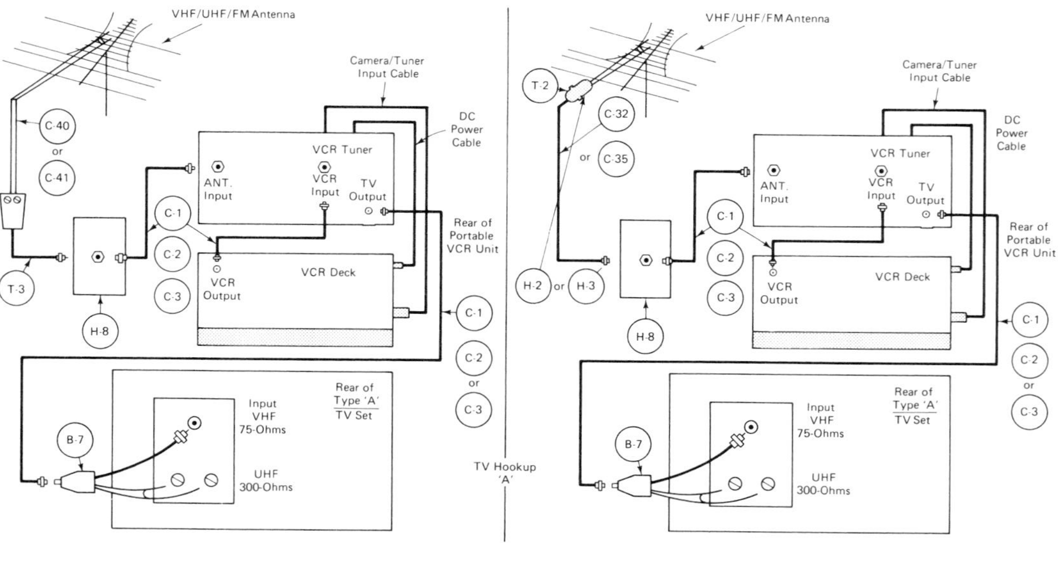

(B)

Figure 4–27B. Connecting a portable VCR to a single TV set. (*Courtesy GC Electronics*)

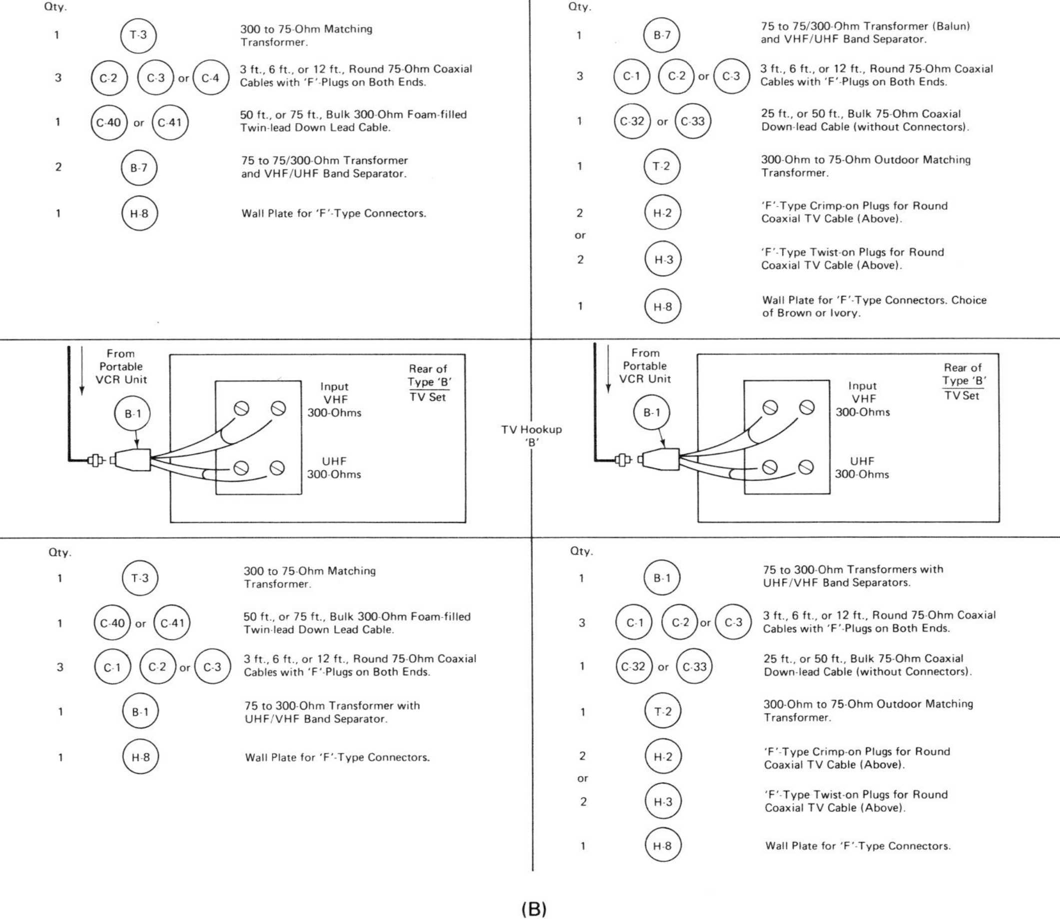

(B)

Figure 4-27B. *(continued)*

VCR, it can be watched on both TV sets when the A/B switch is in its A position. It is also possible to watch a prerecorded videotape on one receiver or both.

Connecting a Portable VCR to a TV Set

A portable VCR used outdoors in connection with a video camera can also work indoors in association with a tuner/timer (Fig. 4–27B). These two components, the tuner/timer and the portable VCR, operate as a single integrated VCR.

Converter Box Tuning

Every superheterodyne receiver intended for AM or FM reception, and every television set, is equipped with a converter. Every VCR similarly contains a converter, and an outboard component such as a converter box (as its name indicates) is also a converter; the process of signal conversion is a common one.

It is important to remember that any converter, no matter where it is used, has only one function, and that is to change the frequency of the carrier to some other frequency, either higher or lower than the original. The modulating signal—the audio or video voltages superimposed on the carrier—is not changed by the conversion process. Consequently, when a signal is brought into a converter box, it undergoes its first conversion. When it is delivered to a VCR, it is converted again. And when it is put into a TV set, it is converted still once more.

Connecting Two VCRs

One of the problems with the wiring arrangements described previously is loss of remote control of the VCR. This can be recovered with the use of two VCRs, following the connections shown in Fig. 4–28.

The signal outputs of VCR 1 and VCR 2, identified by the letter C, are both brought into the input terminals A and B of the A/B switch. This means that the TV set has access to each of these VCRs, with the selected VCR depending on the setting of the switch. However, only one of these VCRs is connected to the cable converter box, and that is VCR 2. VCR 1 does not make use of the cable converter and is wired directly to the cable signal via the signal splitter.

With this wiring setup, it is possible to record a channel on either VCR while watching the same channel. It is also possible to record a program with one VCR while watching a different channel on TV or watching a tape through the other VCR.

VCR 1 cannot be used to watch a scrambled signal, as it has no way of

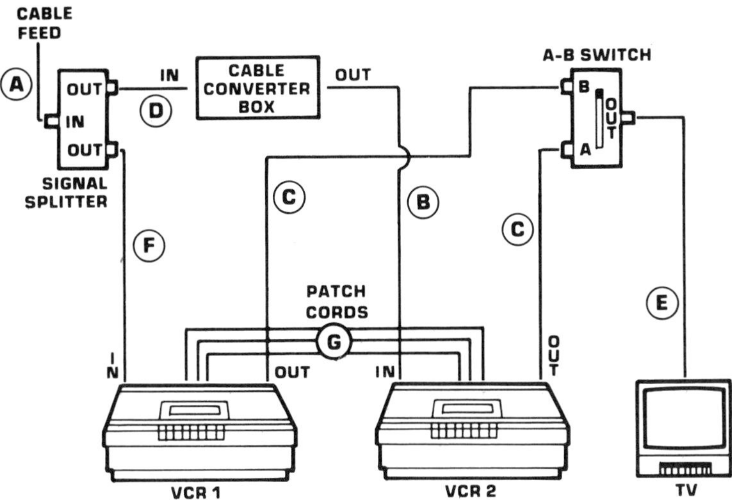

Figure 4–28. Wiring arrangement for recording two channels at the same time. (*Courtesy Discwasher, Div. International Jensen, Inc.*)

decoding that signal. Thus when the A/B switch is set to its B position, the only cable programs that can be watched will be those that are not scrambled. This setup also has restricted remote control. VCR 1 can be handled this way, as it does not work through the cable converter box.

Either VCR can be used for recording a channel with that channel displayed on the TV set. It is also possible to record a program with one VCR while watching a different channel on TV or else watching a prerecorded videotape through the other VCR. Using patch cords (G) it is possible to dub from one VCR to the other while watching a different program on TV, assuming the VCRs have video and audio composite outputs in addition to RF and VCR jacks.

A VCR will have a number of jacks for receiving and delivering signals, including a coaxial RF jack. The output of this jack will be a modulated signal that includes video, audio, and various synchronizing pulses. This is the type of signal that can be fed directly into the antenna terminals of a TV set, generally the VHF terminals with the TV selector control set to channels 3 or 4.

There are also two pairs of jacks marked "Video In" and "Video Out"; "Audio In and Audio Out." These terminals can be used for receiving or delivering video and audio signals that are not modulated. The audio output terminals could be used for connections to a high-fidelity system. If you use a monitor instead of a TV receiver, the audio and video jacks could be used for connections to the input of that monitor. That is also one of the reasons a monitor can supply a better picture than a TV receiver. The signal does not undergo the modulation process, often a necessary technique, but one that helps degrade the signal. Not only video cassette recorders, but videodisc players, video games, and home computers have built-in RF modulators, so the outputs of these units can be connected directly to the antenna VHF input terminals of a television receiver.

This is also true of cable TV, as it supplies an RF signal via a converter box. The terminals on a TV receiver can accept only an RF signal; a video signal will not do. The audio and video output terminals of the VCR bypass the modulation section.

The sound going into a VCR is recorded at the same time as the video signal, whether the VCR is used for off-the-air taping, taping from a video camera (whether that camera uses its built-in microphone or an accessory microphone), or the signal is being dubbed in from another VCR. It is not necessary to keep the original sound track. If the VCR has a dub jack, a different sound track can be supplied, without affecting the picture. The new sound occupies the track used by the old sound, and the new sound can be supplied by a microphone, a phono record, a compact disc, or an audio cassette player.

Connecting a Converter/Unscrambler

If a scrambled signal is supplied by a cable company, an unscrambler must be used before the signal reaches the VCR, as shown in Fig. 4-29. The unscrambler in this example is combined with the cable converter box. The A/B switch permits the selection of unscrambled or scrambled signals, but

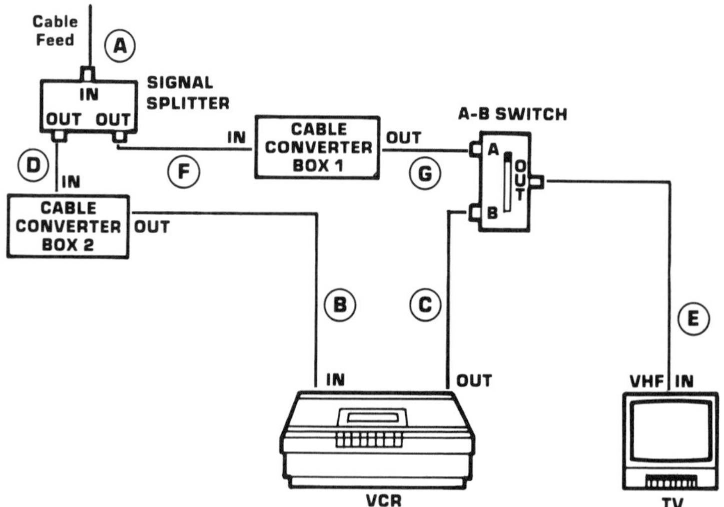

Figure 4-29. With this wiring arrangement it is possible to watch basic cable programs using cable converter box 1 or premium cable programs using cable converter-decoder box 2. (*Courtesy Discwasher, Div. Intenational Jensen, Inc.*)

since the converter contains the decoder, the picture shown on the TV screen will always be in viewable form.

As is shown in the illustration, the cable signal is divided by a signal splitter, with the signal divided between two cable converter boxes. One of these, box 2, is equipped with a decoder. With this setup it is possible to watch and record an encoded channel. With the A/B switch in its A position, it is possible to watch a basic cable program. You can also watch or record an unscrambled channel while watching a different channel.

Connecting a Non–Cable-Ready TV Set

Having both the TV set and the VCR cable ready simplifies connections, but if the TV set is an older one, it is quite likely it will not be cable ready. Figure 4–30 shows the connections that can be used if the VCR is cable ready but the TV set is not. The problem with this arrangement is that two inde-

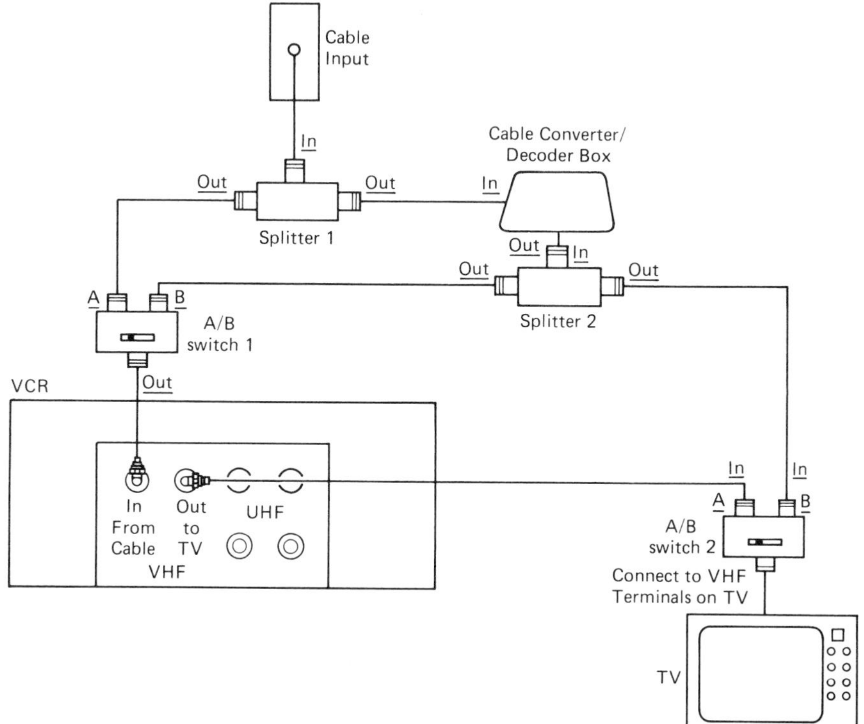

Figure 4–30. Arrangement using a cable-ready VCR and a TV set that isn't cable ready. With these connections it is possible to watch and record the same scrambled channel, or to record an unscrambled channel while watching a different channel. That channel can be scrambled or unscrambled.

pendent A/B switches are needed; consequently, it would be advisable to write a card and put it in some convenient place, possibly the top of the TV set, to indicate the different switching possibilities.

Whenever a signal is to feed a VCR and a TV set, the first accessory required will always be a signal splitter, and that is the case here. Part of the cable signal is supplied to the VCR when A/B switch 1 is in its A position. That signal is then delivered to terminal A of A/B switch 2 and if that switch is in its A position, the signal will be received by the TV set. The VCR, as indicated earlier, is cable ready. However, with this signal path, only unscrambled cable signals can be used.

The second path of the signal from the splitter is to a cable converter box, equipped with a decoder. This signal is brought into a second signal splitter. One of its outputs is to the second A/B switch. When this switch is in its B position, the signal is delivered directly to the TV set where the picture can be watched on the screen. This picture can be scrambled or unscrambled.

The signal is also delivered to the VCR and can be used by the VCR when it is in its B position. The signal can then be recorded.

This hookup permits watching and recording the same scrambled signal. To do so, set the first A/B switch to its B position and the second A/B switch to its A position.

Three component controls must be adjusted. The first is to make a channel selection using the cable converter box. The VCR channel selector must be set to receive the cable signal and the TV set must be adjusted to receive the signal from the VCR.

It is also possible to watch and record a pair of channels, recording the one that is unscrambled and watching still another channel whether that channel is scrambled or not. To be able to do so, set both A/B switches in their A positions. Since the channel to be recorded is unscrambled, it can be selected by using the tuner function of the VCR. It is now possible to move ahead to watch the scrambled channel. Set the second A/B switch to its B position, and use the converter box for channel selection. Since the signal will be passing through the decoder in the converter box, a scrambled signal will be viewable.

Cable TV Problems

One of the problems associated with cable TV is the lack of program standardization among the different cable companies. Some of these supply programming only on twelve channels and these are the standard VHF channels from 2 to 13. Some cable companies not only supply additional channels but scramble some of them. The channels beyond channel 13 are identifed by letters instead of by numbers (Fig. 4-31). Thus, channel 14 is A, channel 15 is B, and so forth. These are the channels identified by letters on the cable converter box and they range from A (channel 14) to W (channel 36). Channels A through I are the midband channels, indicated earlier in Fig. 4-16. They

Channel											
A	–	14	G	–	20	M	–	26	S	–	32
B	–	15	H	–	21	N	–	27	T	–	33
C	–	16	I	–	22	O	–	28	U	–	34
D	–	17	J	–	23	P	–	29	V	–	35
E	–	18	K	–	24	Q	–	30	W	–	36
F	–	19	L	–	25	R	–	31			

Figure 4–31. Channels A through I are the midband channels. The others are the superband channels.

are called midband, as they are positioned between VHF channels 6 and 7. The superband channels are those that follow channel 13. The superband channels were so named because their frequencies are higher than the highest VHF frequency. However, neither the tuner in a TV set nor the one in a VCR is capable of tuning in these specific frequencies. That is why a converter is needed, either as a separate component or as a special circuit for VCRs and TV sets, producing the so-called cable-ready components.

Who Owns the Accessory Converter?

Subscribing to a cable TV service does not carry ownership of the converter along with it. The reason for this is that the cable companies charge according to the service supplied. Some converters have a decoding function, others supply only twelve channel operation, while others supply thirty-six channels. Thus the kind of converter used determines the kind of service a subscriber receives.

The UHF Connection

Every TV set, by law, is required to have a UHF tuner. That tuner can be used to select cable channels, and it does so by converting all signals, including VHF, midband, and superband channels to UHF, using an outboard converter (Fig. 4–32).

Unlike the usual converter, this one has two outputs for all channels except the usual VHF, and these include the superband channels. The UHF output of the converter is brought into a splitter, with part of the signal delivered directly to the UHF terminal of the TV set. That same signal is also delivered to the VCR, so the cable program can be watched while it is being recorded.

The second output of the converter is VHF, channels 2 to 13. These signals are delivered to the converter and from the converter as a VHF input to the VCR. Station selection is made by the converter, with the VCR converting all the VHF signals to the frequency of either channel 3 or channel 4, determined by a switch on the rear of the VCR. The TV set can receive these signals when its tuner is set to the corresponding channel, that is, either 3 or 4.

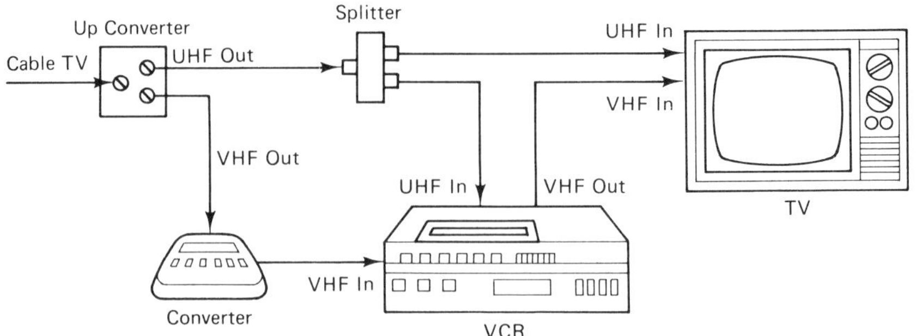

Figure 4–32. Wiring arrangement using a block upconverter.

This hookup has a number of possibilities. The same channel can be watched and recorded, or one channel can be watched while another is recorded.

Precautions in Connecting Converters

Connecting a converter to a VCR or TV set is more than just plugging in some cables. These cables are coaxial, and they are shielded, but it is possible to get interference effects, particularly if the shield consists of wire wrap instead of braid or if cables are adjacent to each other and are long, possibly as long as 5 feet. The result could be picture waviness, or possibly a herringbone pattern. With the TV set turned on, move the cables, separating them, until the condition disappears.

The problem may not exist on all channels. Select the channel that produces the worst case of interference and then try to eliminate it by moving cables. Do not use connecting cables that are any longer than necessary. Also, try substituting a different cable.

Another possible cure is to cover the cables with aluminum foil, a common household item. Wrap a bare copper conductor securely around the foil at one end and then ground it.

The Wall Plate Connection

Both cable TV and master television antenna systems (MATV) deliver their signals to homes with their respective transmission lines ending in a wall plate. The concept is the same as the delivery of AC power to an outlet. For cable TV, the connection to the wall plate is via coaxial cable. For MATV broadcast television reception in a high-rise apartment, either coaxial cable or 300-ohm twin lead is used as the connection to the first component that is to receive the signal. For cable TV the jack is an F-receptacle, and all that is required is a suitable length of cable terminating in F-plugs at both ends. The same procedure is followed if the wall plate is for a master antenna TV system (MATV). If the MATV wall plate is connected to its master antenna via 300-ohm line, the connection will be via a short length of twin lead.

Twin lead is usually connected to components by wrapping the wire ends around a pair of machine screws, but in the case of MATV, a special 300-ohm connecting plug is used. The plug can be disassembled and the twin lead connected by small machine screws inside the plug. The wires at the end of the twin lead must be stripped. Twirl the strands to supply the equivalent of a single, solid conductor, making sure not to break or cut any of the strands and see that no strands reach over and touch the adjacent conductor. Although the plug may have three terminals, the center pin is a dummy and isn't used.

Unnecessary Use of Baluns

Because a balun is so inexpensive, lightweight, and easy to install, there could be a tendency to consider it as a make-do device. The time to consider the possible need for baluns is prior to an installation, not afterward. With planning, it is possible to eliminate all such transformers—or at least to keep their use to a minimum.

As an example, consider Fig. 4–33. A balun is used in this case to match the impedance of the downlead to the input impedance of the splitter, but splitters are available with either a 75-ohm or 300-ohm input impedance, so the balun could have been omitted by the proper selection of the splitter. Since no balun is used following the splitter, the two output impedances obviously match the input impedances of the two TV sets.

Connection Choices

Because there are a number of ways of connecting TV receivers and VCRs, a determination should be made before wiring about exactly what is wanted at present and what may be wanted in the future. Further, wiring should not be regarded as unchangeable. Upgrading a VCR, a TV set, or some other

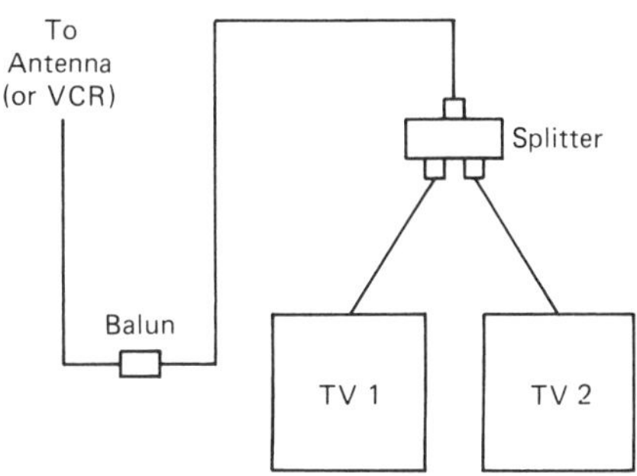

Figure 4–33. Antenna or VCR operating a pair of TV sets.

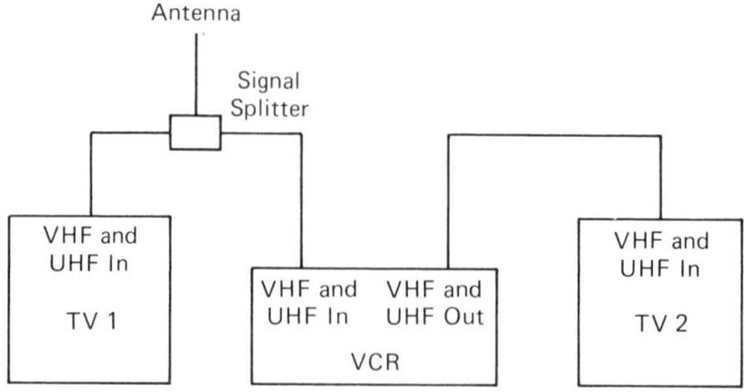

Figure 4–34. With this wiring setup, the VCR can supply signals to TV 2 only. TV 1 gets TV broadcast signals only. TV 1 can be remotely controlled, but TV 2 cannot.

component may not be easy to do because of cost or space limitations, but new wiring systems can be installed without considering these factors.

Figure 4–34 shows two TV sets and a single VCR. With this wiring setup, the VCR can supply signals to TV 2 only. TV 1 gets broadcast signals only. TV 1 can be remotely controlled, but TV 2 cannot.

Two things happen when more accessories and components are added to an existing system: (1) The flexibility of the system increases; that is, the system can function in a greater number of different ways; and (2) the interconnections become a bit more complex, so prior planning is desirable. Such planning can be simplified by starting with a basic system, such as the one shown originally in Fig. 4–34, and then modifying it in a step-by-step manner until the wanted connection arrangement is achieved. Before going ahead with the connections, go over the wiring diagram to determine just what will happen when the various components are activated, at the same time learning if the desired results have been achieved.

Figure 4–35 is a modification of Fig. 4–34 and Fig. 4–36 is a modification

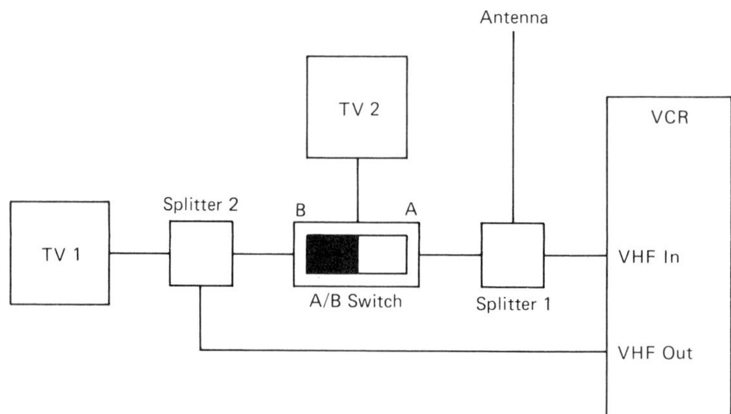

Figure 4–35. This is a modification of Figure 4–34.

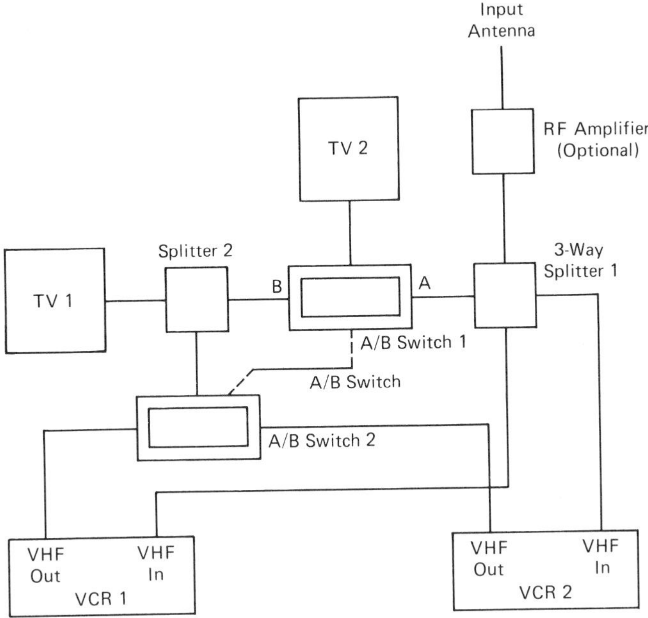

Figure 4–36. This is a modification of Figure 4–35.

of Fig. 4–35. The original TV sets have been retained, but more accessories and components have been added. There are now two VCRs, two signal splitters, and two A/B switches.

With the hookup shown in Fig. 4–35, TV 2 can be isolated from the VCR when the A/B switch is set to its A position. TV 2 is then connected directly to one port of signal splitter 1. The VCR also receives the antenna signal via splitter 1 and delivers this signal to TV 1. Alternatively, TV 1 can watch a prerecorded videotape signal supplied by the VCR.

If we now set the A/B switch to its B position, a videotape can be watched on both TV sets. Both TV sets can be used to watch a broadcast TV program while, at the same time, the VCR can be put in its record mode. This recording can be the same channel being watched on the TV sets or it can be a different channel. Finally, if the VCR is recording, it can be monitored on either one of the TV sets, or on both. Figure 4–36 carries the system growth concept a step further.

The signal, received by the antenna, is delivered to splitter 1, a three-way splitter. The outputs of this splitter move in three different directions: two will head for the two VCRs (VCR 1 and VCR 2) and the third toward A/B switch 1. As a consequence, both VCRs are on line at all times. Now consider TV 2. When A/B switch 1 is in its A position, the antenna signal is routed to that TV receiver and that receiver can function without VCR 1 or 2. The VCRs can be on or off and TV 1 can also be on or off. Thus, TV 2 can be independent of the entire system and can be used for broadcast TV viewing. It can also be manually or remotely controlled.

Both VCRs can use either TV 1 or TV 2 for picture display but the VCRs cannot use the television sets simultaneously. Thus, VCR 1 can display on TV 1 or TV 2, and VCR 2 can operate in the same way. As an example, VCR 1 can show a picture on TV 1 while TV 2 is tuned to pick up some channel on broadcast TV. One of the unusual features of this system is that both VCRs can record at the same time, but this does not necessarily mean using the same channel but different channels if that is what is wanted.

This can be made into a user-friendly system if a written notation is made and kept near the system, unless it is used so often that operating the two TV sets and the two VCRs becomes automatic. It is also desirable to make a sketch of the wiring for two reasons: to make a wiring change or to repair the wiring or system.

SIGNAL CONVERTER SPECIFICATIONS

Not all converters are alike any more than all VCRs or TV receivers or switchers are the same. Most converters, as they are solid state, and use a small number of transistors, require very little operating power—actually tiny compared to the power demands of a TV set. Two watts is typical. But there are some that are power hungry and get quite warm.

Signal converters supplied by cable companies do not include specifications (specs). Alternatively it is possible to buy a signal converter from sources other than cable companies and these usually have specs.

Because these components are broadband units, they should be able to cover the VHF and UHF bands. For VHF, their range should be from 50 MHz to 280 MHz and for UHF from 610 MHz to 866 MHz. For a unit having two output ports, VHF and UHF, the isolation at the output should be a minimum of 20 dB. The converter should reach operating stability in a few minutes after it is turned on.

FREQUENCY CONVERSION

Frequency conversion, used by all converters, should actually be called *carrier conversion.* Conversion is the process of changing the frequency of the carrier wave, but it does not (or should not) alter the frequency of the modulating signals, whether audio or video.

Frequency conversion can be categorized as upconversion, downconversion, single-channel conversion, and block conversion.

Upconversion

Upconversion is the process of changing a carrier frequency to one that is higher. Thus if the original carrier has a frequency of 100 MHz and that carrier is changed to one of 106 MHz, the carrier is then said to have been upconverted.

Downconversion

As you might expect, downconversion is the opposite of upconversion. If the 100 MHz carrier specified above is changed to one of 95 MHz, the process is one of downconversion.

Single-Channel Conversion

Converters supplied by cable companies to their subscribers are single-channel converters. A single-channel converter converts the carrier frequency a single channel at a time. The pushbuttons on a cable converter are used to select the different channels.

Block Conversion

Block conversion involves downconverting or upconverting an entire group of channels, handled as a block, hence the name. Unlike single-channel conversion, the block converter does not have channel selection. All of the converted channels are delivered to a separate tuner, which is then used for making the channel selection. As an example, a block converter can supply an entire group of channels to the UHF tuner of a TV set. The tuner then makes the channel selection.

In this respect, a block converter is the equivalent of a TV antenna. While the antenna does no frequency conversion, it does supply all the signals it receives to a tuner and it is the tuner that makes the channel selection.

CONNECTIONS THAT LIMIT THE VCR

One of the great advantages of a VCR is that it can record in real time, that is, present time, and can also use its time-shifting feature to record at some future time. Another advantage is that it can be used to record one program while a different program (or the same program) is being watched. These advantages, however, can be negated, depending on how the VCR is connected into a system.

One method, for example, is to insert the VCR on line between a con-

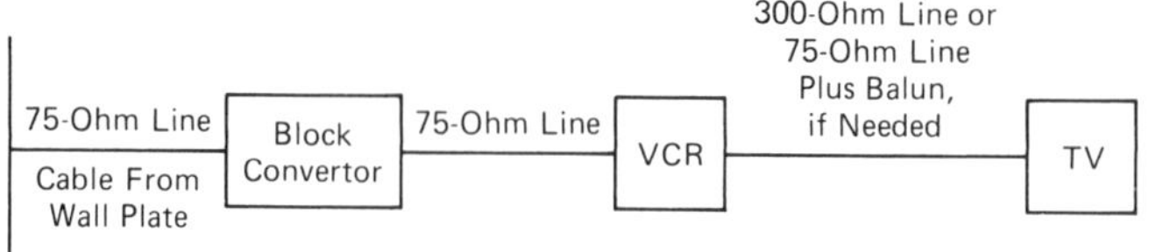

Figure 4–37. Connections using a block converter.

verter and the TV set. The converter then preempts the tuning and the only program that can be recorded is the station selected by the converter. But suppose the two units, the converter and the VCR, are transposed. The VCR now precedes the converter. The VCR will be able to record only VHF signals and these, of course, must not be scrambled.

As an alternative, it is possible to use a block converter (Fig. 4–37). Since this converter is most likely not the one supplied by a cable TV company, it must be bought separately. The block converter is connected via a length of coaxial cable to the cable TV wall plate while its output is wired to the input of the VCR. As a block converter, it changes the midband and superband channels delivered by cable TV to UHF. This arrangement allows watching any channel, or monitoring a channel while recording it, or recording one channel while watching another. However, as the block converter is not one supplied by a cable company, it will not contain a decoder, so scrambled signals will remain that way.

Subscription to a cable TV service automatically means a converter will be supplied, and if a cable company does scramble its signals, that converter can still be used (Fig. 4–38).

All the signals supplied by a cable company travel at the same time through a coaxial cable to subscribers' homes. Each signal, like a TV broadcast signal, has a bandwidth of 6 MHz. The signals are separated, as each has its own video and audio carriers.

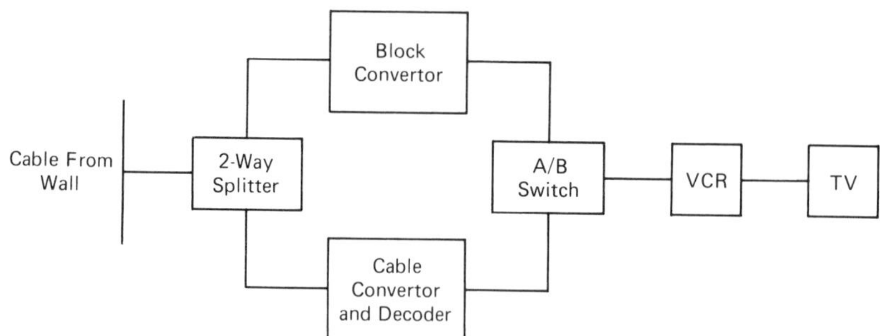

Figure 4–38. This hookup permits recording of either scrambled or unscrambled channels.

Figure 4–38 shows that the cable signal is supplied to an A/B switch. If it is in one position, an entire block of signals is delivered to the VCR. With the A/B switch in its alternate position, the signals are supplied one channel at a time, with the channels chosen by the cable converter-decoder.

When you are using the cable converter, scrambled signals can be watched, as the converter is decoder equipped. That is not the case when using the block converter.

The limitation of this arrangement is that this is a one-channel-at-a-time setup. If a scrambled channel is being recorded, an unscrambled signal cannot be watched. When the A/B switch is set for the use of the block converter, the wiring is the same as that for the connections shown in Fig. 4–37. This means it is possible to record any cable signal, whether VHF, midband, or superband channel, while watching any other channel. However, if the A/B switch is set so signals are to be delivered to the cable converter, the only channel that can be recorded is selected by the converter. It isn't possible under these conditions to record one channel while watching a different channel.

The VCR and Multiple TV Sets

Ordinarily the VCR is considered only in association with a single TV set but it can be used with a number of them. Figure 4–39 supplies the wiring for a VCR/three-TV set hookup while Fig. 4–40 uses four TVs.

DUBBING

Dubbing is the transfer of video and audio signals from one VCR to another. This can be done in two ways, as most VCRs have two input ports and two output ports. An easy way to dub is to connect the RF output of one VCR to the antenna input of the other. However, it is possible to get better results by working with unmodulated signals obtained from the video and audio ports. This direct connection avoids having the signal pass through the tuner section of the VCR, so the signal will not be afflicted by this circuitry. Using the RF output, however, means that only one cable will be required, while a pair of cables will be needed if the direct video and audio outputs are used. When you are using the RF output be sure to set the recording VCR to channel 3 or channel 4. If a TV set is connected to the recording VCR, it will be possible to monitor the transferred signal.

The kinds of connectors to use depend on whether the VCRs are VHS, Beta format, or one of each. VHS format VCRs use RCA jacks on all audio and video inputs and outputs. Precut cables with these connectors mounted are available in 6- and 10-foot lengths with two plugs on each end.

Beta format VCRs have miniature jacks instead of the RCA jacks used

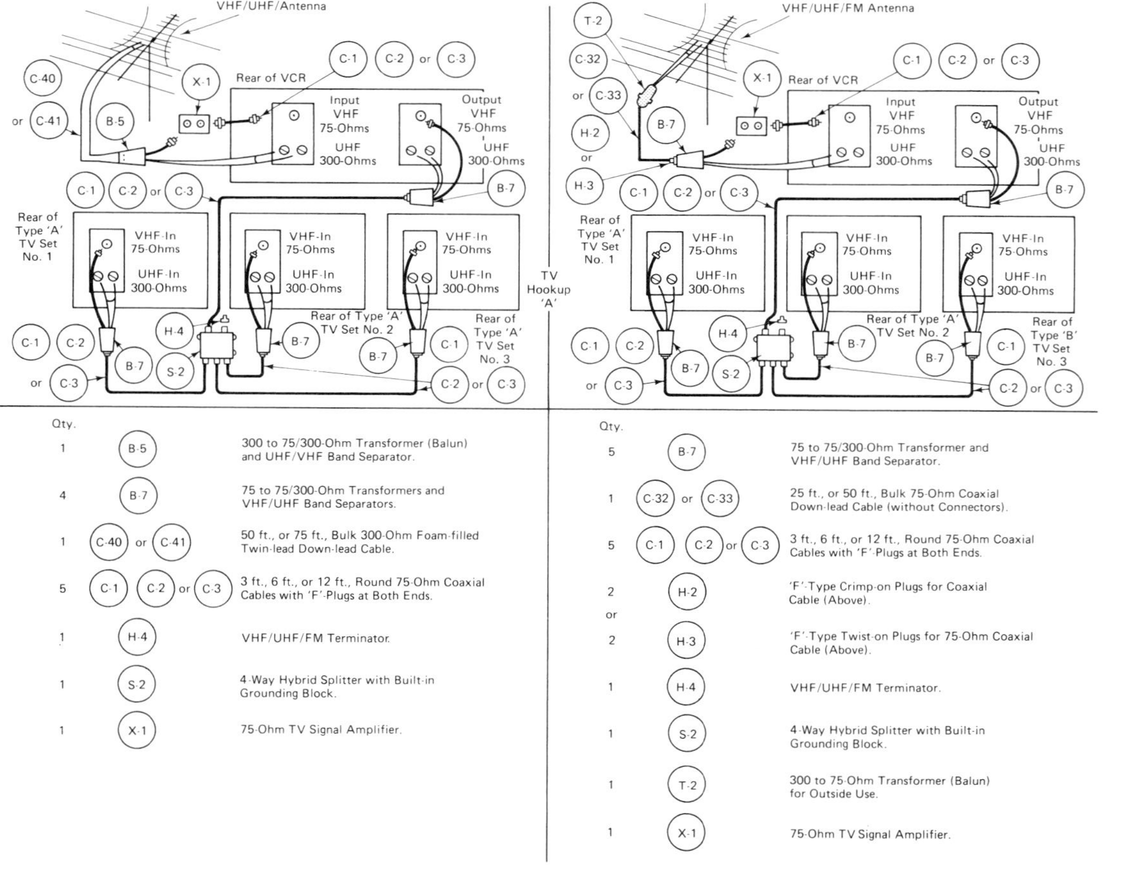

Figure 4–39. VCR hookup to three TV sets. (*Courtesy GC Electronics*)

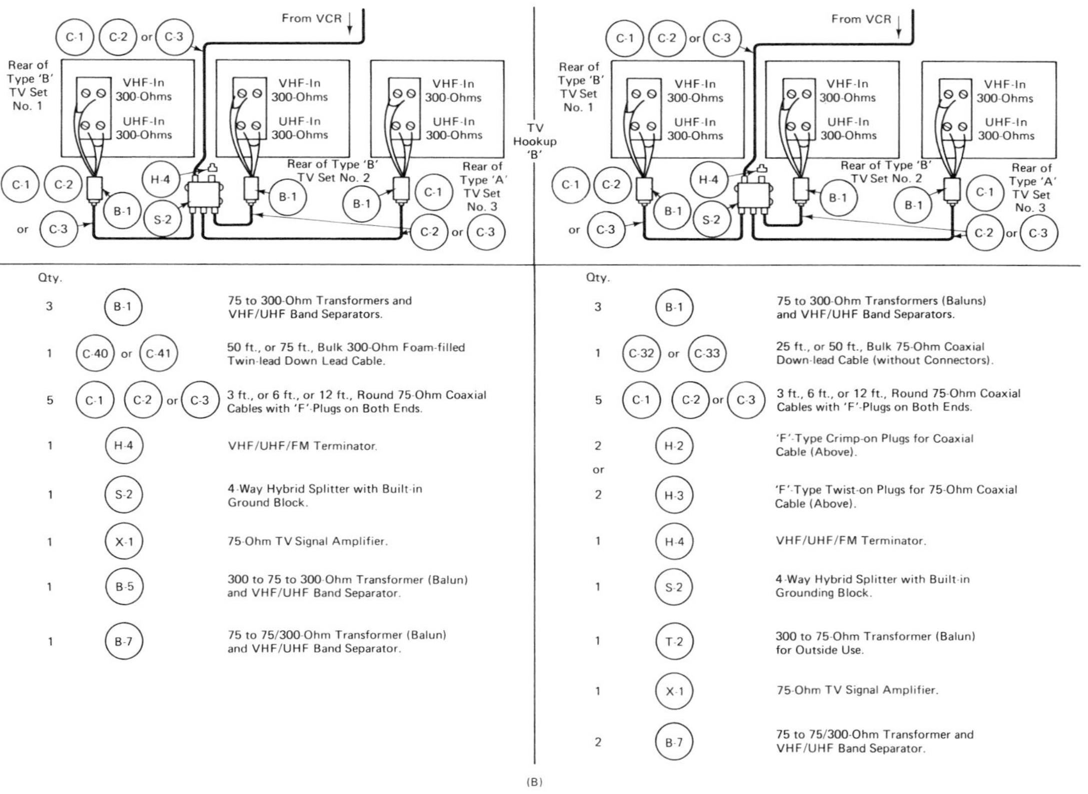

Qty.		
3	B-1	75 to 300-Ohm Transformers and VHF/UHF Band Separators.
1	C-40 or C-41	50 ft., or 75 ft., Bulk 300-Ohm Foam-filled Twin-lead Down Lead Cable.
5	C-1 C-2 or C-3	3 ft., or 6 ft., or 12 ft., Round 75-Ohm Coaxial Cables with 'F'-Plugs on Both Ends.
1	H-4	VHF/UHF/FM Terminator.
1	S-2	4-Way Hybrid Splitter with Built-in Ground Block.
1	X-1	75-Ohm TV Signal Amplifier.
1	B-5	300 to 75 to 300-Ohm Transformer (Balun) and VHF/UHF Band Separator.
1	B-7	75 to 75/300-Ohm Transformer (Balun) and VHF/UHF Band Separator.

Qty.		
3	B-1	75 to 300-Ohm Transformers (Baluns) and VHF/UHF Band Separators.
1	C-32 or C-33	25 ft., or 50 ft., Bulk 75-Ohm Coaxial Down-lead Cable (without Connectors).
5	C-1 C-2 or C-3	3 ft., 6 ft., or 12 ft., Round 75-Ohm Coaxial Cables with 'F'-Plugs on Both Ends.
2	H-2	'F'-Type Crimp-on Plugs for Coaxial Cable (Above).
or		
2	H-3	'F'-Type Twist-on Plugs for 75-Ohm Coaxial Cable (Above).
1	H-4	VHF/UHF/FM Terminator.
1	S-2	4-Way Hybrid Splitter with Built-in Grounding Block.
1	T-2	300 to 75-Ohm Transformer (Balun) for Outside Use.
1	X-1	75-Ohm TV Signal Amplifier.
2	B-7	75 to 75/300-Ohm Transformer and VHF/UHF Band Separator.

(B)

Figure 4–39. *(continued)*

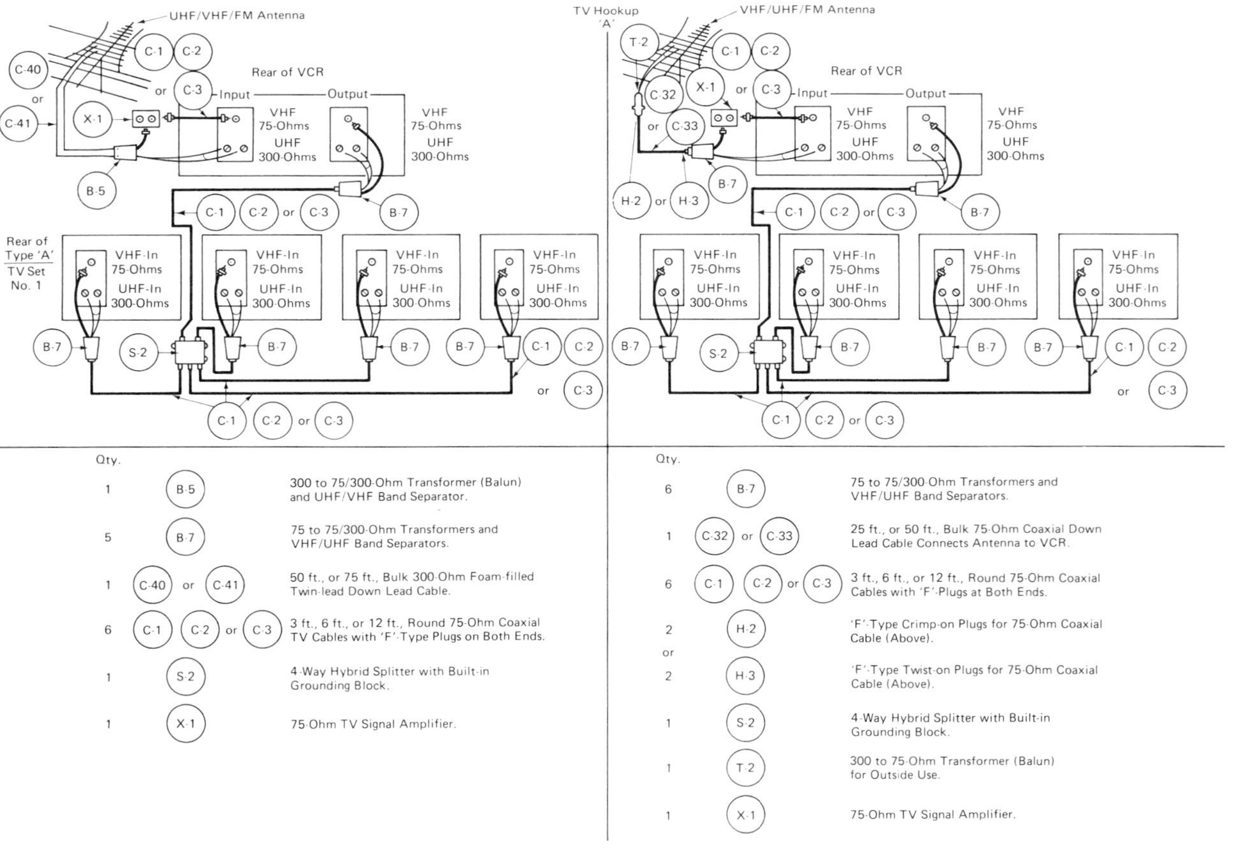

Figure 4–40. VCR hookup to four TV sets. *(Courtesy GC Electronics)*

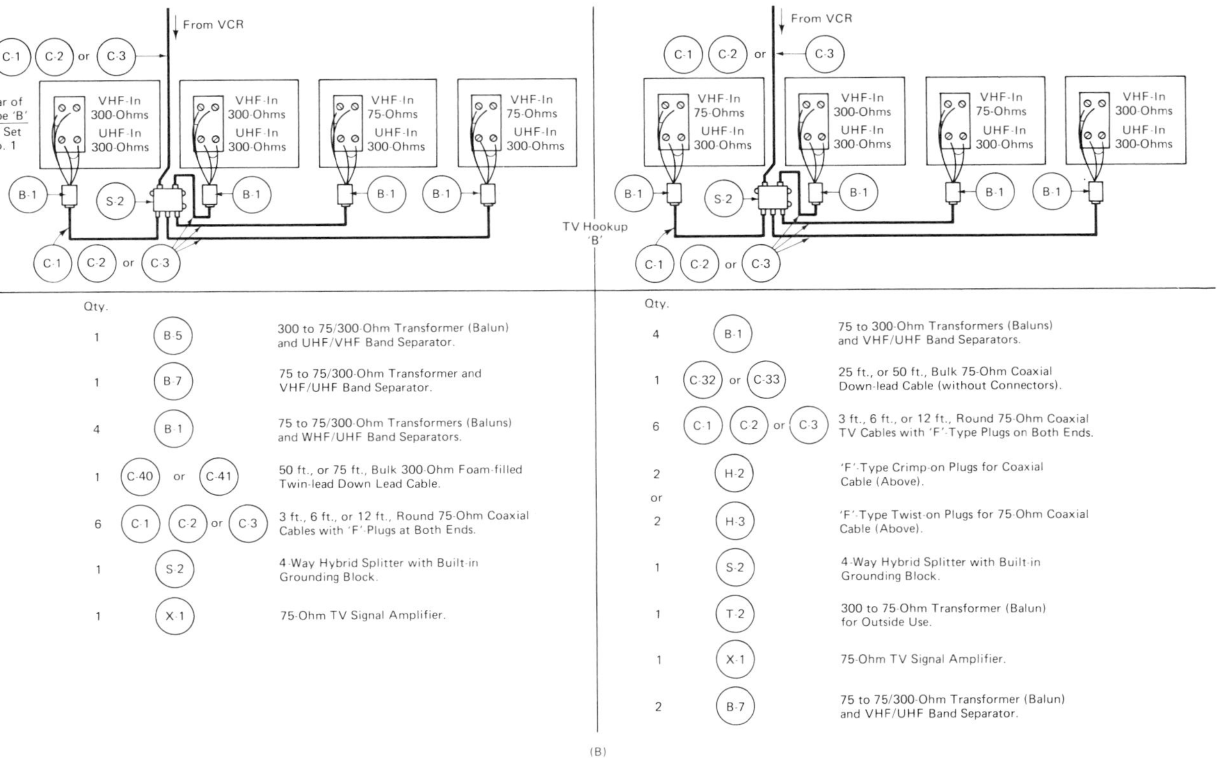

Figure 4–40. *(continued)*

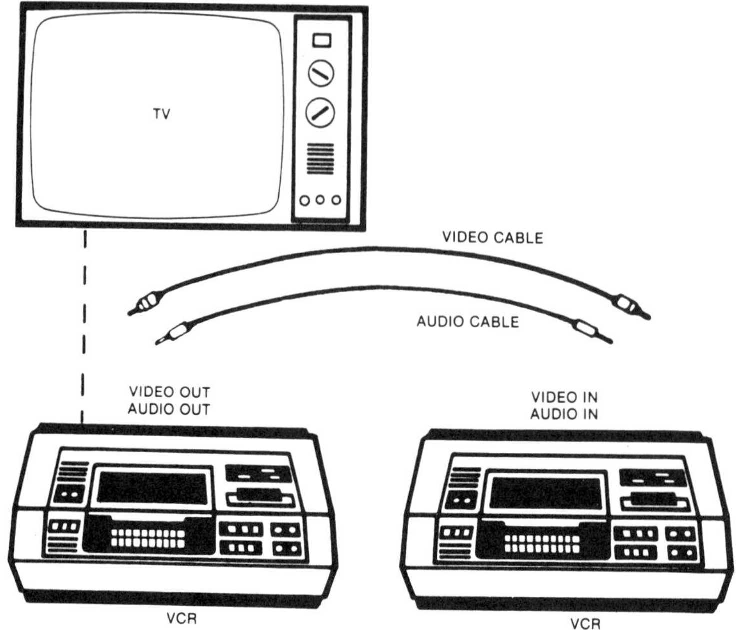

Figure 4–41. Connections for dubbing from one VCR to another. (*Courtesy GC Electronics*)

for VHS. The RCA-to-miniplug cable is intended for dubbing or re-recording between the two different formats.

When you are making the video dubbing connection, set up one VCR for recording. It will not be necessary to set the channel selector on that VCR. The same holds true for the playback VCR. When you are dubbing, it is advisable to monitor the signal transfer on the TV set.

Figure 4–41 shows a single cable used for the transfer of video information. For monophonic audio, a single cable is used as well, but for stereo, a pair of cables will be needed—one for connecting the left sound channel of the playing VCR to the left sound channel input of the recording VCR, and the other to connect the right sound channel similarly.

There are two advantages in dubbing videotapes: (1) a duplicate tape can be obtained, and (2) editing can be done. Watch the monitor and use the pause control on the recording VCR to stop the action. Release the pause control when you want the dubbing action to continue.

VIEWING DISTANCE

Getting the best possible picture on a television screen and obtaining desired operating features requires attention to component quality, correct impedance matching, and planning the connection arrangement. The final step is interfacing the TV receiver with the eyes of the viewer. This can be considered as much of a connection as any wire or cable.

Assuming a person with normal vision, or wearing glasses that produce the equivalent of normal vision, the correct viewing distance is 1500 times the spacing between adjacent pixels (picture elements). If the viewing distance is more than this, picture detail seems to decrease.

Assuming a picture tube having a diameter of 20 inches, the spacing between picture elements is approximately 0.03 inch. The viewing distance can then be calculated by multiplying 1500 by 0.03. This yields a distance of 45 inches. An easier method is to multiply picture height by 4.

The amount of eye movement of a person watching a TV picture depends on two factors—the viewing distance and the total number of picture elements. The central part of the human eye contains about 30,000 cones, short sensory organs of the retina that function in color vision. If the total number of picture elements is 210,500, then 30,000 cones mean we can concentrate on only 30,000/210,500 or 0.1425 or approximately 14 percent. Since the television picture has its main action at the center, but also has movement from side to side, there is substantial eye movement at the optimum viewing distance. If the viewing distance is increased, possibly to two or three times the optimum, eye movement is more limited, but picture detail appears reduced.

5

THE VIDEO CONNECTION

There is one way in which cable TV is eminently superior to broadcast TV, and that is in the matter of responsibility. A TV broadcast station puts its signal into space, but other than trying to have signal lobes reach areas of maximum population density, it has no further responsibility as far as signal strength or quality is concerned. If the signal is weak or snowy, or has ghosts that precede or follow the main image—or both—there is no recourse as far as the broadcasting station is concerned, for picture signal strength and quality are the viewer's responsibility.

The situation is exactly the opposite for cable TV. There the responsibility rests directly with the cable operators. They deliver the cable signal right into the home of the viewer. If signal strength is inadequate or the picture is weak, the viewer can make his disappointment clearly (and loudly) known.

SIGNAL STRENGTH

One of the most important, but often one of the most neglected, areas of broadcast TV for in-home electronic entertainment is from the antenna to the antenna input terminals of the TV receiver. The antenna system comprising the antenna, preamplifier, outside downlead, outside impedance matchers, antenna rotator, and inside run of transmission line, may be poorly installed or badly located, and it is subject to weather. This is unfortunate, for as far as the in-home electronic entertainment system is concerned, this is one of the most important program sources.

Space Loss

Also known as spreading loss, this is the weakening of any broadcast signal, whether transmitted from a terrestrial AM, FM, or TV station or from a satellite. Space loss is a function of distance: the greater the distance, the higher the attenuation of the signal.

Broadcast Television Signal Strength

The strength of a received television signal depends on its distance from the transmitting antenna, the radiation pattern of that antenna, the output power of the transmitter, the type of terrain between the transmitter and the television receiver, and the kind of transmitting and receiving antennas used.

TV signal strength attenuation is also a function of frequency. Thus, a UHF TV signal, such as one on channel 69, has a higher attenuation rate than a VHF TV broadcast signal, such as on channel 2 or channel 3. Consequently, with all other factors being equal, it is more difficult to receive a broadcast UHF signal than one on VHF.

For broadcast TV, the composite signal consists of amplitude-modulated video and frequency-modulated audio. The video carrier attenuates more rapidly than the sound carrier. In a fringe area, it is possible for a TV set to pick up the sound carrier but not the picture.

ANTENNA CONNECTIONS

A good antenna installation consists of a combined VHF/UHF/FM antenna equipped with a rotator, which is advantageous because it permits the antenna to be used as a tuning device with the antenna elements positioned broadside to the signals of a desired station.

Figure 5–1 shows an installation having an output impedance of 300 ohms and using twin lead as the transmission line to the TV set. For unshielded twin lead, this line should be held in place, away from the house by standoff insulators spaced from 4 feet to 6 feet (1.22 meters to 1.83 meters) apart. When coaxial cable is used as the downlead it can be held against the house by clamps made for this purpose.

The antenna discharge unit shown in the drawing is a small device inserted in the downlead between the antenna and the receiver and connected to a grounding wire or strap to discharge static electricity to ground. Static produces electrical noise that can be seen in the picture and can also be heard. The ground wire from the static discharge unit can be grounded in either of two ways. The easiest is to run the wire to the power service grounding terminal or to an interior metal water pipe. This connecting wire, sometimes called a bonding jumper should be at least 10 AWG copper or 17 AWG copper-

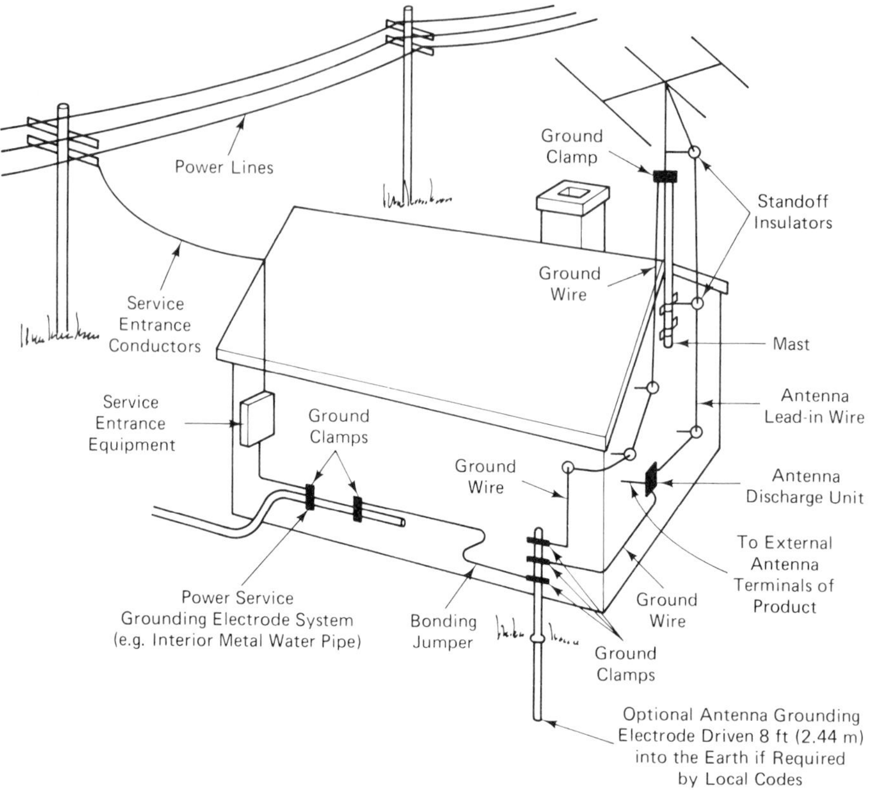

Figure 5-1. Details of antenna installation. Keep antenna as far from power lines as possible to minimize chance of electrical shock and to reduce pickup of electrical noise.

clad steel. If no interior ground connection is available (although this seems unlikely) it is possible to use an antenna grounding electrode driven 8 feet (2.44 meters) into the earth.

The drawing in Fig. 5-1 is an overall view, and succeeding illustrations supply details. Figure 5-2 shows the installation of a dual array, high-gain, multiband antenna equipped with an antenna rotator and a preamplifier. The downlead is coaxial cable that loops around the rotator to supply slack when the antenna rotates. Coaxial cable should be used with all rotor installations to avoid interaction that can occur between the rotor wire and 300-ohm twin lead. If you must use twin lead (Fig. 5-3) keep it at least 3 inches away from the rotor wire and mast for the full length of the installation. This can be done by using in-line double standouts as shown in Fig. 5-4. At the entrance to the home, form a drip loop in the shape of a U in the downlead (Fig. 5-5) to prevent the entrance of water. Drill the hole upward, from the outside in, to accommodate the twin lead or coaxial cable.

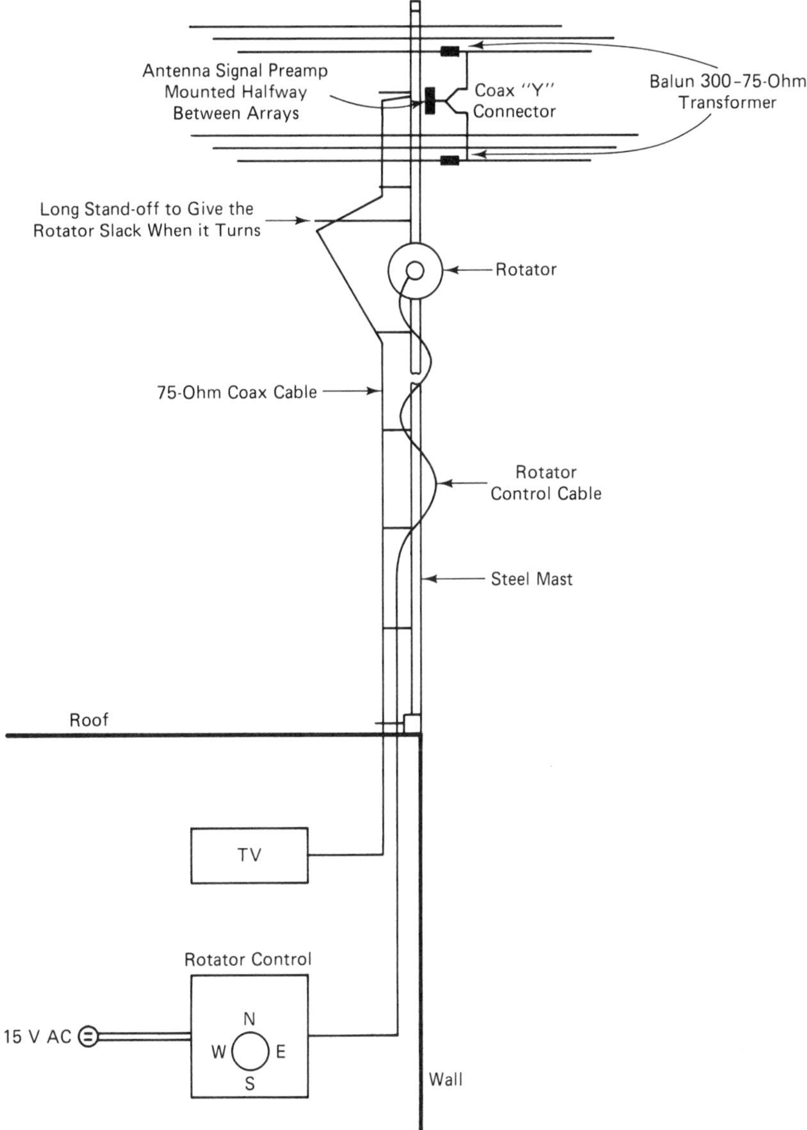

Figure 5-2. Antenna system using preamplifier and antenna rotator. The preamp and the rotator receive AC voltage from an AC line leading to an in-home outlet.

Connecting the Antenna Discharge Unit

It isn't just the height of an antenna that makes it susceptible to lightning. Both antennas and the transmission line can accumulate static electrical charges that also increase the chance of lightning's striking an antenna in-

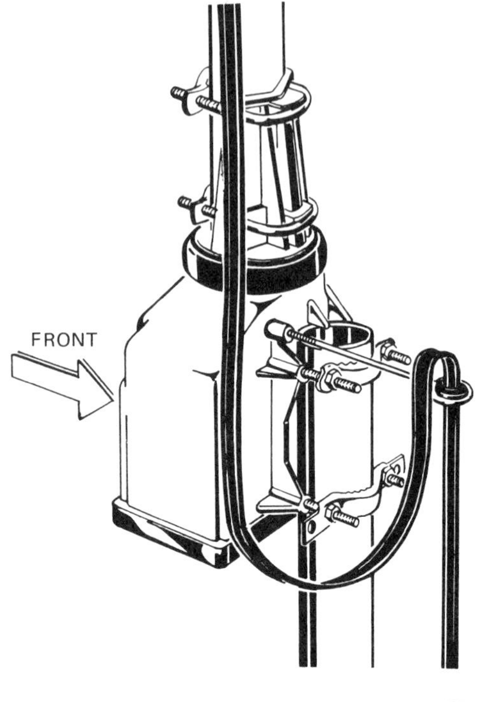

Figure 5-3. Loop downlead when using rotator to supply slack. This applies to coaxial cable as well as to twin lead. (*Courtesy Channel Master, Div. Avnet, Inc.*)

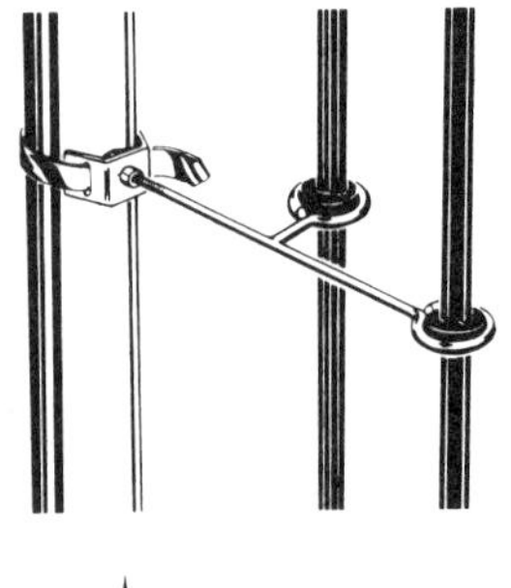

Figure 5-4. Keep twin lead and rotator cables at least 3 inches apart, using double standoffs. This precaution isn't necessary with coaxial cable. (*Courtesy Channel Master, Div. Avnet, Inc.*)

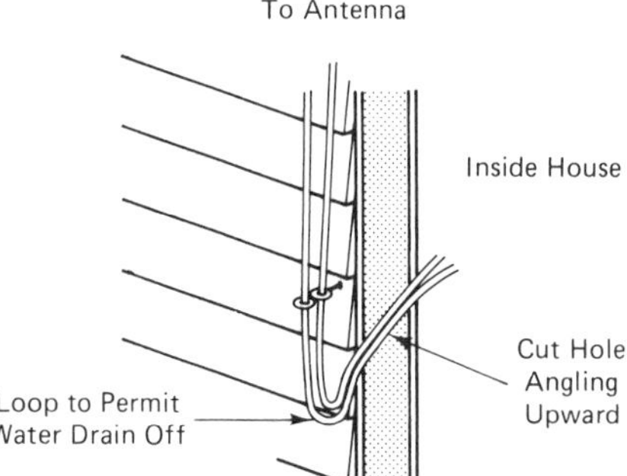

Figure 5-5. Drip loop to prevent water entry into the home. (*Courtesy Channel Master, Div. Avnet, Inc.*)

stallation. To neutralize static electricity, a small device known as an antenna discharge unit (Fig. 5–6) must be included in the installation. Connect it to the transmission line near where it enters the house. The drawing at the left shows how it is connected to twin lead through the use of penetrating washers. To connect the discharge unit to coaxial cable requires the use of an F-connector plug and jack inserted into the line. In both drawings, a thick ground wire leads to the grounding point.

Connecting a TV Preamplifier

Television antennas, whether folded doublet or open dipole, are two-terminal devices. The input to a preamplifier is a small section of twin lead; the output can be another set of machine screws for connecting twin lead or an F-jack for coaxial cable.

The best location for a preamp is as close to the antenna output as possible. A preamp is required if signal strength is too low, indicated by a snowy picture. If the TV signal is less than 1,000 microvolts at the antenna terminals of the TV set, a preamp is required. If a number of stations are being received, some of the signals may have adequate strength, but the criterion is the strength of the weakest signal.

A preamp will also generate a small amount of noise. In areas with extremely weak signals, even a low level of noise in the preamp will be too near the level of the received signal. Because both the received signal and the noise are equally amplified, the difference in their relative levels will never be great enough to permit the received signal to override the noise and eliminate the snow on the screen. There are a number of methods of coping with this problem. Use an antenna having optimum gain. Mount the antenna as high as possible. Orient the antenna so it is broadside to the weakest station. Select a

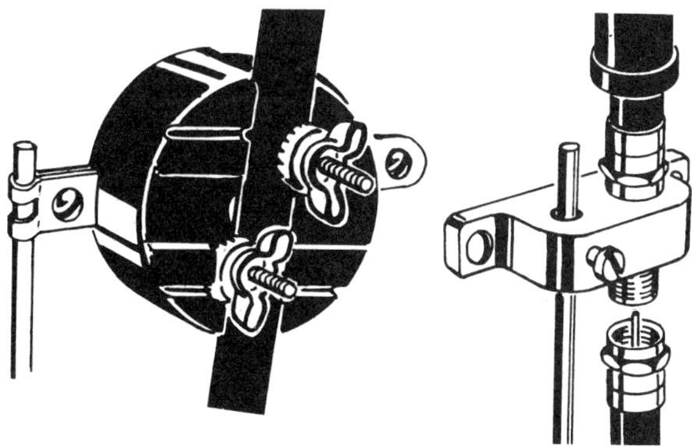

Figure 5–6. Static discharge unit with twin lead (left) and coaxial cable (right). (*Courtesy Channel Master, Div. Avnet, Inc.*)

TV set having high input sensitivity. Try to position the antenna so its run to the TV set is as short as possible. Make sure impedances are matched, both at the antenna and at the TV set. Do not use the antenna for driving more than one TV receiver. Use transmission line having the lowest possible loss per 100 feet. Make sure all connections between the antenna and the receiver are secure.

Connecting the Transmission Line to the Antenna

All antennas, whether open dipole or folded dipole, are two-terminal devices. Connecting twin lead to either is quite simple. The antenna may have a metal standoff like the one shown in Fig. 5-7. This works as a strain relief device. Bring the twin lead through it and then slice down through the center of its plastic jacket. Trim the ends of each conductor, twirl the strands and wrap them around the two antenna screws. These are often wing nuts. After making the connection, spray it with an acrylic insulator—a plastic material used for weatherproofing outdoor antenna system connections. The substance is applied in liquid form, typically by spraying from an aerosol can. Do not use electrician's tape, whether fabric or plastic types, because it can and does unravel.

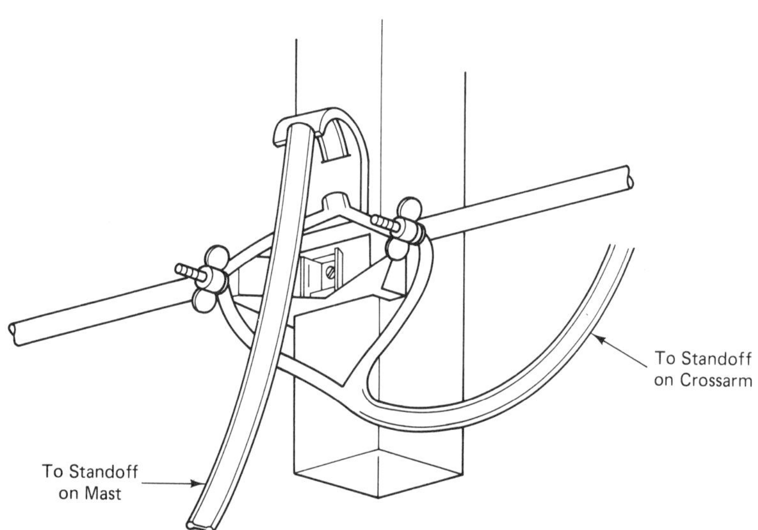

Figure 5-7. Method of connecting twin lead to an antenna.

If the antenna is a vertically stacked array, as shown in Fig. 5-8, equal lengths of twin lead can be connected to each antenna and then joined with a splicing box.

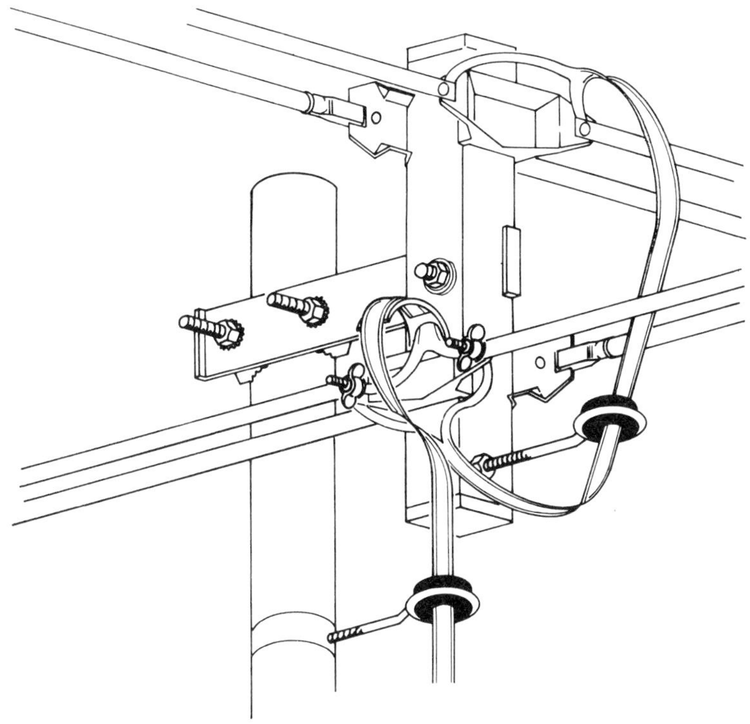

Figure 5-8. Connecting a vertically stacked array to twin lead. (*Courtesy Channel Master, Div. Avnet, Inc.*)

Coaxial cable can be connected to an antenna in several ways. One method, shown in Fig. 5-9, is via a 75-ohm to 300-ohm transformer. The antenna side of the transformer is twin lead and connects directly to the wing nut terminals of the antenna rod. The output side of the transformer is an F-jack, which connects to an F-plug at the end of the coaxial cable downlead. In this case, the balun is an outdoor type and is covered with a weatherboot, a protective covering placed over the transformer.

An antenna connection can also be made when you are using an antenna-mounted preamp. In Fig. 5-10, the preamp has a 300-ohm antenna input and a 300-ohm output for connection to twin lead transmission line. For coaxial cable, the output of the preamp would be an F-jack.

A major consideration when selecting a preamp is the possible sources of interference in the area. Local FM stations, police and fire frequencies, military communications, and other sources of radio-frequency signals can cause interferences that should be trapped at the preamp stage.

Preamps are available with almost every conceivable arrangement of traps (filters). These are either tunable or switchable. Tunable traps can be

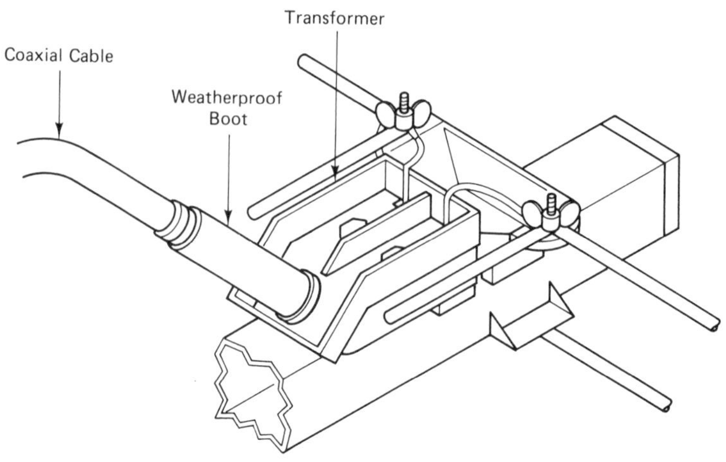

Figure 5–9. Method of connecting coaxial cable to an antenna. (*Courtesy Channel Master, Div. Avnet, Inc.*)

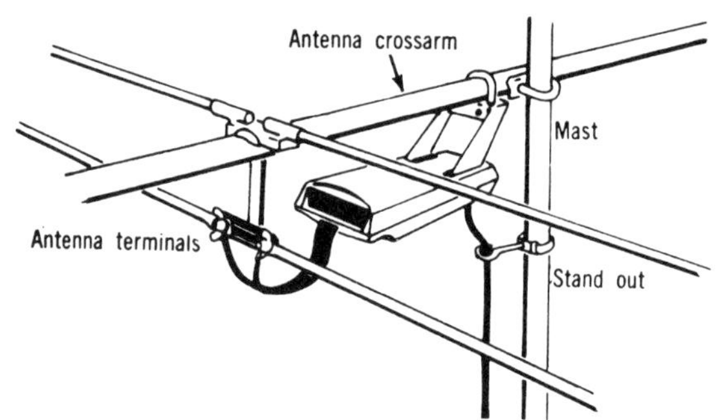

Figure 5–10. Transmission line connected to an antenna via a preamp. (*Courtesy Channel Master, Div. Avnet, Inc.*)

adjusted to eliminate a specific frequency, while switchable traps attenuate an entire band. If, as an example, there is interference from one local station, possibly at 101.5 MHz, a tunable trap can be adjusted so any signals at this frequency are eliminated without attenuating the rest of the FM band. If interference is caused by several FM stations, a switchable trap will attenuate the entire band.

It might seem that eliminating this source of TV interference would also eliminate FM reception. Usually, any FM signal strong enough to require trapping will be strong enough to be picked up by an FM receiver even though it is trapped out of the TV bands. An FM receiver requires a much lower-level signal to operate than does a TV receiver. When a switchable trap is used, however, some of the weaker, more distant FM stations will be lost.

HOOKUP FOR SEPARATE ANTENNAS TO VCR AND TV

The advantage of separate antennas is that each can be permanently oriented for best reception by being positioned broadside to a preferred station or stations; if this direction is the same for both VHF and UHF, then there is no point in using separate antennas. These antennas could be mounted on separate masts, or on a common mast with the antennas independently oriented for best signal reception for their particular signal bands.

Figure 5–11 shows two individual antennas and, of course, both use separate downlead transmission lines. The one at the left is the UHF antenna; the other is for VHF reception. The UHF antenna has a 300-ohm output and is connected via 300-ohm twin lead to the UHF input of the VCR. The UHF output of the VCR is wired with 300-ohm line to the UHF antenna input of the TV set. A scrap length of twin lead can be used here.

The VHF antenna is also 300-ohms and uses a matching transformer (A) to connect to the 75-ohm coaxial cable downlead. This transmission line is attached to the 75-ohm VHF input of the VCR with an F-jack. The VHF

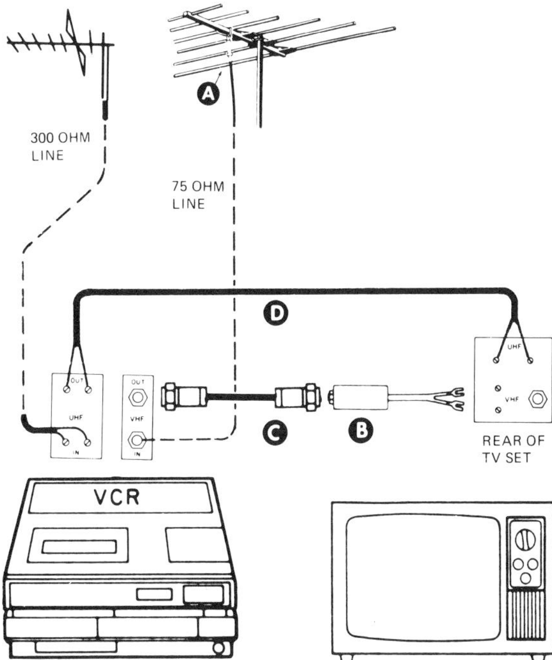

Figure 5–11. Connections for separate VHF and UHF antennas to a VCR: (A) balun; (B) balun—not required if receiver has 75-ohm input; (C) coaxial cable; (D) 300-ohm twin lead. (*Courtesy RCA*)

output of the VCR is 75-ohms and is linked to the TV set via a coaxial cable (C) equipped with a pair of F-connectors at both ends. Because the VHF input to the TV set is 300 ohms, a 75-ohm to 300-ohm matching transformer is required, indicated by B. Because two separate antennas are used, the wiring is actually somewhat simplified. Thus a band separator is not required.

Just about every suggested connection system can be modified to take into consideration the impedances of the components involved. That is why connection systems are referred to as "suggested." It is much better to understand why connections are made rather than to follow a system slavishly.

For example, there are several ways in which the diagram in Fig. 5–11 can be changed. A band combiner could be used near the antennas to permit the use of a single downlead. Whether this would be practical or not could depend on the physical location of the antennas. In an electrically noisy neighborhood, the downlead from the UHF antenna could be coaxial cable but in that case, a balun would be needed at the antenna and also at the UHF input to the VCR. An easier method would be to use shielded 300-ohm twin lead. Diagrams of this kind rarely indicate whether shielded or unshielded twin lead should be used. This can only be suggested, not specified.

The connections to the ports on the VCR and the TV set may not be as shown in the diagram, as the impedances indicated in the drawing may be different. If the components have already been purchased, the user is locked in by the existing impedances. However, if the components are yet to be purchased, input and output port impedances should be considered just as much as any of the more touted features.

CONNECTING A VCR AND A TV SET TO A MULTIPLE ANTENNA

While VCR and TV set connections were described in Chapter 4, the diagram in Fig. 5–12A, with those that follow, supplies more detailed instructions.

The antenna used in Fig. 5–12A is a multiband VHF/UHF antenna having an output impedance of 300 ohms, a type, incidentally, that is commonly used. Its output is connected to a 300-ohm to 75-ohm matching transformer (A) permitting the use of coaxial cable as the downlead. In the home, this cable is F-plug connected to the input of a band separator, B. This band separator has a 75-ohm input, and two outputs, both 300 ohms. The 300-ohm output leads are attached to a 300-ohm connector to enable the quick extension of 300-ohm line. Connector (C) can be omitted if the 300-ohm line from the band separator is long enough to permit the band separator to be wired directly to the UHF input terminals of the VCR. The UHF output terminals of the VCR are wired to the UHF antenna input terminals of the TV set using a scrap length of 300-ohm line. It would be advisable to put open spade lugs on this line, either crimping them on or soldering—preferably both.

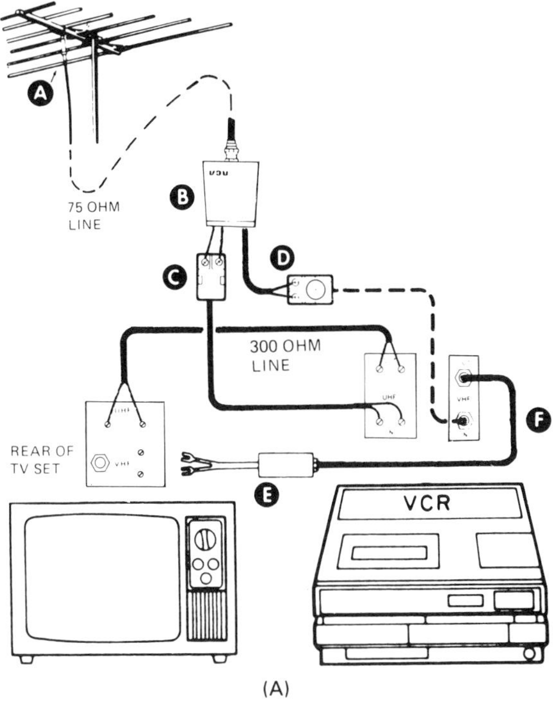

Figure 5-12A. Connecting a VHF/UHF antenna to a VCR. (A) balun; (B) band separator; (C) splice box; (D) balun; (E) balun; (F) coaxial cable. (*Courtesy RCA*)

A matching transformer is indicated at D, but this assumes that the VHF input of the VCR is 75 ohms. If it is, the matching transformer is required, but not if the VHF input of the VCR is 300 ohms. The VHF output of the VCR (F) is connected by coaxial cable to a matching transformer, E, a balun having a 75-ohm input and a 300-ohm output. The 300-ohm terminals of this balun are connected to the 300-ohm VHF antenna input terminals of the TV set.

Before assuming that a system will require a number of baluns, first check on the impedances of the components involved. The best hookup is one that uses as few of these add-ons as possible.

CONNECTING A MULTIBAND ANTENNA TO TWO TV SETS

The hookup in Fig. 5-12B is based on the arrangement of Fig. 5-12A, except that an additional TV set has been included. Because two TV sets are being used, we need a two-way signal splitter (C). A balun (A) is required at the

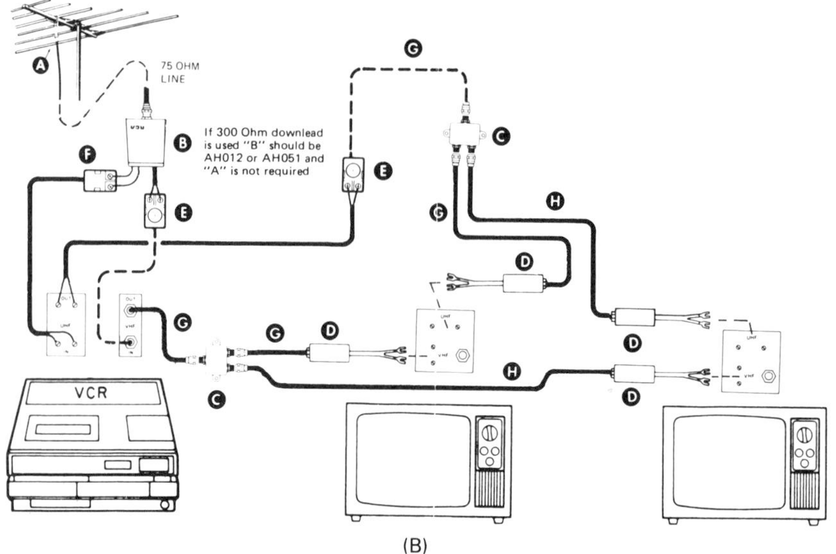

Figure 5–12B. Connecting a VHF/UHF antenna and a VCR to two TV sets. (A) balun; (B) band separator; (C) two two-way splitters; (D) baluns; (E) two baluns; (F) lead extension; (G) four cables; (H) two cables.

antenna to permit the use of coaxial cable, but it can be omitted if you prefer 300-ohm line.

One way of handling this wiring setup is to connect just one TV set and then check the system, using both the VCR and the one TV receiver. If the system functions as it should, add the connections for the second TV set. This will make troubleshooting much easier if for some reason the system does not work as it should.

There is another reason for trying the one-TV-set-at-a-time approach. The TV broadcast signal may be adequate for one TV set, but may supply only a marginal picture when another receiver is included. With two TV sets supplied by the same signal, a preamplifier may be required.

CONNECTING CABLE TV TO MULTIPLE TV SETS

Figure 5–13 is a wiring arrangement that permits the use of broadcast TV or cable TV. If cable TV is not wanted at all, disregard the cable converter and also eliminate the coaxial A/B switch. In that case, the antenna downlead can be connected directly to either a three-way or a four-way signal splitter. Since there are only three TV sets, the four-way splitter will have an unused port and a terminator can be plugged into that port, or a 75-ohm resistor can be connected across its terminals.

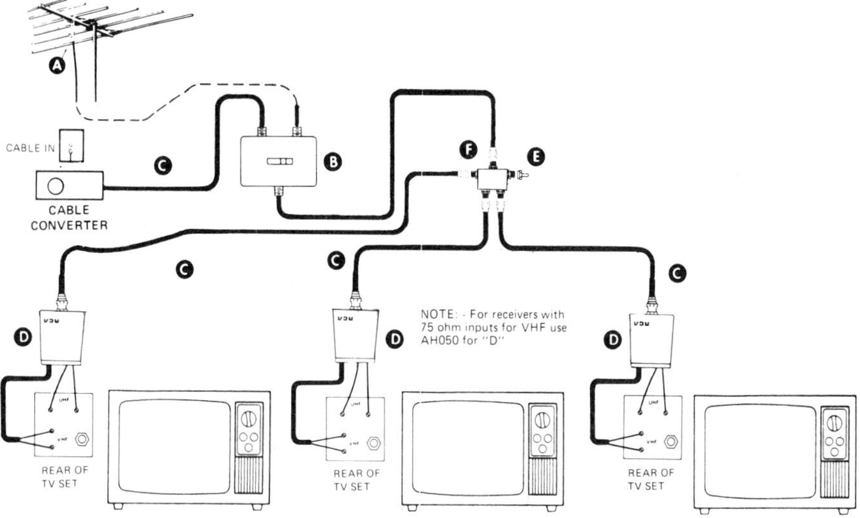

Figure 5–13. Connecting cable TV to multiple TV sets. (A) balun; (B) coaxial A/B switch; (C) coaxial cables; (D) band separators; (E) terminator; (F) four-way signal splitter (a three-way splitter can be used). (*Courtesy RCA*)

If both cable and antenna are available, then the connections will be as shown in Fig. 5–13. The coaxial switch, B, is used to select one of the two possible inputs, either cable or broadcast TV. The A/B switch is called coaxial, as its two input ports and single output port all use F-jacks. The output of the switch is led to the input of the four-way splitter.

There are three separate coaxial lines of suitable length from the splitter with each line going to a different TV set. Note that up to this point the VHF and UHF signals have been traveling together, as the antenna is multiband. Consequently, a band separator must be used before delivering the signal to each of the TV sets. The band separator shows a 75-ohm input and 300-ohm outputs for the VHF and UHF signals. However, use band separators that match the VHF and UHF impedances of the TV sets. It doesn't necessarily follow that each of the band separators will be identical as far as impedances are concerned.

CONNECTING TWO CONVERTERS TO ONE TV SET

Not all cable converters have the same channel-handling capabilities, so, even though an in-home video system is equipped with one, a supplementary converter may be helpful. The wiring arrangement for a two-converter setup appears in Fig. 5–14.

The original converter box delivers VHF signals to the TV set's VHF

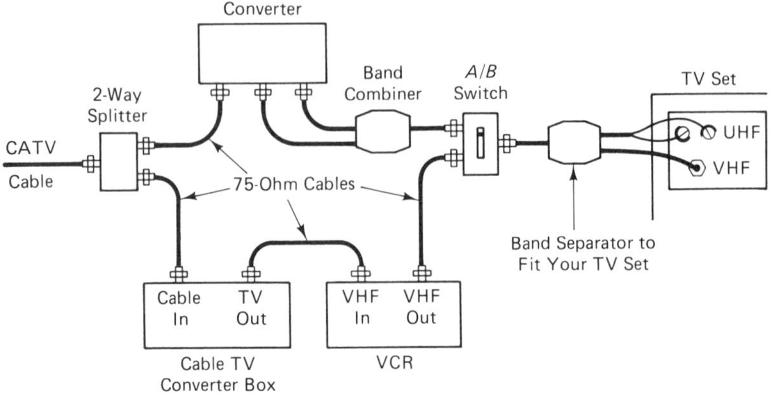

Figure 5-14. Connecting two converters to one TV set. (*Courtesy Gemini Industries, Inc.*)

input. With this converter, the TV receiver's tuning control is set to channels 3 or 4, with VHF channels selected by pushbuttons on the converter. The second converter box is a block tuning unit and receives midband and superband cable channels. This converter box is not a tunable unit and these channels are selected by the UHF tuner in the TV.

Note that this arrangement does not have any connections to a TV antenna, either indoors or outdoors, and depends for its programs solely on cable and a VCR. The cable signal, obtained from a wall plate in the home, is brought via coaxial cable to a two-way splitter. The signal is divided in half, approximately, with one part headed for the first converter box, the other portion for the second converter, shown in the lower part of the diagram. While all the cable signals are supplied to this converter, its output is VHF signals only, and these are brought into a VCR. The VCR is connected to one input terminal of a coaxial A/B switch.

The second converter box, the block unit, also receives a part of the cable signal. Its output consists of midband and superband signals delivered via a pair of ports to a band combiner. The single output of the band combiner is supplied to an input terminal of the A/B switch. The output of this switch now delivers all signals—VHF, midband, and superband—to a band separator. This particular band separator uses coaxial cable for the VHF signals and twin lead for the midband and superband signals, now at UHF frequencies.

The UHF tuning control on the TV set is used for tuning any of the midband and superband channels. The VHF signals are selected by the lower cable TV converter box. The output of this converter is either channel 3 or channel 4, with the TV set also tuned to one or the other of these two channels.

This setup has only two signal sources: programs delivered via cable and prerecorded video tapes supplied by the VCR. Manual tuning only is used.

THE VIDEODISC PLAYER

A videodisc is comparable to the record player used in high-fidelity systems, but electronically its construction and design are far more complex. Typically, such a player will have three output ports: audio, video, and a composite (modulated) video signal output. The audio can be supplied to the TV receiver or brought into the preamplifier input of a high-fidelity sound system.

One of the ports supplies unmodulated video and, using a single length of coaxial cable with an F-connector at the free end, can be plugged into the video signal input port of a monitor. It is not suitable for connection to the antenna input terminals of a TV set, whether VHF or UHF.

The remaining port supplies a modulated video-audio signal for connection to a TV set, with the carrier frequency either channel 3 or channel 4, determined by a slide switch on the player. The output from this port is 75 ohms and if the connection is to be made to a 300-ohm input, a matching transformer will be required. This transformer will have a short length of twin lead attached to its output, ending in open spade lugs, which can then be attached to the screw VHF terminals of the TV set.

One of the advantages of having a signal supplied by a VCR, videodisc player, or camera is that the signal is usually strong enough to preclude the need for a preamplifier. However, it may still be required if the system involves a number of TV sets. A signal splitter will also be needed.

CONNECTING THREE SIGNAL SOURCES

Quite commonly, an in-home video entertainment system follows a certain growth path; it usually starts with a TV set connected to an antenna. Subsequently, a VCR is added, and then cable TV. Not all in-home entertainment systems follow this route, however, as is indicated in Fig. 5-15. Here the signal sources are broadcast TV, cable, and a videodisc player.

The coaxial A/B switch has two inputs: one a 75-ohm line from an antenna (A), the other input from a cable converter. Depending on the position of the A/B switch (G), either of these signals is brought into a suitable length of coaxial cable (E), which terminates in a band separator (B). From the band separator, the VHF signals are routed to the videodisc player and the UHF signals are sent to the TV set.

Line D is a length of twin lead. The small box positioned between points B and D is a twin-lead connector (a splice box) described in Chapter 3, and used for connecting one length of twin lead to another—much more convenient for joining twin lead than cutting and splicing.

The input and output ports of the videodisc are F-jacks designed for coaxial cable. If the VHF output of the band separator for VHF signals is

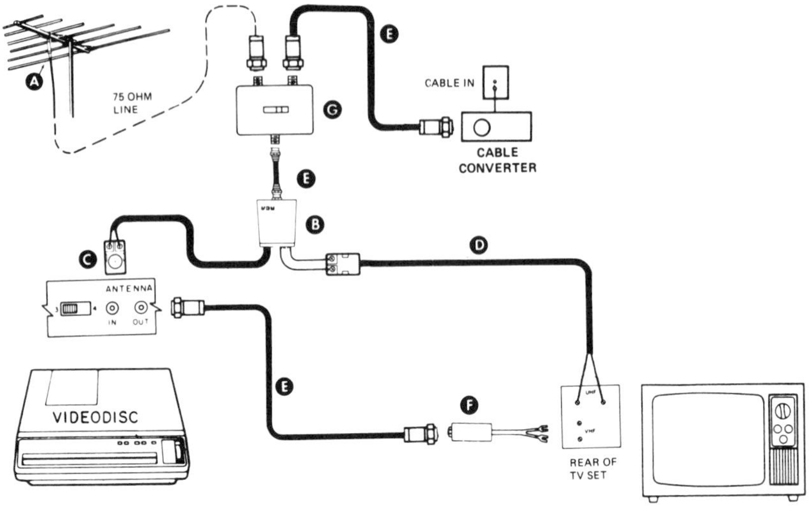

Figure 5-15. Connecting three signal sources to a TV set. (A) balun; (B) band separator; (C) balun; (D) 300-ohm line; (E) coaxial cables; (F) balun; (G) coaxial A/B switch. (*Courtesy RCA*)

twin lead, a matching transformer (C) will be needed prior to the input of the VCR.

The output terminals of the VCR are connected by coaxial cable (E) to the VHF input terminals of the TV set. If those terminals are for 300-ohm line, a matching transformer (F) will be required. If not, then the transformer can be omitted and the coaxial cable from the videodisc connected directly. The interesting feature of Fig. 5-15 is that although there are three possible signal inputs, just a single A/B switch is used.

Figure 5-16 is a connection diagram also, using three signal sources: a TV antenna, a TV game, and a home computer terminal board. However, unlike Fig. 5-15, it requires two A/B switches.

Start by examining hookup A in the upper part of the illustration. The antenna is a multiband VHF/UHF/FM antenna, using 300-ohm twin lead in the drawing at the left. This transmission line leads to a TV/video game switch (an A/B switch), X3. For the reception of TV broadcast signals, the antenna signal output terminal of this switch is brought into a 300-ohm to 75-ohm matching transformer whose output cable is connected to the 75-ohm VHF input terminal on the antenna block of the TV set. If that input is 300 ohms, the matching transformer is omitted and the TV/video game switch is connected directly to the 300-ohm antenna input terminals as indicated in the lower partial hookup drawing, hookup B.

The TV game and the home computer terminal keyboard are both connected to another A/B switch identified as X2. The output port of this switch

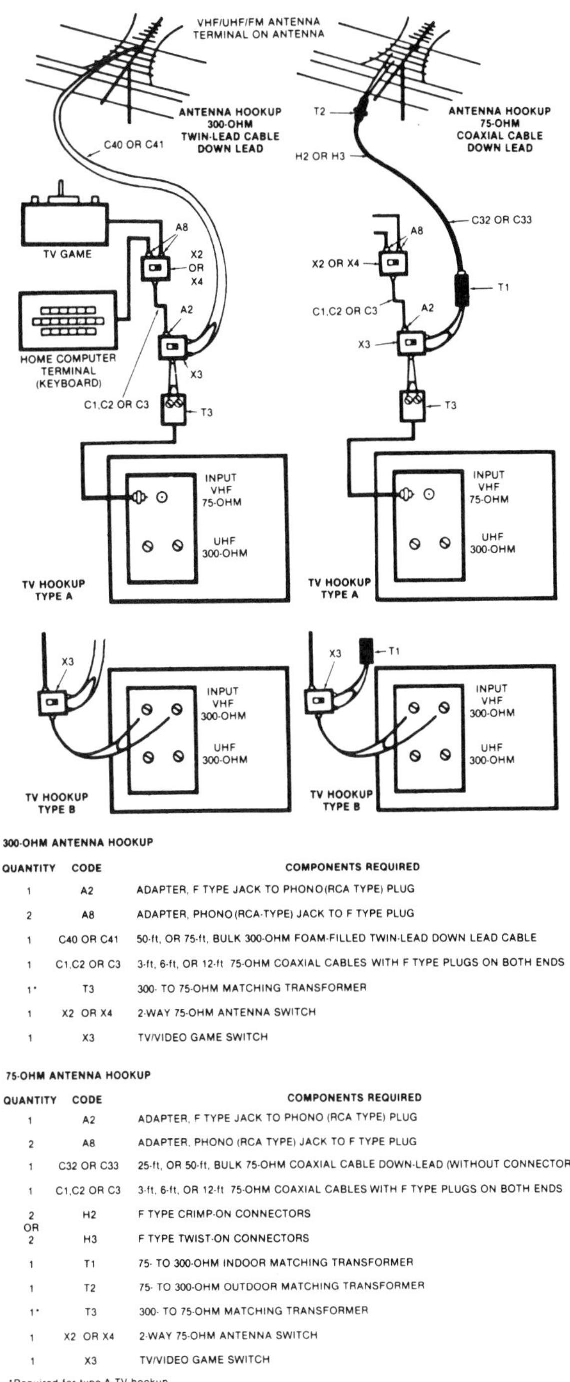

300-OHM ANTENNA HOOKUP

QUANTITY	CODE	COMPONENTS REQUIRED
1	A2	ADAPTER, F TYPE JACK TO PHONO (RCA TYPE) PLUG
2	A8	ADAPTER, PHONO (RCA-TYPE) JACK TO F TYPE PLUG
1	C40 OR C41	50-ft, OR 75-ft, BULK 300-OHM FOAM-FILLED TWIN-LEAD DOWN LEAD CABLE
1	C1,C2 OR C3	3-ft, 6-ft, OR 12-ft 75-OHM COAXIAL CABLES WITH F TYPE PLUGS ON BOTH ENDS
1*	T3	300- TO 75-OHM MATCHING TRANSFORMER
1	X2 OR X4	2-WAY 75-OHM ANTENNA SWITCH
1	X3	TV/VIDEO GAME SWITCH

75-OHM ANTENNA HOOKUP

QUANTITY	CODE	COMPONENTS REQUIRED
1	A2	ADAPTER, F TYPE JACK TO PHONO (RCA TYPE) PLUG
2	A8	ADAPTER, PHONO (RCA TYPE) JACK TO F TYPE PLUG
1	C32 OR C33	25-ft, OR 50-ft, BULK 75-OHM COAXIAL CABLE DOWN-LEAD (WITHOUT CONNECTORS)
1	C1,C2 OR C3	3-ft, 6-ft, OR 12-ft 75-OHM COAXIAL CABLES WITH F TYPE PLUGS ON BOTH ENDS
2	H2	F TYPE CRIMP-ON CONNECTORS
OR 2	H3	F TYPE TWIST-ON CONNECTORS
1	T1	75- TO 300-OHM INDOOR MATCHING TRANSFORMER
1	T2	75- TO 300-OHM OUTDOOR MATCHING TRANSFORMER
1*	T3	300- TO 75-OHM MATCHING TRANSFORMER
1	X2 OR X4	2-WAY 75-OHM ANTENNA SWITCH
1	X3	TV/VIDEO GAME SWITCH

*Required for type-A TV hookup.

Figure 5–16. Connections using three signal sources and two A/B switches. (*Courtesy GC Electronics*)

leads into the second switch, X3. When this switch is in its proper switching position, the signal from either the TV game or the computer is routed to the VHF input of the TV set. Since there are two switches and three possible signal sources, it would be advisable to make a written or typed record of what happens when both switches are operated.

The two drawings at the right side of Fig. 5–16 are supplied here to emphasize impedance matching; otherwise the wiring is unchanged. The same 300-ohm output antenna is used and a matching transformer, T2, impedance matches the antenna to the coaxial cable downlead, C32. The downlead can be bulk coaxial cable, that is, cable supplied without connectors. This type of cable is often available in lengths of 25 feet, 50 feet, 75 feet, and so on. F-connectors will be required. When doing such an installation, tailor the length of the cable so there is no excess, forming unused loops.

As in drawing A, the transmission line is connected to X3, the TV game/home computer terminal keyboard. This switch, however, has a 300-ohm input for the antenna downlead, so a matching transformer, T1, is used. This transformer was not required in drawing A.

Other than the use of two matching transformers, one at the antenna and the other at the A/B switch, this hookup (B) is the same as that shown in A. If you will compare both drawings marked B, the one at the left and the other at the right, you will see they are identical. The only difference is that the 300-ohm output leads of T1, the impedance-matching transformer, are connected to X3, the TV/video game switch.

THE BLOCK DIAGRAM APPROACH

Even with a simple home entertainment setup, but especially with one that uses more than two or three components, a block diagram is helpful. The block diagram is an overall view and is beneficial for indicating the path followed by one or more signals.

The block diagram doesn't indicate impedance-matching points, but it does include components such as TV sets and VCRs—and add-ons such as splitters, A/B switches, and converters. Since the block diagram is a general plan, it could be followed by a more specific diagram.

Figure 5–17A shows such a diagram with cable input, using a VCR plus a TV set. The cable signals are first supplied to a two-way splitter with the divided signal input shared by a pair of converters: a cable company-supplied unit and a separate block converter. The UHF output of the block converter is supplied to a VCR and the output of the cable company's converter is fed to one of the input terminals of a coaxial A/B switch.

Figure 5–17B shows a wiring diagram along the lines of the block diagram of Fig. 5–17A. It is somewhat simpler, as the A/B switch has been eliminated. The incoming cable signal is supplied to the input port of the converter.

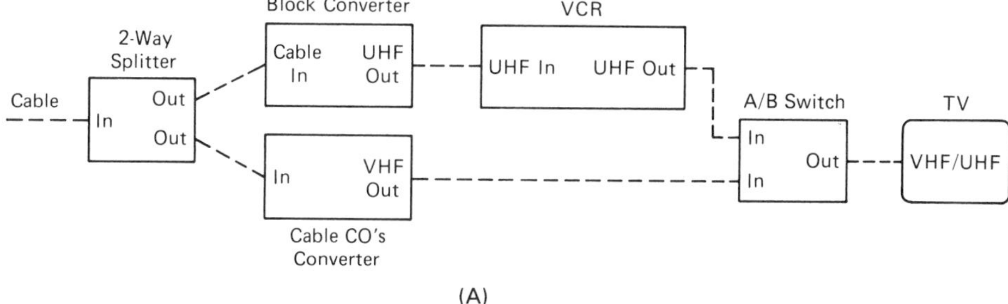

Figure 5–17A. Block diagram of double converter arrangement.

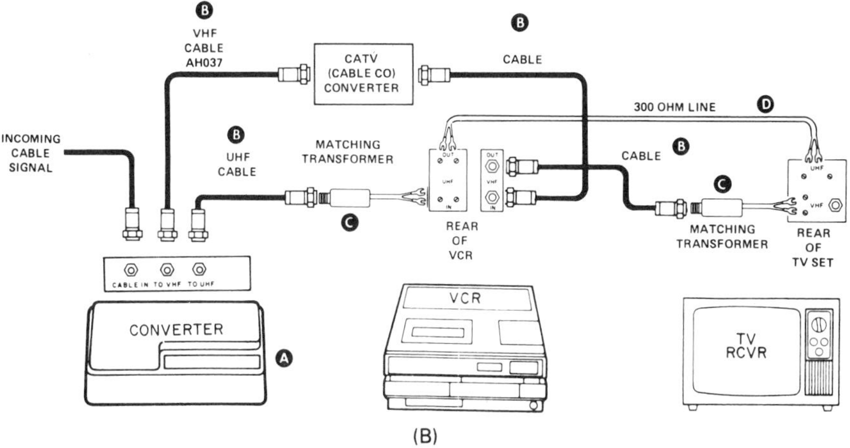

Figure 5–17B. Circuit arrangement using two converters. (A) cable converter; (B) four cables—two furnished with converter; (C) two baluns; (D) 5 feet of 300-ohm line. *(Courtesy RCA)*

This converter has two outputs: VHF and UHF. The VHF and UHF signals ultimately reach the VCR where they are demodulated and are then remodulated onto a channel 3 or channel 4 carrier, which is then supplied to the two input ports of the TV receiver.

The cable company may supply a pay TV converter, one that contains a decoder for handling scrambled signals, with the hookup shown in Fig. 5–18. Note how similar this circuit arrangement is to that illustrated in Fig. 5–17A, yet the A/B switch has been eliminated. The UHF output of the block converter is brought into the UHF input terminals of the VCR. The pay TV converter handles VHF signals and from the output of that converter, the connections are led to the VHF input terminals of the VCR. The outputs of the VCR are VHF and UHF and these are connected directly to the corresponding antenna input terminals on the TV set.

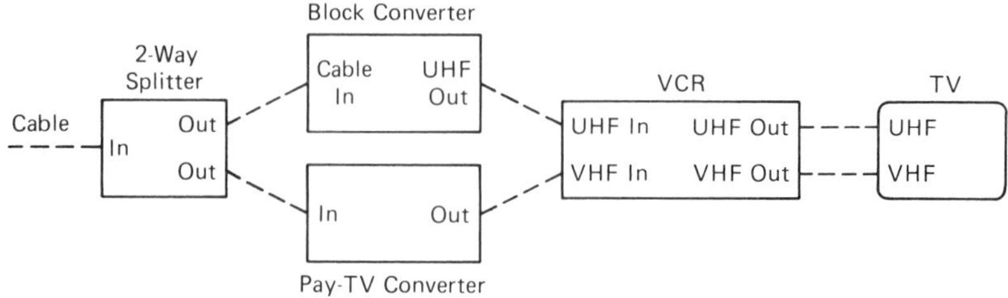

Figure 5–18. Connections for a pay TV converter.

In this arrangement, the UHF tuner of the TV set selects cable midband and superband channels and the VHF tuner is used for VHF broadcast signals.

The second converter is a pay TV unit. Pay TV, also known as subscription TV or STV, usually consists of the transmission of programs not interrupted by advertising with the converter supplied by the TV station making the broadcasts. The pay TV converter not only changes the frequency of the carrier to one in the VHF band but also contains a decoder, as STV signals are scrambled. Subscribers to STV make monthly payments.

The STV signals are brought into the VHF input of the VCR and are then routed to the VHF antenna terminals of the TV set. Tuning of the STV signals can be done by having the VCR convert the STV signals to the carrier frequencies of either channel 3 or channel 4, whichever is not active, with the TV set tuned to the selected channel.

The block diagrams shown in Fig. 5–19 were drawn with the assumption that the TV set is cable ready and has a 112-channel or 130-channel TV capability. The simplest hookup is that shown at the left. Here, the F-connector in the cable TV wall plate is connected directly to the TV set, using a suitable length of coaxial cable. No converter is required. Program tuning can be handled manually right at the TV receiver or else by a remote control unit.

If one or more cable channels are scrambled, a special converter/decoder supplied by the cable company will be required. However, this is only if the scrambled channels are wanted. Not all channels are encoded, and with a cable-ready TV set it is still possible to view cable channels that aren't scrambled. Using the converter-decoder, the block diagram in the center of Fig. 5–19 gives general details of the hookup. The connection from the cable TV wall plate to the converter will be via a short length of coaxial cable. The output of the converter will also be coaxial cable. A balun may be required between the converter and the TV set, depending on the antenna input impedances of the receiver.

The block diagram at the right in Fig. 5–19 gives the owner of a cable-ready TV set the option of using a converter/decoder or not, as desired. The cable signal from the cable TV wall plate is brought via a length of coaxial cable to the input of a splitter. The two outputs of the signal splitter, both 75

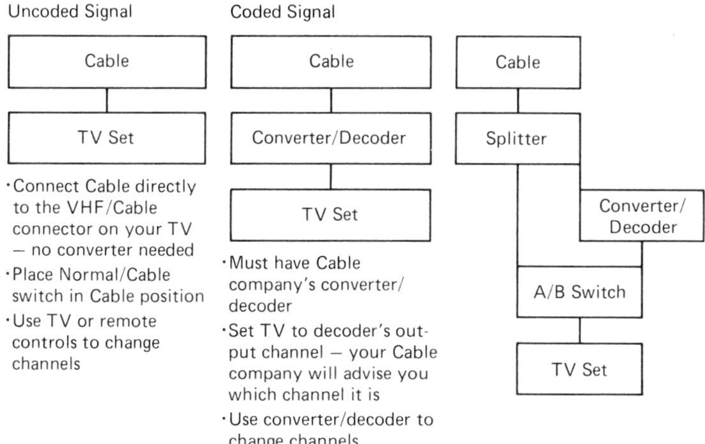

Figure 5-19. Cable TV connections for 112-channel and 130-channel cable-ready TV set. (*Courtesy General Electric*)

ohms, are supplied to a converter-decoder and also to an A/B switch. The other input terminal of that switch is connected to the output of the converter-decoder. The output of the A/B switch is wired to the antenna input of the TV set.

With the switch in one position, the converter/decoder is eliminated as a factor in delivering cable signals to the TV set. Reception, then, is directly from cable and is for unscrambled signals only. Under those circumstances the converter used is the one built into the TV set. With the A/B switch in the opposite position, however, signals are received via the converter-decoder and are unscrambled by that unit.

Tuning is done in two ways with this arrangement. When unscrambled signals are being received, the TV set can be operated manually or by using a remote control unit. With the A/B switch in its opposite position, it is necessary to use the converter-decoder for channel selection. The TV set is adjusted for channel 3 or channel 4 reception, and neither manual nor remote control is possible.

If the TV set is cable ready but has only an 82-channel capability, its options are limited (Fig. 5-20). As is shown in the block diagram at the left, one possibility is to use the cable company's converter. The connection from the cable TV outlet, usually a wall plate, is via coaxial cable to the 75-ohm input of the converter. The output of the converter is also 75 ohms, but if the VHF input of the TV set is 300 ohms, a 75-ohm to 300-ohm balun will be needed between the converter and the TV receiver.

The TV receiver must be set to the output channel of the converter, usually VHF channel 3 or channel 4. The converter is used to change channels,

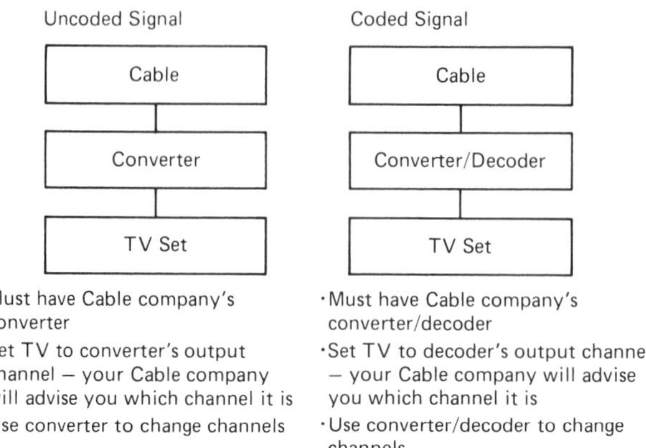
Uncoded Signal
Cable
Converter
TV Set
•Must have Cable company's converter
•Set TV to converter's output channel – your Cable company will advise you which channel it is
•Use converter to change channels
Coded Signal
Cable
Converter/Decoder
TV Set
•Must have Cable company's converter/decoder
•Set TV to decoder's output channel – your Cable company will advise you which channel it is
•Use converter/decoder to change channels

Figure 5-20. Cable TV connections for 82-channel cable-ready TV set. (*Courtesy General Electric*)

and with this arrangement neither manual nor remote tuning of the TV set is possible. Unless otherwise indicated, the converter being used does not have a decoding function.

An alternative arrangement is shown in the block diagram at the right in Fig. 5-20. This setup is identical to the one at the left and so are all the connections. The only difference is that the converter contains a decoder circuit, and with this setup it is possible to watch scrambled programs.

From the block diagrams shown in Figures 5-19 and 5-20, it must be fairly obvious that if a new TV set is to be purchased, it would be advisable to get one having the maximum cable-ready facilities. Cable-ready sets are made with their own converters, but none of these have a decoding capability. The reason for this is that there is no standardization for the scrambling of TV signals, as there are a number of different encoding techniques. There is also a question about the legality of using an add-on decoder for scrambled signals, something that could lead to a charge of program piracy.

VIDEO VERSUS TELEVISION

It is important to make a distinction between video and television. Television is broadcast or cable TV, and the use of a receiver for the display of pictures. Video is much more than that, for it not only includes television, but has also an interesting variety of additional components: first of all, the video cassette recorder, and also videodiscs, video enhancers, video cameras, video stabilizers, converters, signal boosters, distribution amplifiers, and so on.

CONNECTING A VIDEODISC PLAYER

There is more than one way to connect a videodisc player to a TV set, one involving an A/B switch, one doing without it, and one using different kinds of switches. The first illustration of this video connection is in Fig. 5–21A.

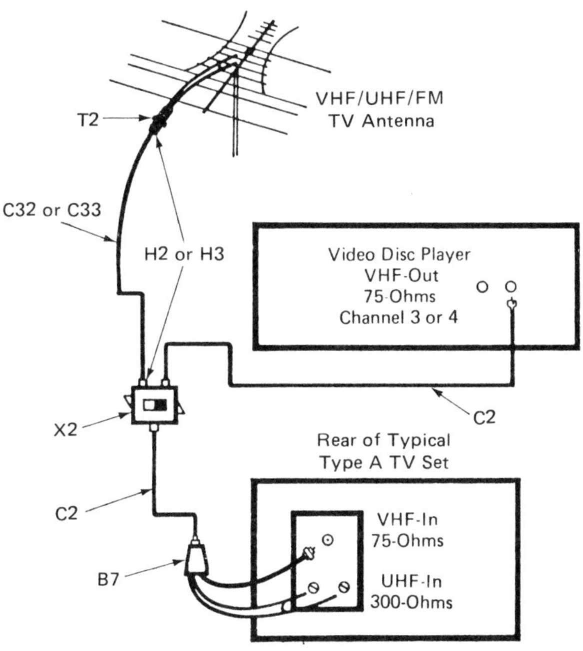

Some Types of Videodisc Players (Pioneer and Magnavision, to Name Two) do not Allow UHF Signals to Pass Through to your TV Set. In Order to use your Set for UHF Reception and for Viewing Videodisc Player Programs, you will Need a Hookup Similar to the Kind Used for TV Games. An X2 Two-Way Switch in the Signal Transmission Circuit Lets you Select Regular TV Reception or a Videodisc Player Program.

Quantity	Code	Components Required
1	T2	300- to 75-Ohm Transformer (Balun) for Outside Use
1	C32 or C33	25-ft, or 50-ft, Bulk 75-Ohm Coaxial Down-lead Cable (without Connectors)
2	H2	F Type Crimp-on Connectors for 75-Ohm Coaxial Cable (Above)
or		
2	H3	F Type Twist-on Connectors for 75-Ohm Coaxial Cable (Above)
1	X2	2-Way 75-Ohm Antenna Switch
2	C2	6-ft 75-Ohm Coaxial Cables with F Plugs at Both Ends;
1	B7	75- to 75/300-Ohm Transformer (Balun) and UHF/VHF Band Separator

(A)

Figure 5–21A. Connecting a videodisc player. (*Courtesy GC Electronics*)

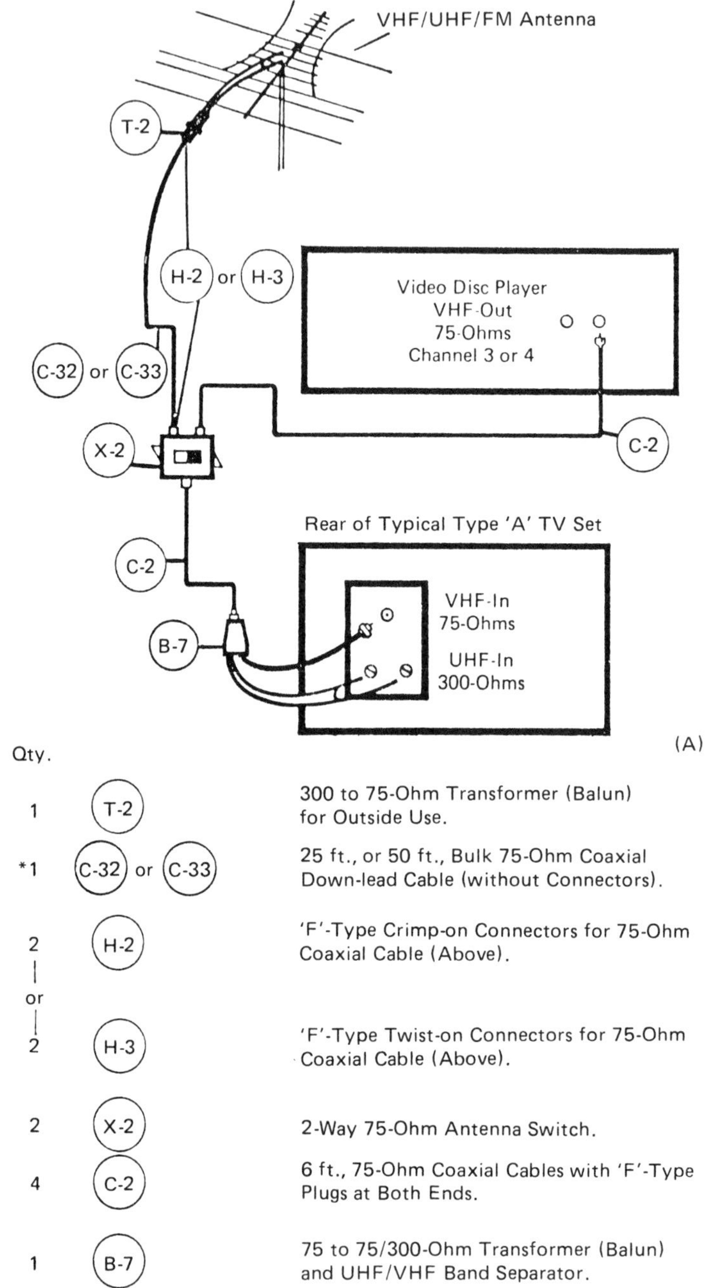

Figure 5-21B. Alternate methods of connecting a videodisc player. (*Courtesy GC Electronics*)

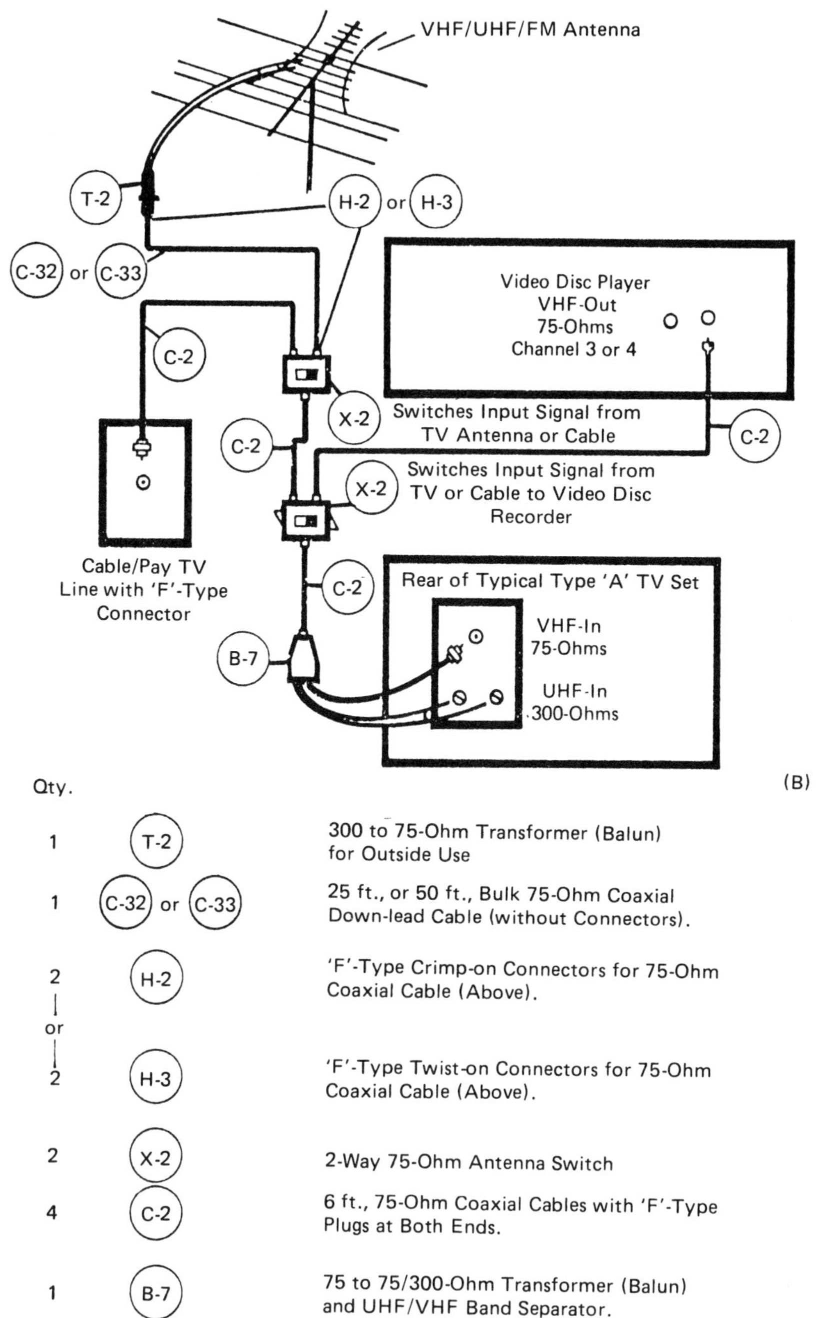
VHF/UHF/FM Antenna
T-2
H-2 or H-3
C-32 or C-33
Video Disc Player
VHF-Out
75-Ohms
Channel 3 or 4
C-2
X-2
Switches Input Signal from
TV Antenna or Cable
C-2
C-2
X-2
Switches Input Signal from
TV or Cable to Video Disc
Recorder
Cable/Pay TV
Line with 'F'-Type
Connector
C-2
Rear of Typical Type 'A' TV Set
VHF-In
75-Ohms
B-7
UHF-In
300-Ohms
(B)
Qty.
1 T-2 300 to 75-Ohm Transformer (Balun) for Outside Use
1 C-32 or C-33 25 ft., or 50 ft., Bulk 75-Ohm Coaxial Down-lead Cable (without Connectors).
2 H-2 'F'-Type Crimp-on Connectors for 75-Ohm Coaxial Cable (Above).
or
2 H-3 'F'-Type Twist-on Connectors for 75-Ohm Coaxial Cable (Above).
2 X-2 2-Way 75-Ohm Antenna Switch
4 C-2 6 ft., 75-Ohm Coaxial Cables with 'F'-Type Plugs at Both Ends.
1 B-7 75 to 75/300-Ohm Transformer (Balun) and UHF/VHF Band Separator.

Figure 5–21B. *(continued)*

Using an A/B switch, the user has a choice of broadcast TV programs or those supplied by the disc. The antenna, with an output of 300 ohms, is connected via a 300-ohm to 75-ohm transformer to the coaxial transmission line. The transmission line and videodisc output are wired to the two input terminals of the A/B switch. The output of the switch leads into a suitable length of coaxial cable equipped with F-type twist-on connectors. A matching transformer, identified as B7, having a 75-ohm input, and 300-ohm and 75-ohm outputs is connected to the 75-ohm VHF and 300-ohm UHF antenna terminals of the TV set.

With the wiring arrangement shown in Fig. 5-21A, the TV set can be tuned to any channel, and—as long as the A/B switch (identified as X2) is in its correct setting—the TV set is completely independent of the disc player and any channel can be selected, either manually or via remote control.

Figure 5-21B shows other ways of connecting a videodisc player. Drawing A shows how to connect a videodisc player to a TV system that has an outdoor VHF/UHF TV antenna. Drawing B shows how to connect a videodisc player to a TV system that has an outdoor VHF/UHF TV antenna and a cable TV line.

An alternate setup is shown in Fig. 5-22 with an arrangement that eliminates the A/B switch. The antenna uses a matching transformer at point A (should such a transformer be needed), with the transmission line connected to a band separator at B. The UHF signals are brought out of the separator

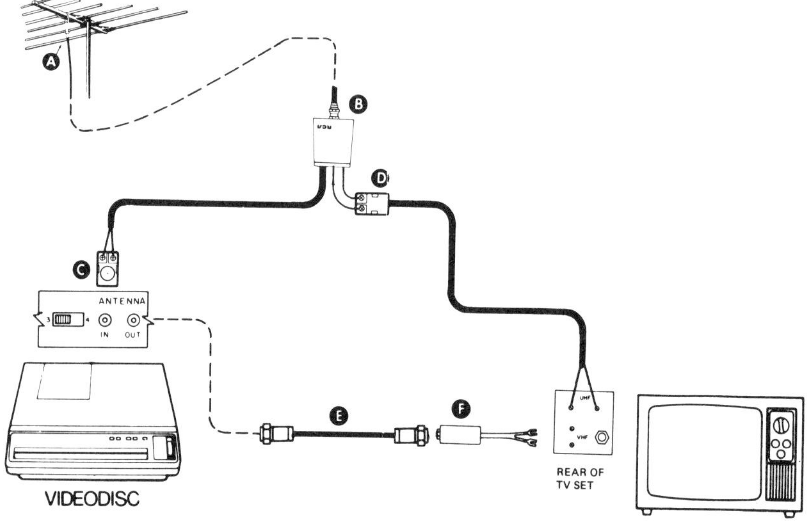

Figure 5-22. Connections for an antenna and videodisc player to a TV set without an A/B switcher. Add-ons include an outdoor balun (A); band separator (B); balun (C) twin lead splicer (D); coaxial cable equipped with F-connectors (E); 75-ohm to 300-ohm matching transformer (F). Not all these may be required. (*Courtesy RCA*)

via a short length of twin lead. This can be connected directly to the 300-ohm UHF antenna terminals on the TV set. Since the twin lead from the band separator is so short, just a few inches, an additional length of twin lead will probably be needed to connect the band separator's UHF output to the TV set. This is indicated by part D and can be a twin-lead connecting block like the one described in Chapter 3.

The VHF output of the band separator is brought to the VHF antenna input terminal on the back of the videodisc player. The output of the disc player is connected, via a length of coaxial cable, F-connector equipped at both ends, to the VHF input of the TV set, using a balun (F).

With this setup, the disc player must be set to either channel 3 or channel 4, whichever is not used for broadcast TV reception. If, for example, this is channel 3, the disc player is set to this channel and so is the TV set when the videodisc player is to be used. As far as the TV set is concerned, the videodisc is just another signal. The TV set can be tuned to all VHF and UHF channels, either manually or via a remote control device. Since the videodisc player utilizes an unused channel there is no program loss.

The connections in Figures 5-21 and 5-22 emphasize an important point—there is sometimes more than one way to interconnect video components.

Figure 5-23 shows the basic arrangement for connecting a videodisc player to a TV set. All other inputs, such as an antenna signal, TV game, or personal computer, have been omitted, and for this reason no A/B switches or baluns or signal splitters have been included.

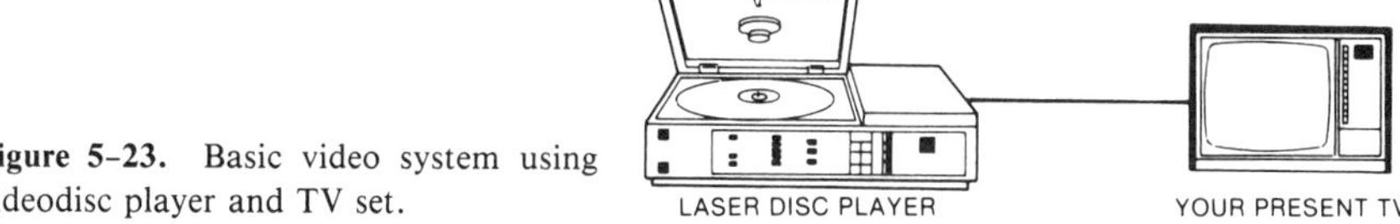

Figure 5-23. Basic video system using videodisc player and TV set.

In this diagram, the modulated signal output of the disc player is connected directly to the VHF antenna input terminal of the TV receiver. The channel is selected by a slide switch on the rear of the player, and is either channel 3 or channel 4; the tuner of the TV set must be set to the same channel. Once this is done, no further adjustments are needed except for the usual operating controls on the TV. Neither remote control of the TV set nor manual switching is required.

Another technique for using the disc player is illustrated in Fig. 5-24. The modulated signal is brought into the VHF antenna input terminal of the TV set. In addition, the audio output is brought into the input terminals of a preamplifier or an integrated amplifier. A stereo receiver can also be used if it has audio input terminals. Some do; some do not.

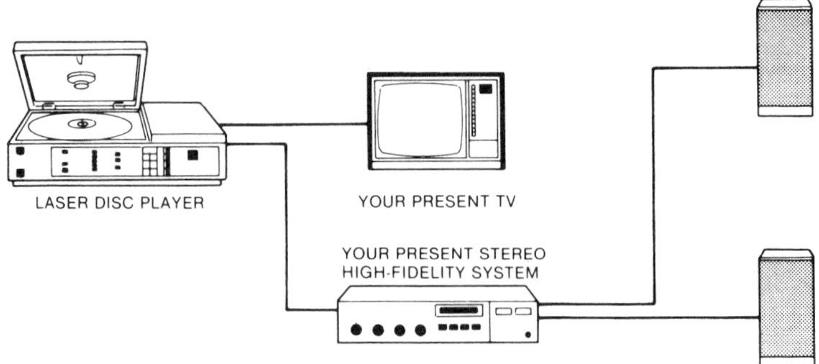

Figure 5–24. Video system using videodisc player and TV set combined with stereo high-fidelity system.

There is one minor problem with this setup: sound will also come out of the TV receiver's speaker. To avoid that possibility simply turn down the volume control on that receiver.

Figure 5–25A is an overall view of a system using not only a disc player but a VCR and a color monitor. Since the monitor has no RF tuning section, it uses a separate outboard tuner. The combination of tuner and monitor is the equivalent of an integrated TV set, but there are a number of differences. The monitor, combined with the outboard tuner, has far more inputs than a TV set, and unlike a TV set, is also equipped with output terminals. Further, the tuner is not only capable of signal selection, but works as a control unit, that is, as a switcher for the connection of signal sources. It can, for example, switch in the high-fidelity system for sound output from the disc player, the VCR, or broadcast TV—although broadcast TV is not indicated in the drawing. Consequently, while a picture is being watched on the screen of the monitor, the sound of a TV broadcast can be heard via the high-fidelity speakers.

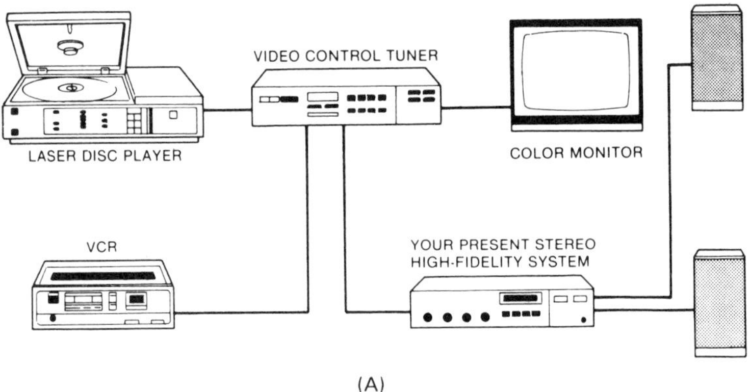

Figure 5–25A. Audio-video system using video disc player and VCR.

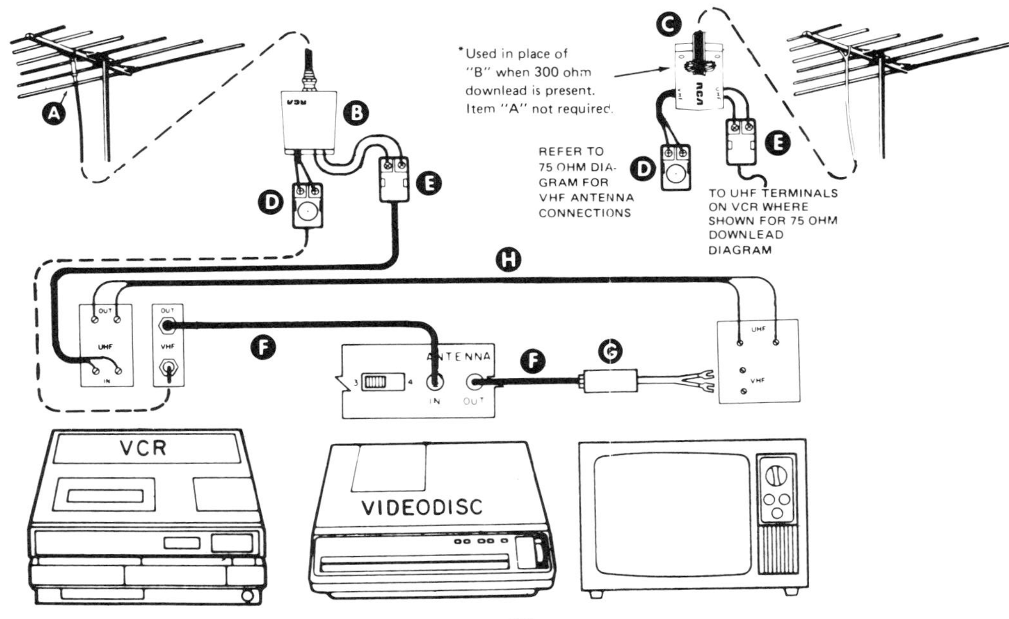

(B)

Figure 5–25B. Connections for a VCR, videodisc, and antenna. The drawing at the left is for 75-ohm downlead: (A) balun; (B) band separator; (C) band separator; (D) balun; (E) lead extension; (F) two cables; (G) balun (not required when TV receiver has 75-ohm input); (H) approximately 10 feet of 300-ohm twin lead. (*Courtesy RCA*)

The wiring diagram in Fig. 5-25B shows the connections when a videodisc, a VCR, and a broadcast TV antenna are used. The drawing at the upper left indicates the use of coaxial cable as the downlead; that at the right uses 300-ohm twin lead. Since the output impedance of the antenna is 300 ohms, no matching transformer is required for the antenna hookup at the right.

From the antenna the VHF and UHF signals are brought to the input terminals of the VCR. The UHF signals are delivered directly from the VCR to the UHF input side of the antenna block on the TV set. The VHF signals, though, from the VCR are first supplied to the antenna input of the videodisc player and are then brought to the VHF antenna terminals of the TV receiver using a 75-ohm to 300-ohm balun.

With the addition of a videodisc player to a system consisting of broadcast TV, one or possibly two outboard converters, a VCR, and cable TV, we are well on our way to a component-style in-home entertainment center. These can be quite varied and the block diagram in Fig. 5-26 is just one concept.

This system has as its center feature a projection television set (PTV) although a direct-view receiver, a receiver/monitor, or a monitor could be used instead. While this block diagram does indicate the components of the system, it has no great value other than that of an overall view. It does not show, for example, how the various components are to be switched, nor does it supply any information about how the components are to be connected. Further, al-

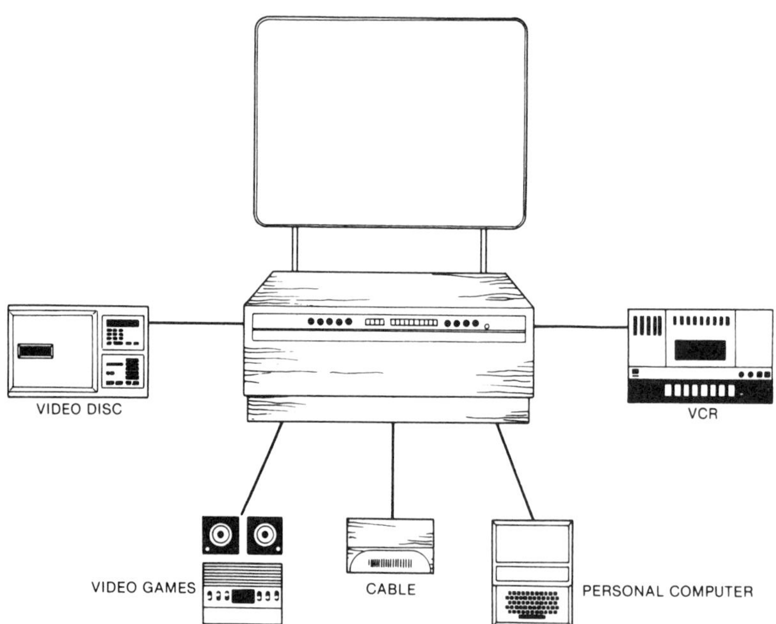

Figure 5-26. Home entertainment center using PTV.

though this system shows the use of a personal computer (PC) it is rather unlikely that a PTV would be used as the display.

Although they are not shown in the block diagram, there could also be additional components such as a video fader, a guard stabilizer, an image enhancer, or an advertising commercial eliminator. These components are intended for improving the fine detail in a picture, for improving color, or for the automatic elimination of commercial advertising.

Newer videodisc players have stereo output instead of mono. The connections from the player are the same with the exception of two terminals; one for left-channel sound (L), the other for right-channel (R). These terminals are wired to the L and R sound terminals on the connector block of a TV receiver/monitor or to the aux input terminals of a high-fidelity system's preamplifier.

Connecting a Three-Way Switcher and a Videodisc

A three-way switcher is a stopgap measure between an A/B switch and a multiple port switcher. An important spec with these switchers is the amount of leakage between signal sources. All of the input signals to the switcher must be RF, for the unit does not demodulate and then remodulate. Remote control can be used with the TV set when the switcher is set to TV broadcast, but not when cable TV or videodisc signals are being used. Although it is not shown in Fig. 5-27, a balun may be required between the output of the switcher and the VHF input to the TV set. The input ports of the switcher are all F-type and so a balun may also be needed between the antenna downlead and the terminal used on the switcher for broadcast.

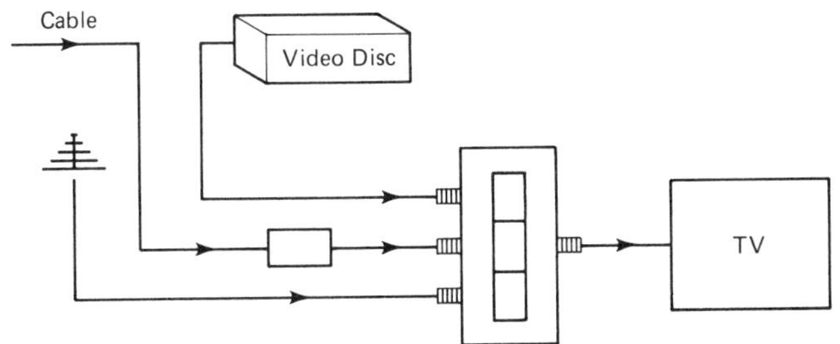

Figure 5-27. Connections for three-way switcher. Signal sources are videodisc, cable TV, and broadcast TV antenna.

Connecting a Videodisc Player and an Impedance-Matching Switcher

A multiple-impedance switcher can be used with a videodisc player (Fig. 5-28). No balun is required in the antenna downlead, for the switcher can accept either 75-ohm cable or 300-ohm twin lead at its input ports. The video-

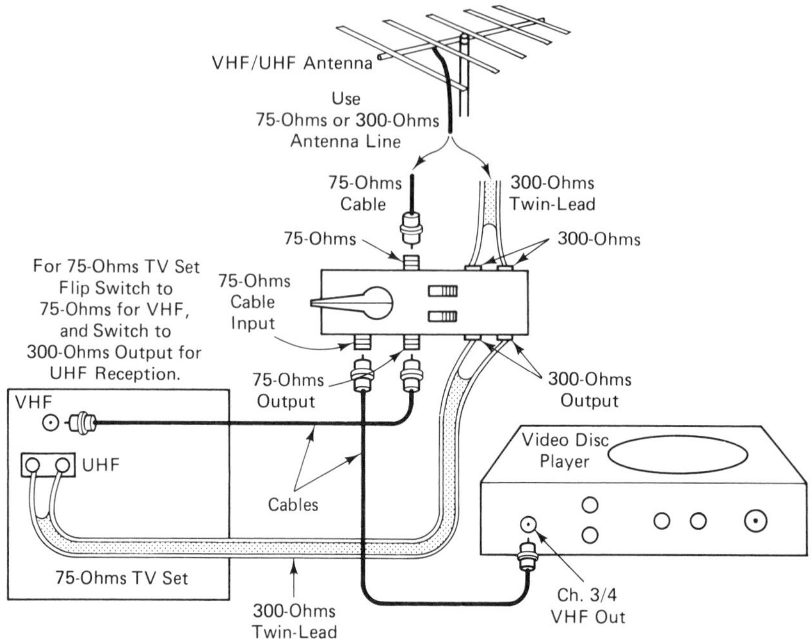

Figure 5–28. Connections for videodisc player with impedance-matching A/B switch.

disc player supplies either channel 3 or channel 4 RF signals connected by coaxial cable to the 75-ohm input port of the switcher. The switcher has a 300-ohm output port connected by a length of twin lead to the 300-ohm UHF input of the TV set.

Connecting a Videodisc Player, TV, and Cable Using an Impedance-Matching Switcher

The A/B impedance switcher can be used with three signal sources, including a videodisc player, cable, and broadcast TV (Fig. 5–29). Although the switcher is the same as that shown in the preceding drawing, its use is different. The antenna input must be 300 ohms. If coaxial cable is used as the downlead, a 75-ohm to 300-ohm balun must be inserted into that line. The switcher uses three input ports to accommodate the three signal sources. For broadcast TV, it is 300 ohms, but it is 75 ohms for cable and videodisc. If the TV set has a 75-ohm input, flip the switch output to 75 ohms for VHF reception or to 300 ohms for UHF.

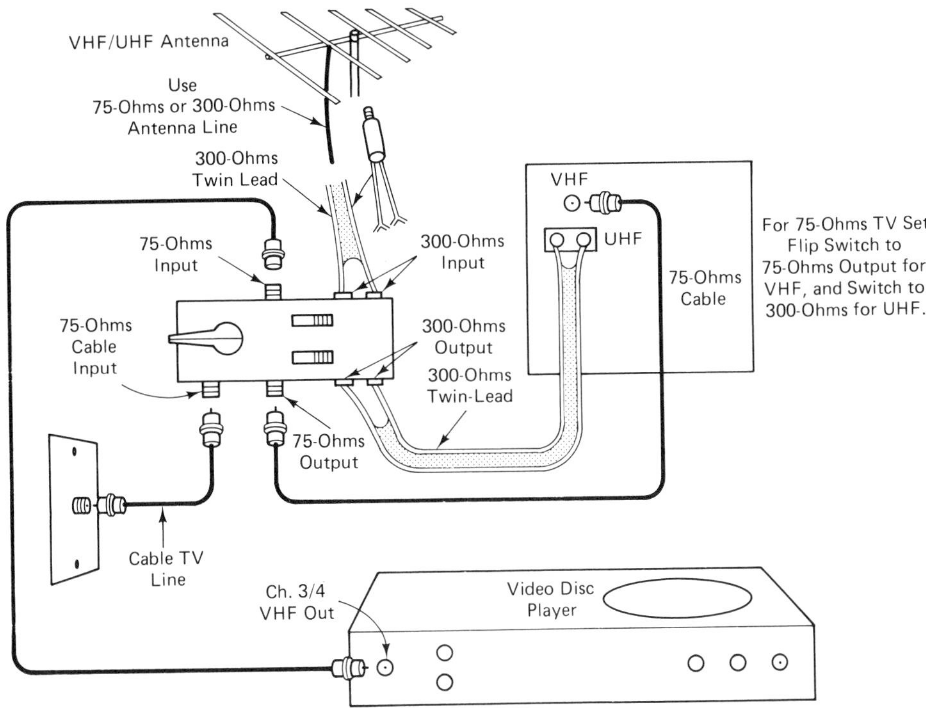

Figure 5-29. Antenna, cable TV, and videodisc player used with impedance-matching A/B switch.

Connecting a Portable TV Set to a Videodisc Player

A portable TV set can be connected to outboard components, but the problem with making such a wiring arrangement is that both the player and the TV set must be carried (Fig. 5-30). While this isn't impossible, it could be awkward. The alternative is to disconnect the videodisc player if the TV set is to be used as a portable.

Connect the leads of the rabbit ear antenna to one end of the 300-ohm extension line (point B) and the other end of that line to a 300-ohm to 75-ohm balun (A) for connection to the antenna input terminal of the videodisc player. The output of the player is connected by a length of coaxial cable (C) to the VHF input terminals of the TV set via a 75-ohm to 300 ohm balun (D). For broadcast UHF reception, the small bowtie antenna (or circular UHF antenna) can remain connected to the UHF antenna terminals on the TV set. When you are using the videodisc player, set the TV set to either channel 3 or channel 4. The telescoping antenna remains internally connected to the TV set's VHF input. To receive broadcast VHF signals, turn the videodisc player off.

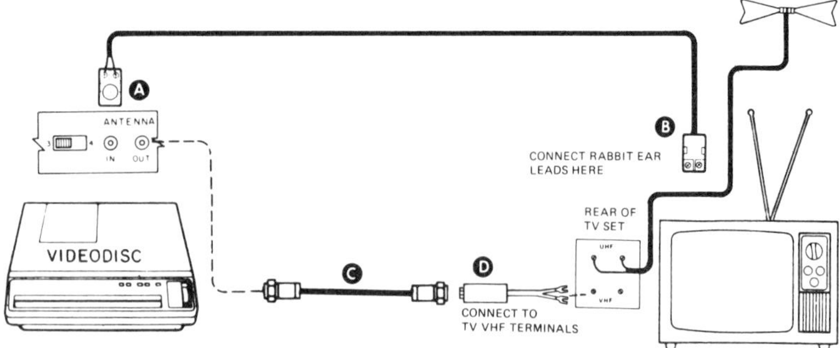

Figure 5–30. Connecting a videodisc player to a portable TV: (A) matching transformer; (B) 300-ohm extension line; (C) coaxial cable; (D) balun, 75 ohms to 300 ohms. This add-on isn't required if the TV set has a 75-ohm VHF input. (*Courtesy RCA*)

PROJECTION TELEVISION CONNECTIONS

There are various ways of getting a larger picture. The most obvious is to use a direct-view TV set having a large screen. The largest of these has a screen diameter of 30 inches. Another method is to mount a Fresnel lens in front of the screen. Unlike earlier oil-filled lenses, the Fresnel is lightweight and flat, and it is supplied with a mounting frame. The lens is put in front of the screen, and has no connections to the TV set. The third method is to use a projection TV (PTV) receiver.

The problem with all picture-magnifying methods is that they enlarge picture faults as well as the picture. Thus you need a quality high-gain antenna, rotator equipped. Pay careful attention to impedance matching, using coaxial cable as the downlead, plus noise filters (if required).

There are five types of picture display units that can be used as the central focus of an in-home system: the direct-view TV set, the combined TV receiver/monitor, the monitor, a projection TV (PTV), or a PTV/monitor. The advantage of a monitor is that it has a larger number of inputs than a direct-view TV set, and it has the capability of better horizontal resolution. Some PTVs or PTV/monitors have more signal input possibilities and supply a much larger picture than either direct-view or monitor sets. Other PTVs are like direct-view sets in their input signal limitations, and as is shown in drawing A in Fig. 5–31, have only 300-ohm twin-lead inputs for VHF and UHF signals. (The exception is a PTV/monitor, similar to a TV receiver/monitor but having a much larger screen.)

Drawing B illustrates coaxial cable input for VHF with twin lead used

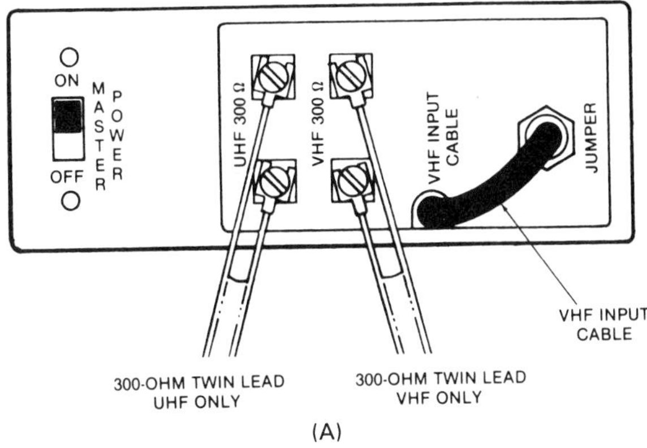

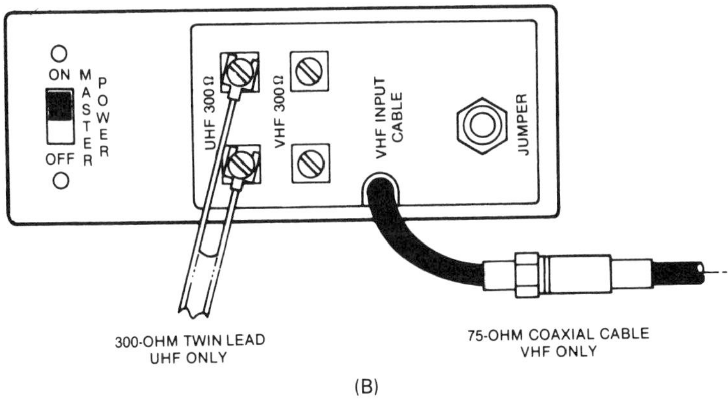

Figure 5-31. Antenna input connections for a projection TV receiver. (*Courtesy Kloss Video Corp.*)

for UHF. Figure 5-32A shows some of the possible signal sources that can be used with a PTV having multiple input terminals, and Fig. 5-32B illustrates a PTV with a videodisc player.

Unlike an ordinary TV receiver, the PTV is equipped with an input/output panel instead of a limited input arrangement only. Further, it permits the connection of outboard components and in Fig. 5-32B these are shown as a video cassette recorder, and a videodisc player. There are also connections for an outside antenna. The advantage of this arrangement is that it eliminates the need for an external switcher.

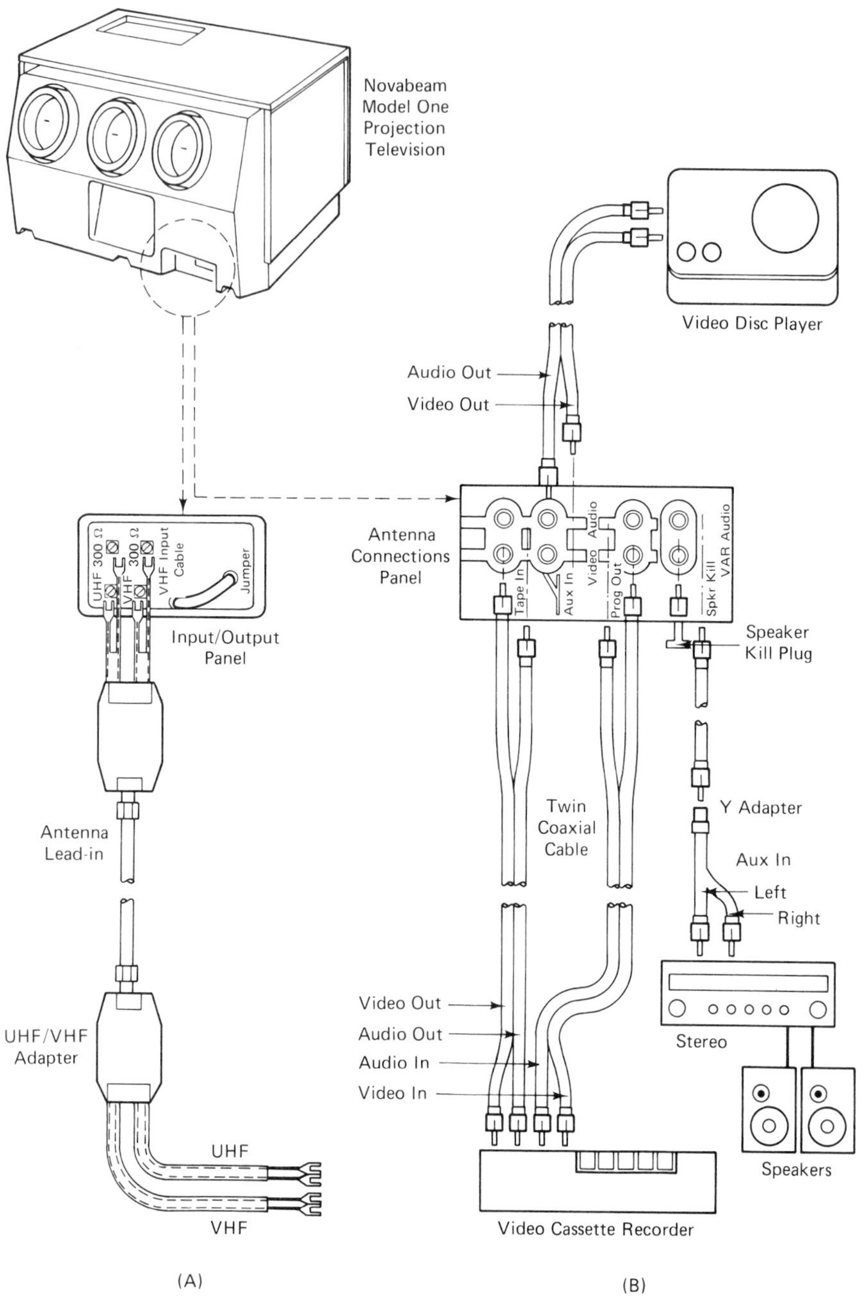

Figure 5-32. Antenna connections for a PTV (A); PTV as part of a video/audio system (B). (*Courtesy Kloss Video Corp.*)

Connecting the PTV to a High-Fidelity System

The PTV may have monophonic sound, but in later units it has a stereo sound capability. Figure 5-33 shows how to connect left and right channel sound to an external high-fidelity system. The connecting cables used are standard audio cables, using shield braid as the ground lead. The connections are made to the audio input terminals of a high-fidelity receiver, a preamplifier, an integrated power amplifier, or an audio tape recorder.

If the audio output of the PTV is monophonic, use a Y-adapter (as shown in Fig. 5-32B) to deliver synthetic stereo to the high-fidelity system. With either type of sound, mono or stereo, turn the PTV's speaker to its off position if the PTV is equipped with a sound-off switch.

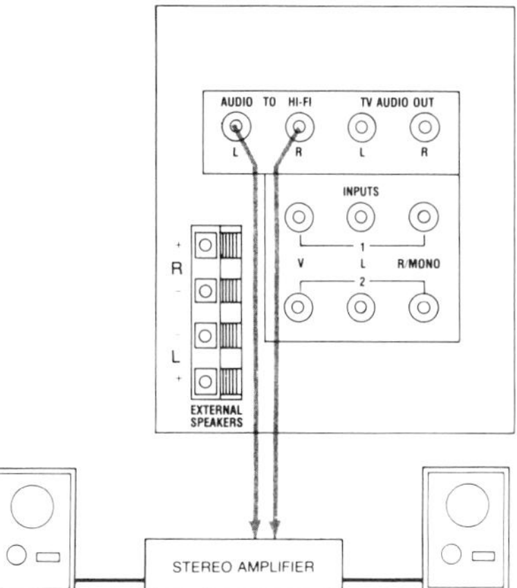

Figure 5-33. When a PTV has a stereo amplifier the audio's left and right sound channels can be delivered to the aux input of a stereo amplifier. (*Courtesy RCA*)

Connecting a PTV to External Speakers

A PTV capable of delivering stereophonic sound (Fig. 5-34) is equipped with a pair of left/right audio power amplifiers. In some PTVs there are terminals for connecting this audio to external speakers. However, because of the low level of the audio power output of the PTV, it is advisable to use high-efficiency speakers. The output impedance across the external speaker terminals is 8 ohms, so the left and right speakers should have a voice-coil impedance of this amount.

The connecting wires to the speakers can be 18-gauge insulated multi-stranded wire. No special connectors are needed. All that is required is to strip the wire ends and use the connectors provided on the PTV and the speakers, and often these are springloaded. The PTV may have a switch to be set to "external speakers."

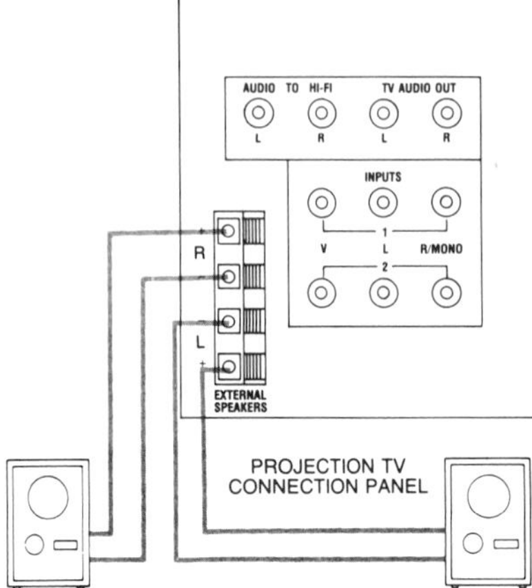

Figure 5-34. Connecting a PTV to external speakers. (*Courtesy RCA*)

Each of the external speakers will have some identification on the terminals indicating plus and minus. This can consist of a plus symbol (+), a red dot, or the abbreviation "pos." Connect this terminal to the corresponding plus terminal on the PTV audio output terminal. For external speakers always connect plus to plus and minus to minus.

Because of the low-power output of the PTV, it is inadvisable to use multiple speakers, that is, two or more speakers for left-channel sound, and a similar number of speakers for right-channel sound.

PTV Surveillance Connections

Like a monitor, a PTV has input terminals for video signals (unmodulated) and can accept signals directly from a video camera without using a VCR or an external modulator. Figure 5-35 shows how a pair of video cameras can be used either for surveillance in a business or for picture taking in the home. The AC-operated camera power supply comes equipped with the nec-

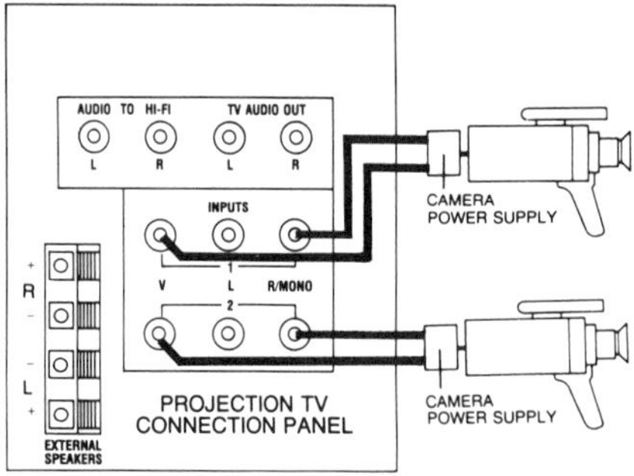

Figure 5-35. PTV for surveillance using two cameras. (*Courtesy RCA*)

essary cables, and if these are compatible with the PTV's input ports no additional wiring will be required. If not, then a camera cable adapter will be required. Of the pair of cameras shown in Fig. 5-35, one or the other, or both, can be used. Further, there is a greater choice of cameras, as they can deliver color signals, or black-and-white, or a mix of the two. The usual camera surveillance system (closed-circuit TV or CCTV) uses monochrome cameras only. The cameras can be mounted on an oscillating plate support to supply a sweep picture, or they can be in a fixed position.

Connecting a PTV to a Computer

If the computer has a regular NTSC (National Television Systems Committee) video output (an unmodulated signal), it can be connected to the same video inputs as a video camera (Fig. 5-36). The outputs of the computer, including video and audio, are wired to the V (video) terminal and to one of the two audio terminals, marked L and R (left and right). For monophonic sound, either of these two sound terminals can be used. For stereo sound, both the L and R terminals must be connected to the input sound signal. For monophonic audio, it is preferable to use the R/mono input terminal, as with this connection, both of the PTV's speakers will operate.

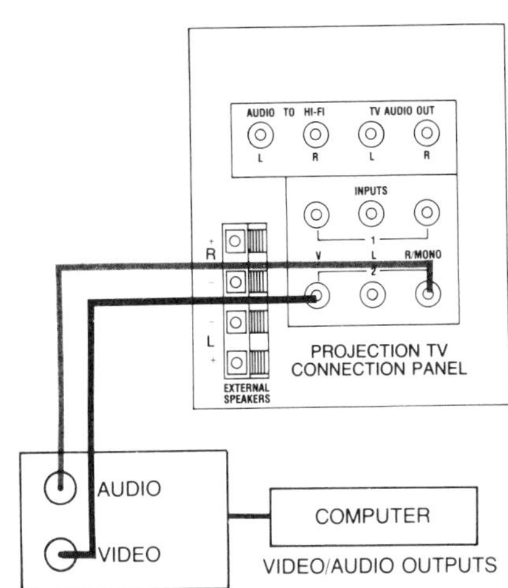

Figure 5-36. Connecting a computer to a PTV. (*Courtesy RCA*)

Connecting the PTV to an A/B Switch

An A/B switch can be used with a PTV unit just as it is with direct-viewing TV sets. Figure 5-37 shows how the signals from a TV game or an antenna signal (or cable TV) can be selected. The rectangle at the left represents the antenna input terminal of the PTV. This means all signals delivered

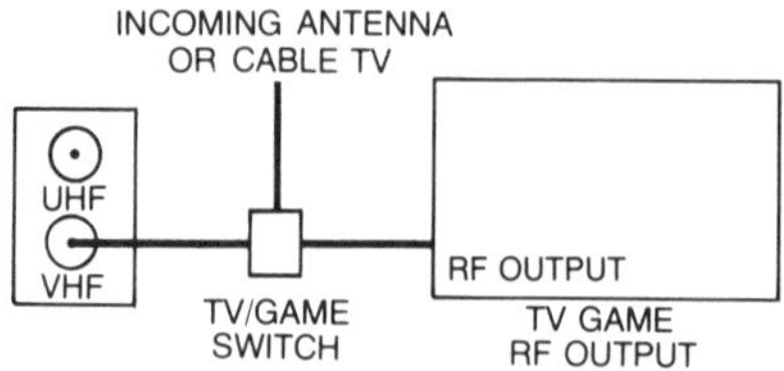

Figure 5-37. Using an A/B switch with a PTV. (*Courtesy RCA*)

to this port must be RF, a modulated signal. The VHF antenna terminal on the PTV is connected to the output terminal of the A/B switch, identified here as a TV/Game Switch. The connection between the switch and the VHF terminal is usually a short length of coaxial cable. A matching transformer between the output port of the A/B switch and the VHF input of the PTV may need to be connected, depending on the impedance of the VHF input and the A/B switch output.

One of the input ports of the A/B switch is connected to the output terminal of the TV game. This output must be RF; if it is not, it must be brought into a modulator. This modulator could be a separate component, or a VCR could be used.

The second input to the A/B switch is from an antenna, and as this signal is always RF, no signal modulation is required. The antenna connection assumes a VHF antenna only. A separate downlead from a UHF antenna could also be used and would then be connected to the UHF antenna terminal.

If the computer has an ouput that is RF (modulated video), it can be connected to the antenna input terminals of the PTV. An impedance-matching transformer may be required, depending on the output impedance of the computer and the input impedance of the PTV. If both have the same impedance, often 75 ohms, then a suitable length of coaxial cable, possibly F-connector equipped, should do.

Connecting a PTV to a VCR

The usual VCR has two types of output signals—modulated and unmodulated. The modulated signals are used for direct-view TV sets, but a PTV is more like a TV receiver/monitor and can accept modulated or unmodulated signals.

Figure 5-38 shows this in more detail. The VHF broadcast signal is brought into the VCR's VHF antenna terminals and if a separate UHF antenna is used, its signal output is delivered to the UHF input terminals of the VCR. In the VCR, the UHF signals are remodulated and are then delivered to the PTV's UHF antenna terminals. The VHF signals, however, are not remodulated and are supplied as video to the video input terminal (V) on the PTV's connection panel. The stereo sound signal is supplied from the L/R ports of the VCR to the left (L) and right (R) audio input ports on the connection panel of the PTV.

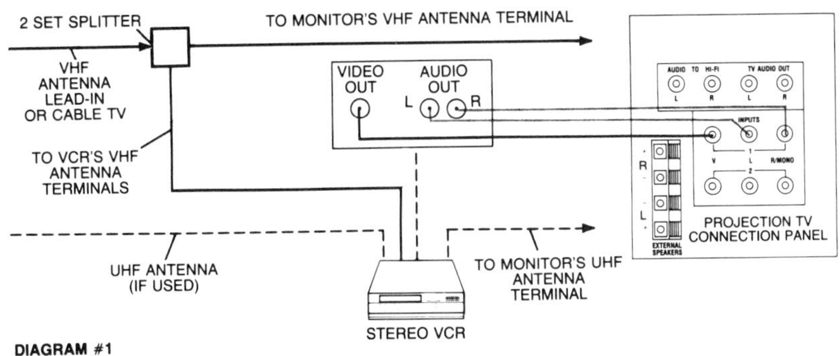

Figure 5-38. Connecting a PTV to a VCR. (*Courtesy RCA*)

Connecting a PTV to an Audio Tape Recorder

The TV "Audio out" left and right sound channels on the PTV supply a sound signal that can be recorded on tape. The connections are shown in Fig. 5-39. For making these connections, as well as those in Fig. 5-33, use audio cables equipped with RCA jacks. With the connections in Fig. 5-39, the sound level will not be affected by the volume and mute controls on the TV receiver.

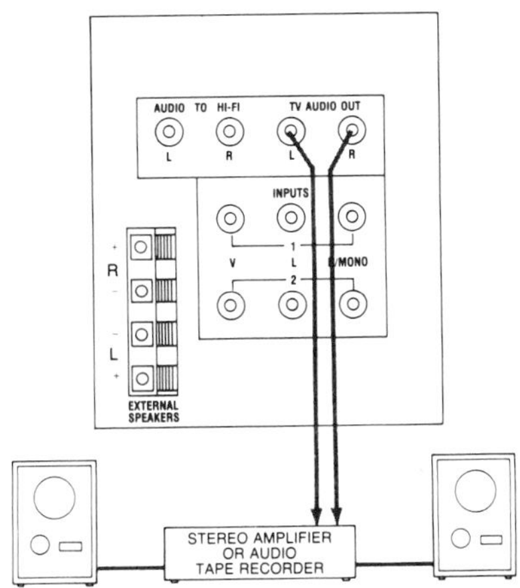

Figure 5-39. Connecting a PTV to a tape recorder. (*Courtesy RCA*)

CONNECTING A HOME COMPUTER OR A VIDEO GAME

When a household decides to become a two-television-set residence, the question sometimes arises as to what to do with the original, and now outdated, TV set that is still working well. That first TV set may be a black-and-white unit, perhaps not too desirable for TV, but well suited as a display device for a home computer. Without color, it is not as desirable for a video game, but if it is a color TV set—even though it may have a small screen—it can serve well. It will also release the main TV set for its primary purpose of watching either broadcast or cable TV.

Figure 5-40 shows a simplified wiring diagram. With this arrangement the user has a choice of using either a home computer or a video game, but not both. The assumption is made that both outboard units, the video game or the home computer, can supply an RF signal (a modulated signal) suitable for input to the TV set. Signals are also supplied by a VCR, but a broadcast TV antenna could be used in its place. A single two-way A/B switch is used, identified as CV95. Ordinary audio shielded cable can be the connecting link between the home computer or video game, with the wire ending in an RCA plug for insertion into the input jack of the switch.

The other input to the switch is from the VCR. The UHF and VHF outputs of the VCR are brought into a band combiner, shown as CV67. The output of this add-on consists of the VHF and UHF signals from the VCR delivered via a short length of 300-ohm twin lead. Thus the A/B switch can choose either input from the VCR or a home computer, or a video game instead of the computer. The single output of the switch is fed into a band separator and from there to the UHF and VHF antenna terminals of the TV set.

Not shown in the drawing is the input to the VCR. This can be the VHF and UHF signals from an antenna. If separate downleads are used, the connections to the input of the VCR can be made directly. With a single downlead, a band separator will be required. To monitor a broadcast TV program being

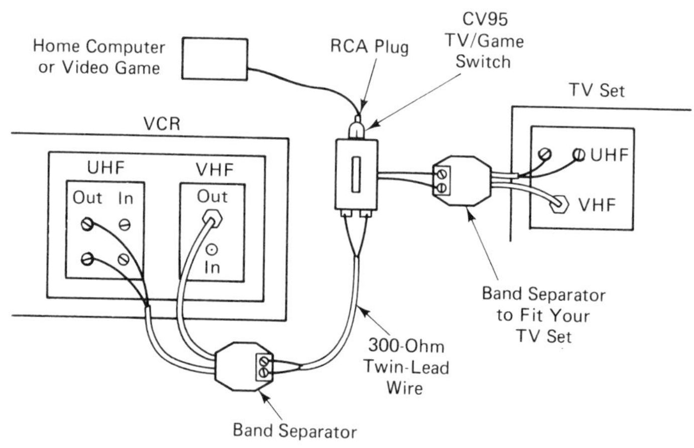

Figure 5-40. Connections for home computer or video game. (*Courtesy Gemini Industries, Inc.*)

recorded, set the switch to its TV position. To play a video game or use a home computer, set the same switch to its "game" or "computer" position.

With this setup, tuning of the broadcast signals is done by the VCR, with the TV set arranged for either channel 3 or channel 4 pickup.

A TV set, possibly a black-and-white unit, no longer being used for broadcast TV reception can be used as a dedicated monitor for a home computer and a video game by following the diagram in Fig. 5–41A.

Figure 5–41A actually shows four different hookups, with the two upper ones marked A, the two lower drawings B. The basic differences are in the kinds of downleads used and the differences in input ports of the TV sets.

The TV game (upper left drawing) and the home computer are both connected to individual input ports of a coaxial A/B switch. The output of this switch (X2) is connected to one of the input ports of a second A/B switch (X3). The remaining input port of that switch is wired to the twin lead transmission line from the antenna. The signal output of X3 is wired to the VHF input of the TV set via a 300-ohm to 75-ohm matching transformer, T3.

The drawing at the upper right uses a coaxial cable downlead and requires a matching transformer, T1. It also uses a matching transformer, T2, at the antenna. Other than these minor differences, the two hookups are the same.

Another hookup along these lines is illustrated in Fig. 5–41B. The signal sources are the same and consist of TV broadcast, a personal computer, and a TV game. With this suggested arrangement, just a single A/B coaxial switch is required. There is a disadvantage, though, for the home computer and the TV game must be connected every time they are to be used. It is this repeated manual connection and disconnection method that replaces one of the coaxial A/B switches.

Not shown in Fig. 5–41B are impedance-matching transformers, and while their omission may simplify the hookup, they may be required.

CONNECTING AN RF MODULATOR

The antenna input terminals of a TV set can accept only one type of signal and that is radio-frequency (RF) modulated video and sound. This consists of picture and sound modulated onto a carrier whose frequency is either in the VHF or UHF TV broadcast bands.

However, there are a number of components whose signal outputs are not modulated, such as a video enhancer or video camera, thus presenting the problem of how to get their outputs into a TV set. A VCR is often used, as this component supplies modulated output, generally using the carrier frequency of either channel 3 or channel 4, while a few do use channels 5 or 6.

An RF modulator is an outboard component, containing, as its name indicates, a modulator circuit so that the TV set can accept direct video and

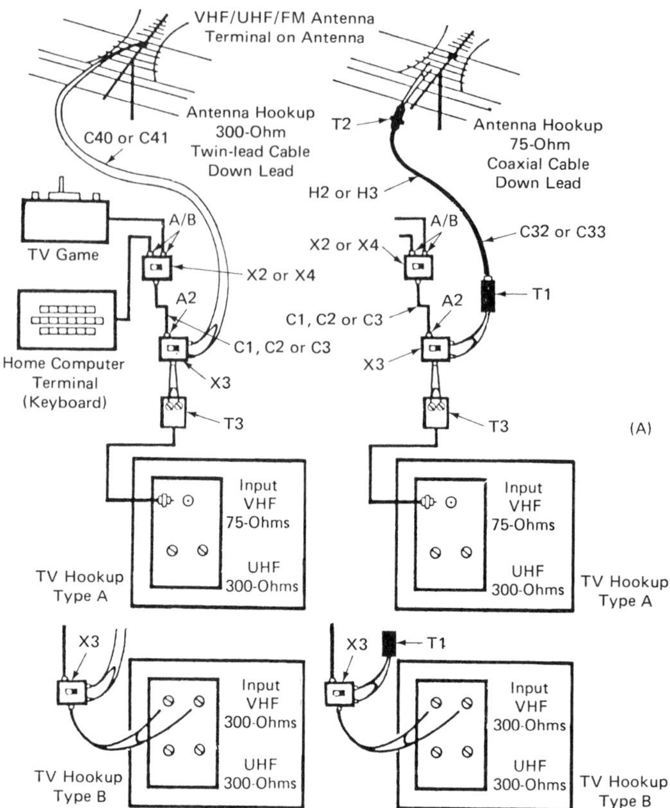

300-Ohm Antenna Hookup

Quantity	Code	Components Required
1	A2	Adapter, F-Jack to Phono (RCA) Plug
2	AB	Adapter, Phono (RCA) Jack to F-Plug
1	C40 or C41	50-ft, or 75-ft, Bulk 300-Ohm Foam-filled Twin-lead Down-lead Cable
1	C1, C2 or C3	3-ft, 6-ft, or 12-ft., 75-Ohm Coaxial Cables with F-Plugs on Both Ends
1	T3	300- to 75-Ohm Matching Transformer
1	X2 or X4	2-Way 75-Ohm Antenna Switch or A/B Switch
1	X3	TV/Video Game Switch

75-Ohm Antenna Hookup

Quantity	Code	Components Required
1	A2	Adapter, F-Jack to Phono (RCA) Plug
2	AB	Adapter, Phono (RCA) Jack to F-Plug
1	C32 or C33	25-ft, or 50-ft, Bulk 75-Ohm Coaxial Cable Down-lead (without Connectors)
1	C1, C2 or C3	3-ft, 6-ft, or 12-ft, 75-Ohm Coaxial Cables with F-Plugs on Both Ends
2	H2	F-Type Crimp-on Connectors
or		
2	H3	F-Type Twist-on Connectors
1	T1	75- to 300-Ohm Indoor Matching Transformer
1*	T3	300- to 75-Ohm Matching Transformer
1	X2 or X4	2-Way 75-Ohm Antenna Switch or A/B Switch
1	X3	TV/Video Game Switch

(A)

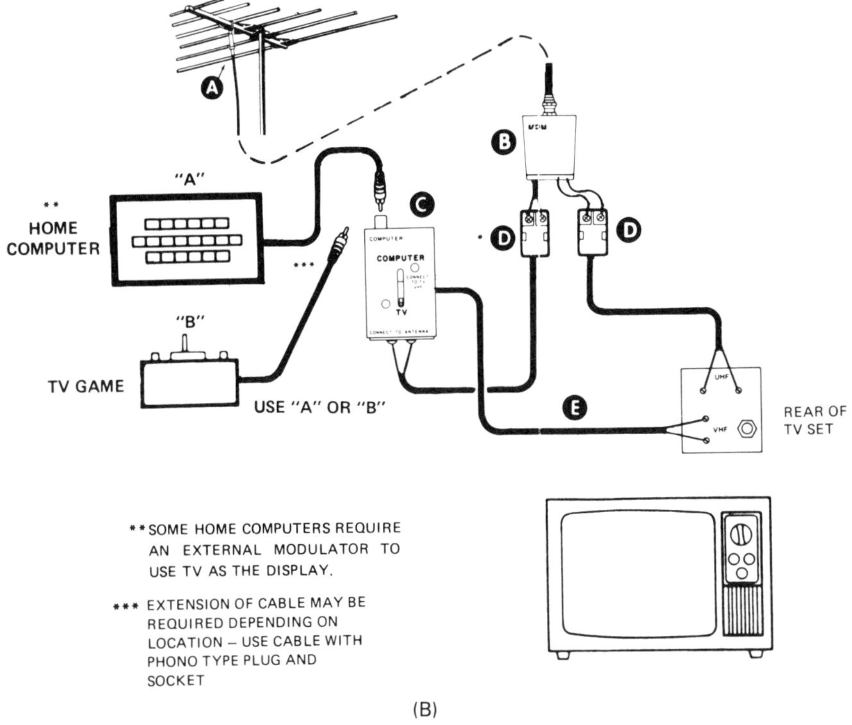

Figure 5–41B. Connections using home computer, TV game, and TV antenna: (A) balun; (B) band separator; (C) A/B switch; (D) lead extensions; (E) cable. (*Courtesy RCA*)

audio inputs from any video component. This permits connecting components such as a camera, portable VCR, video game, or computer directly to the TV (Fig. 5–42).

The RF modulator is equipped with a switch to give the user an option of channel frequencies, usually channel 3 or channel 4. The unit is equipped with 75-ohm input and output ports. The output of the video component is connected via a short length of coaxial cable to the input of the RF modulator, while the output is coaxial cable connected to the VHF input of the TV set. If the VHF input of the TV is 300 ohms, then, as is shown in Fig. 5–42B, a 75-ohm to 300-ohm balun is required between the modulator output and the TV set's input. A signal switcher whose input is a number of unmodulated signals can be used to make direct connections to the TV set.

Figure 5–41A. Hookups for home computer, video game, and TV broadcast. (*Courtesy GC Electronics*)

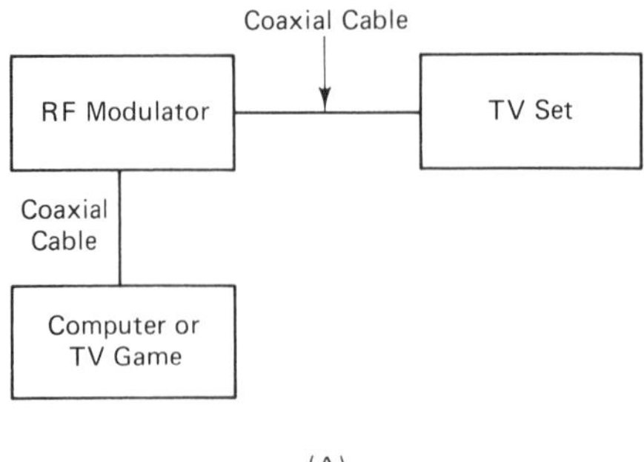

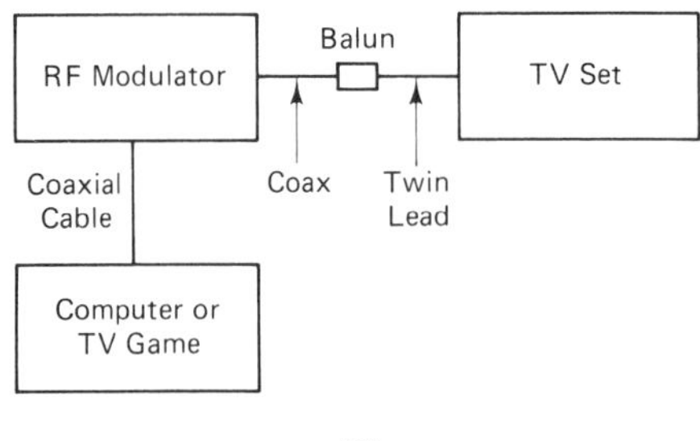

Figure 5–42. Connections for a separate RF modulator.

The RF modulator can also be used to permit two TV sets to be driven by a single VCR. The program signal is brought to the input of the VCR. That signal, however, is delivered by the VCR's output in two ways—modulated and unmodulated. The modulated signal can be delivered to the antenna input terminals of the first TV set, while the unmodulated signal can be supplied to the RF modulator, whose output is supplied to the second TV set.

The modulated output of the VCR could be brought into a signal splitter instead of using the RF modulator, but with the RF modulator, there is little or no signal loss. The splitter, of course, cuts signal strength in half.

In either case, whether a splitter or RF modulator is used, the advantage is that the two TV sets can be used in different locations with viewers watching the same taped VCR program.

HOW TO CONNECT A MULTIPLE-SIGNAL INPUT SYSTEM

The average in-home entertainment system is in a growth pattern as users realize the possibilities of using an in-home picture display unit as the central component, and that includes direct-view TV sets, monitors, PTVs, and integrated monitor/receivers.

Figure 5–43 shows a system using cable TV, broadcast TV, a home computer, a TV game and a videodisc player. Because of the large number of

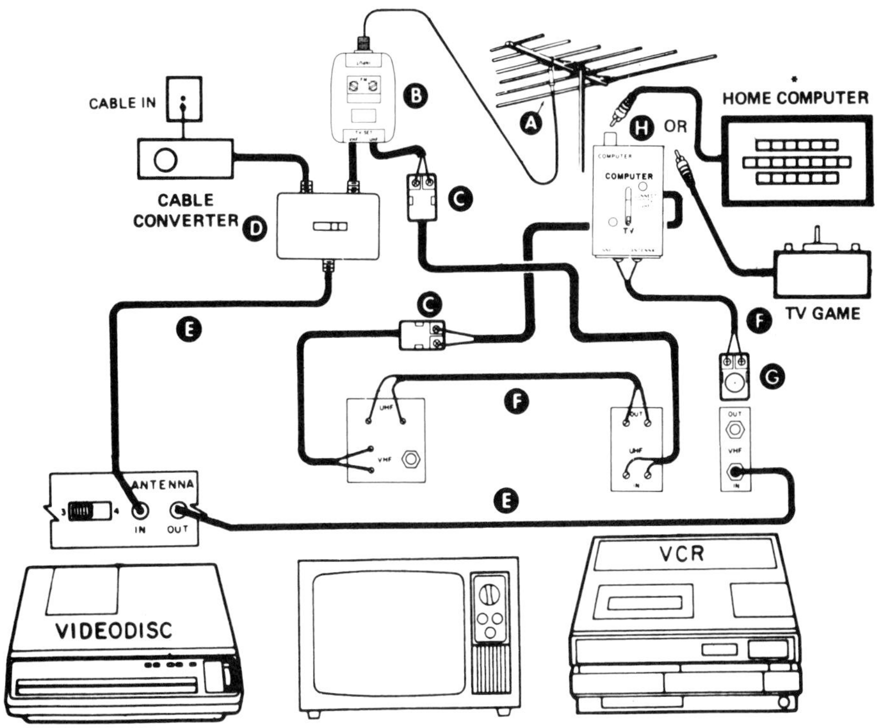

Figure 5–43. Multiple signal input system: (A) balun; (B) band separator; (C) splicing box; (D) coaxial A/B switch; (E) cables; (F) suitable length of twin lead; (G) balun; (H) antenna/computer switch. (*Courtesy RCA*)

inputs, two separate switches are required. Only one converter is used, one that is supplied by a cable TV company.

The antenna is VHF/UHF, with an output impedance of 300 ohms. It is connected via a 300-ohm to 75-ohm matching transformer (A) to a suitable length of 75-ohm coaxial cable, which, in turn, is inputted to a VHF/UHF band separator (B). This band separator has three ports; the input port and the VHF port are both 75 ohms; the UHF output is 300 ohms.

The UHF output of this band separator is brought, via a short section of twin lead to an add-on unit (a splicing box), which will connect two lengths of 300-ohm line without the need for stripping the ends of the line. This is necessary because the piece of twin lead out of the band separator is just a few inches long, and the distance to the UHF input of the VCR may be considerably more. The splicing box shown at C is not an impedance-matching device, has no signal losses, and is used solely to join one length of twin lead to another. From the connector, a suitable length of twin lead connects the

UHF signal of the antenna to the 300-ohm input terminals of the VCR. The UHF terminals of a VCR are usually 300 ohms, but if they are 75 ohms a 300-ohm to 75-ohm matching transformer would be needed somewhere in the line from point C to the VCR.

The VHF output of band separator, B, is 75 ohms, and this signal is connected to one of the inputs of a coaxial switch, D. The other input to this switch is from a cable converter supplied by a cable company, and this switch is used to select either TV broadcast VHF or cable TV signals. The output of this switch is also 75 ohms, and a length of coaxial cable connects it to the antenna input terminal of the videodisc.

The antenna output of the videodisc is delivered, via 75-ohm coaxial cable (E) to the 75-ohm VHF input terminal of the VCR.

The 75-ohm VHF output of the VCR is joined to a matching transformer, G, whose 300-ohm output leads to one of the input terminals of the computer/TV game switch (H). At the other end of this switch, either a home computer or a TV game can be connected. This means that either the home computer or the TV game can use this input port. If both the home computer and the TV game are used regularly with the TV set as the display device, the user is faced with the nuisance of regularly connecting and disconnecting the two outboard components. Possibly a better setup would have been to use a three-way switch at H instead of a two-way switch. This would have eliminated the need for disconnecting cables. Still another choice would have been to use a multiterminal switcher, possibly having as many as five or six input ports. There are advantages and disadvantages to everything. An A/B two-way switch has only two input ports; the three-way switch is a little more complicated to use; a multiport switcher, unlike the two- and three-way switches cannot be fastened to the rear of the TV set, out of sight. It is not only highly visible but its connecting cables can easily be seen. Further, with a multiport switcher, there is a greater chance of signal leakage from one input signal to another, particularly at high signal frequencies. This is one example of why wiring diagrams are often modified. Still another is the differences in component inputs.

The UHF output of the VCR is supplied to the UHF antenna terminals of the TV receiver via a length of 300-ohm twin lead (F). The UHF output of the VCR is 300 ohms and so is the UHF input of the TV set, hence no balun is required.

The videodisc is not only a program source, but it also contains a demodulator and a remodulator. Signals received by the videodisc, whether from the cable TV connection or VHF from the antenna, are stripped of their carrier waves and are then modulated onto a carrier having the frequency of channel 3 or channel 4, selectable by a slide switch on the rear of the videodisc player. The VCR also contains a demodulator/remodulator, so the input to that component, whether a cable TV or VHF signal from the antenna, is once again stripped and then remodulated onto a carrier in the UHF band. This means these signals undergo this demodulation/remodulation process twice before reaching the UHF input to the TV set.

The output of the two-way game/computer switch (H) is twin lead connected to a 300-ohm line add-on, which conveniently joins various lengths of twin lead. This line continues on to the 300-ohm input at the antenna terminal of the TV set.

A VCR and a videodisc player are capable of modulating video signals, but the same isn't necessarily true of home computers or TV games. In this diagram, the assumption is made that the outputs of these outboard units can be brought right into the antenna terminal of the TV set. That is possible only for modulated signals. If the home computer and the TV game aren't modulator equipped, an external modulator will be required.

VIDEO CAMERA CONNECTIONS

The output of the video camera is a composite video signal, but unlike a broadcast TV signal, it is unmodulated. The VCR modulates the video signal supplied by a camera (including sound as well as picture) onto a carrier wave. The signal is then suitable for input to the antenna terminals of a TV receiver. However, if a monitor is being used instead of a TV set, it will accept the camera's signals directly without modulation.

When you are connecting a video camera to a VCR it is not necessary to disturb any of the connections to the antenna input terminals of the VCR, whether VHF or UHF, as the camera does not make use of these ports. The camera uses the unmodulated signal inputs of the VCR, as is shown in Fig. 5-44. The camera cable (G) is connected to the AC operated in-house camera power supply. Separate cables from this supply are connected to the audio input and video input terminals of the VCR. The left side of the illustration shows how the camera is hooked up to the VCR, and the right side shows the connections of an antenna to that same VCR, with the output of the VCR to the TV set.

At the antenna there is a 300-ohm to 75-ohm matching transformer (A) and VHF/UHF band combiner with the coaxial cable downlead connected to another pair of transformers. Transformer D has a 75-ohm output and supplies the VHF signal to the input of the VCR.

From the VCR, the VHF output is coaxial cable connected (F) to a 75-ohm to 300-ohm matching transformer, which is connected to the 300-ohm VHF terminals of the TV set. The UHF output of the VCR is wired directly to the UHF input of the TV receiver. No matching transformer is needed for this connection.

With this arrangement, the camera cannot be used at the same time that broadcast TV is being received. In either case, though, whether broadcast TV

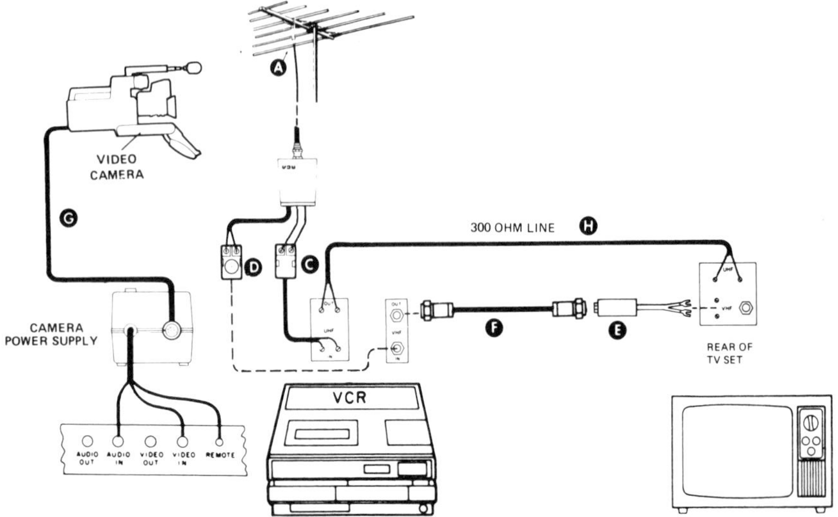

Figure 5–44. Connecting an antenna, a VCR, and a video camera to a TV set: (A) balun; (B) band separator; (C) 300-ohm lead extension; (D) balun; (E) matching transformer, not required when receiver has 75-ohm input; (F) cable; (G) camera cable; (H) 10 feet of 300-ohm twin lead. (*Courtesy RCA*)

or a camera signal is brought into the VCR, the TV receiver's tuning control must be set to either channel 3 or channel 4, corresponding to the same channel selection on the VCR. Further, all broadcast TV tuning is done by the VCR and a remote control unit cannot be used in connection with the TV set.

Figure 5–45 shows more details of the connections to the camera's in-

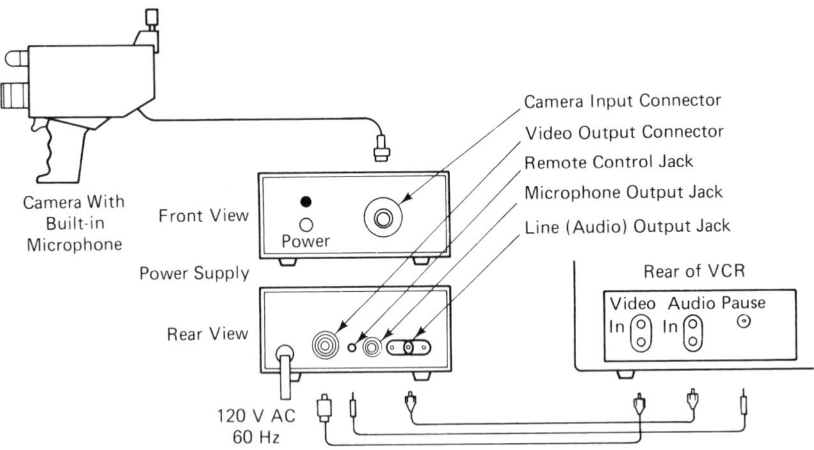

Figure 5–45. Connection of video camera to in-house power supply.

home AC power supply. The type of multiconnector cable connecting the video camera to the power supply was described in Chapter 1, with this connection to the front of the unit. The video and audio signals are wired to the video and audio inputs of the VCR. These signals are modulated onto a channel 3 or channel 4 carrier and then delivered to the VHF input terminal on the TV set.

Video Camera DIN Connector

The audio and video signals are brought out of the video camera (Fig. 5-46) and are delivered to the camera's power supply unit with the use of a DIN cable, also called a multicore cable. These signals are unmodulated and can be brought directly to the audio and video input terminals of a monitor. The sound input to the camera can be from a built-in microphone, usually boom mounted, or the camera may have a port for accepting audio from an outboard microphone.

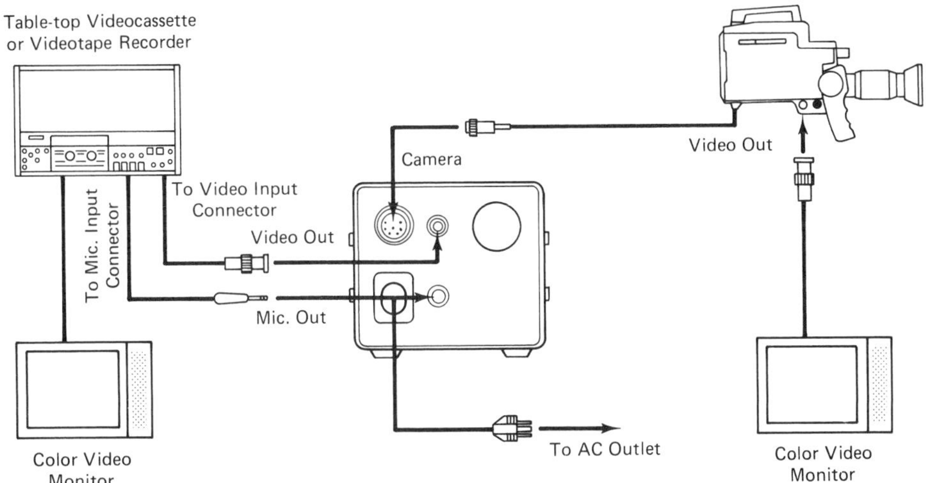

Figure 5-46. Video camera connections.

The wiring diagram in Fig. 5-47 shows a video camera for in-home use. The cable connecting the camera to the power supply unit (A) can be an extension cable with a length of 20 feet to 25 feet. While an additional extension cable can be used, a cable of 50 feet or more isn't recommended because of high-frequency signal losses. The effect of this loss is a reduction in picture detail.

The output of the power supply is delivered by a pair of video cables (C) to the aux inputs on the TV receiver/monitor's connection panel. One of these cables supplies monophonic audio; the other the video signal. The output

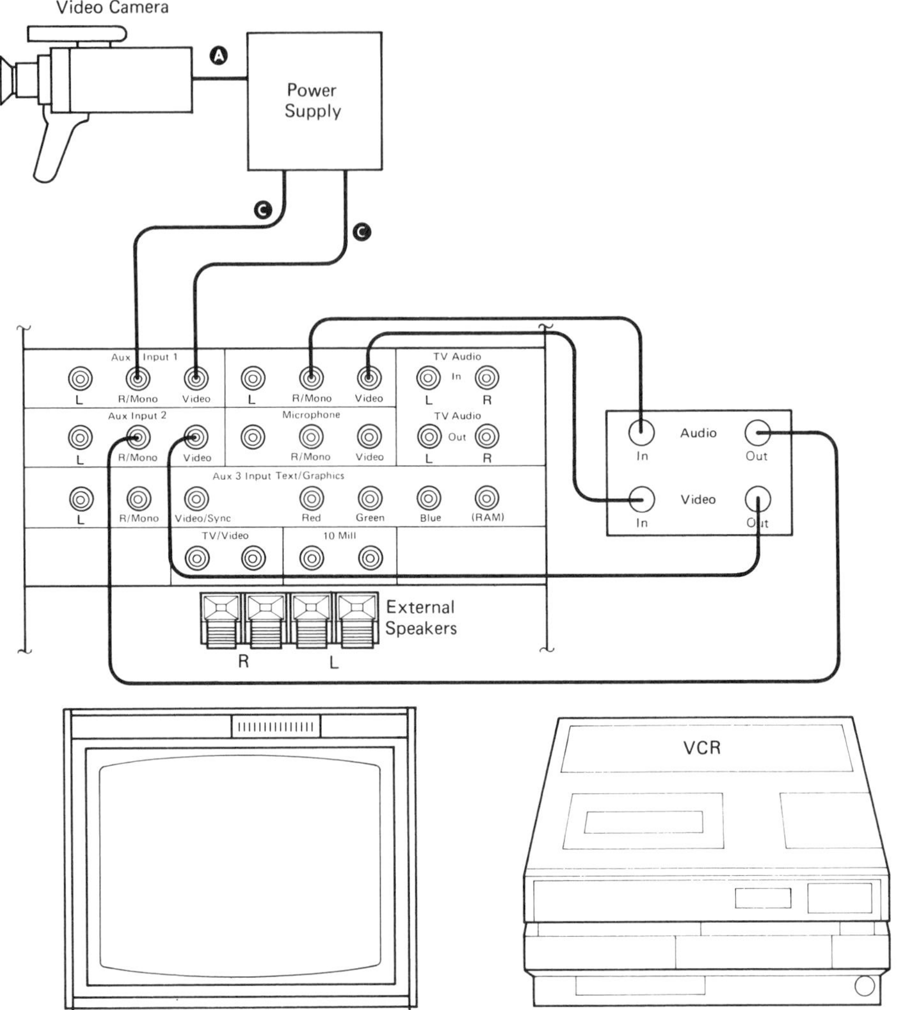

Figure 5-47. Connections for a video camera, a VCR, and a monitor. (*Courtesy RCA*)

delivering these two signals to the VCR is via the bridge aux terminals, which are connected to the audio and video input terminals on the VCR. The output terminals of the VCR are wired to the audio and video aux 2 inputs on the connection block of the TV receiver/monitor.

Not shown in the drawing is the power cord from the power supply to the AC power line.

With this setup, the picture being taken can be viewed on the screen of the receiver/monitor in addition to that seen on the viewfinder of the camera. However, there is quite a big difference between these two. The viewfinder on the camera is small and supplies a monochrome picture only. Not only is it difficult to see details, but since it is black and white only, it supplies no clues as to color quality. The monitor, however, has a large screen and displays a picture in color, and it can be used as an excellent check on the quality of camera work. This enables the user to make camera adjustments or to rearrange lighting.

Video Camera Adapter Cables

When a video camera and a portable VCR are purchased from two different manufacturers, there is always the possibility that the cable supplied with the camera will not fit into the portable VCR's camera input port, and even if it does fit, will be wired incorrectly. This interfacing problem is caused by the lack of standardization in home video equipment. However, it is possible to use an adapter for almost any camera to VCR combination, with almost thirty different types available. The manufacturers of adapters supply a convenient cross-reference chart on each adapter package. To use the adapter, connect the existing camera cable to the adapter's camera input and the adapter directly into the VCR. Then operate the camera and the VCR normally, as instructed by each individual manufacturer. Cable adapters have an overall length of 1 foot and do not add significant weight to a portable VCR system. As more camera models and VCRs are introduced, you can expect new adapters to accompany them.

Despite the general availability of adapter cables, it is always less of a problem to buy a video camera and a portable VCR from the same company, but even then it is advisable to get some assurance that the cable link between the camera and VCR is correct. The camera cable may terminate in a 10- or 14-pin plug, depending on the manufacturer. Even if the cable can be plugged into the camera jack on the VCR, there is no assurance that the wiring inside the cable is correct.

Camera Extension Cables

The operating range of a video camera not using a zoom lens is limited by the length of the cable connected to the portable VCR. In field work, the camera is wired to the VCR by a fairly short length of cable since the VCR is portable. However, there may be occasions when carrying the VCR isn't practical or is awkward. If a tripod is used, carrying the tripod plus the video camera may make it difficult to carry the VCR as well. In that case, an extension camera cable can be used. This may also be applicable when the camera is used indoors.

CONNECTING A MICROPHONE TO A VCR

A microphone, independent of the microphone that is boom mounted on a video camera, can be used for making sound recordings on a video tape. The microphone comes equipped with a cable, possibly 5 feet long (extension cables are available), with one end permanently attached to the microphone's output and the other end terminating in a plug. Insert the plug in the jack marked "mic" or "audio in" on the front panel of the VCR.

The connector at the end of the audio cable from the microphone may or may not be suitable for the audio jack on the VCR. Quite likely it will be a phone plug or a mini plug. Beta VCRs use a mini plug; VHS uses a phone plug or possibly a phono (RCA) plug. If necessary, use an adapter that will permit the connection to be made. The audio jack takes priority over the audio signal received from the tuner on the VCR.

TV RECEIVERS, MONITORS, AND RECEIVER/MONITORS

There are three types of display devices that can be used in an in-home entertainment system: a TV receiver, a monitor, and a receiver/monitor. A TV set is an integrated unit, consisting of an RF or tuning section and a video amplifier section, including the picture tube and its associated circuitry. A monitor is essentially half of a TV receiver, for it does not contain an RF section. A monitor/receiver is a combination of a tuner and video amplifier sections. While a monitor/receiver would appear to be the equivalent of a TV set, it is different in its signal input and output arrangement. No TV set has an output port, with the possible exception of a jack for headphones. The receiver/monitor can accept RF signals at its front end or video signals at its video amplifier input. A monitor and a receiver/monitor sometimes have better-grade picture tubes and have circuitry that may have a wider picture bandwidth, hence they are capable of supplying better picture definition. However, the fact that a component is a monitor or a receiver/monitor does not automatically mean picture quality will be better, for there are quality grades in these components just as there are in TV receivers.

Because of its construction, a color monitor/receiver can function either as a television receiver or as a monitor. Instead of an antenna input panel, as on TV sets, it has a connector panel. It can use 8-pin BNC connectors for video in and out, and mini connectors for audio in and out.

A receiver/monitor (also called a monitor/receiver) can handle unmodulated signal playback from a VCR; or direct feed from a video camera, some videodisc players, TV games, and home computers; or it can be used to view off the air signals. One advantage of a monitor's having direct feed from a video camera is that it displays the picture in color, something the viewfinder on the camera cannot do. The video signal has practically a direct path to the picture screen, after passing through a video amplifier, so there is much less chance for picture distortion.

Like a direct-view TV receiver, or a projection TV, a receiver/monitor or a monitor can be cable ready.

The color monitor/receiver has its counterpart in an AM/FM receiver equipped with jacks for audio input. The modulated signal is received by the antenna and is ultimately demodulated and used to drive two or more speakers. However, the receiver may also have a pair of input ports for supplying an unmodulated audio signal to the audio amplifier in that receiver. Thus, like a monitor/receiver, the AM/FM receiver is capable of handling two types of signal inputs—modulated and unmodulated.

The Connector Panel

The connector panel on a monitor is quite different from that used on a TV set. The back of a TV set is quite sparse as far as connections are concerned and consists only of the antenna block to which VHF and UHF connections are to be made. The only other connection is the power line cord. This is permanently connected and is plugged into the nearest available power outlet.

Typically, the connector panel for a monitor has an 8-pin plug BNC connector for video in and out and RCA connectors for audio in and out or individual ports (Fig. 5-48). Like TV sets, the monitor may have a built in speaker, but as this is often a 4-inch type, it isn't used so much for its sound quality as for monitoring. The audio output terminals can be used for connection to a high-fidelity sound system. The monitor requires a signal input of 1 volt peak-to-peak, plus/minus 10 percent, NTSC composite video.

Aside from the possibility of improved horizontal resolution, the greatest difference between a TV receiver and a monitor is the much larger number of inputs. The only inputs for a TV set are its VHF and UHF antenna terminals. A monitor does not have these, but they are included with a direct-view TV receiver/monitor or a PTV receiver/monitor. Both types, along with a dedicated monitor (a component that functions as a monitor only), also have a video/audio connection panel located on the rear of the component. The one shown in this illustration has twenty-three signal inputs and four outputs for speakers.

The TV receiver/monitor is more flexible in the matter of signal inputs for it can accept RF (composite) signals as well as audio/video (unmodulated). Hence, no matter what type of outboard component is used, a connection can be made. In many instances, it eliminates the need for using outboard modulators or avoids the use of modulation in outboards. Since unmodulated signals are not connected to the tuning section of the TV and proceed directly

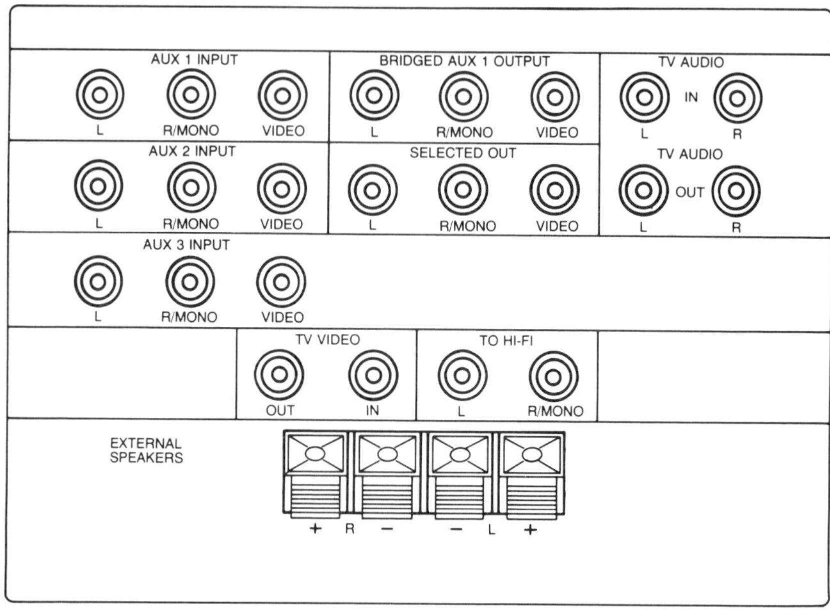

Figure 5–48. Monitor connection panel. (*Courtesy RCA*)

to the video/audio amplification circuits, they are less likely to endure the effects of excessive signal processing. This results in picture and sound of better resolution, in the case of pictures, and better audio quality.

The six ports shown at the upper left in the illustration of the connector panel identified as aux 1 input and aux 2 input are intended for unmodulated audio and video signals. The inputs marked L and R/mono are both used for left and right channel stereo. If only monophonic sound is available, use the center port (R/mono). The terminal at the right (video) is for the input of unmodulated picture information.

Both sound (monophonic or stereo) and video can be supplied simultaneously. All six ports can remain connected at all times, although only one group of three is used at any one time. There is also an aux 3 input having the same ports. Switching is handled by the TV receiver/monitor, eliminating the need for external 2-way, 3-way, or multiport add-on switchers. Further, all of the aux inputs, as well as all the other inputs on this connector panel, are uniformly 75 ohms. This is a step toward input port standardization and will help eliminate or reduce the need for baluns.

On the fourth row are two pairs of terminals marked TV Video and Hi-Fi. These ports are one of the more unusual aspects of a TV receiver/monitor or of a monitor. They permit delivery of these signals to another receiver/

monitor or monitor. Thus it is possible to have two display units driven by the same signal. Both displays, that of the first monitor unit and that of the second, will show the same picture. The terminals marked "to Hi-Fi" are for connection to the receiver, preamplifier, or integrated amplifier of a high-fidelity sound system. For stereo sound, both ports, L and R, are to be used. For mono sound, just the right port marked R/mono is necessary.

A TV receiver/monitor does not usually contain any speakers and so all sound for such units is external.

Below these ports are the left/right audio connections for a pair of speakers. These should be high-efficiency types since the audio power output is quite low.

The aux 1 output, marked "Bridged," supplies output audio and video signals so that these can pass through the monitor without supplying sound or a picture on the monitor's display tube. These can be delivered to a second monitor with the first monitor soundless and pictureless, or to a VCR for recording. The ports identified as "Selected out" work the same way as the bridged aux output and are used for delivery to another TV receiver/monitor or a monitor. When these ports are used, the picture is displayed on the original TV receiver/monitor and the sound is reproduced.

The remaining four ports are for broadcast TV stereo sound. When stereo audio signals are transmitted, a monitor may have provisions for two-channel stereo, plus a third channel or audio B channel transmitted by the TV station. This might be a bilingual sound track. The selection of audio B is from a control panel on the front of the component.

CONNECTING AN ANTENNA AND A VCR TO A RECEIVER/MONITOR

Some in-home entertainment systems are unable to take advantage of an outdoor antenna and rely on cable TV or a master antenna system. One advantage of these two is that there is no need to be concerned about impedance matching at the antenna nor about the kind of downlead to use. Because of this, one variable is removed, and in this respect the connections may be less complicated. Broadcast reception, though, when possible is still highly popular.

Figure 5–49 shows two identical antennas in the sense that both are 300-ohms. The one at the left uses a 300-ohm to 75-ohm matching transformer (A), which is connected by coaxial cable to a band separator, B. The input to this add-on is 75 ohms, but its two outputs are both 300 ohms. One of the outputs is brought into a 300-ohm to 75-ohm balun whose output is fed into the VHF terminal of the VCR. The VHF output terminal of the VCR is coaxial cable (F) connected to the VHF input of the TV receiver/monitor.

The UHF output of the band separator (B) uses a splice box (E), with

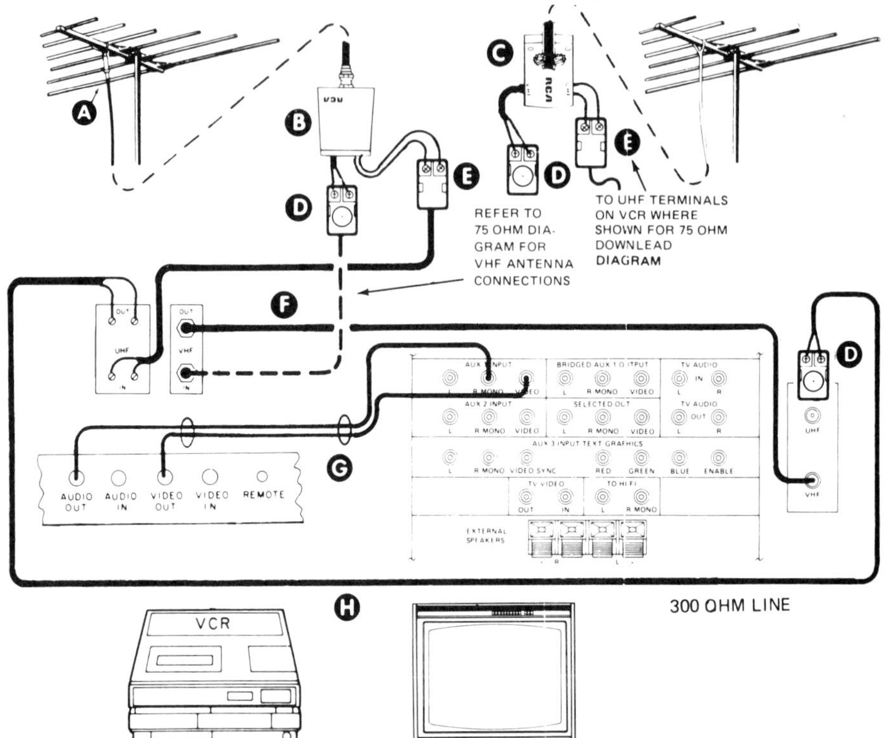

Figure 5-49. Connections of an antenna and a VCR to a video monitor. The hookup at the left uses a 75-ohm downlead, that at the right 300-ohm downlead: (A) balun; (B) band separator; (C) band separator; (D) two baluns; (E) 300-ohm lead extension; (F) cable; (G) dubbing cable; (H) 10 feet of 300-ohm twin lead. (*Courtesy RCA*)

the twin lead on the other side of this box continuing on to the UHF input terminal of the VCR. The UHF output of the VCR is then twin lead connected to the UHF input terminal of the receiver/monitor.

The VCR can deliver two kinds of output signals—modulated and unmodulated. The audio and video outputs are connected via audio cable (dubbing cable) to the aux inputs of the receiver/monitor. The audio is monophonic sound.

The right side of the same illustration shows the wiring connections, using the same antenna connected to 300-ohm downlead. The matching transformer (A) is omitted. The band separator, C, is different from the other band separator, B, in that it has a 300-ohm input instead of 75 ohms. Its outputs are also 300 ohms. From this point on, though, all the connections are the same, including the use of a pair of splice boxes, D and E.

CONNECTING AN ANTENNA, A VIDEODISC PLAYER, AND A VCR TO A MONITOR

The wiring diagram in Fig. 5–50, a split illustration, shows how to connect an antenna, a videodisc player, a VCR, and a video monitor, using the monitor's connection panel illustrated in Fig. 5–48.

Both drawings assume the antenna to be 300-ohms. At the left, the antenna uses a matching transformer (A) 300 ohms to 75 ohms for impedance matching to the coaxial cable downlead. This cable is connected to band separator B, having a 75-ohm input and a pair of 300-ohm outputs. Note that the impedance outputs of this separator are determined by the antenna input impedance of the videodisc player and the UHF input terminals of the VCR. If both are not 300 ohms as in the drawing, the band separator to be selected should have impedances to match.

Following the band separator, the first output is twin lead, connected to a 300-ohm to 75-ohm matching transformer, D. The 75-ohm output of this transformer is connected to the 75-ohm input terminal of the videodisc player. The output of the videodisc player is connected to the VHF input terminal of the VCR. The VHF output of this component is wired to the VHF input on the antenna block of the TV receiver/monitor. Both cables marked F are coaxial and have F connectors at both ends. No baluns are needed or used in these lines.

The second output from band separator B is brought to a splicing box E with the twin lead out of the splicing box continuing on to the UHF input terminals of the VCR. The UHF output of this component is wired via a length of twin lead (H) to a 300-ohm to 75-ohm transformer for connection to the UHF antenna terminal of the receiver/monitor. A balun is shown here, but it may not be necessary to use it if the UHF input is 300 ohms.

The alternate antenna connection is shown at the right in the drawing. There are just a few differences. The downlead is 300 ohms, so the balun (A) isn't needed. The band separator C is the same as B except that its input is 300 ohms instead of 75 ohms. Except for these changes, the rest of the wiring remains the same.

If the VCR is to be used for the playback of prerecorded videotapes, its audio output terminal is connected to the aux input (R/mono) on the connector pad on the receiver/monitor. This is monophonic sound. The video output of the VCR is joined to the video input terminal on the receiver/monitor's connection block. These connections are handled by two wires marked G, a paired group sometimes called dubbing cable.

CONNECTING CABLE AND A VCR TO A MONITOR

With a cable-ready TV receiver/monitor and only one outboard component, such as a VCR in this example, connections are very simple (Fig. 5–51). No

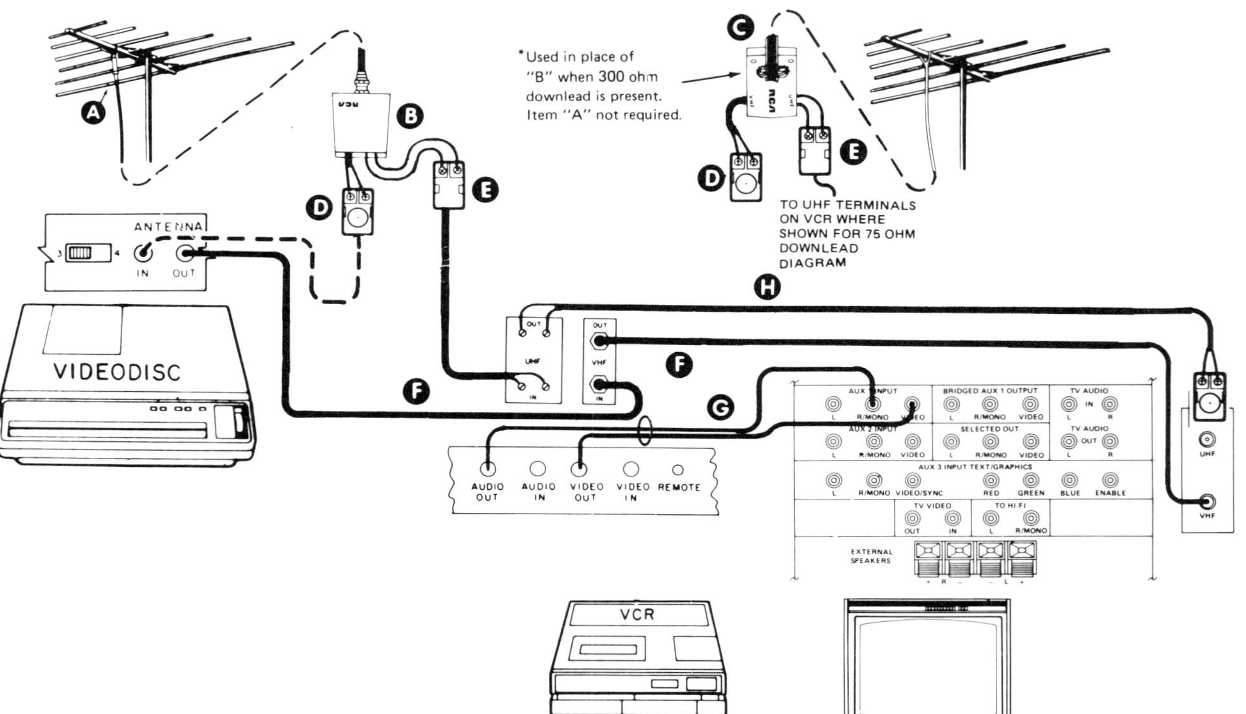

Figure 5–50. Connections for an antenna, a videodisc, and a VCR to a receiver/monitor: (A) balun; (B) band separator; (C) band separator; (D) baluns; (E) twin lead splice box; (F) coaxial cables; (G) dubbing cable; (H) twin lead. (*Courtesy RCA*)

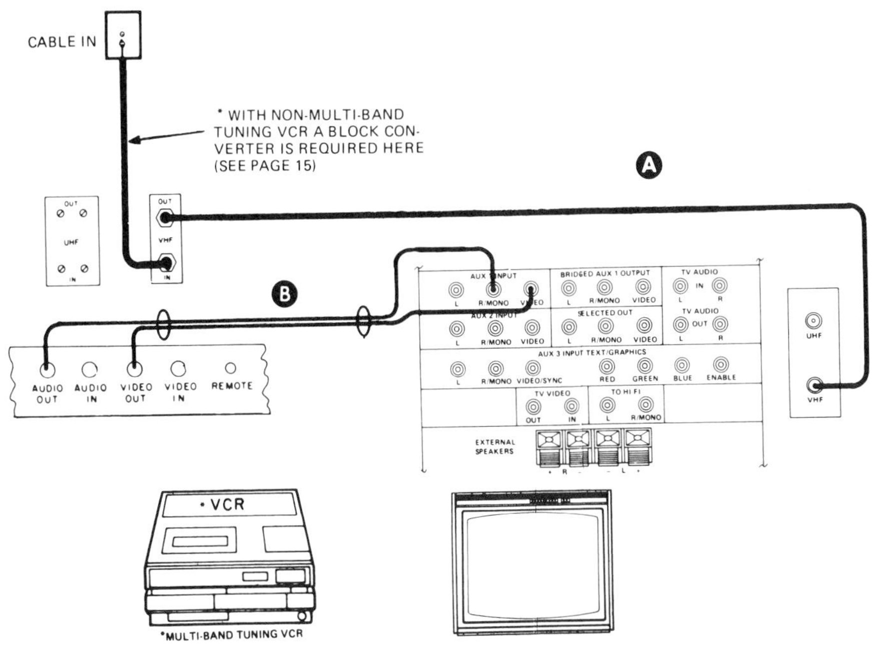

Figure 5–51. Connections for cable TV, a VCR, and a video monitor: (A) cable; (B) audio/video cable; (C) converter. (*Courtesy RCA*)

cable company block converter is used and only nonscrambled cable pictures can be viewed. There is no external antenna, nor are MATV signals available. This system is very limited, but there are two program choices—cable and VCR.

The cable TV wall plate is coaxial cable connected to the VHF input of the VCR; its VHF output is also cable connected to the VHF input on the receiver/monitor's antenna input block. This wiring is 75 ohms throughout, so no baluns are required.

When the VCR is used to supply tape playback, an audio/video cable combination is connected from the audio and video output terminals on the VCR to the aux input terminals on the receiver/monitor. Monophonic sound only is being played back with this setup.

Ordinarily, with the usual TV set, an external A/B switch would be needed. This wouldn't complicate the wiring by much, but installing and using (particularly using) such a switch is a nuisance. In this example, the switch is built into the monitor/receiver, and further, the switching positions are identified. Whenever add-on functions are taken over by the viewing device, wiring is simplified. This wiring setup is similar to those shown earlier in which the VCR is positioned between the signal input, whether cable or antenna, and the TV receiver.

CONNECTING CABLE, A MONAURAL VIDEODISC PLAYER, AND A VCR TO A RECEIVER/MONITOR

Figure 5–52 has a videodisc player included as one of the signal sources. Since the disc player and the VCR supply prerecorded programs, these two components put program selection in the hands of the viewer. Cable TV can also yield program variety but the viewer must accept what is supplied.

The cable TV signal is delivered by coaxial cable to the VHF input of the VCR, with the VHF output directed toward the antenna input terminal of the videodisc player (A). From here, the signal is coaxial cable connected to the VHF input terminal on the receiver/monitor's antenna block. For VCR playback, an audio/video cable is used, connected to the audio and video output terminals of the VCR and then to the corresponding terminals on the connection block of the TV receiver/monitor. Again, as in the preceding example, no external switcher is used, even though three input signal sources are available.

The connections in this illustration are somewhat simplified by the fact that wiring from the speaker output terminals to a pair of speakers isn't shown, nor is there any wiring to a high-fidelity system. It may take a little while to get accustomed to the fact that TV receiver/monitors are most often not equipped with built-in speakers and, like any high-fidelity radio receiver, need external sound drivers.

CONNECTING CABLE, A STEREO VIDEODISC PLAYER, AND A VCR TO A MONITOR

Figure 5–53A shows the connections to be made when a stereo videodisc player is substituted for the mono player shown earlier in Fig. 5–52. The left and right sound channels are brought, via a pair of audio cables using RCA connectors to the left (L) and right (R) audio input terminals on the connector panel. Although connections to the external speakers aren't shown in this illustration, all four of the connections to the speaker terminals would be used—one pair for the left speaker, and the other pair for the right speaker. Two speakers could also be used for the mono videodisc player in Fig. 5–52, but the sound would still be monophonic.

CONNECTING TV/CABLE/PAY TV WITH AND WITHOUT A DECODER

An external decoder isn't always necessary when receiving cable TV or pay TV. Figure 5–53B shows some possible hookups with and without a decoder.

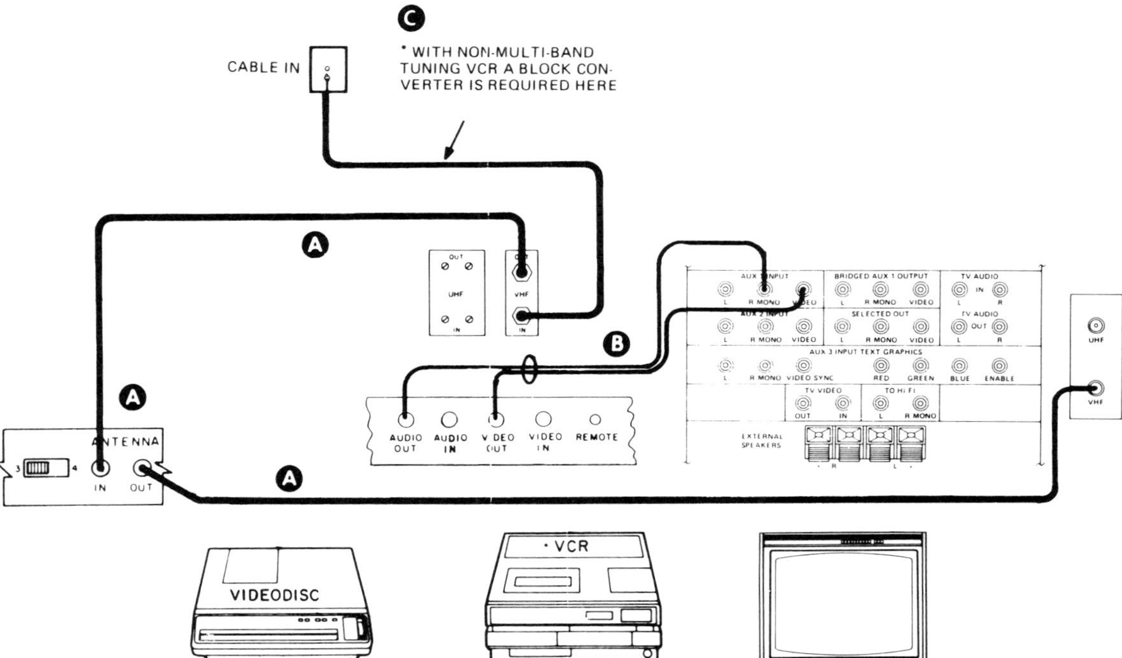

Figure 5–52. Connections for cable TV, a monaural videodisc, and a VCR to a video monitor: (A) three cables; (B) audio/video cable; (C) converter. (*Courtesy RCA*)

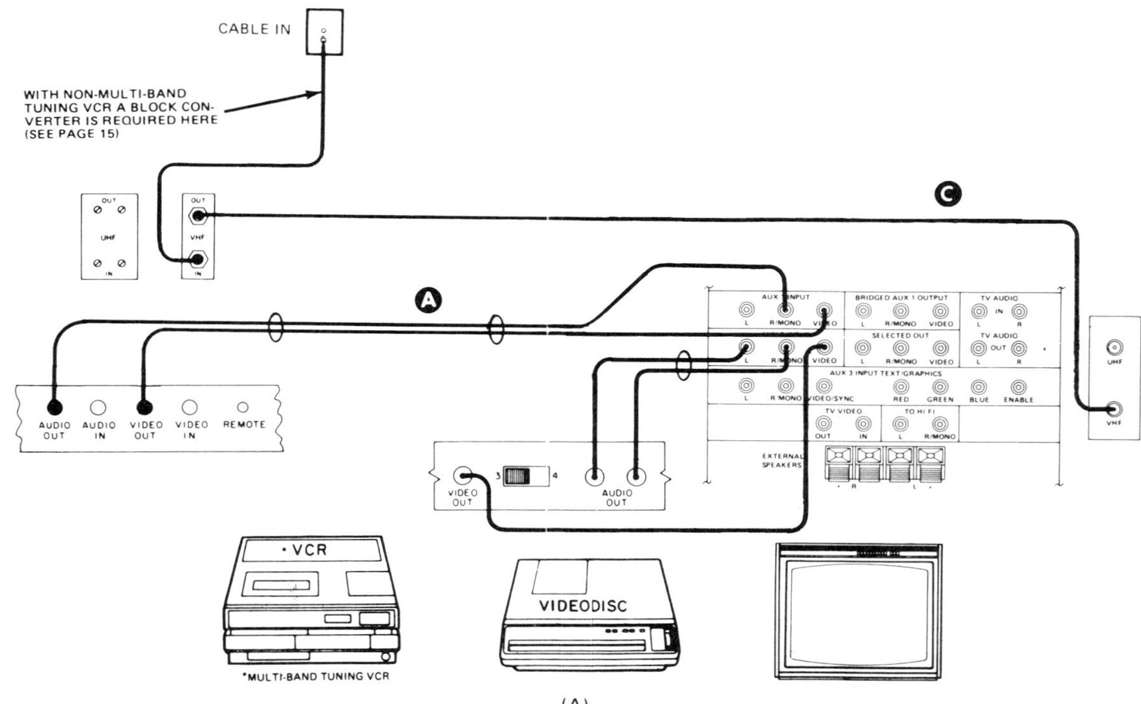

Figure 5–53A. Connections for cable TV, a stereo videodisc, and a VCR to a video monitor: (A) two audio/video cables; (B) coaxial cable; (C) cable; (D) converter. (*Courtesy RCA*)

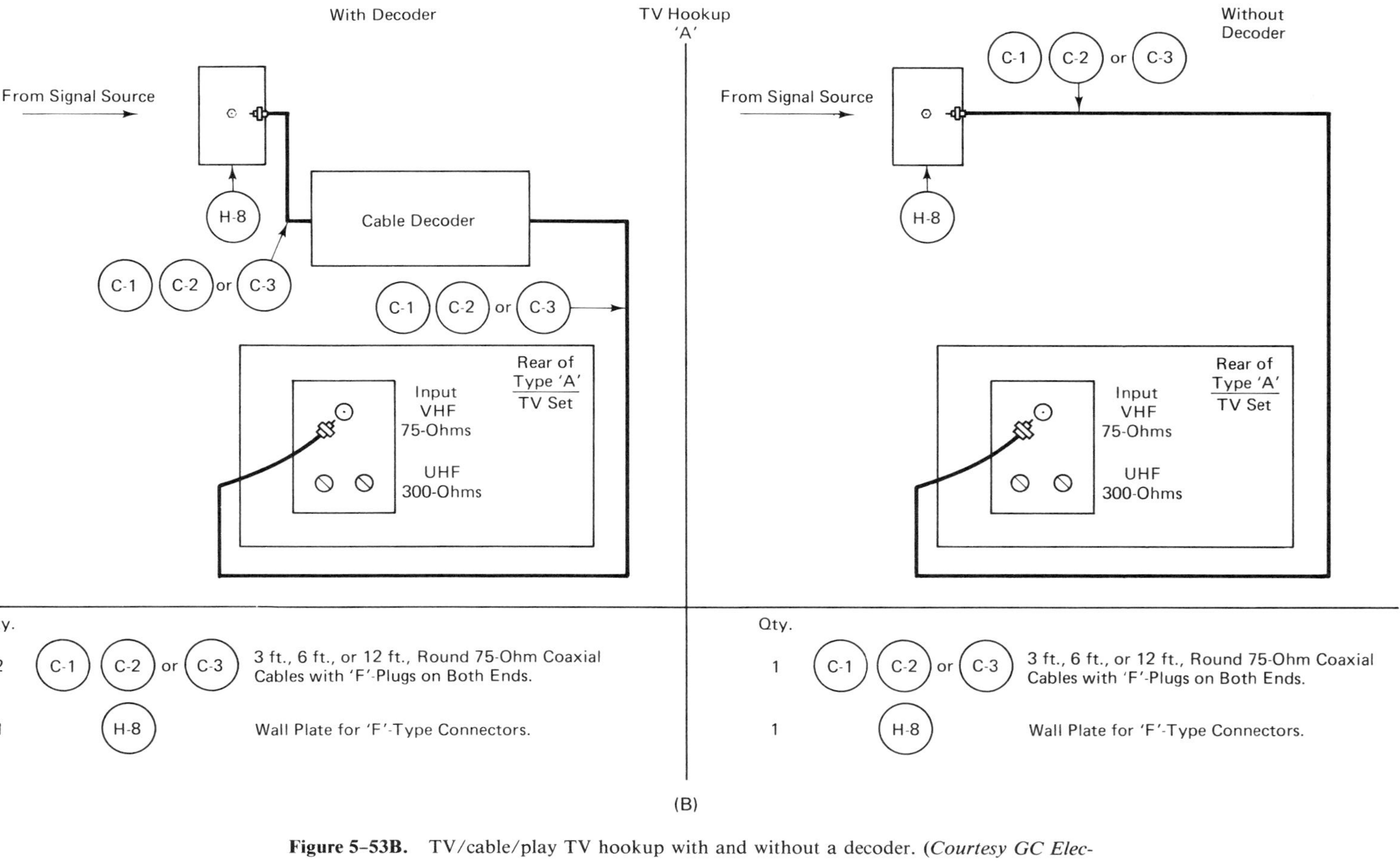

Figure 5–53B. TV/cable/play TV hookup with and without a decoder. (*Courtesy GC Electronics*)

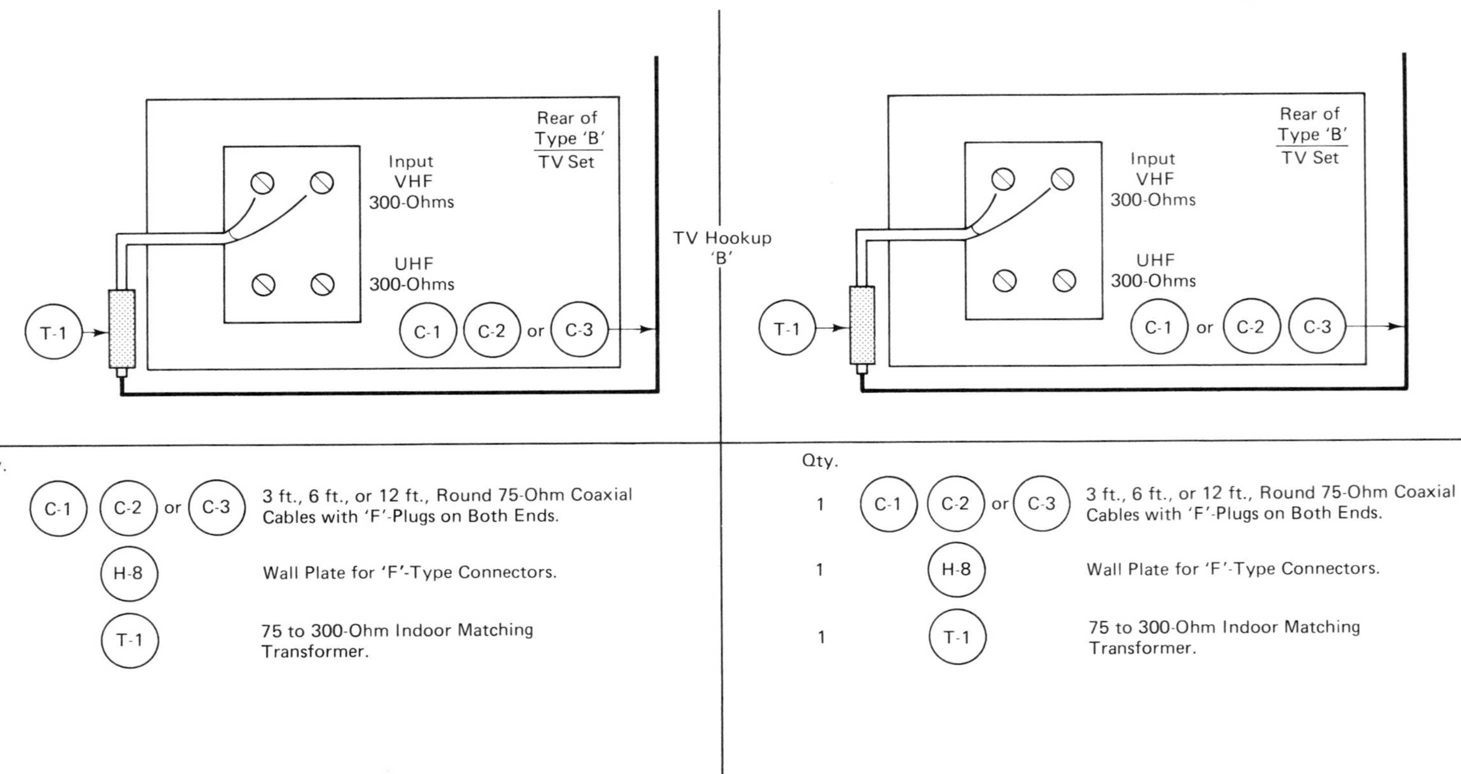

Figure 5–53B. *(continued)*

MAKING BRIDGING CONNECTIONS

Various wiring diagrams have been supplied showing the connection of two or more TV receivers. A somewhat similar technique is used for interconnecting TV receiver/monitors, except the wiring approach is much easier and simpler because no VHF/UHF band splitters are needed nor are any baluns used.

The hookup is shown in Fig. 5-54, with three monitors wired. The same connections are used throughout. The audio and video outputs of the VCR are wired to the bridged aux input ports, with the audio lead connected to the R/mono terminal and the video to the video terminal. In this wiring diagram, we are working only with monophonic sound.

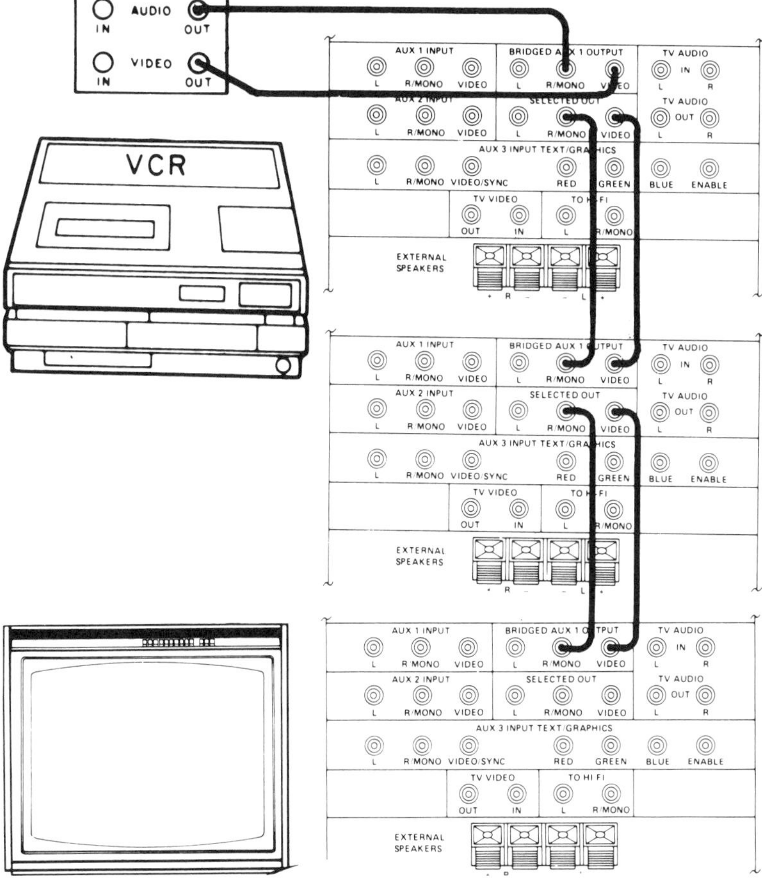

Figure 5-54. Monitor bridging connections. Three dubbing cables are required. (*Courtesy RCA*)

The audio and video output of the first TV receiver/monitor is taken from a pair of terminals identified as "selected out," with these connected to the bridge aux input terminals of the second TV receiver/monitor. With only two such units used there would have been no further connections. For the third TV receiver/monitor, the connections continue in the same way.

The interconnecting cables can be audio/video shielded cables specifically designed for video and audio use with video cameras and VCR equipment. These cables are generally 5 feet long. Another group of cables could be dual video/audio cables with color-coded plugs, the kind used for dubbing tape from one VCR to another. The advantage of the dubbing cables is that they are twinned, making it less likely for one of the connecting wires to become lost or mislaid.

CONNECTING A MONITOR FOR SURVEILLANCE

Just as a monitor and a video camera can be used for surveillance, it is also possible to use one or more such cameras with a TV receiver/monitor. The pictorial in Fig. 5-55 shows how the connections are made.

Each of the video cameras has its own power supply with connections from that supply to a TV receiver/monitor. The cameras can be as much as 50 feet away from the connector panel of the receiver/monitor by using an extension cable (A). Usually, 50 feet is about the limit for a picture that is to be viewed, but that is for entertainment purposes. For surveillance, good picture detail may not be necessary, so the camera cables could be extended, depending on the purpose of the surveillance and the picture quality required.

There is also some signal loss in the cables and so the final possible lengths of the cables depends on the sensitivities of the camera pickup tube (picture tube).

The wiring to the connector panels of the TV receiver/monitor are to the aux 1 and aux 2 inputs with one of the wires carrying monophonic sound, and the other the video signal. The cameras can be in a fixed position or mounted on a motor-operated plate whose planar movement is in a limited arc. Unlike the usual video camera surveillance arrangements operated in closed-circuit TV systems (CCTV), these monitors show the object being viewed in color. The wiring in Fig. 5-55 can be extended to a VCR so a taped record can be made of the scene being scanned.

CONNECTING MATV/CABLE

A high-rise apartment house, or a motel or hotel may be equipped with a master antenna TV (MATV) system, but this does not exclude the use of cable TV (Fig. 5-56). The difference is that a MATV system is intended for the

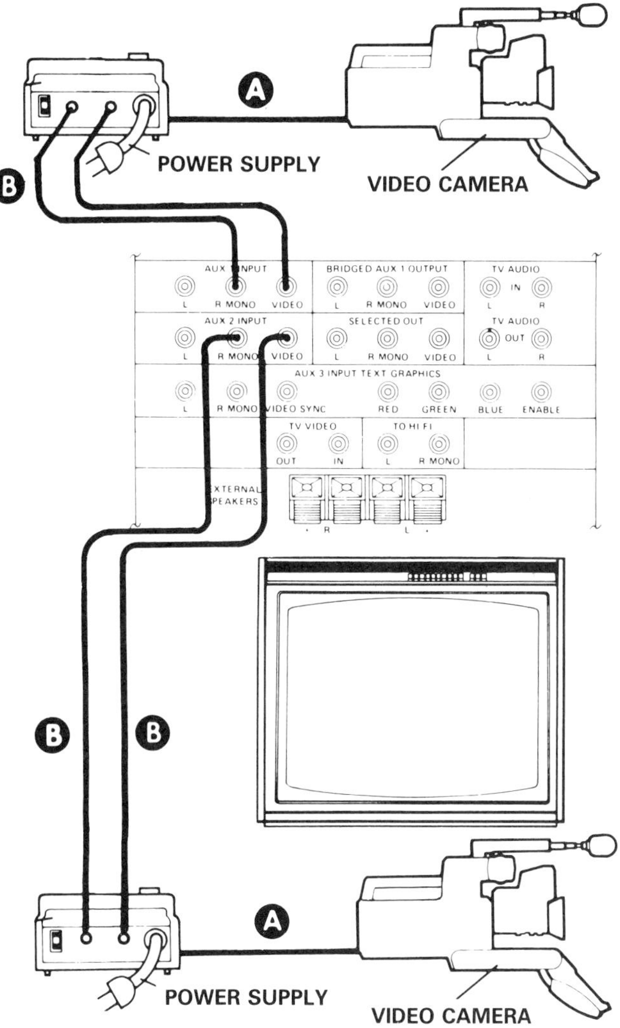

Figure 5–55. Monitor connection using two cameras for surveillance. (A) camera cable; (B) four video cables. In some cameras these cables are part of the camera power supply. (*Courtesy RCA*)

reception of broadcast TV, using a high-gain antenna/amplifier system for the distribution of programs to different apartments or rooms. The cable-ready feature of TV sets is of no use when MATV is the sole program source, as cable reception is available only to customers subscribing to the service. Cable-compatible models of TV sets will be able to tune in most nonscrambled cable channels without the need for an external converter box. However, as there is

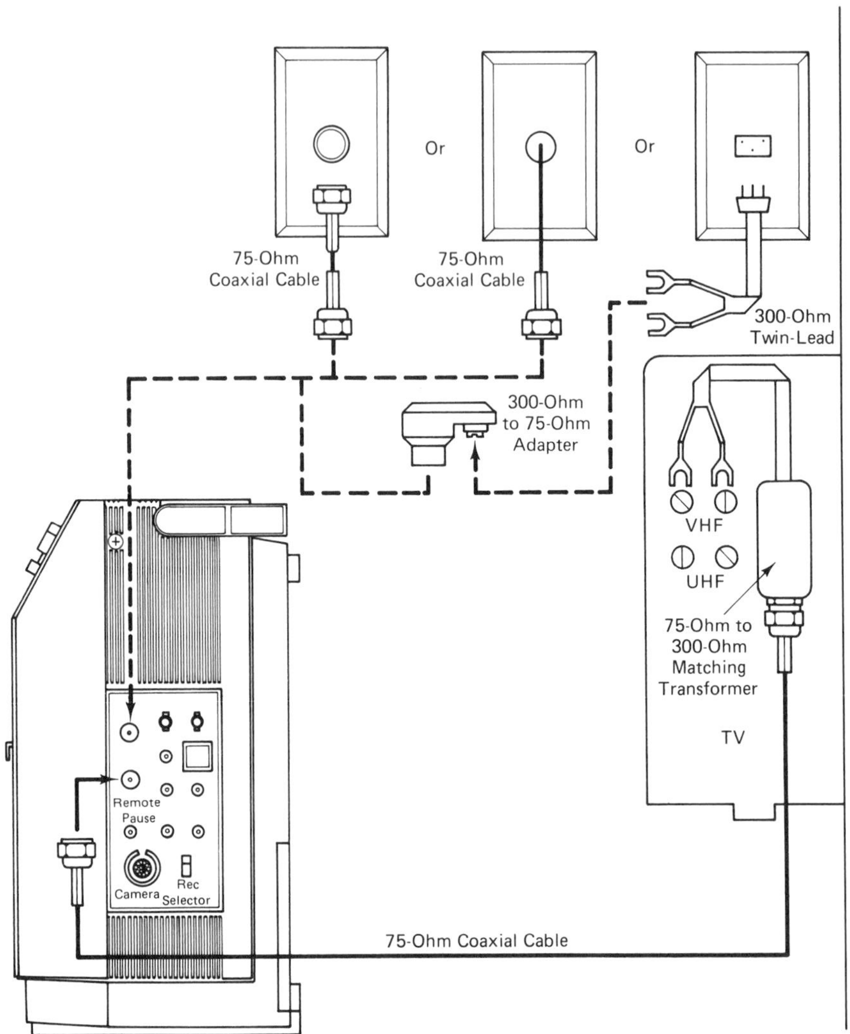

Figure 5–56. Cable or MATV connections. (*Courtesy Sharp Electronics Corp.*)

no assurance that a cable-ready TV set will be able to convert all the cable channels available, it is better to check with the local cable company on channel compatibility and any additional requirements. Cable-ready TV sets are in a numbers race, with some claiming as many as 181 channels. Presumably, the larger the cable-ready capability, the greater the likelihood that an external converter will not be required. However, no matter how great the cable capability of a TV set may be, an external converter box will be required for decoding scrambled cable signals.

The two hookups in Fig. 5–57 show two possible ways of making con-

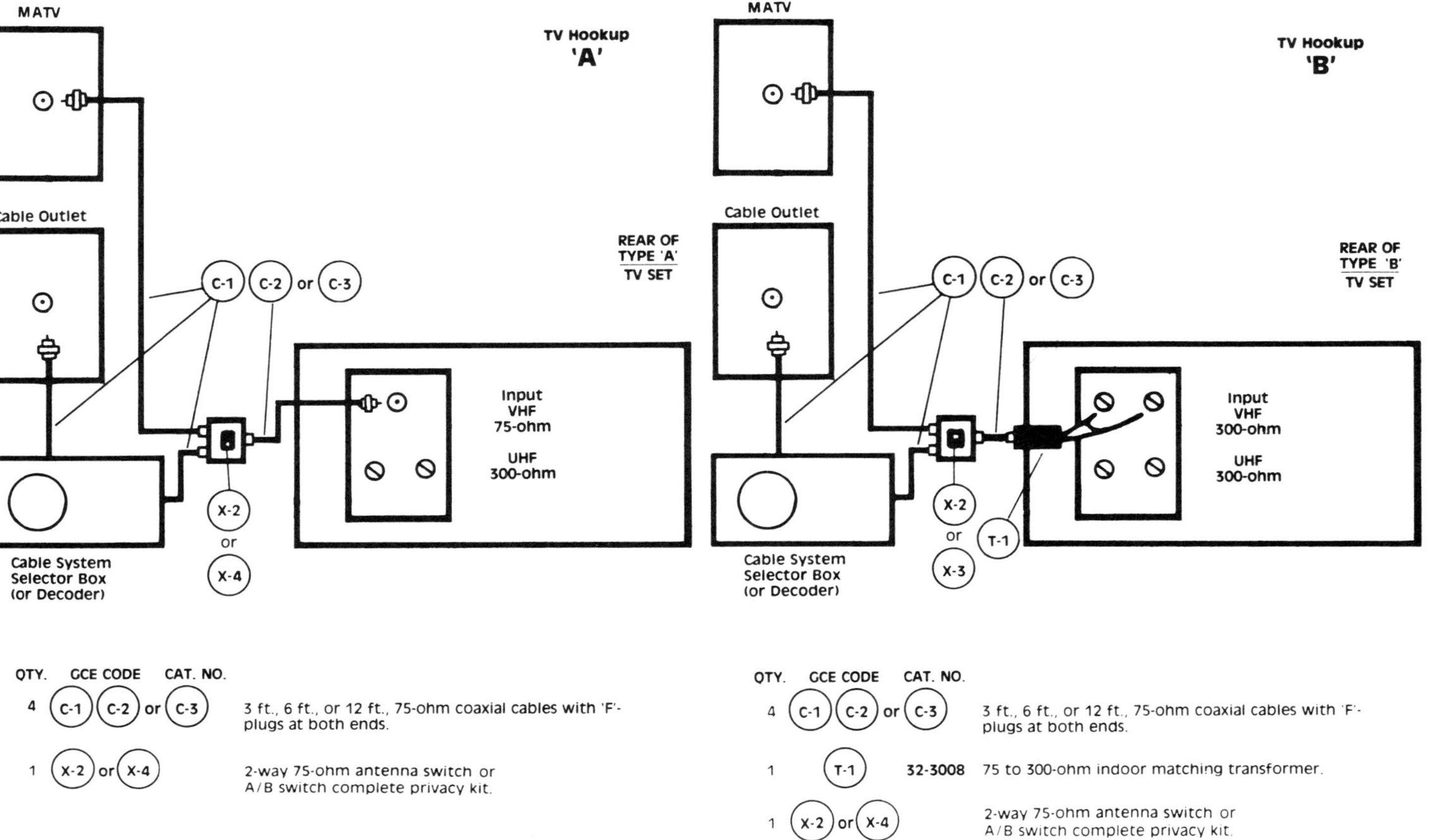

QTY.	GCE CODE	CAT. NO.	
4	C-1 C-2 or C-3		3 ft., 6 ft., or 12 ft., 75-ohm coaxial cables with 'F'-plugs at both ends.
1	X-2 or X-4		2-way 75-ohm antenna switch or A/B switch complete privacy kit.

QTY.	GCE CODE	CAT. NO.	
4	C-1 C-2 or C-3		3 ft., 6 ft., or 12 ft., 75-ohm coaxial cables with 'F'-plugs at both ends.
1	T-1	32-3008	75 to 300-ohm indoor matching transformer.
1	X-2 or X-4		2-way 75-ohm antenna switch or A/B switch complete privacy kit.

Figure 5–57. Two possible connections for MATV and cable. (*Courtesy GC Electronics*)

nections when MATV and cable are to be used. In both illustrations a decoder box is used not only for signal frequency conversion but also for unscrambling. The TV set may or may not be cable ready.

Both the MATV system and cable programming are brought into the home via coaxial cable terminating in a wall box containing an F-jack. The connecting cable is a suitable length of coaxial cable equipped at both ends with F-plugs. The plugs may be either push-on or screw-on connectors.

The two program sources, MATV and cable, are joined to the two input terminals of a coaxial A/B switch. In the upper drawing, the VHF antenna input of the TV set is 75 ohms, so the output of the switch is brought directly into that input.

In drawing B, the antenna input to the TV set is 300 ohms, so a 75-ohm to 300-ohm matching transformer is required. If the switch is a combined switch/balun having a 300-ohm output, the balun is not needed.

The balun has no moving parts and it is lightweight, so it can be suspended directly from the antenna input terminals of the TV. However, the switch is operative and should be screw-fastened to the rear panel of the TV.

Connecting Cable and MATV to a VCR and TV

The use of a MATV system doesn't exclude the possibility of also having cable TV facilities. The connections for these two program sources to a VCR and a TV receiver are shown in Fig. 5–58A. This setup requires the use of two

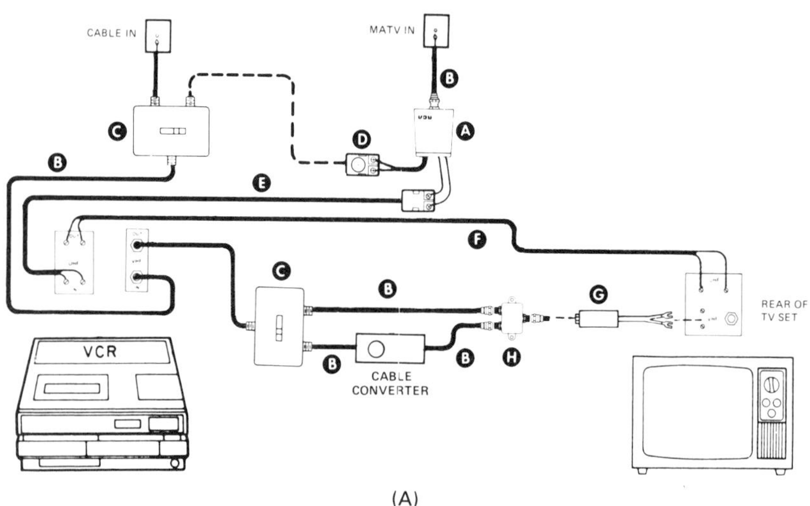

(A)

Figure 5–58A. Connections for cable TV and MATV with inputs to a VCR and TV receiver: (A) band separator; (B) six cables; (C) two coaxial A/B switches; (D) balun; (E) cable extension; (F) 10 feet of 300-ohm twin lead; (G) balun—not required when receiver has 75-ohm input; (H) two-way splitter. (*Courtesy RCA*)

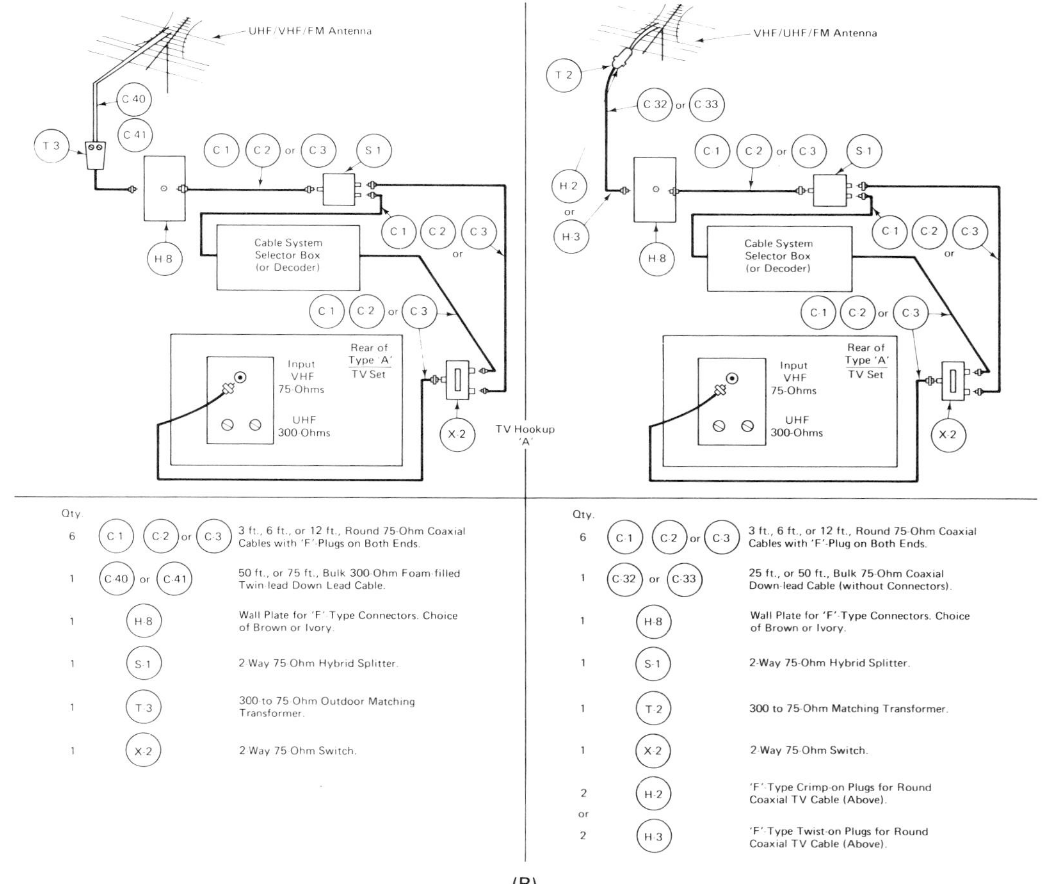

Figure 5–58B. MATV hookup without a VCR. (*Courtesy GC Electronics*)

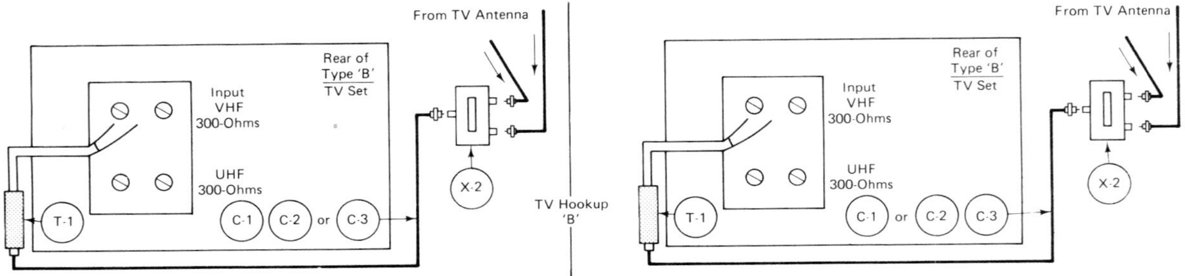

Qty.		
6	C-1 C-2 or C-3	3 ft., 6 ft., or 12 ft., Round 75-Ohm Coaxial Cables with 'F'-Plugs on Both Ends.
1	C-40 or C-41	50 ft., or 75 ft., Bulk 300-Ohm Foam-filled Twin-lead Down Lead Cable.
1	H-8	Wall Plate for 'F'-Type Connectors. Choice of Brown or Ivory.
1	S-1	2-Way 75-Ohm Hybrid Splitter.
1	T-3	300 to 75-Ohm Matching Transformer.
1	X-2	2-Way 75-Ohm Switch.
1	T-1	75 to 300-Ohm Indoor Matching Transformer.

Qty.		
6	C-1 C-2 or C-3	3 ft., 6 ft., or 12 ft., Round 75-Ohm Coaxial Cables with 'F'-Plugs on Both Ends.
1	C-32 or C-33	25 ft., or 50 ft., Bulk 75-Ohm Coaxial Down Lead Cable (without Connectors).
1	H-8	Wall Plate for 'F'-Type Connectors. Choice of Brown or Ivory.
1	S-1	2-Way 75-Ohm Hybrid Splitter.
1	T-2	300 to 75-Ohm Matching Transformer.
1	X-2	2-Way 75-Ohm Switch.
1	T-1	75 to 300-Ohm Indoor Matching Transformer.
2	H-2	'F'-Type Crimp-on Plugs for Round Coaxial TV Cable (Above).
or		
2	H-3	'F'-Type Twist-on Plugs for Round Coaxial TV Cable (Above).

Figure 5–58B. *(continued)*

coaxial A/B switches with one of these used for the selection of signal input (either cable or MATV) to the VHF input of the VCR. The cable converter is in line between the VCR and the input to the TV set. The MATV signal is brought into a band separator. When MATV signals are received, program selection is handled by the receiver. For cable TV, program selection is by the converter. It is also possible to connect to a MATV system without using a VCR. (Fig. 5–58B)

Dubbing Mono and Stereo VCRs Using a Video Monitor

Figure 5–59A shows the connections for VCR dubbing, using a mono VCR, and drawing B illustrates the wiring for a stereo VCR. Both setups use the connection panel of a monitor. In drawing B, the cables at A are video cables and three of them will be required. The cables at B are stereo (audio) cables.

Both arrangements make use of the aux input terminals of the monitor, except, as indicated by the dashed lines in drawing B, the stereo arrangement makes use of the left sound channel aux input.

In both, the VCR at the left is the source or master (play) unit while that at the right is the copying (record) unit. The stereo VCRs have left and right sound channel inputs and outputs. Although not indicated in the drawings, external speakers would be connected to their respective terminals.

Connecting External Speakers to a Monitor

The speaker connections on a monitor can be wired directly to a pair of speakers, but these speakers must be high-efficiency types as the audio power output of the monitor is often just a few watts (Fig. 5–60). The wires joining the monitor to the speakers need not be equipped with connectors since the monitor and the speakers may both have spring-loaded jacks. The speaker terminals on the monitor and the speakers will be marked in some way to indicate polarity. The connecting wires should run plus to plus and minus to minus. The polarity symbols may be plus and minus signs, or the plus terminals may carry a red dot.

Placing some speakers too close to the monitor could affect the picture, depending on the distance and the strength of the permanent magnets in the speakers. A separation of several feet is advisable. The impedance of the speakers should be 8 ohms unless the monitor's instruction manual indicates otherwise. It would be quite unusual to have 4-ohm speakers, as this would impose a fairly heavy load on the amplifiers in the monitor. Do not use 4-ohm speakers unless the instruction manual indicates approval of such a connection. Do not try to operate speakers in parallel; this would lower the impedance and increase the load on the monitor.

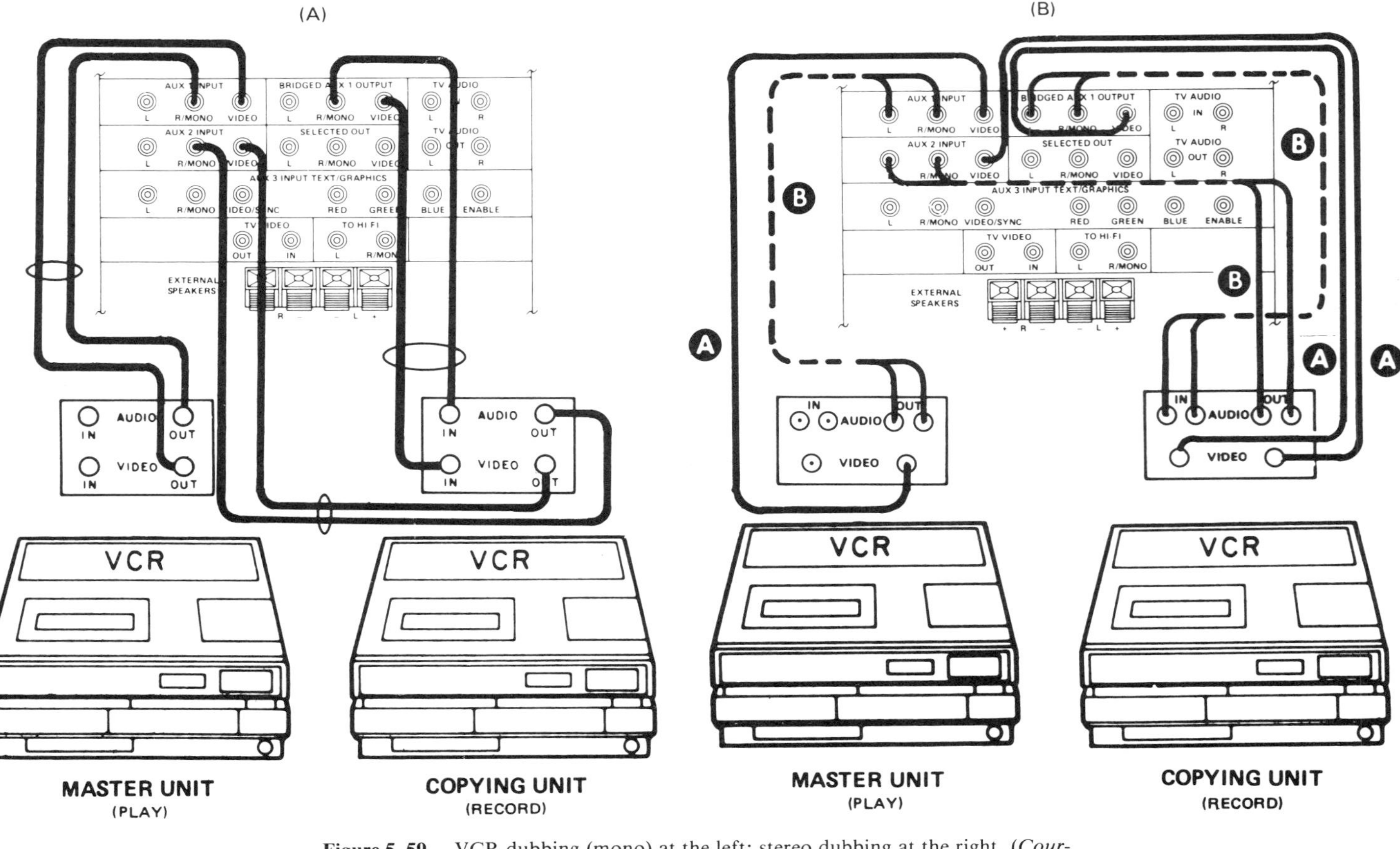

Figure 5–59. VCR dubbing (mono) at the left; stereo dubbing at the right. (*Courtesy RCA*)

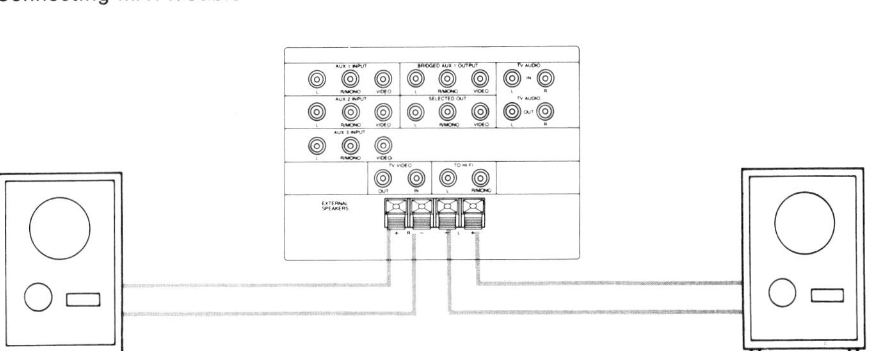

Figure 5–60. Connecting external speakers to a monitor. (*Courtesy RCA*)

Connecting a Stereo Amplifier to the Monitor

The audio power output of the monitor can be augmented by supplying the audio signal to a stereo amplifier, as shown in Fig. 5–61. The connecting wires from the monitor to the amplifier are standard audio cables equipped with RCA plugs.

The required impedance of the speakers is determined by the output impedance of the stereo amplifier and is generally 8 ohms. The connecting cables from the stereo amp to the speakers can be zip cord or special speaker cable.

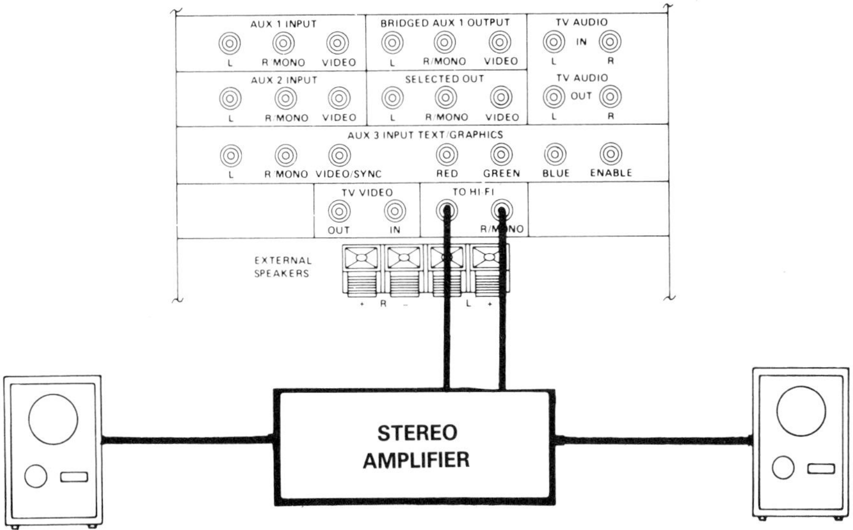

Figure 5–61. Connecting a monitor to a cassette recorder. (*Courtesy RCA*)

Connecting a Cassette Recorder to a Monitor

The sound output of the monitor can be taped on a cassette recorder using the connections shown in Fig. 5-62. If you use the connections in this illustration, the sound will be stereo, assuming stereo output from the monitor. The connecting wires can be equipped with RCA plugs on both ends. The audio output of the recorder can be zip cord wired to the two speakers.

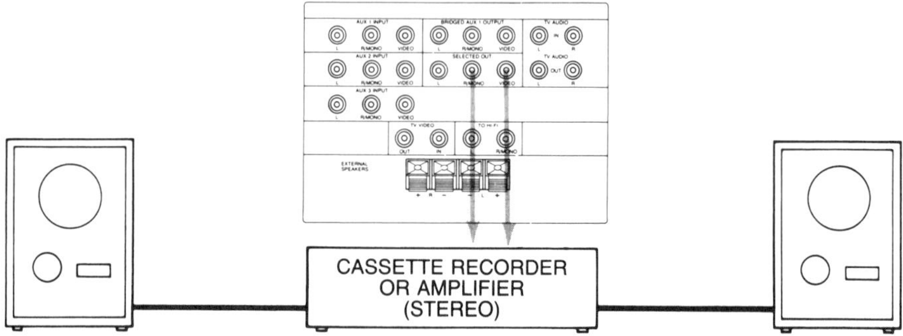

Figure 5-62. Connecting a monitor to a cassette recorder. (*Courtesy RCA*)

CONNECTING AN IMAGE ENHANCER

The faster a video tape runs, the better the picture. A tape that requires two hours from start to finish can be made to record for six hours by operating at one-third speed with some sacrifice in picture quality. A second-generation tape made by dubbing may also lose some of the detail of the original.

Picture quality can be restored (at least to some extent) by a video image enhancer, an outboard component that amplifies the high-frequency end of the video signal.

There are various ways of connecting an enhancer. Figure 5-63 shows the component wired for tape dubbing. The video output of the VCR is connected to the video input of the enhancer, which is equipped with two video output terminals. Either one of these, or both, can be used to drive a single or a pair of recording VCRs. The playback VCR can be one that supplies playback only or it can be a recorder/playback VCR. The connections are determined by the impedances of the components. For the VCR and the image enhancer, these are 75 ohms, so a suitable length of coaxial cable, equipped with F-connectors at both ends, can be used. Impedance-matching transformers can be used as required.

An alternative arrangement for making four tape copies instead of two would be to use a signal splitter in each of the video output lines. This would, of course, require four recording VCRs. The image enhancer will also have a

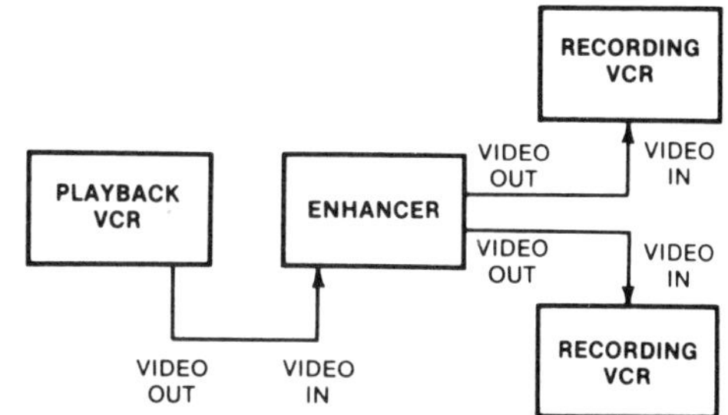

Figure 5-63. Enhancer used for tape dubbing.

number of inputs, often three, so that many playback VCRs can be connected at the same time, with each input selected by a switch on the front of the image enhancer.

Another method of connecting the enhancer is shown in Fig. 5-64. Here the playback VCR is connected to the enhancer, which, in turn, is wired to a converter. Up to the converter the picture signal is video. In the converter a modulator puts the video signal onto a carrier. The modulated video signal can then be connected to the antenna input terminals of a TV set.

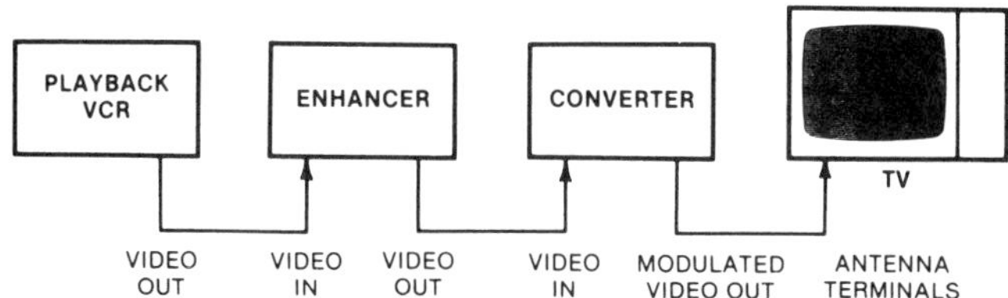

Figure 5-64. Enhancer with separate converter.

Some enhancers are supplied with a built-in converter, thus simplifying the circuitry of Fig. 5-64 so it appears as shown in Fig. 5-65. The video signal output of the playback VCR is connected to the video signal input of the enhancer. In this component, the signal is modulated onto a radio-frequency carrier which is then delivered to the antenna input terminals of a PTV.

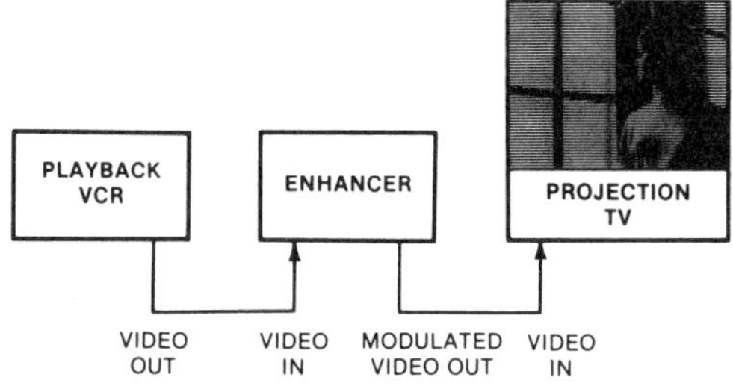

Figure 5-65. Enhancer with built-in converter.

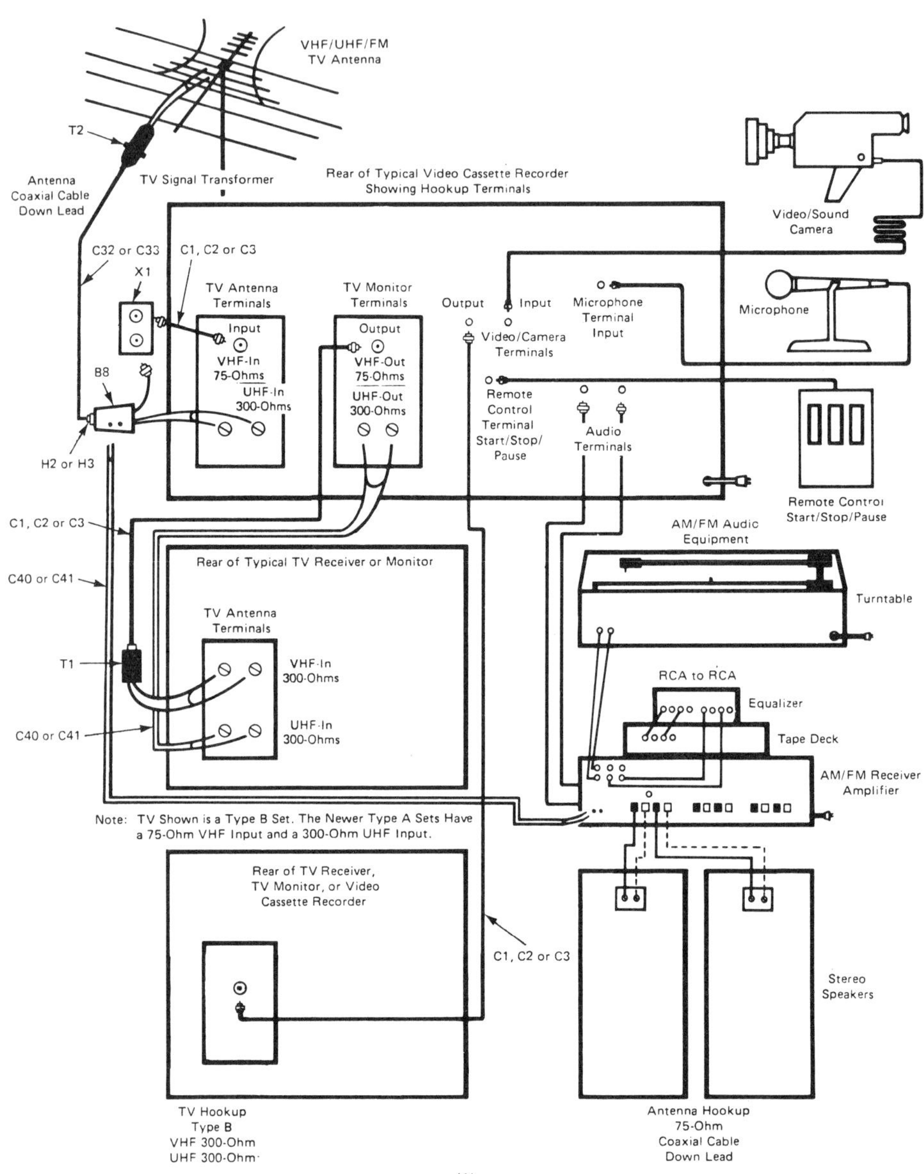

Figure 5-66. Connections for a combined video/high-fidelity system. (*Courtesy GC Electronics)*

A PTV is used in Fig. 5–65, but a direct-view TV set could be used instead. Since the output of the enhancer can also be unmodulated video, this signal could be fed into the video input terminals of a monitor or monitor/receiver.

COMBINED AUDIO/VIDEO

A TV receiver/monitor lends itself well for connection to a high-fidelity system. Unlike a TV set requiring a Y-connector for pseudo stereo, the monitor has outputs for either mono or stereo sound.

The audio amplifier system in a TV set consists of a single channel of sound. If two speakers are used in such a receiver, as is sometimes the case, both speakers will deliver monophonic sound. While there are no speakers in a TV receiver/monitor or in a monitor, there are two audio amplifiers, one for left-channel sound, the other for right-channel. Output sound can be either monophonic or stereophonic and can be delivered via audio cables equipped with RCA plugs to the preamp of a high-fidelity system or to the sound input ports of an integrated amplifier.

The sound delivered to the high-fidelity system can be from whatever program source is supplied to the TV receiver/monitor. This can be from a broadcast TV antenna, cable TV, a VCR, or a videodisc player. If only mono sound is supplied, that is what will be heard from the left and right speakers of the high-fidelity system.

CONNECTING A COMPLETE ENTERTAINMENT SYSTEM

The wiring diagram in Fig. 5–66 shows the connections for a combined video/high-fidelity entertainment system. This is just one of a number of different possibilities, for it does not involve various other components. It does not

Quantity	Code	Components Required
1	B8	75- to 75/300-Ohm Transformer (Balun) and VHF/UHF Band Separator with FM Tap
2	C1, C2, or C3	3-ft, 6 ft, or 12 ft, 75-Ohm Coaxial Cables with F Type Plugs on Both Ends
1	C32 or C33	25-ft, or 50-ft, Bulk 75-Ohm Coaxial Down Lead Cable (without Connectors)
2 or	H2	F Type Crimp-on Plugs for 75-Ohm Coaxial Cable (Above)
2	H3	F Type Twist-on Plugs for 75-Ohm Coaxial Cable (Above)
1	C40 or C41	50-ft, or 75-ft, Bulk 300-Ohm Foam-filled Twin-lead Down Lead Cable
1	C40 or C41	50-ft, or 75-ft, Bulk 300-Ohm Foam Filled Twin-lead Down Lead Cable. Connects FM Tap on B8 with Antenna Terminals on FM/AM Receiver
1	T2	300- to 75-Ohm Transformer (Balun) for Outside Use
10	T2	Phono Plug (RCA) to Phono Plug (RCA) Connector Cables
2	12, 14, or 16-Gauge Two Strand Speaker Wire	Cut to Required Length Connect Stereo Speakers with FM/AM Receiver

(B)

Figure 5–66. *(continued)*

include a videodisc player, a compact disc player, or a multiport switcher. It does not show a block converter/decoder.

The antenna is a combined VHF/UHF type having an output of 300 ohms. The short length of twin lead from the antenna connections are brought into an outdoor (weather protected) 300-ohm to 75-ohm matching transformer, T2. The downlead, C32, is a length of coaxial cable, tailored for this particular installation, and equipped with F-plugs at both ends. One end is plugged into the TV matching transformer, T2; the other end into a band separator, H2. The band separator has UHF, VHF, and FM outputs.

The 300-ohm UHF output is connected to the UHF input of a VCR. The 75-ohm output of the band splitter is brought into a preamplifier, X1, whose amplified output is connected to the 75-ohm VHF input of the VCR.

The FM output of the band splitter, H2, is wired to the FM antenna terminals of the AM/FM receiver. The output terminals of the VCR are joined to the antenna input terminals of a TV receiver or a TV receiver/monitor. The UHF connections of both components are screw types, indicating that the impedances are 300 ohms. Consequently, the UHF output of the VCR can be connected to the UHF antenna input terminals of the TV receiver or TV receiver/monitor, using a length of 300-ohm line. While this line can have its ends stripped for making these connections, it is preferable to mount open spade lugs on both ends, either crimping them on or soldering. The best way is to use both methods; crimping for the mechanical connection, and soldering for the electrical.

A rack is desirable for high-fidelity or video use, but the problem is that most racks are designed for one or the other, seldom both. Even if you can find a rack having enough shelves, it will rarely be suitable for including additional components. When you are looking for a rack, make sure it is mounted on the best casters available. Racks on display in a store have everything in their favor. They are positioned on a hardwood floor; in the home they will probably be on a rug. In the store the rack may not be loaded with equipment; in the home it will be. It is important to be able to move the rack easily, loaded, and on a rug.

A rack with a glass door can be a nuisance, for it will show finger marks and will have to be opened and closed. However, dust is a serious enemy of audio and video components, and while the rear of the rack may be open to dust, having a glass door on the front will at least make the components less accessible to dirt.

With regular use of a system, most owners know the front side, but they know little or nothing about the rear, as it isn't visible. Most connections are made to rear ports, and it is essential to know how many there are, their functions, and their impedances. When you are making an installation plan, possibly in block diagram form, it is the rear view that is important, not the front.

A complete audio/video system can easily cost as much as a new car and more in some cases. Economizing on cables is highly inadvisable. Get the best, preferably those having a well-known brand name.

Cable length is important. Do not make the cables so short that they are barely long enough to permit connections to be made, nor so long that they form loops behind the system. There should be enough slack in the cables so the user can pull a component forward for examination of the rear ports. The rack may be rotated, but it may be more convenient to turn the component to be inspected.

If you want to use tie cords to hold cables together, be sure not to associate input and output cables. Do not make the tie so tight that the cables are bound together. Use tie cords that can be easily undone, as you may, at some time, wish to remove them.

If you use a balun at the antenna, make sure you cover it with a boot—a weatherproof covering—or buy a balun intended for outdoor use. If you use twin lead you are probably aware it is available in rolls of 25 feet, 50 feet, and 100 feet, and at a variety of prices. Use foam-filled twin lead; it is less susceptible to weather and has less capacitance. Shielded twin lead or coaxial cable is preferable in electrically noisy neighborhoods.

A VCR or TV set has a very limited number of input ports. This presents a problem when more than one signal source is used. Signal input cables can be switched every time a new signal source is wanted, but an easier method is to use a video control center.

CONNECTIONS FOR CLOSED CAPTIONING

There are two types of captioning used in television, open and closed. With open captioning the picture is viewed and the text material is at the bottom of the screen, but is not under the control of the viewer. With closed captioning the written material can only be seen if an add-on component is used that will make the captioning visible. Closed captioning is used as an aid for the hearing impaired. Figure 5–67 shows how to connect a closed-caption unit to a TV set.

CONNECTING OLD COMPONENTS

The loyalty of some system owners to their old components is astonishing. Some prefer antiquated FM receivers that use vacuum tubes to solid-state components, claiming that tubes supply better sound. The problem with such sets is that many of them have predated the use of present-day plugs and jacks, and are equipped with internally threaded binding posts.

Figure 5–68 shows how to connect coaxial cable to the 75-ohm antenna

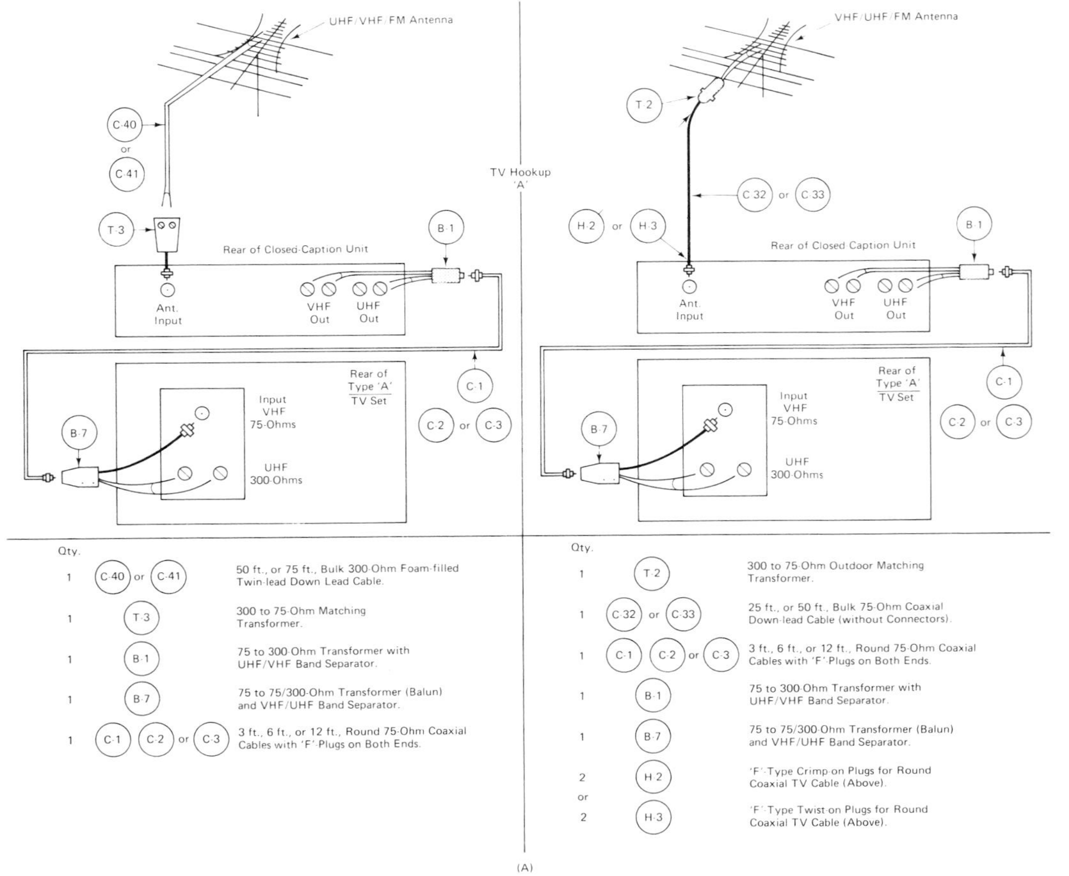

Figure 5–67. Connections for closed caption unit. (*Courtesy GC Electronics*)

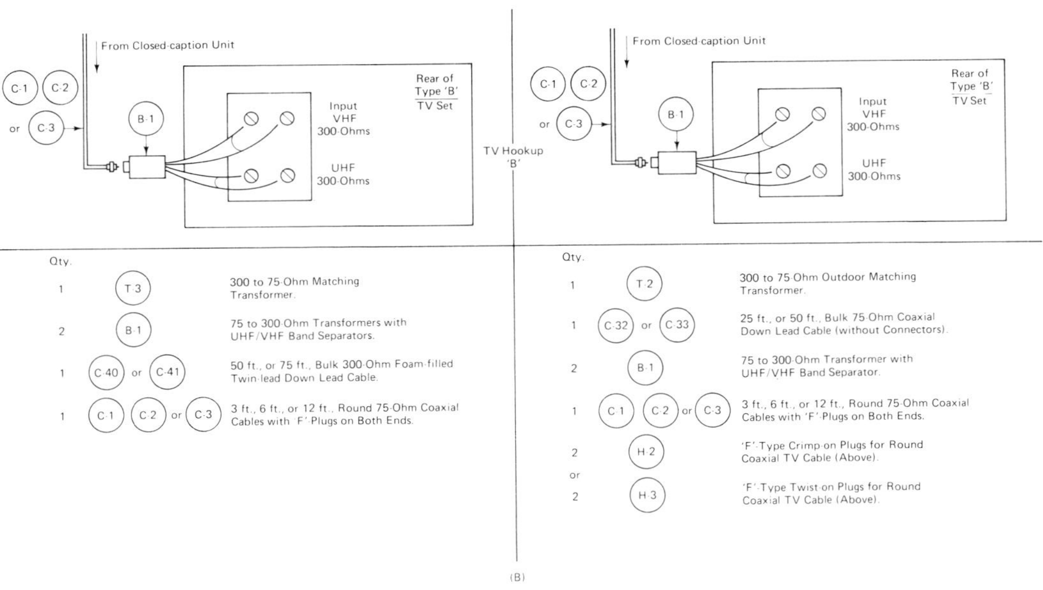

Figure 5–67. *(continued)*

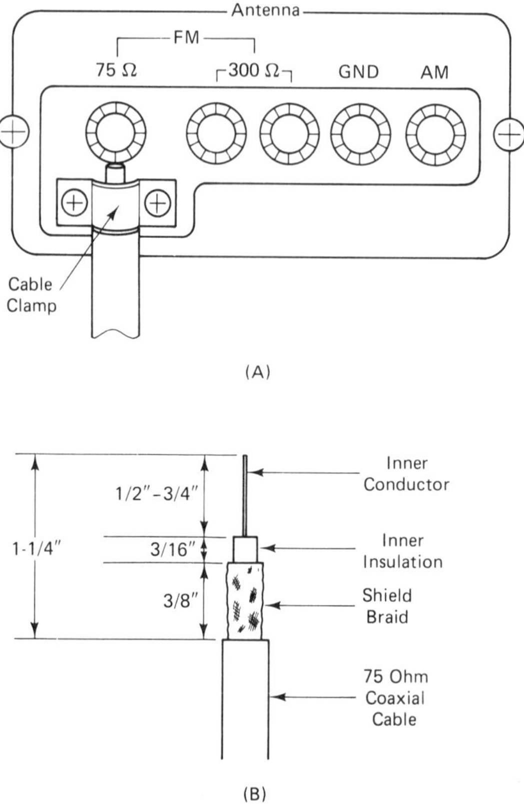

Figure 5-68. Connecting coaxial cable to an old FM receiver.

input of an old-time FM radio. Strip the coaxial cable as indicated in drawing B. Hold the coaxial cable in place with a cable clamp, with the clamp wrapped around the shield braid. This will provide the ground connection to the chassis or metal frame of the receiver. After mounting the cable, wrap the center conductor around the binding post in a clockwise direction, and then tighten the post.

An alternative technique would be to drill a hole in the rear apron and mount an F-jack. This would require not only mechanical mounting but connecting the terminals of the jack to the correct input of the receiver. Although this is the preferred method of connection, it is considerably more work.

To prepare the cable in drawing B, remove approximately 1-1/4 inch of the outer jacket from the cable. Use a new single-edge razor blade. Expose about 3/8 inch of the braid and then expose 3/16 inch of the inner insulation. The center hot lead should be 1/2 inch to 3/4 inch long.

INSTALLATION PRECAUTIONS

Before you decide to set up a complete video/high fidelity system, consider the arrangement as a two-part setup, for that is exactly what it is. Get half the system working to your satisfaction, and then the other half. There is nothing more exasperating or time consuming than having an in-home entertainment system working poorly, intermittently, or not at all.

The picture display unit will be the central component of the system, and the best to use is a cable-ready TV receiver/monitor, with maximum cable readiness preferable. A TV receiver/monitor will supply a display unit having far more input and output ports than an ordinary TV set. From the viewpoint of connections, it is more desirable than a separate tuner and monitor.

An in-home system requires more power outlets than the usual home or apartment is capable of supplying. A baseboard multiple outlet with a master switch will be helpful, but even here it is best to select high-fidelity components having as many switched and unswitched convenience outlets as possible. These outlets are fairly standard with audio equipment, but not with video.

6

THE HIGH-FIDELITY CONNECTION

A high-fidelity system is an audio system, but not all audio systems are high fidelity. An AM receiver with a single built-in 3-inch speaker is an audio system; it is not high fidelity. High-fidelity sound is a goal; a continuing effort is being made to obtain as accurate a reproduction as possible of an original sound source, including an imitation of the acoustic environment in which the original sound was produced. Audio is easy to obtain. High-fidelity sound can come close to perfection, but close is not complete attainment.

There are two approaches to a high-fidelity system: the compact, or integrated, and the component, or modular, form. Compacts are available in various arrangements, commonly a receiver, a record changer and a pair of speakers, built into one console. It is often put together by an assembler, not a manufacturer, with speakers from one source, receiver from another, and the turntable from still another. The result can be loud sound, but high fidelity it is not. Aside from price, its advantage is that it requires no connections, but low fidelity is the price paid for this advantage.

The simplest high-fidelity system consists of a not-so-ordinary AM/FM/MPX integrated receiver and a pair of external speakers. An AM/FM/MPX receiver is capable of receiving monophonic or stereophonic AM sound, FM monophonic sound, and stereo FM sound as indicated by MPX, an abbreviation for multiplex. All tuners are stereo, and any FM receiver or tuner that gets stereo (and they all do) also responds to mono signals. "FM mono" does not mean the component will respond only to FM stations broadcasting monophonically. It does mean, when the front panel control is set to FM mono, that all programs will be received in single-channel form, including those that

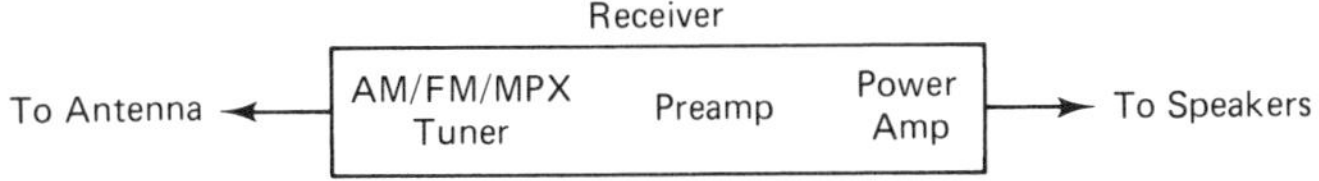

Figure 6–1. Receiver is an integrated unit.

are stereo. In its FM auto mode, the tuner or receiver will automatically switch to FM stereo when tuned to a stereo broadcast. Even an integrated receiver (Fig. 6–1) is a component system, as it uses the receiver as one component and the speakers as another.

High-fidelity component systems can become somewhat complex as more and more units are added. There is no change, though, in the cables that are used and the connections that are made. Shielded audio cables, using RCA pin plugs (phono plugs) are the connectors.

Building a system is more than just getting components and cables, for the problem of just how the components are to be interfaced remains. A component is always equipped with input and/or output connections, but one main unit, such as a receiver or a preamplifier, is the entry for a number of sound sources. This means the receiver or preamplifier, also working as a signal switcher, must be able to accommodate all the extra signal sources. The more entry ports available, the easier it will be to add components in the future. These could include a tuner, a preamplifier, one or more power amplifiers, one or more turnables, a compact disc player, an equalizer, two or more speakers, and possibly other sound sources as well.

There are five possible sound sources: AM and FM broadcasts; phono records; compact discs; cassette and open-reel tapes; and microphones. Other components, such as equalizers, sound expanders and compressors, and noise reduction units, are sound modifiers, altering existing sound but not producing it.

THE CONNECTION PROBLEM

Connecting audio components is much less difficult than video connections—audio cables and their connectors are easy to use and there is less variety of plugs and jacks than in a video system—but still there are problems.

Connecting cables are so ordinary looking, so electronically unexciting, and they will be hidden from view behind the components, so it is easy to overlook the effect they can have on the sound. The way in which the cable is made, its length, its resistance, and its capacitance, can all result in a change in sound quality. It does not pay to spend big dollars on high-fidelity components and then try to economize on cables and connectors. When you buy cables, get them from a manufacturer who specializes in producing them as a main item, not as a sideline.

When you are building a component system, the rear panel—and that is where most of the connections are made—is the area of the component that gets the least attention when a unit is purchased, yet whether an outboard component can be added at some later date depends on the availability of ports, terminals to which units can be connected.

Avoid limitations on the growth of a system. Even an inadequate number of AC outlets, switched and unswitched, on a rear panel can be a cause for aggravation. It is possible to make a wiring diagram in advance of purchasing a component only to find there is no way of connecting it directly to a system.

Adding a component may involve nothing more than connecting the cables of a turntable. You may wish to add a second turntable only to note there is no suitable terminal on the integrated receiver or preamplifier. You may want to add a compact disc player, and discover that there is no input provision for it. A precautionary step, then, prior to making a purchase, is to make a drawing of the inputs and outputs of each component and plan accordingly.

In some instances, a component such as a signal processor, can be connected in a number of different ways, and while one of these may be a compromise, it may be better than no connection of the unit at all. Not all similar components are identical, either in the number of their features, or in the number of components to which they can be connected.

ROUTING THE AUDIO SIGNAL

As long as a high-fidelity system is basic, such as an integrated receiver, routing the signal to its destination is practically automatic, involving nothing more than selecting AM, FM mono, or FM stereo. As a system moves from an integrated to a component system, and as more units are included, the interconnections require more care and prior planning. The routing of the audio signal to its destination requires the use of more controls, and these may be scattered among several units. It isn't always easy to remember these settings, so it is helpful to put them down on paper in their proper sequence. It is also helpful to draw a line diagram showing the flow of the signal, using rectangles to indicate the components involved in the flow.

The Interrupted Signal Path

The easiest movement of the signal, as far as the user is concerned, is one in which the signal moves from a source directly on its path toward the speakers, but the signal may be interrupted in that movement to receive some sort of processing. In effect, what we are doing is breaking into the chain from original signal output to final signal usage to do something to the signal, to modify it in some way.

The Better Connection

Not all cables, connector equipped or not, are alike, even though a physical examination may not reveal any differences. Poorer-quality cables may have a spiral wire wrap instead of braid. The plugs may be more subject to corrosion and the cables may have a low tolerance to flexing. The hot lead of the cable may simply make a force fit inside its cable. A better-quality cable will have the contact tip of its plug solder dipped to ensure good electrical contact with the hot lead. The braid will not only be mechanically secure to its plug, but will be soldered to it to minimize contact resistance.

A quality cable will have minimum DC resistance from one end of the cable to the other. It will also have low capacitance between its center conductor and the shield braid measured in picofarads (pF) per foot. It is advisable to avoid cables whose specs indicate a capacitance of 25 pF or more. Cable capacitance acts as shunt and "steals" treble tones in high-fidelity equipment.

A better-grade cable will also have a noncompressible insulating material between the center conductor and the braid. With a compressible insulating material, crimping the cable may permit the central conductor to cut through the insulating material, producing a short circuit.

Cables for high-fidelity systems use a hot lead made of stranded copper wire. Copper is a good electrical conductor, but it does lack strength if the cable is flexed. This is not a problem for the usual in-home installation, as the cables remain in a fixed position once a connection has been made.

SYSTEM GROUND

An AM receiver, AM/FM/MPX receiver, satellite receiver, or other components in a high-fidelity system will work without a ground connection. All the components are ground connected by the shield braid of the interconnecting cables, consequently it is necessary to ground only one component, usually the turntable.

Finding a ground isn't always easy. If the junction box of a wall-mounted twin outlet is metal (some are plastic), ground could be one of the machine screws attaching its front plate to the junction box. To check if it is really grounded, use a VOM set to read 150 volts AC. Attach one test lead to the plate's holding screw, and insert the needle probe of the test instrument into one, then the other, opening of the outlet. A reading of zero volt on both tests indicates the screw is not grounded. A water pipe is always a good ground connection, although not always conveniently located. If a component does not have a ground terminal, connect the ground wire to any accessible screw that makes contact with its chassis.

NAMES OF PORTS

There is no standardization in the names used for ports on high-fidelity or video equipment. To make sure you understand what the manufacturer is trying to say, consult the owner's operating manual that comes with the components and learn just what the port or ports are supposed to do. Using self-stick labels, put new names on the ports, names that mean something to you or that are consistent with the names of the ports used on your other components.

The Aux Input

The word "aux" (auxiliary) means the manufacturer of the component has supplied an optional port whose function will be determined by the user. Since a high-fidelity system has a growth capability, it would seem that a manufacturer would install as many ports as possible, but this means more than drilling a hole for a jack. That jack must be connected to the input of some circuit. There are also economic considerations. That is why, on some receivers, preamplifiers, or integrated amplifiers, you may not find an aux input; it may have been relabeled CD (for compact disc input) or some other designation.

AUDIO CABLES

The audio cable joining high-fidelity components may be too short or too long. If it is too short, there are two options. The easier is to buy a cable of the right length, saving the original for some subsequent use. Another is to buy raw cable, cut it to a suitable length, and then mount connectors on each end.

Unneeded length adds to the "cable confusion" that exists behind equipment, and the longer the cable, the greater the opportunity of having the cable work as an antenna—picking up extraneous signals and hum, or bypassing treble tones because of the additional cable capacitance.

Cable Confusion

When it becomes necessary to interconnect a number of components, or to reconnect them at some later date when one or more new units are added, the large number of connecting leads, particularly if they are similarly color coded, can be confusing, making it possible to join components that should not interface. A solution is to put a numbered tag or a self-stick label on each connector, that is, at both ends of the cable. To remember the significance of each of the numbers, keep a master list, plus a description of the components that are connected, and include a wiring diagram. When you prepare the wiring diagram, identify the connectors by color as well as by function: "phono ground—black"; "speaker plus—red," and so on.

THE AM RECEIVER

Although not high-fidelity components, AM receivers (Fig. 6–2) are used extensively and can be individual units or available in combination with an AM/FM/MPX receiver. The receiver may have one or more built-in speakers, in which case they do not require connecting wires, or the speakers may be external.

The AM receiver or the AM section of the AM/FM set may or may not need an outside antenna. These receivers are equipped with a loopstick, a polyiron coil mounted on the rear outside the receiver and equipped with a hinge so the loopstick can be moved to its best pickup position.

If the loopstick is inadequate, an outside antenna will be helpful. With the increased use of AM stereo, an outdoor AM antenna would be desirable to get the best signal-to-noise ratio. The antenna can be any length of wire and is often continuous with the lead-in. The lead-in is connected to the AM antenna terminal of the receiver, which may or may not also have a terminal for a ground connection. The indoor or outdoor antenna can be a length of antenna wire, stranded instead of being a single, solid conductor. The lead-in should be stranded, insulated wire. A professional installation would have a wall plate mounted behind the receiver on the baseboard molding. Run a suitable length of insulated wire from the wall plate to the receiver. If the receiver has an external speaker (or speakers) connect them following the instructions described later in this chapter.

At the antenna, strip the lead-in back about one inch and wrap it around the bare, uninsulated antenna. The best arrangement is to solder the lead-in to one end of the antenna and then cover the connection with shrink wrap. For AM, there is no need to be concerned about impedance matching, either at the antenna or at the receiver. The signal is picked up by the antenna and also by the lead-in wire. No special plug is needed for the antenna lead-in. The AM terminal will be a captive machine screw. Strip the insulation of the lead-in by about 3/8 inch and wrap the exposed wire clockwise around the screw shaft, then tighten the screw. Twirl the stranded wires before doing so,

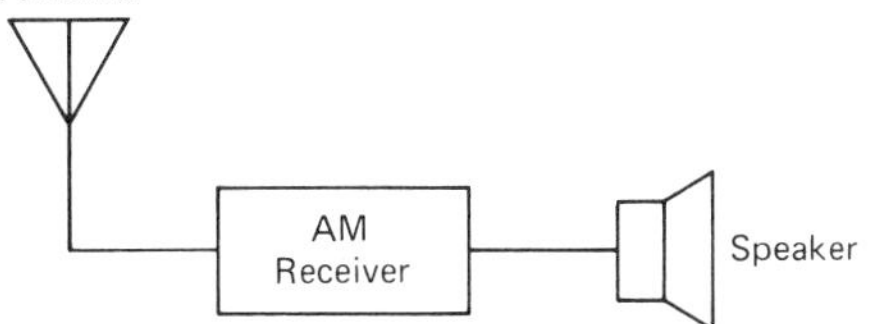

Figure 6–2. The simplest in-home entertainment system. Two speakers will be needed if the receiver is stereophonic.

to let the conductors work as a single wire. Make sure no strands reach any other antenna terminals. None of the copper strands should extend beyond the screw head.

The Two-Speaker AM System

In-home monophonic radios may have two speakers (Fig. 6–3) but if they are built into the set, no connection, other than that to an outdoor antenna, is required. If the receiver has enough audio power to drive two speakers and these are external, make the connections using zip cord. The receiver will have two terminals, A and B, or speaker 1 and 2. The polarity of the speaker outputs will be identified by plus and minus symbols or by a red dot to indicate plus. Connect these to the correspondingly marked terminals on the speakers.

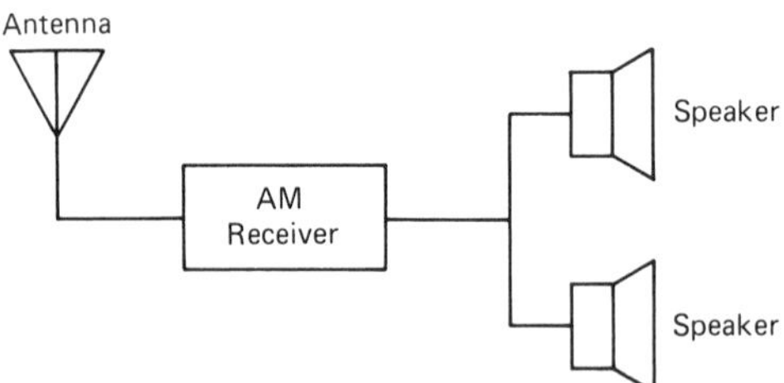

Figure 6–3. Two-speaker system for mono or stereo AM receiver.

THE FM-ONLY RECEIVER

Some receivers are used for FM only and usually have two outboard speakers. Connect these, using either lamp cord or speaker wire. It may be desirable to solder the stranded wire ends to make a more solid connection to the receiver and speaker terminals. If the receiver has machine screw terminals, solder open spade lugs on the wires. The best lugs to use are those in which the wire ends can be secured mechanically by crimping, prior to soldering. The lamp cord from the receiver to the speakers can be tacked against a baseboard, hidden under rug ends, or enclosed in a metal channel fastened to the baseboard.

THE FM ANTENNA

The metallic rods of an FM antenna, sometimes called elements, may be confusing, because there are so many of them. Known as directors and reflectors, they have no physical or electrical connection to the antenna itself. This is usually a short, horizontal rod, or it can be a folded dipole to which the downlead is connected.

There are several connection possibilities right at the antenna. The antenna can be 300-ohms, permitting the direct connection of twin lead, or a balun may be required if the 300-ohm antenna is to be connected to coaxial cable, or if the 75-ohm antenna is to be connected to twin lead.

At the other end of the transmission line there may also be impedance-matching problems. The input to the FM set is often 300 ohms, but if coaxial cable is used as the downlead, a 75-ohm to 300-ohm matching transformer will be required. Thus, a downlead installation may require two transformers, one at the antenna, the other at the antenna terminal of the receiver. It is possible that no transformers, or just one, will be needed.

In electrically noisy environments, there are two downlead choices: The first is to use shielded twin lead, especially if the antenna and the receiver are both 300 ohms. The other is the use of coaxial cable, possibly requiring a balun at the antenna and another at the receiver.

If a combined antenna is used instead of a separate FM-only antenna, a band separator will be needed at the receiver end of the transmission line. The output of the band separator for the FM signal is usually 300 ohms and is indicated by a small section of twin lead coming from the separator. The twin lead ends with spade lugs, so the component can easily be connected to the two machine screw terminals of the FM receiver's antenna signal input block.

MPX RECEIVER

This integrated receiver (Fig. 6-4) is the first step to a high-fidelity system. Unlike the in-home AM receiver, it is a move toward the use of ports for connecting other signal sources, such as a turntable, a cassette deck, and possibly an open-reel deck. Unlike the AM receiver, it will also have convenience outlets, switched and unswitched.

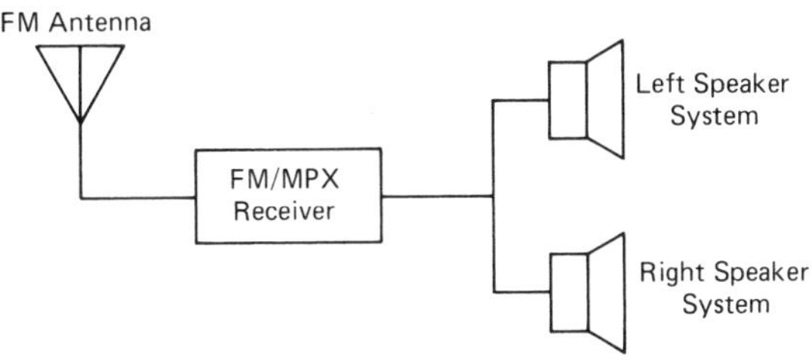

Figure 6-4. FM (mono)/MPX (stereo) receiver uses minimum of two speakers.

As far as the AM section of the receiver is concerned, an external antenna can be connected in the same way as described for the AM receiver.

Figure 6-5A shows the possible antennas for an AM/FM/MPX receiver. Although four antennas are shown, only two, and possibly only one, will be

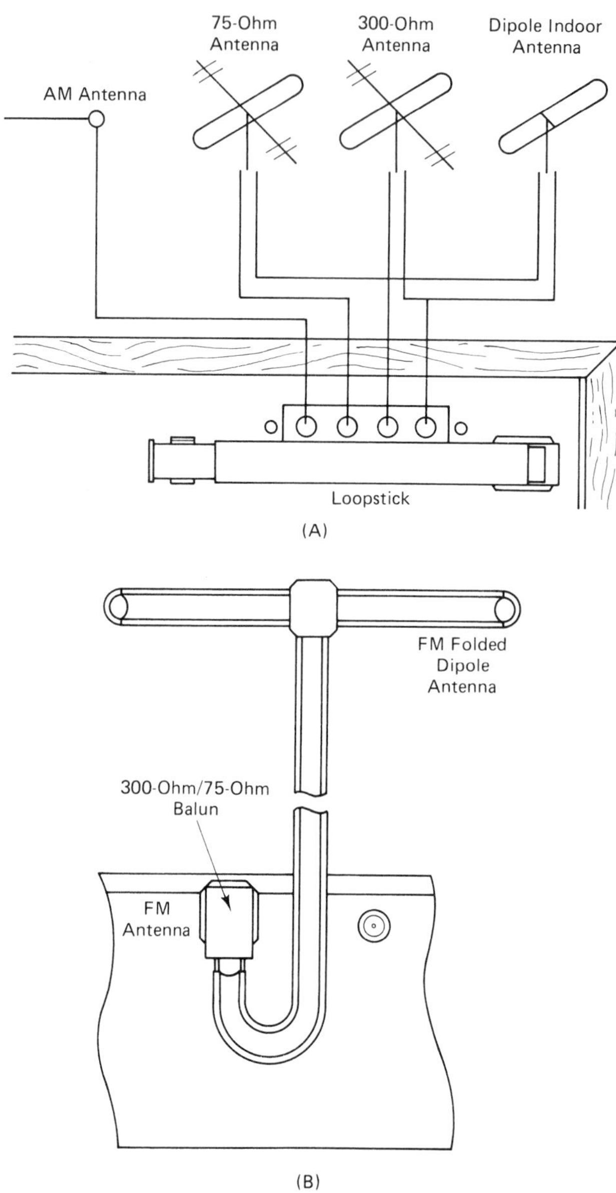

Figure 6–5. Antenna connections for AM/FM receiver (A). Twin lead uses right-angle balun for connection to FM receiver (B).

used. An outdoor AM antenna may be wired in as indicated if the loopstick is inadequate for signal pickup. The FM antenna may be a folded dipole or an open dipole, or it may consist of an indoor dipole, a length of twin lead supplied with the receiver and used indoors.

Quite often the antenna block on an FM receiver will have screw-type terminals indicating a 300-ohm input to which twin lead can be connected. In some receivers, though, the port has a 75-ohm jack. If the downlead is 300-ohms, a 300-ohm to 75-ohm balun will be required, as indicated in Fig. 6–5B.

At the other end of the AM/FM/MPX receiver, the output is connected to a pair of stereo speakers, one for left-channel sound, the other for the right channel (Fig. 6–6).

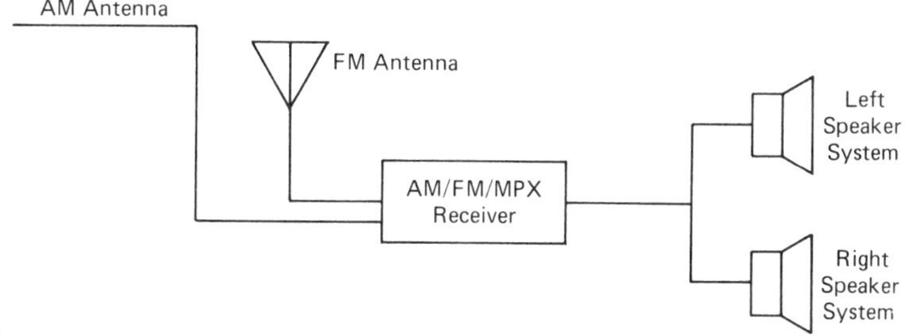

Figure 6–6. Speaker connections for AM/FM/MPX receiver.

The description of the receiver, AM/FM/MPX, is an outgrowth of the original designation for such sets prior to the introduction of stereo. At that time they were known as AM/FM sets with both bands transmitting monophonic sound only. When FM stereo finally came along the receivers were called AM/FM/MPX to distinguish them from monophonic-only sets. "MPX" is an abbreviation for multiplex, the technique used for obtaining stereo sound in FM broadcasts. Monophonic FM sets are no longer being made, as all these receivers can now pick up either mono or stereo FM, but the description AM/FM/MPX has been retained.

SYSTEM GROWTH

Figure 6–7 shows three possible steps in the growth of a high-fidelity system. In drawing A, an integrated receiver is used. An integrated receiver consists of three individual components on a single chassis: a tuner, a preamplifier, and a power amplifier. In a component system these units are separate. An integrated receiver also works as a control center, for it has a selector to determine which of a number of sound sources is to be used. This control can choose AM broadcasting, FM mono, FM stereo, a turntable, and a tape recorder.

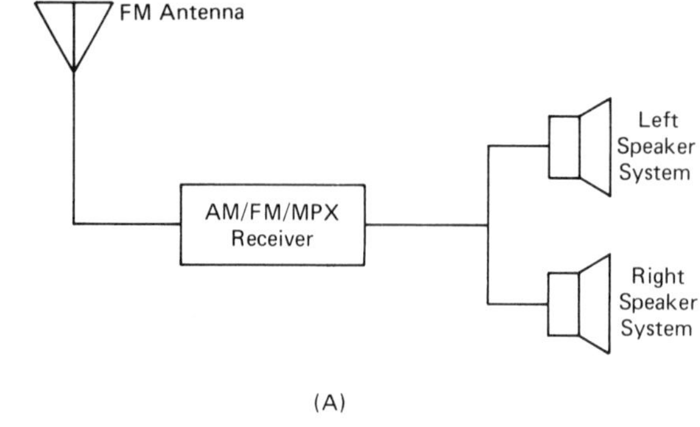

(A)

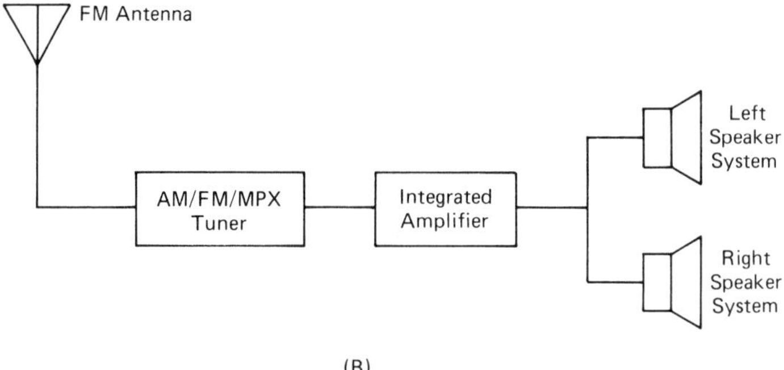

(B)

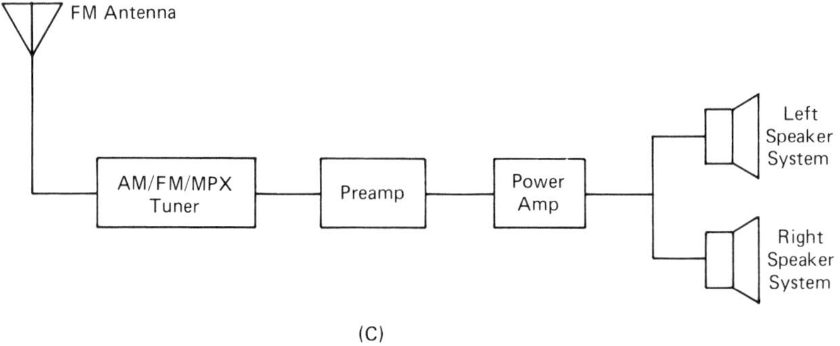

(C)

Figure 6–7. Steps in the formation of a component system.

In drawing B, the combined preamplifier and power amplifier has been removed from the receiver, and the receiver—minus these components—is now designated as a tuner. The system now makes its appearance as an integrated amplifier consisting of these two units, combined, preceded by the tuner. The final step is the separation of the integrated amplifier into its component sections comprising a preamplifier and power amplifier, as shown in drawing C. Again, all the other components remain the same. However, in the process of going from an integrated to a component arrangement, more connections and more cables will be required. Further, there will also be an increase in the number of controls, and these will appear on the tuner and the amplifiers. Basically, the tuner will be used for station selection; it will choose the type of broadcasting (AM, FM, and FM stereo). It may have a station memory, and on the rear of the unit there will possibly be both switched and unswitched AC power outlets. The amplifier may have a control for sound source selection, a volume control, one or more tone controls, a tape monitor control, a muting control, a speaker balance control. This may seem like a large number, but many of them are one-time selections.

With the movement of the integrated amplifier out of the tuner, the additional sound sources such as a turntable (or turntables), a cassette deck, an open-reel deck, and a compact disc will need ports. The number available will depend directly on the amplifier. Better-grade integrated amplifiers often have ample provision for system expansion; budget integrated amplifiers have less.

THE MULTISPEAKER SYSTEM

The growth of a high-fidelity system can move in a number of different directions. Figure 6–8 illustrates an AM/FM/MPX tuner followed by a preamplifier and a power amplifier, with the last amplifier driving two pairs of speakers. These speakers are subsystems, with one pair often identified as speaker system A, and the other as B. The systems can be in the same room

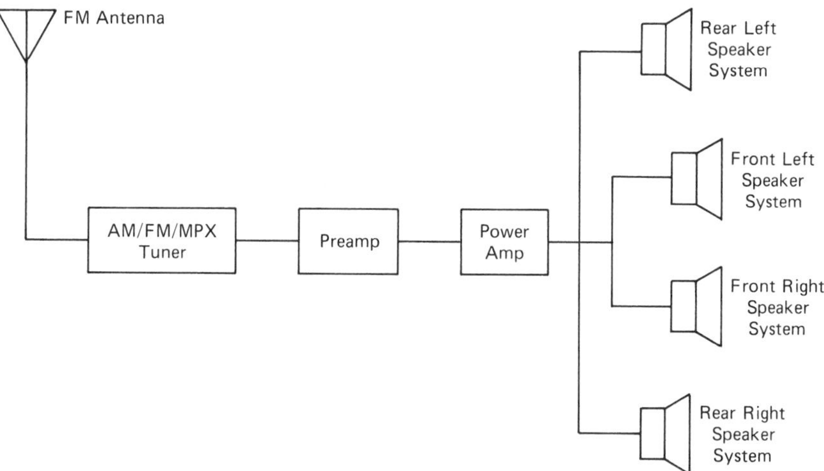

Figure 6–8. System using two pairs of speakers.

or one pair can be in another room. Speaker system selection is usually from a control on the power amplifier, marked "A, B" and "A + B."

HOW TO CONNECT AN AM/FM TUNER

A tuner is just one section of an integrated receiver and as such can be used separately in a component high-fidelity system. Connecting the tuner (Fig. 6–9) is simply a matter of using audio cables from the tuner's output to the input of the following preamplifier or power amplifier. As the amplifier's power supply may generate a certain amount of radio-frequency noise, position the tuner so its AM antenna loopstick is well away from the amplifier.

A tuner is a sound source, just like a turntable or a compact disc player. Every tuner has an input (an antenna) and an output (a baseband audio signal—unmodulated—the modulation signal having been separated from the audio signal in the tuner, and discarded). The input to the tuner from the antenna is quite different and consists of a modulated signal—an audio signal plus a radio-frequency carrier.

For AM reception, connections are the same as for the AM-only receiver described earlier. The tuner will be equipped with a loopstick antenna. No separate connection is required and the loopstick is an integral part of the tuner. The loopstick can be adjusted for best AM reception, since it is mounted on a swivel bracket. For better signal pickup, an outdoor antenna can be used. Connect the lead of the AM antenna to a terminal marked "AM Ant" on the

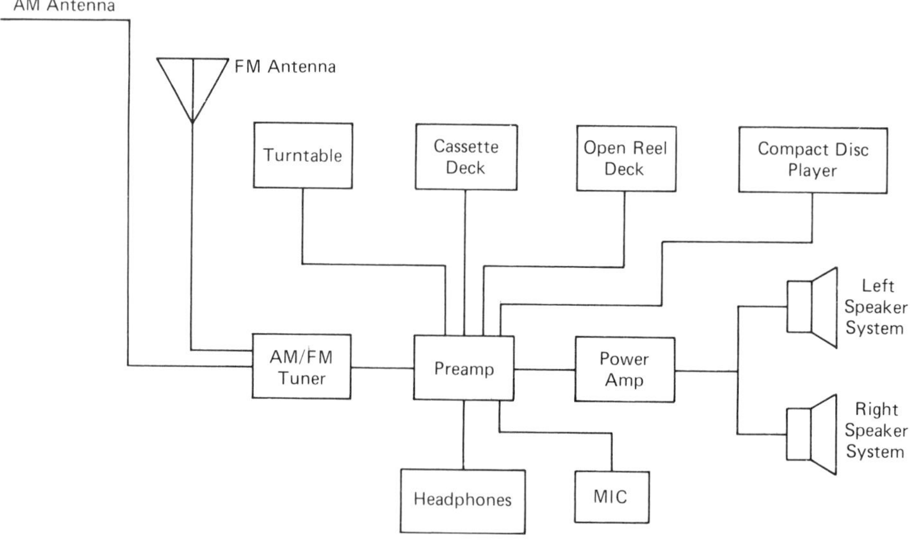

Figure 6–9. Component high-fidelity system using an AM/FM tuner.

back of the set, usually a captive machine screw. Before making this connection, make sure the receiver connection end of that wire is bright and clean.

The tuner is equipped with a ground terminal. Connect a wire from this post to the same grounding point as that of the turntable. Grounding the tuner will also ground the following preamplifier or power amplifier automatically via the shield braid of the connecting cable.

THE PREAMPLIFIER

The component following the AM/FM tuner (Fig. 6–9) or the FM-only tuner is a preamplifier (preamp), a voltage amplifier with a double function. It is used to amplify the audio signal delivered by the tuner and it also works as a control center. The preamp can have a large number of inputs and one output for delivery of the signal to the following power amplifier. The preamplifier can also determine the ultimate arrangement of the high-fidelity system, depending on the number of its input ports.

The preamp accepts audio signals only in unmodulated form, and that is the way the signals are delivered, not only by the tuner but by all the other sound sources as well.

The sound source inputs can be on the front panel as well as the back panel of the preamp. The preamp could have one or two microphone (mic) ports, and these are front panel jacks. These jacks are different from those on the rear and are designed to accommodate the plugs on the microphone cable. The connectors at the rear of the preamp are RCA phone jacks. Headphones that connect to the front of the preamp also have their own plugs. If the plugs on these two components, microphones and headphones, do not fit, use jack adapters.

The turntable (there may be two), cassette deck, open-reel deck, compact disc player, equalizer, and sound processor can be connected to the rear of the preamplifier, using audio coaxial cable. Their plugs will be RCA phono plugs (pin plugs).

The preamp will often have switched and unswitched AC power outlets. The line cords for the power amplifier should be plugged into the switched outlet so it is activated every time the preamp is turned on. The preamplifiers and power amplifiers are basic to the entire system and unless they are active none of the sound sources will be heard.

ADDING MORE COMPONENTS

The system in Fig. 6–10 shows two turntables, which are desirable for nonstop music. Two pairs of headphones are used. Ports for these headphones will be available, as they may be supplied by the tuner or by the preamplifier. Even

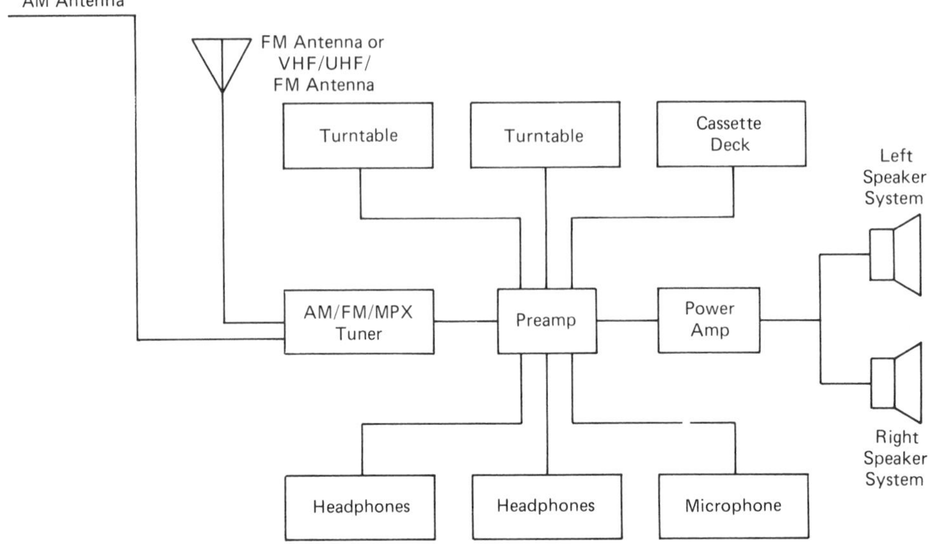

Figure 6–10. High-fidelity system using two turntables.

if there is just one port, a headphone adapter is available to permit the use of two.

Although only one pair of speakers appears in Fig. 6–10, we could have more than one pair, depending on speaker sensitivity and output power of the power amplifier. Each speaker enclosure could house one or more woofers, speakers for bass response; one or more midrange speakers; and one or more tweeters, speakers for treble response. To avoid having a multiplicity of wires running from the power amplifier to the speakers, speaker systems contain crossover networks within their enclosures. These networks divide the audio band into two or three parts: bass, midrange, and treble. Consequently, even though a speaker enclosure might contain two or more speakers (drivers), the input to the speaker system could be just two conductors.

Frequency division takes place in this system following delivery of the audio signal to the speaker input terminals on the outside of the enclosure. Crossover networks in audio could be compared to the band separators used in a transmission line downlead for the separation of VHF/UHF/FM frequencies.

COMPONENT DUPLICATION

In some systems, there is component duplication. Thus, in Fig. 6–11, the system includes two turntables, two tape decks, two pairs of speakers. The setup consists of an AM/FM stereo tuner, followed by an integrated amplifier. This

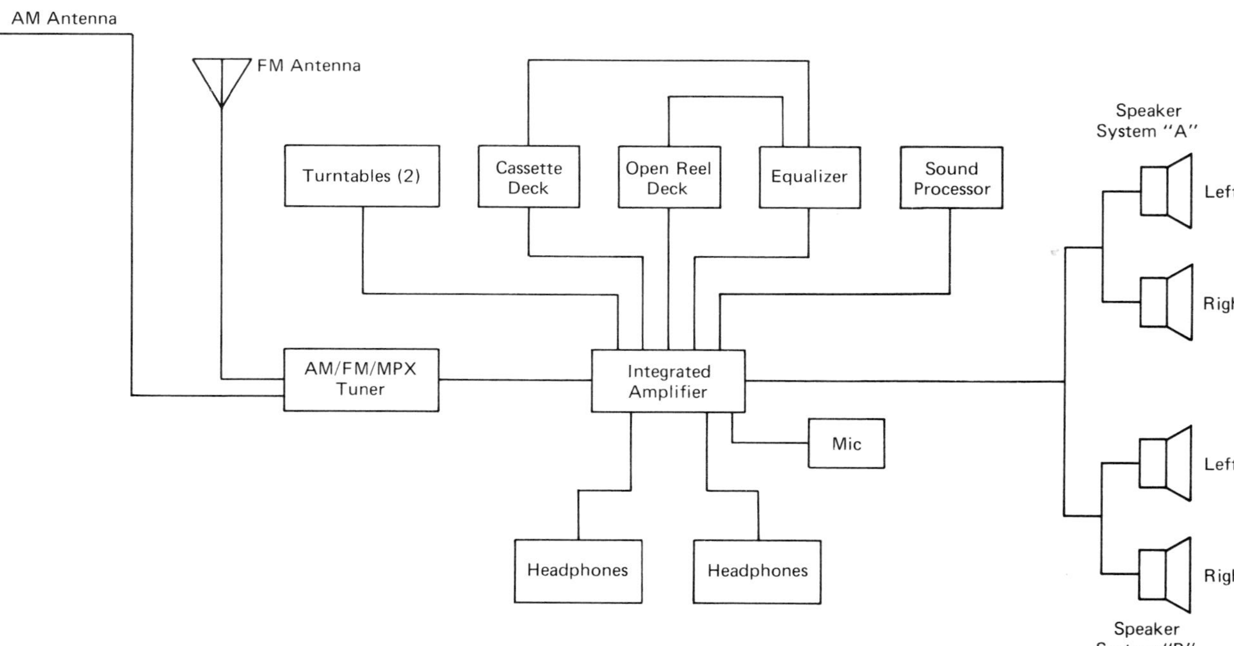

Figure 6–11. High-fidelity system with component duplication.

amplifier is equipped with ports for all the input cables—those from the tape decks, the tuner, and the turntables. The headphones and microphones are plugged into the front panel. Although only a single microphone is shown, the amplifier has front panel ports for two of them. This system uses a large number of units, but it is still not a complete component setup, for the amplifier is integrated.

SIGNAL PROCESSING

The signal path in a high-fidelity system can be directly from the sound source to the speakers as the output of this direct chain. However, along the way the signal may be modified by a component such as an equalizer or a sound processor. Figure 6–11 shows the inclusion of these in addition to the other components. All of these are individual components, but note that we still have an integrated amplifier, the only integrated unit in this system.

As a final step toward a total component system, the integrated amplifier, as shown in Fig. 6–12, can be separated into its individual units, which, in this example, consist of a preamplifier, or voltage amplifier, and a following power amplifier.

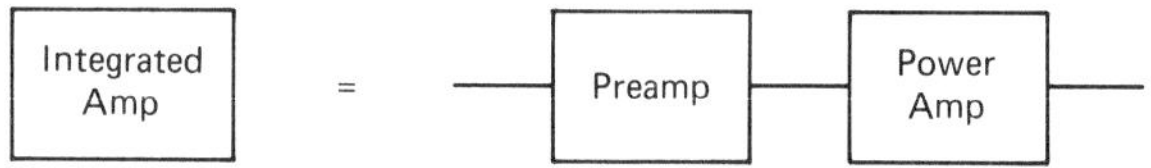

Figure 6–12. Integrated amplifier consists of a preamplifier (voltage amplifier) and a power amp.

THE TOTAL COMPONENT SYSTEM

The basic component system shown in Fig. 6–7 can be expanded into the more elaborate arrangement illustrated in Fig. 6–13. Note that practically all of the components—with the exception of a sound processor and the speakers—are connected to the preamp, which functions not only as a signal voltage amplifier but as a source selector. Whether it will be able to supply such control depends on the number of input ports and a suitable switching arrangement. The preamp has only one output port and that is connected to the power amplifier. The power amplifier has only two input ports, and while only one pair of speakers is shown, it may have provision for connections to another pair.

The Connections

A block diagram indicates only the relationships of the components to each other and supplies only an overall view; it does not yield any connection information. Each line shown in such diagrams represents not one but a pair

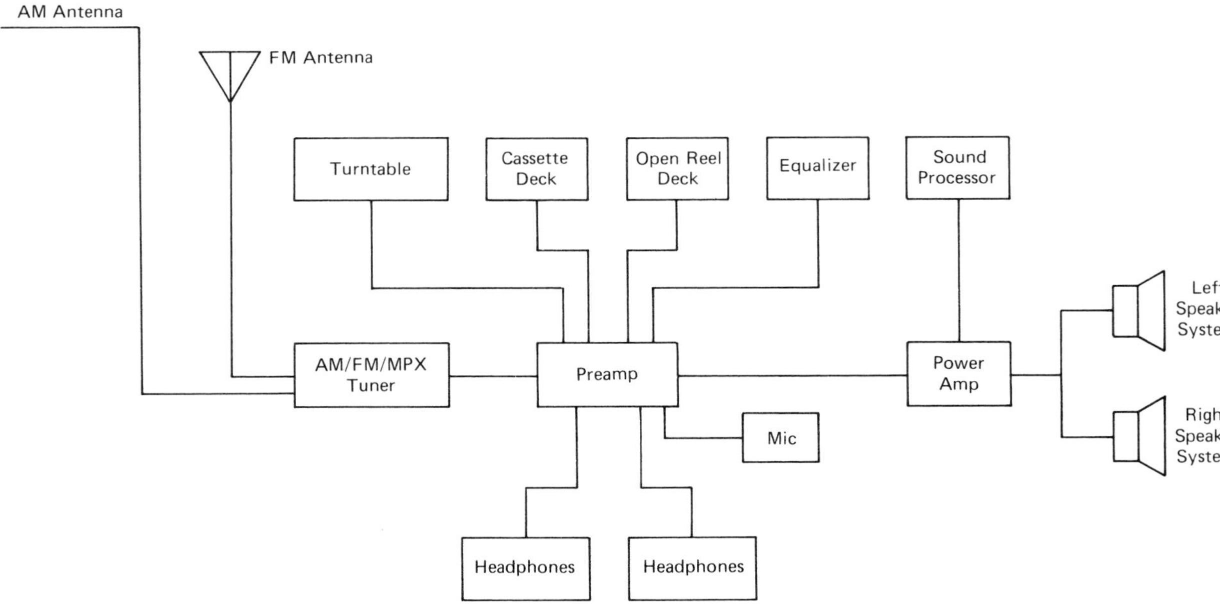

Figure 6–13. With the exception of the headphones and the speakers, all these high-fidelity components are AC line powered.

of wires. In a high-fidelity system, the interconnections are made using audio cable, described in Chapter 1. This cable consists of a center conductor covered with insulating material surrounded by an outer layer of shield braid. The signal is not delivered by the center conductor alone but by that center conductor plus the shield braid. The connectors used at the ends of the audio cables are most often RCA phono plugs. As described previously these consist of a center pin connected to the hot lead, and a cylindrical four-leaf outer shell, connected to the cold, or ground, lead. The plugs are housed in plastic, often colored red and white, although other colors are used as well.

AC Power

All active components, unless they are battery operated, have a power-line cord, which must be connected to an AC outlet, whether that outlet is on another component or is mounted along the baseboard in the listening room. Any outlet used for supplying power to a high-fidelity system, a video system, or an audio/video system should be a dedicated outlet, that is, not used for any other purpose. There are a number of reasons for this: The first is not to overload the power line. While an individual component may not impose a heavy load on the line, the total power needed is the sum of the individual component power requirements. The second is to minimize the possibility of the transfer of line electrical noise; and, finally, outlets are all double receptacles, so a dedicated outlet means both receptacles should be available for the sound and/or video systems.

The components in an in-home high-fidelity system are powered by the AC line with the connections made by a power-line cord terminating in a power plug. The power plug may be polarized or nonpolarized. The nonpolarized plug has two metal extensions identical in size and shape. Consequently, this plug can be connected to an AC outlet in two ways. This is convenient as one possible method for reducing hum; if some hum is present, try reversing the power plug.

A polarized plug can be inserted into the AC outlet in one way only, as one blade of the plug is wider than the other. This is a safety feature. If the plug does not fit, the outlet is obsolete and should be replaced. If it is replaced, the more desirable outlet is one that will accept a three-wire grounding plug.

For supplying power to various components, it is advisable to use as many outlets on components as possible. These outlets often indicate their power-handling capability in terms of volt/amperes or in watts. Components equipped with convenience outlets should have at least two, both switched and unswitched, with as high a volt/ampere or wattage rating as possible. A switched outlet is one that requires the on/off switch of the component to be turned on to deliver AC power.

Do not use cube taps either on a wall outlet or on a component's convenience outlet. In an ideal arrangement, there should be only one line cord coming from the system to an outlet. If the home entertainment is such that a single power outlet is inadequate, consider the installation of a multiple outlet. These come equipped with a red light whose glow indicates that power is on, plus a switch to deactivate line power. Not only does this supply the convenience of extra outlets, but the on/off switch can be turned to its off position, thus deactivating the entire in-home entertainment system.

When inserting the plug of a power cord it should slide into its jack smoothly, although some pressure will be required. If the plug will not go into the jack, do not try to force it, as the plug may be polarized. Remove the plug by grasping it; do not remove the plug by pulling on the power-line cord.

The metal extensions of the plug may be of different sizes, or the plug may have a third metal extension resembling a small metal tube. This is the grounding pin.

Quick Power Check

The line cord is one of the least suspected troublemakers in any system, audio or video, or combined audio/video. It can be responsible for poor system results under two conditions: the line voltage is lower than normal, and there is too much of a voltage drop not only across the power cord, but also at the plug itself. As a quick check, turn on all the components of the system, even though the system is not normally used this way; it still represents a possible operating technique. After the system has been on for some time, possibly an hour, disconnect the line plug and touch its blades. It should be no more than moderately warm. If the blades are hot to the touch, and if the line cord connected to that plug feels warm, there may be trouble. The problem may be in poor contact at the outlet, or the wrong wire gauge, if an extension cord is being used, or an overload condition in one of the components. To determine if a component is at fault, turn off the components one at a time, and then repeat the check on the plug and cord.

THE ELECTRONIC CROSSOVER

A high-fidelity system using an electronic crossover need not be much more complex than one with passive units. In Fig. 6–14, two power amplifiers are used. There are two speaker systems with each supplying left- and right-channel sound. One power amplifier delivers bass and midrange tones while the other is responsible for treble frequencies. An external electronic crossover separates the woofer/midrange frequencies from the treble. The tweeter speakers may have a built-in low-pass filter screening any bass/midrange tones that may still be present.

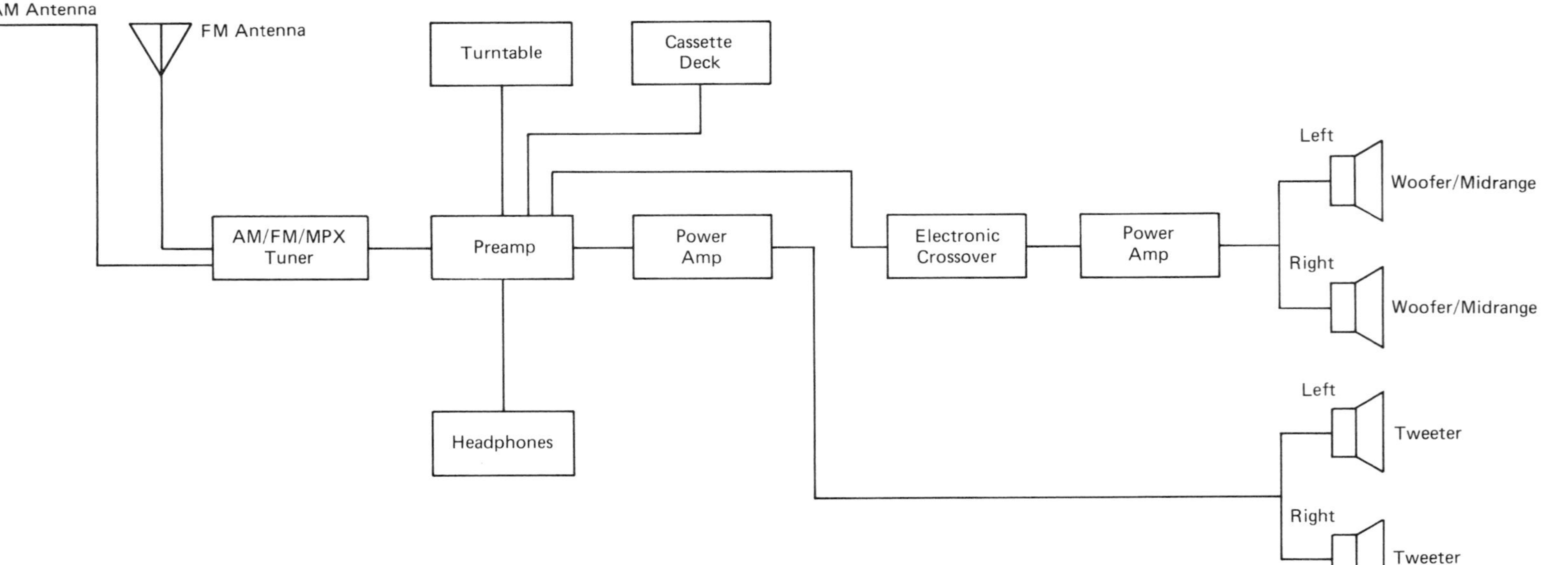

Figure 6–14. System using an electronic crossover.

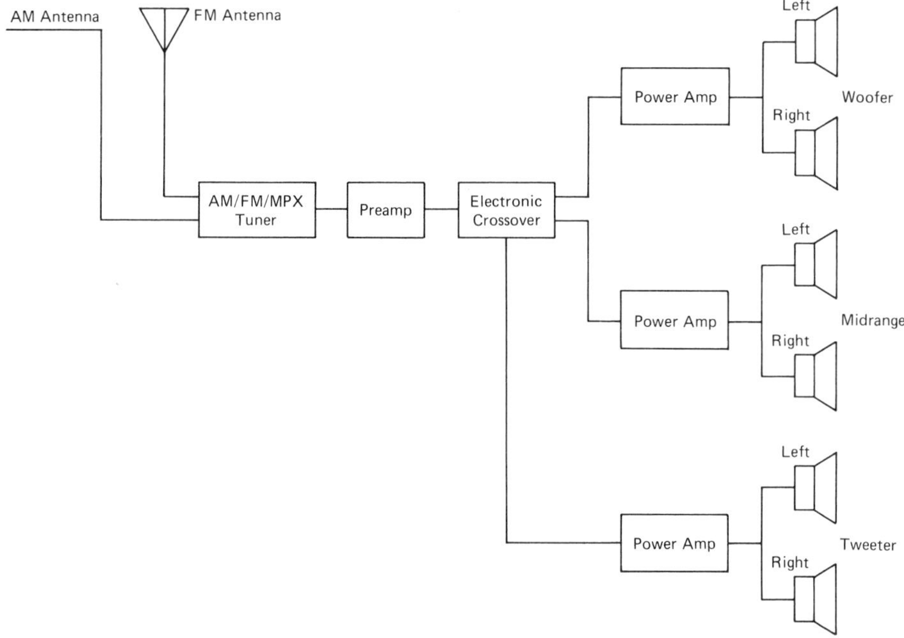

Figure 6–15. System using separate speakers for bass, midrange, and treble tones.

Figure 6–15 shows another system using an electronic crossover, but now there are separate speakers for bass, midrange, and treble tones. The crossover divides the audio spectrum into two audio ranges—treble, and bass/midrange. There are three power amplifiers in this system, and, as in the preceding system, the amplifiers need not have the same power output capability. The midrange and woofer speakers have built-in bandpass filters.

A combination of multiamp operation, plus the addition of a number of sound sources, produces the rather elaborate setup shown in Fig. 6–16. This system has no less than seven sound sources: a tuner, a turntable, two tape decks, a compact disc player, and a pair of microphones. Although a common line connection to the preamp is shown for the microphones, each of these would have its own cable. The headphones are shown connected to the preamp, assuming it has ports for two. The cassette deck and the open-reel deck also have their connections indicated by single lines, but both of these sound sources have a record/playback facility, so there would actually be two cables running between the decks and the preamp.

The multiamp system is somewhat simplified if an integrated amplifier (sometimes called a pre-main amp) is used instead of a separate preamplifier and power amplifier (Fig. 6–17). Although the drawing shows just one pre-main power amplifier preceding a dividing network, an electronic crossover, followed by a separate power amplifier, is used to drive the bass speaker. In

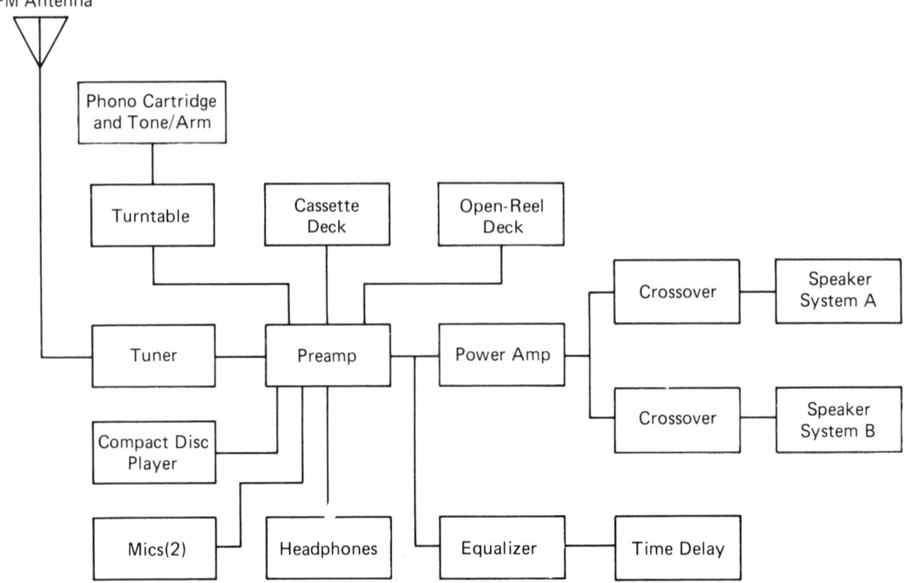

Figure 6–16. High-fidelity system using a pair of external crossovers for the speaker systems.

this case, the crossover filters the bass tones, delivering only the midrange and treble to the high and mid speakers.

The setup in Fig. 6–17 is apparently more economical, as it eliminates one component—and also simplifies the connections—but it is not as desirable as the use of a separate preamp and power amplifier. The trouble is that the

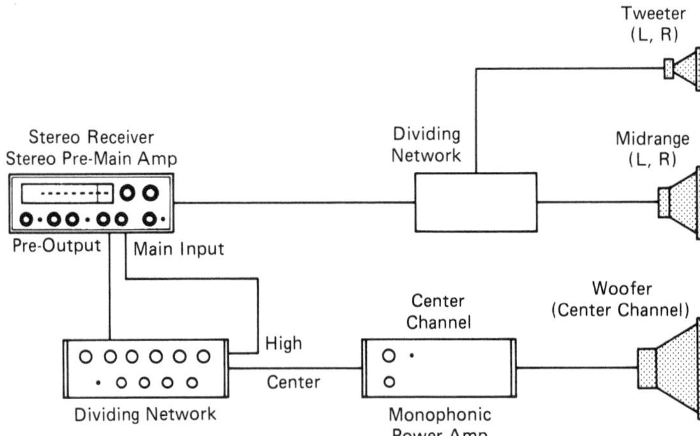

Figure 6–17. Center channel connections for electronic crossover.

integrated amplifier, despite the filter it uses, still delivers some treble and midrange sound to the bass speaker.

EVOLUTION OF THE MULTIAMP SYSTEM

Like an integrated amplifier, a combined preamplifier and power amplifier, a speaker is also integrated, consisting of a filter or crossover network, plus the drivers (speakers), as shown in Fig. 6-18. The crossover in such an arrangement is purely passive and consists of resistors, capacitors, and coils. The problem with this combination is that tonal separation is seldom as good as it should be, and can result in intermodulation distortion (IM), producing

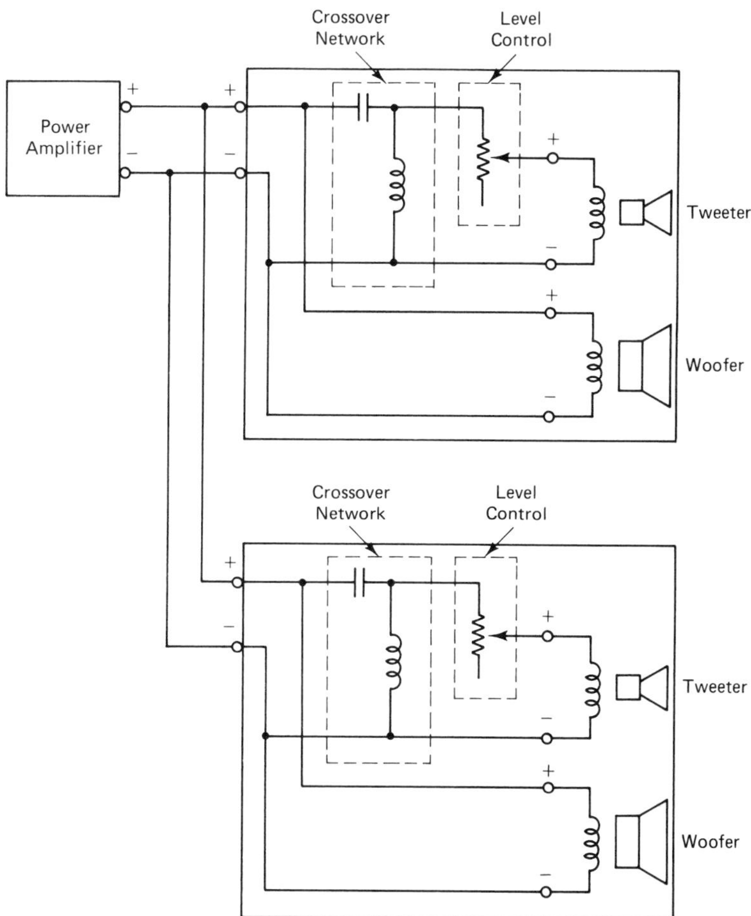

Figure 6-18. Passive crossover network in speaker system.

"muddy" sound. The electronic crossover, a transistorized active network, is helpful in eliminating IM and permits a wider dynamic range.

Figure 6–19 shows five possible steps in the development of a multiamp system. The ultimate, and most desirable (and most costly) arrangement is the use of separate power amplifiers for bass, midrange, and treble tones.

As a start in this electronic evolutionary process, drawing A shows a widely used hookup consisting of a single power amplifier driving a speaker system. The power amplifier contains not just one but two amplifiers, one for left-channel sound, the other for right-channel sound. Although a single-speaker system is shown in the drawing, there are actually two, with one speaker system omitted for the sake of drawing clarity, hence all the setups shown in these drawings are stereo, not mono.

In the next drawing, B, a separate power amplifier is used for driving the bass speaker. An electronic crossover supplies midrange and treble tones, via a power amplifier, to the mid and treble speakers. While this is an improvement of the setup in drawing A, it is still not as good as it should be, as there is no tone separation prior to signal delivery to the bass driver. For that reason, this speaker would need to use a filter network inside its enclosure.

Drawing C shows the use of a separate power amplifier for the bass speaker. This is an improvement over the hookup in drawing B for several reasons. One of these is that the internal crossover for the bass speaker has been removed, with the filtering handled by the electronic crossover. The other is the use of a separate power amp for the bass, a driver that requires substantial signal energy. However, there is still an undesirable feature; the midrange and treble tones travel together until they reach the passive crossover in the enclosure.

Drawing D is interesting since, for the first time, all passive crossovers have been eliminated. Also, individual power amplifiers are now available for all the drivers. A pair of separate amplifiers are used for the midrange and treble speakers, while signal power for the bass driver is obtained from the pre-main unit.

The setup in drawing D is the best of all those shown. It can still be modified, however, by eliminating the integrated power amplifier and substituting a separate preamplifier and power amplifier for it as in drawing E. However, the functioning of the systems in D and E is the same.

Not all of the power amps in E need be identical, nor do they all have the same power output rating. The amplifier for the treble tones can have the least power output, for the midrange more, and still more for the bass driver. This is because each of the speakers has different power requirements. A good rule of thumb is to use power amplifiers having as high a power rating as your budget can tolerate, especially if more than one speaker system is to be included.

All the power amplifiers should be stereo, and, if their output power is adequate, capable of driving two pairs of speakers, that is, an A and B speaker

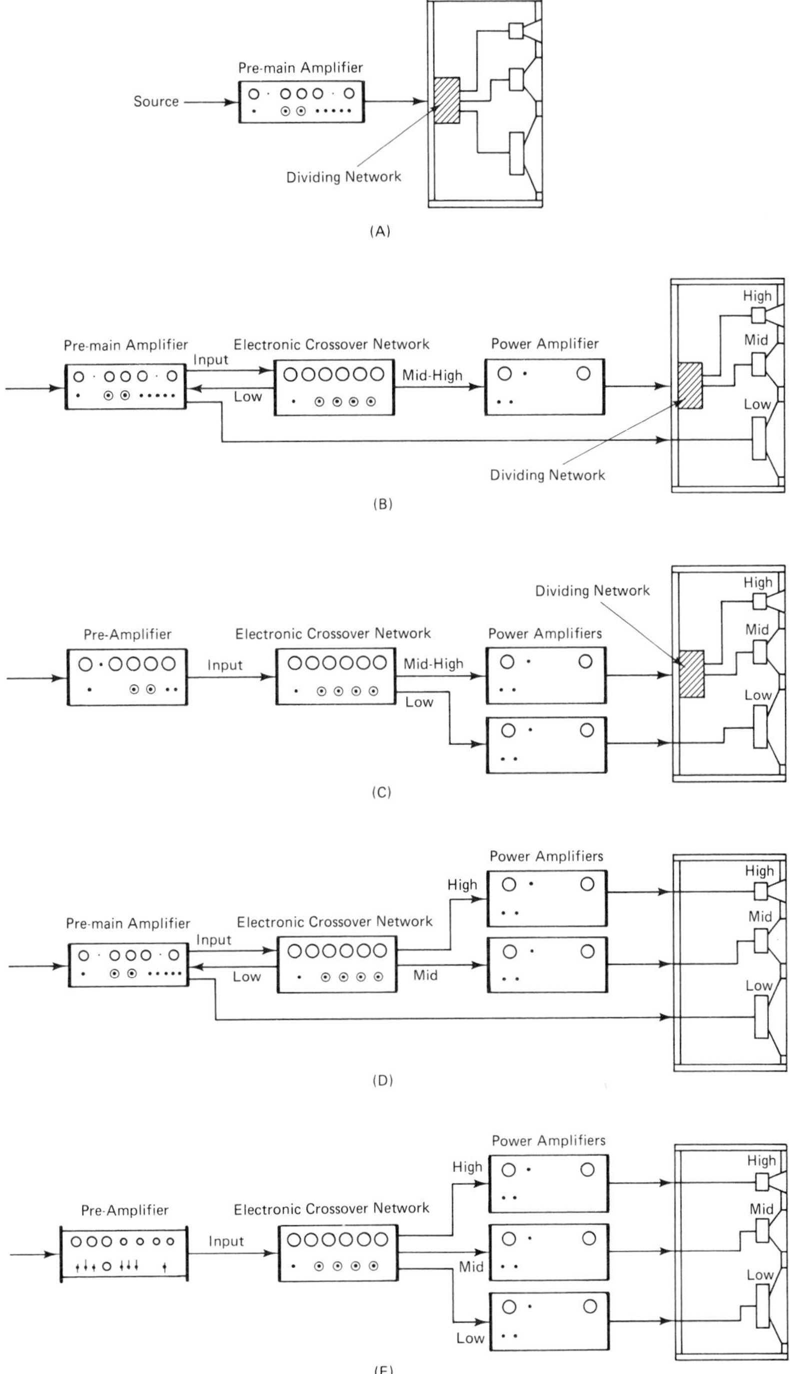

Figure 6–19. Connections for multiamp systems.

system. The power amplifiers should be equipped with a control permitting the selection of either speaker system A, or system B, or both.

CONNECTING THE STEREO POWER AMPLIFIER

The stereo power amplifier precedes the loudspeakers and is directly connected to them. The purpose of the power amp is to deliver electrical power in the audio range to the speaker system.

The power amp is a true component, unlike an integrated amplifier containing both a preamplifier and a power amplifier. Figure 6–20 shows the diagram for connections to such an amplifier. While this drawing shows the wiring to three pairs of left/right speakers, implying a large power output capability, many cannot drive more than one pair.

The input signal for the power amplifier is supplied via an audio cable, RCA plug equipped, by the connected preamplifier, sometimes called a control amplifier. The preamplifier selects the signal source—open-reel deck, cassette deck, turntable, or compact disc—and it is the signal of the selected sound source that is delivered to the input of the power amp.

The power amplifier also has a ground connection terminal. This terminal may need to be connected to ground if there is any hum output from the speakers. This can be determined by turning up the gain control but with no input signal being used. If there is any hum, connect a wire to the ground terminal used by the turntable.

The power amplifier in Fig. 6–20 has just one convenience AC outlet, an unswitched outlet, although some power amplifiers have several outlets, both switched and unswitched. In this example, as the outlet is unswitched, it has AC power as long as the power amp is connected to a live power outlet, whether or not the power amp is turned on.

Note that the AC plug of the power amplifier should be connected to an AC outlet and not to the convenience outlet on the preamp. The reason for this is that the peak current drawn by the power amplifier can be several times the normal operating current, as it would be momentarily when the unit is first turned on, or when the power amplifier is driven by a large input signal from the preamplifier. This precaution does not apply to other components, such as a tuner or preamplifier.

The arrangement of the speaker systems, A, B, and C, is a matter of personal choice. Speaker system A can be in the front of the room, with the left speaker positioned at the left, and the right speaker at the right. Speakers for system B could be placed in the rear of the room, and speaker system C in another room. A control switch on the front panel of the power amp gives the user a choice of operating just one speaker system, or two, or all three. The amplifier must have a power output capable of driving the three speaker systems simultaneously.

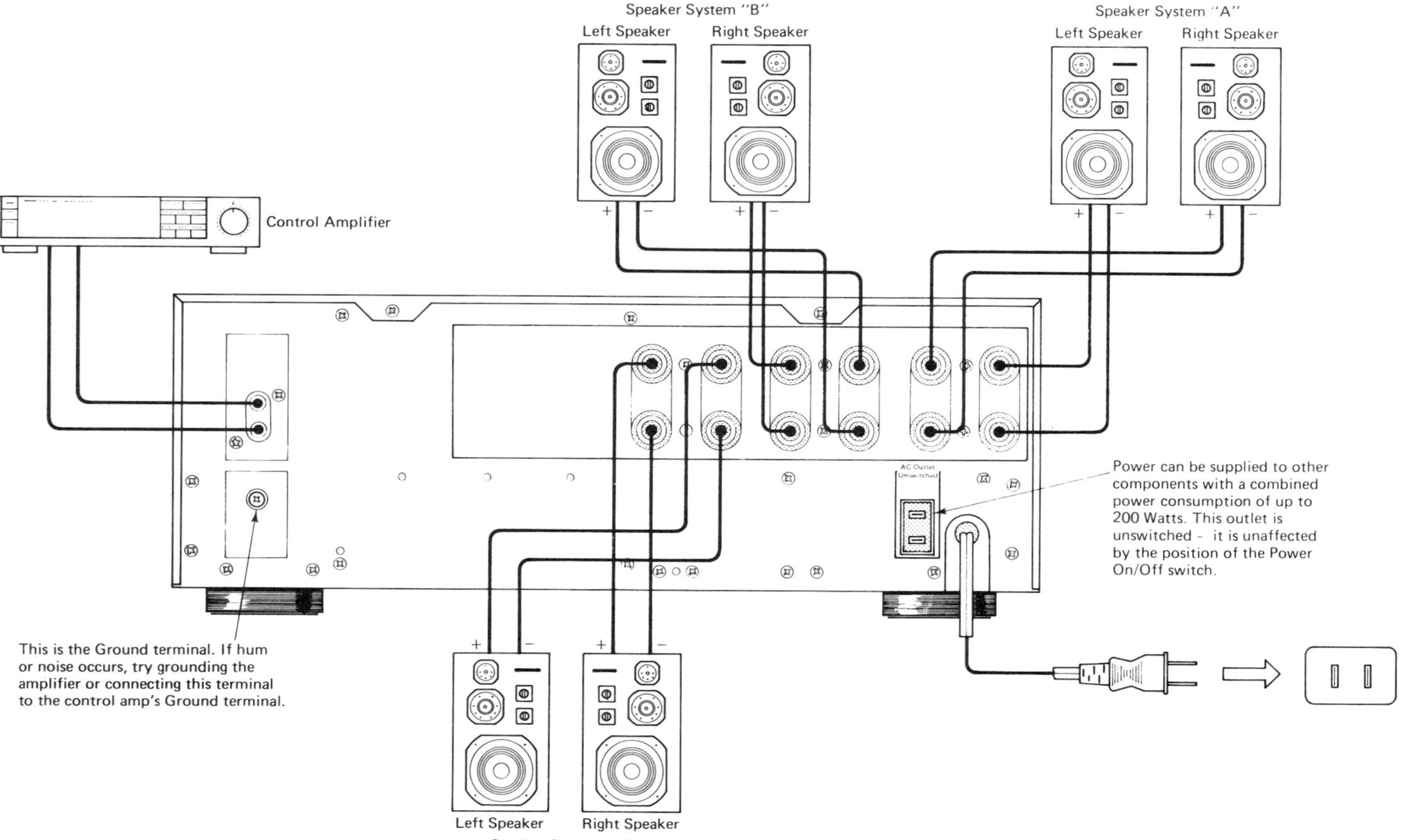

Speaker System "B"
Left Speaker
Right Speaker
Speaker System "A"
Left Speaker
Right Speaker
Control Amplifier
AC Outlet
Unswitched
Power can be supplied to other components with a combined power consumption of up to 200 Watts. This outlet is unswitched - it is unaffected by the position of the Power On/Off switch.
This is the Ground terminal. If hum or noise occurs, try grounding the amplifier or connecting this terminal to the control amp's Ground terminal.
Left Speaker
Right Speaker
Speaker System "C"

Figure 6–20. Connections for a power amplifier. (*Courtesy Yamaha Electronics Corp.*)

Connecting Speakers

While it is desirable to have speakers located equidistant between the amplifiers that supply them with audio power, the distances need not be identical, and the connecting cables can have different lengths. If the cable lengths (Fig. 6–21) are considerably different, the longer length of cable may need to be of a smaller wire gauge (that is, a thicker wire). Stranded wire is commonly used for speaker cables, and while 18-gauge wire is readily obtainable, wires having lower gauge numbers are special items if you want them twisted. Wire gauges 16, 14, and 12 are available in electrical supply stores, but if they are solid conductors, they will not have the flexibility of stranded wire and will be difficult to handle.

The best cable for connecting speakers is one that is as thick as possible or practical. The instantaneous peak current produced by a transient can be many times more than the average current. Whether this peak signal will reach the speakers depends on the voltage drop across the speaker cable. That cable has signal priority in the sense that its voltage drop takes place prior to signal delivery to the speakers. Special cables are made for speaker connections but these are more costly than zip cord.

Guidelines for Connecting Speakers

Aside from impedance matching, there are certain guidelines to follow when you are connecting speakers. It is always satisfactory to use a wire gauge

Speaker Impedance	Maximum Length of Wire From Power Amplifier	Wire Gauge	Speaker Impedance	Maximum Length of Wire From Power Amplifier	Wire Gauge
4 Ohms	11 Feet	24	8 Ohms	23 Feet	24
	30 Feet	20		60 Feet	20
	47 Feet	18		95 Feet	18
	75 Feet	16		150 Feet	16
	120 Feet	14		240 Feet	14
6 Ohms	16 Feet	24	16 Ohms	47 Feet	24
	35 Feet	20		118 Feet	20
	75 Feet	18		190 Feet	18
	110 Feet	16		300 Feet	16
	180 Feet	14		475 Feet	14

Figure 6–21. Suggested wire gauges for various speaker distances and impedances.

having a smaller number than that recommended by the manufacturer of the power amplifier or receiver.

If the polarity of the speaker connections is transposed, no electrical damage will be done, but either one or the other of the speakers will deliver sound that seems unnatural. Bass tones may be weak.

In some instances, speaker cords may be of considerable length, but in any event, they should be no longer than necessary. Do not coil excess speaker wire, but trim the wire to the approximate length needed. Because of the large currents they carry, speaker wires are surrounded by a strong magnetic field so do not bundle them with wires of other components, particularly wires carrying input signals.

Before you connect your speakers, it is advisable to make certain that the integrated receiver or power amplifier is turned off. Since these depend on illuminated power on/off lights that can be defective, a safe method is to disconnect the power-line cord. Speakers can be damaged by accidental connect or disconnect from live power amplifiers.

Speakers are current-operated devices and the connecting lines between them and the output terminals of the receiver or power amplifier must have an adequate thickness. What this should be will depend on the peak audio power output of the power amp, the distance to the speakers, and the impedance of the speakers. The connecting wires can be in the range from 14-gauge to 24-gauge. The wire can be single, solid conductor but stranded wire is preferable and is used more often. Special speaker wire is also available, and some of these have a heavier gauge than ordinary lamp cord. There are some practical limitations. Thicker wires are more difficult to handle and may be more difficult to keep out of sight. It may also be harder to connect the wire to the power amplifier and speaker terminals. As a general rule, though, the thicker the speaker wire—that is, the smaller the wire gauge number—the better.

Any kind of copper wire can be used, provided it is insulated to prevent accidental short circuits. The question, however, is how well the wire conducts current to the speakers. If the resistance of the wire is excessive, it will limit the amount of audio power the receiver or power amplifier is capable of delivering. A 30-watt amplifier, for example, could become the equivalent of one that is 28 watts, with 2 watts lost in the connecting lines (in the form of heat), leaving only 28 audio watts for delivery to the speakers. The connecting lines always get the first share of the power to be delivered.

The flow of current to a speaker isn't constant; it can vary considerably. A low-amplitude, smoothly occurring treble tone may require little current flow. A sharply peaked, high-amplitude, percussive bass tone may demand a large, instantaneous value of current, far exceeding average values. This could produce a large voltage drop along the connecting cable, with the result that less of it would reach the voice coil of the speaker, with that bass tone attenuated.

Speaker Connectors

There are many ways of connecting speaker wires to the speakers and these are all dependent on the kind of connectors the manufacturer has used. Figure 6–22 shows several methods. In drawing A, the speaker knobs are first turned counterclockwise, and the speaker leads, whose ends are stripped about 3/8 inch, are inserted at the bottom of the knob, which is then rotated clockwise. In drawing B, the speaker terminals are spring loaded. Press down, insert the speaker wire in the through hole, and then release. Make sure the speaker wire strands do not extend beyond the connector and do not nick or cut any of the strands.

Another type of spring-loaded connector is shown in drawing C. Depress a small lever below the connector and insert the stripped wire end of the speaker cable; then release the lever.

Drawing D illustrates the use of a polarized speaker plug. The connecting wires are equipped with open-end spade lugs, which are then fastened to the machine screw terminals of the speakers. The lugs should be crimped and soldered to the wires.

If the wires are stranded, and this is most likely, twirl them before inserting them into the terminal knobs. Soldering the cable ends will help make a better connection and will also minimize the danger of having a stray strand of wire reaching over and touching the adjacent terminal. The resulting short circuit could damage the power amplifier.

Polarization

Speakers and the output terminals of power amplifiers or receivers are polarized, marked with plus and minus symbols, or with a red dot to indicate plus and a black dot to indicate minus. These colors are commonly used, but there is no standardization and manufacturers use any color they wish. In some instances you will find (+) and (−) symbols. The input connections to speakers are similarly marked. The positive and negative terminals of a speaker should be connected to the similarly identified terminals on the receiver or power amplifier.

There are other polarity indicators. Some speaker, receiver, and power amplifier terminals are marked L (left channel) and R (right channel).

Wire Coding

To make sure the positive and negative terminals on the output terminal board of the receiver or power amplifier are correctly connected to the speakers, it is advisable to use color-coded connecting wire. Lamp cord is available as uncoded or coded. If uncoded lamp cord is used, it will be difficult to make correctly polarized connections, especially if the speakers are at some distance

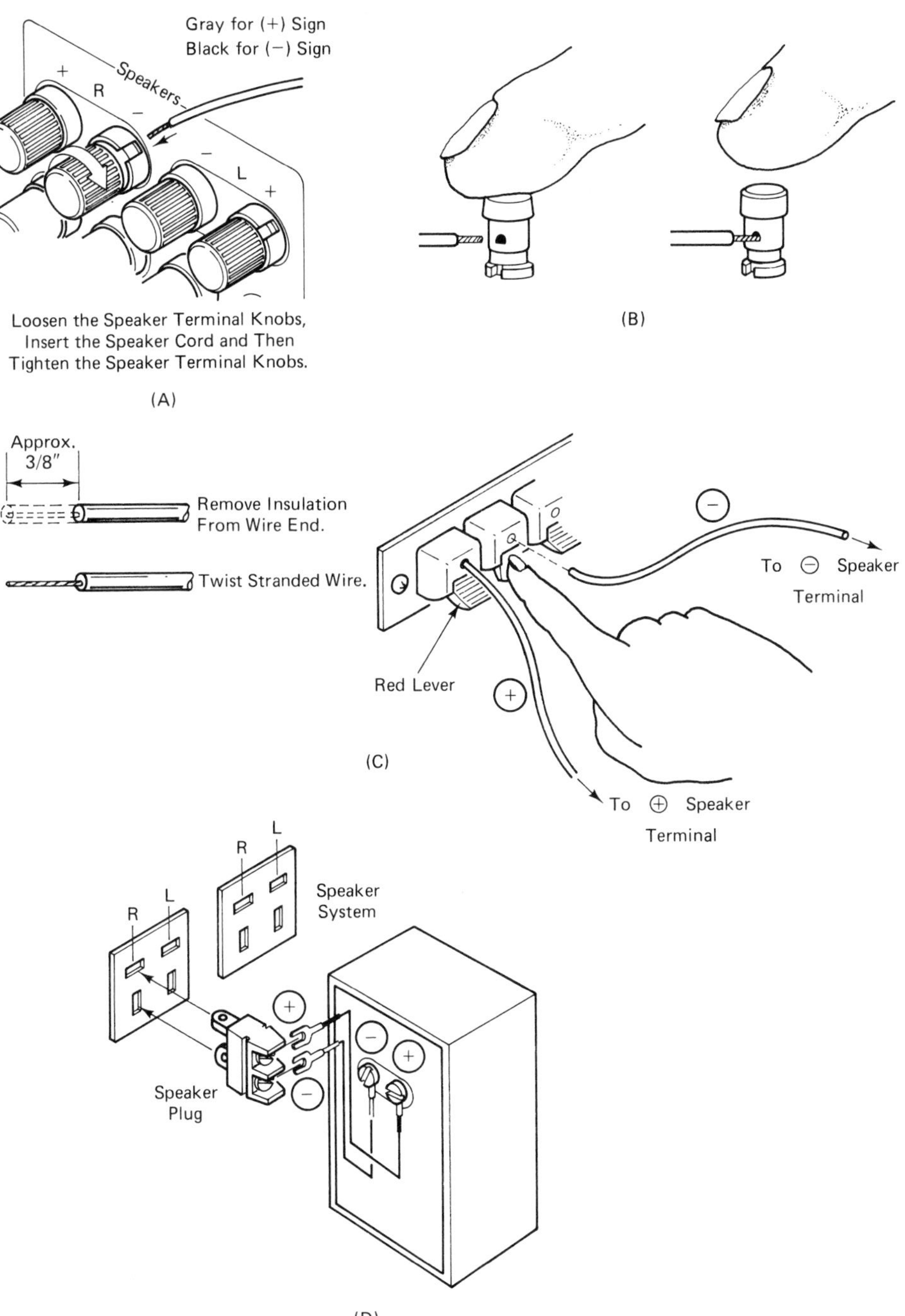

Figure 6–22. Speaker connections: (A). Spring-loaded terminals on rear of speaker. Button end of terminal is pushed down and stripped wire end inserted. Spring pressure maintains good contact on the wire (B). Spring-loaded speaker connectors (C). Polarized speaker connections (D). (*Drawing A courtesy Yamaha Electronics Corp.; drawing D courtesy Pioneer Electronics,* [*U.S.A.*] *Corp.*)

from the receiver or amplifier. In coded lamp cord, one of the conductors may be silver, the other copper colored with these clearly visible through the plastic. Use either for the plus connection, the other for minus. Some speaker cords have a tracer string accompanying one of the leads. The two conductors in all these connecting cords have the same gauge, so either wire can be used for plus and the other for the minus lead, but there are several precautions. There may be a plus sign, the word "plus," or a red color dot for the plus terminal. There may be no marking at all for the minus terminal, or there may be a black dot or a minus sign. Make sure the connecting wire you have selected as the plus conductor is attached to the plus terminal.

The designations "Left" and "Right" on the output terminal block of the receiver or power amplifier refer to the speakers as you face them. Left-channel sound should be connected to a speaker positioned to your left as you face the speaker; right-channel sound to the speaker at your right.

Some systems come equipped with a control on the front panel of the receiver or amplifier permitting switching of receiver sound. Ordinarily, speakers face the listener, but this may not always be possible, with one of the speakers in front, the other to the rear. In that case, either speaker can be left; the other considered right. Figure 6–23 shows the speaker connections of a receiver. Polarization on the speakers is marked by plus and minus symbols and the speaker terminals on the receiver are similarly marked. The connecting cord is polarized by color, and in this case, the white wire has been selected for the plus connections.

Speaker Impedance

There are a number of connecting points where impedance is important: at the antenna; at the antenna intput terminals of an FM receiver, a TV set, or a VCR; at the output of a receiver or power amplifier; and at the input of a speaker.

Impedance can be designated as input and output. A receiver or an amplifier receives a signal at its input and delivers a signal at its output; consequently, it has both an input and an output impedance. A speaker receives a signal but has an input impedance only. An antenna has an output impedance only.

The impedance of a speaker, actually the impedance of its voice coil, has a range between 2 ohms and 16 ohms, although most speakers are rated at 4 ohms and 8 ohms. The lower the impedance of a speaker, the greater the load it imposes on the output of a power amplifier or receiver; that is, the greater the amount of current that will move into the voice coil.

Figure 6–24A shows the connections for a single speaker from a source such as an amplifier. The impedance of this speaker's voice coil is 8 ohms and so is the output impedance of the power amplifier. With impedances matched, as in this case, we get the maximum transfer of audio energy from the am-

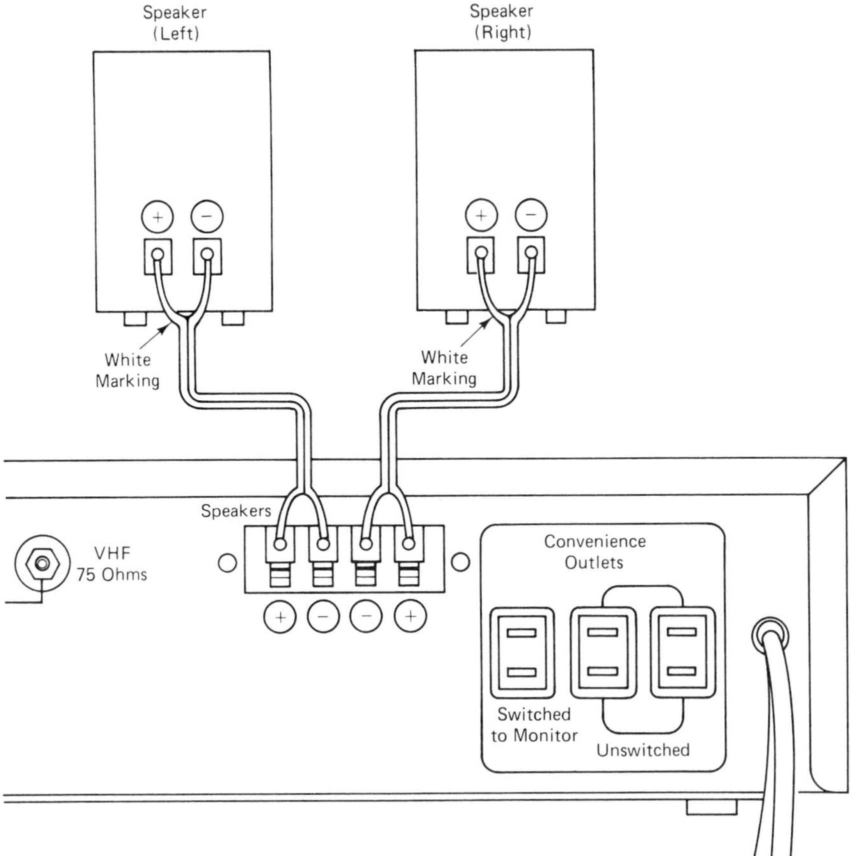

Figure 6–23. Right and left speaker connections. This is view facing the speakers.

plifier to the speaker. When impedances are mismatched, the capability for the transfer of audio energy is reduced.

Like batteries, speakers can be connected in series, in parallel, or in some series-parallel arrangement. Figure 6–24B shows a pair of speakers in series. In such an arrangement the equivalent impedance is double that of the individual speaker impedance. In this example, it is 16 ohms, assuming that each speaker is rated at 8 ohms. The requirement here would be an amplifier having an output impedance of 16 ohms. Some amplifiers and receivers are constructed so the user has an option of using outputs of either 8 ohms or 16 ohms.

Drawing C shows a pair of 8-ohm speakers wired in parallel. When impedances are of equal values, the overall impedance is one-half that of each

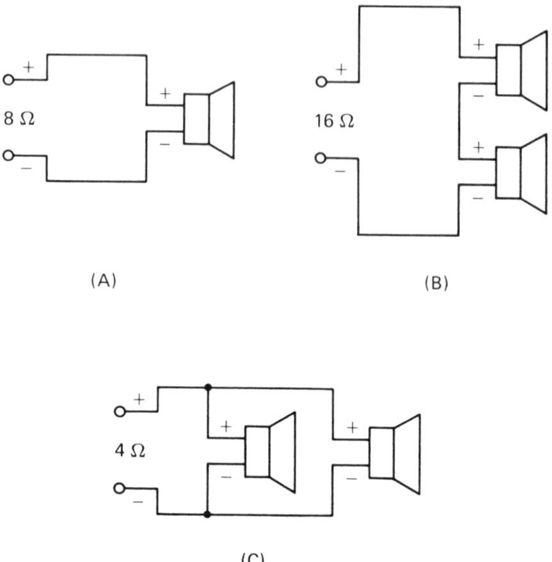

Figure 6–24. Single-speaker connections (A); two 8-ohm speakers in series (B); two 8-ohm speakers in parallel (C).

speaker, consequently in this case a total of 4 ohms. The speakers can then be connected to the speaker output of an amplifier or receiver rated at 4 ohms.

Speaker Connection Precautions

There are a number of precautions when adding speakers to a high-fidelity sound system, including size, placement, and speaker efficiency. Speaker impedance is another important consideration. Do not intermix speaker impedances, that is, do not set up a system using 4-ohm, 8-ohm, and 16-ohm speakers. Doing so will make it difficult to properly impedance-match speakers to receivers or power amplifiers. Further, the speaker having the lowest impedance will make the greatest current demand.

Speaker Connections and Power Delivery

The audio power delivered to speakers is limited by the maximum power output capability of the power amplifier in a receiver or that of a separate power amplifier. If a power amplifier has a maximum rated power output of 100 watts, that is the most it can supply to a speaker (or speakers) under full load conditions. If a single 4-ohm speaker is wired to a 50-watt power amplifier whose output impedance is also 4 ohms, the full power output can be delivered to that speaker. If two 8-ohm speakers are connected in parallel to that same power amplifier, the power will distribute itself equally between the two, with each receiving 25 watts. If four 4-ohm speakers are used, wired in a series-parallel arrangement, as shown in Fig. 6–25, each of the speakers would receive 12-1/2 watts. The overall impedance of the four speakers would be 4 ohms, connected to a 4-ohm source.

Drawing B shows a single 8-ohm speaker connected to a source whose output impedance is 8 ohms. The amplifier, rated at 50 watts, can deliver its full output to this one speaker. Instead of using a single 8-ohm speaker, the equivalent speaker impedance can be obtained by wiring two 4-ohm speakers in series. Each speaker would then receive one-half the maximum output power

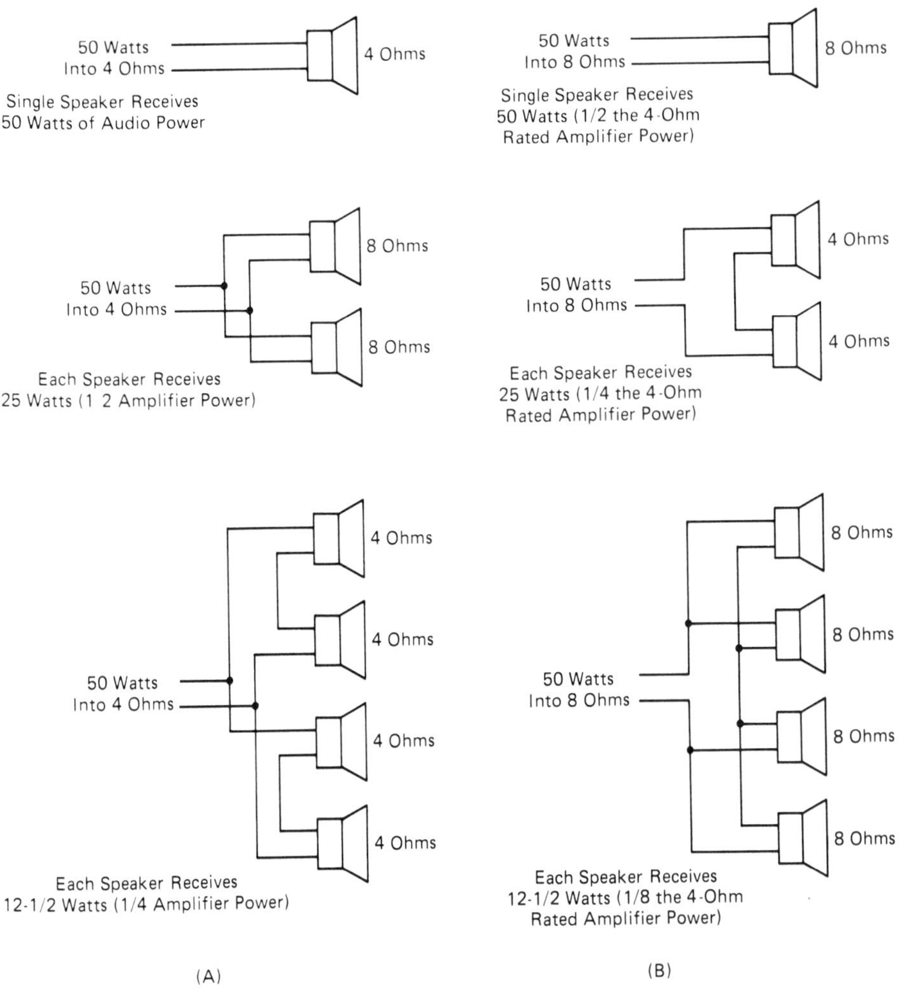

Figure 6–25. Audio output power distribution for 4 ohms (A); 8-ohm speaker configuration (B).

of the amplifier, or, in this case, 25 watts. A series-parallel combination of four 8-ohm speakers could be wired, and the impedance presented to the amplifier would be 8 ohms. In this example, each of the speakers would receive 12-1/2 watts maximum.

Connecting A and B Speakers

Some amplifiers have enough output power to drive A and B speakers. Such speakers are not wired in parallel or in series, but operate independently from the output of the power amplifier. However, this does not mean the load impedance cannot change. It can do so if additional speakers are wired in series or in parallel with the original speakers.

The A/B System

Figure 6–26A shows a pair of 4-ohm speakers controlled by a single-pole, three-position switch. When the switch arm is at position 1, the bottom speaker is shorted, but the upper speaker is operative. When the switch is at position 2, the speakers are in series and the total impedance is 8 ohms. When the switch is at 3, the upper speaker is shorted and the bottom speaker is operative. Figure 6–26B shows a better arrangement using four speakers. The switches are ganged so all their armatures move at the same time. If the speakers are 4 ohms, all the resistors shown should be 4 ohms; if speakers are 8 ohms, all the resistors should be 8 ohms. In the diagram, the two upper speakers are in series, and as each is 4 ohms, they present a total impedance of 8 ohms. The same applies to the two lower speakers.

EXPANDING THE HIGH-FIDELITY SYSTEM

A cassette deck, an open-reel tape deck, one or more turntables, a compact disc player, or an equalizer or other signal processor can be connected to the preamplifier, the integrated amplifier, or a receiver, using pin connectors throughout. These are sometimes supplied by the manufacturers with their equipment, and the pin connectors are often color coded.

It is important not only to connect components correctly but also to connect them at the right part of the audio chain. The more components there are in a system, the more difficult this becomes. Components can interact, depending on how and where in the reproduction chain they are connected. This isn't as applicable to through signal components such as a tuner, preamplifier, power amplifier, and speakers, for with these the movement of the signal is straightforward. With components such as cassette decks, open-reel decks, and particularly with signal processing equipment, however, connections can sometimes be variable. Thus, in the case of an equalizer, you may

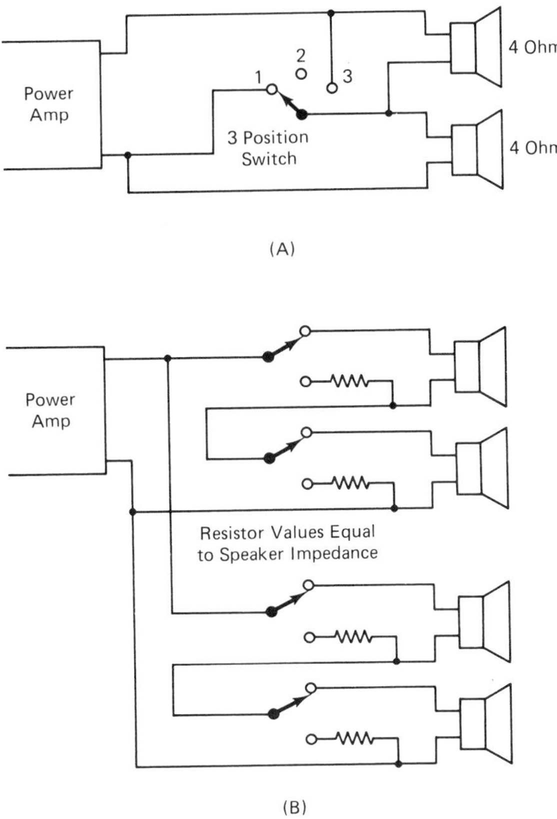

Figure 6–26. Speaker switching using 3-position switch (A); single-channel, multiple-speaker switching (B).

want to equalize the signal going into a tape deck or the signal coming out of it.

CONNECTING MICROPHONES

A microphone, a transducer, changes voice or instrumental energy to its electrical equivalent. The resulting signal can be brought into an amplifier and from there into one or more speakers. It can also be connected to a receiver, a cassette deck, or an open-reel deck for recording onto tape or into a mixer.

For stereo sound, two microphones are required. Microphones (mics) usually come equipped with a cable connected internally and held in place mechanically, with the cable terminating in a phono plug. If a component has inputs for a pair of microphones, stereophonic sound can be recorded (Fig. 6–27). The microphone positioned at the left, as you face the stage, will supply

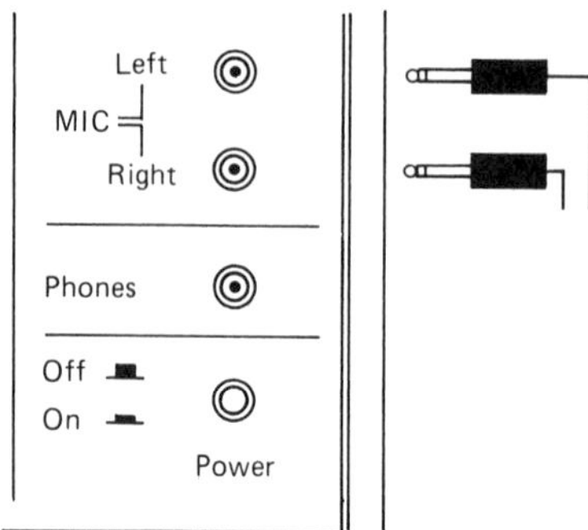

Figure 6–27. Left/right microphone inputs. (*Courtesy Pioneer Electronics [U.S.A.] Corp.*)

left-channel sound; the other microphone, right-channel sound. Cable extenders can be used if the wiring supplied with the microphones isn't long enough.

Microphones have an output impedance across the two points at which the signal is being delivered to a connecting cable. Their impedances range from 50 ohms to 250 ohms and from 20,000 ohms to as much as 50,000. However, actual impedance values are seldom specified, so microphones are usually indicated as either low or high impedance. Any microphone can be manufactured as a low- or high-impedance device. The advantage of a low-impedance microphone is that the connecting cable is less susceptible to hum and electrical noise pickup, especially important if the cable is to run a long distance from the mic to the input of the audio preamplifier. The advantage of a high-impedance mic is that it supplies a greater signal output for a given sound level input. High-impedance mic cables are suitable for distances of 20 feet or less. Longer runs mean a loss of high-frequency response due to cable capacitance.

Connecting a Mic Mixer

For the amateur in-home recordist, the choice of microphone to use, and consequently the cable, is governed by the impedance of the preamplifier or cassette deck to which the mic is to be connected. If these inputs are low impedance, a better selection is a low-impedance mic. If they are high, the system should be high-impedance throughout.

A VCR can be used to record sound, as shown in Fig. 6–28, using a microphone mixer. The mixer, depending on its construction, can have a larger number of inputs than the three in the drawing with phono jacks used for the mic connections. The output of the mixer is via a cable, phono-plug connected at the mixer end and at the VCR.

One or more microphones, plus associated amplifiers and speakers, is called a sound reinforcement system. When such a system is in position tem-

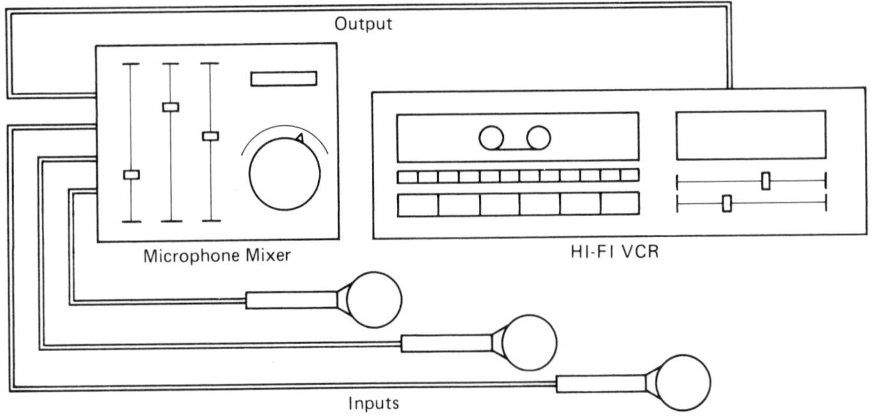

Figure 6–28. Mixer for multiple microphone inputs.

porarily, the connecting cable may extend across the stage and possibly along the floor of an orchestra pit. If the mic is to be used by an artist who must move across the stage, the connecting cable must trail the performer. To overcome this problem, wireless mics are used with a small transmitter built into the microphone housing and a receiver for picking up the signal. The sound produced by the mic is used to modulate an FM carrier with the receiver tuned to its frequency. Several wireless mics can be used at the same time, but these must all be on different frequencies, with separate receivers tuned to those frequencies.

When the sound system is a permanent installation, a suitable jack can be wall-plate mounted with the connecting cable run from that wall plate to the sound amplifiers. This has the advantage of clearing the stage of cables, but it does limit the movement of the microphone unless extension cables are used.

The cable is an integral part of the mic, and the wall connector must house a jack that will match the plug on the free end of the mic cable. If an extension cable is used, one end must have a jack that mates with the free end of the mic cable. The other end of this cable has a plug that must mate with the wall jack.

Even if an extension cable mates with the mic cable and the jack on the wall plate, a connection is not automatically made. The wiring arrangement in the extension cable may not correspond with the wiring arrangement in the mic cable, nor necessarily with the wiring arrangement from the wall plate to the amplifier.

When a number of microphones are used, it is helpful to select those that follow the same cable connections, so the cable system used in sound reinforcement is standardized.

CONNECTING THE TURNTABLE

The turntable comes supplied with its connecting leads, including a ground wire, individual or twin signal leads, and an AC power cord. The connections are shown in Fig. 6–29A, and in more detail in drawing B. The ground lead

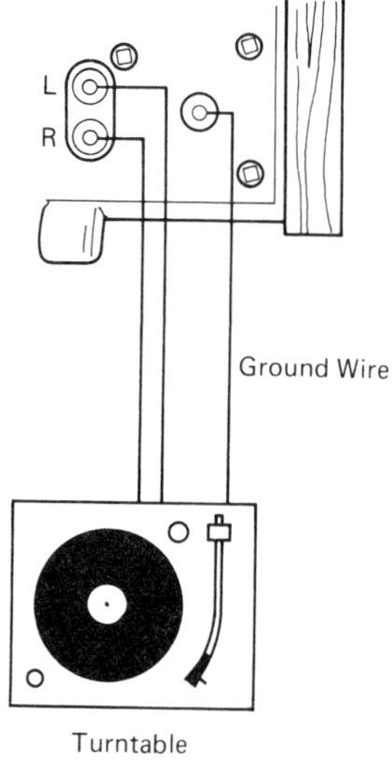

Figure 6–29A. Connections from turntable to receiver, pre-amplifier or integrated amplifier. Line cord of the turntable is not shown.

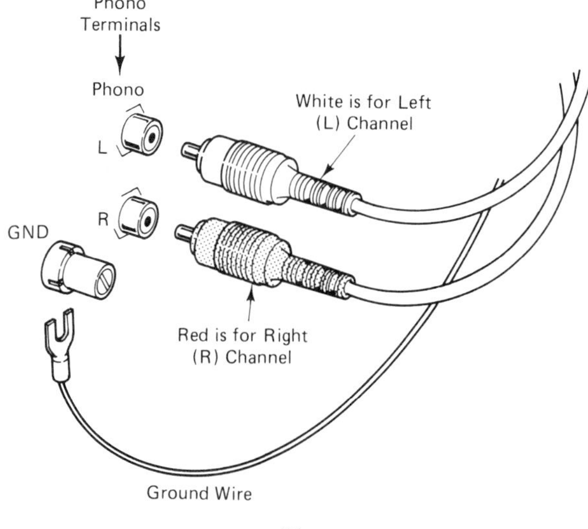

Figure 6–29B. Connections for a turntable. *(Courtesy Yamaha Electronics Corp.)*

can be a bare length of wire, or insulated wire, and it may be color coded by using black or green insulating material. In some instances, the ground lead isn't a separate wire but is combined with the signal leads. The advantage is that having just one cable means fewer connecting wires behind the unit, hence a neater installation. The connecting cords end in a phono pin plug, also known as a phono plug or RCA connector.

Figure 6–30 shows the connections from the turntable to a receiver. At the turntable end, the audio cables and the ground wire are permanently connected to the turntable. Connections by the free ends of the audio cable are by phono plugs, with these connections to phono jacks identified as L (left channel) and R (right channel).

While manufacturers use different color connectors to identify these channels, white is commonly used for the left channel, red for the right.

Phono Connection Precautions

The connection panel on a receiver, preamplifier, or integrated amplifier may have a number of ports identified as "Phono," but not every turntable can be connected to them. The important factor is the kind of phono cartridge used. Nor can one input port be arbitrarily substituted for another. Thus, an aux input terminal should not be substituted for a phono input, as the phono port leads to an internal RIAA (Recording Industry Association of America) equalization circuit designed specifically for phono records.

Ports on equipment intended to receive turntable input may be marked MM (moving magnet) or MC (moving coil) or IM (induced magnet). The signal output of the MC type is so low that a special amplifier or transformer is usually required. This may be supplied by the component having the phono input jack, or it may be used separately.

How to Connect Two Turntables

In some instances, a high-fidelity installation will use two turntables. Two are sometimes used if continuous music is wanted, so that as soon as one turntable is finished, the other is started, with the first segueing into the second. The two turntables can be connected to the phono input terminals of a preamplifier or an integrated amplifier, or a receiver, assuming that these components have provision for accommodating two turntables.

Figure 6–31 shows how the connections are made. Although the illustration does show two phono inputs, it does not follow that they are suitable for all types of cartridges. The two jacks at the top are for moving magnet or moving coil cartridges. However, for the second phono input, intended for turntable 2, use only an MM cartridge, rated at 47,000 ohms, 220 picofarads (pF). The two ground wires of the record players should be connected to the common ground terminal. The ground wires terminate in open spade lugs for

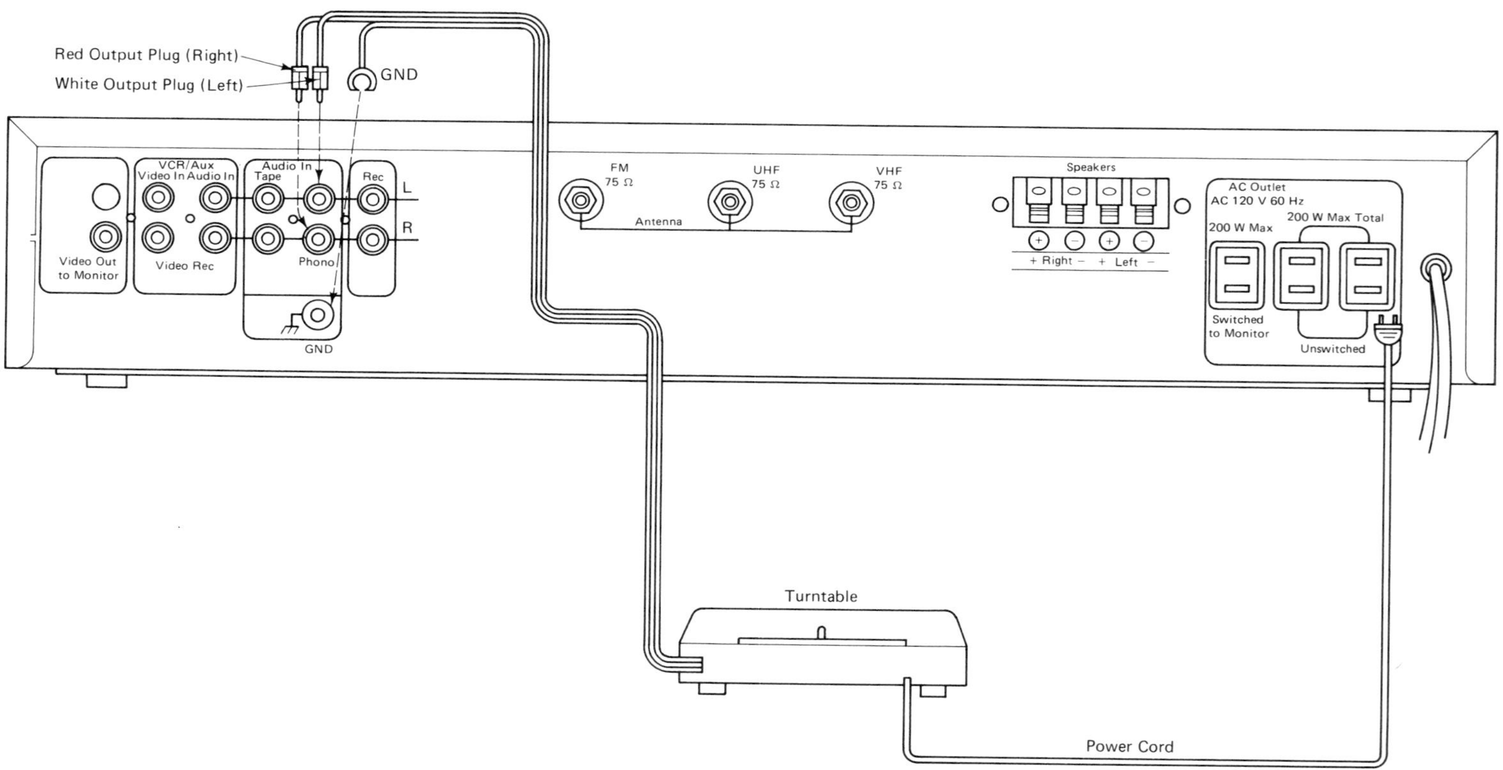

Figure 6–30. Turntable connections.

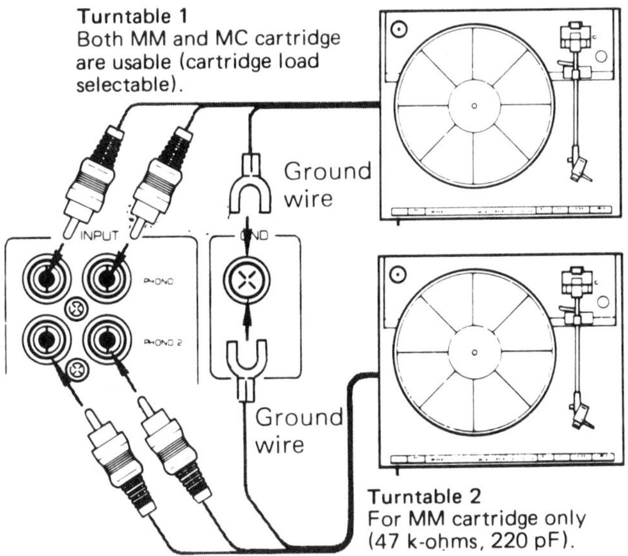

Figure 6–31. Connections for two turntables. (*Courtesy Yamaha Electronics Corp.*)

connection to a machine screw connector. For minimum hum pickup, keep the phono signal output cords, usually several feet long, away from any power-line cords and not near any wires connecting the power amplifier to the speakers. If hum persists, try disconnecting one or the other of the ground leads, and then both at the same time. Also make sure the ground connection is really a ground. If it is a cold water pipe there can be no doubt it is. If it is some other presumed ground, check with a VOM (volt-ohm-milliammeter) set to read 150-volts AC. Touch the ground terminal with one test lead, and insert the other lead, successively, into the two inputs of an AC wall plate. With one connection, the meter should read zero. With the other, it should read the full line voltage. If both positions of the test lead result in a zero reading, the supposed ground is not a ground at all.

Powering the Turntable

Connect the AC plug of the turntable to an AC outlet along the baseboard, but preferably use one of the convenience outlets on the preamplifier or power amplifier. Since the turntable will never supply sound by itself, it would be better to plug it into a switched outlet. If the turntable has its own on/off switch, it will need to be turned on to be used, so power availability to the turntable will still be independent of any other component. If you connect to an unswitched outlet, you will be able to operate the turntable, but since it must work through an amplifier or receiver they will need to be turned on as well.

Turntable Problems

Turntables can be plagued by problems of hum, buzz, and howling, and in some instances by complete failure. Hum is usually considered the same as that of the power-line frequency, 60 Hz, but it is more likely to be the second harmonic, 120 Hz. The problem is usually the result of a poor ground connection, a loose connection, or no connection at all. Make sure the ground is actually a ground. The signal wires of the record player should not be near a power cord. If the signal cords of the turntable are cabled (tied together) with other wires, remove the cable tie and separate the conductors. Move the signal output wires of the turntable to various positions, to learn if the hum is eliminated or attenuated. Hum can be caused by a poor connection between the turntable and the amplifier. Try replacing the cables. Try to avoid using cables longer than 3 feet. If the plugs on the cables are tarnished, clean them, or, preferably, replace them.

Try wiggling the connectors. They should make a snug fit; if not, replace them. The connector (an RCA plug) has a ground connection consisting of an assembly of four metallic leaves. They may be loose, and if so, tighten them with pliers. If the center pin of the plug seems to be loose, replace the entire cable, plus connectors.

One of the trouble spots is the point at which the cable enters the plug. Put a record on the platter and turn the system on. With the system operative, move the cable at the entry point to the plug. If this action results in hum, a crackling noise, or intermittent sound, get rid of the cable. Moving the cable itself should result in no change in sound. An even easier test is to replace the cable with a new one.

Make sure the phono cartridge connection is clean and tight. Try using a different phono cartridge. The old one may have an internal short or may be poorly connected.

A buzzing sound could be caused by the wires in the tone arm working as an antenna and picking up high-intensity television signals even though the television set may be in an adjacent room. To check, have someone turn the television set on and off while you listen to a phono record. Sometimes turning the TV set or the turntable to a different angle will help. Howling is caused by acoustic feedback from an output to an input. It is sometimes caused by signal leakage from the speaker system to the tone arm or cartridge. Try increasing the distance between the turntable and the speakers. Keep speaker cables away from the turntable.

If the problem is one of no sound, first make sure the sound-source selector control is properly set. Do not touch the stylus or move it in an effort to see if it produces sound, as doing so could damage the stylus assembly. First try to determine if some other sound source is operative. If the speakers operate, the system is functioning except for phono input. Try connecting a different sound source to the phono input, disregarding equalization requirements. If sound comes through, you have localized the problem to the turntable. Check the phono cartridge connections or substitute a cartridge known to be in good working order.

Phono Cartridge Connections

It may sometimes be necessary to replace one or more of the four wires used in a phono cartridge—possibly because of wire breakage or corrosion (Fig. 6–32). To do so, first remove the headshell. Beneath that covering you will find four delicate wires color-coded blue, white, red, and green. Carefully remove these wires and replace them. You might also wish to use a better grade of connecting wire than those being replaced. A top-quality connector would consist of 120 strands of solid silver Litz wire with gold-plated terminals. These are made with tiny tubular connectors on each end, so wire replacement isn't difficult but does require patience. Since these wires are thicker and heavier than those they replace, recheck the tracking force.

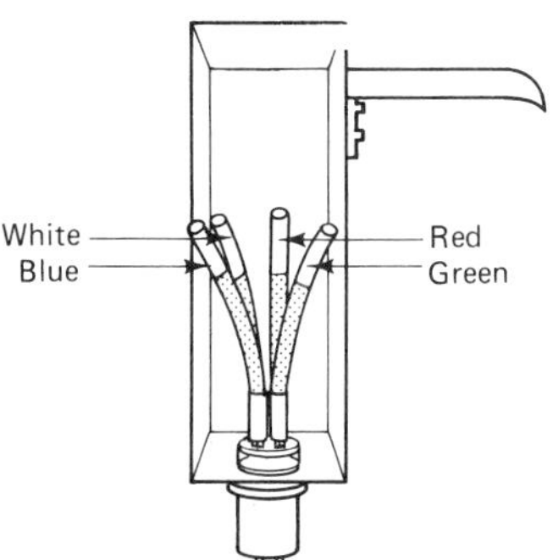

Figure 6–32. Standard headshell wiring pattern.

CONNECTING THE PREAMPLIFIER TO THE POWER AMPLIFIER

The output of the preamplifier is connected to the input of the power amplifier via shielded audio cables with both ends equipped with RCA plugs. If the connecting cables aren't long enough, use an extension cable equipped with a phono jack at one end and a phono plug at the other.

Before making the connection, be sure the plugs on both ends of the audio cable are clean—this means sparkling clean, with no trace of corrosion. If the plugs have any trace of rust, remove it by burnishing with a rough cloth or a pencil eraser.

Another method is to insert the plug into its jack and rotate the plug a number of times, permitting the cable to rotate freely at the same time. The opposite end of the cable should also be free. If it is impossible to clean the plugs, replace the entire audio cable and its connectors. If the plugs connecting the cable to the jacks of the preamp and power amp do not make firm, positive contact, the result can be noisy sound, intermittent sound, or no sound at all.

The preamplifier and power amplifier should always be turned off when you are connecting or disconnecting cables. A large-amplitude, sudden signal surge caused by connecting and disconnecting cables could damage the speakers.

CONNECTING THE COMPACT DISC PLAYER

Figure 6–33 shows how to connect a compact disc player (CD), also called a digital audio disc or DAD, to a preamplifier or integrated amplifier. These components should have a pair of input terminals marked CD or DAD. If not, use the aux input terminals, and if these are not available, use the tape input jacks.

The line output of the compact disc player is connected to the preamplifier or integrated amplifier by a pair of audio cables ending in phono plugs. On the rear of the compact disc player are a single pair of jacks marked "Line Out." These are the output signal terminals. The audio cables are usually supplied with the compact disc player.

The terminals at the output of the CD and the input of the receiver or integrated amplifier will be marked to identify polarity: either L and R, plus and minus, or a red dot to indicate plus. The plugs may be colored red and white. The L-terminal of the disc player should connect to the corresponding L-jack of the receiver or integrated amplifier. Similarly, the R-terminal of the CD should be cable connected to the corresponding R-jack.

Compact Disc Player Problems

The laser mechanism in a CD is "equivalent" to the cartridge assembly on a turntable, but both work in completely different ways. Unlike a turntable, though, a laser beam can emit hazardous radiation and can cause eye damage. The laser beam is invisible, so it is important to avoid any direct exposure to it. If a CD is defective, return it to the manufacturer or the authorized service station.

A compact disc player can be compared to a turntable, but only in the sense that both are sound sources. Beyond this point there is no comparison. The pickup of the CD is inside a disc tray opening. To avoid the collection of dust on the pickup, keep the tray closed except when it is to be used. The CD uses a lens, along the lines of those used by cameras. If the lens becomes dirty, clean it with a soft brush or use a lens brush or an air blower brush of the type sold in camera stores.

If the CD player produces no sound, check the amplifier's input ports by connecting a different sound source, such as a turntable.

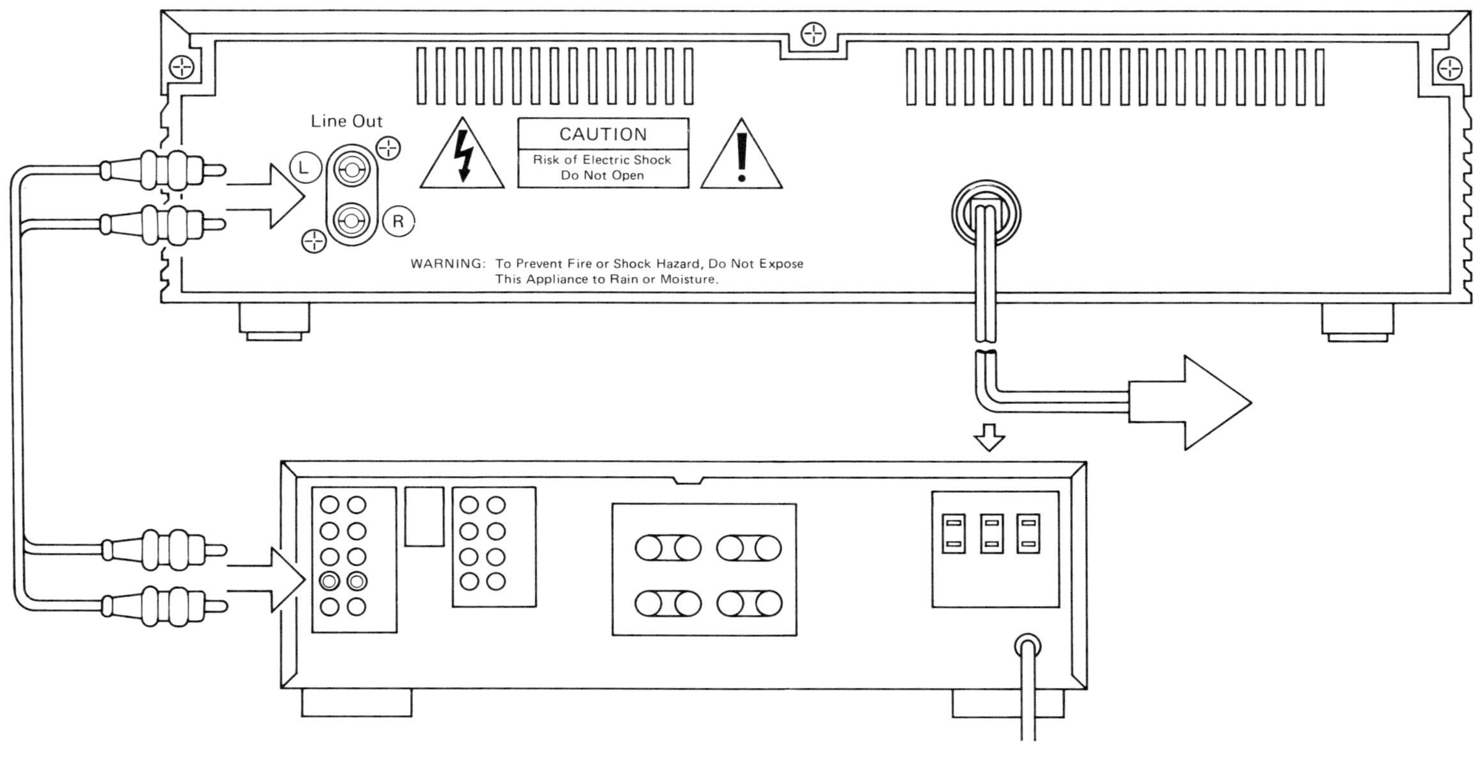

Figure 6–33. Connections for a compact disc player. (*Courtesy Yamaha Electronics Corp.*)

CONNECTING AN OPEN-REEL TAPE DECK

Unlike other components such as a turntable or CD, tape decks have two pairs of connecting cables instead of one. The easiest and best arrangement is to use a 5-pin DIN connector, a single cable with keyed plugs for recording and playback. With this type of connector, other cables aren't required.

If the DIN connector isn't used, a pair of input and output audio cables will be needed. While single cables can be used, that is, a total of four individual cables, a simpler arrangement is to use a double (twin or joined) cable as shown in Fig. 6-34. The tape deck has a pair of double jacks, one marked "Line in," the other "Line out." The line output is audio signal output and is connected to the tape monitor jacks of the receiver or separate audio amplifier, whichever is used. If the receiver does not have terminals marked "Tape monitor" or "Tape input," use the aux input instead. The line input of the tape deck is connected to the tape rec (tape recorder) input of the receiver or amplifier.

When the tape deck is set to its play mode, the audio signal exits from the tape deck via its line output terminals and is delivered to the tape monitor terminals of the amplifier (if a separate unit) or to the amplifier in a receiver. For input, the audio signal is delivered to the audio amplifier, and from that amplifier is supplied to the line input of the tape deck for recording.

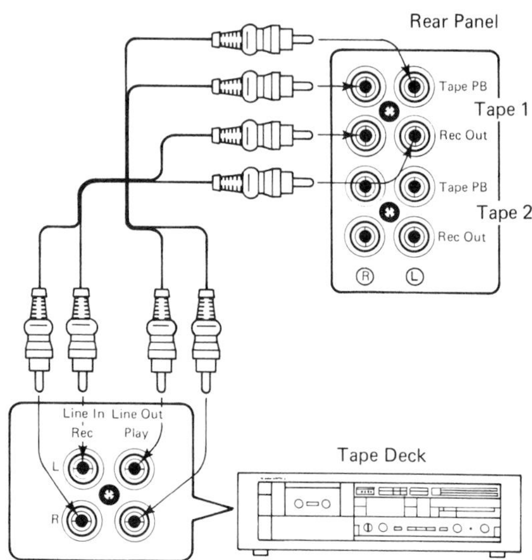

Figure 6-34. Connections for open-reel or cassette tape deck. (*Courtesy Yamaha Electronics Corp.*)

CONNECTING AN AUDIO CASSETTE DECK

The connections for these two components, an audio cassette deck or an open-reel tape deck, are the same. Unlike a turntable or a CD, a cassette deck or an open-reel deck has a pair of cables, one for bringing an audio signal into the deck for recording, and the other for delivering the recorded signal to the input of an amplifier. It can also use a DIN connector (Fig. 6–35). The cassette deck can obtain its AC power from an unswitched AC convenience outlet on the rear of a receiver or preamplifier (see Fig. 6–36).

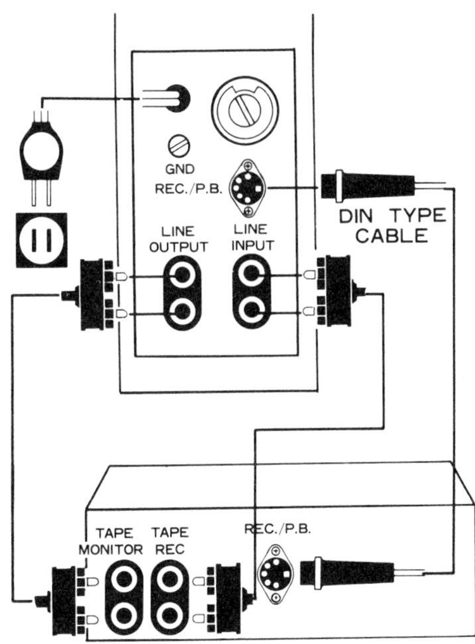

Figure 6–35. Details of connections of a tape deck to a receiver or amplifier. (*Courtesy Pioneer Electronics,* [*U.S.A.*] *Corp.*)

The problem with connecting a tape deck is that manufacturers use different designations for the jacks positioned on a preamplifier or receiver; the jacks may be labeled "Line output" and "Line input" or they may simply be marked as "Tape" and "Audio in." *Line in* means that the equipment has an input for unmodulated audio. That input could be supplied by a microphone, a turntable, a compact disc player, or a tape deck.

Line out means the port is an exit point, also for unmodulated audio. In some instances a line-in port may be used for a special reason. Consider a low-cost mixer, for example. It receives the audio signal from a number of microphones, can be made to adjust the sound level produced by each, delivering a composite of all the inputs to an open-reel or cassette deck.

The mixer, on its rear apron, has a jack for the insertion of a plug that

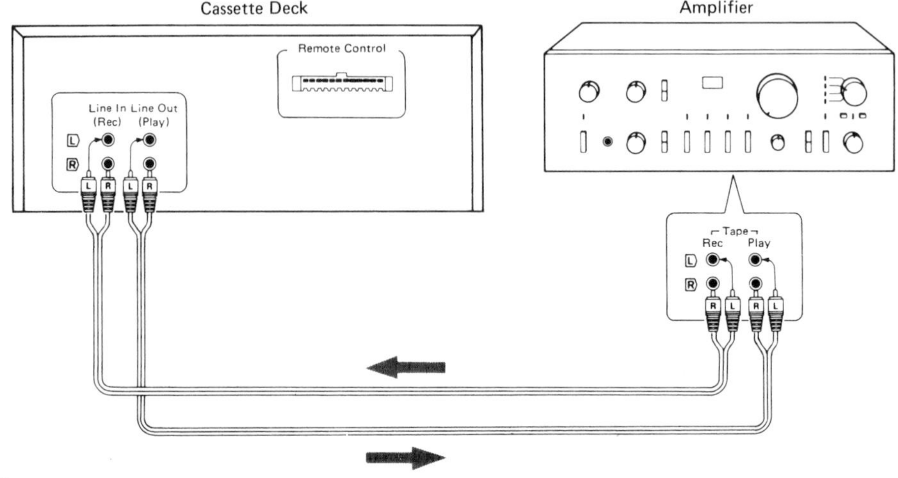

1. Connect the Input (R/L) Terminal on the Cassette Deck to the REC (R/L) Terminal on the Receiver.
2. Connect the Out (R/L) Terminal on the Cassette Deck to the Tape (R/L) Terminal on the Receiver.
3. Insert the Cassette Deck's Power Plug in an AC Socket Marked *Unswitched* on the Receiver.

Figure 6–36. Cassette deck connections. (*Courtesy Pioneer Electronics* [*U.S.A.*] *Corp.*)

is cable connected to the microphones. There is a jack for each microphone. On the same rear apron there are also a number of inputs identified as line in. Each of these line-in inputs is also for a microphone. The only difference is that the mic input and line input use different kinds of plugs. The advantage is that the user isn't confined to one particular plug, but has a choice of cables using two plug types. Plug-to-plug adapters could be used, but if a mixer has a ten-microphone input, for example, that would mean that ten plug-to-plug adapters are needed. Switches on the front of the mixer select either mic in or line in, depending on which ports are being used. Since the audio jacks are most common for audio work, it is quite possible they will mate with one or the other of the most often used plugs.

Pin Jacks versus Standard-Size Mic Jacks for Tape Decks

On some tape decks, standard-size microphone jacks are used instead of pin jacks. The mic jacks have a much larger surface contact area, ensuring more positive contact and a lower contact resistance.

Better-grade decks also have two pairs of audio input/output terminals and may also have a DIN jack, as in Fig. 6–35, thus giving the user a choice of cables to use. The DIN connector combines the input and output cables into one and makes a neater installation. There is also less chance of making a connection error, for two reasons: All input and output connectors are plugged in simultaneously, and since the DIN connector is keyed, there is no possibility of transposing connectors accidentally. For this application, the DIN connector is a five-pin connector.

The Difference Between Mic Input and Line Input

On the back of a tape deck you may find two types of inputs—mic and line. They are alike in the sense that they are both unmodulated audio inputs. One of the differences is in the type of jacks and plugs used for both. The line plugs and jacks may be pin types; the mic input, standard phono jacks. This isn't obligatory on the part of the manufacturer and there may be variations. The input sensitivity for these two inputs is also different; it is greater for the microphone input. Typically, a mic input can be as low as 0.2 millivolt, and that of a line input 60 millivolts. The impedance of the microphone input is 20,000 ohms, and that of the line input 470,000 ohms.

Connecting a Time-Delay Unit

Any musical performance in a closed room, theater, auditorium, or concert hall supplies two kinds of sound—direct and reverberant. Direct sound, also called dry sound, is delivered to the listeners directly from the musical instruments, or—if a sound reinforcement system is used—directly by the speakers. The sound also strikes the floor, ceiling, and surrounding walls, and is reflected to the listener. This sound, called reverberant sound, differs in time of delivery by the amount of time it takes the sound to travel to the reflecting surface and then to the ears of the listener. At that point, the direct and reverberant sounds combine, supplying a total sound that is rich and enjoyable. To supply the acoustic illusion that the in-home listening room is the concert hall, auditorium, or theater, a device called a time delay or ambience synthesizer can be used.

The time-delay component requires the use of a pair of additional speakers. If, as is likely, the sound system is stereo, two speakers positioned in front will supply direct sound and another pair of speakers, placed at the rear, will deliver reverberant sound. Not only is an extra pair of speakers required, but a stereo amplifier for the reverberant sound is needed as well. Since reverberant sound has a smaller amplitude than direct sound, a lower sound wattage power amplifier can be used.

The four speakers must be connected to the power amplifier outputs of the two separate stereo amplifiers. The connecting wires, as described earlier, can be 18-gauge zip cord, or a better and heavier gauge, with the wires attached to the speaker outputs of the amplifiers and to the input terminals of the speakers. There are eight output terminals on the dual stereo amplifiers and a total of eight connections to the speakers.

The speaker output terminals on the amplifier and the input terminals on the speakers can be the same. No plugs or mating jacks are used. The speaker wire is stripped at its ends and is fastened directly to the terminals. These can be spring-loaded or screw terminals, with small knobs as the fasteners.

VCR STEREO SOUND

The FCC permits television broadcasters to transmit stereo signals just as though they were FM stations. The problem is that TV receivers do not contain the circuitry to handle stereo audio and even if they could, the audio amplifier and the speakers in TV sets could not do justice to such a signal.

However, even though television sound may be on its way to stereo, present-day monophonic sound can be considerably improved by routing it through a separate sound system. One way of doing this is by obtaining a synthesized two-channel sound signal from a VCR and routing it as shown in Fig. 6–37. If the VCR is of a Beta format type, use a 1/8-inch mini or earphone plug at the VCR, with the plug inserted in the audio output jack at the back of the VCR. The connecting cable is a standard audio cable. At the other end of the cable, a phone or RCA plug can be connected to the aux input jack at the back of a receiver, preamplifier, or integrated amplifier. Use the same connection technique for VHS recorders, except that the audio connecting cable will have standard RCA plugs at both ends.

This arrangement does not produce stereo sound, but the sound will still be more enjoyable for two reasons: Any signal processors in the high-fidelity system can be used to help improve the sound; and the sound will be better coming out of high-fidelity speakers than out of a TV speaker. When more than one speaker is used, there is some resemblance (possibly only psychological) to stereo sound.

If the VCR does not contain a sound synthesizer, the same results can be obtained with the monophonic sound from the VCR brought via a single audio cable to the input of an outboard synthesizer. The sound is put through a delay circuit providing a delay of about a half millisecond. The delay circuit supplies the signal to a phase splitter, with two output signals separated in phase by 180 degrees. In operation, the delayed signal is added to the right channel and subtracted from the left channel.

VCRs that feature dual audio channels for stereo sound are now available. These allow the user to add stereo to video recordings or permit stereo input directly to a high-fidelity system.

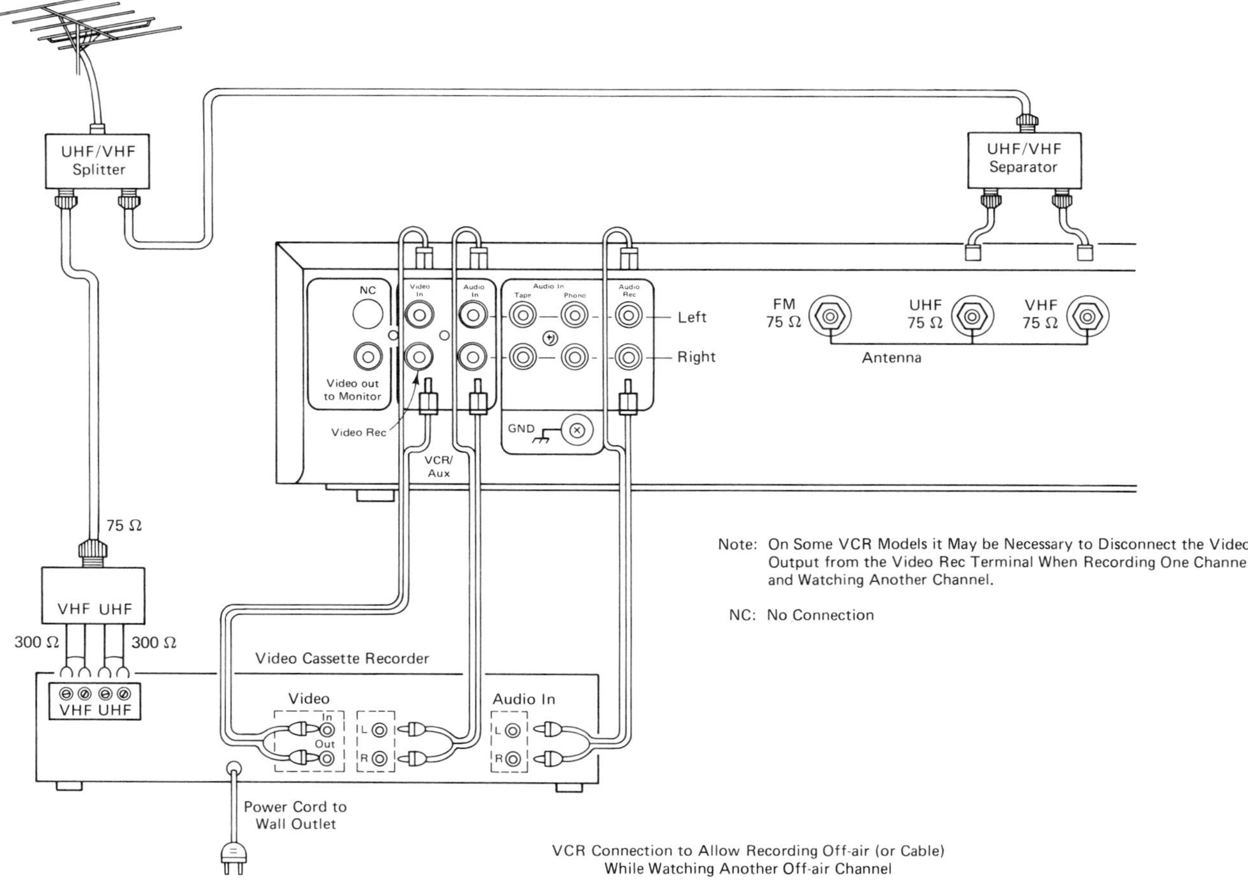

Figure 6–37. VCR stereo audio connections. (*Courtesy Pioneer Electronics* [*U.S.A.*] *Corp.*)

Connecting Headphones

Headphones are easy to connect, as they come equipped with a flexible connecting cord having an attached phone plug. The cord can be straight or coiled, with the cord ranging in length from as little as 5 feet to as much as 25 feet. The coiled cords are more convenient, as, when not stretched, they take up little space.

In some units, the act of inserting the headphone plug into its jack automatically cuts off the speakers. In others, the speakers are controlled by a switch that can turn one pair of speakers, or a different pair, or both, on or off simultaneously.

Not all receivers or amplifiers are equipped with one or more phone jacks. If this is the case, you can use a phone junction box (Fig. 6–38). Use shielded audio cable and strip the ends to connect to the screw terminals on the junction box and also to the speaker terminals on the receiver or other component.

The phone junction box may have provision for connecting just one pair of headphones. If two are wanted, use a Y-cord, as shown in the illustration. If the headphone cord isn't long enough, use an extension cord.

Headphone plugs are stereo plugs designed to transfer left-channel sound to one earpiece, and right-channel sound to the other. If the sound is mono, the plug can still be used.

CONNECTING AN EQUALIZER

The problem with tone controls is that the adjustments they make are broad. Inexpensive receivers have a single control—for the entire audio frequency band from 20Hz to 20kHz, an impossible task. Somewhat better is the use of separate bass and treble tone controls and still better is the addition of a third, midrange control. Even three tone controls are too gross in their settings to do much about room acoustics. That is the specific job of an equalizer—to give the high-fidelity system user an opportunity to compensate for the particular acoustic characteristics of a listening room.

There are two types of equalizers—graphic and parametric. The parametric is better, but more expensive. An equalizer can be used for adjusting bands of sound frequencies from phono records, compact discs, or sound broadcasts—either for listening to these sound sources or for recording them, for tape recording and playback, or for the reduction of tape hiss. It can be used in a home high-fidelity system or in a car sound system.

These outboard components may have connections for the equalization of tape sound only, or for the equalization of all sound sources. If tape is equalized, it is only for the sound characteristics of the room in which the recording has taken place. When these tapes are used elsewhere, they may need

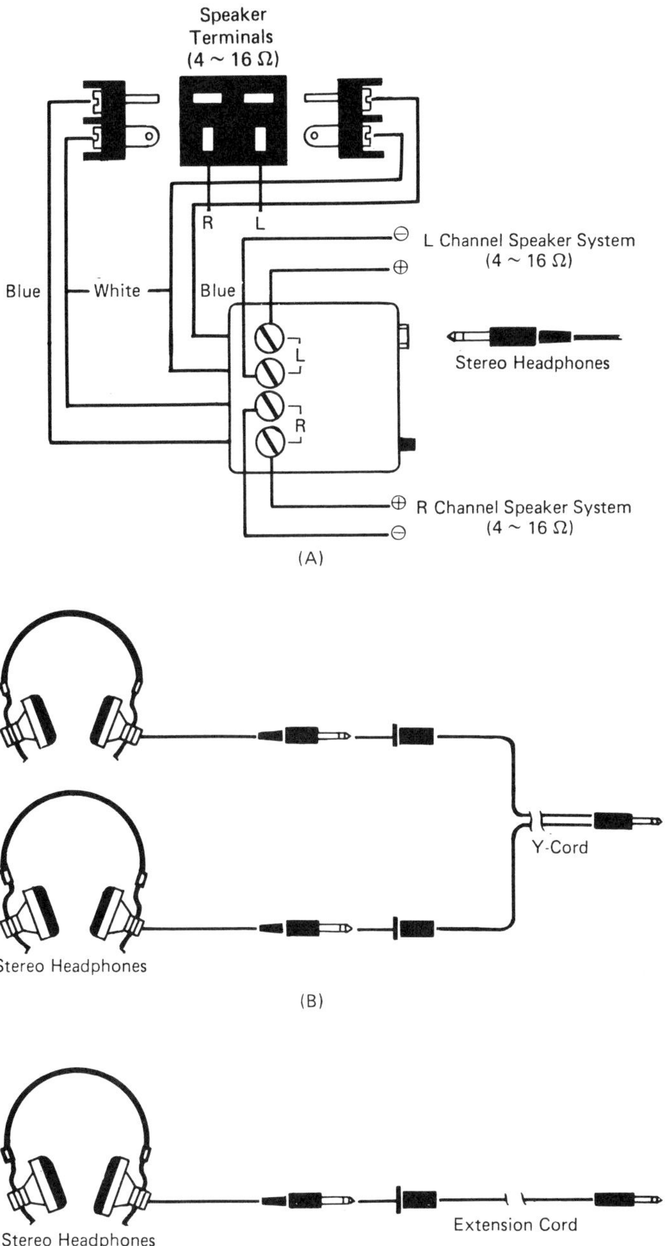

Figure 6–38. Headphone junction box (A); connections for a pair of headphones using Y-cord (B); headphone extension cord (C). (*Courtesy Yamaha Electronics Corp.*)

to be re-equalized, as the acoustics will probably be different. As long as the tapes are played back in the same room, they will not require the further use of the equalizer. This could be called *fixed equalization*. When the equalizer is used for other sound sources, such as the tuner, a turntable, or a compact disc, equalization is not fixed, that is, it is not recorded, and the equalizer and its settings will need to remain in active use in the system. Further, the equalizer may need to be readjusted for the type of music played back.

Figure 6–39 shows a connection diagram, with the equalizer as the center component. This component has eight jacks, connected by audio cables equipped with phono plugs to an amplifier (either a preamp or a power amp) and to a tape deck (either a cassette deck or an open-reel deck). Although single, individual cables can be used, it is more convenient to work with twin (joined) cables. Observe left-right channel polarity when making the connections.

Locate the line-in (record) and line-out (play) terminals on the back of the tape deck. Connect the line-in terminals to the corresponding record (rec) terminals on the equalizer. Connect the line-out cable to the play terminals of the equalizer.

The rear panel of the amplifier or receiver should be equipped with two pairs of tape jacks: tape pb (playback) and rec (record) out (output). Connect the line-in (input) of the equalizer to the tape rec-out jacks and the line-out jacks to the tape playback jacks. After completing the connections, check them just to be certain they are correct, as with this number of connections it is easy to transpose a pair of cables. The power-line cord of the equalizer can be connected to a switched outlet on the amplifier or receiver. The line cord of the amplifier or receiver should not go to a component outlet, but directly to an AC power outlet external to the system, possibly on a baseboard. The tape deck shown in the illustration can also have its line cord plug inserted into the unswitched outlet on the amplifier or receiver, or to the unswitched outlet on the equalizer.

The rear of the equalizer has a total of eight ports, or four double jacks. Two of these are input and output terminals. The other two are monitor and record output. These are plug-in jacks, designed for phono plugs. As indicated in Fig. 6–39, the equalizer is connected to the tape deck, so the sound recorded on that deck is equalized. However, these are not the only possible equalizer connections. The input and output terminals can be connected as shown in Fig. 6–40. The equalizer is still connected to the cassette deck or the open-reel deck via ports on the receiver. However, it is also connected to the input and output terminals of the power amp. Thus, output-only signal sound, such as that supplied by a tuner, turntable, or microphone can have the sound equalized. When the tape decks are switched out of the system by the front panel input sound control, and one or the other of the sound sources is switched in, the equalizer is still included in the system.

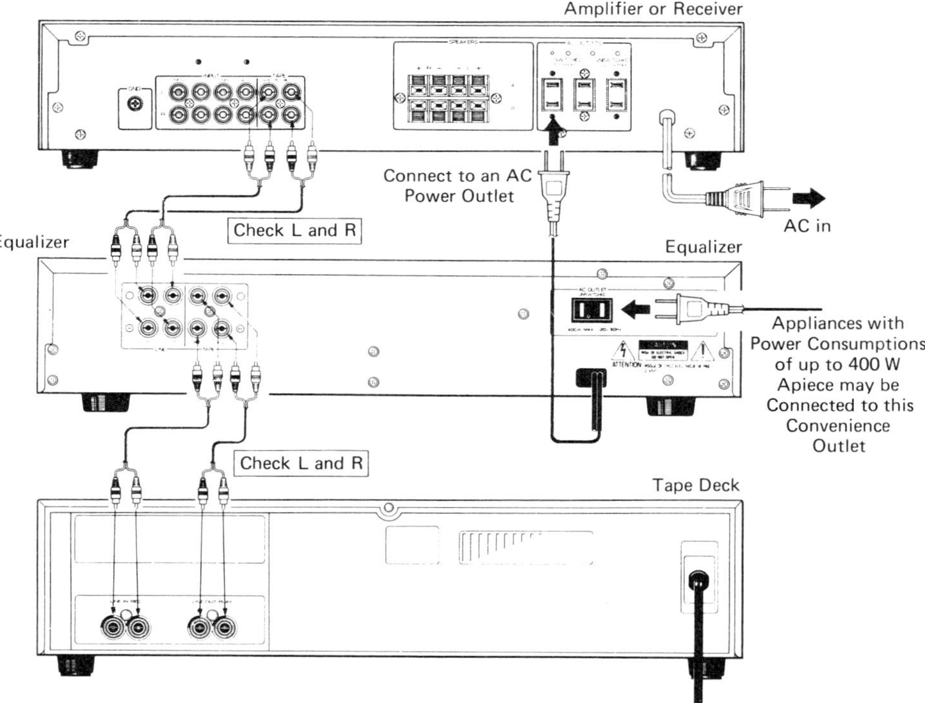

Figure 6–39. Equalizer connections. (*Courtesy Yamaha Electronics Corp.*)

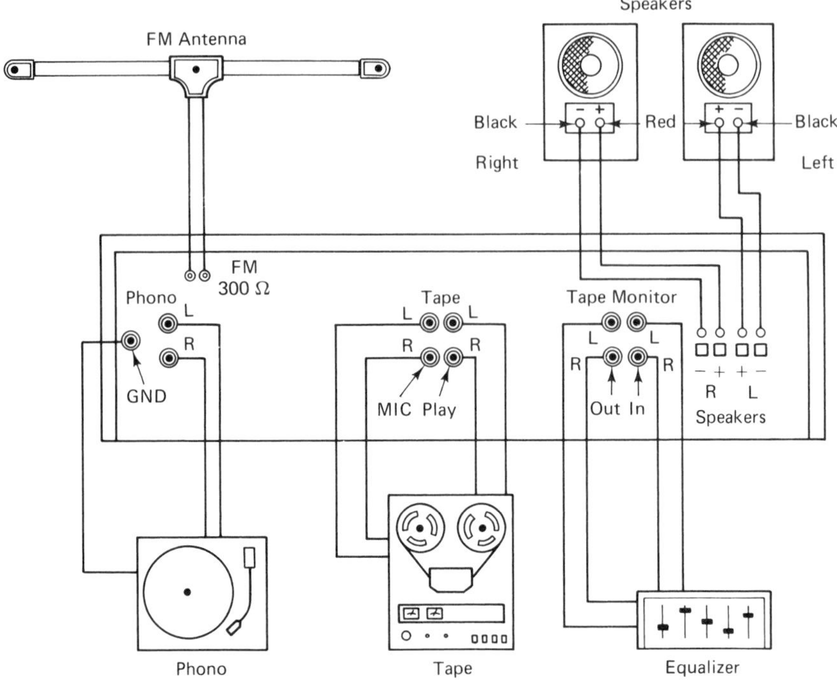

Figure 6–40. Connections for a high-fidelity system using an indoor FM antenna, a turntable, an open-reel or cassette deck, an equalizer, and a pair of speakers.

CONNECTING A SOUND-PROCESSING AMPLIFIER

The equalizer is one, but the most widely used, of a family of sound- (or signal-) processing amplifiers. Others include dynamic range enhancers, ambience simulators, switching systems, noise reduction components, surround stereo-processing amplifiers, and sound expansion and compression components.

A sound-processing amplifier can supply surround stereo sound, and it can be used to drive rear speakers, supply bass tone emphasis, simulate stereo, or operate a super woofer. A sound-processing amplifier does not replace a system's existing integrated or component amplifier or the amplifier in a receiver. It can be connected in the same way as an equalizer. It can help recreate the reverberant sound heard in a live sound situation. To do this, an additional pair of speakers is required, positioned to the rear of the listener. Positioning and connections of existing speakers need not be changed.

There are a number of ways in which a sound processor can be connected into a high-fidelity system. The simplest is to insert the processor between a separate preamplifier and its following power amplifier, as shown in Fig. 6–

41A. As indicated, the audio output terminals of the processor are connected to the input terminals of the power amplifier. In making these connections there are certain precautions. Make sure all electrical power to the high-fidelity system is turned off. Observe polarity and if you have previously set up a color code, such as using black connectors for minus and red connectors for plus, be consistent and follow this approach. Identify the connectors by using self-stick labels on all connectors (not the cable) and modify the wiring plan of the system accordingly.

The sound-processing amplifier can be connected through a tape loop (Fig. 6–41B), using the tape terminals on an integrated amplifier or receiver. Use joined cables to avoid a wiring maze. These cables, of course, will have separate connectors.

Some integrated amplifiers and receivers (Fig. 6–41C) are equipped with a rear panel accessory output loop, which sends and receives a source signal for external processing by a graphic equalizer or sound processor. Such terminals are sometimes referred to as *pre-main coupling terminals.* Instead of being identified as "In" and "Out," they are marked "Send" and "Receive."

If the integrated amplifier or receiver has such terminals, connect the send (out) terminals to the input terminals on the processor and connect the receive (in) terminals to the output terminals on the processor.

The problem with connecting a sound-processing amplifier to an integrated amplifier or receiver through a tape loop is that you cannot use the tape loop for its intended purpose—tape deck connections. However, the sound processor will have its own terminals and they can be used to connect a tape deck to the amplifier or receiver. The tape deck, whether open reel or cassette, will then function as though connected to the receiver or amplifier. The simplest way to do this is to disconnect the tape terminals from the receiver or amplifier and to connect them to the corresponding terminals on the sound processor. It is not necessary to remove the connectors from the tape deck.

The processor will drive a pair of left/right speakers. It may also have an output for an additional monophonic speaker from terminals identified as mono. This mono speaker can be a woofer to supply additional bass emphasis. However, the mono output isn't connected directly to a speaker, but to a separate power amplifier. A single audio cable is required from the mono output of the processor to the input of the power amp and another cable from the power amplifier to the input of the speaker. The cables connecting the sound processor to the high-fidelity system are typical audio cables equipped with phono plugs as connectors. Use cable extensions if the cables supplied with the sound processor aren't long enough.

It is also possible to use a processing amplifier that will not only enhance conventional stereo sources but will help supply pseudo stereo from mono sources such as a TV receiver or VCR. A processing amplifier may be equipped with selectable high-frequency filters and may be capable of supplying bass boost.

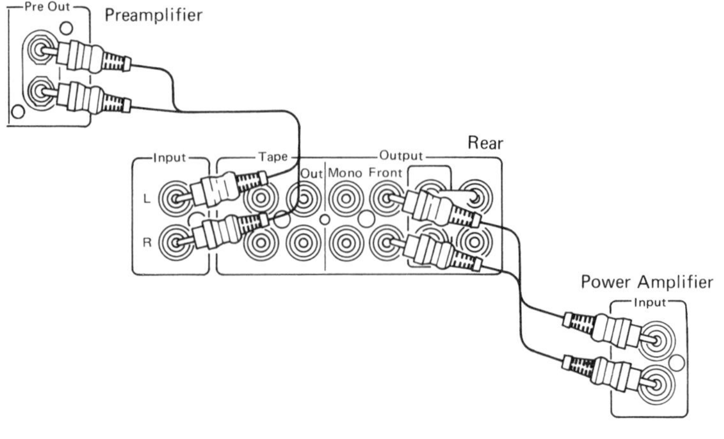
Pre Out
Preamplifier
Rear
Input
Tape
Output
Out
Mono
Front
L
R
Power Amplifier
Input

(A)

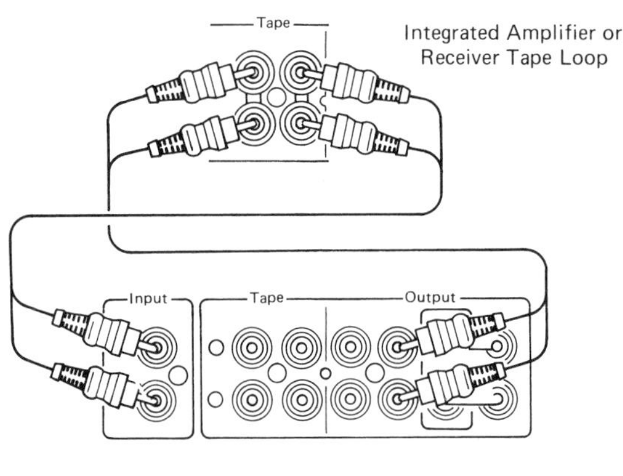
Tape
Integrated Amplifier or
Receiver Tape Loop
Input
Tape
Output

(B)

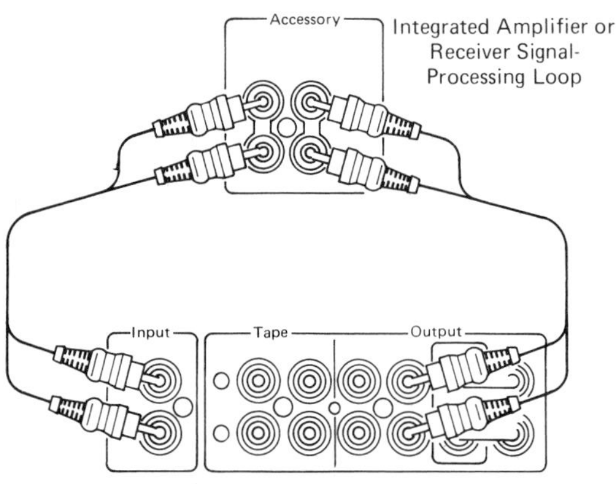
Accessory
Integrated Amplifier or
Receiver Signal-
Processing Loop
Input
Tape
Output

(C)

CONNECTING A COMPANDER

One of the problems of high-fidelity equipment is that as it gets better, it can also get worse. This isn't as paradoxical as it sounds, for as equipment improves it becomes more sensitive and responsive to noise.

Noise is more than just hum and hiss; it is a combination of all noise. It can be produced outside high-fidelity equipment or in it—usually both.

Hum belongs to the noise family, but unlike other kinds of noise that may have sudden starts and stops, it is a regular noise. Hum can exist for a number of reasons. When filter capacitors in the power supply get old and somewhat dry, or when they develop leakage, the result is an increase in hum. An improperly shielded phono cartridge can produce hum. As a high-fidelity system is expanded, and more components are included, the patch cord connections joining the components become more numerous. Hum can develop if these are too close to power-line cords.

Electrical noise is distracting, and the signal-to-noise ratio decides the dynamic range of a high-fidelity system. Dynamic range is the separation, in decibels, between the softest sound in a composition and the loudest.

Various techniques are used for the reduction of tape hiss. One of the most widely known is the Dolby B system, more often just referred to as *Dolby*. This system must be used during recording and playback. During recording, treble tones are boosted if their signal strength is low. At playback, these same tones must be weakened to the same extent to which they were originally boosted, so what we have is a system of compression/expansion. Certain parts of the frequency range are compressed during recording, and these same portions are expanded during playback.

Sound expansion and compression isn't a new idea, for it is used in cutting records. The width of a record groove depends on the frequency of the tone being cut in. Bass tones produce wide swings in the cutter; treble tones rather narrow movement. To keep the cutter from going through the wall of the groove, bass tones are deliberately weakened. Treble tones do not require as much audio power. As the cutter moves through the record material it also produces noise, and to avoid this, treble tones are boosted. This means that during manufacture, records have weak bass and strong treble. The bass is compressed, the treble expanded.

A compander is used to supply either expansion or compression of sound. Figure 6–42 shows two ways in which a compander can be used. Drawing A illustrates how to connect the compander in a fully component system using a separate preamplifier and power amplifier. The audio output of the preamp is connected, via shielded audio cable equipped with RCA plugs, from the

---

Figure 6–41. Processor connected between preamp and power amp (A); processor connected through a tape loop (B); processor using accessory output loop (C). (*Courtesy Yamaha Electronics Corp.*)

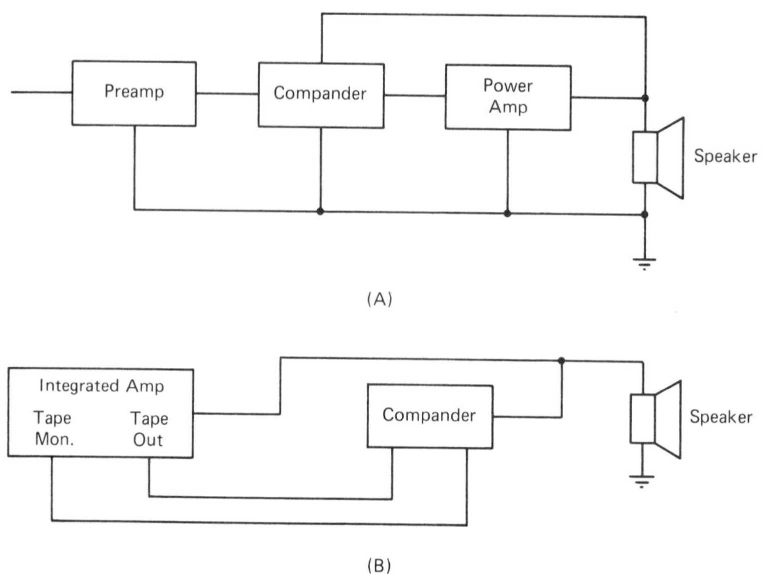

Figure 6–42. Compander connections for separate preamp (A) and compander connected to integrated amp (B).

output of the preamp to the input of the compander. The compander has two inputs. One is for a sample of the signal from the speaker while the other is an input jack for connection to the preamplifier. The output of the compander is connected, using the same kind of cable, to the input of the power amp.

Although a ground connection is shown, this is accomplished via the shield braid of the audio cable. Not shown in the drawing is a connection from the preamp to a turntable, and it is this component that has a separate ground wire.

The speaker is also shown with one side of its voice coil grounded. More often, the power amplifier has a pair of speaker output terminals and these are connected to the speaker by zip cord or special speaker wires. No ground connection to the speaker is required. However, such a connection is sometimes used for auto radio speakers, described in the next chapter.

Drawing B shows how to make the connections when an integrated amplifier is used. The tape monitor and output terminals of the integrated amp are wired to the compander. As in drawing A, there is a feedback loop from the hot lead of the compander back to the integrated amplifier.

ROUTING THE SOUND SOURCE

In the early days of high-fidelity sound, the preamplifier was used not only as a signal voltage amplifier but as a sound source selector. As systems became more complex this function was divided among a number of other components, including the tuner and the power amplifier. The lack of a central control unit makes operation of a system more difficult. Signal switchers have become quite common in video systems, but they have not had extensive use in audio.

For complicated high-fidelity—complicated in the sense that a relatively large number of components must be interconnected—a signal switcher/preamplifier and power amplifier such as that in Fig. 6–43 is helpful. It makes it possible to connect two tape decks, two turntables, a compact disc player, and a sound processor through a single tape-monitor loop. The unit also has enough power output to drive a pair of A/B speaker systems.

HIGH-FIDELITY SYSTEMS

It is possible to set up a variety of high-fidelity sound systems, ranging from an AM/FM/MPX receiver with a single pair of speakers to one utilizing a number of outboard components. Whatever system is used, it should allow for future expansion.

Figure 6–44 is just one possible arrangement of many. This setup is designed with just one sound input source, a pair of microphones, with the sound reproducible by stereo headphones or a pair of stereo speakers. A tape deck is used for recording and playback. The DIN connector is optional and can be used to replace the pin cords shown in the drawing. One or the other is used, but not both. The tape deck receives its operating power from a convenience outlet on the back of the stereo amplifier, a switched type so that turning on the power amplifier also activates the tape deck. The deck will have its own on/off switch, to defeat AC power input if that is what is wanted.

A pair of microphones is used—one for left-, the other for right-channel sound. These are connected to microphone jacks on the front panel of the tape deck.

Another possible system is illustrated in Fig. 6–45. The setup is dominated by a three-way crossover system whose low, mid, and treble tone outputs drive three separate power amplifiers, which, in turn are connected to a pair of speaker systems. The sound sources include a stereo tuner, either AM/FM/MPX, or an FM-only unit. The tuner, with a tape deck and a turntable, supplies sound signals to a stereo preamplifier. A control on the face of the preamplifier is used to determine which of these sources will be selected as the input signal to the three-way crossover. The ground terminal on the crossover can be connected to the same ground point used by the turntable.

One of the desirable features of the crossover is the four convenience power outlets, two of which are switched, two unswitched.

The system shown in Fig. 6–46 is quite elaborate and has an integrated amplifier as the central component. A pair of tuners is used, with one connected to the tuner input jacks, the other to the aux 1 input. There is also a

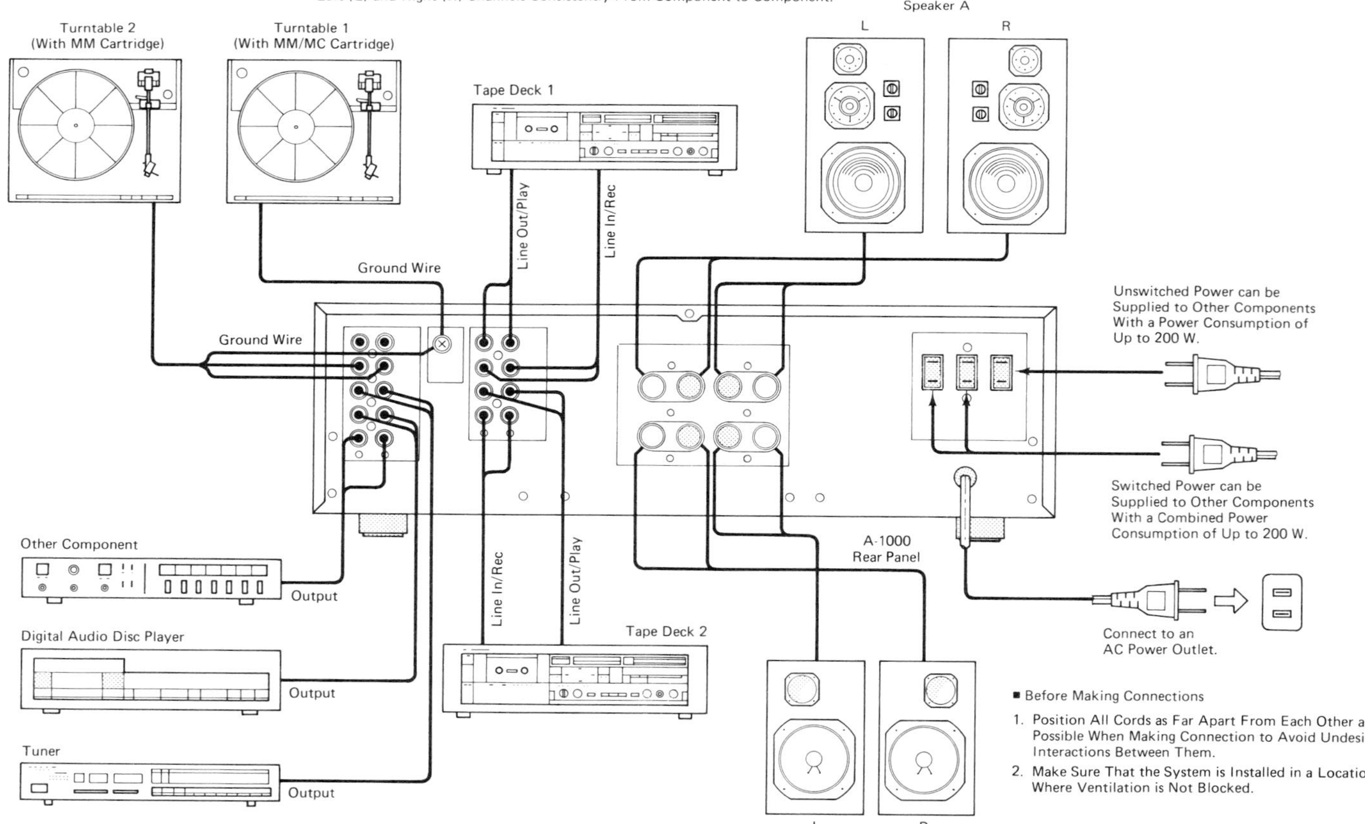

Figure 6–43. Multiple-input high-fidelity system. (*Courtesy Yamaha Electronics Corp.*)

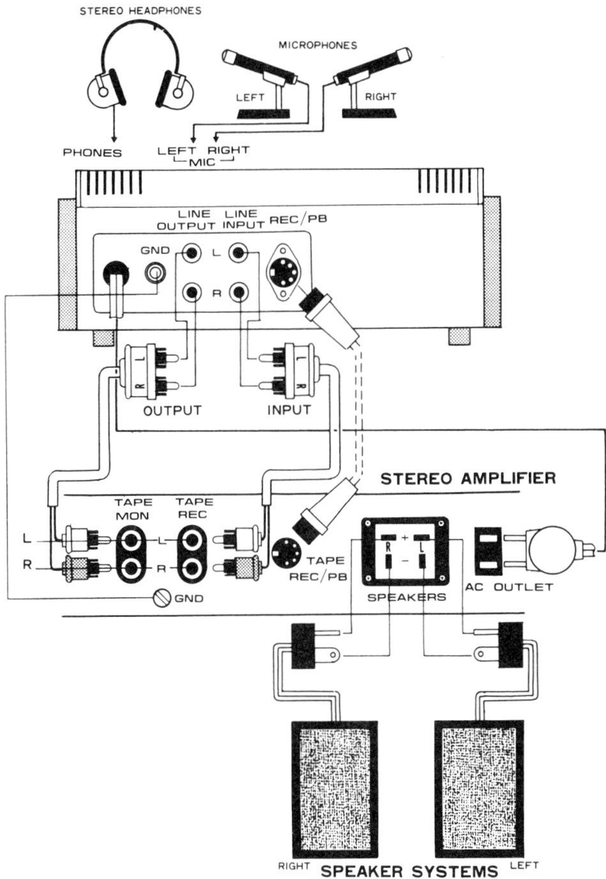

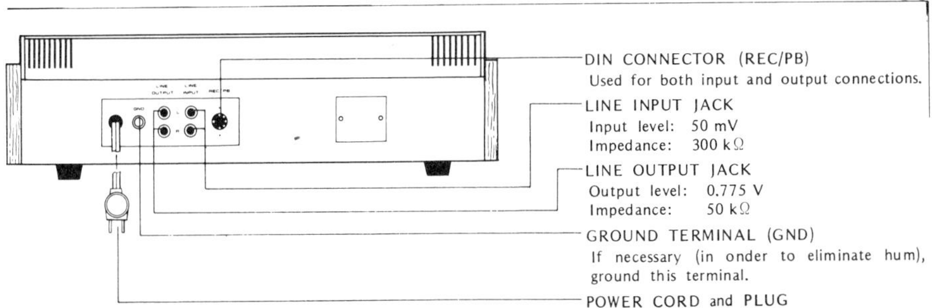

Figure 6–44. Stereo microphone sound system. (*Courtesy Pioneer Electronics [U.S.A.] Corp.*)

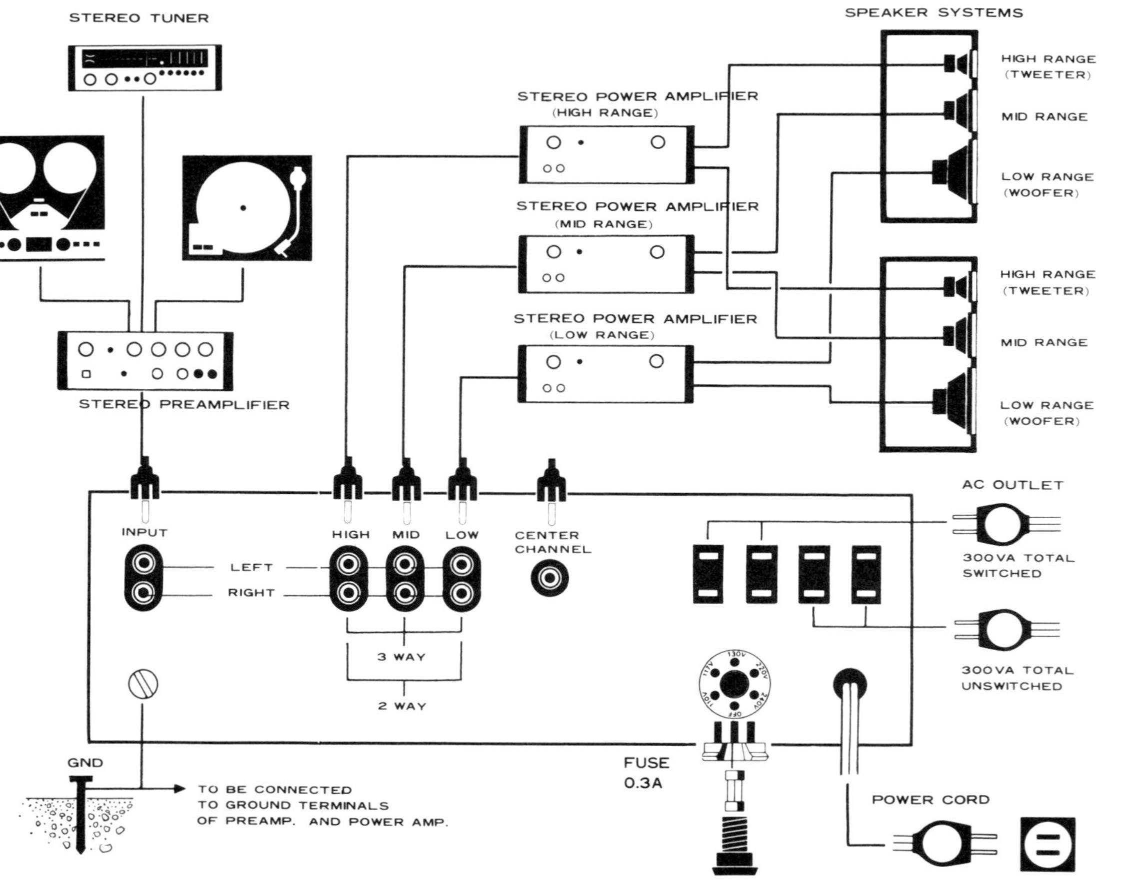

Figure 6–45. Electronic crossover system. (*Courtesy Pioneer Electronics* [*U.S.A.*] *Corp.*)

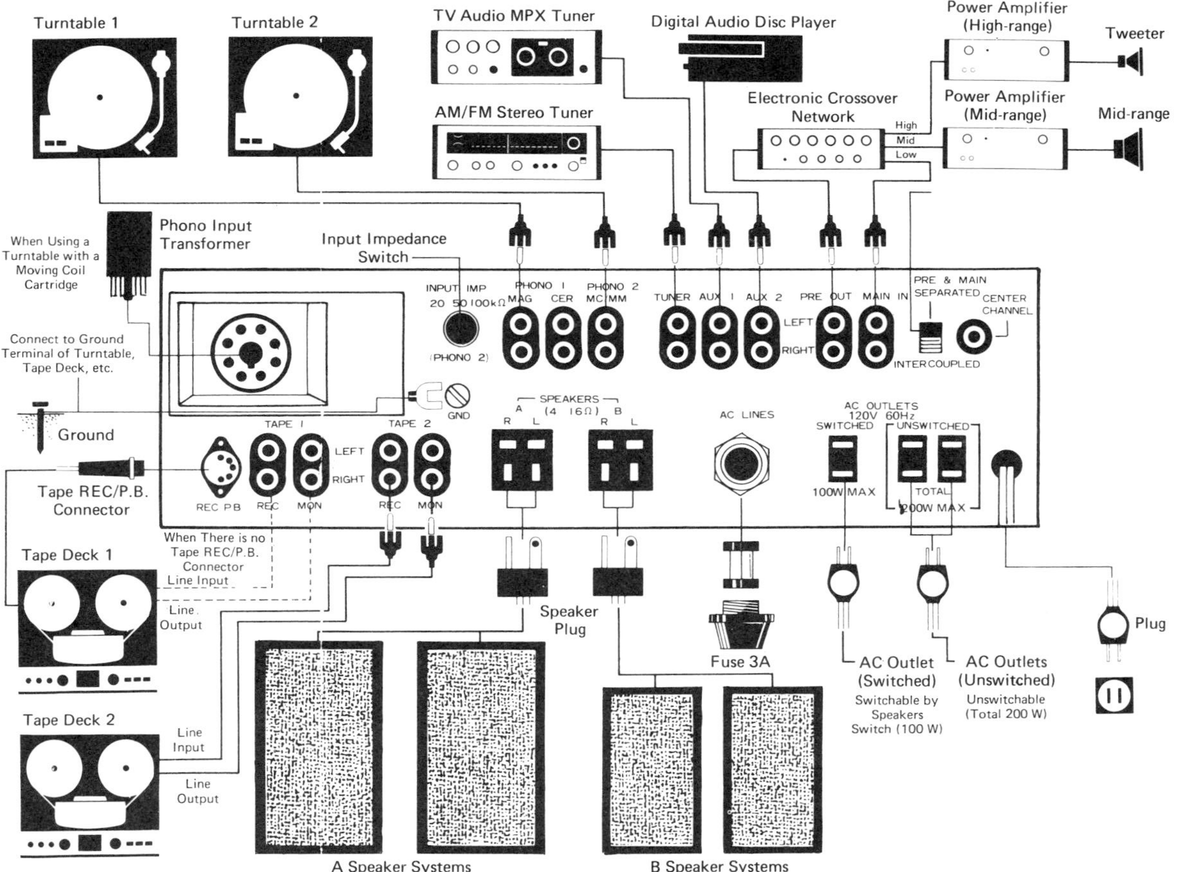

Figure 6–46. System connections for a high-fidelity system. Compare with the sound system shown in Figure 6–43. (*Courtesy Pioneer Electronics [U.S.A.] Corp.*)

pair of tape decks, one of which could be a cassette recorder/player, the other an open-reel unit. The deck in the lower left corner uses RCA plug-equipped cables for connection to the integrated amplifier. Tape deck 1 can use a tape record/playback connector—a DIN type—or if this cable isn't available, individual audio cables—RCA plug equipped. The connections for the individual cables are shown as dashed lines.

There are two turntables, but note that there are three phono input terminals, for a magnetic pickup, a ceramic, and one for a moving coil (MC) or a moving magnet (MM) phono cartridge. There is also a keyed 8-pin socket for a phono input transformer to be used with a turntable having a moving coil cartridge.

This system also has provision for accepting signal input from a digital audio disc player, which makes use of the aux 2 input jacks. Note that although there are two ports for each sound source, only one of them shows a connecting line. Each sound source has a pair of cables, but the second cable has been omitted for the sake of drawing clarity. Thus, the TV/audio MPX tuner, used for bringing in television sound, shows just a single cable leading to the aux 1 port, although there are actually two such cables.

Another feature of the integrated amplifier is that the output voltage of the preamplifier section can be obtained separately. This is controlled by a switch on the back panel of the unit. When the switch is in its up position, the preamplifier and power amplifier of this integrated amplifier are disconnected and the preamplifier voltage can be obtained as an output signal source.

The system also uses an electronic crossover network. In effect, it is connected between the preamplifier and the main (power) amplifier. The input to the electronic crossover is the output signal from the preamp. The bass tone output of the crossover is brought to the main input of the amplifier. Consequently, the power amplifier section of the integrated amplifier is used to drive the woofers. The midrange and tweeter frequencies have their own power amplifiers. The individual outputs of these amplifiers are used to drive the tweeter and midrange speakers.

There are four drivers, two left/right speakers shown as speaker system A, and another speaker system shown as B. The different speaker sizes shown in the drawing are simply to indicate that the A speaker system uses a higher amount of audio power. This could be the case if the A speaker system is to be used in front, while the B speaker system could handle rear channel sound, possibly reverberant sound.

The integrated amplifier is equipped with three convenience outlets, one of which is switched, the remaining two unswitched.

Note that practically every jack on the rear of the integrated amplifier has been used, and while this is quite a substantial system, there is no equalizer or processing amplifier.

7

CAR RADIO SOUND SYSTEM CONNECTIONS

A car radio sound system is very much like an in-home high-fidelity system. It uses an antenna, a radio receiver or a tuner, and an audio amplifier. It may have a tape deck, and it has speakers. The car's sound system does not use a turntable, although efforts were made many years ago to adapt them to the car. In its place, there are compact disc players. The in-home system has a choice of tape decks: open-reel or cassette, but the car system uses a cassette deck only. The in-home system depends on the AC line for its fundamental source of power, but the auto system uses DC power input supplied by the car's battery.

A car is an extremely hostile environment for any electronic entertainment system. Noise signals are not only generated by the engine, but also produced by car movement, by the body of the car, by passing cars, by equipment in buildings being passed, and by street lights and advertising signs. Signal strength is variable, as the distance from the station keeps changing. Changes in terrain can cause the signal to become weak or variable, or to disappear.

Installation is a problem, as the amount of room in the dash, or under it, is not only seriously limited but already occupied by car wiring. The components of the car's audio system and its connecting wiring are subject to severe vibration. Further, the system must undergo extreme changes in temperature.

The voltage for a car sound system is supplied by the battery. As the internal resistance of that battery increases, as it will when the battery ages, its impedance rises, so the battery can form a common element between the various auto radio components. As a result, it supplies an unwanted signal path, causing problems that are difficult to trace. For this reason, it is advisable to shunt the battery with a low-voltage electrolytic capacitor having as high a value of capacitance as possible. Since such a capacitor is polarized, the connections are plus to plus, minus to minus. To avoid the heat of the engine, mount the capacitor on the passenger's side of the firewall. No special plugs or cables are needed, and any insulated wire, gauge 22 or thicker, will do.

CAR SOUND SYSTEMS

Car sound systems can follow the same general outlines suggested in Chapter 6, but there are some differences. In a home system, it is common to have just a pair of up-front left/right speakers. In a car or recreational vehicle, front and rear speakers are commonly used. There are no phono turntables in car systems, but a cassette deck is generally included with the AM/FM receiver, eliminating the external connections needed between the two. Further, the cassette deck in the car system is a playback type only; in the home it is a recording/playback unit. The use of station memory, supplying the ability to recall wanted stations at the push of a button, is much more common in auto radio receivers than in home receivers. As far as speakers are concerned, the ground system of the car, that is, the car's metal frame, is often used as a means of simplifying speaker wiring.

Figure 7-1 shows one of the simpler, but more commonly used, car sound systems. It consists of a pair of front speakers and a pair for the rear. The front speakers supply midrange/tweeter tones, while bass notes are furnished

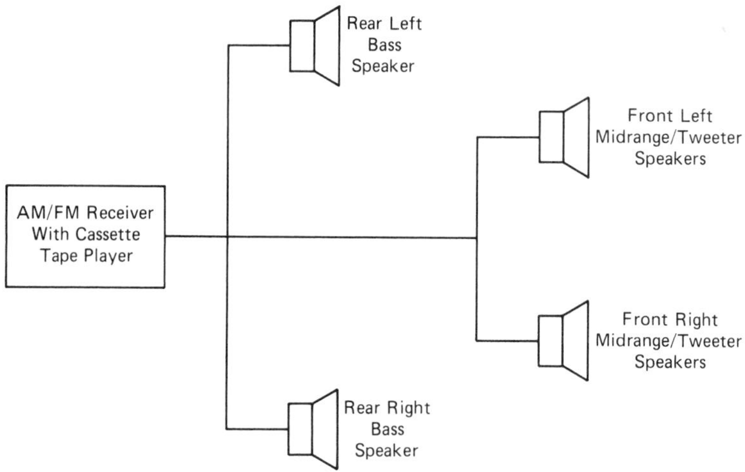

Figure 7-1. Basic auto sound system.

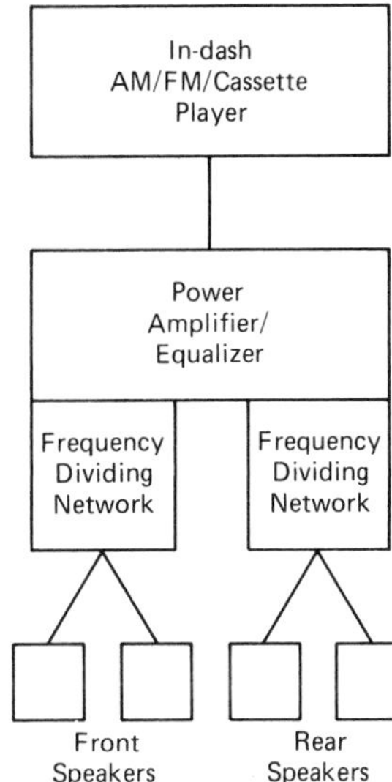

Figure 7–2. Integrated system using combined receiver/cassette player and combined power amplifier/equalizer.

by those mounted at the rear. This diagram, like others of its type, does not supply actual connection information—only a general overview.

Figure 7–2 shows a somewhat more sophisticated arrangement. The receiver is an in-dash AM/FM receiver, with a built-in cassette player. Not all car radios are of this kind, as some have no cassette player, which is often a separate unit mounted under the dash. The audio output signal, whether cassette or radio, is front-panel-switch selected and is supplied to an integrated amplifier/equalizer. In some high-fidelity systems, the equalizer is most often a separate add-on component.

Following the amplifier/equalizer, the signal is supplied to a pair of frequency-dividing networks. These passive types are included in the amplifier/equalizer. This also supplies an example of one of the differences between home and car setups. In a home system, passive frequency dividers are included inside the speaker enclosure. In the car system, they may be positioned inside the power amplifier. In some installations, the frequency divider is an outboard component and is situated between the output of the power amp and the input to the speakers. For the front speakers, the frequency-dividing network usually bandpasses the tweeter and midrange tones for the front speakers, and the bass tones for the rear-mounted drivers.

Figure 7–3 is a block diagram for yet another auto sound system. In this arrangement, the integrated amplifier/equalizer has been separated into two individual components, an equalizer and an output power amplifier. Only a single frequency divider is used and just a pair of speakers. There is no great advantage in separating the equalizer and amplifier, but this arrangement is used if an equalizer is to be added to an existing system that doesn't have one.

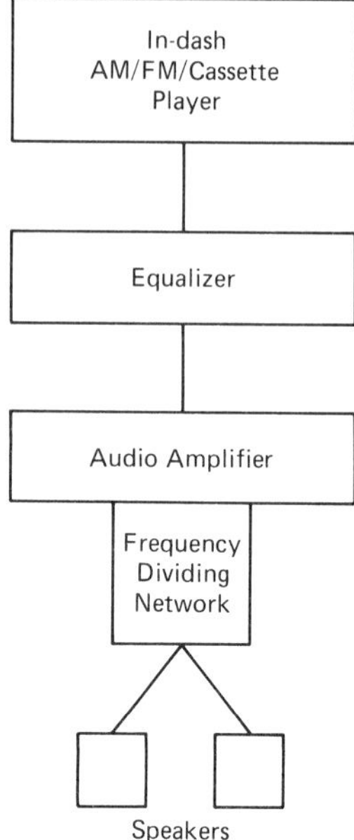

Figure 7–3. Component approach in auto sound system.

The speaker arrangement in Fig. 7–2 is preferable to that shown in Fig. 7–3 and could be the upgrading routine used for the setup in Fig. 7–3.

THE RF PREAMPLIFIER

As a way of improving the signal-to-noise ratio for car radios, some systems may include an RF (radio frequency) preamplifier. This outboard component is an untuned broadband amplifier and is inserted in the signal line between the antenna and the input to the radio receiver. No adjustments are ever required, and as the unit is untuned, there are no operating controls. Figure 7–4 shows an auto radio system using this component.

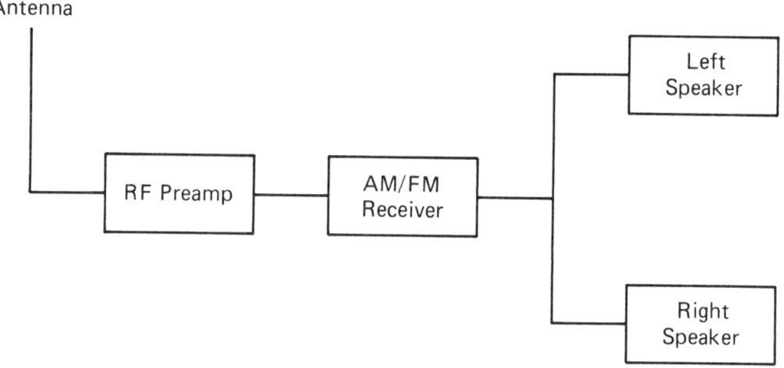

Figure 7–4. Auto sound system with preamplifier.

THE ANTENNA SYSTEM

Auto antennas range from the lowest-cost single-element whip to power-operated antennas. Included in the list of possible antennas are the single-element type coated with fiberglass, an advantage since it makes the antenna more rigid and reduces wind whipping.

Connecting the Antenna

Antennas are supplied with a flexible length of coaxial cable. At the antenna end, the cable may be fixed to the antenna and at the receiver end, it is equipped with a pin plug for insertion into a jack in the receiver. Unlike in-home components, the jack is not part of the rear apron but is connected to a short length of coaxial cable extending out of the receiver and fastened to it by a clamp. This makes it easier to insert the plug attached to the antenna cable. Similarly, there is no rear-mounted jack for other connections, such as those to the speakers. Instead, short lengths of color-coded flexible wires are used, extending several inches from the rear of the component.

Antenna kits may supply the cable with a coaxial connector for attachment to the antenna. To keep the cable from vibrating while the car is in motion, it is helpful to fasten the cable to the car's body by using clips or fasteners. The best location is to have the cable as far from the car's engine as possible, running the cable along the firewall.

The Motorized Antenna

One of the problems with whip antennas, whether a single, fixed whip or a telescoping type, is that they are subject to vandalism. There are several ways of minimizing this problem. One is to avoid the telescoping type, using instead a highly flexible antenna that can be repeatedly bent but that will not break. The other is to use a motorized antenna. Some are activated simply by turning on the ignition switch—a step that automatically delivers DC power to a motor that elevates the antenna. Turning off the ignition recesses the antenna into a well on the right front fender, or close to it.

The motorized antenna is connected to a DC voltage point inside the receiver, which leads to a relay box. This voltage activates a relay that controls current to the antenna motor.

The best location for an antenna, whether motorized or not, is as close to the receiver as possible. This means a short connecting cable, which is desirable because even small amounts of electrical noise picked up by the cable will be amplified.

Coaxial cable (Fig. 7-5) is used for connecting the antenna to the receiver since the car's engine is an electrical noise generator. The shield braid, or

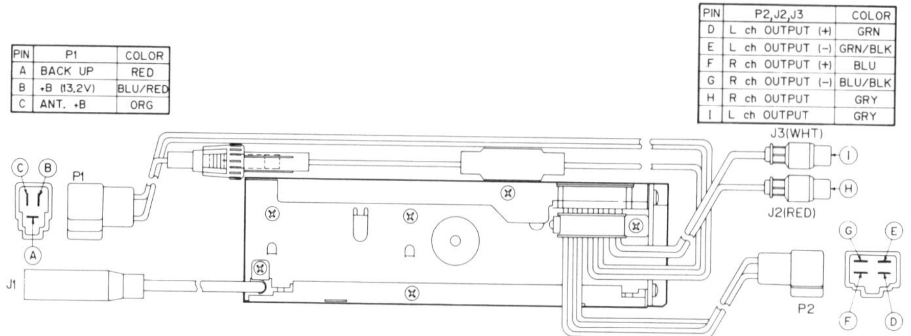

PIN	P1	COLOR
A	BACK UP	RED
B	+B (13.2V)	BLU/RED
C	ANT. +B	ORG

PIN	P2,J2,J3	COLOR
D	L ch OUTPUT (+)	GRN
E	L ch OUTPUT (−)	GRN/BLK
F	R ch OUTPUT (+)	BLU
G	R ch OUTPUT (−)	BLU/BLK
H	R ch OUTPUT	GRY
I	L ch OUTPUT	GRY

Figure 7–5. Antenna jack (J1) is connected to receiver with a short length of shielded cable. (*Courtesy Fujitsu Ten Ltd.*)

ground lead, is connected to the body of the car through the antenna's mounting assembly. A poor grounding contact at this point will result in a high noise level. If there is any doubt about the effectiveness of the ground connection, strip a small section of the outer covering to expose the shield braid of the cable. Wrap some uninsulated copper wire tightly around the braid and then connect the wire to the car body.

The cable connecting the antenna to the receiver or RF amplifier should be as short and direct as possible. Before deciding on cable length, determine the path the cable will follow. To avoid drilling through the firewall, take advantage of any existing holes. If the cable has a small amount of slack, pull the excess through the hole so the wire is on the driver's side of the firewall. If the original cable isn't long enough, use an extension equipped with a plug at one end and a jack at the other.

Connecting the AM, FM, or CB Antenna

A single antenna can be used for AM, FM, and CB. AM and FM are for reception only; CB is for reception and signal transmission. Connection of a single multiband antenna requires the use of a coupler (Fig. 7–6). Since the antenna may be located at the rear of the vehicle, an extension cable may be needed to connect it to the coupler. The pin plug of this cable fits tightly into the extension jack of the coupler. This unit has two outputs, one for connection to the CB transceiver, and the other for connection to the radio receiver. The coupler supplies separation of AM, FM, and CB frequencies, works automatically, and does not require switching. The coupler is a passive device and does not require any connection to the car's battery.

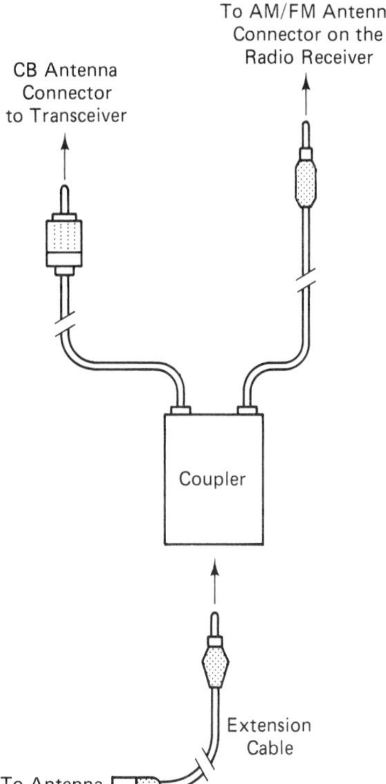

Figure 7–6. Single-antenna operation for AM/FM receiver and CB transceiver.

THE GROUND CONNECTION

Unlike an in-home high-fidelity system, where a ground connection may or may not be required, auto radios are equipped with a ground wire, usually color-coded black, which should be connected to the frame of the car. If necessary, drill a small through hole in the fire wall and use a small self-tapping machine screw and nut to anchor the ground lead. Make sure the area around the hole is clean and free of rust or paint, using steel wool if necessary. Wrap the bare end of the ground wire around the screw and tighten securely. Simply wrapping the ground wire around a convenient extrusion of the firewall isn't adequate. It is important to remember that ground also represents the negative terminal of the battery and that the battery supplies DC operating power for the car's sound fidelity system.

The entire radio receiver is enclosed in a metal housing that not only acts as ground but also helps avoid noise pickup by the wiring inside the set. Grounding the receiver is secured in several ways. It is obtained by the metal straps that hold the receiver in place, and also when the antenna is connected, as the wire joining the antenna to the receiver uses shield braid. When the antenna is connected, the shield braid makes contact with the body of the car.

Floating Ground

The frame of the car is a convenient ground, simplifying auto radio connections, but there are some systems that do not use this ground exclusively. For some power amplifiers and speaker systems, a separate ground wire is used instead. The car frame ground simplifies connections, but it isn't always desirable, for the assumption is made that the car frame is unitary construction. In some instances it is made of several parts that are joined. These may rub or move against each other, producing electrical noise. The use of a separate wire as a ground, known as a floating ground, is superior. This ground lead should avoid any connections to the car frame.

The car frame and the separate floating ground wire can both be used as ground; the shield braid of the antenna-connecting cable is grounded to the car frame, but a power amp and its associated speakers may use a ground wire.

THE BATTERY CONNECTION

Coming out of the receiver are a number of color-coded wires leading to a multipin connector. These pins—and their colors—are not standardized, but black is generally used for ground, and this wire is connected to the car body. The color red is used for battery plus. It does not go directly to the battery but somewhere along its length is a "quick disconnect" consisting of a plug and a jack. These can be a twist lock or a tight fit, but they have no resemblance to plugs and jacks used in home fidelity systems. The purpose of the quick disconnect is to open the wire leading to the battery plus terminal.

The red battery plus wire, following the quick disconnect, leads to a fuse on the fuse block on the engine side of the firewall and from that fuse to a terminal on the ignition switch. This arrangement has a double purpose. The fuse protects the receiver against accidental short circuits. With the ignition switch connection, the receiver cannot be turned on unless the ignition switch is activated. This keeps the receiver from being left turned on when the driver of the car leaves the vehicle. However, there are installations in which the ignition switch is bypassed and the receiver can be turned on and left on regardless of the setting of the ignition switch. In this case, the on/off action is controlled only by the on/off switch on the front panel of the receiver. The wire used for making this connection is color-coded red with a white tracer. The purpose of this connection is to maintain a DC voltage input to the receiver so that clock logic and station memory will continue to function even though the receiver is turned off.

Color-Coding Record

Whether you do your own installation or have it done for you, keep a record of the color coding and the connection points of each wire. This will make servicing faster, as it will not be necessary to trace wires from their start to their destination.

THE FUSE BLOCK

The purpose of a fuse is to protect the receiver but that fuse can be defeated in two ways: by using a fuse having a larger current-carrying capacity than that indicated by the manufacturer, or by shunting the fuse with a short length of wire. Fuses can be checked easily for an open circuit condition by removing them and just looking at them. In cases of doubt, double check with a VOM set on any resistance scale, or simply replace the suspected fuse with one known to be in good condition.

JOINING WIRES

The wires coming out of the receiver have a length of about 4 inches to 6 inches, certainly not enough to reach to the components to which they are to be connected. The manufacturers of car radios have no way of knowing just how far the components, such as speakers, will be from the receiver.

The add-on wires can be solid-conductor wires or twisted, but in either case, they must be insulated. Single-conductor wire is not as flexible as stranded wire, but it does not have the disadvantage of possibly cutting through one of the strands. The wires are not audio cables, and are not equipped with shield braid.

These wires can be connected to the color-coded speaker wires by using a wire nut (Fig. 7–7). All that is necessary is to insert the bare ends of the two wires, the color-coded speaker wire and the extension wire, into the wire nut and then to turn that nut until it is tight. This is a solderless connection. If

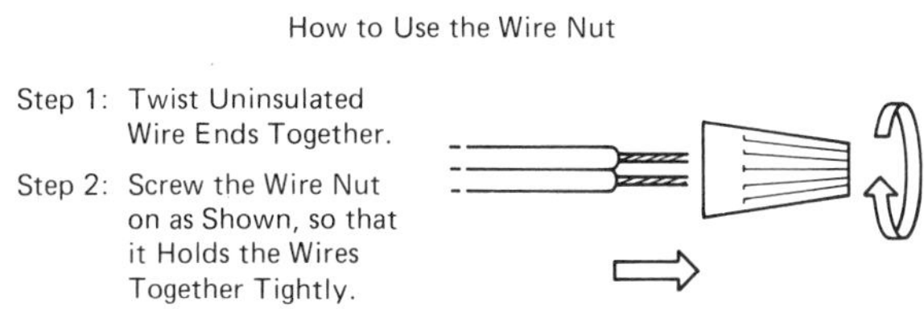

How to Use the Wire Nut
Step 1: Twist Uninsulated Wire Ends Together.
Step 2: Screw the Wire Nut on as Shown, so that it Holds the Wires Together Tightly.

Figure 7–7. Method of using a wire nut. (*Courtesy Yamaha Electronics Corp.*)

you wish, you can wrap electrician's plastic tape around the wire nut to make sure it does not come loose.

AUTO HIGH-FIDELITY SYSTEMS

The simplest auto high-fidelity system is an AM/FM receiver. Very early models were AM only and had a built-in speaker, but these have long since been bypassed in favor of AM/FM sets using a minimum of two external speakers. These sets aren't designated as AM/FM/MPX, as are in-home receivers, but they can receive stereo broadcasts. They lost their popularity because they did not include a cassette deck forcing that component to become an outboard unit, mounted beneath the dash. Just about all car receivers today have a built-in cassette deck (although there are exceptions as shown by the block diagram in Fig. 7-8), so external connections from the cassette deck to the receiver are no longer needed.

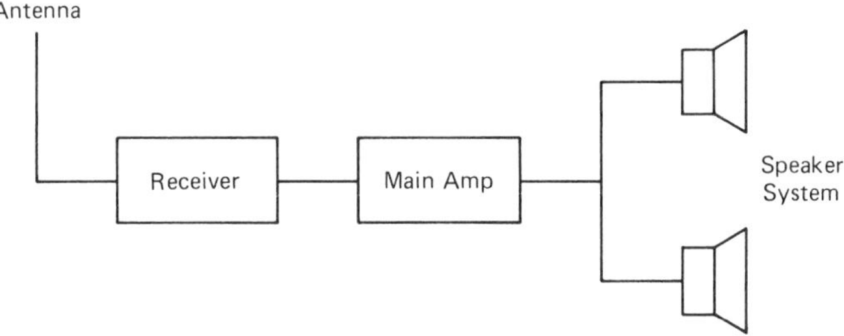

Figure 7-8. Some auto receivers do not contain a cassette player.

Every receiver has a number of connections with these going to ground, the battery or ignition key, an antenna, and one or two pairs of speakers (Fig. 7-9).

CONNECTING A RECEIVER

A TV receiver or monitor is the central component of a video system, and the receiver is the main unit in auto hi-fi setups.

The wiring to an auto radio can be somewhat extensive, as shown in Fig. 7-10, a system using a single pair of speakers. Operating power is obtained from the battery via the fuse block, with the minus terminal of the battery wired to the car body. Note that there are two DC inputs to the radio receiver, via a red wire and a red wire with a white tracer. Both of these DC plus lines are fused. Since this receiver is an integrated unit, it has its own power amplifier, a section that requires more operating current than the tuning circuitry.

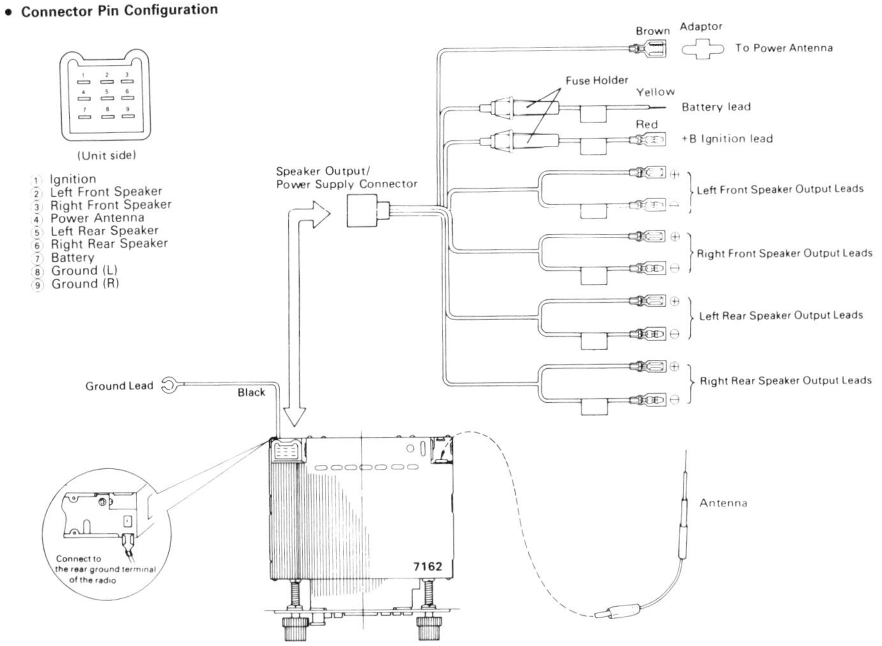

• **Connector Pin Configuration**

(Unit side)

1. Ignition
2. Left Front Speaker
3. Right Front Speaker
4. Power Antenna
5. Left Rear Speaker
6. Right Rear Speaker
7. Battery
8. Ground (L)
9. Ground (R)

Speaker Output/ Power Supply Connector

Brown Adaptor To Power Antenna

Fuse Holder Yellow Battery lead

Red +B Ignition lead

Left Front Speaker Output Leads

Right Front Speaker Output Leads

Left Rear Speaker Output Leads

Right Rear Speaker Output Leads

Ground Lead Black

Connect to the rear ground terminal of the radio

7162

Antenna

Figure 7-9. Connections for an auto radio receiver. (*Courtesy Alpine Electronics of America, Inc.*)

The two fuses are not the same, with one probably rated at 3 amperes, the other at 7 amperes.

The yellow wire out of the receiver is a plus voltage line going to the relay box and is used to supply operating potential to the motorized antenna. The plus line from the relay to the antenna motor is a white wire while the ground connections from the relay box and the motor are black, with both attached to the car frame.

The only other connections are to the two speakers. The speaker wires are not grounded, although in some systems they are. Speaker wires are usually color coded. Some wires may have two colors or may have wires that are the same color, with one wire having a tracer. The coding of the wires is necessary to phase the speakers properly. Phasing the speakers assures maximum bass response.

Receivers with Four Speakers

Figure 7-11 is a wiring arrangement for a receiver driving four speakers. The various connections to the relay, the antenna motor, and the fuse block are the same as those shown in Fig. 7-10. The left speakers are wired in series,

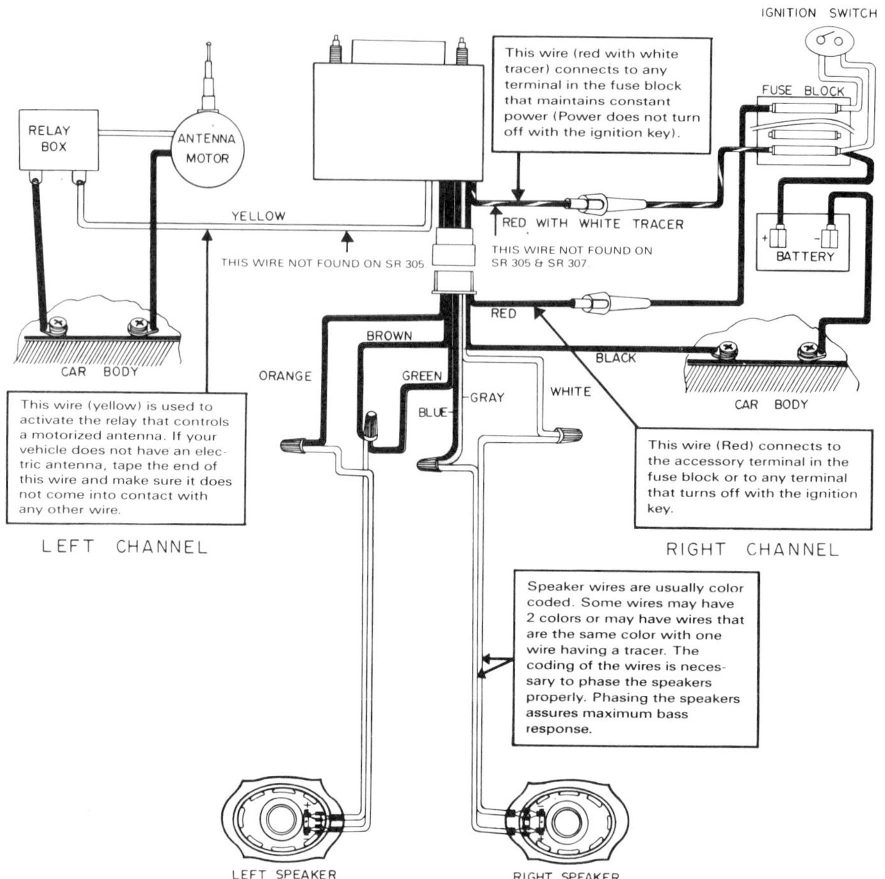

Figure 7–10. Wiring for a receiver using a motorized antenna and two speakers. (*Courtesy Sparkomatic Corporation*)

and so are the right speakers. If the output impedance of the receiver is 8 ohms, then the series speakers should be 4 ohms each. The two front left and right speakers should be identical, and so should the rear left and right speakers. However, the front and rear speakers are seldom the same. If the rear speakers are used to supply bass tones, they will generally be physically larger than the front speakers.

Figure 7–12 shows still another wiring arrangement for an auto radio receiver used with four speakers. Although red is commonly used as a color indicating a wire connected to DC plus, and black as a ground conductor, there is no standardization on color coding for speaker wires.

There are two DC plus lines going into the receiver, with both fused.

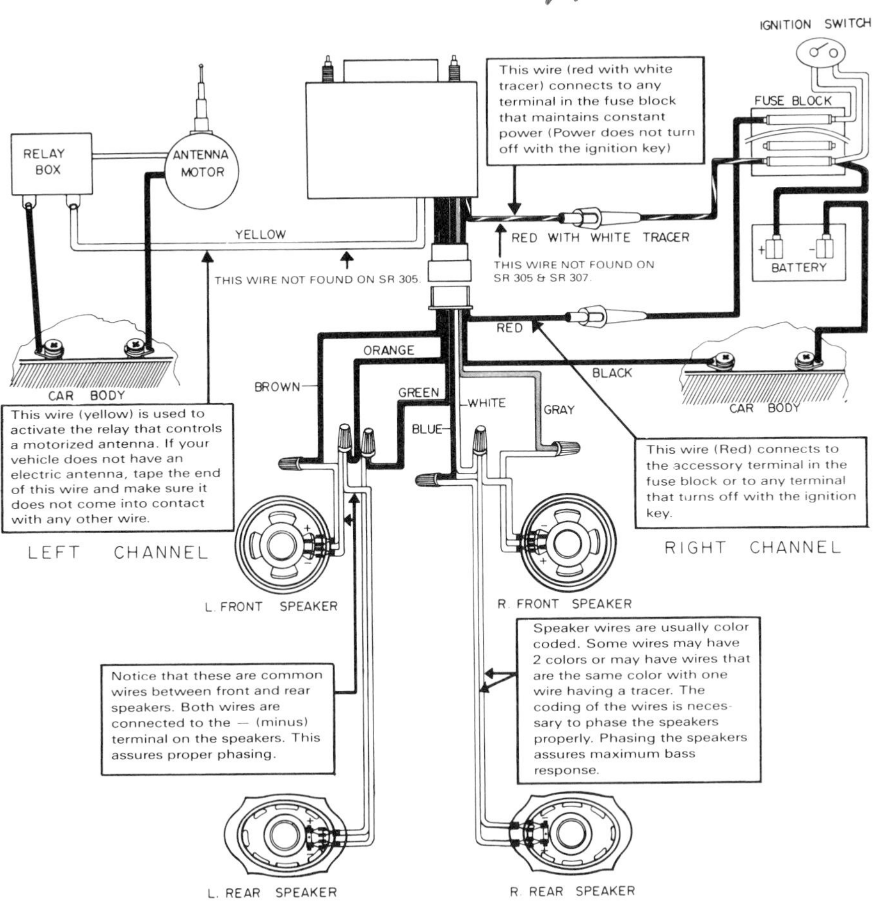

Figure 7-11. Connections for a four-speaker receiver with signal pickup by a motorized antenna. (*Courtesy Sparkomatic Corporation*)

One of these is a 1-ampere fuse for the line that will power the tuner section of the receiver; the other is a 7-ampere fuse for the power amplifier section.

The speaker system uses individual wires for the voice coils and none of these is grounded. This receiver also features a noise suppressor inserted in series in the DC power line going to the receiver.

CONNECTING A CASSETTE PLAYER/RECEIVER

Auto sound systems make extensive use of separate components, but lack of space often forces the formation of integrated units. This is usually not a problem for an in-home high-fidelity system, so a cassette deck is always an in-

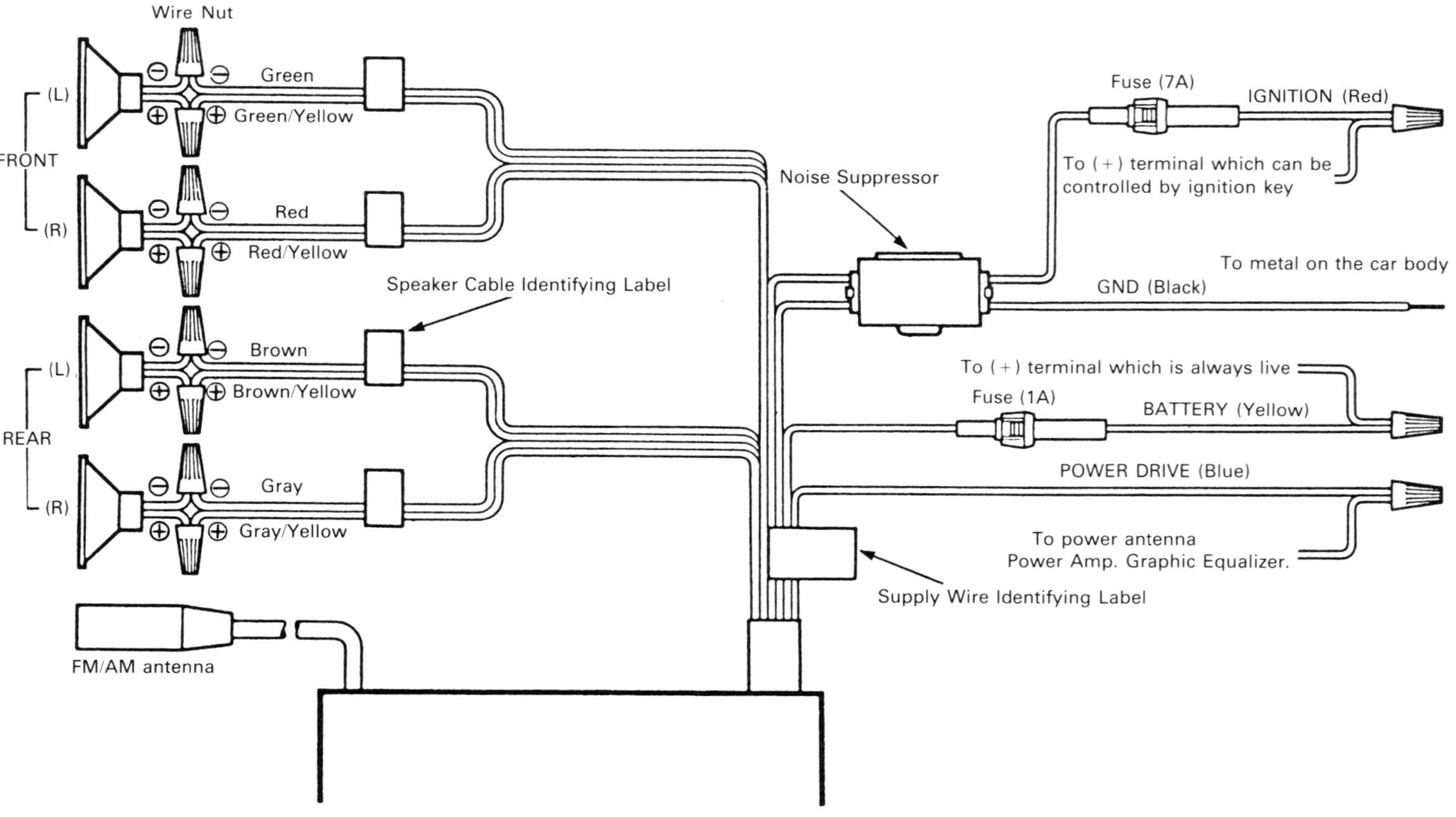

Figure 7–12. Wiring arrangement for a receiver with four-speaker output.

dividual component. In an auto sound system, the cassette deck has been made an integral part of the tuner or receiver, whichever is used. Because of this arrangement, no wiring is indicated between the cassette deck and the amplifier of the receiver. The diagrams previously shown for two- and four-speaker radio receivers may (or may not) include a cassette deck and no wiring is shown for these units.

The cassette player/receiver is supplied with a ground lead and this should be connected to the frame of the car or to any component whose wiring leads to a ground. When you make this connection, be sure the ground lead makes positive contact and there is no rust, dirt or paint between the connection and the car frame.

The ground lead of the cassette player/receiver is usually color-coded black and equipped with an open spade lug for connection to the body of the car.

CONNECTING AN UNDER-DASH TAPE PLAYER

A cassette tape player can be added to a car sound system using an AM/FM receiver that does not have one. Usually mounted under the dash, the unit is equipped with a pair of plus and minus (ground) DC voltage leads. The ground lead is a length of wire terminated in an open spade lug (Fig. 7–13), for con-

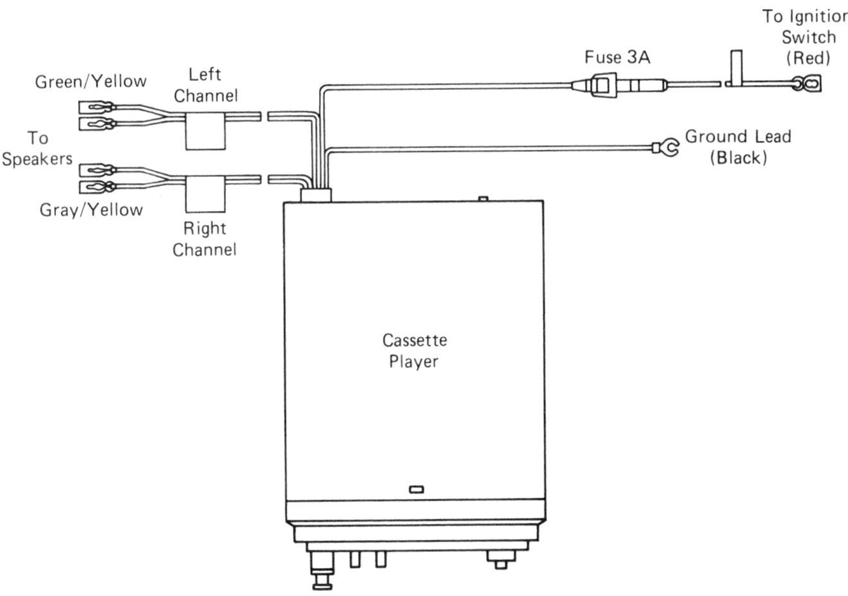

Figure 7–13. Connections for an under-dash cassette tape player.

nection to the car body. The DC plus lead is often a red-coded wire and is connected to the ignition switch through a 3-ampere fuse.

The sound signal isn't delivered to the receiver but is wired directly to the input terminals of a pair of left/right speakers, usually those located in the front of the car. The under-dash player is equipped with its own audio power amplifier and can drive the speakers directly. In some installations, the stereo signal output leads are connected to the input of a separate integrated power amplifier, using it in common with a radio receiver or a tuner.

Cassette decks, whether built into the receiver or mounted under the dash, are immune to signal fading, do not require tuning, and are not subject to electrical signal interference. The prerecorded tapes they use also do not carry commercial advertising. The cassette player does have a few problems, although these are minor. Like other electronic components in the car, it is subject to vibration, a possible cause of tape breakage. Since longer-playing tapes, such as the C-120 use a thinner tape, it is advisable to limit tapes to the C-60 and C-90 types, preferably using a deck equipped with automatic reverse.

The Space Problem

Auto sound systems may be integrated or consist of individual components. For auto radio systems, though, there is always the problem of where to put it. That is why so many auto installations include a receiver combined with a cassette player, with an equalizer included. The receiver, plus the other components all contained within the one unit, is a high-fidelity system in itself.

CONNECTING A TUNER

Figure 7–14 illustrates a tuner mounted in the dash. The unit has a small section of shielded cable to connect to the lead from an antenna. The output to

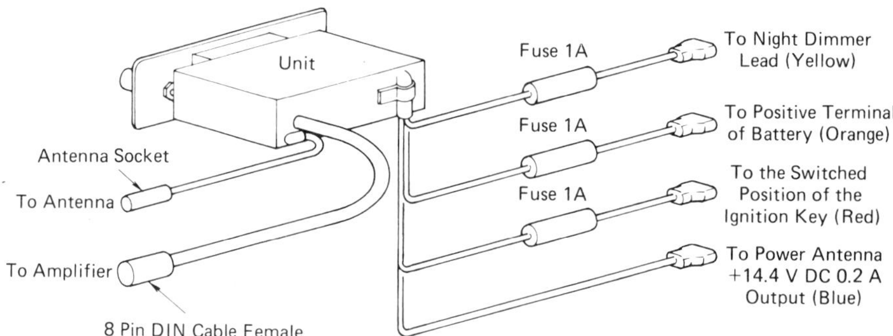

Figure 7–14. Connections for a tuner.

the power amplifier, which can be mounted under the dash or positioned in the trunk, is by an 8-pin DIN connector. This cable not only delivers the DC operating voltage from the tuner to the amplifier, but it supplies the stereo signal voltage. The amplifier is connected to a pair of left/right front speakers.

This system uses a pair of 5-ampere fuses (not shown)—one in the power line going to the amplifier, and the other in the DC plus line from the receiver to the amplifier.

The tuner is unusual in that it has three leads that connect to the battery via separate 1-ampere fuses. The one shown at the top (color-coded yellow) supplies DC voltage for a night dimmer lamp. This supplies illumination for the cassette door and tuning panel of the unit. The second connector (color-coded orange), the one in the center, is wired directly to the positive terminal of the battery to supply a permanent voltage for the memory of the unit. The third wire (color-coded red) via the 1-ampere fuse, connects to the switched position of the ignition key. The bottom wire (color-coded blue) is used as a DC line to supply 14.4 volts DC at 200 milliamperes for a forward-reverse drive motor for a power antenna.

A tuner may have a single audio output to be connected to a power amplifier for driving a pair of speakers. However, some tuners have two audio outputs, one for direct connection to speakers, the other for driving a separate power amplifier whose output, in turn, operates a second pair of speakers.

MAIN AMPLIFIER VERSUS POWER AMPLIFIER

There are a minimum of two audio amplifiers in an in-home high-fidelity system. One of these is a preamplifier, a voltage amplifier followed by a power amplifier. There may be more than one power amplifier, but in this system, the signal voltage from the preamplifier drives the input of one or more power amplifiers. The preamp and power amps may be components, that is, separate units, or they may be integrated into a combined preamplifier and power amplifier.

This arrangement is somewhat different in an auto radio sound system. Here an additional amplifier—variously termed a main amp, a power booster, or a booster amp—is used to supplement the power output of the amplifier in a receiver. Another setup is that in which a tuner supplies its output signal to a power amplifier, which, in turn, uses its output to drive a main amplifier.

There are various combinations that can be used with either one or both of these amplifiers. The power amplifier can drive a pair of speakers whether it is a separate unit, as it would be in a tuner installation, or incorporated in a receiver. In some instances, when the power output of the receiver isn't adequate, it is followed by a main amplifier.

Connecting the Power Amplifier

Unlike an in-home high-fidelity system, in which controls may be scattered among a number of components or which may be equipped with a switcher, the controls for a car system are on the front panel of the tuner or receiver. The power amplifier, sometimes mounted in the trunk of the car, has no controls, as it is often out of the reach of the user.

Figure 7–15 shows the connections to a main amplifier. To minimize the number of separate cables needed for supplying the component with signal and DC voltages, a single cable is used, terminating in a DIN connector. The power amplifier isn't equipped with an on/off switch. When the ignition is turned off, the DC power to the amplifier is shut off automatically.

The power amplifier is equipped with a ground lead, color-coded black. This lead, ending in a spade lug, can be attached to the car body using a Phillips head self-tapping screw. Make sure the area beneath the lug is clean, free of paint or rust. The speaker leads for connection to the left/right speakers end in tabs. These should make a tight fit into corresponding tab holders on the speakers. Soldering to the speaker connections isn't necessary. Polarity on the speakers is often indicated by a red dot adjacent to the positive terminal. The connector pin for the speaker and DC power leads is a 9-pin connector, but only six of the pins are used.

Unlike the DIN cable in which all the wires are housed in one jacket, those used for battery voltage and the speakers are individual wires. The reason for this is that these wires may sometimes need to be extended. If the wires contained in the DIN cable aren't long enough, use an extension cable. Since the function of each of the wires in that cable is assigned by the manufacturer, it will be necessary to get the extension cable from one of that manufacturer's dealers. The fact that a DIN plug fits into a jack does not mean the wiring is

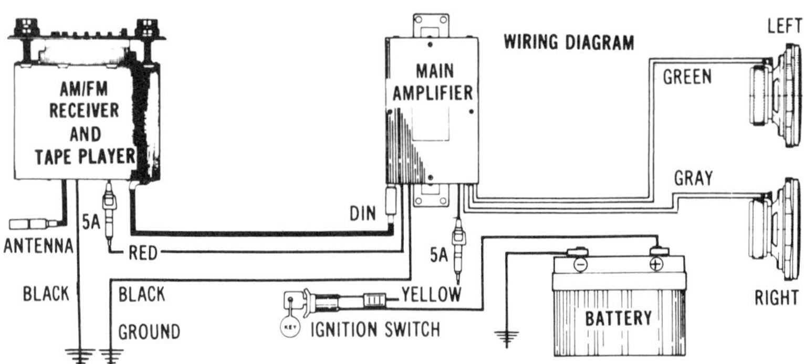

Figure 7–15. Connections for a main amplifier. (*Courtesy Alpine Electronics of America, Inc.*)

correct. It is the option of the manufacturer to use any wiring arrangement desired. Do not try to cut the DIN cable in an effort to lengthen the wires.

Fusing the Power Amplifier

Figure 7-16 supplies details of connections to a main amplifier and also shows the wiring arrangement of the DIN connector, which is not necessarily the same as the arrangement used in the DIN connector of Fig. 7-15—or that of any other receiver. The fuse ratings are different and include an extra fuse for an active equalizer, a tuner, a radio receiver, or a cassette deck.

Fuses for power amplifiers are inserted in fuse holders in series with the wires connected to the DC power source. These are lock, spring-loaded units designed to hold the fuse securely in place, yet permitting easy replacement. On some power amplifiers, the fuses are mounted in block form on the rear of the component, and they are snap-outs. Fuse replacements should always have the same current carrying-capacity as the originals.

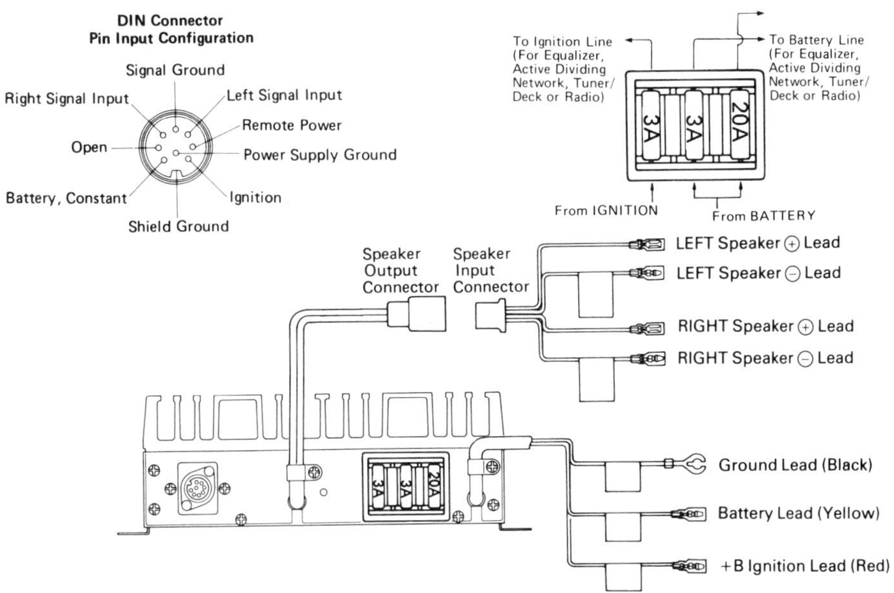

Figure 7-16. Connection details of a DIN cable and a triple fuse block. (*Courtesy Alpine Electronics of America, Inc.*)

Connecting Multiamplifier Systems

In some auto radio systems, the main amplifier is followed by one or more additional amplifiers. The main amplifier in Fig. 7-17 is unusual, as it is an integrated unit containing not one but two power amplifiers.

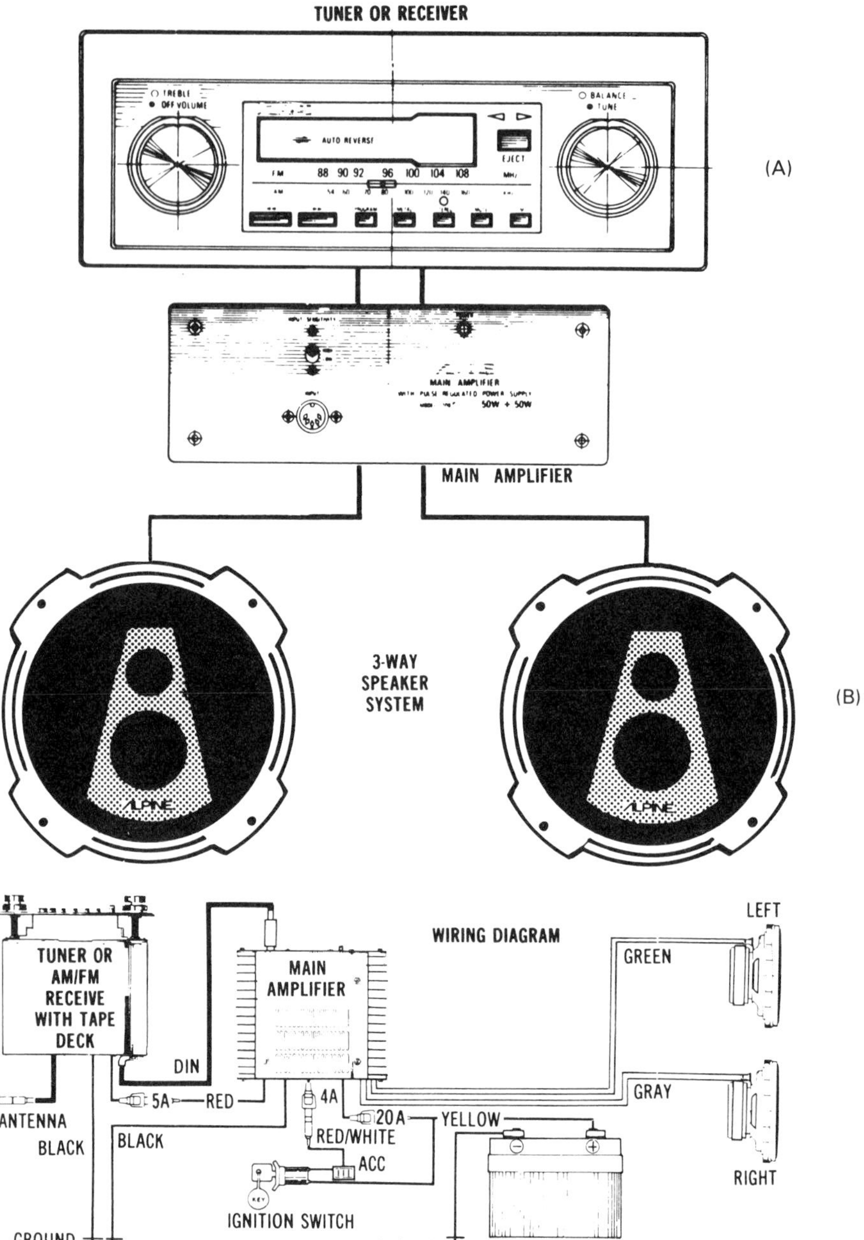

Figure 7–17. Pictorial (A) and wiring diagram (B) of a multiamplifier system. (*Courtesy Alpine Electronics of America, Inc.*)

The main amplifier is connected to the tuner or receiver via a DIN cable. This cable contains wires that carry the left/right signal voltages utilizing four of the five wires in the cable. The fifth wire is unused. The DIN connectors are keyed to avoid the possibility of making a wrong connection. The tuner or receiver has a short length of antenna cable ending in a connector, to be joined to the wire leading from the antenna. There is also a ground wire and a DC power lead, usually color-coded red, with a series-connected, 5-ampere fuse. Thus the tuner or receiver gets its DC operating voltage from the main amplifier.

The main amplifier has four signal output wires leading to two speakers. These are three-way, another way of indicating that the speaker system consists of a woofer, midrange, and tweeter. The crossover is a speaker-mounted capacitor.

Like the tuner or receiver, the main amplifier has its own ground connection. It is preferable for this ground to be at the same connecting point as that used for the tuner or receiver. This may be difficult to do if the amplifier is in the trunk of the car. In that event use any convenient ground point, provided it is clean and free of rust or paint.

There are two DC voltage-input points for the main amplifier. One is via the ignition switch, so that turning this switch off removes this source of DC from the main amplifier. The separate connection to the battery is required as a nonremovable source voltage for the tuner or receiver's memory. This DC voltage is on at all times, but the current drain is very small.

Adding More Power

Using more speakers in an installation that originally had only two does not mean the sound will be stronger. It does mean that the audio output, formerly divided between two speakers, will now be split among four or more. Since no speaker is 100-percent efficient, the actual effect will be a reduction of sound and this may be noticeable. Aside from a possible reduction in sound volume, there will be a greater distribution of sound in the car.

To solve the problem of insufficient audio power, an amplifier can be used (Fig. 7–18). The receiver does have its own power amplifier, so this system will now be equipped with two such units, one internal, the other external. The external unit, a booster amplifier, should have a substantially greater power output than the one in the receiver, especially since it is to drive four speakers. In an installation of this kind, the power amplifier in the receiver might have a 20-watt capability. An output power of 50 watts per channel would be typical for the booster.

Coming out of the booster amplifier are eight independent wires that connect to the drivers. The booster gets its DC power through a fused line wired to the ignition key, and the minus lead is attached to a convenient point on the car's chassis.

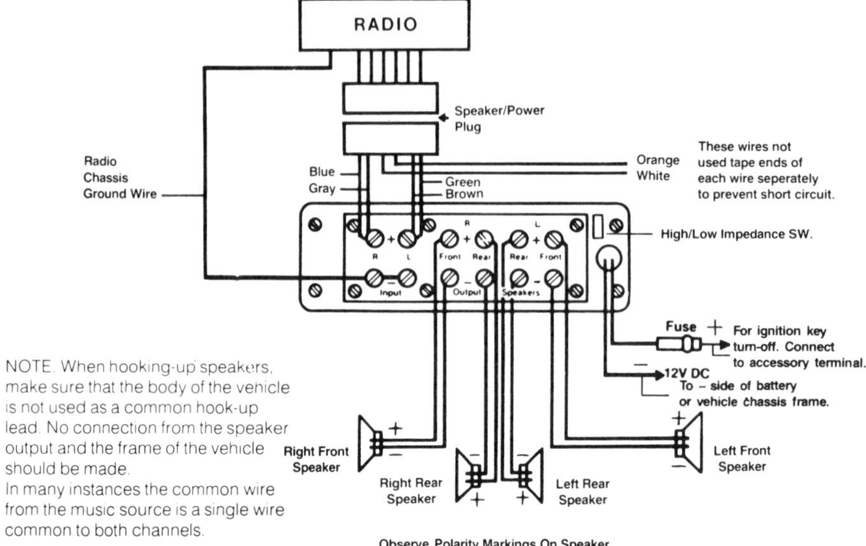

Figure 7–18. Connections for a booster power amplifier. (*Courtesy Sparkomatic Corp.*)

The sound output of the receiver is supplied to the booster via four wires in a six-wire cable with two of the wires unused. The speaker plug connected to this cable mates with a jack. The plug extends a short distance from the radio via wires, and the booster jack is wired the same way.

Multiamp Variations

A multiamp system can have a number of variations. The receiver may contain one power amplifier while another main amplifier is used externally. A multiamplifier may be an integrated unit containing not just one, but two main amplifiers. Finally, the auto radio sound system may have two separate main amplifiers, plus an in-receiver power amplifier, an arrangement shown in Fig. 7–19.

The receiver in this drawing is bilevel and has two signal outputs. These outputs are identical except for signal amplitude, because one of the main amplifiers will require less signal-driving voltage than the other. The main amplifier connected to the bass speakers will need more signal input. Drawing A is a pictorial of this system; drawing B shows the wiring connections.

The main amplifier can have various locations in an auto sound system. Figure 7–20A is a typical arrangement, in which the main amplifier follows the power amplifier and is used to supply the audio power needed to drive the two speakers. Drawing B shows a four-speaker system, with the main amp

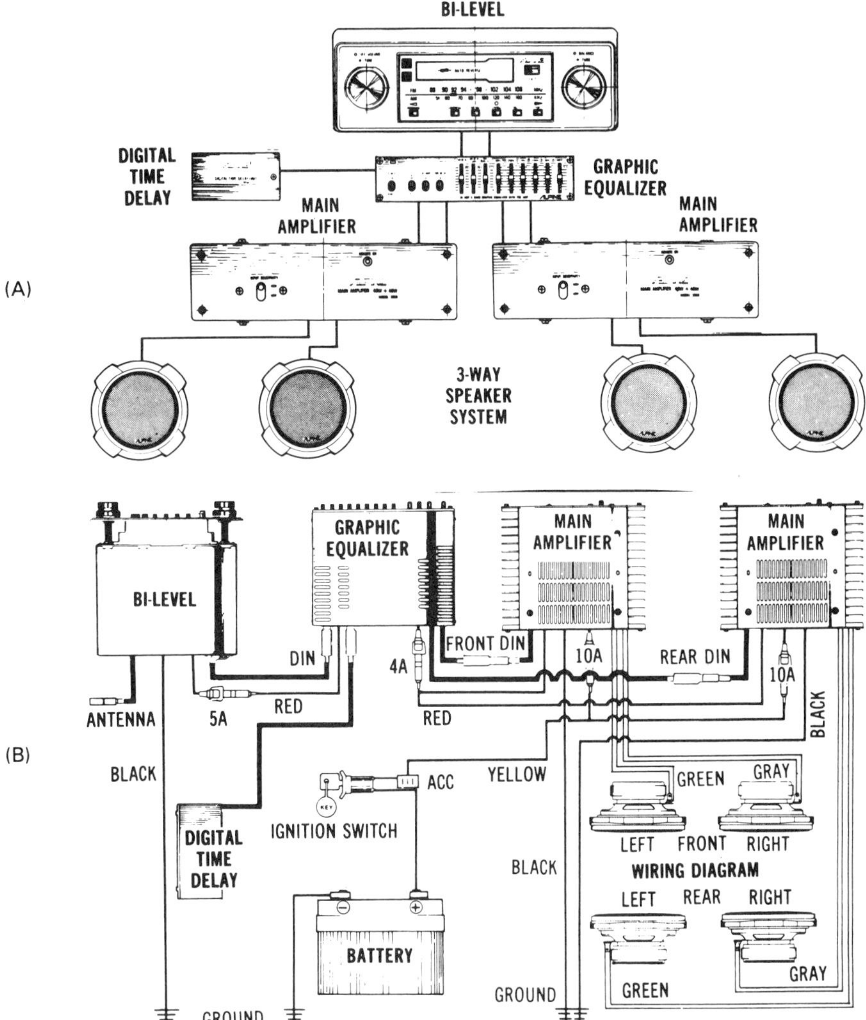

Figure 7–19. Bilevel receiver driving a pair of main amplifiers. (*Courtesy Alpine Electronics of America, Inc.*)

receiving its signal-driving voltage directly from the preamplifier. Two of the speakers are connected to the power amplifier; the other two to the main amplifier.

Main Amplifiers for Tuners and Receivers

Figure 7–20 shows a number of components, but it doesn't necessarily follow that a main amp is used only with extensive auto sound systems. A

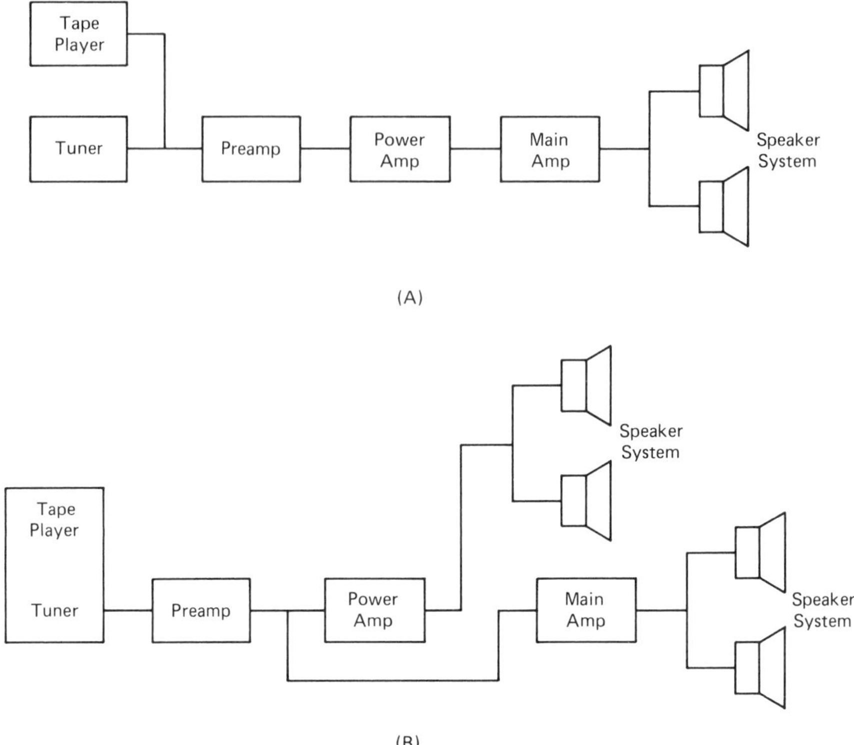

Figure 7–20. Possible connections for a main amplifier.

main amp can be used with either a tuner or a receiver and Fig. 7–21 shows the connections when just a tuner and a main amp are used.

Although the main amp is often referred to as a *power booster,* it is quite unlike the power amplifiers used for in-home systems. For auto radio, the main amp can be regarded as a combination of preamplifier and power amplifier. It can accept the comparatively modest signal output of a tuner and can then be used to drive a pair of speakers. To make the connections indicated in Fig. 7–21, the tuner must have enough signal output to drive the main amplifier. Looked at another way, the main amplifier must have sufficient input sensitivity to make use of the output of the tuner.

Figure 7–22 uses a similar wiring setup except that a receiver is used instead of a tuner. Since the receiver has a built-in amplifier, its signal output should be sufficient to supply the main amplifier with adequate signal-driving voltage. In both drawings only two speakers are used.

In Figures 7–21 and 7–22, a DIN cable is used between the tuner, or receiver, and the main amplifier; however, this does not mean that a DIN cable

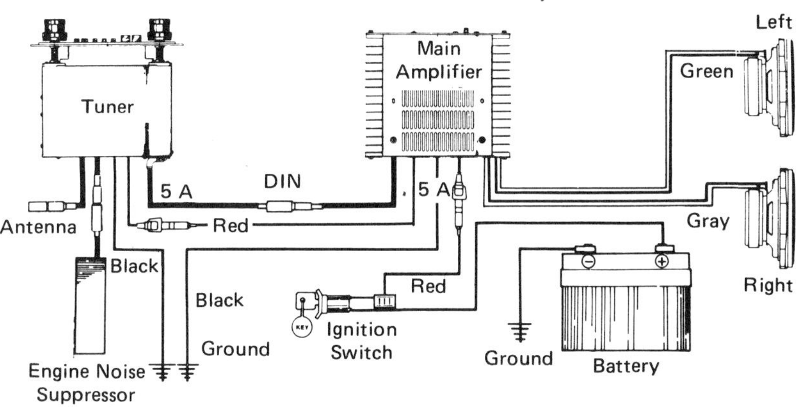

Figure 7–21. Main amplifier used with a tuner. (*Courtesy Alpine Electronics of America, Inc.*)

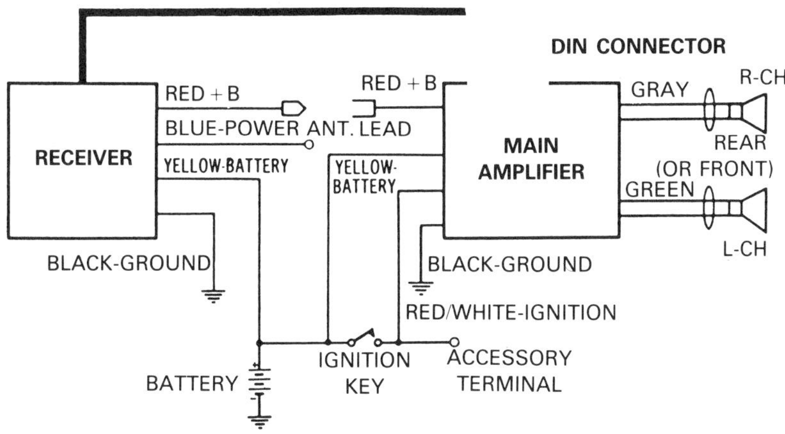

Figure 7–22. Main amplifier used with a receiver. (*Courtesy Alpine Electronics of America, Inc.*)

is always required. Figure 7–23 illustrates a wiring setup with individual wires connecting the main amp and a tuner or receiver.

SPEAKER SYSTEMS

Speakers used for in-home high-fidelity systems are equipped with enclosures, so it is possible to mount the drivers anywhere within that enclosure, supported by the inside framework. The speaker system may include tweeter (treble tones), midrange (once called a squawker), and woofer (bass).

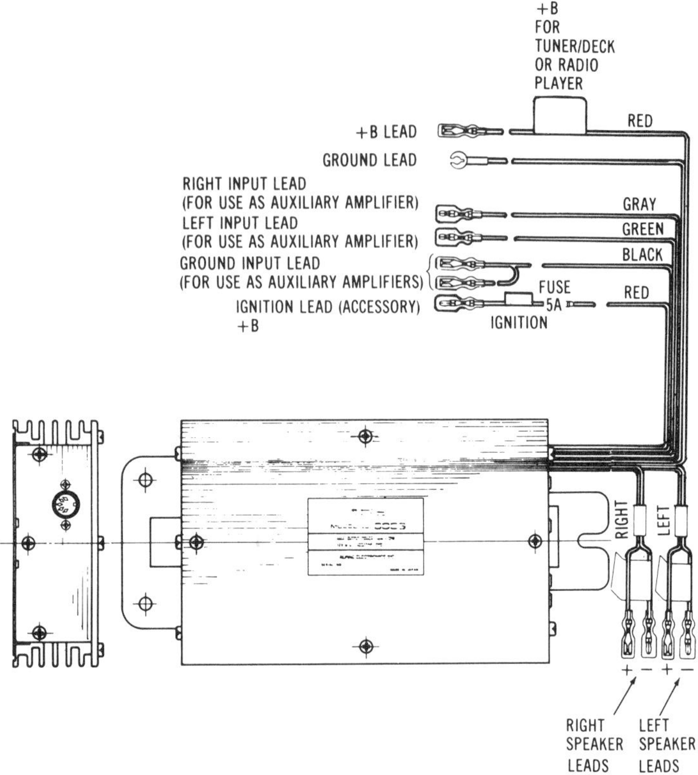

Figure 7-23. Individual wire connections to a main amplifier. (*Courtesy Alpine Electronics of America, Inc.*)

Sound signal frequencies are separated by a crossover network, a passive arrangement using resistors, coils, and capacitors, but often enough, nothing more than a single capacitor is used. In some systems the crossovers are electronic.

Because auto radio speakers have no enclosure, they are mounted separately, coaxially, or triaxially. A coaxial arrangement is one in which one speaker is mounted axially in front of the other, with the larger speaker at the rear. A triaxial setup consists of three speakers, with the smallest in front. In some arrangements, two speakers—a combined woofer/midrange and a separate tweeter—are mounted on a flat plate with the speaker cones covered with a metallic mesh. The speakers, however, are still "raw," that is, not equipped with a separate enclosure.

The External Passive Frequency Divider

An external audio-frequency divider, or crossover—a passive type—can be used with raw speakers, as shown in the connection diagram in Fig. 7-24. The stereo outputs of the two main amplifiers are brought into a pair of dividing networks. The two cables from the amplifier deliver the full audio range to the input terminals of the divider. One terminal will be marked plus (+); the other minus (−). The output of the dividing network consists of treble tones and bass/midrange tones. The treble frequencies are brought into a tweeter, and the bass/midrange into a speaker marked "Woofer," although that speaker covers the midrange as well. The connectors are the same as those used for speakers, a solid lug that slides into a matching open lug. This is a force fit and no soldering is required.

Speaker Impedance

The audio output of the power amplifier of a car radio or that of a main amplifier is usually 4 ohms or 8 ohms. As in the case of a home high-fidelity system, it is advisable to have the impedance of the speakers match the impedance at the output of the amplifier.

If you plan to use just two speakers, impedance matching should be no problem. If the amplifiers' impedance is 8 ohms, the left and right speakers should each have an impedance of 8 ohms. When you use four speakers, the impedance doubles for each pair of left/right speakers, if they are wired in series, and it is halved if they are connected in parallel, assuming speakers of identical impedance. Thus two 4-ohm speakers in series have an overall impedance of 8 ohms, but the impedance is only 2 ohms when wired in parallel.

The simplest impedance-matching arrangement is shown in Fig. 7-25A—a stereo hookup that uses just two speakers, one for left-channel sound, the other for the right channel. These speakers are not wired in series or in parallel, for each is operated by a separate amplifier. All that is required here is that each speaker's impedance match that of its particular amplifier.

In the diagram of Fig. 7-25B, the two 8-ohm speakers are wired in parallel, producing the equivalent of a single speaker of 4 ohms.

Connecting speakers in parallel imposes a heavier load on the power amplifier, as the load impedance is reduced. For best results, the parallel speakers should not only have the same impedance; they should be the same models made by the same manufacturer.

Further, wiring a pair of 4-ohm speakers in parallel isn't recommended, as the total impedance would drop to a nominal value of 2 ohms, dangerously close to a short circuit. Speaker impedances do not remain constant but fluctuate with the frequency of the sound. Under certain circumstances, the total

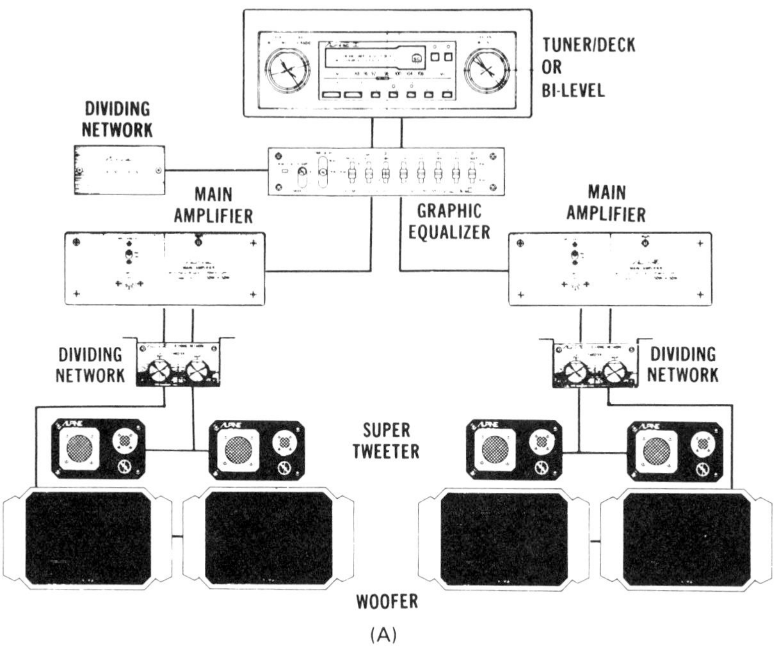

(A)

Figure 7–24. System using external crossovers: pictorial (A); connection diagram (B). (*Courtesy Alpine Electronics of America, Inc.*)

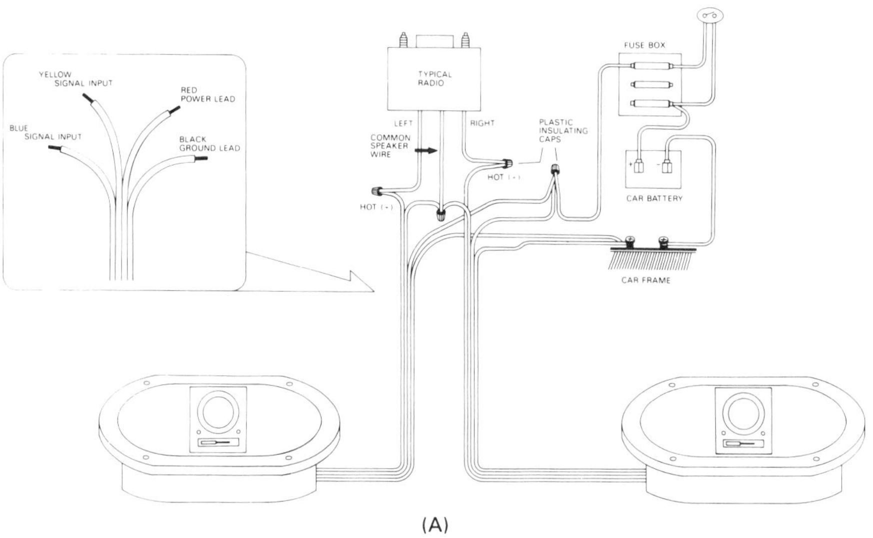

(A)

Figure 7–25A. Connections for single left and right speakers. (*Courtesy Sparkomatic Corporation*)

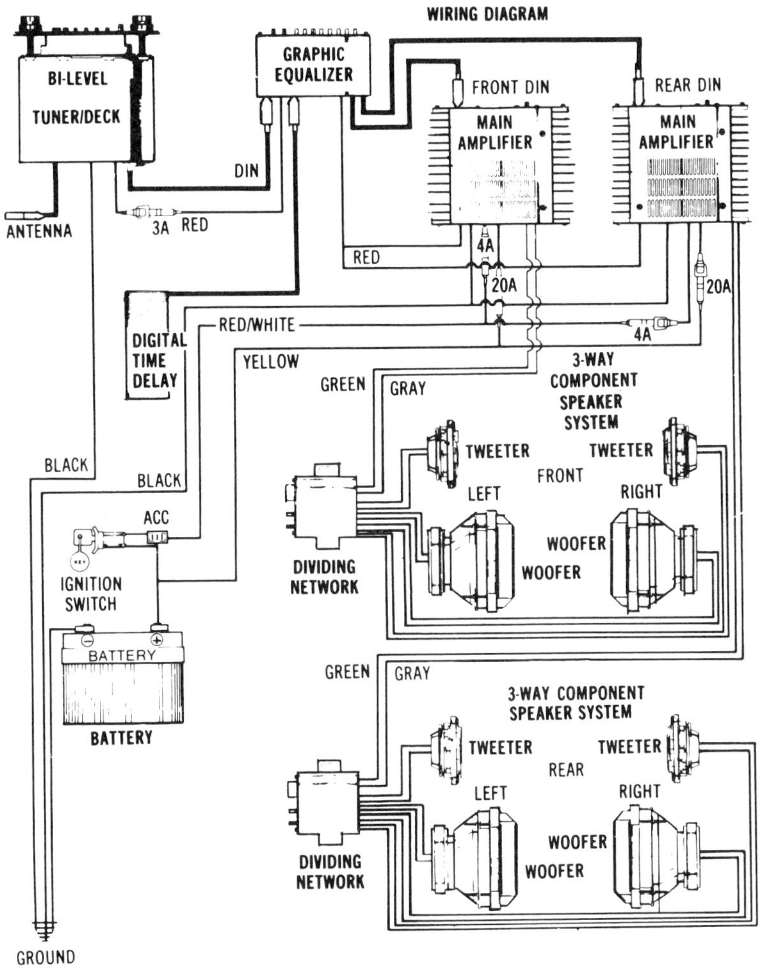

WIRING DIAGRAM
BI-LEVEL TUNER/DECK
GRAPHIC EQUALIZER
FRONT DIN
REAR DIN
MAIN AMPLIFIER
MAIN AMPLIFIER
DIN
ANTENNA
3A RED
RED
4A
20A
20A
4A
DIGITAL TIME DELAY
RED/WHITE
YELLOW
GREEN
GRAY
3-WAY COMPONENT SPEAKER SYSTEM
TWEETER
TWEETER
FRONT
LEFT
RIGHT
WOOFER
WOOFER
DIVIDING NETWORK
BLACK
BLACK
ACC
IGNITION SWITCH
BATTERY
BATTERY
GREEN
GRAY
3-WAY COMPONENT SPEAKER SYSTEM
TWEETER
TWEETER
REAR
LEFT
RIGHT
WOOFER
WOOFER
DIVIDING NETWORK
GROUND

(B)

Figure 7–24. *(continued)*

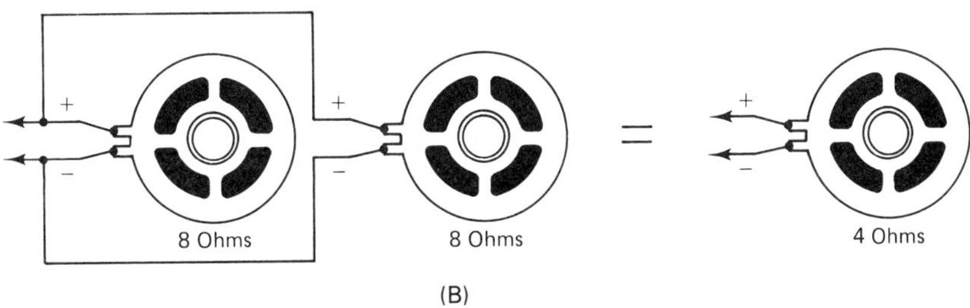

(B)

Figure 7–25B. Eight-ohm speakers wired in parallel—plus to plus, minus to minus—have an equivalent impedance of 4 ohms.

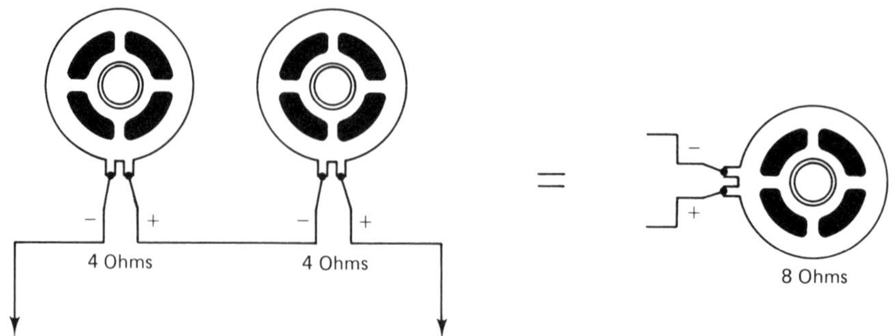

Figure 7–26. Two 4-ohm speakers in series have an equivalent impedance of 8 ohms.

speaker impedance could drop so low that the increased current demand could either blow the speaker fuses or damage the power amplifier. If the fuses do not open fast enough, or if there are no fuses, the output power transistors in the power amplifier or the speakers' voice coils could burn out. Two or more speakers can be wired in series, as shown in Fig. 7–26, with the connection arrangement the same as batteries in series. The impedances are additive. If both speakers have an impedance of 4 ohms, the total speaker impedance is 8 ohms and the wires can be connected to an amplifier having an output impedance of 8 ohms.

With the exception of a subwoofer, car speakers are usually operated in pairs, but in exceptional car systems there may also be two subwoofers.

Although it is customary to use four individual wires for a pair of left/right speakers, a three-wire system can also be used (Fig. 7–27). The minus terminals of the speakers are joined and the single wire can be connected to the body of the car or to the minus terminal of the power amplifier if a floating

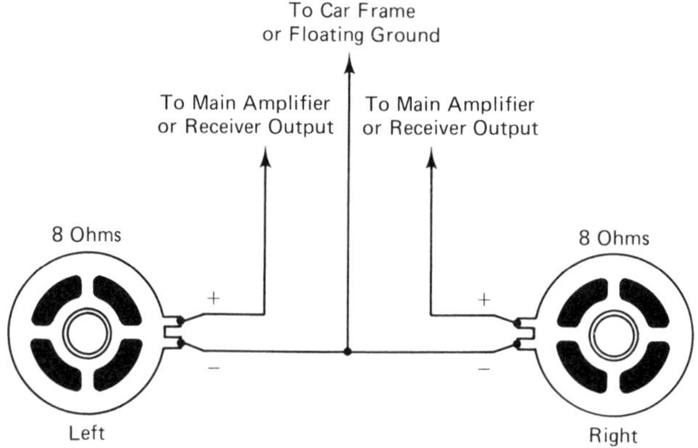

Figure 7–27. Three-wire system for connecting two speakers.

ground is used. The plus leads, one from each speaker, are individually connected to the power amplifier.

Four speakers can be connected to the power amplifier (Fig. 7–28A), or three wires will do, as indicated in Fig. 7–28B. If you trace the wiring you will see that the left front and left rear speakers are in parallel, and that the right front and right rear speakers are also shunt wired. This means that in effect we can consider the left speakers as a single unit and the right speakers the same way.

Bring the separate minus leads to the power amp, or use a three-wire arrangement.

A single capacitor is sometimes used as a crossover, a device for separating the entire spectrum of audio frequencies into bands. Figure 7–29 shows the wiring for a four-speaker system—two front speakers and two rear. The front speakers are intended to handle the midrange and treble tones; the rear speakers bass tones. The drawing shows that this is a four-wire system using a floating ground.

Speaker Enclosures

Raw speakers—speakers without enclosures—are commonly used in cars. In this instance, the car's trunk and doors are available as enclosures. For recreational vehicles, speakers like those in home high-fidelity systems are sometimes used.

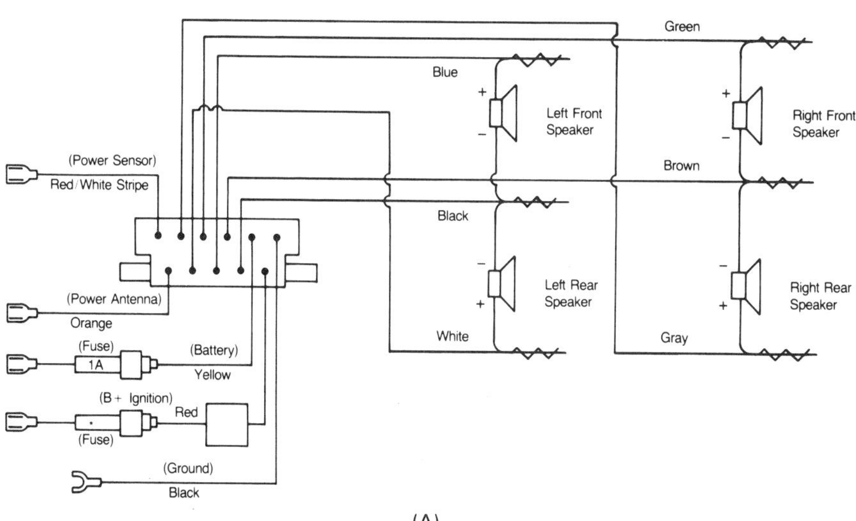

Figure 7–28A. Connections for four speakers.

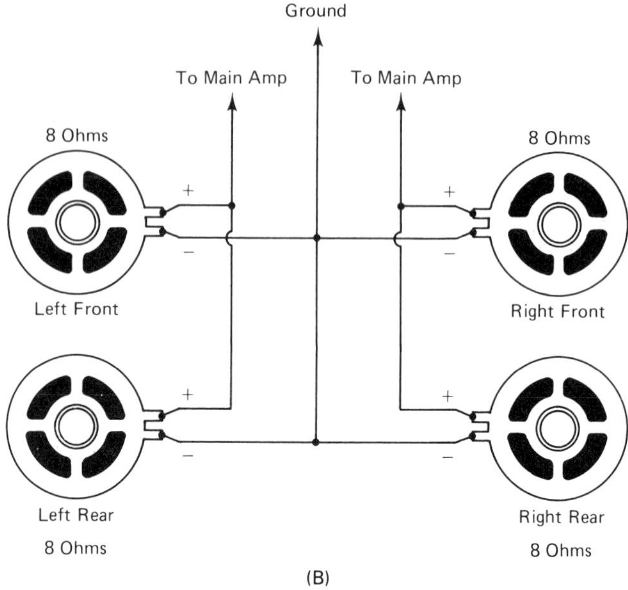

Figure 7–28B. All of these speakers have an impedance of 8 ohms. The left front and rear speakers are in shunt and have an equivalent impedance of 4 ohms. The right front and rear speakers are wired the same way.

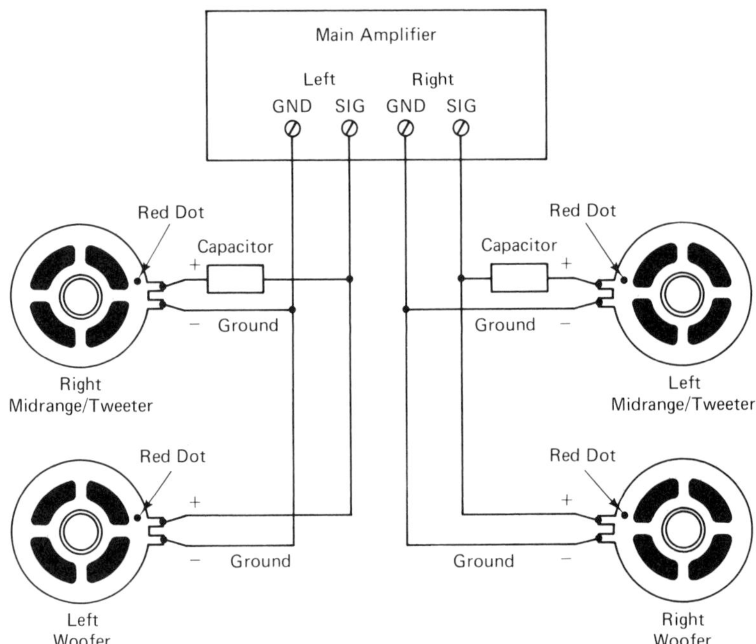

Figure 7–29. Four-speaker system using single capacitor as a crossover.

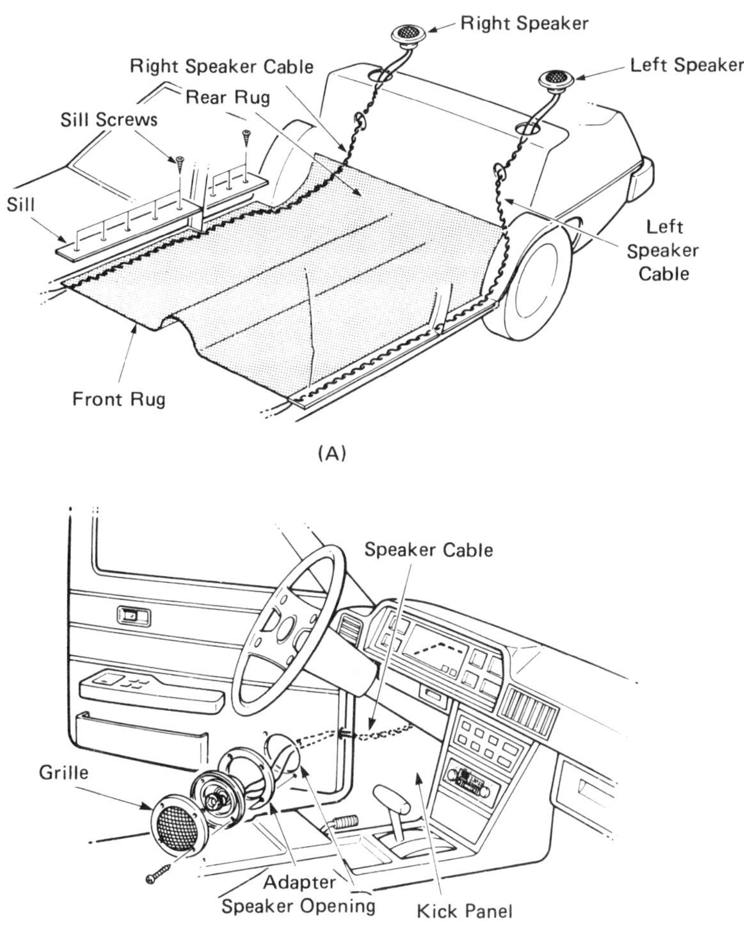

Figure 7–30. Wiring for rear (A) and front speakers (B). (*Courtesy Yamaha Electronics Corp.*)

Woofer/midrange speakers are often mounted on the car's rear deck (Fig. 7–30A). Sometimes one lead of each speaker's voice coil is grounded to the car frame, so only one wire is run from each speaker, possibly to an amplifier located in the trunk. This is not permissible with all systems, and the drawing in Fig. 7–30A shows two wires for each speaker connected to the audio output of an up-front receiver. Wire the leads on the left and right sides through and beneath the rear deck. Remove the door sills and continue the wires under the edges of the rug, and then replace the sills. Continue the leads, concealing them behind the side kick panels and under the dash.

The wires need not be shielded cable, but they should be the thickest that can be handled comfortably. For up-front door installations, and these are usually tweeters, run the wires across the door hinge areas by clamping the leads under the edge of the door and kick panels. In some cars, there are access holes in the front edge of the door, near the hinge, that provide a convenient way of running the leads. In either installation, form a loop in the leads long enough to allow the door to open completely without pulling the connecting wires. Be sure to arrange them so they aren't pinched when the door is closed.

Connecting a Subwoofer

The subwoofer is a speaker used for the reproduction of extremely low audio frequencies. There is still some question whether such frequencies can be stereo separated to supply left- and right-channel sound, so ordinarily just a single driver is used. In the subwoofer system shown in Fig. 7-31, there are two subwoofers and also a pair of power amplifiers, with the assembly housed in a plastic enclosure. The wires leading from the subwoofer/amplifier subsystem are connected to the wires leading from the receiver by wire nuts (plastic insulating caps). There are four signal wires, none of which is grounded.

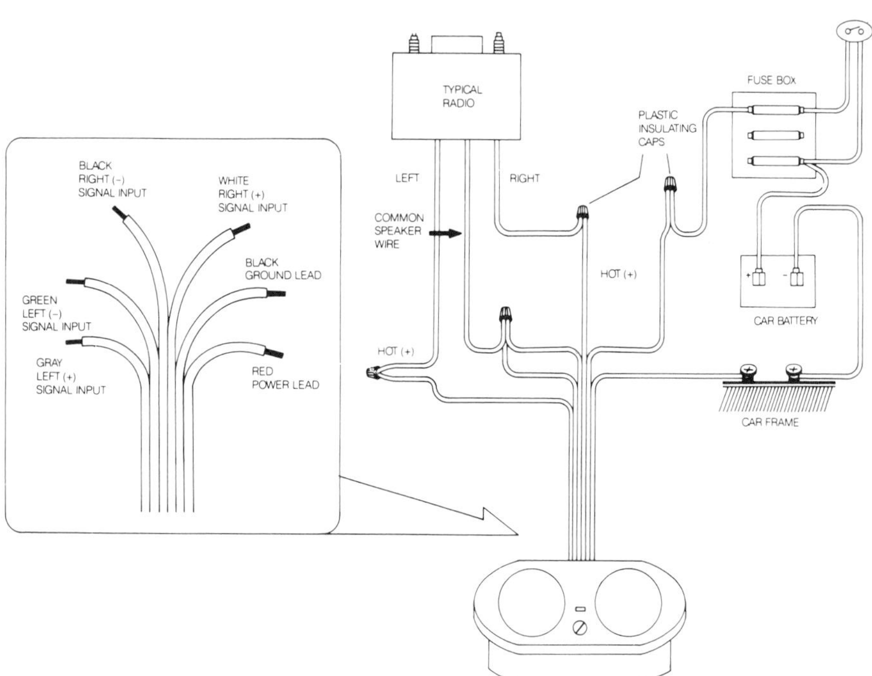

Figure 7-31. Dual subwoofer with built-in power amplifiers. (*Courtesy Sparkomatic Corporation*)

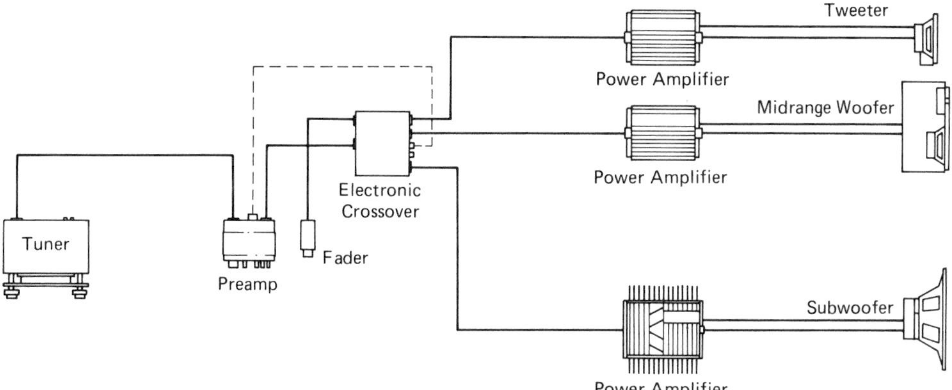

Figure 7-32. Connections for a subwoofer.

There is a black ground lead and a red DC power lead, but these are used to supply operating power to the amplifiers.

Another setup, using a single subwoofer, is shown in Fig. 7-32. Although just a single tweeter and midrange/woofer are shown, there are actually two of these for stereo operation. Each of the speaker systems has its own power amplifier, which receives signals via an electronic crossover. The fader is used to control the amount of sound output from the rear or front speakers.

THE GRAPHIC EQUALIZER

The acoustics of a car are subject to considerable variation, causing peaks and dips in the audio-frequency range. These not only include the auto's interior but factors such as speaker location and type, the number of passengers, and whether the windows are open or closed.

The purpose of a graphic equalizer is to compensate for the acoustic environment inside the car. Because the car uses padding and carpeting extensively, with few reverberant surfaces other than the windows and windshield, there can be extensive tonal absorption. Treble tones may disappear and bass tones may be weakened considerably. While the receiver is equipped with a tone control there is usually just one such adjustment, inadequate for an audio range extending from below 120 Hz to 15 kHz and higher. An equalizer can be used to overcome this deficiency. Another method of frequency control is to use six or more speakers in various locations.

The equalizer has a number of slide adjustments. These may be set as a preliminary for the car's acoustics, but the slides will have to be positioned, depending on the type of music being received. The sound-control engineer at a broadcast station may emphasize treble tones in an effort to achieve signal brilliance, or bass to obtain special musical effects. What the sound engineer does is a reflection of his or her own musical tastes and may not be agreeable to the listener. An equalizer can modify sound amplitude, attenuating or boosting certain tonal frequencies. Since adjustments are often required, the equalizer—unlike the power amplifier—must be close to the receiver. In some installations the equalizer is built into the receiver, but more often it is an add-on component.

Figure 7–33 shows the connections to be made to the equalizer. The rear of the unit has a DC power cable for supplying voltage input. A fuse, identified as F1, is put in series with this line. There are two cables marked "Line in" for connection to a tuner. These are for left- and right-channel sound. There are four outputs for connection to a pair of power amplifiers. These are identified as line out wires and are left-channel and right-channel connections for the power amplifiers. The conductors are color coded, red for line in, white for line out. The input impedance of this unit is approximately 10K ohms, and the output impedance is about the same. The load impedance is in the range of 10K ohms to 20K ohms, typical of the input of most auto power amplifiers. Impedance matching between the equalizer and the tuner, and the equalizer and its following power amplifiers isn't critical, as it is with speakers.

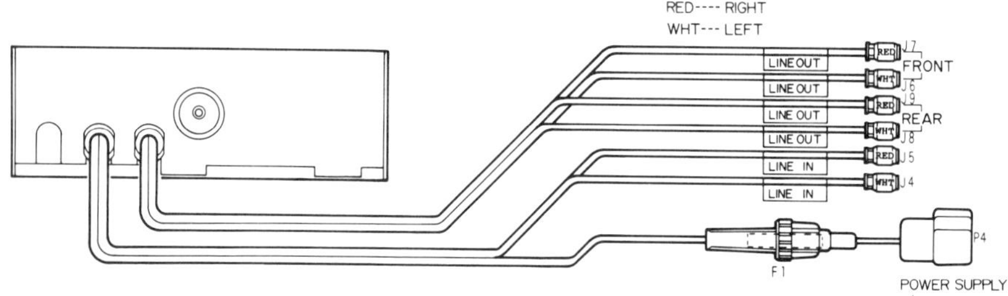

Figure 7–33. Equalizer connections. (*Courtesy Fujitsu Ten Limited*)

The equalizer is an active, not a passive device, so there is no signal loss in the unit. Although the drawing in Fig. 7–34 is for two pairs of speakers, the equalizer can also be used with just one pair—a left speaker and one at the right. Ignore the connectors for the second set of speakers. Figure 7–34 shows the relationship of the equalizer to the other components of an auto sound system, and the connections required.

Figure 7–35 shows the specific connections for an equalizer. The unit is wired to the sound outputs of a receiver using a common ground connection. The receiver and the equalizer have fused DC lines, but these fuses may not have the same rating. The receiver and the equalizer are wired to the ignition switch, and are automatically turned off by that switch. However, these com-

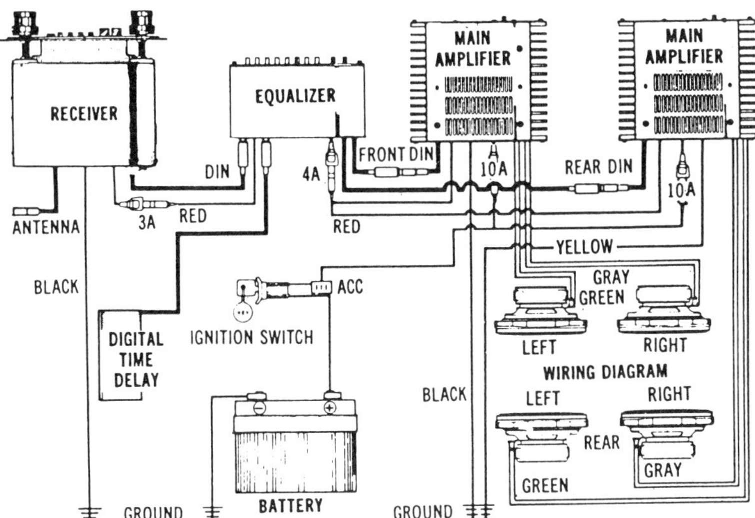

Figure 7–34. Equalizer wiring in a four-speaker system. (*Courtesy Alpine Electronics of America, Inc.*)

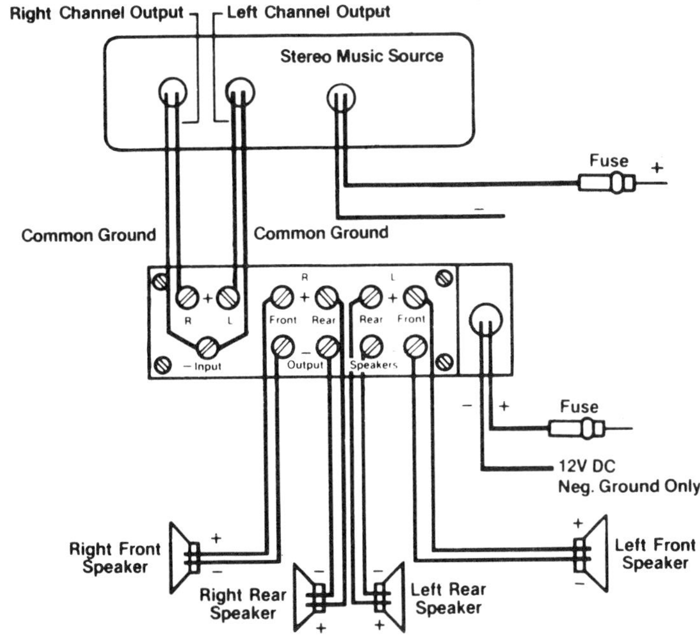

Figure 7–35. Equalizer wiring for a four-speaker system. (*Courtesy Sparkomatic Corporation*)

ponents have their own on/off switches. In this system none of the speaker leads is grounded.

CONNECTING THE COMPACT DISC PLAYER

Early efforts some decades ago to introduce a record player as part of an auto sound system weren't successful. Now attempts are being made to introduce the compact disc (CD) player. These are outboard components or are combined with an AM/FM receiver. For those that are built into a receiver, no external wiring is required. Outboard units must be wired into the car's DC line and their audio outputs connected to the input wires of a preamplifier or main amplifier. No signal inputs are required, for the CD is its own signal source.

Connecting a compact disc player in the home is much easier than in a car. The signal output of the player is audio and can be connected directly to the aux input of a receiver, preamplifier, or integrated amplifier of the home sound system. Car radio receivers and their main (integrated) amplifiers do not have ports for additional sound sources.

One method is to connect the CD player to its own amplifier with the output of that amplifier wired to the car system's speakers. The CD player must be connected to the battery plus lead of the car's ignition switch, usually via a fuse contained in a fuse holder. Connect the metal frame of the CD player to the car's frame to supply the ground connection.

There are other options. If there is no room for an in-dash or under-dash player, use a portable player. No antenna is required and the player will work as well inside the car as anywhere else. The portable CD player, though, will not sound as good as a player that works through the car's amplifiers and speaker sound system.

Another method is to use a CD player adapter. The adapter makes it possible to access the audio system of the radio by transmitting an FM stereo signal directly through the antenna of the radio. The radio is tuned to the transmission frequency of the adapter the same way any other station is tuned in.

The car's antenna is connected to an input port on the adapter; the output of the adapter is connected to the antenna input terminals of the receiver. The adapter also has a port so it can receive audio signals from the compact disc player. The adapter frequency modulates the audio signals from the player, and as far as the car radio is concerned, the signal it gets from the CD player, via the adapter, is just another FM signal.

CD players have now been made small enough and rugged enough to perform reliably despite the shocks, shakes, and temperature extremes of the car's environment. New, advanced laser optics and large-scale integrated (LSI) technology have made this possible.

SOPHISTICATED SYSTEMS

An auto sound system can consist of nothing more than a receiver and a pair of speakers, but systems can also be elaborate as shown in the three drawings, Fig. 7-36A, B, and C. In some installations, a separate battery is used, housed in the trunk, to supply the DC operating power required. The main amplifiers are also housed in the trunk. Even these arrangements do not represent the limit of car sound fidelity, for none of those shown in the three illustrations uses a compact disc player. Such a unit could be installed under the dash, but it must be easily available for the insertion and removal of the discs. A solution is to use a disc changer, mounted in the trunk and operated by a control pad near the driver. Digital time delay is used to supply artificial sound reverberation and is often wired in connection with the rear speakers. The dividing networks can be active or passive and are positioned externally with reference to the speakers to which they are connected.

None of the systems in Fig. 7-36 uses a subwoofer. This could be handled

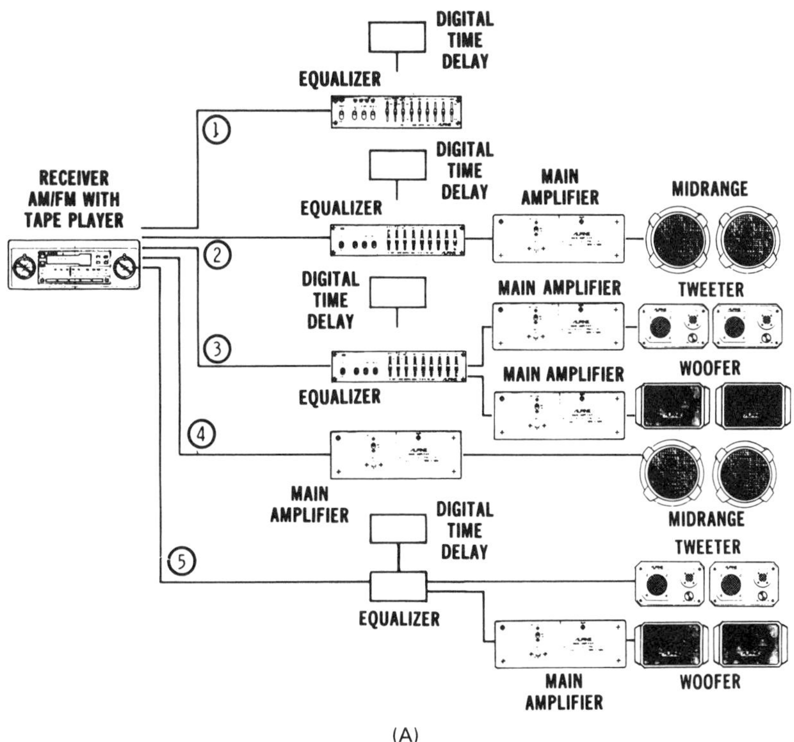

Figure 7-36A, B, and C. Advanced auto sound systems. (*Courtesy Alpine Electronics of America, Inc.*)

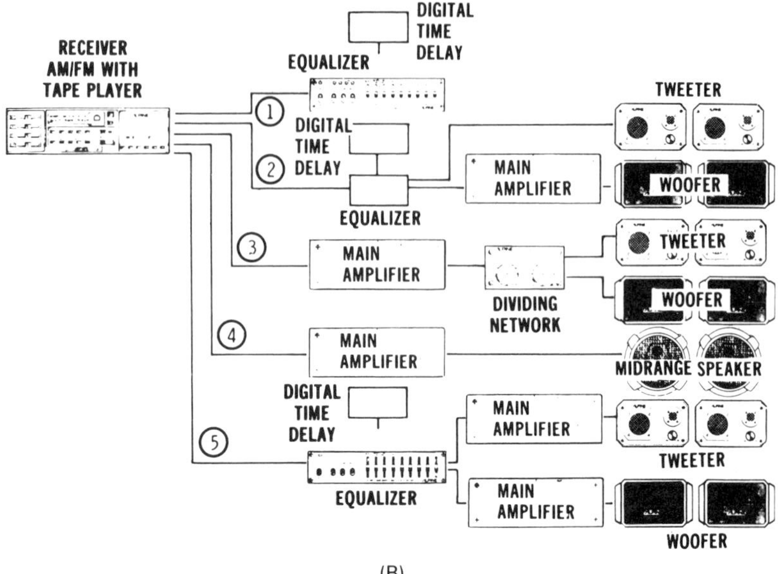

(B)

Figure 7-36B.

by installing another power amplifier, using it solely for the subwoofer. However, there are always two important considerations—cost and room. It is easy enough to plan a system, but paying for it and finding the space for it are another matter.

WIRING PRECAUTIONS

Anticipating problems means less work in finding causes of trouble when a system is finally made operative. Keep sound system wires away from potential noise sources such as electric motors, gauges, and high voltage areas such as those around ignition wires. Keep all wiring away from moving parts, sharp edges, seat tracks, door hinges, and cut metal. Keep wires neat and channeled through available runners, trim, and channels of the car.

If wires are connected to a moving component, as when speakers are mounted in doors, make sure the wires have enough slack to permit maximum opening of the door, and that these wires do not touch sharp metal edges. Front-door speakers should be clear of the door window opening and closing mechanism.

Cover tab connections to speakers and wing nut connections with plastic electrician's tape. For long lengths of wire, supply some support by fastening

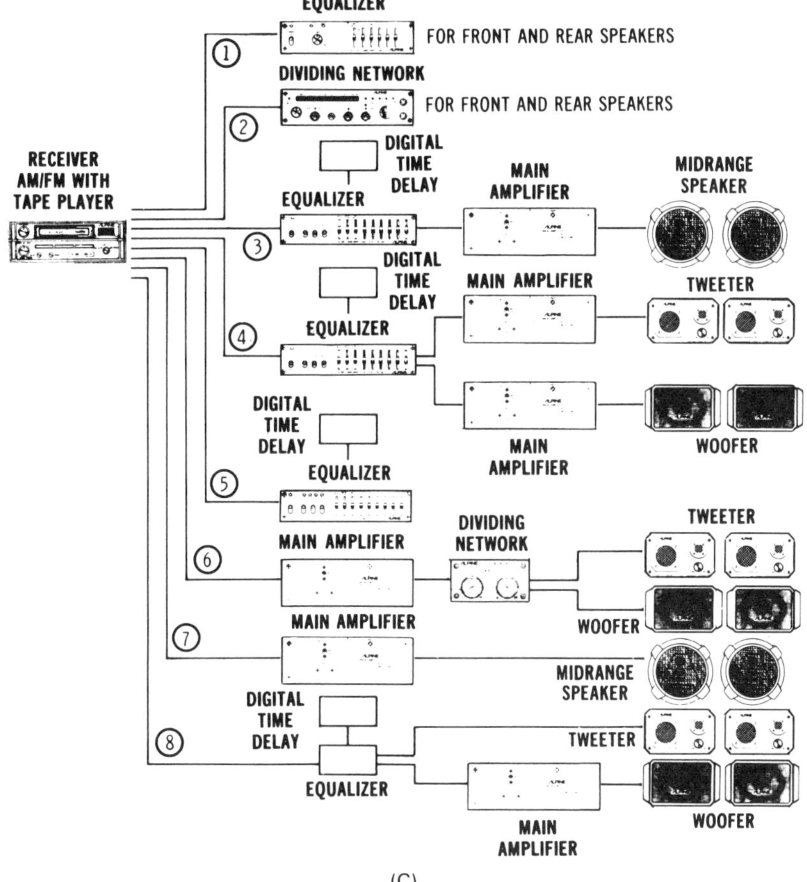

Figure 7–36C.

to the car body. Speakers may have one terminal grounded to eliminate one wire running to an amplifier, but many systems use two wires. Follow the manufacturer's recommendations on the connection method to be used.

Many rear speakers are mounted in the rear deck and are suspended in the trunk, used as a speaker enclosure. Keep the area around such speakers free and clear. Some speakers are supplied with an enclosure and are positioned above the rear deck. Make sure these are securely fastened to that deck. Do not use raw speakers above the rear deck. These are difficult to fasten, and the lack of an enclosure can only cause sound deterioration. Some states do not permit mounting speakers above the rear deck, claiming interference with the driver's vision.

When you start a car in winter, be sure the sound system is turned off, to avoid imposing a load on the battery when it is operating under difficulties. An old battery can also result in poor operation of the sound system, particularly if that system has a number of active components.

Keep the connecting lead of the antenna to the tuner or receiver as far from the engine as possible. Use shielded cable only.

8

CONNECTIONS FOR SATELLITE TV

There are a number of ways in which television viewers can access video programs, and the most widely used are broadcast TV's VHF and UHF channels. There are some variations, one of which is multipoint distribution service (MDS). An MDS system picks up broadcast television signals using high-gain VHF/UHF antennas mounted on towers positioned on or near the top of a hill or mountain. The received signals are converted to microwave frequencies, increased in strength by preamplifiers, and then retransmitted. This enables viewers within the area to watch broadcast TV signals that would otherwise be unavailable. To pick up the microwave signals, the user must install a microwave antenna, which is then connected to a downconverter and then to a TV receiver or VCR. The signals may be scrambled, so an integrated downconverter/decoder—or separate components—may be used. From the output of the downconverter to the TV set or VCR, the connections follow the same procedure previously described for VHF/UHF broadcast TV reception.

Another way of receiving broadcast television signals is via a master antenna television system (MATV). In this technique, the broadcast TV or satellite TV signals are picked up by an antenna, which is sometimes mounted on a tower or on the roof of a high-rise apartment complex. The signals are preamplified and delivered to the viewers via coaxial cable, terminating in a wall plate in the home. From that plate, signals are connected to the antenna input terminals of the TV receiver, either directly via coaxial cable or with 300-ohm line via a balun.

Companies that supply cable TV services get their signals from satellites or broadcast TV and then deliver these signals to their subscribers via coaxial cable. As in the case of MATV, the coaxial cable terminates in a wall plate, with the subscriber using one or more converters, with or without decoders as described in Chapter 4.

SATELLITE TV

One of the problems of broadcast television is that the high frequencies used are quasi-optical, and as such can be reflected from buildings and high terrain. What is needed is a clear line of sight between the transmitting and receiving antennas, with both positioned as high as possible. Even under ideal conditions, the satisfactory limit for good reception is about 60 miles.

In the early days of TV, attempts were made to use airplanes for broadcasting TV, but limitations on flying time made this proposal short-lived. A more practical arrangement was to put satellites in orbit 22,300 miles above the earth's equator. This distance was selected because at that height the rotation of the earth and that of the satellite are synchronous. Consequently, a satellite at that height appears to be stationary and is referred to as geosynchronous. Actually, the satellites have a wobble of about 60 miles.

It is the line-of-sight signal transmission requirement that has encouraged the use of satellite TV. Because of their tremendous height, it is estimated that just three satellites, equally spaced in orbit, could cover the entire earth, with the possible exception of the polar areas.

TV programs are originated in earth stations and are beamed to a selected satellite using frequencies in the range of 5.925 to 6.425 GHz (gigahertz). These uplink signals are received by the satellite and retransmitted by transponders, combined receiver/transmitters. Before transmission by the transponder, the signals are downconverted, with the carrier frequency lowered to a range of 3.7 to 4.2 GHz. The audio and video signals, both frequency modulated, remain unchanged in the downconversion process.

On earth, these signals are picked up by a television receive-only (TVRO) system and then processed for ultimate display on a home television receiver.

DEDICATED VERSUS INTEGRATED COMPONENTS

A dedicated component is one that performs a specific function. A tuner is a dedicated component, for its work is signal selection. It becomes an integrated component when combined with an amplifier, and is then called a receiver.

Signals from satellites in space are reflected by a dish, a dedicated unit representing the initial component in a TVRO system.

OVERALL VIEW OF A TVRO

A TVRO system consists of a number of dedicated or integrated components, or some combination of the two. In this sense it is very much like a video or a high-fidelity system. To understand the connections needed by the units of a TVRO, it is helpful to have at least a general idea of the signal path from a satellite.

The downlink signals (Fig. 8–1) from a transponder aboard a satellite strike a dish, a passive device having a parabolic shape. Although often referred to as an antenna, the dish is just one part of the antenna system, working solely as a reflector, but with no wired connections to any of the other components in the TVRO. The purpose of the dish is to collect and concentrate the signals onto a device called the feed.

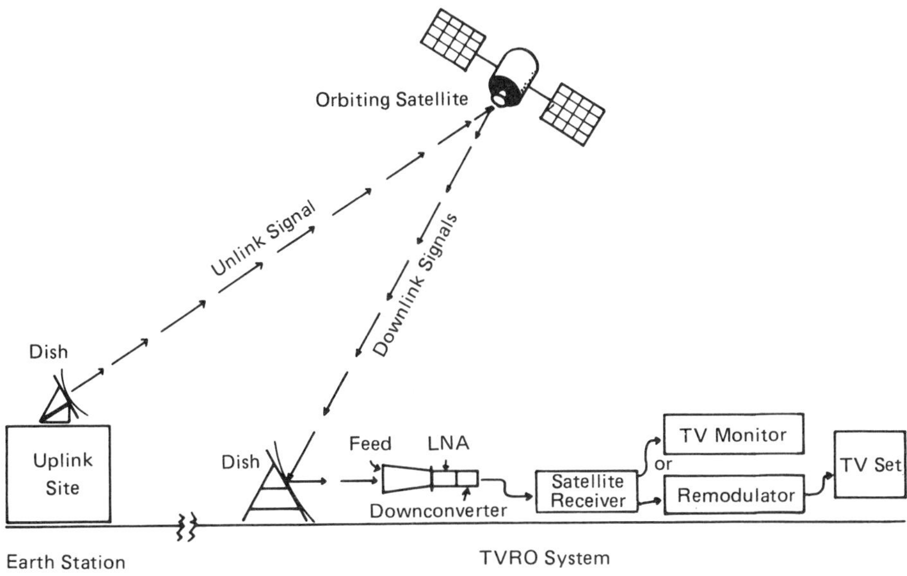

Figure 8–1. Signal path of a satellite TV system. (*Courtesy McCullough Satellite Equipment, Inc.*)

The feed is simply the entrance to a small section of waveguide described in Chapter 1 and illustrated in Fig. 1–40. Waveguide (Fig. 8-2) belongs to the transmission line family, although it does not resemble twin lead or coaxial cable. There is an interesting difference in the way waveguide is used, as compared with twin lead or coax; the latter two bring the signal from an antenna to a receiver or tuner input, but in a TVRO system the waveguide brings the signal to the antenna.

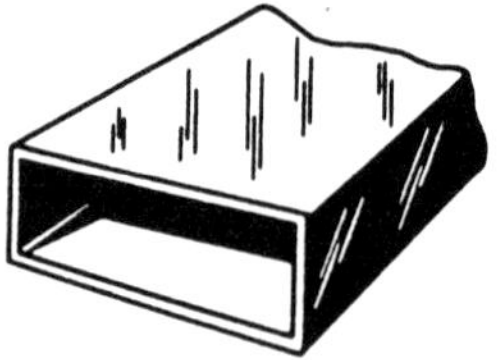

Figure 8–2. Rectangular waveguide.

The actual antenna, a very short length of solid conductor, either straight or in the form of a loop, extends into the rear of the waveguide, and it is from this antenna that the signal is finally delivered to the first component of the system, a low-noise amplifier (LNA). The connection from the small loop is via a very short length of coaxial cable, as shown in Fig. 8–3A. Sometimes, as in Fig. 8–3B, the coaxial cable is formed into an antenna. A very short length of the cable is stripped, with the center conductor of the cable inserted into the open space of the waveguide. The outer shield braid of the coax is soldered (not just mechanically fastened) to the bottom portion of the waveguide.

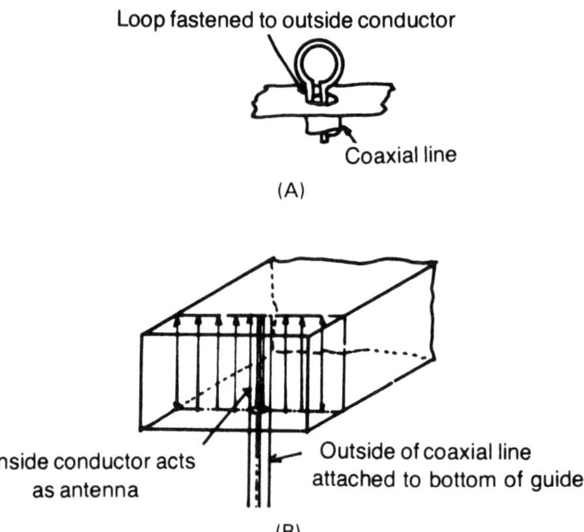

Figure 8–3. Satellite TVRO antennas: loop (A); coaxial cable conductor (B).

Because of the very high frequencies involved, the connection from the antenna to the input of the LNA is kept extremely short. To effect this, the LNA is mounted on the rear of the waveguide (Fig. 8–4). The waveguide and the LNA are mounted on a structure supported by the dish. These are outdoor components, with the connections from the antenna to the LNA made by the manufacturer.

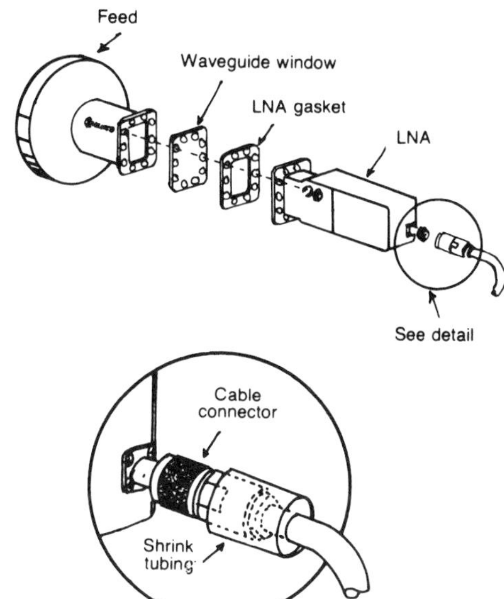

Figure 8–4. Exploded view of waveguide and LNA assembly. The lower drawing illustrates the connection between the LNA and its following downconverter. (*Courtesy Avantek, Inc.*)

The output of the LNA consists of frequencies in the gigahertz region, and at these frequencies, line losses in the connecting coaxial cable would be intolerable. For this reason, the LNA is followed at an extremely short distance by a downconverter. The output of the downconverter is typically 70 MHz, with the frequency-modulated audio and video signals not affected by the downconversion process. Figure 8–4 shows connection details between the LNA and the downconverter.

Sometimes the LNA and downconverter are integrated, but they are also sold as separate units and then must be connected using a short length of RG-8U coaxial cable. The connectors to be mounted on this cable will be determined by the kinds of jacks used on the output of the LNA and the input of the downconverter. It may be possible to buy a suitable length of RG-8U equipped with the correct connectors, but if not, purchase the cable and the connectors separately and mount them following the cable-connector procedures outlined in Chapter 2.

The connection between the LNA and the downconverter is one of the most important in a satellite system and ideally should be as short as possible. To make the connection, use RG-8U, RG-142 or RG-213 coaxial cable. As a protection against the weather, cover the connection with shrink tubing to supply a watertight seal (Fig. 8–4). When you make such a connection, use a heat gun until the tubing is securely bonded to the cable. Instead of a heat gun, you can also try a match or a cigarette lighter.

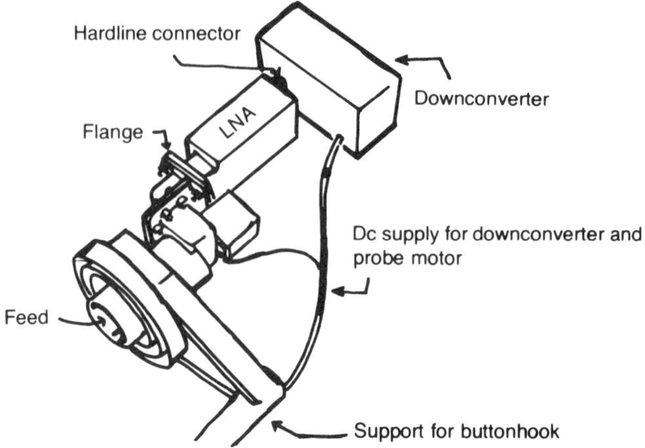

Figure 8–5. Positioning of the LNA with reference to the downconverter. (*Courtesy Winegard Co.*)

Because the carrier frequency of the signals being amplified by the LNA are so extremely high, getting these signals into the home presents a problem especially when the dish is at some distance from the home, as is usually the case. At one time a connecting cable known as *Heliaz* was used, but this cable was expensive and had intolerable signal losses. The simple solution is the use of a downconverter. The downconverter is mounted immediately adjacent to the LNA (Fig. 8–5) to keep the connection between the two as short as possible. In some instances, the LNA and the downconverter are contained in the same housing as indicated in Fig. 8–6, an arrangement known as a low-noise converter (LNC).

The downconversion process is along the same lines as frequency downconversion used in a superheterodyne receiver with the downconverter referred to as a mixer or converter. The output is known as the intermediate frequency (IF). The signal output of the TVRO's downconverter is also an IF and can be any frequency decided upon by the manufacturer. As indicated earlier, the frequency selected is often 70 MHz.

The LNA and the downconverter must be housed in a waterproof enclosure. Both are active units and require a DC voltage source, which can be supplied by a cable leading to a DC voltage tap in the satellite receiver in the home.

Downconverter/Satellite Receiver Connections

The signal output of the downconverter, consisting of frequency-modulated audio and video on a 70-MHz carrier, is brought into the home by coaxial cable. The 70-MHz modulated carrier can be carried by RG-59 coaxial

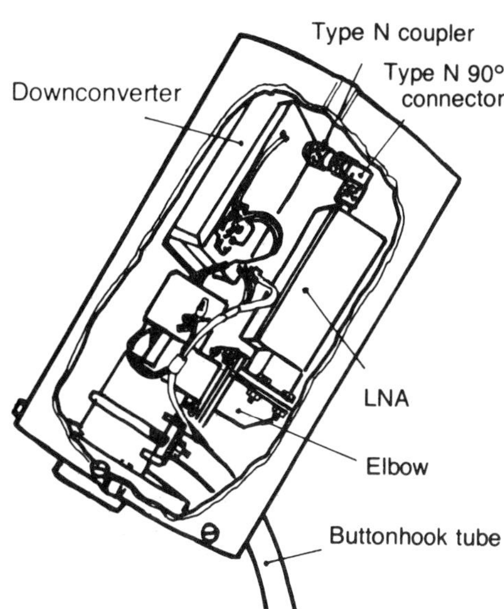

Figure 8-6. LNC consists of LNA and downconverter in a single, weatherproof housing. (*Courtesy Winegard Co.*)

cable for distances of up to about 300 feet. Whether such a distance can be tolerated depends on the efficiency of the dish, the strength of the original signal, and the gain of the LNA. Three hundred feet is a fairly long run of coaxial cable, but if the signal is too degraded, a preamplifier (line amplifier) can be inserted somewhere along the length of the cable.

The longer the connecting cable between the downconverter and the receiver, the greater the possibility of picking up microwave interference. Whether this will happen depends on the length of the cable, the type of shielding used by the cable, and the nearness of the interfering source. The most commonly used coaxial cable uses copper braid as the ground, or cold lead. A more interference-resistant cable has a surrounding layer of metallic foil in addition to the braid, and this type of coax is doubly protected against the pickup of unwanted extraneous signals. A variation consists of two layers of braid with the braid coated with a layer of silver, an extremely low-resistance conductor. This type of coax is highly desirable because of its effective shielding, but it is also more expensive than the other types. Whichever one of these cables is used, it must be terminated in a coaxial connector suitable for insertion into the mating jack on the rear of the satellite receiver.

A convenient way to make the connection between the outdoor downconverter and the in-home satellite receiver is to dig a shallow trench in as straight a line as possible. The cable can then be brought to the home through a succession of 10-foot lengths of polyvinyl (PVC) tubing. This tubing should have a diameter large enough to accommodate the coaxial cable, generally about 1/2 inch.

The open ends of the tubing and the cable can be protected against weather and water seepage by using a commercial sealant at both its ends and also at all tubing joints. To bring the coaxial cable into the home, attach it to outside walls using coaxial cable fasteners. Since the cable must be brought through the wall, drill a through hole to accommodate the cable. This hole should be at a downward slant from inside the home to the outside. One method is to use a suitable length of plastic tubing. Use a dab of plastic cement at the entrance and exit points of the tubing and then bring the coaxial cable in through it. Inside the home, bring the coaxial cable through inside walls, or along a baseboard, or along the cove molding near the ceiling. If you plan to use the inner wall spaces, you will find it helpful to get the services of an experienced electrician. When you bring the line into the home, do not put its terminating connector on until the cable has reached a point close to the satellite TV receiver. At that time, you can bring the cable up to the input of the satellite receiver, or if it is coming through a wall, to the wall plate. The wall plate technique is more professional looking; the direct connection approach is easier.

SIAMESE CABLE CONNECTIONS

To be able to receive signals from a selected satellite, the dish must be pointed directly at it. Since there are about eighteen satellites, with their number increasing, the dish must be repositioned every time reception is wanted from a different satellite. You can change the position manually, and you will find it a nuisance, but it can also be done electrically, by a motor drive.

The motor drive can be remotely controlled by a DC voltage, supplied by the satellite receiver. To eliminate the need for running a separate wire out to the dish, use a type of cable known as *Siamese cable.* This cable was described in Chapter 1 and illustrated in Fig. 1–27. That illustration is repeated here, in Fig. 8–7.

Siamese cable consists of coaxial cable for bringing the signal from the downconverter to the receiver, plus a pair of single, insulated wires for delivering the above-ground motor voltages. These DC voltage wires are color-coded white and supply voltages of opposite polarity. One of these voltages produces clockwise rotation of the motor; the other, counterclockwise rotation. A third wire, color-coded black, is included; it works as a ground lead

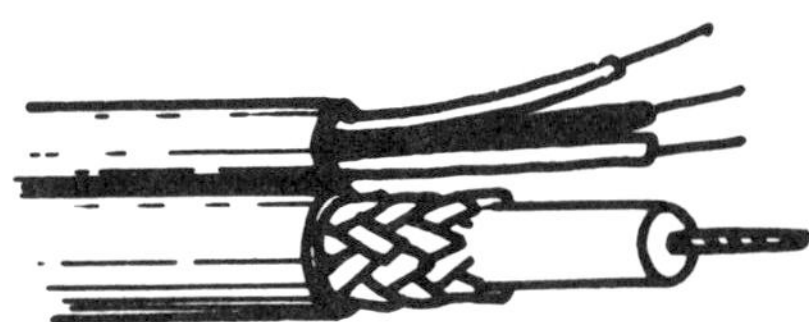

Figure 8–7. Siamese cable used to carry satellite signals plus DC voltages for dish motor, LNA and downconverter. The coaxial cable is RG-59. (*Courtesy Precision Satellite Systems*)

and is the common or ground lead for the two DC voltages. The wires are connected to a terminal block mounted on the dish, and at the opposite end they are connected to a motor terminal block on the satellite receiver.

MESSENGER CABLE CONNECTIONS

A somewhat more economical wiring arrangement for operating a dish motor is messenger cable, shown in Fig. 8-8. This cable was described in Chapter 1 and illustrated in Fig. 1-26. That illustration is repeated here.

Like Siamese cable, messenger cable includes coaxial cable to carry the satellite TV signals into the home satellite TV receiver from the downconverter. It includes a single wire, usually solid-conductor and is covered with an insulating material. This conductor, called the messenger wire, and the shield braid of the coaxial cable form the plus and minus conductors for the DC voltage required by the dish motor. Since the coaxial connector at the dish motor terminal makes a ground connection automatically, all that is required is to attach the single-motor conductor to the appropriate terminal on the motor block at the dish.

At the satellite receiver, the shield braid makes automatic connection to the negative or ground side of the receiver, which is also the minus of the DC voltage supply. As at the motor block at the dish, the single conductor is connected to the plus terminal of the motor block on the receiver. In both instances, no special connector is needed for the motor wire. The connection at the dish and also at the receiver is via a screw terminal; just wrap the wire around the screw and tighten it.

The voltage used for operating the dish motor drive is quite low and is typically 18 volts. This voltage is produced by a power supply in the satellite receiver and is also used in the receiver for its own solid-state circuitry.

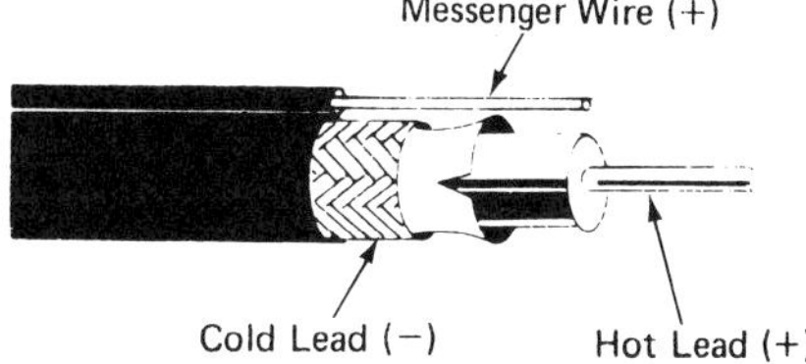

Figure 8-8. Messenger cable. (*Courtesy Precision Satellite Systems*)

POLAROTOR CONNECTIONS

The remaining cable from the in-home satellite TV receiver to the dish is a three-wire cable supplying DC voltage to a polarotor. With a polarotor, either vertically or horizontally polarized waves can be received.

In the United States, broadcast television signals are horizontally polarized, hence the receiving antennas are in a horizontal position. In Great Britain, broadcast television signals are vertically polarized, and the receiving antennas are vertical. By using both types of polarization, the transponders in a satellite, typically twenty-four, can make use of twenty-four transmission channels instead of twelve. In this way, the bandwidth occupied by twelve channels can be used for the transmission of twenty-four.

One method of receiving both vertically and horizontally polarized signals is to rotate the antenna so it is either horizontal or vertical.

The satellite TV antenna positioned inside the waveguide, near its end and close to the LNA, is very small, generally about an inch or so, and can be turned quite easily by a small motor.

A polarotor achieves the same result as turning the antenna simply by rotating the received magnetic field of the satellite's television signal. This is done by a coil surrounding the fixed-position antenna. Applying a positive current to the coil selects vertical polarization; a negative current, horizontal polarization. Short pulses of current can be used to fine-tune the selection.

REMODULATOR CONNECTIONS

In the satellite receiver, the video and audio signals are amplified and then delivered to a demodulator, with that circuitry removing the 70 MHz carrier. These signals can be delivered directly to an audio and video signal input panel on a TV receiver/monitor or a monitor, but not to a TV set. For the TV receiver the video must be amplitude modulated and the audio must be frequency modulated, with both signals using a channel 3 or channel 4 carrier.

Modulation is accomplished by a remodulator, and this circuitry can be incorporated into a satellite receiver or it can be an external component. Whichever method is used, it is essential for delivering signals to a TV receiver, but can be omitted for a receiver/monitor or a monitor.

The signals delivered by the downconverter to the satellite receiver are frequency-modulated audio and video. However, in this form they are not usable by a TV set. The receiver/monitor or monitor can accept either unmodulated signals or those that have been remodulated. It is preferable, if there is a choice, to use audio and video signals that have not been remodulated, as remodulation cannot improve signal quality but can only degrade it.

The satellite receiver can be connected to a remodulator positioned between the satellite receiver and the TV set by a suitable length of coaxial cable and the right connectors on both ends. We cannot assume that these connectors will be identical, because the satellite receiver and the external modulator can be made by different manufacturers.

The satellite receiver and the remodulator can be an integrated unit. In that case the output of the satellite receiver will be a video signal, amplitude modulated, and a sound signal, frequency modulated, onto a channel 3 or channel 4 carrier and, as a result, will be ready for direct input to the antenna VHF terminals of a TV set.

Figure 8–9 shows the various connections that have been described. The

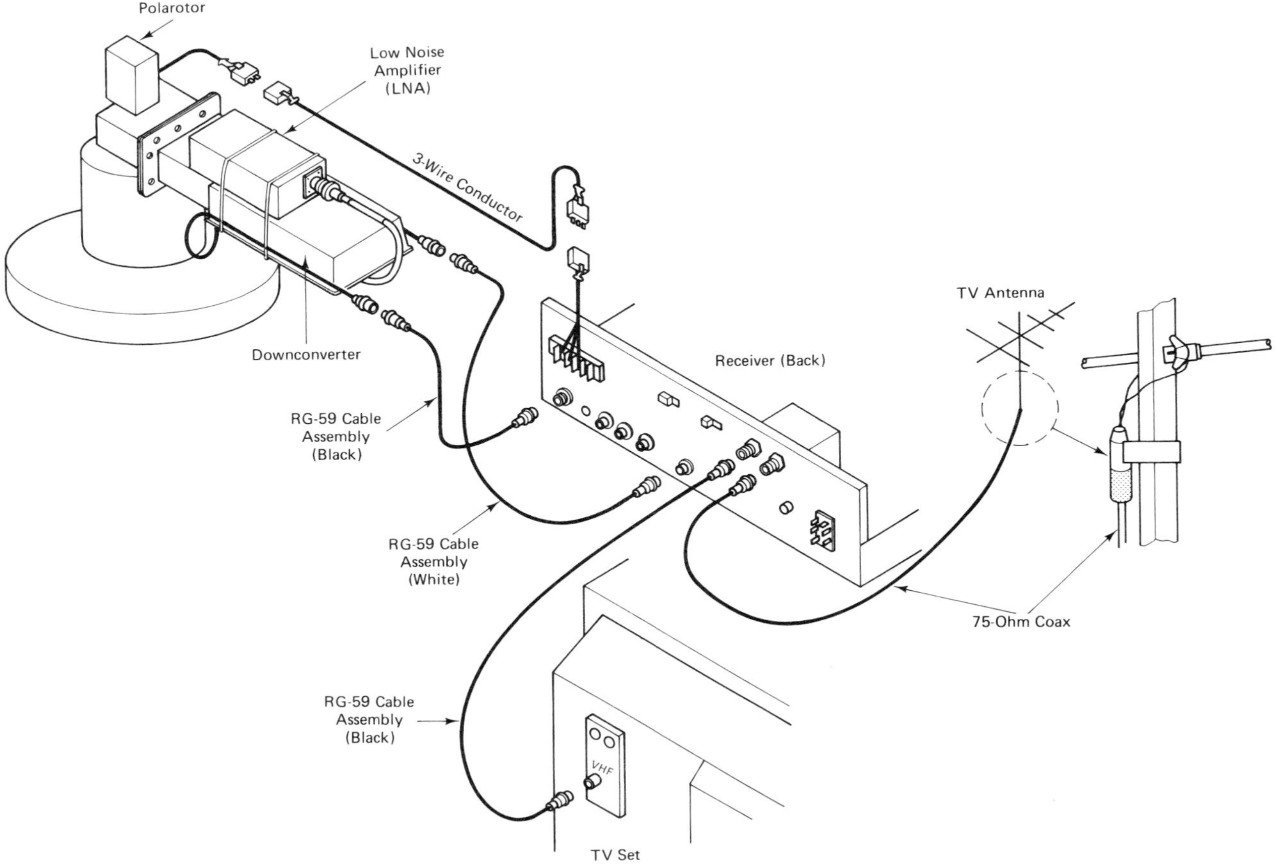

Figure 8–9. Satellite components and TV receiver connections.

LNA is wired to the separate downconverter by a short length of coaxial cable. Coming into the polarotor is a three-wire conductor from the satellite receiver using a terminal block. The individual wires are attached to the terminal block and from there to a three-wire in-line connector. While the three wires could have been brought individually to the polarotor, it is more convenient to use a three-wire cable. Near the polarotor, the cable is brought into a three-wire in-line jack. This jack mates with a three-wire in-line plug coming out of the polarotor. Inside the polarotor, the three wires are separated and connected to the polarotor terminals.

The output of the downconverter is connected to an RG-59 coaxial cable assembly. The length of this cable is determined by the distance of the downconverter to the satellite receiver in the home. That distance is not only from the downconverter mounted on the dish assembly to the outside of the home but includes the distance from the point of entry, through the wall, and possibly up or down in it, to the satellite receiver. Because this distance is such a variable, for no two satellite installations are alike, this cable must be tailor-made for each TVRO. It is advisable to install the cable first and then to mount the connectors at each end. Still another wire assembly is used to bring DC voltage for the LNA and downconverter from the satellite receiver to these dish-mounted components.

TVRO WIRE SIZES

The chart in Fig. 8–10 shows the wire gauges for supplying DC operating power and also for the type of coaxial cable to be used, depending on distance. To connect the output downconverter to the satellite receiver, use RG-59 coaxial cable for distances up to 300 feet; RG-6 cable for distances between 300 feet and 600 feet, and RG-11 for 600 feet to 800 feet. For long distances, it is helpful to choose coaxial cables having the least amount of attenuation. This chart is based on the assumption that the output frequency of the downconverter is 70 MHz.

CABLE USAGE	Distance Between Receiver and Antenna									
	0–100'	100'–150'	150'–200'	200'–250'	250'–300'	300'–400'	400'–500'	500'–600'	600'–700'	700'–800'
Power for LNA, Down Converter Polarotor, 5 or 6 conductor	20 Ga.	20Ga.	18 Ga.	16 Ga.	16 Ga.	16 Ga.	14 Ga.	14 Ga.	12 Ga.	12 Ga.
Actuator Drive Cable 5 or 6 Conductor	20 Ga.	18 Ga.	16 Ga.	14 Ga.	14 Ga.	12 Ga.	12 Ga.	10 Ga.	10 Ga.	10 Ga.
Output Down Converter 70MHz Coaxial Cable	RG-59	RG-59	RG-59	RG-59	RG-59	RG-6	RG-6	RG-6	RG-11	RG-11

Figure 8–10. Recommended TVRO wire sizes (gauge). (*Courtesy Winegard Co.*)

The satellite TV receiver shown in Fig. 8-9 is designed to supply either satellite TV signals to a TV set or television broadcast signals. If the antenna has an output impedance of 300 ohms, and this is quite usual, a 300-ohm to 75-ohm balun will be required. The broadcast TV signals can then be delivered to the rear of the satellite TV receiver. That receiver has a single-output terminal for switchable satellite or broadcast TV, with the connection to the VHF input of the TV set. For satellite TV signals, the channel selector on that receiver should be set to either channel 3 or channel 4. For broadcast TV, the channel selector should be set for VHF reception.

Figure 8-9 shows an arrangement for VHF reception only, but a band separator can be used at the TV set's antenna terminal board. The antenna, of course, would have to be multiband. Alternatively, the UHF terminals of the TV receiver could be connected to an indoor or outdoor UHF antenna.

BLOCK DOWNCONVERSION

The downconverter described previously produces, as a signal output, just one channel at a time. As a result, even though two or more TV sets are connected to the satellite TV receiver or to an outboard remodulator, there is no channel selection other than that made by the satellite receiver. Consequently, all of the TV sets will display the same picture. While this may be satisfactory for an in-home TVRO system, it is not suitable for use in a motel, a high-rise apartment house, or any other set of living accommodations housing more than one family.

To permit individual selection of satellite TV programs, we can use an alternative method known as *block downconversion.* With this technique, instead of the downlink frequency of a single transponder being downconverted, the entire downlink band, from 3.7 GHz to 4.2 GHz is downconverted at the same time. The bandwidth is equal to $4.2 - 3.7 = 0.5$ GHz or 500 MHz. This means that the heterodyning process that takes place in the downconverter produces a band that is 500 MHz wide, accommodating all the channels produced by a single satellite.

The satellite receiver used isn't quite the same as the one mentioned earlier, for it must be capable of accepting a signal having a 500-MHz bandwidth. Since all the channels of a satellite's transponders are presented at the input of the receiver, it can select any one of them for display.

MULTIPLE TV CONNECTIONS FOR A TVRO

Two, three, or four TV sets can be operated in a TVRO system (Fig. 8-11). The techniques for making these connections will follow the arrangements described in Chapter 5. Whether these methods will be successful depends on

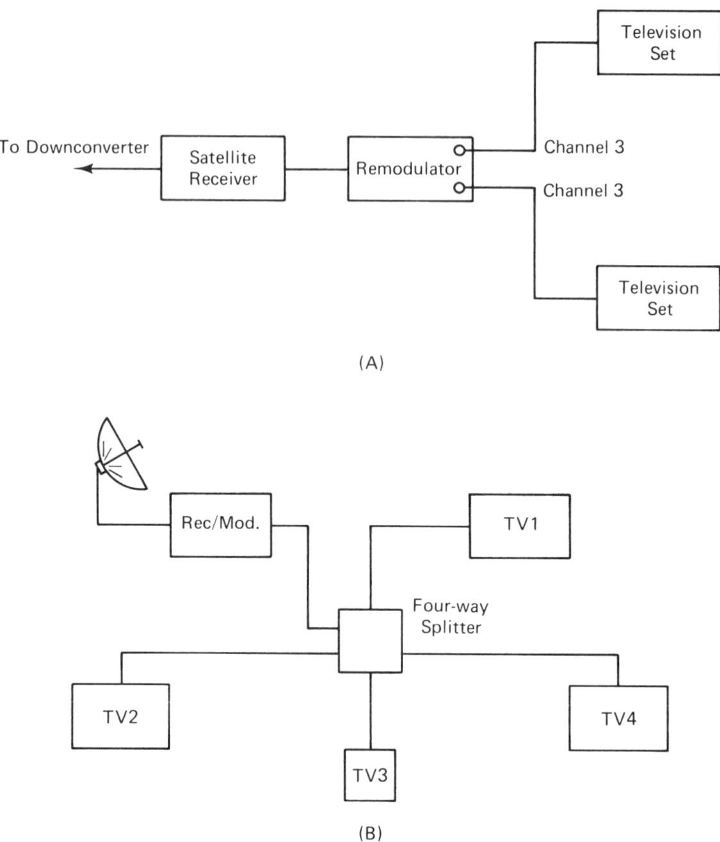

Figure 8–11. Two TV sets operated from a single remodulator (A); operating four TV sets from a single receiver equipped with an integrated remodulator (B).

the strength of the satellite signal, the distance from the dish to the satellite receiver, and the number of TV sets being supplied with the signal. It may be necessary to use a line amplifier, and possibly a preamplifier as well, with one or more of the TV sets.

If an outboard remodulator is being used following the satellite receiver, it may contain a pair of independent modulators so that the output ports can supply signals for more than one TV receiver. Outboard remodulators sometimes contain switchable output channels, giving the user a choice of channel frequencies. In some instances, these are channels 3,4,5, and 6. However, the same satellite program will be seen on all the TV sets that are connected. To give independence of program choice to all the TV sets in a multi-TV arrangement, we can use a block demodulator.

Figure 8–12 shows the connections and components for a TVRO block

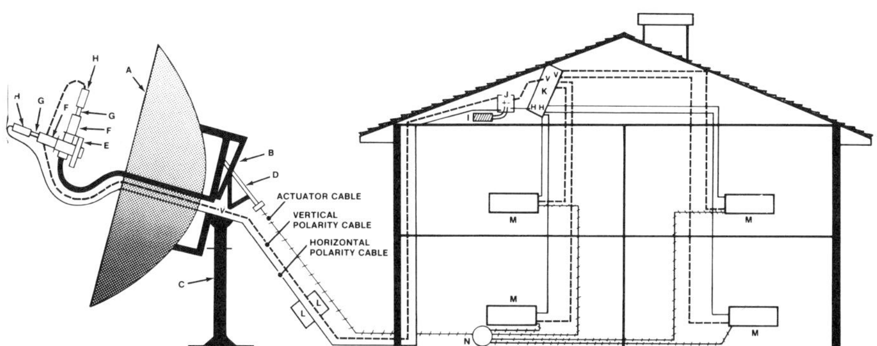

Figure 8-12. Block downconversion system. Frequency range is 1108–1608 MHz. All coax cables throughout the system, from dish to receivers, are RG-6/U foam. No A/B switches or relays are required. (A) dish; (B) backup structure; (C) pedestal mount; (D) actuator; (E) dual feed; (F) two LNAs; (G) double N connectors; (H) block downconverters; (I) 24-volt DC power supply; (K) dual input four-way splitter for 900–1650 MHz, four vertical, four horizontal outputs; (L) 900–1650 MHz line amplifiers; (M) block converter receivers; (N) actuator coupling block. (*Courtesy Winegard Co.*)

downconversion system. The signals from a selected satellite's transponders, from twelve to as many as twenty-four, are reflected by the dish (A) onto a feed, E, (the entrance to the waveguide) and are delivered to the antenna at the far end of that waveguide. The antenna is connected to the input of the LNA (F), and from there the signals are supplied to the block downconverter (H). The signals are strengthened by a pair of line amplifiers (L) and are delivered to four block converter receivers (M). Each satellite receiver is connected to its own TV receiver, with the satellite receivers capable of tuning in any one of the transponders for a selected satellite. Program independence refers only to the programs transmitted by a selected satellite. Satellite selection can only be done by one satellite receiver equipped with a remote motor control.

Each of the satellite receivers is equipped with a control (V and H) to select satellite signals that are horizontally or vertically polarized. A 24-volt DC separate power supply (I) is used for the voltage requirements of a polarotor.

The block downconverter has its own selected intermediate frequency, ranging in bandwidth from 1108 MHz to 1608 MHz (1608 − 1108 = 500 MHz). All the coaxial cables used in this system, from the dish to the receivers, are RG-6/U foam. The four-way amplifier/splitter (K), the line amplifiers (L), both LNAs (F) and the block downconverters (H) are all powered from the 24-volt DC power supply (I). Two downconverters are used, one for horizontally polarized signals, the other for vertically polarized.

Connecting Two Receivers, Single Polarity

Since satellite transponders can transmit signals that are either vertically or horizontally polarized, the satellite receiver must be equipped with an H (horizontal), V (vertical) polarity control, to allow the selection of either vertically or horizontally polarized signals.

Figure 8–13 shows a block diagram of two TV receivers in a TVRO system, a single-feed, two-receiver hookup. Only one of the satellite receivers can make use of its polarity control. Thus, while there is program independence for the two TV sets, it is limited to signals of the polarity selected by just one TV set. Within that limitation, each set can choose its own programs.

The block converter is connected to a two-way integrated amplifier/splitter. The intermediate frequency is a band extending from 950 to 1450 MHz and is delivered to the two-way amplifier/splitter by RG-11U coaxial cable that is approximately 250 feet, or less. The splitter is equipped with an amplifier, so the signal will be boosted but note that signal boost is at the end of the cable that follows the block converter. This means that the cable has a signal voltage drop before the signal reaches the amplifier/splitter. For this reason, an additional preamplifier may be required immediately following the block converter.

The two output ports of the amplifier/splitter are wired to the TV receivers with RG-11/U coaxial cable.

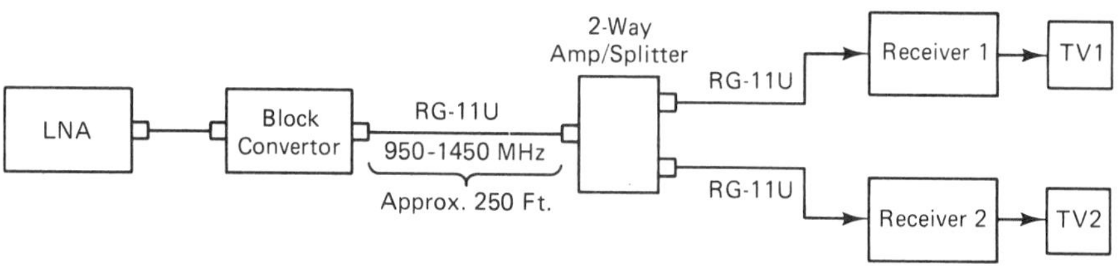

Figure 8–13. Two receivers, single polarity. Typical single-feed, two-receiver hookup.

Connecting Six Receivers, Single Polarity

Figure 8–14 shows another setup using six receivers, but once again only one receiver is designated for polarity control. This block diagram indicates that three amplifier/splitters are used. The first splitter is a two-way splitter following the block downconverter connected by RG-11/U coaxial cable. The two output ports of the splitter supply signal inputs to a four-way amplifier/splitter and also to a two-way amplifier splitter. These splitters, using RG-11/U coaxial cable, connect each of the satellite receivers to the output ports of their respective splitters.

As in Fig. 8–13, since only one of the TV sets is in charge of polarity

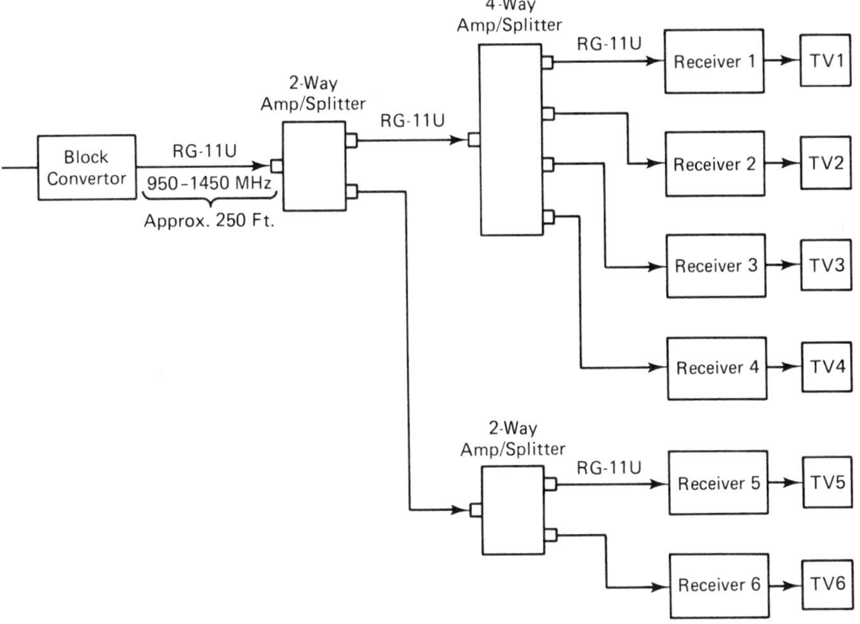

Figure 8–14. Six-receiver operation, with one receiver assigned polarity control.

control, some restrictions are imposed on channel selection. The TV sets can all watch horizontally or vertically polarized signals, but they can watch only those signals whose polarization is selected by the V/H control TV set.

Connecting Two Receivers, Dual Polarity

If both of the TV sets are to use their polarity controls, each will be able to watch horizontally or vertically polarized satellite signals, completely independent of each other, of any single-selected satellite. To make this possible, some changes must be made, and these are shown in Fig. 8–15—a block diagram of the modified setup.

Two low-noise amplifiers are used, one for vertically polarized signals, the other for those that are horizontally polarized, with each supplying satellite signals to a pair of block downconverters. The signal outputs of the two splitters consist of vertically and horizontally polarized signals and these are delivered to each of a pair of V/H switches. Although these are shown external to the satellite receivers, they are positioned inside the sets with a V/H control extending from the front panel. These switches can both be set to either the V position or the H position, so the TV sets have all of the channels of a satellite, regardless of the polarity of their signals.

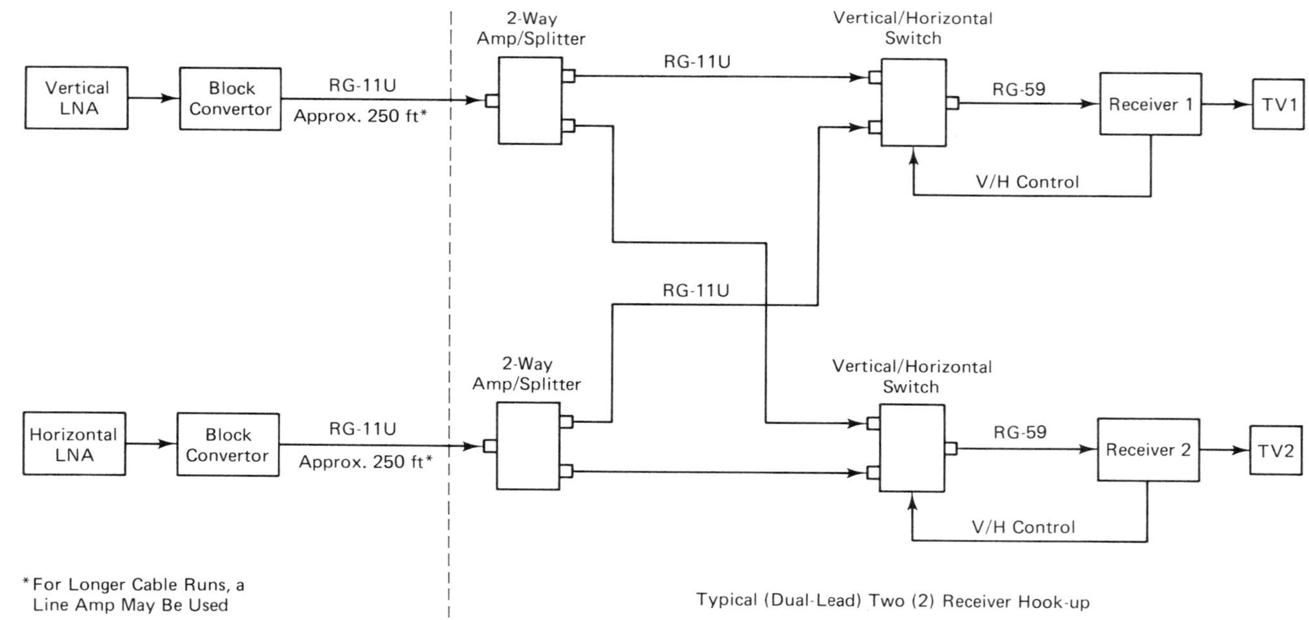

Figure 8–15. System using two satellite receivers with both having polarity control.

Connecting Six Receivers, Dual Polarity

If two TV sets can be arranged to have independent viewing of all satellite signals, any number can be wired. The block diagram shown in Fig. 8-16 for six TV sets may look complex, but it is simply a repetitive form, based on the arrangement shown in Fig. 8-15. Actually, it is much more detailed than necessary because the V/H switching is shown external to the satellite receivers.

The two-way amplifier/splitters are active units and require a source of DC voltage. These could have their own power supplies operated from the AC power line, but a more practical way would be for them to get their DC operating potential from the satellite receivers. This is shown in Fig. 8-16, in the blocks marked "Pwr blk." It is done this way to emphasize the delivery of 18 volts DC obtained from the receiver and does not mean the use of an outboard component. These power blocks, like the blocks used to indicate V/H switching, make the connections seem more complex.

SATELLITE STEREO

For a terrestrial broadcasting station, the single sound carrier is 4.5 MHz above the frequency of the video carrier. For satellite transponders, the sound carrier can have a 5.6-MHz, 5.8-MHz, 6.2-MHz, or 6.8-MHz separation from the picture carrier. Because of these different sound carrier frequencies, the satellite receiver must have an audio tuning control.

A satellite can use either one or a pair of sound carrier frequencies. Further, a pair of these carrier frequencies can be used for one program and a different pair for another.

The monophonic audio and video outputs of the remodulator, as described earlier, are delivered to the VHF antenna input of a TV set. For stereo sound, the left/right sound signals can be supplied by the satellite receiver, if it has ports for this purpose, with these signals delivered to a stereo processor (Fig. 8-17).

The connecting cables can be audio cables like those used in a high-fidelity system. The stereo output of the processor is usually supplied to the aux input of a preamplifier in a high-fidelity system. The audio signals can also be used to drive a speaker directly if the speakers are high-efficiency and if the stereo processor has an adequate audio power output.

A transponder can transmit a number of audio programs, either monophonic or stereophonic. As an example a satellite's transponder can transmit a pair of stereophonic subcarriers, with one having a frequency of 5.94 MHz and the other at 5.40 MHz. The frequency separation between these two is 0.54 MHz. This frequency difference need not be the same for other audio subcarriers. Thus a transponder aboard the same satellite can transmit a pair

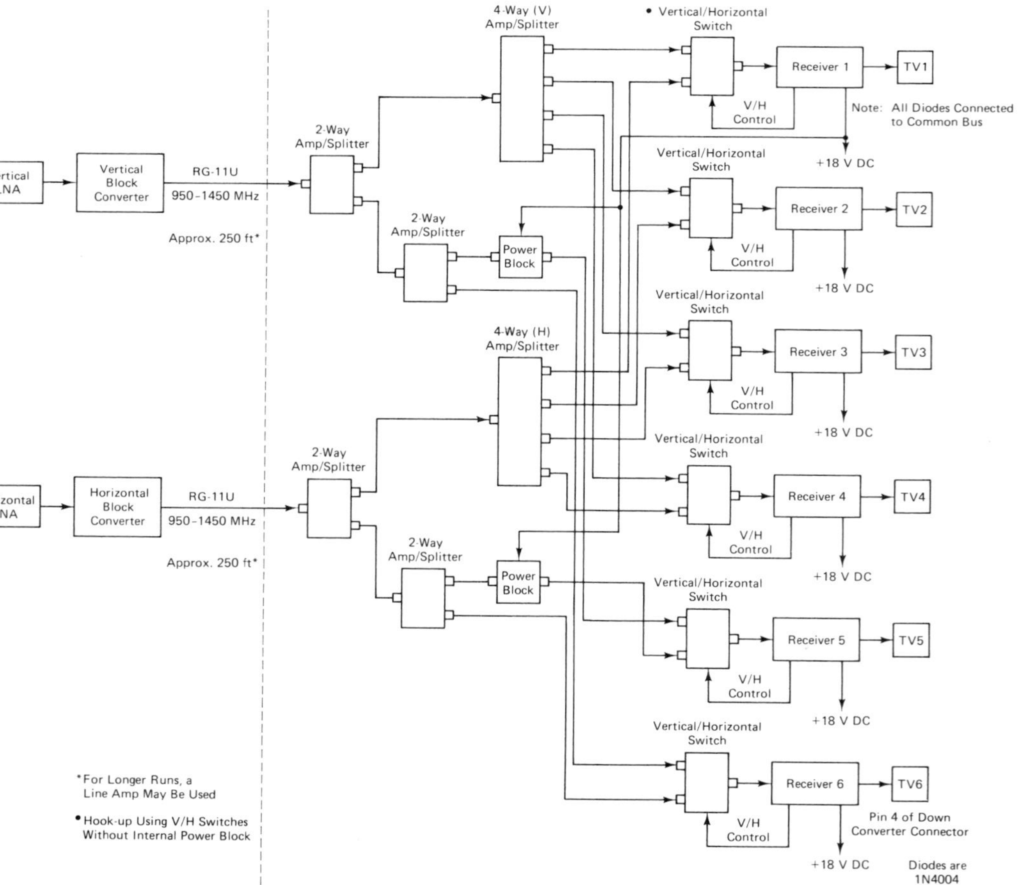

Figure 8–16. TVRO system with six receivers, all equipped with polarity control.

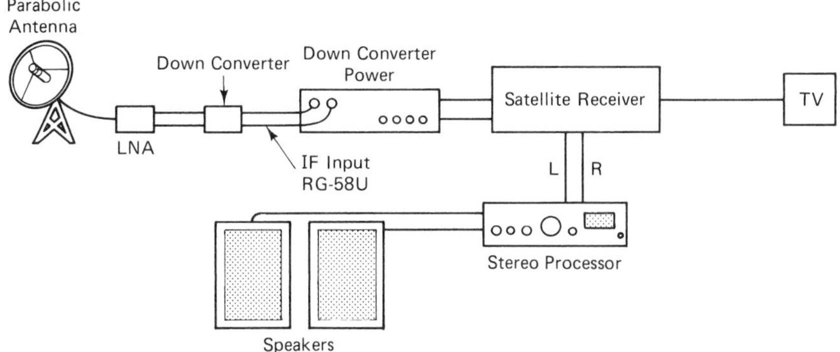

Figure 8–17. Satellite TV stereo sound system.

of audio signals with one at 5.76 MHz and the other at 5.58 MHz, with a frequency separation of 0.18 MHz. Even though a satellite transmits stereo sound, the TV set receiving the modulated video and audio signals at its VHF input terminals may well be designed for monophonic sound only, and that is what will be reproduced.

To take advantage of double subcarrier sound transmission, the audio must be delivered to a TV set having a stereo sound capability or else to a high-fidelity system. There are several ways of doing this. If the satellite receiver has stereo audio output ports you can connect these to the aux audio input terminals of a preamplifier in the sound system.

Another method, as shown in Fig. 8–17, is to use a stereo processor, an outboard component. The input to the stereo processor is taken from the left/right output ports of the satellite receiver, assuming that it has such ports. These output ports may be identified as stereo processor, audio processor, or unfiltered/composite video. Connect these terminals using RG-59 coaxial cable to the "Video in" jack located on the rear panel of the stereo processor.

If your satellite TV receiver does not have such output jacks, connect the video input jack on the stereo processor to the video output jack of the TVRO receiver. Then connect the video output jack on the stereo processor to the video input jack of your VCR or monitor. Finally, connect the left and right audio output jacks of the stereo processor to the aux inputs of your high-fidelity preamplifier.

As is the case in terrestrial TV broadcasting, the transmission of monophonic sound by a satellite requires just a single subcarrier, but for stereo sound a pair of subcarriers is required. These subcarriers need not be the same for different satellites and further, aren't necessarily the same for each program transmitted by the same satellite. When a single audio subcarrier is used it is called *subcarrier A*. If two are used for stereo transmission, they are called *A and B* or *A + B*.

The transmitted sound subcarriers may or may not have the same signal amplitude. When the signal strengths of both subcarriers are the same, the transmission is referred to as *discrete stereo*. If one of the subcarriers is substantially stronger than the other, it is called *matrix stereo*. In either case, whether discrete or matrix, it isn't always necessary to make the connections to a high-fidelity system. If the stereo processor is equipped with an internal stereo amplifier setup, connect a pair of left/right speakers to the speaker A and B terminals on the processor. This is convenient as far as connections are concerned, but you may find the audio power output of the processor inadequate.

SATELLITE TV CONNECTOR PROBLEMS

The greater the number of interconnected components, the larger the number of desired features, but this always brings along with it the increased possibility of incorrect or poor connections, connections that may become corroded in time, or that may work their way loose. Connections for satellite TV may present a special operating fault, as not only the dish, but the LNA and downconverter mounted on the dish structure, operate outdoors. While the dish has no direct electrical or physical connection to the LNA, it does receive DC operating voltage for its drive motor via a cable. The LNA and downconverter not only receive DC operating voltages from the indoor satellite receiver but also deliver signals to it.

Outdoor components and their connections must be tight, and they must be protected against the weather. If moisture manages to work its way into any cable connector that carries DC voltage, there will be some development of carbon at the contacts. There is one way to prevent this—and that is to use an outdoor sealant, one that is electrically inert. The presence and growth of carbon particles on the connector contacts can produce a form of picture interference variously called sparkles or sparklies. These may occur intermittently or be continuous.

INDEX

B

C

D

E

F

G

H

I

J

L

T

U

V

W